MW00608655

THE BIBLE AND AMERICAN POPULAR CULTURE

THE OXFORD HANDBOOK OF

THE BIBLE

AND

AMERICAN

POPULAR

CULTURE

Edited by

DAN W. CLANTON, JR.
and TERRY R. CLARK

OXFORD

UNIVERSITY PRESS

OXFORD
UNIVERSITY PRESS

Library of Congress Cataloging-in-Publication Data
Names: Clanton, Dan W., Jr., editor. | Clark, Terry Ray, editor.
Title: The Oxford handbook of the Bible and American popular culture /
edited by Dan W. Clanton, Jr. and Terry R. Clark.
Description: New York : Oxford University Press, 2020. | Includes
bibliographical references and index.
Identifiers: LCCN 2020023223 (print) | LCCN 2020023224 (ebook) |
ISBN 9780190461416 (hardback) | ISBN 9780190077471 (epub)
Subjects: LCSH: Popular culture—Religious aspects—Christianity. | Popular
culture—United States. | Bible—Criticism, interpretation, etc.
Classification: LCC BR517 .O9 2020 (print) | LCC BR517 (ebook) | DDC
261.0973—dc23
LC record available at https://lccn.loc.gov/2020023223
LC ebook record available at https://lccn.loc.gov/2020023224

1 3 5 7 9 8 6 4 2

Printed by Sheridan Books, Inc., United States of America

Contents

PART III BIBLICAL THEMES IN POPULAR CULTURE

PART IV BIBLE IN POPULAR CULTURAL GENRES

PART V "LIVED"/PERFORMATIVE EXAMPLES OF THE BIBLE AND POPULAR CULTURE

PART VI THE STATE OF THE FIELD

Acknowledgments

Steve Wiggins approached us at the end of 2013 to say he felt "it is about time for a Handbook dedicated to the Bible and Popular Culture." Since then, he's been an invaluable resource and guiding hand in this massive project. Many, many thanks to you, Steve!

I (Dan) would like to thank Jeffrey Mahan and Leonard Greenspoon, my mentors in the study of Religion and Popular Culture for their advocacy and guidance. Thanks also to Oxford University Press for all its support for this *Handbook*. I'd also like to express my abiding appreciation for the work and friendship of my co-editor Terry Ray Clark, without whom this project would've fallen apart several times. Trust me, y'all: Terry's one of The Good Ones. Finally, as always, none of this could've been possible without the love and help and tolerance of my family. Missy, Danny, and Hannah, this is for y'all.

I (Terry) would like to thank Dan Clanton, my friend, colleague, and on-going mentor in all things related to Religion and Popular Culture for first introducing me to research, writing, and teaching in this field. The breadth and depth of his expertise, as well as his dedication and diligence, are at times breathtaking. I would also like to thank my wife (Natalie) and my boys (Corwin and Wesley) for patiently enduring the many hours I've spent glued to my laptop while working on this project. And finally, I'd like to thank Oxford University Press for giving me the opportunity to participate in such exciting and interesting academic work.

CONTRIBUTORS

James S. Bielo Department of Anthropology, Miami University of Ohio
bielojs@miamioh.edu

Caroline Blyth Department of Theological and Religious Studies, University of Auckland
c.blyth@auckland.ac.nz

Dan W. Clanton, Jr. Department of Philosophy and Religious Studies, Doane University
Dan.Clanton@doane.edu

Terry R. Clark Department of Religion, Georgetown College
Terry_Clark@georgetowncollege.edu

Matthew A. Collins Theology and Religious Studies, University of Chester
m.collins@chester.ac.uk

Elizabeth Rae Coody Department of Religious Studies, Morningside College
coodye@morningside.edu

Scott S. Elliott Department of Philosophy and Religion, Adrian College
selliott@adrian.edu

Deane Galbraith Religion Program, University of Otago
deanegalbraith@yahoo.co.nz

David G. Garber, Jr. McAfee School of Theology, Mercer University
GARBER_DG@mercer.edu

Greg Garrett Department of English, Baylor University
Greg_Garrett@baylor.edu

Michael J. Gilmour Biblical Studies and Practical Theology, Providence University College
Michael.Gilmour@prov.ca

Kathryn Gin Lum Religious Studies Department, Stanford University
kgin@stanford.edu

Leonard Greenspoon Klutznick Chair in Jewish Civilization, Creighton University
ljgrn@creighton.edu

David M. Gunn Texas Christian University, Emeritus
d.gunn@tcu.edu

Carol A. Hebron School of Theology, Charles Sturt University, Brisbane
revheb@hotmail.com

Scott M. Langston Department of Religion, Texas Christian University
s.langston@tcu.edu; sclangston@charter.net

Katherine B. Low Departments of Philosophy; Religious Leadership and Ministry, Mary Baldwin University
klow@marybaldwin.edu

James F. McGrath Department of Philosophy and Religion, Butler University
jfmcgrat@butler.edu

Andrew Moss PhD candidate, Department of Theology and Religion, Durham University
a.d.moss@durham.ac.uk

Tina Pippin Religious Studies, Agnes Scott College
tpippin@agnesscott.edu

Katja Rakow Department of Philosophy and Religious Studies, Utrecht University
k.rakow@uu.nl

Gregory Allen Robbins Department of Religious Studies, University of Denver
Gregory.Robbins@du.edu

Theresa M. Sanders Department of Theology and Religious Studies, Georgetown University
sanderst@georgetown.edu

Linda S. Schearing Department of Religious Studies, Gonzaga University (retired)
schearing@gonzaga.edu

Robert Paul Seesengood Theology Department, Eastern University
rburnett@eastern.edu

Shayna Sheinfeld Sheffield Institute for Interdisciplinary Biblical Studies, The University of Sheffield
Shayna.sheinfeld@gmail.com

Eric Thurman Department of Religious Studies, Sewanee, The University of the South
etthurma@sewanee.edu

Rachel Wagner Department of Philosophy and Religion, Ithaca College
rwagner@ithaca.edu

Jane S. Webster Department of Religion and Philosophy, Barton College (retired)
jwebster@barton.edu

Valarie H. Ziegler Department of Religious Studies, DePauw University (emerita)
vziegler@depauw.edu

PART I

INTRODUCTION

INTRODUCTION

DAN W. CLANTON, JR. AND TERRY R. CLARK

LET's start with why. Why a volume like this? Why ask all these wonderful scholars and writers to talk to us about Bible and American popular culture? Why is that an important relationship to explore?

Let me (Dan) try to answer that question by describing a trip I took recently to Washington, D.C. I was there in April 2019 for the annual meeting of the Popular Culture Association/American Culture Association. In between sessions, I managed to sneak away and visit the Museum of the Bible (MotB). The MotB—which opened in November 2017—is one of several museums, theme parks, and exhibition spaces funded by evangelical Christian organizations for the purpose of disseminating specific narratives about Christianity, history, science, and the Bible. Other examples include the Holy Land Experience in Orlando and the Creation Museum and Ark Encounter in Kentucky (the latter of which James Bielo and Valarie Ziegler examine in their essays in this volume).

One of the most important things to note about the MotB is that it's owned and funded by the Green family, the folks who own Hobby Lobby. This is the family behind the 2014 Supreme Court case *Burwell v. Hobby Lobby Stores, Inc.*, which upheld the rights of privately owned companies to be exempt from otherwise generally applicable laws due to religious beliefs.[1] This is also the family that in May 2018 had to pay a $3 million fine and return to the Iraqi government around 3,800 cultural and religious artifacts it unethically acquired.[2] Even more recently, the MotB admitted that it had purchased thirteen manuscript fragments from a professor at Oxford, when in fact these fragments

---

[1] See SCOTUSblog, *Burwell v. Hobby Lobby Stores, Inc.*, https://www.scotusblog.com/case-files/cases/sebelius-v-hobby-lobby-stores-inc/.

[2] See Peggy McGlone, "Hobby Lobby's Illicit Artifacts Are Returned to Their Iraqi homeland," *Washington Post,* May 2, 2018, https://www.washingtonpost.com/entertainment/museums/hobby-lobbys-illicit-artifacts-are-returned-to-their-iraqi-homeland/2018/05/02/3f59842a-4e44-11e8-84a0-458a1aa9acoa_story.html.

(all from the Oxyrhynchus Collection) belonged to the Egypt Exploration Society. At the time of this writing, the MotB has agreed to return the fragments.[3]

Another important thing to note about the MotB is that it claims to be "nonsectarian," i.e., it doesn't seek to advance any specific theological position. Instead, they describe themselves neutrally as "an innovative, global, educational institution whose purpose is to invite all people to engage with the Bible."[4] Even though scholars like Candida Moss and Joel Baden have shown that claim to be inaccurate in practice, the MotB still maintains its nonsectarian stance publicly.[5]

For the sake of space, let me talk about one specific exhibit I visited, "The World of Jesus of Nazareth," located on the third floor, all of which is titled "The Stories of the Bible."[6] "The World of Jesus of Nazareth" is a semi-immersive walking tour. As you enter, you're surrounded by real, large, stone walls, and there are Bible verses etched into these walls (e.g., Luke 8:1, "Jesus traveled about from one town and village to another, proclaiming the good news of the kingdom of God"). Overhead, one hears the sounds of bleating animals and soft harp music.

The entry opens wide into a replica of a first-century village in Nazareth, with a large tree in front of you, bearing a plaque about wine and wine-making. To the right is a facsimile of a small dwelling with a brief video presentation titled *Teaching and Parables* (e.g., the Lost [aka Prodigal] Son in Luke 15:11–32). An adjoining room to the right of this is a display titled "Flocks," highlighting the image of Jesus as a shepherd. To the left of the entry are more of these small rooms and large trees with more informative plaques (e.g., "Water"), and each room has a different topic. In the room labeled "Hospitality," guests learn about "daily life at home" courtesy of an actress playing a character from "biblical times" talking to children seated at a table stacked with food.

There's an courtyard adjoining this room where the kind "biblical times" lady explains "preserving water" and "bread." Next to the courtyard there's a mikvah, a ritual bath for purification purposes. In the building next to the mikvah one can enter a "synagogue" and chat with an actor playing a character named Jeremiah, a "historical Jew." Jeremiah

---

[3] See Candida Moss, "Hobby Lobby Scandal Widens as Museum of the Bible Admits Oxford Prof Sold Illicit Papyri to Green Family," *Daily Beast*, October 17, 2019, https://www.thedailybeast.com/ hobby-lobby-scandal-widens-as-museum-of-the-bible-admits-oxford-prof-sold-illicit-papyri-to-green-family.

[4] See Museum of the Bible, "About Museum of the Bible," https://www.museumofthebible.org/ museum/about-us.

[5] In their chapter "The Museum of the Bible," in *Bible Nation: The United States of Hobby Lobby* (Princeton, NJ: Princeton University Press, 2017), 137–75, Candida Moss and Joel Baden have shown that the label "nonsectarian" has a specific meaning, viz., it "is not a synonym for either 'nonreligious' or 'open to all approaches.' On the contrary, the nuances of the term imply both Christian and Protestant" (145). That is, these scholars claim that the MotB gives the impression that "the Bible does not need interpretation, commentary, or scholarly explanation," which is a specifically Protestant view of the Bible (149).

[6] What follows is adapted from a segment from a podcast I cohost with my friend and colleague Dr. Tim Hill titled *Impolite Conversation*. For more about my visit, as well as pictures, see *Impolite Conversation*, "Dan's Trip to the Museum of the Bible," http://impconvo.blubrry.com/extra-stuff/ museum-of-the-bible/.

tells the visitors—several of whom take a seat on the stone stairs, as "historical Jews" might have done—that lots of villages had synagogues like these and that they served as schools, courts, and meeting places. He also claims that synagogues started to be built in Babylon after the first Temple was destroyed but admits there's no proof for the building of synagogues during this period. Jeremiah explains the importance of the sacrificial system in Jewish worship, that it's an atonement for sin, and that Jews atoned three times a year in the Temple. As one moves on, there are more scenes from rural life, like an olive press and a woodworking room. The exhibit ends on the left in a serene room filled with quiet ocean sounds, situating one on the banks of the Sea of Galilee (even though Nazareth is something like thirty kilometers from the Sea of Galilee).

My impression was that the intended effect of this semi-immersive experience is, obviously, to give a sense of participation, a heightened contextualization and historicity to one's understanding of the Bible.[7] There's a clear emphasis on authenticity and realism in the exhibit, as if the MotB wants to reassure visitors of the historical verisimilitude of biblical stories and scenes. To this point, it's important to note Stephen L. Young's description of museums as sites in which the "meaning or significance of an exhibit is animated by the interaction between the museum's physical space and the cognitive landscape of visitors, the backgrounds or discourses or memories they bring."[8] The significance of this point lies in the way(s) in which a museum, here the MotB, reinforces and even reifies the views of some visitors while leaving others confused or bemused. I admit that I fall into the latter category, as it's obvious that I—as a Jewish scholar of religious studies—am not the target visitor.

My impressions fit nicely with Young's focus on another section of the MotB, the second-floor exhibit titled "The Impact of the Bible," which depicts "the Bible's presence around you, often in unexpected places, hidden in plain sight" and, more specifically, "its significant impact on American culture."[9] Here one finds artifacts and posters detailing the influence the Bible has wielded in American and world history, including foci on slavery, the US Civil War, human rights, science, education, art, comic books, and even fashion. The exhibit ends in a circular room titled "Bible Now," in which visitors "will discover the Bible's dynamic presence in a spectacular live-feed of global data." In the center of this room stands a small circular enclosure called the "Joshua Room," where guests are invited to participate in and testify to this ongoing influence; you're asked to "record your story" of "how the Bible has impacted" you.

While no one would deny that the Bible has influenced historical events and movements, one gets the sense from "The Impact of the Bible" exhibit that it has exerted a singular, dominant influence on the unfolding of human history. In his work, Young notes this as well, and claims that the MotB "promotes the exceptionalism of the Bible."

---

[7] This kind of immersive experience is also discussed in Bielo's chapter in this volume.

[8] Stephen L. Young, "The Museum of the Bible: Promoting Biblical Exceptionalism to Naturalize an Evangelical America," in *Christian Tourist Attractions, Mythmaking, and Identity Formation*, ed. Erin Roberts and Jennifer Eyl, Critiquing Religion: Discourse, Culture, Power (London: Bloomsbury, 2019), 25–41, here 26.

[9] This quote is found on the welcome sign for this exhibition.

However, he goes further in that he sees this use of the museum's "physical space" as targeting specific visitors; i.e., the exhibit produces a discourse that will be especially welcome by certain kinds of guests because that discourse will resonate with and reinforce their "cognitive landscapes." Young writes that this exhibit—and even all of the MotB— views the Bible "in a way that makes normative influence of evangelical culture in the United States seem natural and desirable." Put differently, by "deploying the rhetoric of the impact of the Bible, the museum promotes the idea of the Bible as a catalyzing force for values, institutions, and societal changes encoded as positive—or progress—in the imaginations of visitors. But this biblical exceptionalism blends into a Christian iteration of American exceptionalism . . . a narrative about national origins that gives evangelical visitors a past that orients their posture toward the present."[10] In essence, Young is describing what he and other scholars of religion refer to as "mythmaking." What evangelical Christians experience when visiting the MotB is an extended, material, pleasurable reminder of who they are, what they believe, and how history has led to them. Myths, after all, help us explain ourselves to ourselves.

In this interaction between discourses, between (a) the ideas, experiences, and memories that constitute the "thought-world" or ideology of the visitor and (b) the physical space, objects, and "official" words and information found in the MotB, one can see clearly the *impact* that Bible has on American popular culture. The Bible not only shapes the identity of the Christian guests before they visit the MotB by being "mediated" through the language of prayer and song and such things as physical Bibles and T-shirts and bumper stickers and childhood toys and hundreds and hundreds of hours of music and TV and films, but it also reinforces and reifies that identity by the choices the MotB staff make in terms of how to gather and display physical artifacts and items and words in the museum itself, the kind of story they want to tell the visitor. Visitors recognize aspects of that story, that discourse, that ideology, because of their prior experience(s) of narratives and images and characters in and from the Bible, and the story the MotB tells is obviously predicated on Bible. One story can't exist without the other.

As you can see, this *impact* is reciprocal. That is, Bible and American popular culture are inextricably linked in the example of the MotB, and this linkage returns us to our initial question: Why spend time on a book like this? The question is answered by two simple observations. First, no one comes to the Bible in an absolute or unmediated fashion. The biblical text is filtered to us in myriad ways in multiple genres and settings. For example, in his chapter in this *Handbook*, David Gunn examines illustrated fictional retellings of the story of David and Bathsheba (2 Sam 11) found in children's Bibles. Just as in the MotB, the authors and illustrators of children's Bibles have to make hard choices about what needs to be included and excluded, given their target audience, as well as what kind of ideological story they want to buttress. Similarly, the authority that lies behind both the presentation of artifacts in the MotB as well as the words that accompany those displays functions to validate the kind of ideology that Young notes. It's this

---

[10]   Young, "The Museum of the Bible," 25–6.

same implied authority that Matthew Collins explores in his chapter on television, in which he discusses Bible documentaries and dramatized renderings of Bible narratives. Collins also notes that TV makes Bible more accessible, often serving as the viewer's first point of contact for biblical content. In this way, these televisual interpretations condition viewers' understanding of what the Bible "says."

The second observation stems from the work of Jeffrey Scheuer. In his 1999 book, *The Sound Bite Society: Television and the American Mind*, he explores the impact television has had on American politics and observes, "Television doesn't just affect society; to a great extent, it *is* society."[11] We can extend that metaphor and claim that popular culture isn't simply one aspect of our society; it constitutes society as we know it. That is, the language, imagery, issues, characters, and even the genres of popular culture are the beans we grind daily to make the coffee of our society. For example, in their respective chapters Katja Rakow and Rachel Wagner examine the way(s) in which biblical content and the very idea of Bible have impacted two of the most important aspects of our society today: the "transition from print culture to digital culture" and video games. The former affects virtually every field one can think of, from literature to healthcare and car repair to education, and is related more broadly to what industry experts term "digital transformation" or "digitization," which not only has revolutionized business practices but has also changed the way we garner and process information. Relatedly, video games have likewise had an enormous effect on our society. In an episode of his Netflix series *Patriot Act*, the comic Hasan Minhaj claims that "gaming culture is popular culture. It's the new social currency." Minhaj also points out that in 2018 video games were a $139 billion-a-year business.[12] Obviously, digitization and gaming culture drive so much of our society that it is difficult to conceive of our modern world without them. The significance of these discourses is reflected in the chapters already mentioned: Rakow focuses on how evangelical and Protestant communities are affected by this "digital" shift in the medium by which they access "God's word" via scholarship on material culture, while Wagner discusses the ways apocalyptic ideology, language, and images influence video game design and play. Both understand implicitly how important it is to examine the mutually influential relationship that exists between Bible and popular culture, as we've noted.

These are just a few examples of how the chapters in our *Handbook* address the reciprocal impact Bible and American popular culture have on one another. In what follows, we'd like to outline what readers can find in this *Handbook* and why we chose to include (and exclude) what we did.

[11] Jeffrey Scheuer, *The Sound Bite Society: Television and the American Mind* (New York: Four Walls Eight Windows, 1999), 1–2.

[12] Hasan Minhaj, "The Dark Side of the Video Game Industry," *Patriot Act*, vol. 4, episode 1, August 4, 2019. The episode is also available on Netflix's YouTube channel at https://www.youtube.com/watch?v=pLAi_cmly6Q.

First, though, let us say what we're not going to do in this introduction. We're not going to talk about theory or method. This isn't to say that theory isn't important. It is.[13] And we've both profited from engaging various theories related to the subject of religion or Bible and popular culture. However, what we've learned the hard way is that discussions of theory have a tendency to devolve into specialized lingo and terminology that wind up being unhelpful and even prohibitive. And if readers aren't enthusiastic about getting elbow-deep in theory, they're not likely to grasp the subtleties of that theory and will simply choose not to engage. Put differently, it won't be useful to them. In our *Handbook*, one of the guiding principles has been just that: *usefulness*. As such, we didn't decree any specific theory or methods for our authors, which has resulted in a pleasant plethora of approaches. Readers who are interested in perusing theoretical works about religion or Bible and popular culture have many options, and we'll include a few important works in the notes.[14] We're proud to say that one of these options is now Scott Langston's chapter on "Methodologies," which we'll say more about later.[15]

Second, we're not going to engage in lengthy detailed descriptions of the key terms in the title of this *Handbook*, such as "Bible," "American," and "popular culture." This is because we agree with Timothy K. Beal when he writes:

> There never has been a time when we could really talk about the Bible in the singular. There is no such thing as the Bible in that sense, and there never has been. The Bible has always been legion, a multiplicity of forms and contents, with no original to be found. In early Judaism and Christianity, there were many different scrolls and codices, variously collected and shared in many different versions, with no standard edition. Even in the early centuries of the print era, after Gutenberg, we find a burgeoning Bible-publishing industry with literally thousands of different editions and versions.[16]

---

[13] For an accessible overview of the importance of theory in the academic field of religious studies, see Bradley L. Herling, *A Beginner's Guide to the Study of Religion*, 2nd ed. (London: Bloomsbury, 2016).

[14] We both have profited immensely from the theoretical work of Conrad Ostwalt, *Secular Steeples: Popular Culture and the Religious Imagination*, 2nd ed. (London: Bloomsbury, 2012). Two absolutely fundamental collections of essays on religion and popular culture are Bruce David Forbes and Jeffrey H. Mahan, eds., *Religion and Popular Culture in America*, 3rd ed. (Berkeley: University of California Press, 2017), and Eric Michael Mazur and Kate McCarthy, eds., *God in the Details: American Religion in Popular Culture*, 2nd ed. (London: Routledge, 2011). For Bible and popular culture, see Philip Culbertson and Elaine M. Wainwright, eds., *The Bible in/and Popular Culture: A Creative Encounter*, Semeia Studies 65 (Atlanta, GA: Society of Biblical Literature, 2010). See also the work of Chris Klassen, *Religion and Popular Culture: A Cultural Studies Approach* (New York: Oxford University Press, 2014).

[15] In that chapter, Langston also notes the danger of the study of Bible and popular culture turning into an elite academic discipline via the proliferation of advanced theory and methodological approaches.

[16] Timothy K. Beal, *The Rise and Fall of the Bible: The Unexpected History of an Accidental Book* (Boston: Houghton Mifflin Harcourt, 2011), loc. 312, Kindle.

Even so, for our purposes, when we or one of our authors says or refers to "Bible," we almost always mean the library of ancient texts collected in the Christian Bible, which many consider to be a sacred text.

What we mean by "American" refers not only to geography but also to influence. That is, in most cases the examples of "popular culture" our authors examine are the product of an American or were created in America. In some instances, though, other geographies are examined, as in my (Dan's) chapter on cosplay, in which I focus on certain Holy Week practices in the Philippines. Because cosplay is most often focused on comic book characters and because comics are one of *the* paradigmatic forms of American popular culture, I felt justified in my choice of geography. By and large, though, it's easy to understand what our authors mean when they refer to "American" examples of "popular culture."[17]

Finally, what do we mean by "popular culture"? Again, our intention is not to engage in nebulous, impractical discussions of terminology, and defining a term like "popular culture" is notoriously difficult. It reminds us of an excerpt from A. A. Milne's *Winnie the Pooh*. As a preface to their famous hunt for the mythical Woozle, Pooh and Piglet have the following exchange:

"Hallo!" said Piglet, "what are *you* doing?"
"Hunting," said Pooh.
"Hunting what?"
"Tracking something," said Winnie-the-Pooh very mysteriously.
"Tracking what?" said Piglet, coming closer.
"That's just what I ask myself. I ask myself, What?"
"What do you think you'll answer?"
"I shall have to wait until I catch up with it," said Winnie-the Pooh.[18]

Similarly, it seems to us too abstract to attempt to define "popular culture" in isolation from specific examples. As a result, like our approach with theory, we didn't saddle our authors with a strict definition of "popular culture," and as you'll see, they chose a variety of suitable and fascinating examples. Not to belabor the point, but our goal was to provide an accessible, useful resource for readers interested in the reciprocal impact Bible and American popular culture have had, and continue to have, on one another. So, as with theory, we're happy to provide some excellent resources on how other scholars have

---

[17] Further, we're actually referring to US popular culture. The clarification is important, as we don't want to give the impression that—*contra* South Americans and Canadians—the US considers itself the owner of, or the only important referent for, the term "American."

[18] Quoted in A. A. Milne, *The Pooh Book of Quotations*, comp. Brian Sibley (New York: Dutton Children's Books, 1986), 30.

thought deeply about what "popular culture" is, but for our purposes in this *Handbook*, a discussion like that won't really help us achieve our goal.[19]

Now that we've discussed what's *not* going to be in this introduction, let's move on and tell you what you'll find in this *Handbook* and why we chose to organize it as we did. Obviously, there's no way we could cover or examine every single issue, topic, story, genre, character, etc. in just one book, even one as large as this one. Proof of this is that the *Encyclopedia of the Bible and Its Reception* (published in print and online by Walter de Gruyter) is expected to run to thirty volumes once it's finished.[20] As such, from the start we thought about this *Handbook* as a representative—not exhaustive—sampling of quality and accessible scholarship focused on specific topics within larger thematic or topical areas. As you'll see from the table of contents, we tried to create spaces for a specific textual focus ("Biblical Characters in Popular Culture") as well as a more thematic survey ("Biblical Themes in Popular Culture"). In the former section, we selected key characters from biblical literature that enjoy robust interpretive afterlives. For example, Theresa Sanders examines how the story of Adam and Eve in Genesis 2–3 is used in popular cultural ruminations on the role(s) of women in society and arguments among creationists and evolutionists. In her chapter on Moses, Linda Schearing tracks the function of Moses as "a multivalent [popular] cultural artifact" in film and humor, as well as how Moses is used metaphorically. Caroline Blyth engages one specific popular cultural example—the 1996 film *Samson and Delilah*—to ask questions about interpreting and rendering Bible in popular cultural discourses and the "reading strategies" employed by producers thereof. We've already mentioned David Gunn's contribution to this section; in her chapter on Esther, Katherine Low similarly focuses on literature. More specifically, Low examines Christian novelistic retellings of Esther and details how the paradigm of Disney princesses has colored their rendering. She then contrasts these

---

[19] I (Dan) address the issue of defining popular culture in my entry, "Pop Culture and the Bible," in *The Oxford Encyclopedia of Biblical Interpretation*, 2 vols., ed. Steven L. McKenzie (New York: Oxford University Press, 2013), 2:114–23. Therein I engage two kinds of definitions: one propositional, from Chandra Mukerji and Michael Schudson, "Introduction: Rethinking Popular Culture," in *Rethinking Popular Culture: Contemporary Perspectives in Cultural Studies*, ed. Chandra Mukerji and Michael Schudson (Berkeley: University of California Press, 1991), 1–61; one more open, from John Storey, "What Is Popular Culture?," in *Cultural Theory and Popular Culture: An Introduction*, 5th ed. (Essex, UK: Pearson Education, 2009), 1–15. I concluded that neither was particularly helpful, and instead advocated a "pragmatic" or "useful" approach, one in which there is a "focus on specific genres within what we might call popular culture, such as film, novels, television, comic books, and the like, so that in-depth theoretical discussions of how to define popular culture are absent in favor of a more focused examination of its ingredients or manifestations" (115). In addition to these works, interested readers can consult the useful anthologies Raiford Guins and Omayra Zaragoza Cruz, eds., *Popular Culture: A Reader* (London: Sage, 2005) or Harold E. Hinds Jr., Marilyn F. Motz, and Angela M. S. Nelson, eds., *Popular Culture Theory and Methodology* (Madison: University of Wisconsin Press/Popular Press, 2006) or one of the standard introductions to the subject, such as Dominic Strinati's overview, *An Introduction to Theories of Popular Culture*, 2nd ed. (London: Routledge, 2004); John A. Weaver's *Popular Culture Primer* (New York: Peter Lang, 2005); or John Storey's well-regarded *Cultural Theory and Popular Culture*, 8th ed. (London: Routledge, 2018).

[20] For more information, see de Gruyter's announcement of the publication at https://www.degruyter.com/dg/page/ebr.

works with Jewish retellings to highlight the ideological, interpretative differences. Switching to New Testament characters, Eric Thurman focuses on Jesus and how stories and images associated with him are adapted and ultimately satirized in the Adult Swim television series *Black Jesus* (2014–15). Finally, Carol Hebron tracks the changing depiction of Judas in film through a dizzying array of silent and sound, black-and-white and color, American and foreign films, and finds an equally variegated characterization of the apostle everyone loves to hate. As is obvious, we didn't include some central figures, such as Jeremiah, Ruth, Paul, or Mary Magdalene, and these were difficult decisions shaped by practical considerations, like the overall length of the *Handbook* and the availability and interest of potential writers. However, as with our other sections, we feel we've included (a) enough evidence for the reciprocal relationship between Bible and popular culture as well as (b) representative examples of how one might conduct such research and (c) bibliographic resources so that interested readers can follow up on these examples.

In the third section, "Biblical Themes in Popular Culture," we attempted to create a list of themes one can find in American popular culture that were clearly influenced by biblical literature. For example, James McGrath's chapter examines a wide array of interpretations of "Creation" in popular culture, focusing particularly on the reception of Genesis 1–3 in songs, folktales, fantasy and sci-fi television, and film. McGrath's kaleidoscopic approach is exemplary for this section and is echoed in my (Terry's) chapter on covenant. Therein, I examine the concept of divine covenant as understood in the ancient world and in the Bible, the founding period in American history, and finally in *Captain America* comics. David Garber follows suit and examines prophets and prophecy in examples ranging from *The Matrix* films to *Game of Thrones* and the rebooted series *Battlestar Galactica*, finding a wide array of appropriation and innovation. Obviously, apocalyptic imagery and language has suffused American popular culture, and Shayna Sheinfeld chooses four key examples—Terry Pratchett and Neil Gaiman's novel *Good Omens*; the TV series *Supernatural*; the 2009 movie *2012*; and Margaret Atwood's *MaddAddam* trilogy—to argue that the use of apocalyptic imagery has been affected significantly by the "turn toward environmental concerns in contemporary Western culture." Deane Galbraith takes a different tack and argues that popular cultural conceptions of Heaven are attempts to compensate for what he sees as the loss of the symbolic Heaven as found in Judaism and Christianity, i.e., pop-culture "Heavens" are best seen as "ways of coping with our loss of the traditional concepts of heaven." Since we can't talk about Heaven without talking about Hell and the Devil, Kathryn Gin Lum traces how early Christian readings of biblical literature resulted in understandings of Hell and the Devil and how these morph and appear in modern discourses like evangelical comic tracts and Hell Houses. Similarly, Tina Pippin examines the biblical and Dispensationalist roots of the Rapture and demonstrates how it pervades evangelical popular culture via books like the *Left Behind* series and the 1972 didactic Christian film *A Thief in the Night*, as well as numerous examples from more mainstream literature, television, and film. And we can't have an End of All Things without examining an afterlife. In his chapter on that topic, Greg Garrett explores how popular culture has created figures like zombies and vampires and used them alongside biblical figures such as angels and demons as ways of contemplating our postcorporeal existence.

Part IV, "Bible in Popular Cultural Genres" is the largest section in this *Handbook*, as we wanted to give authors permission to cast their nets wide to explore how generic limitations foster creativity among content producers. Some of these genres are familiar, like film and television, but we also included genres that haven't enjoyed as much critical examination, such as comics and jazz. An example of the former is Matthew Collins's aforementioned entry on television. In his chapter on another familiar genre, film, Gregory Robbins focuses on an example that's probably unfamiliar to most biblical scholars, Godfrey Reggio's *Qatsi* trilogy—consisting of *Koyaanisqatsi*, *Powaqqatsi*, and *Naqoyqatsi*—and examines them using the film theorist Etienne Souriau's layers of "reality" in film. Michael Gilmour discusses the ways in which Bible is used and adapted in the music of such rock bands as Stryper and Iron Maiden as well as the ways in which musical poets like Bob Dylan and Leonard Cohen have employed biblical language and imagery in their works. Moving from the familiar to the (perhaps) unfamiliar, Andrew Moss discusses the parallels between jazz and biblical interpretation by focusing on key artists (Louis Armstrong, Duke Ellington, John Coltrane, and Sun Ra) as well as the subgenre known as sacred jazz. The next three chapters focus broadly on comic art, beginning with Elizabeth Rae Coody's examination of comic books and graphic novels. She deftly surveys how "comics in America engage the Bible" as well as "the biblical and secular and religious understandings of the Bible," analyzing how nonbiblical comics treat the miracles of Jesus. Next, Scott Elliott discusses the "visual narratology" of graphic Bibles—works that render biblical stories into the medium of (most often sequential) comic art—by investigating four modern graphic adaptations: *Testament*, *The Manga Bible*, *The Action Bible*, and *The Lion Comic Book Hero Bible*. This triad of comic art chapters concludes with Leonard Greenspoon's exploration of newspaper comic strips and how they depict the divine, render specific Bible texts, and situate themselves as sites of religious controversy. This section concludes with the chapters by Katja Rakow and Rachel Wagner, mentioned earlier.

Since, as I (Dan) recounted at the outset of this introduction, the relationship of the Bible and American popular culture is a dynamic one that plays out in real time in public settings, we felt it was important to include a section on lived and performative examples. In addition to my (Dan's) chapter on "Participatory Fan Cultures," in which I explore cosplay and Filipino Holy Week practices, there are excellent entries from James Bielo and Valarie Ziegler. Based on firsthand field research, Bielo sees the Ark Encounter in Kentucky as an example of the phenomenon of theme parks buttressed by the ideology of "the modern creationist movement." Ziegler too focuses on the Ark Encounter, but she considers it from the vantage point of a "creation museum" that puts "young-earth creationism" ideology on display and as such functions as a kind of "pilgrimage site" for creationists.

We decided to conclude this *Handbook* with three metachapters that we're calling "The State of the Field" (in full recognition that by the time this *Handbook* is published the "field" will probably have an entirely new "state"!). In his chapter on methodologies,

Scott Langston discusses the pitfalls and profits of methods scholars have used to examine Bible and popular culture. Langston doesn't advocate any specific approach but illustrates the utility of a popular method called "reception history" by showing how it can be used to examine "Gilded Age– and Progressive Era picture postcards of the Ten Commandments." Jane S. Webster addresses the practical issue of pedagogy and outlines a "backwards design" model of course construction that incorporates an engagement with Bible and popular culture as a way to capture student interest and demonstrate the ongoing relevance of Bible. Finally, Robert Paul Seesengood discusses the issue of publishing in his chapter and surveys the impact of works on Bible and popular culture on academic publishing focused on biblical studies.

In addition to this macro-organization of the *Handbook*, we tried to provide a useful framework for each author's work, a common structure or paradigm for each analysis. So each chapter consists of five sections: an introduction; an overview of the topic (which includes a brief history of inquiry along with definitional and methodological issues); specific example(s) and/or foci (which can include original research that demonstrates how scholarly investigation in this field is performed and also the significance of such research); future prospects and questions; and suggested readings with an annotated bibliography. Again, it should be obvious that our goal is usefulness, i.e., by making the volume more internally coherent we hope to avoid a common pitfall of volumes of this length: they can veer into disjointedness. Also, and more important, a microstructure of this kind will make the volume more accessible to neophyte readers, for whom this specialized field might be daunting. This concern is precisely why we asked authors to include the final two components in their essays; by identifying future prospects, authors can demonstrate to readers that there's still work to be done in a given area, and the additional questions prod readers to think critically about how *they* can contribute to the field. Similarly, we asked authors to compile a list of four or five key sources with annotations so that interested readers could follow up on the work in a given chapter. In this way, we hope this *Handbook* serves as an invitation to the reader to engage the incredible variety of popular cultural examples and dialogue with the erudite yet accessible scholarship displayed by the talented authors represented herein.

As we said, we never viewed this *Handbook* as exhaustive; we knew going in that we wouldn't be able to cover every topic we wanted to cover. At the same time, we came to recognize the additional limitations based on the availability and interest of relevant experts and learned that such is the challenge of recruiting for and editing any such volume. What this means practically is that the *Handbook* we originally envisioned isn't exactly the one we ended up with. That's the case with any large project. However, we're extremely proud of the finished product and grateful for the hard work of all of our authors, and we hope that readers are enthused and excited enough after engaging their terrific and *useful* work to launch out on work of their own.

PART II

BIBLICAL CHARACTERS IN POPULAR CULTURE

CHAPTER 1

THE IMPACT OF ADAM AND EVE ON POPULAR CULTURE'S UNDERSTANDINGS OF WOMEN'S ROLES AND EVOLUTION

THERESA M. SANDERS
DEPARTMENT OF THEOLOGY AND RELIGIOUS STUDIES, GEORGETOWN UNIVERSITY

INTRODUCTION

ADAM and Eve are everywhere. The first biblical couple shows up in movies,[1] television shows,[2] comic strips,[3] comic books,[4] novels,[5] advertisements,[6] and pop music.[7] An online search for their names yields millions of hits (many for erotic toys and clothing),

---

[1] See Theresa Sanders, "In the Beginning: Adam and Eve in Film," in *The Bible in Motion*, ed. Rhonda Burnette Bletsch (Boston: De Gruyter, 2016), 17–34.

[2] See, for example, the opening credits of *Desperate Housewives*, USA, ABC, 2004–12).

[3] A classic example is Whitney Darrow Jr.'s cartoon in *The New Yorker* on March 9, 1957.

[4] R. Crumb, *The Book of Genesis Illustrated by R. Crumb* (New York: W. W. Norton, 2009).

[5] Recent novels include William Paul Young, *Eve: A Novel* (New York: Howard Books, 2015); Gioconda Belli, *Infinity in the Palm of Her Hand*, trans. Margaret Sayers (New York: HarperCollins, 2010); and Elissa Elliott, *Eve: A Novel* (New York: Bantam, 2009).

[6] See Katie B. Edwards, *Admen and Eve: The Bible in Contemporary Advertising* (Sheffield, UK: Sheffield Phoenix Press, 2012).

[7] Songs include Pink's "Leave Me Alone" (2006); 10,000 Maniacs' "Cherry Tree" (1987); Bob Marley's "Adam and Eve" (1970); Elvis Presley's "Adam and Evil" (1966); and Bob Dylan's "Talkin' World War III Blues" (1963).

and the two stand at the center of heated debates about sexual ethics, marriage, and how science should be taught in public schools. In short, Adam and Eve are as popular as ever.

As the Bible's first man and woman, Adam and Eve serve as proxies for ongoing discussions about what it means to be a person or to be a woman or to be a man. They teach us how we should interact with animals and with the environment and what significance work has. They illustrate the struggle that we (seemingly alone among all other species) have with moral decision-making, and they show us the perils of the quest for knowledge. They show us why we fear death and why we fear each other. By telling us where we came from, they tell us who we are.

The problem with all of this, however, is that the biblical story is structurally complicated and linguistically sophisticated. Versions in English differ widely, and scholars argue vehemently about how to translate particular words.[8] Moreover, even if everyone could agree on how to render the text in English, there are radical differences of opinion regarding how to *interpret* the story. For example, in Genesis 3:16, after the man and woman have eaten the forbidden fruit, God says to the woman, "Your desire shall be for your husband, and he shall rule over you." When God speaks these words, is God explaining what *should* happen (in other words, what God wants), or is God merely explaining the consequences of the couple's disobedience? The nineteenth-century abolitionist and suffragette Sarah Grimké thought the latter. She opined, "Our translators having been accustomed to exercise lordship over their wives, and seeing only through the medium of a perverted judgment, very naturally, though I think not very learnedly or very kindly, translated it *shall* instead of *will*, and thus converted a prediction to Eve into a command to Adam."[9]

Still further questions arise regarding the genre of the story. For some, Genesis 1–3 is the inerrant word of God; it was spoken by God to humans, and God expects us to believe that the world came about precisely as the story says it does. For others, the story is an ancient tale that represents the worldview of a primitive people; it is no more relevant than the belief that the earth is flat, or that, as the atheist biologist Richard Dawkins puts it, "the moon is an old calabash tossed into the sky, hanging only just out of reach above the treetops."[10] For still others the story is a profound mythic exploration of the meaning of human life; it does not explain how we came to be, but it gives voice to existential truths.

---

[8] For a summary of varying translations of Gen 2:4–4:2, see Kristen E. Kvam, Linda S. Schearing, and Valarie H. Ziegler, *Eve and Adam* (Bloomington: Indiana University Press, 1999), 26–38. See also Phyllis Trible, *God and the Rhetoric of Sexuality* (Philadelphia: Fortress, 1978), 72–143; Robert Alter, *Genesis* (New York: W. W. Norton, 1996); and Mary Phil Korsak, *At the Start: Genesis Made New* (New York: Doubleday, 1992).

[9] Sarah Grimké, *Letters on the Equality of the Sexes, and the Condition of Woman* (Boston: Isaac Knapp, 1838), 7.

[10] Richard Dawkins, *River Out of Eden* (New York: Basic Books, 1995), 31.

In other words, the story of Adam and Eve endures precisely because it is so difficult to determine what it means. It is a strange tale that raises more questions than it answers, and thus it mirrors and models the strangeness of being human. We are not simple creatures, and we do not live simple lives. The story of our origins should capture, and does capture, the messy complications of that fact. An origin story that were any less complex would not have the enduring relevance that Genesis does.

OVERVIEW OF TOPIC

There are two areas in particular where the biblical couple show up again and again in popular culture. The first is society's continual rethinking of the role of women, and the second is the ongoing dispute between evolutionary biologists and creationists (those who believe that the world and its creatures came into existence precisely as the Bible says they did). Before we can address those two issues, however, it is necessary first to figure out what precisely we mean when we talk about "the story of Adam and Eve." Most biblical scholars contend that Genesis 2–3 (the story of the Garden of Eden) was written by an author called "the Jahwist" between the tenth and sixth century BCE. By contrast, even though it appears earlier in the Bible, Genesis 1 was probably written by the "Priestly" author, quite possibly as a response to and an alternative version of what the Jahwist had written.[11] And yet many interpreters, particularly moviemakers, tend to conflate the two stories.[12]

Likewise, most popular uses of the story end with God's casting the couple out of Eden; they neglect to mention the births of Adam and Eve's children in Genesis 4:1–2 and 4:25, and they leave out the death of Adam, which takes place in Genesis 5:3–5. Interestingly, stories about Adam's last days figured prominently in antiquity and up through the Middle Ages, but they are virtually absent in popular presentations today.[13] Like popular culture itself, then, we will concern ourselves here primarily with Genesis 2:4–3:24. That is, we will focus on the creation of the first two people, their disobedience, and their expulsion from Eden.

---

[11] On the question of biblical authorship, see Richard Elliott Friedman, *Who Wrote the Bible?* (New York: Harper Collins, 1989). As Friedman notes, the J author uses the name Yahweh or Jehovah for God (24). Friedman also explains that the man most responsible for the contemporary idea that the first five books of the Bible were written by four different authors is Julius Wellhausen (1844–1918). See Friedman, 25–7.

[12] For example, *The Bible . . . In the Beginning*, directed by John Huston, USA, Italy, 1966, jumps from Gen 1:26 ("Let us make man") to 2:7 ("The Lord God formed man") and then back to 1:27 ("So God created man in his own image").

[13] See Brian Murdoch, *The Apocryphal Adam and Eve in Medieval Europe: Vernacular Translations and Adaptations of the* Vita Adae et Evae (New York: Oxford University Press, 2009).

Specific Examples and/or Foci

For the most part, when movies, songs, and advertisements address the disobedience of the first couple, all eyes turn to one figure: Eve. Katie B. Edwards observes that "for popular culture and for so many interpreters over the centuries, Eve is the star of the story."[14] Eve is the site where battles are waged over women's roles in society at large, in the home, and in the intimacy of the bedroom.

Indeed, in the Bible itself, one of the most difficult passages to translate describes the creation of Eve. Genesis 2:18 tells us, "Then the LORD God said, 'It is not good that the man should be alone; I will make him a helper as his partner.'"[15] However, the words "helper as his partner" can be translated in any number of ways, including "a partner suited to him," "a power equal to man," and "a helper against him."[16] One ancient Jewish commentator, reflecting on 2:18, opined that if a man is fortunate in his mate, then "she is a help; if not, she is against him."[17] The medieval Jewish scholar Rashi put responsibility for the woman's role on the man, commenting, "If he is worthy she shall be a help to him; if he is unworthy she shall be opposed to him, to fight him."[18] The difficulty of translating and interpreting the text is mirrored in the difficulty of determining women's "rightful place" in society.

As far back as the 1920s, the question of Eve's relation to Adam (and thus woman's relation to man) was being explored in the movies. Howard Hawks's silent film *Fig Leaves* (1926) is something of a classic that relies on traditional gender norms to make its point. Its opening sequence is set in the distant past ("896 or 7 million years" ago, explain the on-screen titles) and portrays the life of Adam and Eve in the Garden of Eden. We first see the couple in their beds, asleep; Eve then wakes Adam from his slumbers by throwing a coconut at his head and asking, "How do you expect to amount to anything if you don't get up in the morning?" After Eve preens herself while looking at her reflection in a water basin, she gets dressed. The screen informs us, "In the beginning, Woman had three problems: 'I haven't a thing to wear.' 'I haven't a thing to wear.' 'I haven't a thing to wear.' " At the breakfast table, Eve tries to cajole Adam into giving her money for a new fig leaf, but he refuses: "Ever since you ate that apple you've had the gimmies—first twin beds and now it's clothes." The argument ends only when a Stegosaurus-drawn commuter train arrives, and Adam rushes off to work. As he boards the conveyance, he demands that a female passenger give up her seat to him. Miffed, the passenger grumbles to a companion, "Mark my words, dearie—someday we'll get our rights." The com-

---

[14] Edwards, *Admen and Eve*, 65.

[15] Unless otherwise specified, all English translations are taken from the New Revised Standard Version.

[16] Kvam, Schearing, and Ziegler, *Eve and Adam*, 28.

[17] H. Freedman and Maurice Simon, trans. and eds., *Midrash Rabbah: Genesis 1* (London: Soncino, 1951), 133.

[18] Rashi [Shlomo ben Yitzhaki], "Commentary on the Pentateuch," in Kvam, Schearing, and Ziegler, *Eve and Adam*, 209.

ment must have seemed to audiences like a wry joke, as women's right to vote in the United States had been ratified only a few years earlier, in 1920.

In the next scene, a serpent arrives at the house to gossip with Eve. The action then shifts to the present day; the serpent has become a slinky blonde neighbor named Alice, Adam has become a plumber, and Eve is a housewife who is still dissatisfied with her wardrobe. Alice visits Eve, and as Eve bites into an apple, Alice tells her, "My advice to you is to get all the pretty clothes you want, regardless of Adam." Meanwhile, down at the plumbing shop, Adam's coworker also has advice to offer; he tells Adam the best way to handle acquisitive wives: "Treat 'em rough—but don't kill 'em; you might want her for somethin' someday."

Soon after, Eve approaches Adam and explains that she wants to get a job. His response: "Don't be silly—no wife of mine can ever work." And yet despite Adam's warnings, Eve *does* get a job—as a fashion model, no less. In doing so she threatens Adam's economic superiority as well as his control of her body. After he sees his wife modeling skimpy negligees, Adam complains to Eve, "Every man's right is to respect his wife and not have her parade around half naked. You cared more for clothes than you did for me." He is upset both by the thought that she is not dependent on him for money and by the thought that she might offer herself sexually to another man. As Jeanne Thomas Allen observes, the movie's comedy "is based on gender stereotypes and the threat of role reversal... female greed exceeding patriarchal loyalty."[19] By the end of the movie, all is forgiven and Eve and Adam are together again. However, Eve is still complaining that she has nothing to wear, and thus audiences know that the battle will continue.

Fig Leaves is only one of many explorations of women's roles in both the home and the workplace. Perhaps the smartest and most amusing rehearsal of the "battle of the sexes" is the 1949 comedy *Adam's Rib*, which stars Katharine Hepburn and Spencer Tracy. In the film, Hepburn and Tracy play Amanda and Adam Bonner, two lawyers who wholeheartedly enjoy being married to each other. They are attractive, sophisticated, and witty, and their affection for one another is obvious.

All goes well for the couple until they end up on different sides of the same trial. The case involves a woman who shot her husband when she found him in the arms of his mistress. Amanda has herself appointed as counsel for the defense and argues that her client is being unfairly punished. After all, says Amanda, if the roles were reversed and a man had shot his adulterous wife, society would merely shrug its collective shoulders and not bother prosecuting; they would think that the unfaithful woman deserved what she got. Why is there a double standard? Why is it more acceptable for a husband to avenge his spouse's infidelity than for a wife to do so? Why are men held to lower standards when it comes to the use of violence, and women held to higher standards when it comes to sexual purity? Declares Amanda, "For years, women have been ridiculed, pampered, chucked under the chin. I ask you, on behalf of us all, be fair to the fair sex."

---

[19] Jeanne Thomas Allen, "*Fig Leaves* in Hollywood: Female Representation and Consumer Culture," in *Fabrications: Costume and the Female Body*, ed. Jane Gaines and Charlotte Herzog (New York: Routledge, 1990), 124, 128.

Adam does not buy his wife's argument that justice discriminates against women. "The law is the law, whether it's good or bad," he counters. Predictably, as the trial progresses, it begins to disrupt the Bonners' happy household. What had seemed a marriage of equals is now tested by hidden assumptions about the roles of husband and wife. At one point Amanda calls to the stand several female witnesses, including a scientist, a factory supervisor, and a circus performer, in order to show that women can be just as intelligent, hardworking, and strong as men. That evening, irritated by his wife's courtroom strategies, Adam complains, "Just what blow you've struck for women's rights or what have you, I'm sure I don't know. But you certainly have fouled us up beyond all recognition." He continues, "I'm old-fashioned. I like *two* sexes! Yeah, and another thing, all of a sudden I don't like being married to what is known as a new woman. I want a wife, not a competitor.... If you want to be a big he-woman, go and be it—but not with me!"

Like *Fig Leaves, Adam's Rib* is a comedy, and so a happy outcome is guaranteed from the start. Toward the end of the film, just when divorce seems imminent, Adam uses tears to win Amanda's sympathy and to convince her to give the marriage another chance. When he later reveals that his crying was a ruse ("Oh yes. There ain't any of us don't have our little tricks, you know!"), Amanda takes this as evidence that she was right all along: "What I said was true. There's no difference between the sexes. Men. Women. The same." Adam demurs, and so Amanda concedes, "Well, maybe there is a difference, but it's a little difference." At this point Adam puts on a roguish smile and, drawing the bed curtains closed around himself and his wife, says, "Well, you know, as the French say... *Vive la difference!*...Hurray for that little difference!"

Thus the movie ends without really solving the riddle of how men and women ought to negotiate the tricky and treacherous path between them. It asserts an equality without specifying how that can be achieved and without pretending that it can be easily maintained. Indeed, in one of the final scenes, when Adam announces with pride that he has been asked to run for a county court judgeship on the Republican ticket, Amanda congratulates him but then asks slyly, "Adam—Have they picked the, uh, Democratic candidate yet? I was just wondering." Like the Genesis story itself, the ending of *Adam's Rib* opens up more questions than it resolves. In doing so it reflects the ongoing struggle to define precisely what it means for the woman to be the man's "helper."

Questions about Eve's relation to Adam, and women's rightful relation to men, remain contentious to this day. No less contentious are debates about how to read the Genesis story as a whole. Is it history? Science? Myth? The publication of Charles Darwin's *On the Origin of Species* in 1859 brought a crisis in biblical interpretation because it argued that animal species had not been created directly by the hand of God but rather had evolved over time. The publication of Darwin's *The Descent of Man* in 1871 went further and suggested that not only animals but humans themselves had evolved from earlier life forms. The possibility that people were not specially created as the crown of God's creation but had emerged through a process of natural selection sent shockwaves through Bible-believing American culture, and these shockwaves continue to this day.

One of the most famous and most important confrontations in the long-running argument about human origins was the 1925 court battle known as the Scopes Monkey

Trial. When John T. Scopes agreed to contest the Tennessee law that forbade the teaching of evolution in public schools, he had no idea what he was getting himself into. The football coach and substitute biology teacher later admitted that he was not even sure that he had ever actually taught Darwin to his students.[20] Nonetheless the case became a turning point in American history. On the one hand, it provided a staging area for many of the cultural skirmishes that had been taking place for decades. On the other, it provided fuel for conflicts that would last all the way into the twenty-first century.

The Monkey Trial was as much theater as it was a legal battle. Media flocked to the small town of Dayton, Tennessee to witness the spectacle, which pitted the famous Christian politician William Jennings Bryan against the equally famous agnostic Clarence Darrow. Special telephone and telegraph wires were installed so that reporters could transmit their stories, and a radio network was set up so that listeners around the nation could follow the court's proceedings. The Scopes affair was the first time in American history that a trial was broadcast in real time.

Near the Dayton courthouse vendors sold stuffed monkeys while musicians performed songs written specially for the occasion, including one titled "You Can't Make a Monkey Out of Me." The owner of a drug store in Dayton dressed a chimp in a three-piece suit, complete with polka-dot bow tie, fedora, and white spats, and had him sip sodas alongside the human customers. Other chimps were dressed in specially tailored soldiers' costumes and marched in formation carrying toy rifles; still others performed on piano and banjo while amused crowds looked on.[21]

Meanwhile comedians and satirists took full advantage of the occasion. A cartoon in the *Nashville Tennessean* showed two monkeys reading a newspaper filled with headlines about cruelty to animals, auto accidents, child labor, murder, alcohol abuse, and short skirts for women. The monkeys in the cartoon worried that their reputation would be sullied by Darwin's associating them with human beings. In New Jersey, members of a local Rotary Club staged a mock version of the trial in which the judge used a monkey wrench for a gavel; the hearing broke up when a man dressed as an ape appeared in the courtroom and leaped from table to table. In London, a newspaper held a contest to see who could write the best limerick about the trial. The ten-dollar prize was awarded to a poem that questioned the intelligence of people in Tennessee by speculating that perhaps monkeys were evolved from humans rather than the other way around.[22]

In popular culture, the actual proceedings of the Scopes trial (which ended with Scopes's being found guilty, though the fine imposed by the court was never paid) have been practically eclipsed by Hollywood's portrayal of the famous conflict. The most

[20] John T. Scopes, *Center of the Storm* (New York: Holt, Rinehart and Winston, 1967), 60.

[21] To hear a recording of "You Can't Make a Monkey Out of Me" and other songs about the Scopes trial, see "Monkey Trial," *American Experience*, PBS, accessed May 17, 2017, http://www.pbs.org/wgbh/americanexperience/monkeytrial/sfeature/sf_music.html. See also Edward Caudill, *The Scopes Trial: A Photographic History* (Knoxville: University of Tennessee Press, 2000), 48–9.

[22] "English Versifiers Contest on a Scopes Trial Limerick," special cable to the *New York Times*, July 26, 1925.

influential of these portrayals is the 1960 movie *Inherit the Wind*, which was based on a play written by Jerome Lawrence and Robert E. Lee.

Despite the similarities between the Scopes trial and *Inherit the Wind*, the authors of the play were clear when they published the drama that they were not presenting history. In their introduction, Lawrence and Lee stated, "*Inherit the Wind* does not pretend to be journalism. It is theatre. It is not 1925. The stage directions set the time as 'Not too long ago.' It might have been yesterday. It could be tomorrow."[23] The director of the 1960 film, Stanley Kramer, echoed this sentiment and remarked that he was not concerned with the past so much as with the present. When the movie was released he issued a statement in which he explained, "The spirit of the trial lives on, because the real issues of that trial were man's right to think and man's right to teach. These are issues for which the never-ending struggle continues and they constitute the real theme of *Inherit the Wind*."[24] Years later Kramer reiterated his position: "To me at least, the whole story is about freedom of expression, its importance in our society and the challenges to it."[25]

Seen as a vehicle to promote the sacredness of human inquiry and expression, *Inherit the Wind* is spectacularly successful. As the burly agnostic lawyer Henry Drummond (the movie's counterpart to Darrow), Spencer Tracy is powerful and compelling. During the trial Drummond argues that there is nothing holier than the human mind and that "an idea is a greater monument than a cathedral." Questioning Matthew Harrison Brady (the film's version of Bryan) on the witness stand, he demands, "Why do you deny the one faculty of man that raises him above the other creatures of the earth: the power of his brain to reason!" When Brady counters that the Bible should be trusted because God "spake" it, Drummond retorts, "How do you know that God didn't spake to Charles Darwin?"

The very last scene of the film attempts to enact a reconciliation of sorts between evolutionary theory and creationist views. After the trial has ended, when Drummond is gathering his belongings, he picks up a copy of Darwin's book from the defendant's table. Then he spies his copy of the Bible lying there as well, and he picks that up too. Drummond seems to muse to himself, and then he places the Bible squarely on top of Darwin and carries both books from the courtroom.

If the ending of the movie is meant to suggest that Darwinism is compatible with Scripture, then the founder of the Creation Museum in Petersburg, Kentucky, would respectfully disagree.[26] Ken Ham, who also founded the online ministry called Answers in Genesis, has devoted his life to promoting a literal reading of Genesis. His museum was designed to be "a rallying place, calling people back to the absolute truth of the Bible.

[23] Jerome Lawrence and Robert E. Lee, *Inherit the Wind* (New York: Bantam, 1955), preface.

[24] Stanley Kramer, quoted in Donald Spoto, *Stanley Kramer: Film Maker* (Hollywood, CA: Samuel French, 1978), 223.

[25] Stanley Kramer, *A Mad, Mad, Mad, Mad World: A Life in Hollywood* (New York: Harcourt Brace, 1997), 174.

[26] For more on the Creation Museum, see Valarie Ziegler's essay in this volume.

It is a place of revival, a starting point for a new reformation."[27] It sees itself as fighting a battle against the powers of secularism and godless evolution.

By many measures, it is succeeding wildly; in its first year it drew 400,000 visitors, and by 2015 nearly 2.5 million people had walked through its doors.[28] In 2016 it opened a "sister attraction" called Ark Encounter in nearby Williamstown, Kentucky.[29] The Ark Encounter "features a full-size Noah's Ark, built according to the dimensions given in the Bible. Spanning 510 feet long, 85 feet wide, and 51 feet high, this modern engineering marvel amazes visitors young and old."[30] Like the Creation Museum, the second park is built on the premise that the Bible is inerrant. Also like the Creation Museum, it features dinosaurs.

Dinosaurs are, in fact, one of the Creation Museum's biggest draws and are featured prominently in its advertisements and promotional materials. A bumper sticker sold in the museum's bookstore proclaims, "We're Taking Dinosaurs Back!" Though it does not say precisely from whom the dinosaurs are being recovered, the implication is that they are being reclaimed from secular science so that they can take their rightful place in a biblically based worldview.

Dinosaurs, according to the museum, actually lived in peace with Adam and Eve in the Garden of Eden. So why, then, does the Bible not mention them? An informational display inside the museum explains that God created dinosaurs to be among "the beasts of the earth" described in Genesis 1:25. The reptiles lived in harmony with the first people and, because they were vegetarians, with the other animals as well. When God decided to flood the world, pairs of dinosaurs were taken aboard Noah's ark. All of those not on the ark died in the ensuing flood, and this accounts for the many fossil remains that we find today. The dinosaurs that were aboard the ark, as well as their offspring, eventually died out due to disease and starvation after the Flood.[31] Thus, though they do not inhabit our world, says the museum, they roamed the world of Adam and Eve. And thus visitors to the museum roam among animatronic dinosaurs.

Visitors are also presented with the museum's vision of how contemporary culture has forsaken God and chosen sin instead. This idea is most graphically displayed in a section of the museum called "Graffiti Alley." In the Alley, one comes across a brick wall papered over with images of warfare, school shootings, gay marriages, and right-to-die

---

[27] "Answers in Genesis," Creation Museum, accessed February 17, 2009, https://assets.answersingenesis.org/doc/articles/2009/05/creation-museum-rack-brochure.pdf.

[28] Susan L. Trollinger and William Vance Trollinger, *Righting America at the Creation Museum* (Baltimore, MD: Johns Hopkins University Press, 2016), 13.

[29] For an analysis of the Ark Encounter as a performative phenomenon and in the context of other theme parks, see James S. Bielo's essay in this volume.

[30] "About the Ark," Ark Encounter, accessed May 23, 2017, https://arkencounter.com/about. Ham has recently announced plans to build a walled city resembling one from the time of Noah, and a village from the time of Jesus. See Karen Heller, "Envisioning a Flood of Guests," *Washington Post*, May 25, 2017, C1.

[31] Aside from the exhibits at the museum, see also Ken Ham, "Dinosaurs and the Bible," Answers in Genesis, November 5, 1999, https://answersingenesis.org/dinosaurs/dinosaurs-and-the-bible/.

legislation. A sign nearby declares, "Scripture Abandoned in the Culture Leads to ... Relative Morality, Hopelessness, and Meaninglessness."[32]

After passing through Graffiti Alley, visitors enter a Time Tunnel that takes them back six thousand years, to the dawn of the universe. The tunnel leads to a small theater in which a short movie portrays the six days of creation described in the first chapter of Genesis. Following the film, one can exit the theater and enter the Garden of Eden. A life-size Adam, with thick hair and a full beard, kneels under a tree with one arm around a lamb and the other reaching out toward a lioness. Penguins, apes, and a bear loiter nearby, and dinosaurs graze not far off. A sign explains that though Adam was given the job of naming the animals by God, he did not have to name every animal that existed but only "birds, cattle, and beasts of the field," the last of which probably referred to animals that had close associations with humans. Naming these few hundred animals would have taken a few hours at most, according to the sign.

A few feet further along the pathway through Eden stands an exhibit that shows the newly created Eve, whom God made from Adam's rib. Like her man, Eve too has thick dark hair, but she wears it long so as to cover her naked breasts. In one display, Eve and Adam stand in a pool below a waterfall with the lower parts of their bodies covered by pond lilies. They seem to look fondly at each other, and they gesture toward one another with what appears to be affection. A sign states that the creation of Adam and Eve "is the foundation for marriage: one man and one woman."[33]

Sin then rears its ugly head, quite literally. The serpent as depicted in the museum is a devilish-looking reptile with red scaly horns and blazing green eyes. The serpent questions God's word by asking, "Has God really said you shall not eat of every tree of the garden?" It convinces Eve to sin, and she in turn convinces Adam to eat from the forbidden tree. What they eat is not the usual apple but a berry-like fruit that grows in clusters.

The result of Eve and Adam's actions is the world's first death; God kills an animal in order to make garments of skin for the couple. Ever since then, says the museum, humans have lived with pain and toil, and they have faced the inevitability of death. Before the first sin, signs explain, there was no burdensome work. As a result of sin, however, we all have to contend with weeds, blight, poor soil, labor pains, and natural disasters. All of this will be wiped away, though, with the advent of the Last Adam, Jesus Christ. A short film near the end of the exhibit, just before one reaches the museum's chapel, shows how Jesus is the answer to the destruction wrought by Adam and Eve.

Though the Creation Museum attempts to provide visitors with a unified message regarding the Bible's truth, it actually conveys a complicated and ambivalent assessment of our origins. Again, the story of Eden is not simple, and neither is the museum's presentation of it. Its exploration of Genesis 1–3 actually (though perhaps unconsciously) enacts the internal fissure that many people experience when they try to reconcile their faith with their reason, or their religion with their scientific beliefs.

---

[32] *Questioning Darwin*, directed by Antony Thomas, USA, HBO, 2014, 5:45.
[33] Trollinger and Trollinger, *Righting America at the Creation Museum*, 166.

That is to say, throughout its exhibits, the museum consistently preaches that one should trust God's Word over human reason. For example, one sign presents a choice: while reason says that the universe began with the Big Bang billions of years ago, God's word says that God created Heaven and Earth in six days and that creation took place only thousands of years ago. Which authority, asks the sign, should people believe? Another exhibit contrasts scientific reason, which says that humans evolved from an ape that lived twenty million years ago, with God's word, which says that God created people in God's image six thousand years ago. Again, visitors are asked to choose what to believe, but the correct answer is clear. "God's Word is True," proclaims a sign. "Forty authors, writing over two thousand years, spoke the SAME MESSAGE."

However, oddly, the museum buttresses its assertions about God's truth not only by appeals to faith but also by appeals to science. One poster explains that the settling of the earth's rock layers after Noah's Flood is the cause of the earthquakes that we experience today. Another contends that the different nationalities and languages that we have on earth now can be accounted for by God's scattering of the citizens of Babel in Genesis 11:1–9. Still another demonstrates how God must have provided special tools to organisms after the Flood so that they could diversify rapidly.

All of this raises a question: If one should choose the Bible over reason, why would one try to use reason to demonstrate the truth of the Bible? The answer seems to be that the Creation Museum is well aware that there are many skeptics in the world who will want to have their reason satisfied. The museum's "Main Theme and Vision Statement" explains, "Throughout this family-friendly experience, visitors will learn how to answer the attacks on the Bible's authority in geology, biology, anthropology, cosmology, etc. They will also discover how science actually confirms biblical history, and be challenged to consider how the first 11 chapters of Genesis—the first book in the Bible—addresses modern cultural issues such as racism, same-sex marriage and abortion."[34] Thus the appeal to science accomplishes several ends. First, it allows Christians to evangelize more effectively because the faithful will have answers to the questions that skeptics ask. Second, it seems to be a way to give credibility to the Bible. Third, it provides ammunition for the war against what the museum sees as the evils of modern culture. Reason, then, seems to be both a danger to faith and a tool to promote it.

This same ambivalent approach to faith and reason arose when the Creation Museum's founder debated the science educator Bill Nye ("the Science Guy") at the Creation Museum in 2014. The debate was live-streamed on the internet and drew over half a million simultaneous viewers.[35] Titled "Is Creation a Viable Model of Origins?"

---

[34] http://www.creationmuseumnews.com/docs/vision_mission.pdf; site currently inaccessible.
[35] Alan Boyle, "Who Won Bill Nye's Big Evolution Faceoff?," *NBC News*, February 5, 2014, http://www.nbcnews.com/science/science-news/who-won-bill-nyes-big-evolution-faceoff-n22076. A Christian public relations firm estimated that about three million people watched the debate. See Stoyan Zaimov, "Bill Nye, Ken Ham Discuss Humans and Dinosaurs with Piers Morgan: Reactions to Creationist Debate," *Christian Post*, February 5, 2014, http://www.christianpost.com/news/bill-nye-ken-ham-discuss-humans-and-dinosaurs-with-piers-morgan-reactions-to-creationist-debate-114043/.

the confrontation between Ham and Nye showed the different starting points taken by the two. Ham made his position clear: "You see, the battle is really about authority. It's more than just science or evolution or creation. It's about who is the authority in this world—man or God?" He continued, "If you start with naturalism then what about morals? Who decides right and wrong? Well, it's subjective.... We do see the collapse of Christian morality in our culture and increasing moral relativism because generations of kids are being taught the religion of naturalism and that the Bible can't be trusted."[36] Nye, on the other hand, preferred to trust his own senses and intellect rather than religious belief. He countered, "So your view, that we're supposed to take your word for, this book [the Bible], written centuries ago, translated into American English, is somehow more important than what I can see with my own eyes, is an extraordinary claim."[37]

Toward the end of the debate, when Ham was asked by the discussion's moderator what would get him to change his mind, his response was telling: "Well, the answer to that question is I'm a Christian.... The Bible is the word of God. I admit that that's where I start from.... As far as the word of God is concerned, no, no one's ever going to convince me that the word of God is not true."[38] Remarkably, though, much of the material that Ham presented during the nearly three-hour conversation concerned scientific findings. In fact, at the very start of his presentation, he stated, "We're seeing people being indoctrinated to believe that creationists can't be scientists. I believe it's all a part of secularists hijacking the word 'science.'"[39] He then showed a video clip of a creationist scientist who says that he finds creationism to be perfectly compatible with scientific evidence.

For his part, Nye, the scientist, expressed a deep appreciation of religion, though not creationist belief. Observed Nye, "Now I just want to remind us all: there are billions of people in the world who are deeply religious, who get enriched by the wonderful sense of community from their religion. They worship together, they eat together, they live in their communities and enjoy each other's company. Billions of people. But these same people do not embrace the extraordinary view that the earth is somehow only six thousand years old." Later he reiterated, "There are billions of people in the world who are deeply religious, and I respect that. People get tremendous community and comfort and nurture and support from their religious fellows, and their communities, in their faiths, in their churches, and yet they don't accept your [Ham's] point of view."[40] Both men, in sum, did their best to integrate faith with science. Whether or not they succeeded, both attempted on the one hand to respect religion and on the other to value the intellectual capacity that makes humans unique among all species. Their debate thus mirrored and enacted the story of Eden itself. After all, the first couple is warned by God not to eat from the Tree of Knowledge of Good and Evil, but knowledge proves to be too great a

---

[36] Ken Ham and Bodie Hodge, *Inside the Nye Ham Debate: Revealing Truths from the Worldview Clash of the Century* (Green Forest, AR: Master Books, 2014), 313, 314.

[37] "Bill Nye Debates Ken Ham," YouTube, February 4, 2014, https://www.youtube.com/watch?v=z6k gvhG3AkI&feature=youtu.be&t=13m14s, 1:49:08.

[38] Ibid., 2:04:09–2:05:30.   [39] Ibid., 17:53.   [40] Ibid., 26:16 and 1:47:16.

lure, and the couple choose to eat. Ham and Nye, and society itself, continue to wrestle with the same choice.

FUTURE PROSPECTS AND QUESTIONS

- How do readings of Genesis 2–3 affect how we interact with the environment and with animals?
- If, in the not too distant future, intelligent life is discovered in other parts of the universe, how will that affect readings of Genesis 2–3, in which humans have a special role in God's creation?
- In cartoons and ads, Adam and Eve are often shorthand for "man" and "woman." As gender roles in society change, how will those shorthand expressions change?
- In the second season of the television show *The Handmaid's Tale* (Hulu, 2017–), a character named "Eden" is introduced, and the story of Adam and Eve is invoked to support a repressive regime.[41] How similar to or different from traditional interpretations of Genesis 1–3 is this show's use of the story? Additionally, numerous viewers of the television show *Westworld* (HBO, 2016–) see connections between the sci-fi series and the story of Adam and Eve.[42] How does the show call into question what it means to be human and to be made in the image of God?

SUGGESTED READINGS AND ANNOTATED BIBLIOGRAPHY

Edwards, Katie B. *Admen and Eve: The Bible in Contemporary Advertising*. Sheffield, UK: Sheffield Phoenix Press, 2012.

As its title suggests, this book focuses on uses of Eve in advertising. Edwards writes, "Eve now functions as contemporary popular culture's pin-up girl for postfeminist female consumer power" (1) and argues that "postfeminist advertising promotes a kind of pseudo-liberation for female consumers" (10). Among the examples of popular culture that Edwards addresses are the 2004 *America's Next Top Model* competition in which models were dressed as various incarnations of Eve, and the advertising associated with the hit television show *Desperate Housewives* (2004–12).

Feiler, Bruce. *The First Love Story: Adam, Eve, and Us*. New York: Penguin, 2017.

Feiler calls Adam and Eve "the ultimate meme" (11). His primary focus is the relationship of love that he sees between the biblical couple, but his analysis of that theme leads him to explore the Sistine Chapel, Milton's *Paradise Lost*, Mae West's radio impersonation of Eve, the character of Lilith (who, according to some legends, was Adam's first wife), and more.

---

[41] See especially the episode titled "Seeds," directed by Mike Barker, originally aired May 16, 2018.

[42] See, for example, Matthew Meyer, "Beauty, Dominance, Humanity," in *Westworld and Philosophy*, ed. James B. South and Kimberly S. Engels (Hoboken, NJ: Wiley Blackwell, 2018), 196–204; and Christina Wilkins, "Recreating Adam: *Westworld*'s Updated Creation Story," *Nomos Journal*, February 24, 2017), http://nomosjournal.org/columns/screening-belief/recreating-adam-westworlds-updated-creation-story/.

Norris, Pamela. *Eve: A Biography*. New York: New York University Press, 1998.

> Norris traces visions of Eve through myth, folklore, art, painting, and literature. She particularly looks at connections between Eve and "bad girls." As the dustjacket of the book observes, "From Dinah and Delilah, Pandora and Psyche, to the snaky Lamias and Liliths who haunted nineteenth-century painting and literature, centuries of disobedient women have been linked with Eve, the original bad girl, providing ample ammunition for male fears and fantasies."

Schearing, Linda S., and Valarie H. Ziegler. *Enticed by Eden: How Western Culture Uses, Confuses, (and Sometimes Abuses) Adam and Eve*. Waco, TX: Baylor University Press, 2013.

> Chapters in this book address evangelical Christian "purity" movements, which teach young girls to abstain from sexual activity; online Christian dating sites; uses of Adam and Eve in advertising; the Christian Domestic Discipline movement; and the marketing of sex-related products. Throughout the book, the authors trace the ways that Adam and Eve (though primarily Eve) are used to reinforce cultural norms and expectations.

Sanders, Theresa. *Approaching Eden: Adam and Eve in Popular Culture*. Lanham, MD: Rowman & Littlefield, 2009.

> This book explores popular culture's uses of Adam and Eve in terms of gender, sex, death, vegetarianism, nudism, and utopian societies. It also looks at popular portrayals of the famous Scopes Monkey Trial, which took place in Tennessee in 1925 and which pitted evolutionary theory against literal interpretations of the Bible.

CHAPTER 2

··

MOSES AND POPULAR CULTURE

··

LINDA S. SCHEARING
DEPARTMENT OF RELIGIOUS STUDIES,
GONZAGA UNIVERSITY (RETIRED)

INTRODUCTION

IT is not hard to see why Moses is one of the more iconic biblical figures in popular culture. Not only does his biblical narrative span four books (Exodus through Deuteronomy), but he is also associated with powerful religious themes such as freedom from oppression, law, and covenant. However, not all who refer to Moses in popular culture do so to extract *religious* meaning from his story. For many, Moses is important because he is an easily recognizable *cultural* artifact. This is especially true in *American* popular culture. The history of the United States is replete with references to Moses and the Exodus. In his book *America's Prophet: Moses and the American Story*, Bruce Feiler draws attention to the role that the story of the Exodus played for many of the early colonists in North America. He marvels that, after four centuries, Americans still find meaning by seeing parallels between the Moses story and their own struggles.[1]

OVERVIEW OF TOPIC: MOSES IN THE BIBLICAL TRADITION

Within the biblical tradition, Moses is significant for several reasons. To begin with, he is the person through whom the law is given. While laws occupy a large part of Exodus

---

[1] Bruce Feiler, *America's Prophet: Moses and the American Story* (New York: HarperCollins, 2009), 6.

through Deuteronomy, they are often identified as belonging to various collections: the Book of the Covenant (Exod 20:18–23:33); the Deuteronomic Code (Deut 12–26); the Holiness Code (Lev 17–26); and the Priestly Code (excerpts from Exod through Num). In addition to these collections, there are three sets of laws commonly called "Decalogues." There are two ethical Decalogues (Exod 20:1–17 and Deut 5:1–21) and one ritual Decalogue (Exod 34). All of these laws are presented in the text as being given by God to Israel through God's chosen mediator: Moses. These laws will be of tremendous importance in Israel's understanding of its covenantal relationship with God.

Moses is also the person to whom the name of God is revealed. In Exodus 3, while tending sheep for his father-in-law (Jethro), Moses is said to observe the strange sight of a burning bush that is not consumed. A voice from the bush begins a conversation with Moses in which he is commanded to return to Egypt and help free the enslaved Hebrews. In the course of the conversation, Moses displays his reluctance by raising a series of issues and questions, one of which is "Whom shall I say sent me?" In response, the voice says, "I AM WHO I AM" (Exod 3:14).[2]

Another point of significance in the biblical presentation of Moses is that he is the main *human* character in four biblical books: Exodus, Leviticus, Numbers, and Deuteronomy. He is born in Exodus 2 and dies in Deuteronomy 34. No other character in the Hebrew Bible occupies the narrative stage for this length of time. Given that fact, however, it is somewhat ironic that not much information is given about segments of his personal life. A good example of this omission can be found in the account of his birth, early life, and marriage. Moses is born in Egypt to unnamed Levitical parents in Exodus 2. According to Exodus 1:8–22, an unnamed pharaoh decrees the death of all Hebrew baby boys as an attempt at population control. Moses escapes this fate due to the actions of his mother, who sets him adrift in a basket on the Nile River (2:3) while his unnamed sister watches (2:4). The baby is found by an unnamed daughter of Pharaoh whose maid retrieves it from the water. After a period with a Hebrew wet nurse (his biological mother, whose services have been volunteered by his sister), the baby is brought back to Pharaoh's daughter, who names and raises him. Nothing else, however, is recorded of Moses's childhood. Later, after he has grown, Moses intervenes when he sees an Egyptian beating a Hebrew slave, and he kills the Egyptian (2:11–12). That this action is known is clear later, however, when he breaks up a fight between two Hebrew slaves who ask him if he is going to kill them as he killed the Egyptian (2:13–14). Moses then flees Egypt to Midian, where he meets a woman at a well (Zipporah) whom he subsequently marries (2:15–21). Nothing more about the marriage is recorded other than the birth of his son, Gershom (2:22). Looking back over the birth, early life, and marriage of Moses one notices a stark lack of detail. His birth occupies ten verses with only one character named: Moses.[3] Moses's childhood in Egypt is shrouded in mystery, and while the characters in his marriage are named (Zipporah and Jethro) as well as his son (Gershom),

---

[2] All English scripture quotes are from the New Revised Standard Version of the Bible.

[3] Later, in Exod 6:14–24, a genealogy identifies Moses's father (Amram) and mother (Jochebed). Moses's sister (Miriam) is later named in Exod 15:20, as well as in Num 26:59.

nothing of note is said about the personal aspects of his married life. Such paucity stands in stark contrast to the detailed laws that Moses later mediates.

One final point of Moses's biblical significance is the event with which he is so closely associated: the Exodus. The Exodus is replete with examples of God's miraculous powers (the plagues), which exemplify God's willingness to come to Israel's aid. This event—followed by the forty years of wandering in the wilderness—serves as a prelude to Israel's entrance into the Promised Land and is a seminal event in Israel's story. Not only does it represent a story of national renewal, but it is a story that images Israel's God as one who fights against oppression. As the leader chosen by God to be part of this story as well as his mediation of the Law, Moses is tremendously significant to the biblical story. The importance of this leadership provides one foundation for his later role as *American cultural artifact*.

SPECIFIC EXAMPLES AND/OR FOCI: MOSES IN POPULAR CULTURE

The story of Moses occurs in a plethora of popular culture mediums (fiction, songs, films, television, video games, comics, digital internet sources, etc.). This essay examines three themes in which Moses as a cultural artifact plays a crucial role in contemporary popular culture: visualizing Moses (Moses in film), learning from Moses (Moses as metaphor or analogy), and laughing at or with Moses (Moses in humor). Such a survey shows graphically the elasticity of Moses as a multivalent cultural artifact.

Visualizing Moses: Moses in Film

Biblical texts rarely provide a physical description of a character or detail a character's emotions unless it contributes to the literary development of the story. Such information is included solely at the prerogative of the storyteller. The same is true of the linear development of a character's life. If a character's story is being told from birth to death, often whole segments of what might normally be expected (childhood, education, etc.) are missing. Whether or not this information was known or simply left out by the original storyteller remains a mystery. What *is* known is that subsequent retellings of the story for future readers frequently filled in the gaps by supplying information not in the original text. This retelling of the story, known as Midrash and practiced by ancient Rabbis, continues in the twenty-first century.[4]

---

[4] Two discussions of how Midrash functions as interpretation can be found in Norman J. Cohen, "Discovering the Meaning of Torah," in *The Way into Torah* (Woodstock, VT: Jewish Lights, 2004), 71–93; Stephen Wylen, "Mishnah and Midrash as Process: The Evolution of Post-Biblical Jewish Scriptures," in *Reading the Sacred Scriptures: From Oral Tradition to Written Scriptures and Their Reception*, ed. Fiachra Long and Siobhán Dowling Long (London: Routledge, 2018), 51–65.

Movies, when they deal with biblical texts, can be understood as a type of contemporary Midrash.[5] When producers select an actor to play the part of Moses they are making an interpretive decision as to the physical Moses. Moreover, when scriptwriters pull together the story of Moses they not only choose what episodes in his life to portray; they often fill in the gaps found in the biblical text. Sometimes these gaps are filled in by postbiblical literature such as the Mishnah or Talmud, while at other times they are a blatant attempt to appeal to the cultural location of the anticipated audience or to the predilections of the director or producer.

With the advent of the movie industry in the first part of the twentieth century, it is not surprising that the story of Moses and the Exodus story were among its early offerings. In 1923 Cecil B. DeMille directed the silent film *The Ten Commandments*. Later, with sound and spectacle, he remade *The Ten Commandments* (1956), which became a blockbuster biblical film featuring Charlton Heston as Moses and Yul Brynner as Pharaoh.[6] While a succession of movies since then have revisited the theme of Moses, the film *Exodus: Gods and Kings* (2014) is a good example of how popular culture retells the story of Moses in the twenty-first century. Directed by Ridley Scott and starring Christian Bale as Moses, the movie significantly modified the biblical storyline.

The storyline of *Exodus: Gods and Kings* is set in 1300 BCE following four hundred years of Hebrew enslavement in Egypt. The primary setting is the palace of Pharaoh in Memphis, where the viewer meets Pharaoh Seti, Pharaoh's son Rameses, and Rameses's cousin Moses. Both Moses and Rameses are military leaders. In the frames that follow, Moses goes to Pithom, where a Hebrew slave named Nun confronts him with the story of his birth. Moses discounts the story and leaves to return to his men. On the way, two of the local soldiers mistake him for a slave, and he subsequently kills them. When Moses returns to Memphis, the old pharaoh is ill and dies. Rameses, the new pharaoh, is now aware of the story of Moses's birth and confronts Moses with it. Ultimately, Moses is exiled from Egypt and meets a young woman (Zipporah) by a well, gets involved romantically, and marries her. The movie then jumps to nine years later, when we see an older Moses with his son Gershom. Up to this time, it is clear that while Zipporah is of the Hebrew faith, the same is not the case with Moses. One day, when chasing some errant sheep up the mountain (a mountain that is forbidden to climb, as it is the habitation of God), he is the victim of an avalanche. Completely submerged in mud until only his face is visible, he sees a burning bush and encounters a child. When asked his identity Moses tells the child that he is a shepherd. The child responds that he thought Moses was a general and that a general is what the child needs. When Moses asks the identity of the child, the child simply responds, "I am." Moses informs Zipporah that God has told him to go

---

[5] For an interesting discussion of the relationship between Midrash and movies, see Wendy I. Zierler, *Movies and Midrash: Popular Film and Jewish Religious Conversation* (Albany: State University of New York Press, 2017).

[6] For a discussion of both of these films, see G. Andrew Tooze, "Moses and the Reel Exodus," *Journal of Religion and Film* 7, no. 1 (2003), http://digitalcommons.unomaha.edu/jrf/vol7/iss1/3.

back to Egypt. In response, she asks, "What kind of a God tells a man to leave his family?"

When Moses returns to Egypt, he confronts Rameses and then immediately begins training the Hebrew men to fight and prepare for an armed rebellion against Rameses. His plan is to cut off the Egyptians' supplies so that they will force Pharaoh to let the Hebrews go. Once again, however, Moses encounters the child, who is definitely not impressed with Moses's plans and tells him to do nothing but watch. As alligators and crocodiles begin attacking fishermen, the water of the Nile turns red from their blood; this in turn kills the fish and is followed by an onslaught of frogs and then flies. While this is happening, the action shifts to Rameses's court, where a medicine man is explaining the probable source of the troubles they are encountering. As the story progresses, Moses once again confronts Pharaoh, this time to warn him that unless they are allowed to leave something terrible will happen. Ironically, prior to this, Rameses had threatened to drown in the Nile every Hebrew child not yet walking. That evening a darkness passes over the city and Egyptian sons stop breathing. Rameses sorrows over the death of his baby son and orders the Hebrews to leave. Later, a somewhat mystified Moses—who really does not know where he is going—leads the Hebrews to the Red Sea with the Egyptians in hot pursuit. He sees something falling into the waters from the sky and, when he awakes the next morning, the water is withdrawing from the shore. Moses and the Hebrews wade through the water (which is still waist deep). After they reach the other shore, the water returns amid a host of tornado-like storms and destroys the Egyptian forces.

From this summary, it is clear that despite its obvious indebtedness to the biblical account, the move differs significantly at points. One of the most obvious additions is the rivalry between Seti's son Rameses and his "cousin" Moses.[7] Indeed, the conflict between these supposed relatives plays a prominent role in the story. Yet another striking addition is the child that represents God and that only Moses can see. Given the biblical injunction against graven images (Exod 20:4), it is rather startling to see an actor play the part of Israel's God, let alone having it played by a young Caucasian child. The characterization of Moses is rather puzzling as well. In the film, Moses is clearly a soldier who leads the Hebrew army. The burning bush dialogue that occupies two chapters in the Bible (Exod 3–4) is minimal, and completely gone is any *detail* of the laws or covenant established at Sinai. All the viewer is shown is a tablet one assumes is the Ten Commandments. The film seems to end with the passing over of the Red Sea rather than the rest of Moses's story found in Exodus through Deuteronomy. In addition to all of this, the film demythologizes the biblical account by giving naturalistic explanations of the plagues (flies will logically follow dead fish, etc.) and the parting of the Red Sea. At the same time, however, it creates a new ethnic mythology: that all the prominent Egyptians were white.

---

[7] There is a similar dynamic in the animated film *The Prince of Egypt*, directed by Brenda Chapman, Steve Hickner, and Simon Wells, 1998, where Moses is treated as Rameses's brother.

Given these changes, the simple question emerges: What is the producer's intent behind these changes given the audience's twenty-first-century context? Midrash functions as a retelling for a new time and audience. If movies are Midrash, then what does this retelling of the story of Moses intend to convey? Unlike *The Ten Commandments* (1956), which made its political statement about the Cold War of the 1950s clear in its opening frames (it implied the USA was Moses and the USSR was Pharaoh), the film *Exodus: Gods and Kings* gives no such explicit clue to its audience.[8] What are the cultural issues to which it alludes? What message does the film's world-weary action hero Moses, its rational explanations of the miraculous, and Moses's perception of God as a somewhat petulant child intend to convey to its twenty-first-century viewing audience?

In subsequent interviews, the producer Ridley Scott explains some of *his* point of view about the production. When asked, "Why did you use a child for the figure of God?," he explains that, contrary to readers' impressions, the child was *not* God but simply a *messenger* of God. While normally a messenger of God would be angelic, Scott wanted his film to be "reality-based," hence no wings, halos, and so on.[9] As for the plagues and the parting of the sea, once again he aimed for *credibility*, not the *miraculous*. In his own words, "Any liberties I may have taken in terms of how I show this stuff was, I think, pretty safe ground because I'm always going always from what is the basis of reality, never fantasy."[10] As for the moral complexity of the action hero Moses, who sees and talks to a child no one else can see, Brent Strawn, professor of Old Testament at the Candler School of Theology at Emory University in Atlanta, notes: "Our ideal form now, at least in popular mass media, is this kind of muscular, omnicompetent, and virtually indestructible heroes. The power of God is channeled through these heroes, and we see these as proxies which both affirm our cultural values while at the same time identify them with the power of God—even though there's an implicit theology that maybe God is dark and ambiguous, or the people following God are crazy."[11] When movies use the Bible as a foundation for their plots and characters they often elaborate on the biblical text by filling in the gaps found in the biblical stories. While the way in which this is accomplished varies from movie to movie, much is dependent on the cultural context of both the producer and the movie's intended audience.

---

[8] For more on the 1956 Cecil B. DeMille film's ideology, see Melanie J. Wright, "Coming in from the Cold War," in *Moses in America: The Cultural Uses of a Biblical Narrative*, American Academy of Religion Cultural Criticism (New York: Oxford University Press, 2002), 89–127.

[9] Steven D. Greydanus, "Interview: 'Exodus' Director Ridley Scott and Stars Christian Bale and Joel Edgerton," *National Catholic Register*, December 10, 2014, http://www.ncregister.com/daily-news/interview-exodus-filmmakers.

[10] Jonathan Merritt, "Christian Bale and Ridley Scott Talk Religion and 'Exodus': An RNS Interview," *Religious News Service*, December 10, 2014, https://religionnews.com/2014/12/10/christian-bale-ridley-scott-talk-religion-exodus-rns-interview/.

[11] Harry Bruinius, "Moses as an Action Hero? What 'Exodus' Film Says about Society Today," *Christian Science Monitor*, December 12, 2014, https://www.csmonitor.com/USA/Society/2014/1212/Moses-as-an-action-hero-What-Exodus-film-says-about-society-today.

Learning from Moses: Moses as Metaphor or Allegory

Not all popular culture appropriations of Moses and the Exodus seek to *visualize* their use of the story. Some use aspects of the story *rhetorically*, drawing upon metaphor and analogy to glean new interpretations. In this way, they appeal to the story to communicate some type of truth. While examples of such usage of Moses proliferate throughout history, two categories will serve to illustrate and analyze this: Moses as leader and Moses as superhero.

Moses as Leader

It is perhaps not hard to see why Moses became a metaphor for leaders. In the biblical account, he leads the Hebrews to the Promised Land (although he himself is never said to actually enter; Deut 34:4–7). What is surprising is the range and application of this metaphor in popular culture. The multifaceted nature of this appropriation can be illustrated by looking at two types of leaders: politicians and corporate executives.

The Israeli philosopher Yoram Hazony sees Moses as an inspiration for political leadership, as exemplified in his book, *Moses as Political Leader.*[12] In popular culture, however, this association is taken further, when an individual is actually labeled a "contemporary Moses." While a variety of political and social leaders in American history have been associated with Moses (Washington, Lincoln, Martin Luther King, etc.), it is interesting to examine such usage in the twenty-first century.

One such politician frequently called Moses is President Barack Obama. In a 2008 CNN interview with James Presley, an agricultural worker in Mississippi, Presley labels Obama "our Moses."[13] The interview took place just prior to Obama's inauguration. In it, Presley identifies himself as a "church man" and says, "I kind of figured this here is about like it was with Moses with the children of Israel. On that day, when he gets to be president, we're all going to be rejoicing."[14] As Moses freed an oppressed people, Presley sees America's first African American president as a leader for racial equality.

Another example of Obama as a modern-day Moses appears in a 2015 *Huffington Post Blog*, in which the sociologist B. J. Gallagher argues that while Obama "lives by the commandments of Moses," there are other commandments he follows as well, the "commandments of a change leader." Gallaher argues that, although the way will not be easy, Obama's mission will eventually succeed. As he reminds his readers, "It didn't happen in Moses's lifetime and it won't happen in Obama's lifetime either. Nonetheless, Obama, like Moses, is carrying out the mission that God—and the American people—gave him to do. He is leading the charge for hope and change. He is showing us the way to the

---

[12] Yoram Hazony, *Moses as Political Leader* (Jerusalem: Shalem Press, 2005). See also Rabbi Jonathan Sacks, "The Belief of a Leader," in *Exodus: The Book of Redemption*, Covenant & Conversation: A Weekly Reading of the Jewish Bible (New Milford, CT: Maggid Books/Koren, 2009), 29–34.

[13] Wayne Drash, "Grandson of Slaves: Obama Is Our Moses," CNN, January 12, 2009, http://www.cnn.com/2009/US/01/12/grandson.of.slaves/index.html.

[14] Ibid.

Promised Land."[15] Of course, not all saw Obama as Moses, some—using the same Exodus story—saw him as *Pharaoh*. Understood in this way, those who oppose Obama's policies now became "Moses." A good example of such identification is seen in an article that identifies Ted Cruz as an "American Moses." The article suggests that Cruz's opposition to Obamacare makes him a political Moses who, by opposing Obamacare, is opposing the oppressive nature of Pharaoh's (Obama's) leadership. As for Cruz's supporters (Rand Paul, Marco Rubio, Mike Lee, and Jim Inhofe), another source likened them "to antiquity's Joshua, Aaron, and Hur, the men who supported Moses during the battle against the Amalekites."[16]

The American presidential election of 2016 is a good example of the ways in which those who feel oppressed see in candidates a chance for change, and so easily label them "Moses." For example, *Time* magazine referred to the presidential candidate Hillary Clinton as an "American Moses" because, as a speaker in 1969 to her graduating class at Wellesley College, she defined politics as "the art of making what appears to be impossible possible." Thus, *Time* concluded, "In this, she has succeeded. Like an American Moses, she was an imperfect prophet, leading women to the edge of the Promised Land. Now it is up to another woman to enter it."[17] Just as Moses led the Hebrews *to* but not all the way *into* the Promised Land, Clinton did not make it to the office of president, but, *Time* argued, paved the way for a future woman to do so.

Then there is Donald Trump. In the August 2016 edition of *American Thinker*, Fritz Pettyjohn wrote the article "Is Trump an American Moses?"[18] In it, he remarks that in the twenty-eight years since the Reagan presidency, Americans had been wandering in the wilderness. He saw the presidential candidate Trump as a Moses that might lead them out of such wilderness. Nevertheless, at that time Pettyjohn was not quite sure that Trump would ultimately succeed in winning the presidency. A Kindle book, *Trump, the American Moses*, written by Tom Strabo and published a few months later, in October 2016, urged voters to get out and vote for Trump. Strabo argues that the nation was in bondage under "Pharaoh" (the Washington D.C. liberal elite). What the United States needed was an "American Moses" to tell the corrupt leaders "Let my people go!" After all, "Moses did not lead a group of multiculturalists and politically correct liberals and moderates through the desert for forty hard, grinding years. You have understood nothing about Moses and Abraham unless you have understood that people like them are much more reminiscent of Donald Trump than Hillary Clinton."[19] After Trump won the

[15] B. J. Gallager, "Obama Is a Modern Day Moses, Leading with the Paradoxical Commandments," *Blog, HuffPost*, January 22, 2015, http://www.huffingtonpost.com/bj-gallagher/obama-is-a-modernday-mose_b_6516556.html.

[16] Jeannie DeAngelis, "Ted Cruz: An American Moses?," *American Thinker*, September 26, 2013, http://www.americanthinker.com/articles/2013/09/ted_cruz_an_american_moses.html. The biblical battle against the Amalekites to which this refers is in Exod 17:11–13.

[17] Charlotte Alter, "Number 2: The Aspirant," *Time*, December 19, 2016, http://time.com/time-person-of-the-year-2016-hillary-clinton-runner-up/?iid=toc.

[18] Fritz Pettyjohn, "Is Trump an American Moses?," *American Thinker*, http://www.americanthinker.com/blog/2016/08/is_trump_an_american_moses_.html.

[19] Tom Strabo, *Trump: The American Moses* (New Founding Fathers, 2016), Kindle.

election, this association with Moses continued. A good example of this is found in an article that talks about the divisive "Moses effect" often found in the president's rhetoric: "Trump's words don't just reshape Republican attitudes. Just as often they empower and radicalize his critics. One could say that, despite his fondness for gilded touches, Trump evinces not a Midas touch, but a Moses touch—an extraordinary talent for planting a stake in the ground and dividing the landscape before him."[20]

It is remarkable, though perhaps not surprising, that twenty-first-century popular culture often finds Moses an apt metaphor for politicians. Regardless of their political party, these politicians' followers perceive them as leading, or having the potential to lead, them out of what they perceive as their oppressed situations. As such, the promise of liberation found in the Moses story provides fertile ground for such identification.

Another type of the contemporary trend to see Moses as a leader occurs in the world of business. In the book *Moses, CEO: Lessons in Leadership* (2000), Robert Dilenschneider sees Moses as an inspiration to corporate executives.[21] What happens when popular culture likens a corporate executive to a modern Moses? One such example is that of Mark Zuckerberg, CEO of Facebook. Zuckerberg was *Time's* 2010 "Man of the Year" due to the significance and impact of Facebook.[22] In 2011 *Global Macro Monitor* published an article titled "Mark Zuckerberg: Modern Day Moses?"[23] The occasion for this stemmed from an excerpt of an interview by the reporters Anderson Cooper and Wolf Blitzer with the de facto leader of Egypt's revolution, the Google executive Wael Ghonim. Ghonim wrote an anonymous post on Facebook that some credit for starting the revolt:

BLITZER: Wael, this is Wolf Blitzer in Washington. So first Tunisia, now Egypt. What's next?

GHONIM: Ask Facebook.

BLITZER: Ask what?

GHONIM: Facebook.

COOPER: Facebook.

BLITZER: Facebook. You're giving Facebook a lot of credit for this?

GHONIM: Yes, for sure. I want to meet Mark Zuckerberg one day and thank him, actually. This revolution started online. This revolution started on Facebook.

You know, I always said that if you want to liberate a society, just give them the Internet. If you want to have a free society, give them the Internet.[24]

[20] Derek Thompson, "Donald Trump's Language Is Reshaping American Politics," *Atlantic*, February 15, 2018, https://www.theatlantic.com/politics/archive/2018/02/donald-trumps-language-is-reshaping-american-politics/553349/.

[21] Robert L. Dilenschneider, *Moses, CEO: Lessons in Leadership* (Beverly Hills, CA: New Millennium Press, 2000).

[22] Lev Grossman, "Person of the Year 2010: Mark Zuckerberg," *Time*, December 15, 2010, http://content.time.com/time/specials/packages/article/0,28804,2036683_2037183,00.html.

[23] "Mark Zuckerberg: Modern Day Moses?," *Global Macro Monitor*, February 12, 2011, https://macromon.wordpress.com/2011/02/12/mark-zuckerberg-modern-day-moses/.

[24] Ibid.

Thus, for the author of the article, the "liberation" mentioned in the video interview is akin to the liberation of the Hebrews from bondage in Egypt! And who is the "Moses" ultimately responsible for this liberation? Mark Zuckerberg!

Perhaps the most notorious "tech world Moses" archetype in popular culture, however, was Apple's CEO Steve Jobs. In a 2010 article in *Bloomberg*, Bruce Nussbaum asks, "Is Steve Jobs our Moses?" Nussbaum points out that every culture has totems that "define and reify" what people believe to be valuable and important. For Nussbaum, "Nothing is more totemic, of course, than the tablets that Moses brought down from the mountain that contained the Ten Commandments." Nussbaum sees the ordering function of the Ten Commandments as embodying "the top-down, hierarchical movement of message and information of the day."[25] He suggests that the contemporary world was about to experience something similar to the Ten Commandments in the upcoming release of Apple's Tablet.

But not all were entirely happy with the type of Moses that Jobs presented. At an interfaith luncheon following Jobs's death, for example, Lord Jonathan Sacks, chief rabbi of Great Britain, remarked, "The consumer society was laid down by the late Steve Jobs coming down the mountain with two tablets, iPad 1 and iPad 2, and the result is that we now have a culture of iPod, iPhone, iTunes, i, i, i." Later, however, Sacks's spokesperson clarified that Rabbi Sacks "meant no criticism of either Steve Jobs personally or the contribution Apple has made to the development of technology in the 21st century."[26]

Moses as Superhero

For some, Moses was not *just* a leader—he was a superhero! After all, "his people faced destruction. They sent out a baby boy, placing him in a box to ensure his survival. He grew up to be a hero, a savior, able to achieve feats that no ordinary man could do." With these words, Rabbi Nossan Slifkin begins his reflection on Moses and then asks his readers this question: "Was this Moses or Superman?"[27] The question is not as odd as it first appears. The creators of the comic book hero Superman were two Jewish writers, Jerry Siegel and Joe Shuster, who published under the pseudonym Bernard J. Kenton. This was in the late 1930s, when comic books were first getting started. The advent of Superman is considered by some to be the beginning of the contemporary superhero genre. The similarities between Superman and Moses are striking. As one writer notes, "*Superman #1* begins with a brief synopsis of the hero's escape from Krypton, which draws heavily on Jewish sources. Superman's journey closely reflects the story of Moses. Like the people of Krypton who faced total annihilation, the Israelites of biblical Egypt faced the murder of their male offspring. To ensure her son's survival, Jochebed places

---

[25] Bruce Nussbaum, "The Tablet as Totem: Is Steve Jobs Our Moses?," *Bloomberg*, January 25, 2010, https://www.bloomberg.com/news/articles/2010-01-25/the-tablet-as-totem-is-steve-jobs-our-moses.

[26] Simon Rocker, "Chief Rabbi: I Did Not Attack Steve Jobs or Apple," *Jewish Chronicle*, November 21, 2011, https://www.thejc.com/news/uk-news/chief-rabbi-i-did-not-attack-steve-jobs-or-apple-1.29369/.

[27] Noson Slifkin, "HOLY MOSES! Was Moses a Leader or a Superhero?," *Torah from Dixie: Parshat Shmo*, accessed May 18, 2020, http://tfdixie.com/parshat/shmot/016.htm.

Moses in a reed basket and sets him afloat on the Nile. Her desperate decision is clearly echoed by Superman's father, Jor-El, who launches the little rocket ship containing his son into outer space."[28] Superman's origins were recognized by Nazi leaders when, in 1940, Joseph Goebbels denounced Superman as a Jew.[29] While many have written about the similarities between the Superman and Moses stories, the title of one article cements the identification in a novel way: "It's a Bird! It's a Plane! It's Moses!"[30]

But in the years following Superman's comic book debut, not all viewed Superman as Moses; some saw Superman as Jesus. For them it was Jesus who was the original superhero after which Superman was fashioned. Writing on the origins of Superman, Dan W. Clanton, Jr. makes a pertinent observation. Regardless of the *historical* origins of the Superman story, "cultural artifacts like 'Superman' can be *religiously multivalent*, that is, different interpreters find various kinds of symbols and themes when examining the same aesthetic product."[31] Ironically, the same can be said of the biblical Moses as cultural artifact!

Laughing at or with Moses: Moses and Humor

Since Moses and the Exodus are powerful cultural artifacts, it should not be surprising that they are also fertile fodder for humor.[32] Before the advent of the internet, humor depended on oral or media delivery (e.g., radio, television) or print publication. Now internet humor is accessible globally and comes in many forms. Jokes, comics, slide shows, and YouTube productions are just a few of the genres in which it occurs. When such humor deals with Moses, it frequently focuses on one of the iconic events in the Moses story, such as the plagues, the parting of the Red Sea, the burning bush, or the Ten Commandments. However, while humor is often entertaining it can also serve a number of purposes beyond entertainment. The following examples illustrate how such humor can provide environmental, educational, political, and technological statements.

The plagues described in the Bible have long presented problems for interpreters. Are they miraculous? Are they natural phenomena that the storytellers think were from

---

[28] Simcha Weinstein, "Superman: From Cleveland to Krypton, the Man of Steel's Jewish Roots," *My Jewish Learning*, accessed May 18, 2020, http://www.myjewishlearning.com/article/superman-from-cleveland-to-krypton/.

[29] Feiler, *America's Prophet*, 225.

[30] Bruce Feiler, "It's a Bird! It's a Plane! It's Moses!," *Daily Beast*, May 5, 2009, http://www.thedailybeast.com/its-a-bird-its-a-plane-its-moses.

[31] Dan W. Clanton, Jr., "The Origin(s) of Superman: Reimaging Religion in the Man of Steel," in *Religion and Popular Culture in America*, ed. Bruce David Forbes and Jeffrey H. Mahan, 3rd ed. (Oakland: University of California Press, 2017), 33.

[32] Animated television series such as *South Park* (season 3, episode 9, "Jewbilee"), *Family Guy* (season 5, episode 17, "It Takes a Village Idiot, and I Married One"), and *The Simpsons* (season 10, episode 18, "Simpson Bible Stories"), for example, all found in Moses a topic suitable for satire and comedy.

God? Or did they even happen at all? In one joke, a different problem arises. Moses, depressed because of all the terrible things that were happening, suddenly hears the booming voice of God: "You, Moses, heed me! I have good news, and bad news." As the joke continues, the good news comes in three parts. The first: "You, Moses, will lead the People of Israel from bondage. If Pharaoh refuses to release your bonds, I will smite Egypt with a rain of frogs." The second: "You, Moses, will lead the People of Israel to the Promised Land. If Pharaoh blocks your way, I will smite Egypt with a plague of Locust." Finally, the voice concludes, "You, Moses, will lead the People of Israel to freedom and safety. If Pharaoh's army pursues you, I will part the waters of the Red Sea to open your path to the Promised Land." While Moses is understandably happy with this good news, the punch comes when he asks about the bad news. The voice replies, "You, Moses, must write the Environmental Impact Statement."[33]

Using a good news/bad news trope for its format, this joke bypasses the usual questions raised by interpreters and suggests a new one. The last exchange, with its command to write an environmental impact statement, stands in stark contrast to the joyous promises of the first three exchanges: freedom from bondage, traveling to the Promised Land, freedom and safety. The biblical story never attempts to evoke empathy for ecojustice concerns. The joke's final line brings to the listener's attention that neglected detail.

Another important event in the Moses story is his encounter with the burning bush. While the episode is key to the call of the biblical Moses, one joke reminds us that there is more than one way to talk about Moses and a Bush. One day, when George W. Bush is at the airport, he sees a man in a long flowing robe with a staff in his hand. He asks him, "Aren't you Moses?," but the man ignores him. It is only after asking him two more times that the man finally admits his identity. The joke then concludes with this line: "George W. asked him why he was so uppity and the man replied, 'The last time I spoke to a Bush I had to spend forty years in the desert!'"[34] The reference is an artful pun on the bush that is burning but not consumed in Exodus 3–4. Does the reference to the forty years of wandering in the wilderness function as a commentary on his presidency?

Another iconic event in the Moses story is the miraculous parting of the Red Sea as the Hebrews leave Egypt. One joke deals with the event by imagining a young boy reading the Bible and loudly praising God for what he is reading. As he is doing this, a recently university-trained man passing by inquires about the source of the boy's joy. The boy responds by commenting on God's great ability and references the parting of the Red Sea. After "enlightening" the boy concerning modern scholarship and telling him that the Red Sea was only ten inches deep at the time, the man then turns to go when he hears the boy praising God again and asks for the reason. The boy responds by saying, "Wow! . . . God is greater than I thought! Not only did He lead the whole nation of Israel through the Red Sea, He topped it off by drowning the whole Egyptian army in

---

[33] "Passover Jokes," *Kosher4Passover*, accessed May 18, 2020, http://kosher4passover.com/jokes.htm.

[34] While this joke is published on multiple sites, one such site is Daily Strength: https://www.dailystrength.org/group/friends-til-the-end/discussion/george-w-meets-moses.

10 inches of water!"[35] By pointing out an error in the logic of the enlightened man, this joke alludes to what is a scholarly attack on the historicity of biblical accounts. Historians, it suggests, have difficulty accounting for the miraculous without providing a logical explanation. However, as the joke points out, an attack on one aspect of the story's logic may only lead to a problem with another!

The giving of the Ten Commandments is a high point in the Moses story. But what would this event look like if God communicated to Moses in the twenty-first century? The American fiction writer Jamie Quatro authored a slide show on the *Reader's Digest* website that explores what this communication event might have looked like if God had *texted* Moses the Ten Commandments. Each slide features a phone with a thumb hovering over the send button. The slide show underscores how different the *message* might look if the *medium* changed. The ten slides read:

> no1 b4 me. srsly.
> dnt wrshp pix/idols
> no omg's
> no wrk on w/end (sat 4 now; sun l8r)
> pos ok—ur m&d r cool
> dnt kill ppl
> :-X only w/m8
> dnt steal
> dnt lie re: bf
> dnt ogle ur bf's m8. or ox. or dnkey. myob.[36]

The issue of contemporary forms of communication technology also becomes a theme in a humorous Passover YouTube video about Moses entitled "Internet Exodus." The video ponders the question "What if God, Moses, Pharaoh and the Israelites had Google and Facebook?"[37] The video then explores a number of possibilities: (1) Moses logging onto his computer with his password (BasketBaby); (2) Moses asking *Yahoo Answers* why the bush is burning but not consumed; (3) when God tells Moses to go to Egypt, Moses replies that he is on it, and does an immediate Google search for Pharaoh's Palace (not Pharaoh's Pizza Palace or Pharaoh's Palace Bar & Grill); and (4) Moses posting on Facebook "My staff just turned into a snake. Cool."[38] The video brings into stark and humorous contrast just how much communication technology has changed and depicts what the biblical account might have looked like if both God and Moses had been able to use the tools that we take for granted today.

---

[35] While this joke is published on multiple sites, one such site is Christians Unite: http://jokes.christiansunite.com/Bible/10-inches_deep.shtml.

[36] Jamie Quatro, "If God Had Texted the Ten Commandments," *Readers Digest*, accessed May 18, 2020, http://www.rd.com/funny/if-god-had-texted-the-ten-commandments/.

[37] "Google Exodus: What If Moses Had Facebook?," Aish, April 2, 2011, http://www.aish.com/h/pes/mm/Passover_Google_Exodus.html.

[38] Ibid.

As a multivalent cultural artifact, Moses and the Exodus are especially significant in the American understanding of their history and present realities. Why? What is the lasting power of this ancient figure and his story? In an interview about his work on Moses, Feiler explains what he wants his readers to remember. His words speak volumes to the power and promise embodied in Moses as cultural artifact:

> The final point I'd like to leave with my readers . . . is that the Moses tradition is still alive. Just look at white presidents using the Moses story, at a black president using the story in his campaign. Women, blacks, minorities, anyone coming from a place of restriction to a new place, to a better place, is using the Moses story. . . .
>
> Ultimately, the Moses story is the story of making dreams come true, of taking risks. Sometimes dreams don't come true, and that's okay, too. This year we're slaves; next year we'll be free. The Moses story is the story of keeping hope alive.[39]

FUTURE PROSPECTS AND QUESTIONS

- How do novels and short stories explore the Moses story? For example, *The Prince of Egypt* by Dorothy Clarke Wilson[40] became extremely influential in the making of the film *The Ten Commandments*. What more contemporary novels and short stories deal with Moses? What about poetry?
- What music genres utilize the Moses's narrative? How do particular genres of music (opera vs. hip-hop) affect its retelling?
- What of Moses's childhood or his marriage? Little is known of either in the Bible, which makes both fertile grounds for popular speculation.
- How have politicians and their followers made use of the Moses narrative? What aspects of leadership and the story of the Exodus are used in contemporary applications?
- How does the age of the intended reader or viewer affect the story's genre and interpretation? For example, how might a children's cartoon about Moses differ from a Hollywood film intended for an adult audience? What parts of the Moses story might be expanded or eliminated in each?

SUGGESTED READINGS AND ANNOTATED BIBLIOGRAPHY

Feiler, Bruce. *America's Prophet: Moses and the American Story*. New York: HarperCollins, 2009.

A popular examination of the role that the story of Moses plays in United States history. Feiler visits historical sites and interviews historians as he makes connections between

---

[39] Maron L. Waxman, "Review: Bruce Feiler *America's Prophet: Moses and the American Story*," Jewish Book Council, August 24, 2011, https://www.jewishbookcouncil.org/book/americas-prophet-moses-and-the-american-story.

[40] Dorothy Clarke Wilson *The Prince of Egypt* (Philadelphia: Westminster, 1949).

the biblical story of Moses and various historical figures and events. The result is an accessible and interesting journey into how Moses's story has both influenced and continues to influence American culture.

Joselit, Jeanna Weissman. *Set in Stone: America's Embrace of the Ten Commandments.* New York: Oxford University Press, 2017.

An examination of the role the Ten Commandments play in American history. From stained-glass renditions to state laws, this text explores the myriad ways in which the Ten Commandments provided a key ingredient in American consciousness.

Klassen, Chris. *Religion and Popular Culture: A Cultural Studies Approach.* Ontario: Oxford University Press, 2014.

Utilizing the theoretical lens of cultural studies, this book explores ideologies that find voice in popular culture. Through case studies, Klassen provides examples of how theory and analysis can inform the relationship between religion and contemporary popular culture.

Langston, Scott M. *Exodus through the Centuries.* Blackwell Bible Commentaries. Malden, MA: Blackwell, 2006.

A commentary that focuses on the rich history of the book of Exodus's cultural interpretation in both religious and secular settings.

Wright, Melanie J. *Moses in America: The Cultural Uses of Biblical Narrative.* American Academy of Religion Cultural Criticism Series. Oxford: Oxford University Press, 2003.

This book explores three twentieth-century interpretations of the Moses narrative: *Moses in Red*, by Lincoln Steffens; *Moses, Man of the Mountain*, by Zora Neale Hurston; and the film *The Ten Commandments, by* Cecil B. DeMille.

CHAPTER 3

NICOLAS ROEG'S RETELLING OF JUDGES 16 IN *SAMSON AND DELILAH* (1996)

CAROLINE BLYTH
DEPARTMENT OF THEOLOGICAL AND RELIGIOUS
STUDIES, UNIVERSITY OF AUCKLAND

INTRODUCTION

ENCHANTRESS. Seductress. Harlot. Femme fatale. These are just some of the names used by biblical interpreters to describe Delilah's character in Judges 16. Samson, meanwhile, is invariably portrayed as the heroic yet hopelessly smitten Hebrew warrior, who is ultimately destroyed by a treacherous temptress in exchange for cold, hard cash. From the early Christian writings of Augustine and Ambrose to more contemporary interpretive traditions, this biblical pair is repeatedly painted in the hues and tones of danger and desire.

And yet if we read Judges 16 carefully, we will discover that these particular characterizations of Samson and Delilah are not explicitly evoked therein. It is a narrative liberally peppered with tantalizing gaps that leave readers with only the vaguest pencil sketch of this duo's literary personas. We are told very little about the nature of their relationship, or the motivations and emotions that shaped their behavior toward each other. To be sure, the narrator tells us that Samson loved Delilah (16:4), but did she love him in return? Was this couple involved in a (hetero)sexual relationship? And if so, why did Delilah betray her lover to the Philistines? Just as perplexingly, why did Samson appear to facilitate her betrayal? She made no secret of her desire to uncover the means by which he would lose his strength (vv. 6, 10, 13), and demonstrated on three occasions that she had no qualms about using this information to pass him over to the Philistines (vv. 9, 12, 14). So why, after lying to her three times (vv. 7, 11, 13), did he eventually tell her the truth? The narrator does not reveal explicit answers to these questions. This may be a deliberate narrative ploy, inviting the audience to conjure up their *own* creative responses to the story; alternatively, the author(s) may simply assume a certain degree of contextual knowledge on the part of their ancient audience that renders further explication unnecessary.[1] Whatever the reason, as contemporary readers (bereft of such contextual knowledge), we are confronted with a gap-ridden text, whose rhetorical intentions are far from clear. As a result, the Judges 16 narrative offers us a "multi-layered system of realized and unrealized potentialities" that we can engage with imaginatively to construct our own interpretive afterlives for these two fascinating figures.[2] And, more often than not, we choose to fashion these afterlives in ways that reiterate that timeless myth of a strong and heroic man, brought to his knees by a dangerously seductive woman.[3]

Why might this be? Why are these particular tropes used to portray Samson and Delilah in so many of the interpretive traditions of Judges 16? I would suggest that this famous duo's interpretive afterlives have likely been influenced by the dominant discourses within readers' own sociocultural contexts, which repeatedly affirm certain patriarchal and heteronormative ideologies around gendered roles and (hetero)sexuality. All readers of texts rely on more than the words on the page (the world *in* the text) or the sociohistorical context of these words (the world *behind* the text) in order to negotiate the interpretive process. The traditional claim that we can approach a text with "studied neutrality" to uncover its "real" or "original" meaning is increasingly recognized as illusory.[4] As Mieke Bal observes, "Interpretation is never objective, never reliable, never free of biases and subjectivity."[5] Rather, the meanings we extract from the text are also

---

[1] The intentions of biblical authors toward their rhetorical engagement with original audiences is always open to question. Did they write with the expectation that their rhetoric would be deduced unambiguously by the intended readers and listeners of their narratives? Or might they have written with a premeditated degree of ambiguity that actively encouraged audiences to bring their own creative interpretations to the narrative? While contemporary interpretive strategies often prioritize the need to discover the one "true" or "intended" meaning of a text, can we never be certain that this *was* a priority, or even a concern, for ancient writers.

[2] David Fishelov, "Roads Not Taken, Taken by the Adapter: The Case of Biblical Samson," *Connotations* 18 (2008–2009): 28. See also Josey Bridges Snyder, "Delilah and Her Interpreters," in *Women's Bible Commentary*, ed. Carol A. Newsom, Sharon H. Ringe, and Jacqueline E. Lapsley, 3rd ed. (Louisville, KY: Westminster John Knox Press, 2012), 141. I use the term "interpretive afterlife" to refer to exegetical portrayals of biblical characters. These portrayals can take on a life of their own, carrying these characters beyond the pages of the biblical text, into the biblical studies academy and onto wider audiences.

[3] Dan W. Clanton, Jr., *Daring, Disreputable, and Devout: Interpreting the Bible's Women in the Arts and Music* (New York: T & T Clark International, 2009), 65; Mieke Bal, *Lethal Love: Feminist Literary Readings of Biblical Love Stories* (Bloomington: Indiana University Press, 1987), 38.

[4] Eryl W. Davies, *The Dissenting Reader: Feminist Approaches to the Hebrew Bible* (Aldershot, UK: Ashgate, 2003), 101.

[5] Mieke Bal, *Death and Dissymmetry: The Politics of Coherence in the Book of Judges* (Chicago: University of Chicago Press, 1980), 238.

shaped (consciously or unconsciously) by the spaces we occupy as biblical readers situated in the world *in front of* the text (our cultural location)—a world inhabited by our own sociocultural discourses, biases, beliefs, and ideologies.[6] These discourses often insist that there is nothing so dangerous as a seductive and sexualized woman, for she can destroy even the strongest and godliest of men. They warn us that men will always be vulnerable to women's treacherous charm, such is the potency of their erotic allure. So when readers of Judges 16 look at Samson and Delilah through the lens of these discourses, they see what they *expect* to see: a sensuous and irresistible woman whose deadly attraction proves too strong a temptation even for Samson's God-given masculinity. In other words, Delilah the femme fatale and Samson the smitten strongman are not necessarily present in the world *in* the Judges 16 text nor in the world *behind* this text; rather, they are creative products of the patriarchal and heteronormative worlds *in front of* the text, in which creators of their interpretive afterlives are located.[7] At the same time, these interpretive afterlives of Delilah the femme fatale and Samson the smitten strongman also *sustain* these worlds in front of the text, affirming their discursive truth claims about men's vulnerability to women's toxic sexual potential.

Yet it is not only biblical readers and interpreters who creatively fill in the textual gaps and ambiguities with the flavors of female treachery and heroic male vulnerability. Creators of Samson's and Delilah's *cultural* afterlives—in literature, music, and the visual arts—have likewise long employed the tropes of danger and desire to retell this ancient story. Drawing on these same sociocultural discourses of women's lethal sexuality prevalent within their own cultural milieus, they weave together afterlives for Samson and Delilah that *reaffirm* these discourses, rendering the ancient gap-ridden story more understandable to their contemporary audiences.[8] The acts of creating these afterlives, it seems, are never done in isolation from creators' worlds in front of the text, which are inevitably crammed and tangled with various discourses and ideologies that jostle and compete for their interpretive attention.

In this chapter I demonstrate the impact that these competing discourses and ideologies have upon our reading of Judges 16, particularly with regard to our interpretation of Samson and Delilah's relationship. I focus on this duo's relationship because it so often

---

[6] David Rutledge, *Reading Marginally: Feminism, Deconstruction and the Bible* (Leiden: Brill, 1996), 93. The theory underpinning social discourses is articulated beautifully by Michel Foucault, *The Archaeology of Knowledge and the Discourse on Language*, trans. A. M. Sheridan Smith (New York: Pantheon Books, 1972).

[7] Of course, we can never uncover the "real" Samson and Delilah, as intended by the Judges 16 author(s); that has been forever lost in the mists of time. Even if we scrutinize the original language of the text and its historical context, the story remains too gap-ridden to offer anything more than hints and possibilities of narrative "intent." I am therefore interested in the various interpretive afterlives that may be created for these characters, while acknowledging that these are neither definitive nor authoritative.

[8] Clanton, *Daring, Disreputable and Devout*, 65. For further discussion of the creation of cultural afterlives, see J. Cheryl Exum, *Plotted, Shot, and Painted: Cultural Representations of Biblical Women*, 2nd ed. (Sheffield, UK: Sheffield Phoenix Press, 2012); Yvonne Sherwood, *A Biblical Text and Its Afterlives: The Survival of Jonah in Western Culture* (Cambridge: Cambridge University Press, 2000).

lies at the heart of interpreters' attempts to resolve the many gaps and ambiguities in this narrative. First, I offer an overview of some common interpretive traditions surrounding this biblical story, which appear to draw upon those familiar tropes of feminine treachery and masculine vulnerability that I have already outlined. Specifically, I suggest that interpreters' reading strategies for the Judges 16 text are constantly negotiated and shaped by their own heteronormative assumptions and discourses of gender and sexuality. In the subsequent section, I turn my attention to a cultural retelling of this biblical story—Nicolas Roeg's 1996 movie, *Samson and Delilah*—and consider the ways that this contemporary cultural text likewise employs these same tropes, imbued with the cultural flavors of the time, to offer us a portrayal of Delilah as a postfeminist femme fatale, whose erotic allure proved too hot to handle for "new man" Samson. Considering interpretive and cultural afterlives side by side, I demonstrate the complexities of the reading process and the multiple threads—those sociocultural discourses, ideologies, and trends—that occupy and direct our worlds in front of the biblical text.[9]

OVERVIEW OF TOPIC

Let me begin by reviewing some of the imaginative gap fillings used by biblical scholars to construct Samson and Delilah's relationship in Judges 16. Space does not permit a comprehensive survey of the abundant interpretation around this issue, so I am focusing on some of the most ubiquitous fillings that specifically model this biblical duo in the costumes and colors of feminine danger and calamitous male desire. I will interrogate these interpretations, demonstrating that Samson and Delilah's literary relationship is far more ambiguous, leaving space for readers to construct a number of *different* interpretations, crafted from their own alternative worlds in front of this text.

First of all, we need to think about sex. Within the interpretive traditions of Judges 16, there is an oft-voiced hypothesis that Samson's relationship with Delilah was both heterosexual *and* consummated. Samson, we are told, "loved" (*'hb*) Delilah (Judg 16:4);

---

[9] Although I separate "interpretive afterlives" from "cultural afterlives," I am aware that biblical interpretation (as produced in academic classrooms, scholarly books and articles, and the sermons, homilies, and interpretations created within faith communities) are also cultural products. My use of these two terms is primarily to distinguish interpretation that takes different *forms* (interpretive afterlives being primarily oral or written, and creative afterlives being a mix of visual, oral, written, and aural), and within different *contexts* (interpretive afterlives being created primarily within academic and faith communities, and cultural afterlives produced within artistic, cultural, and entertainment contexts, including film, art, advertising, music, theater, and literature). In addition, though, there is often a tendency among creators of interpretive afterlives to consider their interpretive endeavors (rightly or wrongly) as a form of "truth-telling" (rather than a creative exercise), which attempts to seek out the "true" or "original" meaning of the biblical text—the meaning "intended" by the text's original author. This may or may not be a priority for producers of creative afterlives, whose own biblical interpretations may also be guided by current artistic trends, commercial interests, or customer demand.

indeed, Delilah is the *only* woman Samson is said to love. His Timnite wife "pleases" him (Judg 14:1–3), while the prostitute at Gaza evokes no emotional or aesthetic response; we are simply told that he "saw" her and "went into her" (16:1) during their brief encounter. For some readers, this distinction betrays the sexual nature of the couple's liaison. According to J. Cheryl Exum, it may signal that their relationship "is going to be especially important—a fatal attraction."[10]

Moreover, in v. 19 the narrator tells us that Delilah "lulled" or "brought" Samson to sleep "upon her knees" shortly before his hair was cut.[11] Some interpreters seize upon this statement as a demure admission that Samson's snooze was most likely postcoital, the Hebrew dual noun *birkayim* ("knees, lap") being read as a euphemism for female genitals[12] or an allusion to Samson's preference for "knee-to-knee" (or missionary position) sex.[13] Within the interpretive traditions of Judges 16, Delilah is therefore regularly referred to as "Samson's mistress,"[14] his "wife,"[15] and his "lover."[16]

Yet in many biblical scholars' eyes, Delilah is no ordinary lover; rather, she is a *treacherous* lover, who betrayed the smitten Samson by ensnaring him in her sticky web of sensuous duplicity. Thus interpreters often describe her as a "temptress,"[17] a "seductress,"[18] and "Samson's lover-betrayer,"[19] who used her sexuality to intoxicate him for avaricious gain. According to Nancy Tischler, Delilah is a "cynical manipulator of

[10] J. Cheryl Exum, *Fragmented Women: Feminist (Sub)versions of Biblical Narratives*, 2nd ed. (London: Bloomsbury T & T Clark, 2015), 59.

[11] This phrase in the original Hebrew text (known as the Masoretic Text) is *'al birkeyha*; the Hebrew word *birkayim* is usually translated as either "lap" (NIV, NRSV) or "knees" (KJV, NASB).

[12] For example, Gen 30:3; Job 3:12. See Susan Ackerman, "What If Judges Had Been Written by a Philistine?," *Biblical Interpretation* 8 (2000): 39.

[13] Anton Karl Kozlovic, "The Construction of Samson's Three Lovers in Cecil B. DeMille's Technicolor Testament, *Samson and Delilah* (1949)," *Women in Judaism* 7 (2010): 5–6. Other scholars who suggest Samson's sleeping position conveys sexual innuendo include Helen Leneman, "Portrayals of Power in the Stories of Delilah and Bathsheba: Seduction in Song," in *Culture, Entertainment, and the Bible*, ed. George Aichele Library of Hebrew Bible/Old Testament Studies, 309 (Sheffield, UK: Sheffield Academic Press, 2000), 145; Susan Niditch, *Judges: A Commentary*, Old Testament Library (Louisville, KY: Westminster John Knox Press, 2008), 166.

[14] Susan Ackerman, *Warrior, Dancer, Seductress, Queen*, Anchor Bible Reference Library (New York: Doubleday, 1998), 231; Royce M. Victor, "Delilah—A Forgotten Hero (Judges 16:4–21)," in *Joshua and Judges*, ed. Athalya Brenner and Gale A. Yee, Texts @ Contexts Series (Minneapolis, MN: Fortress Press, 2013), 237.

[15] Matthew B. Schwartz and Kalman J. Kaplan, *The Fruit of Her Hands: A Psychology of Biblical Women* (Grand Rapids, MI: Eerdmans, 2007), 53.

[16] James L. Crenshaw, "The Samson Saga: Filial Devotion or Erotic Attachment?," *Zeitschrift für die alttestamentliche Wissenschaft* 84 (1974): 498.

[17] Crenshaw, "Samson Saga," 487; Roger Ryan, *Judges*, Readings: A New Biblical Commentary (Sheffield, UK: Sheffield Phoenix Press, 2007), 121.

[18] Robert Alter, *Ancient Israel. The Former Prophets: Joshua, Judges, Samuel, and Kings* (New York: W. W. Norton, 2013), 191.

[19] Carolyn Pressler, *Joshua, Judges, and Ruth*, Westminster Bible Companion (Louisville, KY: Westminster John Knox Press, 2002), 222.

sensuality" who poses a "real threat to [Samson's] masculinity and his mission."[20] Meanwhile, Royce Victor suggests that the narrator's mention of Samson's "love" for Delilah in v. 4 only serves to accentuate "the intensity of her treachery": she not only betrayed a man, she betrayed the man who *loved* her.[21]

Within these interpretive afterlives, Delilah's character is molded into the shapely form of a classic femme fatale, whose eroticism (and often exoticism) renders her a deadly presence for those unfortunate enough to fall under her spell.[22] What is more, her deadliness is located in her sex, embodied in her gender; she is envisaged as a *sexualized* woman and therefore as a *dangerous* woman. Sometimes she is even a whorish woman, whose apparent willingness to "barter" her sexuality for financial gain marks her out as "promiscuous"[23] and "very prostitute-like";[24] for John Vickery, she is simply a "whore at heart."[25] Samson, meanwhile, is transformed in these interpretive traditions into her tragic quarry, a solitary and spiritual knight with a God-given mission, whose fatal attraction led him blindly into the harlot's snare.

Nevertheless, if we look closer at this biblical narrative, we discern that the narrator is far from explicit in his depiction of this duo's relationship. To be sure, we are told Samson loved Delilah, but it is not clear what form this love took (romantic, sexual, platonic, or otherwise), and we never learn if Delilah loved him in return. We simply do not know if they *shared* a heterosexual attraction to or relationship with each other (however such a relationship could be mapped onto Hebrew biblical conceptions of sexuality), although traditional heteronormative interpretations of this text typically suppose they did. Yet the usual Hebrew euphemisms for sexual intercourse are absent from Judges 16:4–22 (where they appear together).[26] Even the allusion to Samson sleeping upon Delilah's knees (v. 19) need not carry sexual overtones. Knees (*birkayim*) are also mentioned in Hebrew biblical contexts of birthing and parenthood: children are born upon parents' knees; an infant is dandled upon a mother's knees (e.g., Gen 30:3; 50:23; 2 Kings 4:20; Isa 66:12; Job 3:12).[27] Delilah may thus present a horrifying maternal parody here, as she

---

[20] Nancy Tischler, *Legacy of Eve: Women of the Bible* (Atlanta, GA: John Knox Press, 1977), 75, 77, cited in Carol A. Smith, "Delilah: A Suitable Case for (Feminist) Treatment?," in *Judges: A Feminist Companion to the Bible* (Second Series), ed. Athalya Brenner (Sheffield, UK: Sheffield Academic Press, 1999), 112.

[21] Victor, "Delilah," 238.

[22] Delilah's racial identity is another intriguing gap in the Judges 16 narrative, which, as Exum notes, interpreters regularly fill with their own preconceptions about gender and race, fashioning her into a foreign seductress who threatens the hegemonic power of Hebrew masculinity (*Fragmented Women*, 48, 50–5). For further discussion of Delilah's ambiguous racial provenance, see Caroline Blyth, *Reimagining Delilah's Afterlives as a Femme Fatale: The Lost Seduction* (London: Bloomsbury, 2017), 74–9.

[23] Charles Halton, "Samson's Last Laugh: The Ś/ŠHQ Pun in Judges 16:25–7," *Journal of Biblical Literature* 128 (2009): 61.

[24] Ackerman, *Warrior, Dancer, Seductress, Queen*, 231.

[25] John B. Vickery, "In Strange Ways: The Story of Samson," in *Images of God and Man: Old Testament Short Stories in Literary Focus*, ed. B. O. Long (Sheffield, UK: Almond Press, 1981), 69.

[26] For example, "to know" (*yd'*), "to go into" (*bw'*), and "to lie with" (*škb*).

[27] See, for example, Greg Mobley, *Samson and the Liminal Hero in the Ancient Near East* (New York: T & T Clark International, 2006), 91–2.

cradles the bald-headed Samson lying asleep in her lap, weak as a baby.[28] Although this conjures some interesting thoughts about her gender-bending characterization within the narrative (she utterly subverts traditional feminine roles of faithful wife and nurturing mother), the lack of explicit reference to her sexual history with Samson allows us at least the *possibility* that his love for her was unconsummated or even entirely nonsexual.[29]

Alternatively, of course, this literary couple may indeed have entered into an erotic relationship, but one in which traditional (hetero)sexual contours are subverted. As Lori Rowlett suggests, given their predilection for playing games with reeds, ropes, and fibers (vv. 6–9, 10–12, 13–14), it may be that they shared a passion for S/M encounters, with Delilah adopting the role of "femme dominatrix," tantalizing and tying up Samson, the "butch bottom" in their sexualized games of dominance and submission.[30] Similarly, Marco Derks suggests that Samson and Delilah may have engaged in "non-genital erotic play (BDSM),"[31] which fulfilled Samson's apparent penchant for danger.[32]

Furthermore, within these BDSM scenarios, the characters of both Samson and Delilah are not confined to a strictly heteronormative sexual script; BDSM relationships do not necessarily involve sexual intercourse in any form, nor do they presume that participants will share opposite-sex desires.[33] Of course, the sociocultural significances and discourses of sexual desires (be they same-sex, opposite-sex, somewhere in between, or something different altogether) have changed significantly since the biblical texts were written; we therefore have to be cautious about categorizing Delilah and Samson's relationship using contemporary terms.[34] Yet we also need to remember that "heterosexuality" too is one of these contemporary terms, although it is usually mapped unproblematically by scholars onto opposite-sex relationships within the biblical traditions.[35] So while we might be tempted to dismiss Rowlett's and Derks's BDSM scenarios as anachronistic interpretations of this ancient text, readings that assume the duo's het-

[28]   Ackerman, "What If," 39; Jack M. Sasson, "Who Cut Samson's Hair? (And Other Trifling Issues Raised by Judges 16)," *Prooftexts* 8 (1988): 334.

[29]   For further discussion of Delilah's gender-bending potential, see Wil Gafney, "A Womanist Midrash of Delilah: Don't Hate the Playa Hate the Game," in *Womanist Interpretations of the Bible: Expanding the Discourse*, ed. Gay L. Byron and Vanessa Lovelace, Semeia Series (Atlanta, GA: SBL Press, 2016), 49–72; Blyth, *Reimagining*, 62–71.

[30]   Lori Rowlett, "Violent Femmes and S/M: Queering Samson and Delilah," in *Queer Commentary and the Hebrew Bible*, ed. Ken Stone, Journal for the Study of the Old Testament Supplement series 334 (Cleveland, OH: Pilgrim Press, 2001), 106.

[31]   BDSM stands for bondage/discipline, dominance/submission, sadism/masochism.

[32]   Marco Derks, " 'If I Be Shaven, Then My Strength Will Go from Me': A Queer Reading of the Samson Narrative," *Biblical Interpretation* 23 (2015): 553.

[33]   For discussion of the fluidity of gender and sexuality within BDSM relationships, see Robin Bauer, *Queer BDSM Intimacies: Critical Consent and Pushing Boundaries* (Basingstoke, UK: Palgrave Macmillan, 2014).

[34]   See Gerard Loughlin, "Biblical Bodies," *Theology and Sexuality* 12 (2005): 9–27. Contemporary understandings of sexual terms such as "homosexuality," "heterosexuality," and "bisexuality" began to develop only in the nineteenth century within professional discourses (medical, legal, and psychoanalytic).

[35]   Ibid., 11.

erosexuality are equally anachronistic, relying on heteronormative discourses dominant within readers' own worlds in front of the text. The ambiguity of Judges 16 leaves open multiple potentials for the nature of Samson and Delilah's relationship, not all of which need be hetero or sexual, as we define these terms today.

But what about those interpretive claims that Delilah was the treacherous protagonist of Samson's fateful love, sexually manipulating his infatuation in order to wrest from him the source of his strength? Certainly, in v. 5 the Philistine elders do instruct her to "entice" (*pattî*) Samson to reveal this secret. Yet while this verb (*pth*) is used three times in the Hebrew Bible to denote one person's seductive actions toward another,[36] it more frequently conveys a sense of persuasive speech, or "verbal convincing," either honest *or* underhand, which is not inherently seductive in form or content.[37]

Additionally, there is nothing about Delilah's subsequent behavior that suggests she "enticed" Samson in a particularly sexualized manner. To be sure, she appeals to his emotions when trying to persuade him to reveal his secret (v. 15), but there is nothing to suggest her words here convey any erotic undercurrents. "How can you say 'I love you' when your heart is not with me?" she demands; her use of the words "love" and "heart" take the sting out of her complaint that his game-playing belies his claims of love.[38] And while she eventually drives him to submission with her verbal harrying (vv. 16–17), the Hebrew verb used to denote this (*ṣûq*) carries no intrinsically sexualized or gendered inferences.[39] In other words, while Delilah's persistent and persuasive speech acts distress Samson greatly, they bear no explicit overtones of eroticism or sexual perfidy. Samson felt compelled to reveal his secret to Delilah not because he was driven to distraction by her sexual allure but simply because he could no longer stand to hear the sound of her voice. It is Delilah's verbal skills, then, not her sexuality, that constitute the crucial source of her power over Samson; indeed it may have been one of the only sources of power she had at her disposal.[40]

Of course, those interpretive afterlives that paint Delilah in the morally ambiguous hues of Samson's *prostitute* lover can likewise be contested by taking a closer look at the Judges 16 text. As Mieke Bal insists, any connections between Delilah and prostitution are, at best, "superficial."[41] To be sure, Samson has sex with a prostitute at Gaza directly before meeting Delilah, but that does not prove he was attracted *only* to prostitutes. And while it is true that Delilah appears to have access to her own house (vv. 9, 12), the narra-

---

[36] See Exod 22:16; Job 31:9; Hos 2:14.

[37] Tikva Frymer-Kensky, *In the Wake of the Goddesses: Women, Culture, and the Biblical Transformation of Pagan Myth* (New York: Free Press, 1992), 135, 260, n. 3.

[38] Barry G. Webb, *The Book of Judges*, New International Commentary on the Old Testament (Grand Rapids, MI: Eerdmans, 2012), 404.

[39] The verb *ṣûq* literally means "to narrow"; in its causative form, as here, it carries the sense "to press upon." See Francis Brown, S.R. Driver, and Charles A. Briggs, *The Brown-Driver-Briggs Hebrew and English Lexicon, with an Appendix Containing the Biblical Aramaic* (Peabody, MA: Hendrickson, 2003), 847. In Judg 14.17, Samson's Timnite wife likewise "pressed" (*ṣûq*) him to reveal the answer to his wedding riddle.

[40] Frymer-Kensky, *In the Wake of the Goddesses*, 136; also Kozlovic, "Construction," 6.

[41] Bal, *Lethal Love*, 51.

tor never even hints that it serves as her brothel workplace. Perhaps, like Judith, she was a woman of means (Jth 8:1–8), a wealthy widow or business woman whose hard work and political acumen allowed her to enjoy a financially independent lifestyle.[42] Or perhaps she *was* a prostitute; perhaps it was the only means she had of surviving within a literary landscape scarred by seemingly endless Philistine-Israelite wars. As Avaren Ipsen notes, history betrays a timeless proximity between militarism and prostitution, war being an occasion when sexual exploitation (including rape, slavery, and coerced sex work) becomes ubiquitous.[43] Filling the textual gaps around Delilah's character with this in mind (adding it to our own world in front of the text, as it were), we might imagine her being forced into this occupation by the military groups in the region or simply *having* to do it in order to support herself. Again, the Judges 16 text does not explicitly evoke these afterlives, but nor does it reveal, as some biblical scholars aver, that she was a perfidious and self-centered whore.

Thus, despite the ubiquity of interpretive traditions that insist Samson and Delilah were in a (hetero)sexual relationship, the duo's sexual relationship remains a gap in the Judges 16 narrative. While biblical interpreters may fill this gap with images of deceitful female sexuality and ill-advised male desire, these images do not originate in the text itself. Rather, they may inhabit the interpreters' own worlds in front of this text—worlds in which heteronormative and patriarchal discourses shape dominant understandings of gender and sexuality; worlds in which a sexualized woman is a source of both danger and desire for anyone unfortunate enough to fall under her spell; and worlds in which prostitution is evaluated as a sign of women's inherent duplicity rather than their only means of survival. This ambiguous narrative is thus re-created time and again as a cautionary tale about the power of women's sexuality and the risks that it can pose to even the most masculine of men. As Exum writes, "Samson yielded, and look what happened to him, says our story. If even an apparently invincible man like Samson can be undone by a woman, how much more so should the ordinary man be on his guard."[44]

SPECIFIC EXAMPLES AND/OR FOCI

While countless cultural afterlives have been created for Samson and Delilah across the centuries in literature, music, art, and film,[45] I want to consider in more detail one relatively recent cultural retelling of Judges 16: Nicolas Roeg's movie *Samson and Delilah* (1996).[46] Creating a visual retelling of a literary text such as Judges 16 adds new interpretive layers to our characters' afterlives, including such issues as their physical appear-

---

[42] Ackerman, "What If," 38–39; Bal, *Lethal Love*, 51; Exum, *Plotted, Shot, and Painted*, 215.

[43] Avaren Ipsen, *Sex Working and the Bible* (London: Equinox, 2009), 61–2.

[44] Exum, *Plotted, Shot, and Painted*, 252.

[45] For wonderful discussions of the wider reception history of Judges 16, see Exum, *Plotted, Shot, and Painted*, 209–75; David M. Gunn, *Judges* (Oxford: Blackwell, 2005), 170–230.

[46] The movie was part of the Bible Collection mini-series aired by US cable network TNT.

ance, their moods and emotions, and their various verbal and nonverbal interactions. By looking closely at the creative choices Roeg makes in order to fill these textual gaps, specifically around the question of Samson and Delilah's relationship, we can trace the sociocultural and historical discourses that have shaped his *own* world in front of this biblical text. And when we consider these cultural afterlives of Samson and Delilah alongside the interpretive afterlives I have outlined, we see similar gap-filling processes at work, which ultimately sculpt our infamous biblical duo in the familiar contours of female sexual treachery and ill-fated male desire.

In *Samson and Delilah*, Roeg (along with his screenwriter, Allan Scott) retells the Samson narrative of Judges 13–16, from his miraculous birth to his death in the temple of Dagon. To play the role of Samson, Roeg cast the American actor Eric Thal, who offers us a "new man" Samson for the 1990s—a sensitive soul who loves his mother, treats his women with respect, yet remains uncertain about the nature of his life's calling. There are few if any allusions to the impetuous and self-centered Samson in the Judges narrative, who tortures animals (Judg 15:3–5), murders and loots (14:19), and sleeps with prostitutes (16:1–3); nor do we glimpse much of the hot-tempered Samson, whose boastful game-playing ultimately leads to the death of his first wife (14:1–15:8). Rather, as the film's narratorial voice-over insists, Roeg's Samson is "gentle, good, thoughtful, and unsure, as all men are, of the purpose of his life."[47] Reluctant to join his friend Naomi's gang of rebels (who are planning an insurrection against their Philistine oppressors), he prefers to while away his days playing with the village children. Even when Naomi urges him to lead their rebellion against the Philistines, Samson appears reluctant. "A man is what he chooses to be," Naomi tells him. "And I choose nothing," he replies. Indeed, it is only when Naomi deliberately endangers herself that we first see Samson's impressive strength; after she is attacked by a passing troop of Philistine soldiers, Samson is compelled to come to her aid. He dispatches the soldiers easily, causing villagers to hail him as a hero. "You have been chosen," cries Naomi, "how can you doubt it?" Yet Samson *does* doubt it, preferring to turn to God in the hope that the deity will guide his path.

Samson's heroic response, however, brings him to the attention of the Philistine leaders, sparking a chain of events that ultimately lead to his death. In the following scene, we enter the Philistine royal courts, where King Hanun of Gaza (played by Michael Gambon) and his hot-headed son, Prince Sidqa (Ben Becker), argue about how to deal with Samson. Delilah (the king's niece in this retelling) lounges nearby on a divan. This familial connection is absent from the biblical text, but its inclusion here fills the gap about Delilah's social status and ethnicity, identifying her unequivocally as Philistine royalty.

The role of Delilah is played by the English actor Elizabeth Hurley, whose afterlife for this biblical character is a vision of 1990s beauty ideals. Styled according to the supermodel trends of the day, her thinly plucked brows, kohl-rimmed eyes, and full glossy lips coat her character with a glamorous veneer. Her fashionably willowy figure is always draped in sleeveless, wrap-around halter dresses (the height of 1990s minimalist chic),

---

[47] This narratorial voice-over is provided by the actor Max Von Sydow.

accessorized with an elaborate gold headdress, hair ornaments, and chunky costume jewelry. Despite her alabaster skin and Received Pronunciation English accent, she is, nevertheless, a vision of exotic Philistine allure.

With Hurley, Roeg creates an explicitly sexualized Delilah, not only in terms of her appearance but also in her on-screen relationships. When we initially encounter her, she is sitting in the royal court with her friend and confidante, General Tariq (played by Dennis Hopper), the king's right-hand man. Although they have never been lovers, Tariq enjoys a certain intimacy with Delilah, entertaining her with snippets of court gossip and playfully calling her a "loose woman." Delilah laughs at his suggestion about her "looseness," retorting, "And if I weren't, I'd find that remark offensive, General." As the duo continue to parry around this theme, Hurley attempts to imbue Delilah's character with the flavors of sexual promise and seduction (thereby proudly affirming her "loose" reputation), twirling her hair and sucking her fingers as she snuggles against Tariq. Like so many of her interpretive afterlives, Delilah is portrayed here as brimming unambiguously with (hetero)erotic potential.

During their conversation, Tariq suggests to Delilah that no man could ever satisfy her sexually. "Except, perhaps, this Israelite hero," she replies. Before meeting Samson, Delilah has him firmly on her sexual radar; news of his extraordinary strength and propensity for violence seems to excite her. Whereas her character's sexual provenance remains unstated in Judges 16, Roeg's afterlife fills this gap with explicit allusions to her (hetero)sexual penchant for the erotic, while simultaneously labeling her a morally ambiguous "loose woman." In a later scene, this facet of Delilah's character is again confirmed, when she admits to Tariq that she is "excited . . . as a woman" about seducing Samson and hopes he provides an adequate "service" to satisfy her sexual needs. Having witnessed him killing a lion with his bare hands, she appears aroused by his strength.[48] This conflation of eroticism and violence is rendered even more explicit during the scene where Delilah and Samson first have sex (shortly after she has agreed to betray him). Through the use of flashback, Roeg offers us a glimpse into Delilah's inner world; writhing in pleasure, she conjures memories of Samson wrestling the lion, as though both events were tied together by shared themes of aggression and desire.[49] Later, as the couple lie in bed, she licks the scars left by the lion on Samson's chest, as though relishing the memory of this ferocious encounter. The relationship between Samson and Delilah, so ambiguous in Judges 16, is crafted here into an explicitly heteroerotic encounter, seasoned with the spicy tang of violence and danger.

Given her obvious attraction to Samson from the outset, it comes as no surprise when Delilah accepts King Hanun's request that she use her powers of seduction to betray him. Sitting in the royal court, she listens to Tariq, Hanun, and Sidqa evoke that age-old myth of the dangerous power of sexualized women; as Tariq observes, the easiest way to

---

[48] Samson has not yet met Delilah when he kills the lion in Judg 14:5–6. In Roeg's retelling, Samson saves Delilah from the lion, and she watches his wrestling match with a mix of fear and desire.

[49] Reinhold Zwick, "Obsessive Love: Samson and Delilah Go to the Movies," in *Samson, Hero or Fool? The Many Faces of Samson*, ed. Erik Eynikel and Tobias Niklas (Leiden: Brill, 2014), 229.

snare an enemy is to "capture him by that part of his body in which he is the weakest." Delilah smugly agrees to participate in the plan, clearly thrilled by the prospect of sleeping with Samson. Nevertheless she names a hefty price for her services: 1,100 pieces of silver from everyone present in the chamber. Here, Roeg fills the gap around Delilah's motivations for betraying Samson with the flavors of avarice. Later, she attempts to justify her high price to Tariq, telling him, "A girl must look to her future." Yet this obtuse statement is never explained, and we are left unable to fathom her apparent cupidity. And while Roeg's Delilah is never explicitly identified as a prostitute or courtesan, her cool-headed approach to betraying a lover for hard cash evokes our suspicions that this "loose woman" is "on the game," in some sense at least.

As a calculating, sexually adventurous, and avaricious seductress, Hurley's Delilah thus embraces the ethos of (hetero)sex-positive postfeminism,[50] or "do-me feminism,"[51] which seeped into popular culture in the closing decades of the twentieth century and remains a significant cultural presence in the opening decades of the twenty-first century. This is a rebranded, (hetero)sexualized feminism, which claims women's sexuality as the primary (if not sole) source of their social, sexual, and economic liberation by offering pleasure to—and retrieving power from—the heterosexual male gaze. Yet, at the same time, such claims have always been undermined by those ubiquitous sexual double standards woven tightly within dominant sociocultural discourses of the day, which are more likely to "slut-shame" a sexualized woman than acknowledge her sexual and social agency.[52] For, despite postfeminist discourses, women's sexual power is *still* treated with suspicion, its potential to disrupt hegemonic masculinity highlighted as an ever-present threat that requires policing and containment.

These ambivalent responses to (hetero)sex-positive postfeminism are evoked strongly within Delilah's afterlife in *Samson and Delilah*. Hurley's Delilah epitomizes the über-sexy and sophisticated postfeminist woman, whose stamina in the bedroom is a marker of her impressive social and sexual currency.[53] Yet her "sexpertise" and her seeming willingness, for a price, to adopt the role of sexual commodity are the only defining features of her character. And with her moniker of "loose woman" echoing throughout the movie, she personifies the sexual double standards inherent within postfeminist rhetoric; her sexuality is not only a source of her power but also a marker of her immorality and, ultimately, her life-threatening treachery.

[50] For further discussion of postfeminism, and its problematic relationship with feminism, see Sarah Projansky, *Watching Rape: Film and Television in Postfeminist Culture* (New York: New York University Press, 2001), 66–89; Angela McRobbie, *The Aftermath of Feminism: Gender, Culture and Social Change* (London: Sage, 2009).

[51] The phrase "do-me feminism" was coined by the journalist Tad Friend in his 1994 article for *Esquire* magazine, "Feminist Women Who Like Sex." Friend berates previous feminists for being antisex, championing instead a new breed of (post)feminists who express their own brand of feminism through their enjoyment of heterosexual sex. For further discussion of this phrase and the article, see Andi Zeisler, *Feminism and Pop Culture* (Berkeley, CA: Seal Press, 2008), 133–5.

[52] Katie B. Edwards, *Admen and Eve: The Bible in Contemporary Advertising* (Sheffield, UK: Sheffield Phoenix Press, 2012), 45.

[53] Exum, *Plotted, Shot, and Painted*, 268.

Thal's Samson, meanwhile, is Delilah's perfect dupe; as a late twentieth-century "new man," his emotional sensitivities, domesticity, and egalitarian bedroom etiquette leave him horribly vulnerable to this woman's mercenary intentions.[54] This is not the violent, impetuous, prostitute-visiting Samson of the Judges 14–16 text; rather, Roeg's afterlife for Samson is akin to those created by biblical scholars who mourn the heroic Samson's tragic weakness in the face of woman's potent allure. Driven into an erotic fugue by his desire for Delilah, Thal's Samson abandons his God and forgets his divine calling, choosing instead to offer up the secret of his strength as a token of his love. As the narrator pronounces censoriously, Samson's love for Delilah blinded him to his mission, reminding the audience of the power of a woman's sex to wrest a man from his godly vocation.

And while Delilah assures Samson that she reciprocates his love, we are left in no doubt that her "devoted lover" routine is a façade. As in the biblical story, Delilah tries three times to convince Samson to reveal the source of his strength, but on each occasion he lies to her. Increasingly frustrated, she then gives her most convincing performance yet, offering us a master class in treachery. Eyes wide and lips quivering, she promises unending love and loyalty to Samson: "I am you. We're one. . . . I love you . . . the man that you are. Why would I want to change you?" Yet Samson remains uncertain, clinging to the belief that his deepest secret is too important (and too dangerous) to share, even with his beloved Delilah. Nevertheless she wears him down with emotive pleading and accusations that his love for her is wanting. When he warns her that, were he to tell her the truth, she *cannot* test it, she looks him straight in the eye and *promises* her fidelity: "No more tests, just love. The proof of love." The camera dwells here in a close-up of Delilah's face, shot from Samson's perspective; her unwavering gaze attests to the well-practiced skill of her performance, while lie after lie pour from her glossy lips. Samson succumbs, desperate to cling to the intimacy that he believes has flourished between them. Meanwhile we are left despairing at the potency of this woman's allure and the misguided naïveté of the man who has fallen under her spell.

Our worst fears are confirmed in the following scene; after sharing his secret with Delilah, the couple sink onto her bed, before the camera cuts modestly to Samson lying asleep. Clearly, Roeg has reworked the ambiguous scene of Judges 16:19, suggesting (as do a number of biblical interpreters) that Samson's slumber on Delilah's lap is postcoital. Delilah lies beside him, holding a small sickle blade. Clearly, the "proof of love" she spoke of moments before has been tested and found wanting. And although she spends the night fretting tearfully about the task ahead, that blade remains in her hand the following morning, signaling her continued willingness to betray the man who loves her.

When Samson wakes up, he fails to grasp that Delilah's devoted lover performance has been an act. "Why have you been crying, my only love?" he asks. "When you were sleeping," answers Delilah, "I held the power of life or death in my hands." Samson sees the blade but remains under the thrall of her masquerade. "The life or death of the man

---

[54] For further discussion of the new man as a dominant construction of masculinity in the 1980s and 1990s, see Rosalind Gill, "Power and the Production of Subjects: A Genealogy of the New Man and the New Lad," *Sociological Review* 51 (2003): 34–56.

you love," he insists, "but you did not cut." Unmoved, Delilah tells Samson that, nevertheless, she "must" now do the deed, for "when power is given, how can it not be used?" Delilah's power in this retelling is not her power of speech or her political power but sexual power—duplicitous power—which she insists upon using to her financial and social advantage. For is it not, according to her postfeminist ideals, the only power that she has? And while Samson responds that "love is stronger still," she remains unconvinced. "Oh yes, love. Love," she mutters absently, as though she had forgotten what that word actually means. And then, at last, she cuts.

Delilah's first emasculating slice causes Samson to writhe in agony as his strength drains from him; almost immediately the Philistines move in, cutting off the rest of his hair before blinding and imprisoning him. Delilah looks on in shock, although before long she is back in the royal palace, her reputation as a "loose woman" bolstered by her recent sexual adventures. And while she appears a little unsettled after Samson's arrest, Roeg offers no strong evidence that she is experiencing any real remorse. To be sure, she admits to Tariq that, after Samson's arrest, she now knows "the pain of feeling." Yet the film fails to make this claim seem terribly plausible. She moons around a little, staring out of windows and snapping at her maidservants, but otherwise it appears to be business as usual for this disturbingly business-like Delilah.

All in all, then, Roeg's cultural afterlives for Samson and Delilah betray something of the world in front of the biblical text from within which these creations arose. Drawing on late twentieth-century postfeminist discourses of women's sexual power, Delilah is crafted into an erotic (hetero)sex-positive woman, for whom sex is a valuable commodity that can bolster her social and sexual power yet leaves her slut-shamed as a dangerously "loose woman." Samson, meanwhile, exemplifies the iconic new man of the 1980s and 1990s, whose emotion-driven masculinity is rendered fatally vulnerable by women's sexual agency. For all his superior strength and sexual stamina, Roeg's Samson is nonetheless sensitive and unsure of himself, enjoying the intimacy of monogamy. By the mid-1990s, however, the new man brand of masculinity was getting pummeled by a rival, the "new lad," whose sexual bravura, hedonism, and misogyny arose (in part at least) as a backlash to second-wave feminism's "damaging" influence on masculine identities.[55] The virile strongman Samson is ultimately beaten and emasculated by a woman he trusted and loved too much; Roeg's retelling of this biblical tale thus shrieks out a warning to its 1990s audience about the vulnerability of such new man masculinity to the destructive power of sexually liberated ("loose") women.

The film reaches its denouement in the Philistine Temple of Dagon, where a now blind Samson stands chained to the temple pillars. As in Judges 16:22, his hair has grown and his strength returned. He thus wreaks his final revenge on his Philistine captors by pushing down the pillars and killing everyone inside (himself included). Clearly, he has shrugged off his new man persona, preferring self-destruction over the emasculating effects of Delilah's postfeminist power. Unlike Judges 16, though, where Delilah's fate remains unknown, Roeg places her in the temple, and we watch (with a little satisfac-

---

[55] Ibid., 47.

tion, perhaps) as she is squashed by a heavy chunk of falling masonry. As the woman who nearly derailed Samson's godly mission, this "loose woman" is not allowed to escape unpunished; her potent postfeminist sexual currency renders her far too dangerous a presence to remain at large.

Like some of the interpretive afterlives I have outlined, Roeg's cultural afterlives offer his late twentieth-century audience a Samson and Delilah that "make sense" within their worlds in front of the text rather than a Samson and Delilah who are located in the world *in* the text. Whether in the pages of biblical scholarship or on stage, canvas, or screen, the afterlives we create will always betray our own sociocultural location, including our beliefs, ideologies, and values. We are *all* engaged in a creative process, whether we realize it or not, our imaginative renderings of this biblical duo betraying more about ourselves, perhaps, than about the sketchy figures in this ancient biblical narrative.

FUTURE PROSPECTS AND QUESTIONS

- In this chapter, I argue that creators of Delilah's and Samson's interpretive afterlives draw upon discourses of gender and sexuality prevalent within their own worlds in front of the text. While I focus predominantly on contemporary (twentieth-century) biblical scholarship, further studies could analyze earlier interpretations of this text (in Jewish and Christian traditions), considering how the historical, geographical, and cultural locations of biblical interpreters might have shaped the interpretive afterlives created for Samson and Delilah across space and time.

- My choice of cultural text in this chapter (Roeg's *Samson and Delilah*) was drawn from a contemporary Western canon of Judges 16 retellings, as are most retellings that have been the focus of previous scholarly investigation. It would be valuable therefore to explore Samson's and Delilah's cultural afterlives in non-Western art, literature, music, and film, considering how discourses of gender and sexuality dominant within these sociocultural contexts have offered new form and meaning to our biblical duo.

- I noted that cultural and interpretive afterlives of Samson and Delilah often follow heteronormative and patriarchal patterns of thought dominant within their creators' own cultural contexts. What benefits might be gained by utilizing critical theories (particularly gender and queer theories) to challenge both these afterlives and the discourses that create them? And this raises a wider question: Do biblical scholars have an ethical responsibility to contest interpretive traditions and cultural retellings of biblical texts if they appear to perpetuate heterosexist or misogynistic discourses? Should they likewise contest those biblical texts which they believe give voice to the patriarchal and heterosexist ideologies of the authors? And what implications might this have for biblical readers carrying out this interpretive work within a community of faith, where the Bible is regarded as sacred scripture?

- At the start of the chapter, I note that the Judges 16 narrative is full of gaps and ambiguities, which audiences are left to fill using their own knowledge, values, and contextually conditioned creativity. This begs the question: When biblical texts are so ambiguous, can modern readers ever be confident that they can pin down the "original" meaning of these texts, as it was intended by the ancient authors? Or must all Bible readers accept that their interpretations will only ever be guesswork? Related to these last questions, is there a particular way that interpreters need to approach the task of filling gaps in biblical texts? Are they obliged to search for the possible meanings intended by the authors? Or are they at liberty to search for their *own* meaning within these texts, which may or may not cohere with the authors' rhetorical intentions? If we answer yes to this last question, what, if any, authority might such a reading strategy have within the wider canon of biblical interpretation, which typically prioritizes the search for that elusive "original meaning" of biblical traditions?
- Throughout the chapter, I suggest that the discourses dominant in readers' own sociocultural contexts (their worlds in front of the text) have an unavoidable influence on their interpretations of biblical traditions. Future research might explore the implications of this hermeneutical claim for those subdisciplines of biblical scholarship (such as historical criticism and text criticism) whose practitioners insist on the maintenance (and plausibility) of empiricist and essentialist epistemologies.

SUGGESTED READINGS AND ANNOTATED BIBLIOGRAPHY

Blyth, Caroline. *Reimagining Delilah's Afterlives as a Femme Fatale: The Lost Seduction.* London: Bloomsbury, 2017.

This book guides readers through an exploration of Delilah's interpretive and cultural afterlives as femme fatale in both biblical interpretation and popular culture, tracing the sociocultural and historical factors that may have inspired them. Blyth also considers alternative afterlives for Delilah's character, using as inspiration both the Judges 16 narrative and several cultural texts (drawn from literature and visual culture), which, when read together, help to deconstruct traditional understandings of the femme fatale and offer new possibilities for understanding Delilah's characterization in Judges 16.

Clanton, Dan W., Jr. *Daring, Disreputable, and Devout: Interpreting the Bible's Women in the Arts and Music.* New York: T & T Clark International, 2009.

A fabulous book, which draws upon various traditions (including religious texts, music, literature, art, and film) to investigate representations of biblical women in biblical interpretation and popular culture. Drawing from a diverse pool of examples, Clanton demonstrates the power of later retellings to shape readers' interpretation of the biblical traditions, particularly those (in)famous female characters found therein (including Delilah). This book offers a highly accessible introduction to biblical reception studies.

Edwards, Katie B. *Admen and Eve: The Bible in Contemporary Advertising*. Sheffield, UK: Sheffield Phoenix Press, 2012.

Edwards breaks new ground in biblical reception studies by studying the use of biblical characters in contemporary advertising. While she focuses on Adam and Eve rather than Samson and Delilah, her discussion throughout the book is hugely relevant to this chapter in that it accentuates the power of sociocultural discourses to shape our interpretation of biblical texts and to influence the interpretive and cultural afterlives of biblical characters. Highlighting the problematics of late twentieth-century postfeminist discourses, Edwards offers manifold examples of Adam's and (particularly) Eve's afterlives in advertising and considers the social influence that these afterlives continue to have on contemporary gender relations. An engaging approach to studying the Bible in popular culture.

Exum, J. Cheryl. *Plotted, Shot, and Painted: Cultural Representations of Biblical Women*. 2nd ed. Sheffield, UK: Sheffield Phoenix Press, 2012.

This is a classic book that paved the way for meaningful engagement between feminist theory and reception studies within biblical scholarship. Exum lays out clearly her understanding of biblical characters' "cultural afterlives," demonstrating how both biblical texts and their cultural retellings often serve to perpetuate contemporary patriarchal and heteronormative discourses. Her chapter on Delilah offers a thorough review of this character's afterlives in literature, music, and visual culture, woven through with a feminist analysis of the Judges 16 text and its interpretive traditions. For readers keen to learn more about reception studies, this is the book to start with.

Rowlett, Lori. "Violent Femmes and S/M: Queering Samson and Delilah." In *Queer Commentary and the Hebrew Bible*, edited by Ken Stone, 106–15. Journal for the Study of the Old Testament Supplement Series 334. Cleveland, OH: Pilgrim Press, 2001.

This is such a valuable article, demonstrating beautifully how queer theoretical approaches to biblical texts can open these texts up to myriad new interpretations and retellings. Rowlett successfully challenges heteronormative interpretive strategies—so common in biblical interpretations of Judges 16—and offers a convincing (and accessible) argument that invites readers to read this narrative with newly opened eyes.

CHAPTER 4

DAVID AND BATHSHEBA IN CHILDREN'S BIBLES AND ADULT NOVELS

DAVID M. GUNN

TEXAS CHRISTIAN UNIVERSITY, EMERITUS

INTRODUCTION

THE story of David and Bathsheba in American popular culture has often been an uneasy one. In brief, the biblical story tells how King David sees a woman bathing and learns that she is the wife of a soldier, Uriah, who is away at war. He summons her, has sex with her, gets her pregnant, and tries to cover up by furloughing Uriah and encouraging him to sleep with her. When that fails, he has Uriah killed and marries her. Subsequently he is denounced by Nathan the prophet and confesses his sin. As God's punishment, Bathsheba's child dies—though God then gives her another one, Solomon, who will succeed to the throne—and David's family in later years is wracked with strife.

Traditionally in Western culture David was the great biblical hero, slayer of Goliath, king in Jerusalem, composer of psalms, and, for Christians, ancestor of Jesus. His reputation suffered somewhat during the Enlightenment, however, with Deists insisting that his ways were too often less than savory and that the Old Testament was generally an unreliable guide for life.[1] Still, while leading founders of the new American republic were seeped in European Deist thinking, many more ordinary Americans, encouraged by periodic revivals, maintained traditional Christian views of Scripture as the Word of God and unerring guide. That said, the impact of the Deist critics was felt by traditionalists for a long time. Various editions of Josephine Pollard's highly successful children's

---

[1] See W. Neil's discussion of eighteenth-century rationalist critics, "The Criticism and Theological Use of the Bible, 1700–1950," in *The Cambridge History of the Bible: The West from the Reformation to the Present Day*, ed. S. L. Greenslade (Cambridge: Cambridge University Press, 1963), 238–55.

Bible included an introduction by Rev. William Henry Milburn, which starts with an anecdote about a renowned congressman who, in his youth, disavowed his mother's Christian teaching and furnished himself instead with the writings of Voltaire and others, "a whole body of infidelity," with which to scoff at the truths of the faithful wise.[2] But in his old age, gaunt and haggard, he demanded the word "Remorse" be written on a card and, gazing at it in horror, breathed his last. More than a century after Voltaire's death, Milburn was promoting Pollard's faithful account of the Bible against the calumnies of the Deists.

Given that the story of David and Bathsheba is one of illicit sex and proxy murder, it is hardly surprising that it was a favorite target among those who would shake the Bible's status as an infallible source of faith and a godly life. In defense of their biblical hero, supporters of religious orthodoxy would point to David's confession of his sin, arguing that all humans are prone to fail and that David's story illustrates the key to forgiveness, namely recognition and confession of that failure. They pointed to the book of Psalms, traditionally assumed to be written mostly by David, as further evidence of his character. The psalms in general showed, they argued, that David was indisputably a man of great piety, and Psalm 51 in particular, which is headed "A Psalm of David, when Nathan the prophet came unto him, after he had gone in to Bathsheba," reveals the inner thoughts and feelings of a man deeply committed to God and deeply repentant. For those who would retell the story, then, the crucial issue was how to conform the construction of the characters, and David's in particular, to the need for him to come out favorably—sinful, yes, but still at heart the devout champion of God and Israel.

Although the rise of German Higher Criticism (historical-critical scholarship) in the nineteenth century led to scholars disputing David's authorship of the psalms, such biblical scholarship was slow to enter seminaries and universities in the United States, even slower to reach ordinary Bible readers or churchgoers, and even in the twenty-first century Davidic authorship of the psalms is widely assumed among people acquainted with the Bible.

For much of its life in American popular culture, the David and Bathsheba story has been tailored to those who treated the Bible with reverence and expected others to do the same and looked to for a positive message. Hence it often came with a warning. Opening his address, "The Great Transgression," the Rev. William M. Taylor, minister of the Broadway Tabernacle, New York City, declares, "Not without the deepest reluctance do I compel myself to-night to make public allusion to the great blemish of David's career." To pass over it in silence, however, would have meant leaving out the Psalmist's "most solemn lesson" and removed the reason for all the calamities that subsequently came upon David. "Hence," he concludes, "I can see no way of evading the consideration of this painful subject."[3]

---

[2] Josephine Pollard, *Young Folks' Bible* (St. Louis, MO, 1889).

[3] William M. Taylor, *David, King of Israel: His Life and Its Lessons* (New York: Harper & Brothers, 1874), 264.

OVERVIEW OF TOPIC

There are many ways in which the story of David and Bathsheba has found expression in American popular culture. In popular music (whether recognized as such or not), for example, one of its most frequent appearances has been in the song "Hallelujah" (*Various Positions*, 1984) by the Canadian singer-songwriter Leonard Cohen, popularized notably through recordings by the Welsh artist John Cale (*I'm Your Fan*, 1991) and the American Jeff Buckley (*Grace*, 1994). It has been covered by many artists and widely used in films, movies, and TV series. The allusion to David is explicit in the first couplet: "Now I've heard there was a secret chord / That David played, and it pleased the Lord," but depends on knowledge of the biblical story when the song alludes to Bathsheba, "You saw her bathing on the roof / Her beauty and the moonlight overthrew you," and pairs her with Delilah, "She tied you to her kitchen chair / ... and she cut your hair." Cohen wrote and sang differing versions and verses, as did other singers, and conveyed a range of different moods and meanings.

The meaning of the story was probably not uppermost in the minds of moviegoers in the most successful cinematic adaptation, *David and Bathsheba* (1951). It was, after all, a story of passion, adultery, murder, and redemption—and it starred favorites Gregory Peck and Susan Hayward. It was also the most popular movie of the year and nominated for five Academy Awards. Written for the screen by Philip Dunne, the movie was directed by Henry King and produced by Darryl Zanuck, both highly acclaimed veterans of the industry. It stays close to core parts of the biblical plot but adds and expands others, including David and Bathsheba enjoying a romantic interlude, Nathan and the people blaming Bathsheba for a drought and demanding she be stoned, and a dramatic final scene where David offers God an impassioned prayer of intercession, at which point the drought breaks, Bathsheba is saved, and, hand in hand, the lovers can gaze into the falling rain.[4]

My focus here, however, is not on movies but on Bible-based novels for adults and books (compendia) of Bible stories written with a young audience or readership in mind, usually illustrated and often given as gifts or prizes (as book plates attest). While novels are an obvious subject, rewritten Bible stories for children, or for a wider readership of "young and old," may be less so. The genre, which gained popularity in the latter half of the nineteenth century, is clearly conceived to be educational, as many a volume preface is at pains to make clear. At the same time, the object is to provide edifying entertainment

---

[4] See further on this movie Bruce Babington and Peter William Evans, *Biblical Epics: Sacred Narrative in the Hollywood Cinema* (Manchester, UK: Manchester University Press, 1993), 70–90; David M. Gunn, "Bathsheba Goes Bathing in Hollywood: Words, Images, and Social Locations," *Semeia* 74 (1996): 75–101; J. Cheryl Exum, "David and Bathsheba (1951)," in *Bible and Cinema: Fifty Key Films*, ed. Adele Reinhartz (London: Routledge, 2013), 78–83.

either for a young reader alone, a parent reading to children, or family members gathered to enjoy the scriptures in a manner accessible to all.[5]

Hurlbut's Story of the Bible ("The Complete Bible Story... Told in the Simple Language of Today for Young and Old"), by the Rev. Jesse Lyman Hurlbut, sold over 200,000 copies in the first year, went through four subsequent editions and numerous reprints, and was still being reprinted in the 1950s.[6] In the preface to the revised edition of 1932, the last before Hurlbut's death, his son, Charles, claims that wherever he went "people tell me how much these stories have meant to them and their children," adding that he had been told "that the book is to be found in over a million homes in this country alone."[7] Such sales figures are not in the least improbable. Hurlbut's stories were hugely popular.

In the original introduction, Hurlbut explains that not all parents have a gift for storytelling or can find their way through arcane biblical matter inappropriate to childhood. Hurlbut's book, therefore, will tell all the principal stories, each self-contained yet connected into a continuous history, and it will tell them in words that a ten-year-old can understand yet without being childish. Moreover, his book will avoid injecting doctrine into the stories so that "all denominations of Christians may feel at home in the pages of this book."[8]

Few children's story Bibles claiming to include the whole Bible have enjoyed such popularity as Hurlbut's book, but many have been produced, with increasingly sophisticated color illustrations, and readily available, still at modest prices, more than a century and a half after the genre first emerged.

While the study of children's literature is a well-established field,[9] the study of children's Bibles is relatively new[10] and roughly coincides with the growth of interest in "reception history" of the Bible (the term is problematic but has stuck). Without question, the book that provided crucial impetus was Ruth B. Bottigheimer's account of children's Bibles, which appeared in 1996 and remains the classic study.[11] It covers a broad span of history, and while dealing particularly with Europe it includes brief outlines of early developments in the USA and of the David and Bathsheba story.

---

[5] See, for example, the Rev. T. DeWitt Talmadge's introduction to J. W. Buel, *The Beautiful Story* (Richmond, VA: B. F. Johnson, 1889), xix.

[6] Jesse Lyman Hurlbut, *Hurlbut's Story of the Bible* (Philadelphia, PA: John C. Winston, 1904).

[7] Charles C. Hurlbut, preface, in Jesse Lyman Hurlbut, *Hurlbut's Story of the Bible*, revised ed. (Philadelphia, PA: John C. Winston, 1932), v.

[8] Hurlbut, *Hurlbut's Story of the Bible* (1904), 7–12.

[9] See, for example, Gillian Avery, *Behold the Child: American Children and Their Books 1621–1922* (London: Bodley Head, 1994); Peter Hunt, ed., *Children's Literature: An Illustrated History* (Oxford: Oxford University Press, 1995).

[10] See the assessment by Gottfried Adam, "Protestantism and Modernisation in German Children's Literature of the Late 18th Century," in *Religion, Children's Literature and Modernity in Western Europe 1750–2000*, ed. Jan De Maeyer et al. (Leuven: Leuven University Press, 2005), 233–49. Of the twenty-nine papers in this volume, only two, including Adam's, treat children's Bibles. In general, the main growth in research has been in scholarship related to continental European children's Bibles.

[11] Ruth B. Bottigheimer, *The Bible for Children: From the Age of Gutenberg to the Present* (New Haven, CT: Yale University Press, 1996).

At the outset, in the introduction and first chapter ("Definition, Early Models, and History"), Bottigheimer makes some useful choices and distinctions. She declines to use a single term for the genre but uses "Bible for children," "children's Bible," and "Bible collection" more or less interchangeably. She also draws a distinction between studying children's Bibles in order to determine their theological history and (her own goal) viewing the story books in terms of their social history: "The notions expressed in children's Bibles have generally incorporated not divisive religious polemic but shared social values, and these Bibles are thus an important part of the transmission of cultural norms and values from one generation to the next."[12] Accordingly, after a general survey of children's Bibles in Europe and America, she turns first to depictions of the character of God, but then to the way the stories have been used, for example, to reinforce (changing) views about the relationship between parents and children and attitudes toward work, drinking ("the demon drink"), and sex.

Twenty years later, another important book-length study, by Russell W. Dalton, gives a comprehensive account of a particular story, that of Noah's ark, in a particular social setting, the USA.[13] Together, these volumes offer a valuable path into the field for those interested in English-language children's Bibles.

Dalton tends to use the term "children's Bible," but, like Bottigheimer, he does so in an "inclusive and expansive sense." Although he makes a distinction between children and teenagers (or "youth"), he treats books intended for either or both. And he includes books originating outside the USA if they were published by an American publisher and intended for American children.[14] Dalton also starts with depictions of the character of God but then turns to a theological dimension, namely the Noah story as a story about salvation in Jesus Christ. There follow chapters on Noah as a model of virtues and vices—including obedience, hard work, caring for animals, controlling anger, bravery, trust, gender roles, and drunkenness—and the story as history and amusement.

As Dalton observes, while authors of these storybooks often maintain in their introductions (as Hurlbut did) that their goal is simply to make the biblical stories accessible to children, inevitably their selections, revisions, and clarifications will involve significant reframing, reflecting and reinforcing "assumptions, beliefs, and values." He goes on to show both the diversity of approaches authors use in the retelling and the "exceedingly diverse levels of awareness of how they are changing Bible stories."[15] Broadly speaking, however, authors of Jewish children's Bibles like Ellen Frankel tend to be more aware of the nature of their changes than their Christian counterparts who are more inclined to abridge and expurgate in the interests of morality and Christian doctrine.[16] While my own research (of some two hundred books) confirms these observations by Dalton and Frankel, most of the examples of storybooks examined in the following main section are

---

[12] Ibid., xii. [13] Russell W. Dalton, *Children's Bibles in America* (London: Bloomsbury, 2016).
[14] Ibid., 4. [15] Ibid., 7, 31.
[16] See Ellen Frankel, *JPS Illustrated Children's Bible* (Philadelphia, PA: Jewish Publication Society, 2009), 35.

by Christians for Christian readers since they constitute the vast bulk of such storybooks published in the United States.

Research on novels is, of course, well-established and extensive. However, on American popular novels based on a Bible story (as opposed, say, to engaging biblical themes), it is relatively sparse. Whereas the subject of the Bible and American movies has received considerable attention, with publications concerning particular movies as well as broad surveys, compendia, and genres, focus on particular Bible-based novels, let alone broad syntheses, has been more sporadic. It is noticeable that such novels as have received sustained attention have usually been written by celebrated novelists, such as Thomas Mann's *Joseph and His Brothers* (*Joseph und seine Brüde*), Joseph Heller's *God Knows*, and Stefan Heym's *The King David Report* (*Der König-David-Bericht*).[17]

One scholar's work on particular novels and movies is noteworthy in that it deploys an analytical framework derived from Gérard Genette.[18] Anthony C. Swindell has produced two volumes of short studies in this mode, including, on David and Bathsheba, Henry King's movie *David and Bathsheba* (1951), and Joseph Heller's novel *God Knows* (1984).[19] Genette's discriminations are extensive, covering a much wider and complex variety of "reworkings" of the biblical text than is treated in the next section, so that I have not found it useful to adopt here.

Changing Ways and Shifting Treatments

My interest, in the first part of what follows, is to track, over time, ways that authors of children's Bibles published in America have dealt with a major problem, namely, how to recount to children and youth a story of murder and adultery while yet affirming the traditional David, the great king, psalmist, and man after God's own heart, and, for Christians, ancestor of Christ. The general answer has been to paint the king as the epitome of repentance. As will become apparent, however, the nub of the problem in retelling the story leading to repentance has been, for many, not the murder but the adultery, that is, sex.

---

[17] Mann's novel was first published in German in four sequential volumes (Frankfurt am Main: Joseph. S. Fischer Verlag, 1933, 1934, 1936, 1943), and in English translation by Helen T. Lowe-Porter (New York: Alfred A. Knopf, 1948); Joseph Heller, *God Knows* (New York: Alfred A. Knopf, 1984); Stefan Heym, *Der König-David-Bericht* (München: Kindler, 1972), and *The King David Report* (New York: Putnam, 1973).

[18] Gérard Genette, *Palimpsests: Literature in the Second Degree*, trans. Channa Newman and Claude Dubinsky (Lincoln: University of Nebraska Press, 1997).

[19] Anthony C. Swindell, "David and Bathsheba in London and Porto Rico," in *Reforging the Bible: More Biblical Stories and Their Literary Reception*, The Bible in the Modern World, 58 (Sheffield, UK: Sheffield Phoenix Press, 2014), 102–6. See also Anthony C. Swindell, *Reworking the Bible: The Literary Reception-History of Fourteen Biblical Stories*, The Bible in the Modern World, 30 (Sheffield, UK: Sheffield Phoenix Press, 2010). Swindell provides a useful summary of his analytic distinctions, following Genette, in *Reworking the Bible*, 2–5.

In the second part, novels for adults are the focus. Commonly in the nineteenth and twentieth centuries David's life writ large is the primary subject of novels, with the story of adultery and murder but an episode, so that David's behavior in this episode can be subsumed into a broader, positive picture of the hero built up in his defeat of Goliath, his relationships with Saul and Jonathan, the long struggle leading up to his kingship, and, subsequent to this episode, through the emotional drama of his son Absalom's rebellion and its aftermath. From the last decades of the twentieth century and increasingly into the twenty-first, however, Bathsheba has become a subject of novels in her own right, and her treatment by and disposition toward David so much more consequential to the reputation David takes away from the novel. Her development as a character has been particularly important in the romances about biblical women popular in the early decades of the twenty-first century and often targeted to an evangelical Christian audience.

One crux, given the romantic underpinnings of the popular novel, is the question whether the king was motivated by lust or love. The concomitant question, of course, is whether Bathsheba was complicit or coerced. Did she, before or after, actually love him?[20] Whereas children's versions could, and most often did, ignore Bathsheba's motivation and feelings, novels must make choices that may involve not only her reason for bathing where she might be seen but the precise nature of their first meeting and her feelings about David on that occasion and afterward.

The other question increasingly facing authors, from the latter part of the twentieth century on, has been the degree to which the language of the novel may be erotic or explicitly sexual in a story whose plot hangs on a sexual act. As it happens, most say little or nothing about the sexual act itself but rather develop the buildup to the event and then the details of physical and emotional exchange immediately prior to the act.

Children's Bibles: Strategies

The changing ways authors have found to defuse a story of murder and adultery are many and various and make for an interesting story in themselves.

Omit the Story

Children's Bibles that retold stories sequentially through the Bible often solved the problem of the David and Bathsheba story by deftly avoiding it altogether. Josephine Pollard's children's stories were very popular at the end of the nineteenth century and have had a revival in recent times as early readers for home schoolers.[21] In her *Young Folks' Bible*,

---

[20] Note that neither in this story nor elsewhere in 1 and 2 Samuel is David said, unambiguously, to love anyone; an exception is the Greek (LXX) text of 2 Sam 13:21 concerning Amnon, his firstborn. For a discussion of love in David's story, see Danna Nolan Fewell and David M. Gunn, *Gender, Power, and Promise: The Subject of the Bible's First Story* (Nashville, TN: Abingdon Press, 1993), 141–63.

[21] See further Gregory M. Pfitzer, *History Repeating Itself: The Republication of Children's Historical Literature and the Christian Right* (Amherst: University of Massachusetts Press, 2014).

she leads her young readers through the stories of Samuel, Saul, and David to the point where David is king, living in Jerusalem.[22] "He went to war, and took spoils of rich kings, and the Lord was with him, for he sought to do that which was right and just." Here Pollard gives us the essential David. Then comes the crucial jump: "Da-vid had two sons: Sol-o-mon and Ab-sa-lom." Absalom "had a bad heart, and his sins made Da-vid weep." The story of his rebellion follows, illustrating the moral that David's subsequent failure to scold his son as he should have done led to things going "from bad to worse." In this account it is Absalom who sins, and David's weakness as a father stands in for adultery and murder by proxy. Pollard was a proponent of age-appropriate reading for youth (along with the words of one syllable and hyphenated names) and clearly judged the Bathsheba story to be inappropriate.

In a volume written for an older readership, Pollard still avoids telling the story, but this time alludes to it. After becoming king, David won victories, prayed, tried to do what was right, and was just in dealing with his people. "But if at any time he was led into sin, for he was not a perfect man, he would ask God's forgiveness and strive to lead a better and a holier life."[23]

For the 1943 color comic book *Picture Stories from the Bible: Complete Old Testament Edition* from M. C. Gaines, a pioneer of the modern comic book, the jump, like Pollard's, is from David celebrated as conqueror to the story of Absalom's rebellion. The caption reads, "And years passed—David was a great king and had a son Absalom, whom he loved very much."[24] The comic book, replete with endorsements from Christian and Jewish luminaries (Gaines was Jewish), was in its fifth reprinting of 100,000 copies each by 1945, had its eighth printing by 1947, and was reprinted by other publishers as late as 1971 and 1979.

More common is a jump to Solomon. Edith Lindeman Calisch tells of David making preparations for the temple so that Solomon will be able to build it without delay: "Thus, to the very end of his life, David showed his love and thoughtfulness for his people, and his desire to glorify the name of the Lord."[25] She then tells of David as an old man wanting to see Solomon upon the throne.

Shift Emphasis to Nathan's Rebuke

An alternative to completely eliding the story is to give the sordid details of David's dealings with Bathsheba short shrift and move to Nathan's rebuke and an edifying story of repentance. An early example is the Rev. John Howard's *Scripture History for the Young*, published first in the early 1850s and then in upward of twenty editions over the next four decades.[26] Virtue & Yorston in New York specialized in popular histories, in small

[22]   For this section, see Pollard, *Young Folks' Bible*, 172.
[23]   Josephine Pollard, *The Bible and Its Story* (Philadelphia, PA: David McKay, 1890), 190.
[24]   M. C. Gaines, *Picture Stories from the Bible: Complete Old Testament Edition* (New York: M. C. Gaines, 1943), 142.
[25]   Edith Lindeman Calisch, *Bible Tales for Young People*, vol. 2 (New York: Behrman's Jewish Book House, 1957), 59.
[26]   John Howard, *Scripture History for the Young* (New York: Virtue & Yorston, n.d.), 163–4.

format, with fine steel engravings bound in. The illustrated edition of their Bible history was issued in fascicles (twenty-seven parts) sold on subscription, then custom-bound on completion. The writing and format represent a genre popular in Britain since early in the century. Howard himself was English, an Anglican clergyman, and a younger son of the Earl of Carlyle. Like other English writers for children and youth—Charlotte Yonge ("Aunt Charlotte") was another—he found a profitable market in the fast-expanding United States.

The story's title and illustration, "Nathan Reproves David," reinforce the point. The narrator briefly relates that David, now king of Israel, had incurred God's displeasure by causing the death of one of his captains and afterward marrying his wife. (As often in children's Bibles, David's lying with her while her husband still lived is omitted.) Taking pity upon David, the Lord sent Nathan to open his eyes to his sin, which the prophet does skillfully by means of a parable rather than "too severe and bitter language." David, perceiving now his wickedness, confesses that he has "sinned against the Lord" ("Against thee, thee only, have I sinned, and done this evil in thy sight," Psalm 51:4 [KJV]) and listens in repentance and submission as Nathan predicts that troubles will befall his family. Perceiving his sincerity, the prophet assures him that his sin was forgiven and he will not be shut out from communion with God or condemned before the world. The moral of the story, then, is that sin will be found out, but true repentance will bring mercy along with punishment. Neither Uriah nor Bathsheba is named, and Bathsheba has no place in the aftermath of Nathan's intervention. The story is entirely about the repentant king.

Whereas Howard moves rapidly to Nathan's rebuke, J. W. Buel's *The Beautiful Story* (1889) does fill out some details of what occasioned it, but not without causing some confusion in the plot.[27] Titled "David's Greatest Iniquity," the episode tells how David observes a "very beautiful woman" washing herself in a nearby house, and "being infatuated with her appearance" and determined to possess her as wife or concubine, conceives "a heinous plan."

David's taking and lying with Bathsheba is omitted. Instead, the king summons Uriah and receives him with "affected kindness" before straightway sending him back to Joab with the secret instructions to arrange his death. Given no sex and pregnancy, there is no clear reason for summoning him and no enticing him to go home and "wash his feet" (2 Sam 11:8). Later, God instructs Nathan to reprove David for "the infamy of his action in causing Uriah to be slain." The prophet artfully poses his parable, denounces the king, and (confusingly, given the previous account) rehearses to him "the infamy of his act with Bathsheba" (so he lay with her after all?) and how he ordered her husband be slain so that "he might indulge his base and lecherous propensity." Threatened with God's anger and curse against his family, David recognizes the enormity of his sin, is overcome with remorse, and prays for compassion with such earnestness that God finally promises to preserve his life and kingdom.

Buel takes the subsequent episode of the child's illness and death to culminate in David's "most memorable and hopeful of all words, 'I shall go to him, but he shall not

---

[27] Buel, *The Beautiful Story*, 238–42.

return to me,'" words expressing "his belief in the final resurrection" and the most direct reference in the Old Testament to life beyond the grave. In sum, David's contrite spirit regained him God's favor so that when Bathsheba had been "joined to [him] in lawful wedlock," God gave him another child, "afterward the glory of his kingdom." This story of David's repentance and God's forgiveness—and (for Buel) the Old Testament's witness to the resurrection of the dead—is thus capped by Solomon's kingship. Bathsheba is largely ignored.

David Falls in Love with Bathsheba

Three decades later, in a book fashionably designed and illustrated (but not this story) in art deco style, Helen Ward Banks likewise omits reference to David lying with Bathsheba.[28] The plot moves directly from David's seeing Bathsheba to his dispatch of Uriah with the letter to Joab, a deed that was one of the worst of his life. One difference jumps out: when David sees the beautiful woman bathing, he at once falls deeply in love with her. Buel's "lecherous propensity" has given way to being "in love." Uriah is killed because David so strongly wants to marry her. At the end, however, even before Nathan comes to rebuke him, David's guilty conscience knows he has sinned. To Nathan he confesses that he has sinned against the Lord and offers no excuses. The baby dies, teaching David a lesson he never forgot. He pours out his repentance in Psalm 51.

That the king falls in love with Bathsheba on seeing her and so strongly desires to marry her that he plots her husband's death is common in twentieth-century retellings. A particularly long-lived example is *The Child's Story Bible* by Catherine F. Vos.[29] "Oh, if only her husband should be killed in the war! Then I could marry her," says the king who has fallen in love at first sight. As with Banks, the story moves quickly away from Bathsheba and Uriah to David's emotions, to his love for the baby who dies, his deep feelings of sinfulness, and his repentance. At the end, in sorrow for his sin, David writes Psalm 51. The episode, titled "How the Good King Sinned," is not illustrated, though a color picture of David being acclaimed by the crowd appears a few pages later with the caption "The people loved David. He was a good king." First published in 1935, the book went through numerous new editions and reprints to at least 2003. On the fifth edition's back cover (1983), Norman Vincent Peale recommends it as "the best summary of the Bible in story form available anywhere," and Mrs. Billy Graham enthusiastically endorses it as a book she has used for years.[30]

---

[28] See Helen Ward Banks, *Stokes' Wonder Book of the Bible* (New York: Frederick A. Stokes, 1918), 154–6.

[29] See Catherine F. Vos, *The Child's Story Bible*, new ed. (Grand Rapids, MI: Wm. B. Eerdmans, 1951), 310–12.

[30] Another story of love (i.e., David's) gone astray but redeemed through repentance is Manuel Komroff's *Heroes of the Bible* (New York: Golden Press, 1966). It further simplifies the already simplified plot: after the marriage there is no first child (after all, there has been no sex), so no death (96).

The Comic Book Bible

There is no falling in love in a comic book version of the simplified (no sex before marriage) plot, *The Picture Bible* (1979), with a script by Iva Hoth.[31] After seeing Bathsheba sitting (clothed) with her feet in a pool (as is common in early printed Bibles), David sends for her and, seeing her to be even more beautiful than at first sight, thinks, "If only I could marry her!" He proceeds to take steps to eliminate her husband in an amply depicted episode. Bathsheba is then shown mourning for Uriah, though a caption implicates her: "But in her heart she knows that now she is free to marry the king." Thereupon David marries her. David's response to the child's death has its own page. In 2010 David C. Cook brought out a new version of *The Picture Bible*, renamed *The Action Bible*, with essentially the same plot but dramatically updated graphics, influenced by contemporary Japanese manga.[32] The illustrator, Sergio Cariello, had grown up in Brazil with a copy of the 1978 book in Portuguese translation, according to a biographical note. He had earlier worked on the *Avengers*, *Spider-Man*, and *Wonder Woman*, among others. The current cover claims more than one million copies sold.

David Has Sex with Bathsheba

In the second half of the twentieth century, authors become more willing to signal that David had sex with Bathsheba while Uriah was still alive. Some authors avoid more direct language by describing him as "sinning" with Bathsheba. As Sister Mary Theola puts it, with emphasis, "David had lived a just and honorable life but in a moment of weakness he sinned and he sinned seriously. David sinned with the wife of one of his generals, and more than that, he arranged that this general be placed in a precarious position in battle so that he would be killed."[33] The girls in Catholic high school no doubt figured out what this meant. For Sister Mary, however, the story, ultimately, was not about sin but about repentance. After telling of Absalom's rebellion she writes that these sorrowful events were a test of David's repentance and, indeed, proved his greatness of soul and submission to God's will. Hence David faithfully prefigured Christ's eternal kingship. The volume is illustrated, but not this story.

In 1983, Sandol Stoddard felt able to be much more direct about what transpired. Prolific author of the best-selling children's classic *I Like You* (1965), she writes simply (and, as regards Bathsheba, neutrally), that David saw a beautiful woman bathing: "King

---

[31] *The Picture Bible*, illustrations by Andre Le Blanc (Elgin, IL: David C. Cook, 1979), 305–12. Cook reprinted the book many times during the next twenty-five years. A drastically slimmed down version of Hoth's script is written and illustrated by Robb Suggs, *The Comic Book Bible* (Uhrichsville, OH: Barbour, 1995), 80–1. Barbour issued reprints over the next fifteen years. These texts are also known as "graphic Bibles," and Scott Elliott focuses on such texts in his chapter in this volume.

[32] David C. Cook and Sergio Cariello, *The Action Bible: God's Redemptive Story* (Colorado Springs, CO: David C. Cook, 2010).

[33] Mary Theola, *Catholic Bible Stories* (New York: Regina Press, 1960), 122–3.

David was filled with desire for the woman; he sent for her, and she came to his bed while her husband was at war. Soon Bathsheba told the king that she was going to bear his child, and he began to plot a way to get rid of Uriah."[34] The illustration discretely shows a seated woman wrapped in a towel, legs exposed, with one maid drying her calf and a second maid shielding her with another towel.

In Stoddard's account, it is David who desires; what the woman feels is not told. Nor is there any mention of love. A decade later, Selina Hastings uses the phrase "make love." David sees a lovely woman bathing and combing her hair. The illustration foregrounds him watching her, further off in a small pool, only her head and shoulders visible: "David was so struck by her beauty and grace that he gave orders for Bathsheba to be brought before him. He talked to her, courted her, and made love to her. In time she told him she was carrying his child."[35] This David does not simply take Bathsheba but rather, like Gregory Peck in the movie *David and Bathsheba*, he first woos her before "making love" to her. Though whether, having made love to her, he loved her, or she him, we do not learn.

There is neither love nor desire, but there is unmistakably illicit sex, in Ellen Frankel's exceptionally straightforward retelling in *JPS Illustrated Children's Bible*. The illustration foregrounds David gazing across flat rooftops to a partly clothed woman sitting, knees up, washing in a basin. Frankel does not embroider the tale. Having seen the woman and learned her identity, David sends for her and she comes to the palace. "She stayed with him, and then went home. She soon sent word to David: 'I am pregnant with your child.'"[36]

But for Janice Emerson several years later—like Ward Banks and Vos earlier—it is again David's love that drives the plot. Unlike Ward Banks and Vos, however, Emerson follows Frankel in making clear the illicit sex. David's eyes, she tells, are drawn to a beautiful woman bathing (which the illustration does not show) and, filled with love for her, he has her brought to the palace that night. "Soon afterward he learned that she was expecting his child!"[37]

Novels for Adults

In earlier novels, in the nineteenth and twentieth centuries, David's life as a whole tended to be the novelist's central interest, with the Bathsheba story as but one component episode. From the second half of the twentieth century, however, Bathsheba became a prominent focus in novels, and her relationship with David a key to David's reputation.

[34] Sandol Stoddard, *The Doubleday Illustrated Children's Bible* (Garden City, NY: Doubleday, 1983), 136.
[35] Selina Hastings, *The Children's Illustrated Bible* (New York: Dorling Kindersley, 1994), 130. The book having proved very popular, Kindersley published a new edition a decade later.
[36] Frankel, *JPS Illustrated Children's Bible*, 185.
[37] Janice Emerson, *The Complete Illustrated Children's Bible* (Eugene, OR: Harvest House, 2014), 184.

An Episode in the Life of David

Before the mid-twentieth century the story of David and Bathsheba is usually found in novels based on the life of David. An early example is *The Throne of David* by J. H. Ingraham, an Episcopalian priest and sometime writer of dime novels. He wrote a trilogy of Bible-based novels, including this one, which was still being reprinted in the early twentieth century. *The Throne of David*, an epistolary novel, is a series of (verbose) letters written mostly by the Assyrian ambassador to David's court. The last one recounts the David and Bathsheba story as prequel to Absalom's rebellion. David, we learn, saw the beautiful wife of Uriah while, "loosely arrayed and unsuspicious of observation, she was leaving her bath in the seclusion of her garden." He was seized with a desire to make her his own. "With a king, to wish is to will," exclaims the scribe, "and to will is to obtain! Nothing can resist power and will combined!" The virtuous wife of the noble soldier was thus "despised and dishonored." What transpired is left unsaid but obvious to an adult reader. When finally confronted by Nathan, however, David became a changed man, sad and contrite. He composed and recited in public a penitent psalm (Psalm 51), which the scribe includes in his letter.[38] Ingraham's Bathsheba is the object of illicit desire, in no position to resist, and free of censure.[39] Hardly developed as a character, she is accorded one feeling: sorrow. David lets his desire rule him but, as always, is redeemed by contrition and repentance.

An Erotic Romance

Eighty years later what was acceptable as popular writing was hugely different. *David the King* (1946) was a second book from Gladys Schmitt, a professor of English and creative writing at Carnegie-Mellon University.[40] It was reprinted in 1947, 1953, 1973, and 1983, a Literary Guild Selection, and a top bestseller, selling over one million copies.[41] Schmitt writes erotically of love and sex. As David gazes out from the rooftop, a "strange brooding expectancy" comes upon him. And then he sees the woman, "the little Benjaminite," he has met as a guest in Uriah's house, coming out to bathe. Knowing he is about to behold secretly a woman "in her nakedness," he is awed and overwhelmed by feverish excitement: "When the beating of his heart had subsided a little, he wondered at himself that he should be so deeply moved by a slender and somewhat childish young woman. . . . She had been fashioned sparsely, so that every part of her was barely

---

[38] See J. H. Ingraham, *The Throne of David* (Philadelphia, PA: G. G. Evans, 1860), 538–9, 551–3.

[39] In another novel, written by Celia E. Gardner to accompany the International Sunday-School Lessons for 1876, the monarch's power is also acknowledged. But Bathsheba, though mindful of her husband's love, is weak, fascinated by the poet king and deserving to feel guilty. David, though too readily seduced by the sensual license of an oriental monarch, does go on to love the object of his desire. See Gardner, *Every Inch a King* (New York: Nelson & Phillips; Cincinnati: Hitchcock & Walden, 1876).

[40] Gladys Schmitt, *David the King* (New York: Dial Press, 1946). Many of the relevant novels since then have been written by women.

[41] "Gladys Schmitt Collection," Carnegie Mellon Libraries, accessed January 20, 2019, https://www.library.cmu.edu/search/special/schmitt.

sufficient and therefore inestimably precious.... To take her, he thought, to take her in the cool of the evening, with the freshness of the water still upon her.... To take her, to know her utterly, and then to sleep." As Bathsheba steps out of the basin, her body seems to him "even more delicate and slender," her haunches "the small, unripe haunches of a child." But as she draws linen across "the slight globe of her buttocks," he sees her as a "vulnerable child," and his desire to possess her gives way to "a spirit of tenderness." Moving to leave, he makes a noise and her glance finds his face. She stands submissively before him—still, silent, and naked. "And the beating of his heart was suspended within him, because his eyes had encountered her eyes.... It was as if she had said aloud to him, 'Here am I without a veil to hide me. Behold, my spirit rises naked in my eyes to stand before my lord.' And he knew that he also had gone forth unveiled to her in this look. She beheld him now as no other living being had ever beheld him. Nothing in him was withheld from her."[42]

But looks are not enough. David has fallen hopelessly, shudderingly, in love. He sends for her. "As the new moon comes into the sky—foreordained and yet miraculous—so she came, shedding a hush and a radiance before her." With simple words she stands before him in submission (again) and self-dedication. She too that day had been assailed by sweet shuddering, "knowing that the night must find them brow to brow and knee to knee." David speaks then, words such as he has never uttered before to a woman, "pouring out his humility and his gratefulness." He lifts her small hands against his face and kisses her cheeks, her eyelids, her forehead, her hair. "And their love was like strong wine within them, so that they reeled with it and could not stand." And later, when they had "utterly known each other," she tells him that she has loved him since she first beheld him. To David, it seemed then that his cup was filled to overflowing.[43]

Bathsheba: A Romance

One of the first novels to be centered wholly on Bathsheba is Roberta Kells Dorr's *Bathsheba: A Novel*.[44] The author held a degree in religious education from Southern Baptist Seminary and, married to a missionary surgeon, had lived and raised children in the Middle East. The first half of her novel deals with Bathsheba growing up in the family of Ahithophel, in prosperity but then hard times, and being given to Uriah, whom she does not know, as his wife. The novel, which has resonances with King's movie *David and Bathsheba*, enjoyed a measure of success, with subsequent editions (and subtitle changed to *The Love Story That Changed History*) from various publishers, including Tyndale House, Bantam, Monarch, and, in 2013, Moody.

As often with Uriah, he is a burden on Bathsheba. Here he has no interest in sex with her except as the means to an heir, and then the act is abrupt and devoid of pleasure for

---

[42] Schmitt, *David the King*, 336, 436–7, 437.   [43] Ibid., 441.

[44] Roberta Kells Dorr, *Bathsheba: A Novel* (Lincoln, VA: Chosen Books, 1980). An earlier novel, Ari Ibn-Zahav's *David and Bathsheba*, is narrated by David on his deathbed and uses his relationship with Bathsheba (which starts from childhood) to frame a story of his personal life. Published in Hebrew in Palestine before World War II, it appeared (less successfully) in English translation in 1951 (New York: Crown).

her. Her mother-in-law constantly harasses her about her failure to produce a child. Hers is a loveless existence. Bathsheba first sees David arriving from victory in battle, his head thrown back, hair blowing in the wind, his muscles rippling under his skin—though what most attracts her is how he looks "so vitally and recklessly alive."[45] She knows immediately she could lose her heart to him.

Later, David gets to meet her and senses that she is "hauntingly sad." Still later, he sees her ritual bath, though she does not see him. Summoned, she is taken again by his physique and entranced by the rich surroundings while he woos her with his harp and songs and increasingly intimate conversation about her life. When his kiss releases "a frozen, silent pond within her," she is filled with joy and a "wild uncontrollable love," but stops short, saying she must go, do what is right, as her grandfather Ahithophel has taught her. Moved, David says (in rather more words) it is for her to choose. Bathsheba thinks of Uriah and her mother-in-law. "I seem to have forgotten all my fine resolve," she says. "Are you sure?" he asks. She looks at his hair, his beard, his mouth, each "a new discovery of perfection." The air is fragrant around him. She nods, he kisses her gently, then passionately, and, sweeping her up in his arms, he carries her to his couch.

Key developments of Bathsheba are her fears on discovering she is pregnant and what this could mean for her grandfather, for David, for herself and the baby she is carrying, since she might well be stoned to death as an adulteress. Later she has an ongoing struggle both to live with her reputation as a seductress and to hold her own against David's other wives as she protects her son, Solomon. It is she who comforts David mourning for his own son, Absalom. The story ends, however, as many do, not with Bathsheba, who disappears, but with David and Solomon. He will be a great king, David tells Solomon, who will build the temple—and will say of his father, "He was an imperfect man, but one who loved his God with all his heart."[46]

The early twenty-first century has seen a spate of novels written about biblical women, in part inspired by the enormous success of Anita Diamant's story of Dinah, *The Red Tent* (1997).[47] The writing is usually in a romantic vein, emotionally but not sexually explicit, and appealing to a broad readership, particularly women. Some, such as *Unspoken* by Francine Rivers, are more narrowly targeted.[48] Rivers writes as a born-again Christian, and her story of Bathsheba is one of five novellas on the women in Luke's genealogy of Jesus, women of ancient times whose stories, she writes in her introduction, apply to our lives today.

Jill Eileen Smith's *Bathsheba: A Novel*,[49] in another series, "The Wives of King David," is less overtly evangelical in its telling but clear in its underlying Christian message of sin and redemption. Bathsheba longs for a child, and although Uriah loves her, he is frequently gone to the wars and a strict observer of the traditional laws restricting intercourse for soldiers. She is lonely. For his part, David is devastated by Abigail's death in childbirth. Bathsheba sees him first leaning on the parapet of his roof and finds his pres-

[45] Ibid., 149.   [46] Ibid., 149.   [47] Anita Diamant, *The Red Tent* (New York: Picador, 1997).
[48] Francine Rivers, *Unspoken* (Wheaton, IL: Tyndale House, 2001).
[49] Jill Eileen Smith, *Bathsheba: A Novel* (Grand Rapids, MI: Revell, 2011).

ence intoxicating. He speaks to her, declares her very beautiful, and she tells him about herself. They meet briefly again, in public, exchanging significant glances and leaving Bathsheba troubled about her feelings and whether she is betraying her devoted husband.

Bathsheba learns to play the lyre, and it is her soft and haunting music that draws David to the parapet on the fateful night. But it is when she sets aside the lyre, strips, and stands naked while a servant pours water over her that heat spreads through him, "a fire burning and unstoppable." When he sends for her, their words are few—"I share your loneliness," he says—though his actions are unmistakable. She knows she should not be there but "she could not stop the longing, the desperate need to give herself to him, to know him as she was fully known." And so "beneath the gentle pressure of his lips on hers," she whispers to him, "I will stay."[50]

The remainder of the novel stays relatively close to the biblical sequence of events while elaborating upon Bathsheba's sense of guilt and her working past that and the hate she comes to feel for David toward eventual reconciliation. By the end of the novel, as their son, Solomon, is designated successor, both David and Bathsheba have found redemption in the eyes of each other and of God.

Through a Sardonic Lens

While a traditional Christian view of David has dominated popular novel writing well into the twenty-first century, there have been noticeable exceptions. Elmer Davis's *Giant Killer* appeared in 1928 and in serial form in *Collier's Weekly* the same year.[51] With a foreword by Sinclair Lewis, it was republished in 1943 by the Readers Club.[52] By this time the author, a highly accomplished news reporter and editorial writer, was serving in the US government as director of the Office of War Information. In his sardonically perceptive foreword, Lewis points to the underlying reflections of contemporary America in this novel from a reporter become manager of national information who, he says, must obviously have had already in him "the seeds of melodrama and the Inside Dope."[53]

Davis's David is an artist who "loves and liquors and lies" (so Lewis) as well as the ultimate opportunist with the brass and panache to build a kingdom. Bathsheba, likewise, is an opportunist—as well as being articulate, passionate, and beautiful. When she gasps, "I've been sick for you! ... What are we to do?" it is not David she is speaking to but Joab. Dissatisfied with her soldier husband and seeking to advance her social station, she has made a play for a susceptible General Joab who has obligingly fallen for her. But eventually this "gentleman of the old school"—who, as she surmises,[54] probably does not like "the modern attitude to marriage"—cannot get past the betrayal of a soldier by his commander and is unable to go through with the affair. Undeterred, Bathsheba sets her sights higher, on David, commander in chief, who turns out not to share Joab's inhibi-

---

[50] Ibid., 128, 141.   [51] Elmer Davis, *Giant Killer* (New York: John Day, 1928).

[52] Elmer Davis, *Giant Killer* (repr. New York: Press of the Readers Club, 1943).

[53] Sinclair Lewis, foreword, in Davis, *Giant Killer* (1943), v.

[54] Davis, *Giant Killer* (1943), 273, 272.

tions. And so she becomes queen. By the novel's end, she is, true to form, the key player in the coup that puts her son, Solomon, on the throne.

Since the early 1970s other novels not constrained by the traditional frame (devoid of irony) of the "man after God's own heart" have appeared in the US. Among them is *God Knows*, by the author famous for *Catch-22*. Heller's story of David is told in the voice of David on his death bed, a voice that blends the biblical past with twentieth-century Jewish America. He longs to lie with Bathsheba, but he is impotent and she, power-grabber, declines to indulge him until he has declared her son, Solomon, a dim-witted plagiarist, his successor. Very different and enjoying little success in the US, perhaps because it is so radically at odds with prevailing American views of the Bible, though widely translated and reprinted elsewhere, *Bathsheba* is a sophisticated novel by the acclaimed Swedish writer Torgny Lindgren.[55] The plot moves from David's taking Bathsheba in a manic outburst of lust, through Bathsheba's growing maturity in the manipulation of power as David's fortunes wax but mostly wane, to her eventual effective rule as Queen Mother. The novel is about the nature of God, the relationship of holiness and madness, and the terror and cruelty incubated by absolute power.

Stefan Heym, author of *The King David Report*, was born to a Jewish family in Germany but fled Nazi rule. He became a US citizen and served in the military during World War II, writing propaganda targeting German soldiers. A socialist, he became disenchanted with US policy at the end of the war and returned to Germany, to the DDR, where he soon became a critic of the authoritarian government. By the time he wrote (in both English and German) *The King David Report*, he was already an accomplished novelist. Influenced by German historical-critical scholarship, which saw the biblical story of David as a patchwork of different sources, he wrote the novel as the report of a scribe, Ethan, to a commission set up by the new king, Solomon, to promulgate a full account of his father's life in order to justify his succession. As Ethan consults his sources, however, he discovers a darker side to David's life than suited Solomon's purpose, so the report becomes an exercise in conveying inconvenient truths under the constraint of totalitarian political power. The novel abounds in irony and facetious humor, and it demands that the reader constantly read between the lines.

When it comes to the Bathsheba story, which Ethan confesses to have long dreaded having to deal with, we follow him interviewing both Bathsheba and Nathan. The former, now Queen Mother, is tight-lipped except to confirm, with minimal details, that Solomon was indeed David's promised son and heir. Nathan, it turns out, is writing his own reminiscences, which he offers to share. They tell a story that largely features Nathan himself and treats David's affair with discretion. His material is useful, Ethan says, "if one keeps in mind his official rank and the kind of person he is: self-important, self-righteous, self-seeking."[56]

---

[55] Torgny Lindgren, *Bathsheba*, trans. Tom Geddes (New York, Harper & Row, 1989) (Swedish original, 1984).

[56] Heym, *The King David Report*, 155.

A Sardonic View with Musical Redemption

Instead of Ethan, it is the prophet Natan (Nathan) who supplies the voice of the narrator in *The Secret Chord* by Geraldine Brooks.[57] The Australian American author, journalist turned novelist, won the Pulitzer Prize for fiction earlier, in 2006. Like Heym's Ethan, Natan is composing an account of David's life, this time a biography for posterity showing who he was as a man. Natan draws upon his own recollections and interviews with others, mostly women, including David's wives, Michal, Abigail, and Bathsheba, and David's mother (about whom the Bible says little—but "in sin did my mother conceive me" [Psalm 51:5] offers the novelist a jumping-off point).

Natan, in his preface, describes David as "a man who dwelt in the searing glance of the divine, but who sweated and stank, rutted without restraint, butchered the innocent, betrayed those most loyal to him." But, he continues, he also loved and listened, flayed himself for his wrongdoing, built a nation, and made music and poetry for the generations to come. Batsheva's (Bathsheba's) own account, however, is less variegated. "Do you think I did not fear, dragged from my home in the dark, to be debauched and discarded?" Why, asks Natan sarcastically, were you up on the roof? To seek privacy in the dark, in a houseful of male servants, for my ritual ablution, she replies angrily. "Do you have any idea what he was like, that night? He used me like some—receptacle. The bruises on my breasts took a month to fade. I was afraid Uriah would come home on leave and see the marks." David's comment to Natan on informing him a few months later that he had taken a new wife is "Batsheva makes me feel like a man."[58] But then, after the prophet has indicted him and pronounced the curse upon his family, and David has confessed—"I stand guilty before the Name"—and given himself over to penitence and public self-execration, he becomes, reports Natan, a "better man" and a "wiser king." He begins to sing, compulsively, his latest composition, "Purge me with hyssop till I am pure" (Psalm 51).

Later, Batsheva challenges Natan's rosy view but, with Solomon's birth, puts the past behind her in her son's interests. The story now follows Solomon instead of her, though she does make a final contribution to the plot when she takes Natan's advice and lies to a fading David that he has earlier promised the throne to Solomon. Given all that has transpired in the novel, not least in connection with Batsheva, the final paragraphs are something of a tour de force. As David hears the crowd acclaiming the new king, he reaches for Batsheva and kisses her. Then (in the tones of Gladys Schmitt) he hears music irrupting from the city, his music, until "all the music of the heavens and the earth" combine into "one sustained, sublime, entirely glorious chord."[59]

"I bought the book for its title reference to Leonard Cohen," says an Amazon customer reviewer, but soon was reading the biblical account in Samuel and Kings. "I had

---

[57] Geraldine Brooks, *The Secret Chord* (New York: Viking Penguin, 2016).
[58] Ibid., 3, 230–1, 231, 218.   [59] Ibid., 331.

no memory (from childhood Bible stories) of King David as such a violent, dissolute character. Frankly, I prefer my childhood version. And yet I was drawn in."

This reader's comment nicely encapsulates the point of exploring children's Bibles as a prelude to novels. For many American readers of Bible-based novels, childhood Bible stories have indeed been their earliest introduction to the story of David, more often to the story of David and Goliath than David and Bathsheba. As concerns the latter story, I have tried to show how children's Bibles have worked to mitigate precisely that violence and dissolution the reader is surprised at, with illicit sex being the prime target of censorship. Only toward the latter part of the twentieth century does that begin to change. As for novels, this brief survey shows that while murder and illicit sex are always integral to the plot, by the mid-twentieth century the way they are treated have taken some strikingly different paths. They may become the occasion for an erotic romanticism (as in Schmitt's *David the King*), more reticent romanticism (Dorr's *Bathsheba* and Smith's *Bathsheba*), or grist to a more sardonic account of David (as in Davis's *Giant Killer* or Heym's *The King David Report*). Notably, since Dorr's novel (1980), there has been a growth of writing (mostly by women) centered, sympathetically, on Bathsheba; but notable also is the extent to which writers maneuver to create, despite all his failings, a favorable portrait of David.

FUTURE PROSPECTS AND QUESTIONS

- For children's Bibles, the topic needs fuller development,[60] including the social background of authors and readers, closer discrimination regarding the ages of likely readers, patterns of use (for example, what evidence is there that story Bibles given as gifts or prizes were actively used?), and an account of changing attitudes toward children and their education in tandem with changes taking place in the way stories are fashioned.
- A comparative study of the ways the story has been treated for children in more than one country or social environment would be valuable, as Russell Dalton suggests.[61]
- Novels need to be set more explicitly in the context of a broad history of popular literature and the social conditions associated with shifting taste, as also the place of the Bible in American society, particularly views of the Bible as sacred scripture, and, not least, attitudes toward marriage, adultery, and the expression of sex in literature.
- There is need for a more comprehensive inquiry into the treatment of Bathsheba in both children's stories and novels, especially in relation to the women's movement since the historic Seneca Falls Convention on women's rights in 1848.

---

[60] See further Dalton, *Children's Bibles in America*, 265–7.   [61] Ibid., 4n11.

Suggested Readings and Annotated Bibliography

Bottigheimer, Ruth B. *The Bible for Children: From the Age of Gutenberg to the Present*. New Haven, CT: Yale University Press, 1996.

> The classic study of the subject, particularly in Europe, drawing upon a wealth of primary sources, with brief outlines of early developments in the USA and of the David and Bathsheba story.

Coates, Andrew T. "The Bible and Graphic Novels and Comic Books." In *The Oxford Handbook of The Bible in America*, edited by Paul C. Gutjahr, 451–67. New York: Oxford University Press, 2017.

> Starting with an example from *The Action Bible* (2010), Coates reviews theory concerning sequential art and offers a concise "visual history" of sequential art Bibles in America.

Dalton, Russell W. *Children's Bibles in America: A Reception History of the Story of Noah's Ark in US Children's Bibles*. Scriptural Traces, 5; Library of Hebrew Bible/Old Testament Studies, 614. London: Bloomsbury T & T Clark, 2016.

> An extensive study of the Ark story in children's Bibles published in the USA, based on hundreds of examples, examining how they reflect continuities and changes in American culture. It provides a history of the story in social context that offers a model for studies of other Bible stories for children; the concluding chapter, focusing on the multivalency and malleability of Bible stories and religion in America, the pragmatic question for parents of choosing a Bible (if any at all) for their children, and avenues for further study, is itself is a "must read."

Exum, J. Cheryl. "A King Fit for a Child: The David Story in Modern Children's Bibles." In *The Fate of King David: The Past and Present of a Biblical Icon*, edited by Tod Linafelt, Claudia V. Camp, and Timothy Beal, 241–59. Library of Hebrew Bible/Old Testament Studies, 500. New York: T & T Clark, 2010.

> A close analysis of a small international sample, including five retellings of the David and Bathsheba story, with a focus on how the writers deal with the problem of sex for young readers, written by a scholar who has herself authored children's Bible stories.

Gold, Penny Schine. *Making the Bible Modern: Children's Bibles and Jewish Education in Twentieth-Century America*. Ithaca, NY: Cornell University Press, 2004.

> A nuanced account of how changes in twentieth-century Jewish children's Bibles reflected moves (particularly in Reform Judaism) toward acculturation in American society through revised educational models.

Noll, Mark. "The Bible in North America." In *The New Cambridge History of the Bible, Volume 4: From 1750 to the Present*, edited by John Riches, 391–426. Cambridge: Cambridge University Press, 2015.

> A readable, broad account of the place the Bible has held in American society, providing a valuable larger background to the children's Bibles and novels examined here.

Vander Stichele, Caroline, and Hugh S. Pyper, eds. *Text, Image, and Otherness in Children's Bibles: What's in the Picture?* Semeia Studies, 56. Atlanta, GA: Society of Biblical Literature, 2012.

> Includes reflections on what children want by the biblical scholar and children's story writer Cheryl Exum (333–45) and a historical perspective on the discussion, including a succinct account of German-language scholarship on children's Bibles, 1999–2011, by Ruth Bottigheimer (321–32).

CHAPTER 5

··

QUEEN ESTHER
IMAGINED AS A DISNEY
PRINCESS

··

KATHERINE B. LOW
DEPARTMENT OF PHILOSOPHY AND RELIGIOUS
STUDIES, MARY BALDWIN UNIVERSITY

INTRODUCTION

THE biblical book of Esther is a novella set during the time of Persian rule; it contains sexual exploitation, violence, political scheming, deception, and adult drinking parties, hardly the content appropriate for a Disney children's princess story. This chapter argues that a popular love for the Disney princess franchise and the values about womanhood it projects influences modern interpretations of Esther. I will discuss elements of the Disney princess mythology and apply them to five modern Christian biblical novels, all published after the turn of the century, during the height of Disney princess culture. When it comes to how many different views exist regarding Esther, Kenneth Craig states that "interpretation is a culturally influenced social phenomenon."[1] That is, culture influences how people interpret Esther's story. In this case, a culture rampant with Disney princess mythology has influenced the biblical fiction market. The market exploded after the success of Anita Diamant's *The Red Tent* in 1999 and remains lucrative, earning $75 million to $85 million since 2016.[2] Biblical fiction, also called Christian fiction, remains a subgenre of the overall phenomenon known as "romance fiction,"

---

[1] Kenneth M. Craig Jr., *Reading Esther: A Case for the Literary Carnivalesque*, Literary Currents in Biblical Interpretation (Louisville, KY: Westminster John Knox Press, 1995), 27.

[2] Lynn Garrett, "The Business of Christian Fiction," *Publishers Weekly*, May 20, 2016, http://www.publishersweekly.com/pw/by-topic/industry-news/religion/article/70450-the-business-of-christian-fiction.html.

which is the bestselling genre in the United States. This popular expectation of romance is the most influential factor in how Christian authors interpret Esther's life and marriage. After the discussion of Christian novels, Jewish sources will serve in this chapter to show different culturally influenced understandings of Esther's story. As a result, a subtle Jewish-Christian dialogue emerges about the place of Esther in Jewish and Christian imaginations in popular culture.

First, a summary of the biblical story of Esther is necessary in order to capture the complexities of the book and how the Christian novels discussed herein interpret those complexities in light of a Disney princess mythology. While the book is named after the heroine, Esther navigates her experiences in relation to the men in her life in a patriarchal world, whether that be through her cousin Mordecai, who raises her, or the King of Persia, who marries her. Persian rule is opulent, with hyperbolic descriptions, royal court intrigue, and buffoonery permeating the book. King Ahasuerus (biblical scholars think he is probably a reference to Xerxes I)[3] displays great wealth and puts on fabulous banquets (1:5–9). Queen Vashti refuses to come before him at his drinking party (1:12). Furious, he consults his sages, who advise him to release a royal order to banish Vashti. Otherwise Vashti might be an example for other noble ladies to refuse their husbands (1:18–19). Vashti's banishment leaves an opening in the harem so that all young virgins would be sought for the king (2:2–4). In such a patriarchal setting, virgins were being guarded by castrated males, called eunuchs, to ensure that they could not impregnate any possible new queen, thus ensuring the king's paternity of future offspring.

The Jews had been exiled by the Babylonian king and were living in diaspora, the dispersion of the Jewish people from Israel; Mordecai adopts Hadassah after the death of her parents. On Mordecai's advice (2:10) she changes her name to the Persian Esther to reflect a Gentile identity and is taken into the king's palace to prepare with a year's worth of cosmetic treatments to become the new queen (2:17). She listens to Hegai the eunuch's advice, and thus finds favor out "of all the virgins," becoming the queen (2:17).[4]

Mordecai went to the palace every day to ask about Queen Esther. There he overheard a plot to kill the king and reported it to her, who told the king; the action was recorded in the king's annals (2:21–23), an action that saves Mordecai later in the story, when the king cannot sleep and so listens to the annals and remembers to honor Mordecai (ch. 6). The bulk of the biblical story of Esther centers on Haman as a threat to all the Jews living in Persia (chs. 3–10). Haman, an official of the king's court, convinces the king to order an edict to alert the provinces that all Jews will be annihilated, particularly because Mordecai would not bow before him (3:2). All the Jews were in mourning when they heard of the decree (4:1–8). Mordecai sends word to Esther, asking her to convince her husband to stop the order, saying, "Perhaps you have come to royal dignity for just such a time as this" (4:14).

---

[3] See, e.g., Jo Carruthers, *Esther through the Centuries*, Blackwell Bible Commentaries (New York: Blackwell Publishers, 2008), 53.

[4] All biblical quotes come from the New Revised Standard Version unless otherwise noted.

Anyone who appears unbidden before the king in his inner court is subject to death; "only if the king holds out the golden scepter to someone, may that person live" (4:11). The first action Esther makes is to dress her royal part and appear before the king. He holds out his golden scepter, so she lives (5:1–2). Next, Esther uses the tool at her disposal in the royal court, a banquet, inviting both the king and Haman to attend. When the banquet takes place, Esther petitions the king to rescind the edict. She then reveals that she too is Jewish. Haman begs for Esther's forgiveness by grabbing her, and the king mistakes his petition for sexual assault, so Haman is hanged on the very gallows he prepared for Mordecai (ch. 7). The king's honor, reflected in the sexual status of his wife, is the breaking point for the king and the impetus for the rash decision to hang Haman out of anger (7:9–10). But the original word of the king cannot be revoked. Instead the king gives Mordecai his signet ring, which allows Mordecai to write and send out letters allowing Jews to defend themselves with the blessing of the king.

In the end, the Jews fought their enemies, slaughtering them, but they did not take material possessions (9:5). Esther requested that the Jews of Susa witness the hanging of Haman's ten sons (9:11–13). In a reversal from the book's opening royal feast, in the end the Jews feast in triumph, heralding a tradition known as Purim (9:24–32). Purim has become a festival that celebrates Jewish survival as a minority group in a hostile world. Therefore, on the evening and morning of the annual Purim festival, Jews traditionally read aloud the book of Esther.

Esther's story takes place at a royal court in a palace wherein a young woman faces a challenge that she overcomes. Such is the setting of films of the Disney princess franchise that was developed at the turn of the century by Andy Mooney, the chairman of Disney Consumer Products. Since 2017, the line-up of Disney princesses in the franchise has come from animated films: Snow White, Cinderella, Aurora (*Sleeping Beauty*), Ariel (*The Little Mermaid*), Belle (*Beauty and the Beast*), Jasmine (*Aladdin*), Pocahontas, Mulan, Tiana (*The Princess and the Frog*), Rapunzel (*Tangled*), and Merida (*Brave*). The franchise reaches into apparel, home goods, games, dolls, packaged food, media, and plastic toys. And, of course, visitors can meet women dressed as these princesses at Disney theme parks.[5] Since these princesses are marketed as a group (they have an official website with synopses of all the films, www.princess.disney.com), this chapter centers on ideals from only those films.

Disney executives market a "princess mythology" in popular culture in a successful campaign, reaching $3 billion in revenue in 2012 from venues across the globe.[6] Newer initiatives that capitalize on the popularity of the Disney princess franchise include live-action remakes of the animated film versions of *Cinderella* (2015) and *Beauty and the*

---

[5] Many find trips to Disney theme parks as pop-culture pilgrimages. See, for example, Eric Michael Mazur and Tara K. Koda, "The Happiest Place on Earth: Disney's America and the Commodification of Religion," in *God in the Details: American Religion in Popular Culture*, 2nd ed., ed. Eric Michael Mazur and Kate McCarthy (New York: Routledge, 2011), 307–21.

[6] Vincent Ng, "How Disney Princesses Became a Multi Billion Dollar Brand," *MCNG Marketing*, March 18, 2013, http://www.mcngmarketing.com/how-disney-princesses-became-a-multi-billion-dollar-brand/#.WQttpOXyvIU.

Beast (2017). The backstory of Sleeping Beauty in *Maleficent* came a bit earlier, in 2014. The trend of live-action remakes continued with *Aladdin* in May 2019.

A formula emerges for the franchise and the princess mythology it disseminates through the films. The princesses live out a popular expectation of heterosexual marital romance as the culmination of their journey. The following section outlines the princess mythology in more detail, which will allow for an analysis of how modern Christian novels apply such a mythology to Esther.

OVERVIEW OF TOPIC

One aspect of popular culture is the practice of disseminating ideas to as many people as possible for the purpose of influencing values. Marketing those ideas to the masses gives them "popular status." In popular culture, messages about biblical subjects are produced, circulated, consumed, and reproduced, to use the words of Stuart Hall. Hall goes on to suggest that patterns of ideas can be tracked, and preferred messages emerge. These "preferred" or popular messages are political and ideological and often come from institutions.[7]

The Disney princess mythology fits Hall's description of the ways institutions market values to the masses. The values Disney wants us to glean from the princess characters are the values that Americans celebrate about womanhood and/or what Disney wants Americans to celebrate about womanhood. Sarah Rothschild analyzes the princess story as Disney captures and markets it throughout American culture. She argues that *Snow White* (1937), *Cinderella* (1950), and *Sleeping Beauty* (1959) depict the women as passive. The princesses are dependent on the male heroes who save them and then ultimately marry them. Feminist critiques led Disney to superficially counter with princesses who have a thin veneer of independence, yet Disney does not ultimately solve the critique that marriage is valorized as a woman's ultimate life goal. Rothschild calls this superficial counter a "second wave" of films that responds to second-wave feminism: *The Little Mermaid* (1989), *Beauty and the Beast* (1992), *Aladdin* (1992), *Pocahontas* (1995), and *Mulan* (1998). Since Rothschild's analysis, Disney added *The Princess and the Frog* (2009), *Tangled* (2010), and *Brave* (2012) to the franchise. Speaking of the second wave of films released by Disney to respond to feminist criticism, Rothschild notes that each princess defies expectations, shows independence, and at least indicates some ethnic difference from the white women of the first three princess films. Nearly every princess experiences pressure from her father against which she initially tries to rebel. "Yet," she states, "the princesses and their stories, while superficially more adventurous and full of more possibilities than the princesses in older Disney films, are still ultimately reduced

---

    [7] Stuart Hall, "Encoding, Decoding," in *The Cultural Studies Reader*, ed. Simon During (London: Routledge, 1993), 91, 93.

to dreamy, romance-obsessed girls who simply travel from father to beloved."[8] The films open with men in power or powerful men, and end with a marriage or engagement. While a possible exception is Merida in *Brave*, that film does not completely discount that she will eventually marry. Popular culture reflects the need for happiness in a narrative of romance and a love-based marriage. Up until the late eighteenth century, marriage was an economic and political arrangement in the Western world. According to Catherine Roach, Western culture presents the idea of a romantic "happily-ever-after" as the prime goal of life, as if all people are on a "quest for the Holy Grail of One True Love."[9]

The work of Jack Zipes on fairy tales in Western civilization reveals a Disney princess formula of the franchise. An opening song introduces the heroine's inner motivations and yearnings. The young woman is always beautiful, virginal, and sweet. She is victimized, often physically captive, by sinister forces or imposing structures of her society, represented by a witch, a scheming minister, or a dumb brute. At the same time, comical animals or human sidekicks provide comic relief. A male hero is the centerpiece for her ability to escape her situation. She cannot save herself. The male hero sings a solo; the two sing a romantic duet; and he is finally needed for the girl to overcome her situation.[10]

Rothschild builds on Zipes, suggesting that even if some elements are adjusted in the second wave of films from *The Little Mermaid* to *Mulan*, one overall element is that the heroine lacks positive adult women or mother figures. Most of the other strong female characters demonstrate jealousy of the youthful, beautiful woman. This is certainly the case for Rapunzel in *Tangled*, who is captured by a witch and locked in a tower, devoid of her mother's presence in her life. The ultimate message, regardless of the various differences in their stories, is that the beautiful girl, princess by marriage or by blood, adapts herself to a situation that ultimately changes her focus from independence to romance. In *The Little Mermaid*, for instance, Ariel endures mutilation of her body by requesting legs instead of her fin in order to walk on land; in the opening of the film her first desire is independence, until she sees her human love interest, Eric. The expectation for romance is so strong that the Disney versions of *Pocahontas* and *Mulan* emphasize love interests when their historical narratives do not and therefore ultimately undercut feminist ideals of female independence and active roles for women.[11]

---

[8] Sarah Rothschild, *The Princess Story: Modeling the Feminine in Twentieth-Century American Fiction and Film* (New York: Peter Lang, 2013), 136.

[9] Catherine M. Roach, *Happily Ever After: The Romance Story in Popular Culture* (Bloomington: Indiana University Press, 2016), 4.

[10] Jack Zipes, *Fairy Tales and the Art of Subversion: The Classical Genre for Children and the Process of Civilization*, 2nd ed. (New York: Routledge, 2006), 209. For more sociopolitical commentary on the fairy tale, see Jack Zipes, *The Irresistible Fairy Tale: The Cultural and Social History of a Genre* (Princeton, NJ: Princeton University Press, 2012).

[11] See in particular chapter 4, "Disney's 'Feminist' Princess Stories," in Rothschild, *The Princess Story*, 135–68.

Some fans wish Disney would make an Esther film.[12] Esther fits the Disney princess model I just discussed in that her story exists in a patriarchal culture bookended by men; it opens with King Ahasuerus and closes with Mordecai. Esther, being an orphan and raised by her cousin, lacks a mother figure. She is virginal, "fair and beautiful" (2:7). Haman is a scheming villain; Esther's beauty and wit, with Mordecai's guidance along the way, allows her to win the king's favor and devotion. But those connections are minor compared to the overall complexities of Esther's story. A Disney princess mythology from the modern world has trouble applying to the ancient world of biblical Esther in several ways. First, modern-day adaptations have to stretch the imagination to fit Esther into the Disney mold because underlying her story is a struggle for Jewish national identity and agency in a hostile world, and that is not a simple story. The book of Esther is grounded in a Jewish holiday that celebrates survival of a particular body of people who happen to be in the minority among the provinces. Second, the biblical Esther story contains many complexities: an absent God; political and sexual oppression; negotiations of agency, identity, and violence. These elements remain integral parts of the ancient story. Third, there is a long and sordid history of the various ways Jews and Christians have engaged with the biblical story. I briefly discuss these three disparities between Disney princess mythology and the ancient story to set the stage for the overview of the five Christian novels about Esther.

In his commentary, Timothy Beal thinks about the book of Esther in "dislocation. Esther is a writing in diaspora, about identity in dispersion and under threat. It plays between annihilation and Purimfest, between desert and carnival."[13] The complexities of the book rest in the interplays of power and the agency of the characters. Vashti's refusal to come before the king resulted in an opening for Esther in the harem. The beauty of Vashti, meant to be put on display for the king, parallels the beauty of Hadassah (2:7), who was "admired by all who saw her" (2:15). Her Jewish identity is always in flux; Esther is given palace food (2:9), but it remains unknown if she upheld Jewish dietary laws while living in the palace. Mordecai's refusal to bow down before Haman (3:1–6), who built gallows for Mordecai, resulted in an ironic twist of fate for Haman and his family. The king empowers Jews to fight at the end of the story, thus intertwining his own fate with those of the Jews. In all this, God does not intervene, nor does anyone pray to God. The fate of the Jews rests on their own ability to maneuver in a Gentile world.

When it comes to female agency, Esther's character can be seen as a victim of a patriarchal system, as a pawn in Mordecai's plans, or as a hero who stands up for her people.[14]

---

[12] One example comes from the *Disney Confessions* tumblr blog, now closed, where fans posted their secret confessions regarding Disney. One post from February 4, 2015, states, "I'm a little upset that Disney hasn't introduced an openly Jewish Princess yet. I'd love to see . . . the story of Queen Esther. I'd like to see some Jewish representation in the Disney film canon to identify with" (http://waltdisney confessions.tumblr.com/post/110102862922/im-a-little-upset-that-disney-hasnt-introduced).

[13] Timothy Beal, *The Book of Hiding: Gender, Ethnicity, Annihilation, and Esther* (New York: Routledge, 1997), 14.

[14] Esther Fuchs, for instance, dismisses Esther as a "fairy tale, though it presents itself as a piece of political history affecting the main diaspora community" (77). See her "Status and Role of Female Heroines in the Biblical Narrative," in *Women in the Hebrew Bible: A Reader*, ed. Alice Bach (New York: Routledge, 1999), 77–84.

Noteworthy here is the fact that the book of Esther ends with full praise of Mordecai, not Esther (ch. 10). Mordecai was powerful and popular, a model Jew for living in a Gentile world. Agency, the authority to act in any given situation, relates to the identity question. As Beal puts it, "To be Jewish is, in the book of Esther, to know exile as a formative experience." The book of Esther constructs Jewish identity in ambiguous ways. To be in exile means to be "out of place," and the anti-Jewish strategies, represented by Haman, present Jewish identity as "other," on the fringe of society.[15] Yet the farcical way in which the book turns Ahasuerus into a buffoon places power not in public politics but in the body politic. Susan Niditch examines Esther alongside the Joseph saga (Genesis 37–50) and asks compelling questions about whether Esther is not responding about how to be an Israelite (and for Esther, an Israelite woman) in the outside world.[16]

The fierce focus on Jewish identity in a hostile world makes for a complicated relationship with Christianity. A tradition in Christian interpretation dismisses Esther for a lack of morals and a presentation of savagery and vindictiveness.[17] Martin Luther, the Christian reformer, wished the book of Esther did not exist at all, primarily because of its heavy emphasis on Jewish identity, an identity without moral scruples.[18]

Even from the very beginning of its circulation, the book of Esther must have felt unstable since many Greek additions were added to the Hebrew. Six main additions in Greek exist, and all Greek translations and editions of Esther carry nuanced changes. One addition, for instance, inserts Mordecai and Esther praying (Greek Esther, Addition C). This change relates to the need to characterize Mordecai and Esther in more devout ways.[19] From its earliest history, the book of Esther has been adapted to fit the values of its readers. Esther in popular culture remains no different in this regard.

SPECIFIC EXAMPLES AND/OR FOCI

Catherine Roach defines the basic plot or common storyline of a romance: "Find somebody to love, work through problems, be happy."[20] The Disney princess mythology also maintains this expectation for women. Couple the bestselling romance genre with a

---

[15] Beal, *The Book of Hiding*, 33, 51.

[16] Susan Niditch, "Esther: Folklore, Wisdom, Feminism and Authority," in *Feminist Companion to Esther, Judith and Susanna*, ed. Athalya Brenner, Feminist Companion to the Bible 7 (New York: Bloomsbury, 1995), 28.

[17] For a thorough discussion of the historical tensions between Jews and Christians when it comes to understanding Esther, see Elliott S. Horowitz, *Reckless Rites: Purim and the Legacy of Jewish Violence* (Princeton, NJ: Princeton University Press, 2008).

[18] Martin Luther, *Table Talk* XXIV. For more on Martin Luther's strident outlook, see Carey Moore, "Esther, Book of," in *The Anchor Bible Dictionary*, 6 vols., ed. David Noel Freedman (New York: Doubleday, 1992), 2:633–43.

[19] For a discussion of the Greek additions, see Linda Day, *Three Faces of a Queen: Characterization in the Books of Esther*, Journal for the Study of the Old Testament Supplement Series 186 (New York: Bloomsbury, 1995).

[20] Roach, *Happily Ever After*, 4–5.

story involving royalty—a Queen Esther—and interpreters fit Esther into a popular Disney princess mold. Perhaps Tommy Tenney, a Pentecostal preacher and author of *Hadassah: One Night with the King* from 2005, set the trend to manipulate Esther's biblical story into princess mythology. The book was made into a film by Michael Sajbel in 2006 called *One Night with the King.*[21] Reviewers of the film have made the connections very clear, including Dan W. Clanton, Jr., who states that *One Night with the King* "seems interested in portraying Esther as a fanciful girl with a creative imagination and a plucky courage, as a dreamer who is both kind and smart—again, all traits that are associated with Disney princesses."[22] Taking analysis of the Disney princess mythology even further, I introduce five Christian novels, all authored by women and published around the time the Disney princess franchise emerged and expanded (from 2005 to 2016), and focus on three main ways in which the story of Esther is imagined in the Disney princess mythology.

First, the novelists create a romantic love story between Esther and Ahasuerus (Xerxes). This means that, in the words of one of the novelists, "clearly the hero had to have some good qualities that would make Esther fall in love with him."[23] The biblical text gives no physical description of the king and makes no apologies for the existence of his harem. Also, most of the novels discussed here have Haman writing the decree in the king's name so that the king remains oblivious and thus excused from hatred of the Jews.[24] Esther's pregnancy (not mentioned in the biblical text) in many of the novels sets up either a stronger bond or a creative tension between her and the king. Marital sex, however, is highlighted in all the novels. The fact that Esther becomes queen, and thus conjugal sex is assumed, provides an opportunity for interpreters to uphold and celebrate the joys of sex within marriage; this has been a theme in evangelical Christianity since the 1960s.[25] Esther's feelings about being taken to the king and his preferring her to the other virgins are not mentioned in the biblical story (2:16–17). The emphasis on Esther's love story leads novelists to downplay the Jewish violence and minimize Purim, and they all live happily ever after.

Second, Esther faces opposition from other females in a way that is not present in the biblical text. As in *Snow White*, *Sleeping Beauty*, and *Cinderella*, for instance, women

[21] For more on this film and other films about Esther, see chapter 5 in Dan W. Clanton, Jr., *Daring, Disreputable, and Devout: Interpreting the Bible's Women in the Arts and Music* (New York: Bloomsbury T & T Clark, 2009). See also Deborah W. Rooke, "'What Shall We Do with the Tainted Maiden?' Film Treatments of the Book of Esther," in *T & T Clark Companion to the Bible and Film*, ed. Richard Walsh (London: Bloomsbury T & T Clark, 2018), 322–34.

[22] Clanton, *Daring, Disreputable, and Devout*, 129.

[23] Joan Wolf, *A Reluctant Queen: The Love Story of Queen Esther* (Nashville, TN: Thomas Nelson, 2011), 375.

[24] In Esther 3:7–11, Haman convinces the king for the decree about a "certain people" and enhances the deal with a payment of silver.

[25] For more on this issue, see Daniel K. Williams, "Sex and the Evangelicals: Gender Issues, the Sexual Revolution, and Abortion in the 1960s," in *American Evangelicals and the 1960s*, Studies in American Thought and Culture Series, ed. Alex R. Schäfer (Madison: University of Wisconsin Press, 2013), 97–118.

compete for male approval. An older woman is jealous of her beauty and wit. Third, Esther prays to God, whether inwardly or outwardly, something that does not happen in the biblical text but does in some early Greek additions. There is a political element to this third point. Mordecai's words to Esther, "for such a time as this" (4:14), are often used by evangelical Christians as a call to political action. A sense in which an increasingly secular nation is threatening Christian values, and God is calling up leaders to bring the nation back to Christian morals, comes through in many of these interpretations of Esther. For the five novels of Christian fiction mentioned here, Esther needs to demonstrate virtues worthy to be called a woman of God. The Jewish attributes of Esther are often downplayed as a result. This lack of Jewish identity in the novels leads to the final section of this chapter, which is a brief discussion of modern Jewish adaptations of Esther in contrast.

Chosen: The Lost Diaries of Queen Esther by Ginger Garrett (2005)

The young adult novel *Chosen* received an award from the Evangelical Christian Publishers Association in 2006. It was incorporated by David Cook Publishing in 2010 into a series called Lost Loves of the Bible. Published in the wake of September 11, 2001, the novel includes a foreword and an appendix of fake news releases regarding the "war on terror" in 2003 and an earthquake in southeastern Iran that unearthed ancient diaries of Queen Esther. A "new understanding of the war" on women fills the pages at the back of the novel, which states, "We have pursued women's rights until they have become women's whims," including their rights to choose to be sexually active before marriage, to use contraceptives, and even to have abortions.[26] Thus the novel carries a strong message in support of the purity movement, a movement that gained momentum in evangelical Christianity in the 1970s and upholds marriage between one man and one woman and that the importance of marital sex is preserved through abstinence-only sex education.[27]

Generation Esther is a collection of stories compiled by Lisa Ryan, a cohost of the television show *700 Club*, and is an example of a purity message. Playing on the naming of generations as Gen-X or Gen-Y, Ryan introduces Gen-E, the idea that young women should rebel against destructive messages in their society, such as that girls need to be sexy and selfish. She assumes that Esther acts as a biblical role model for godly characteristics to today's young women. Esther is "a young orphan girl from a common background who was suddenly thrust into a beauty contest and quickly elevated to the role of queen of a vast kingdom (kind of a Cinderella story, really)."[28] The "beauty contest"

---

[26] Ginger Garrett, *Chosen: The Lost Diaries of Queen Esther*, Lost Loves of the Bible (Colorado Springs, CO: David Cook, 2010), 284.

[27] Williams, "Sex and the Evangelicals," 97–118.

[28] Lisa Ryan, *Generation Esther: Stories of Young Women Raised Up for Such a Time as This* (Sisters, OR: Multnomah, 2003), 17.

refers to the extensive cosmetic treatments that the virgins had to endure while under guard at the palace to make them presentable to the king (2:12). For Ryan, the assessment of Esther as role model hinges on her purity, which in this case is synonymous with her virginity, because her virginity qualifies her to enter the first round of the "pageant." Her virginity (aka purity) is a virtue of high value, according to Ryan.

Overtones of Esther as spokeswoman for the purity movement exist in Garrett's *Chosen*. Esther enters the harem by force, like the other young girls, and the novel likens the virgin roundup to contemporary sex trafficking and even includes President George W. Bush's address to the United Nations Assembly in 2003 about rescuing women and children from exploitation. In the harem, "the girls who honored seduction as their only asset got only sex. Esther valued herself, and her God above all, and was given the kingdom and the king."[29] Yet it is not so simple for women to "value their purity" when being forced into sexually exploitative situations. They cannot give consent in these matters. It is highly unlikely that Esther and all the other young virgins in the harem who are meant to replace Vashti had given their consent because they were brought to the citadel by the king's decree (2:1–4).

When Esther and Xerxes meet in Garrett's novel, their conversation turns into one about Esther's honor in giving her virginity to Xerxes, that she will do so only in exchange for love. When Esther offers both her body and her heart, Xerxes chooses her to be his queen, calling Esther "my Star" (*esther* is Persian for "star") throughout the rest of the novel. Esther's opportunity to consent in *Chosen* is not afforded to sexually trafficked individuals.

Esther pines for her first love, a man named Cyrus, throughout the novel. Xerxes asks Esther why she never says she loves him. She becomes pregnant and miscarries; tensions exist between Esther's feeling like a prisoner and wanting the attention of Xerxes. She even states, "Discontent shows in a woman's features, making her undesirable to a man. So I will be grateful that I still have the king's heart—although I must share his body— and grateful for my crown."[30] At the end of the novel, Xerxes confesses devotion to Esther's God on his deathbed, but it is not stated whether he converts to Judaism, and Esther confesses that she loved him. Purim is mentioned in a brief footnote.

A Reluctant Queen: The Love Story of Esther by Joan Wolf (2011)

The subtleties of turning Esther into a love story disappear for this novel, given that "love story" is part of its title. The princess mythology too is overt. Joan Wolf states that Esther is "the Cinderella story of this little Jewish girl becoming the queen of the Great King of Persia."[31]

---

[29] Garrett, *Chosen*, 282.   [30] Garrett, *Chosen*, 176.
[31] Joan Wolf, *A Reluctant Queen: The Love Story of Esther* (Nashville, TN: Thomas Nelson, 2011), 373–4.

The novel includes a plot in which Mordecai reluctantly sends Esther to the palace harem as a Jewish emissary. The king will choose her because her beauty was given to her for a purpose from God, the Jewish elders tell her. Esther is inspected to confirm her virginity and she undergoes tedious treatments; the first time she sees Ahasuerus she is smitten: "Living in the strict world of her Jewish culture, she hadn't even known this kind of attraction existed."[32] To explain away the harem to create the love story, Ahasuerus stops going to other women and sleeps exclusively in Esther's bed, to the scandal of the royal court. With plans to dissipate the harem and marry off the rest of the wives, Esther turns the eunuchs into the Queen's Royal Guard.

Haman, the king's boyhood friend, is jealous that Ahasuerus loves Esther. This jealousy leads to his forgery of a declaration against the Jews in the king's name. The king feasts at a royal religious banquet during a Persian holy day in which he has to keep himself away from women. Wolf conflates the appearance of Esther before the throne of the king and a king's banquet by having her appear at the royal religious banquet at which women are excluded.

When Esther enters the religious banquet with all eyes watching her, she faints, only to be caught by Ahasuerus's "strong arms," which sets up Esther as a "damsel in distress" worthy to be saved by her love.[33] Finding out that Haman forged a declaration in his name, Ahasuerus declares another decree: that Jews will not be slaughtered but instead will celebrate with feasts, an easier resolution than in the biblical book. In the end, Ahasuerus comes to Esther's chambers mortified and in tears that his boyhood friend betrayed him and was hanged. Esther is pregnant. As she comforts him with a hug, the baby kicks, and the novel ends in their private embrace. Purim is not mentioned. Incidentally, neither is the name Hadassah. Two important connections to the Jewish identity so strongly emphasized in the biblical book of Esther disappear in the romantic novel by Wolf.

Esther the Queen by H. B. Moore (2013)

This novel by Heather Moore, published by and marketed to a Latter-day Saints audience, inserts an early surprise meeting between Esther and Ahasuerus at the town well (to continue with a biblical motif) before Esther enters the harem to provide a sense that their marriage was "meant to be." Moore drops hints throughout the book that marriage between a man and a woman to create a family is "part of the Lord's plan." Ahasuerus is in love at first sight and calls for Esther directly and only allows for the year of treatments in the harem because of Persian law. In fact, Esther is poisoned by a jealous concubine

---

[32] Ibid., 34, 121.

[33] In several Greek versions of Esther, B and D, she falls or faints or demonstrates physical weakness when appearing before the king. See the discussion in Day, *Three Faces of a Queen*, 174–6. It is not clear whether Wolf is aware of the Greek versions, but a trend in Renaissance art, beginning with Tintoretto (1519–1594) and continuing with Paolo Veronese (1528–1588), popularly depicts Esther fainting before the throne of Ahasuerus. For details, see Carruthers, *Esther through the Centuries*, 196–200.

three days in, and the king helps nurse her back to health. When Ahasuerus asks Esther if she wants to be queen and she consents, they save their first kiss for their wedding day. After their first night together, Esther "understood now the bond created between a man and a woman when they become husband and wife."[34] After pleading for her life as a Jew, Esther tells Ahasuerus that she loves him. Rather than pursue Haman, the king waits to ask Esther if she truly loves him. According to one reviewer who uses princess language to describe the novel, Xerxes acts like "Prince Charming" and Esther gets her "happily ever after."[35]

The "happily ever after" does not come easily when the king keeps concubines. To get around that problem, the king does not have sex with the virgins; he "interviews" them. If he does not like them, he sends them back to their home with a generous dowry to marry someone else. After he marries Esther, he forbids late night feasting and drinking and reduces the number of concubines to five, but he does not sleep with any after he marries Esther. He confesses his love for Esther in the last pages of the novel and the epilogue reveals Esther's pregnancy, thus ensuring an heir and no need for Ahasuerus to visit the harem ever again.

When it comes to the vendetta against the Jews, it is not Haman's background with the Agagites that fuels it. Haman is identified in the biblical text as a descendant of King Agag the Amalekite (Esther 3:1), who was spared by King Saul in battle to God's disappointment (1 Samuel 15), but this tradition is entirely absent in the novel. Instead, Haman had an affair with a Jewish woman, Rebekah, who does not leave her husband in the end because it is not "the Lord's will." Haman becomes bitter. "If your god does not approve, you are worshipping the wrong god," he says to her, which sparks his need for revenge on all the Jews and their fanatical religious beliefs.[36] Rebekah's death during the birth of her husband's child leads Haman to declare that the Jews marry their own kind and live by false ideals. Perhaps a parallel is meant to be drawn between the Jews in this novel and modern Latter-day Saints living in the United States, who have historically often faced discrimination and have struggled with mainstream America.

Esther: Royal Beauty, a Dangerous Beauty Novel by Angela Hunt (2015)

Esther is the first book in Angela Hunt's Dangerous Beauty series. Hunt holds a doctorate in theology and is a member of the Christian Writers' Guild. The novel brings in pseudo-historical names and events from the Greek author Herodotus, chronicler of the

---

[34] H. B. Moore, *Esther the Queen* (American Fork, UT: Covenant Communications, 2013), 117.

[35] Michelle Garrett Bulsiewicz, "Book Review: 'Esther the Queen' Re-tells Old Testament Story from a Mormon Perspective," *Deseret News*, June 16, 2013, http://www.deseretnews.com/article/865581663/Book-review-Esther-the-Queen-re-tells-Old-Testament-story-from-a-Mormon-perspective.html.

[36] Moore, *Esther the Queen*, 75.

History of the Persian Wars from the fifth century BCE.[37] The novel also alternates chapters from Hadassah's perspective and from Harbonah's, a eunuch who contributes his perspectives about Hadassah (who is called Esther by those in the palace).

The novel opens with Hadassah's inner ambition to be a queen, a timeless beauty and flawless like the Persian women. She recalls an incidental meeting with one of the king's wives, whose splendor she envied; this was none other than Vashti. This entry into Hadassah's inner longings reveals a flighty, impatient, distracted girl at the age of thirteen, who dreams of marrying a boy in the market and who will become a mature, wise woman of God by the end of the novel. A few pages in, for instance, Mordecai's wife, Miriam, tells Hadassah that "women should be modest" and "not overly concerned with outward beauty."[38] This stern warning comes because Mordecai and his family are invited to the royal feast and Hadassah longs to order a new dress for the occasion. Hadassah is truly a princess, however, in that she knows she is a descendant of King Saul's royal line.

Hadassah is taken to the harem against her will when slave traders capture her. Every girl the eunuchs approve of will stay and sleep with the king one night, then stay in the harem forever, becoming a possession of the king. The turning point comes when Esther talks with a concubine of Xerxes's father. She gives Esther advice to shelter the king's heart, to "love him for the man he is and the man he could be. Expect greatness of him. And then, perhaps, he will find it in himself."[39] The meet-cute encounter between Esther and Xerxes transpires when Esther bends down to help a slave clean up a spill and gets gravy on her dress. Both laugh. Hadassah falls in love with Xerxes months after their marriage, but mystery remains as to whether Xerxes loves Esther.

Haman does not enter the story until two-thirds of the way into the novel, after five years of Esther's being in the palace. Haman still creates a plot to kill all the Jews, developed in the last part of the novel, but the real threat to Esther throughout is Vashti, who is allowed to stay in the palace to care for her children. When Esther becomes pregnant, Vashti kidnaps one of the king's sons to sacrifice to the gods so Esther will lose her baby. Whether through effective sacrifice to the gods or not, Esther miscarries and continues through several unsuccessful pregnancies, never carrying a child full term. Out of spite and jealousy the threatened Vashti taunts Esther about the king's visiting other women, something Snow White and Sleeping Beauty can understand in regard to older queens wanting to thwart the happiness of the younger princess.

The final chapter, told from the viewpoint of Hadassah, quickly wraps up the reverberations of the Haman edict with a few paragraphs mentioning "episodes of intimidation" from the people of Susa against the Jews.[40] Esther's final thoughts recall her duty to honor, obey, and ultimately love her husband. Two chapters from Harbonah's perspective end the novel. Mordecai tells Harbonah about the coming Messiah, quoting the

---

[37] Several novels incorporate Herodotus's ideas about Persia, although he never mentions Esther. In understanding Herodotus, though, Adele Berlin calls him a "storyteller" rather than a historian. See her "The Book of Esther and Ancient Storytelling," *Journal of Biblical Literature* 120 (2001): 3–14, here 8–9.

[38] Angela Hunt, *Esther: Royal Beauty* (Bloomington, MN: Bethany House, 2015), 30.

[39] Ibid., 165.   [40] Ibid., 328.

prophet Isaiah, and Purim is introduced. The final chapter comes seven years later, when Harbonah recalls the events of the king's assassination and the rise of Vashti's son to the throne. Vashti maintains her power and Esther retires to a room in the harem, although continually loved and admired by both Jews and Persians.

Game of Queens: A Novel of Vashti and Esther by India Edghill (2016)

It does not get any more clear that modern authors relate Esther to Disney princess mythology than when India Edghill states in her notes that Esther is "the Perfect Disney Princess."[41] She says this, however, after noting that authors have created an image of Esther as a poor orphan to increase her "Cinderella-esque qualities." Edghill manipulates Esther's story to recall motifs from Cinderella. For instance, Esther's mother dies in childbirth, after which Esther is raised on a farm as the only child of a loving father. Esther's father raises horses, and she learns the freedom of the countryside before her father dies. A similar depiction of Cinderella riding horses in the countryside exists in the Disney live-action film of 2015.

Also similar to Disney's *Cinderella*, a royal decree is sent throughout the streets declaring that any girl between fourteen and twenty can go to the palace to be judged by the king of kings to become the next queen of queens. A swirl of excitement from the girls of the kingdom ensues. To continue the Cinderella ideas, Esther and Ahasuerus fall in love during their first meeting. They live a happy, love-filled life in the palace until Haman conspires with the queen mother to create the king's edict to slaughter the Jews; thus the evil queen mother would rid the world of Queen Esther. In the novel, Queen Mother Amestris fits the role of the evil queen plotting to get rid of her competition, an uncanny similarity to *Snow White*, *Sleeping Beauty*, and even the wicked sea hag Ursula in *The Little Mermaid*.

Esther trusts that her marital love will allow Ahasuerus to forgive her intrusion of going before the king unsummoned, and it does. The king takes his seal and declares that once a year he can rescind a decree. The Jews can defend themselves as well. Purim is not mentioned, although a *pur* (lot) is utilized by various characters.

All novels noted here elaborate on the eunuchs, an important development and modern commentary on sexual politics beyond the scope of this chapter. In a clever backstory, Edghill creates a situation with Haman, the king's childhood friend, and Hegai, who is captured by Haman and turned into a eunuch. Haman sold Hegai as a sex slave to an older man, thus extending Haman's villain status and Hegai's secret motivation to get revenge on Haman. Also, the first time Esther meets Haman, he is drowning puppies, so it is not hard to hate him. The character of Daniel appears as another biblical character living in the royal court; he saves Hegai in the marketplace, thus explaining how Hegai

---

[41] India Edghill, *Game of Queens: A Novel of Vashti and Esther* (New York: St. Martin's Press, 2015), ix.

ends up as the chief eunuch of the Women's Palace. Then, in another twist, Vashti runs away with Hegai after they fall in love and get married. Earlier in the novel, Mordecai warns Hadassah, "Be glad you are not a queen, Hadassah, for they are never truly free."[42] At the end of the novel, while Esther watches Vashti and Hegai ride away, she acknowledges her restricted role as queen, but the love she has for her husband keeps her satisfied.

Summary of the Five Christian Novels

These Christian novels all contain one central element not in the biblical tale: Esther is in some form or fashion in love with the king, which allows her to suspend her concern for lack of independence and identity. Furthermore, perhaps the most striking addition is the introduction of an evil-plotting woman. Rothschild argues that romance may serve as the primary plot, but a secondary addition to the Disney princess mythology is the lack of positive female presence. The lack of such female role models in princess mythology helps to maintain patriarchy or keeps women competing with one another rather than actively seeking ways to advance in leadership positions. The evil women in the princess mythology seek their own advancement as they get older due to jealousy of feminine youth and beauty—ideal attributes set up for women in a patriarchal world.[43]

Nearly every novelist gives Esther a Jewish love interest early on in the novel to highlight her sense of loss or to teach her a moral lesson about what real love with the king is supposed to look like. The triumph of love over difference recalls the Disney version of *Pocahontas*, in which a dreaming princess falls in love with and saves a man not from her ethnicity. In nearly every case, Esther's inner struggle to reveal her Jewish identity comes with the possibility of disappointing her husband and thus losing his love. This struggle does not exist in the biblical story, in which the primary motivation for Esther's revelation of her identity is saving the Jewish people from annihilation. In the words of Rothschild, any feisty or independent decision made by a Disney princess is "motivated by her romantic relationship."[44]

A romance novel maintains a central love story with a satisfying ending. As Lynn Neal explains, "Evangelicals in the nineteenth, twentieth, and twenty-first centuries have used popular culture to reap the religious rewards of evangelism and edification."[45] For instance, Garrett's *Lost Diaries of Queen Esther* informs *Queen Esther's Secrets of Womanhood: A Biblical Rite of Passage for Your Daughter*, which contains a year's worth of devotions regarding purity standards and a caution against the pursuit of worldly

---

[42] Ibid., 205.   [43] Rothschild, *Princess Story*, 143.   [44] Ibid., 142.

[45] Lynn S. Neal, "Evangelical Love Stories: The Triumphs and Temptations of Romantic Fiction," in *Evangelical Christians and Popular Culture: Pop Goes the Gospel*, vol. 2, ed. Robert Woods Jr. (Santa Barbara, CA: Praeger, 2013), 1–20. A helpful summary of women's edification of reading romance can be found in Rebecca Kaye Barrett, "Higher Love: What Women Gain from Christian Romance Novels," *Journal of Religion and Popular Culture* 4 (2003): n.p.

standards of beauty, yet it lists suggestions for beauty treatments at the end of every chapter and a full list of beauty treatment ideas is at the end of the book![46]

In an analysis of Esther in film, Carl Ehrlich notes an overtly Christian move to downplay the sexual politics involved in the biblical book. With Esther's "girlish dreams of becoming not only a princess but a queen" and a moral story that "faith and purity are rewarded with riches and love," evangelical Christians especially commodify Esther in a Disney princess mythology in order to allow for at least one biblical woman to fit the mold.[47] Putting Esther in this position is highly ironic, especially given that the largest evangelical group in the United States, the Southern Baptist Convention, condemned Disney in the 1990s for losing its moral values.[48]

Esther has become an evangelical Christian version of a Disney princess, a role model for Christian women to use their beauty and purity to gain men's love and respect.[49] As a result, interpretations of her story follow the main guidelines for the Disney princess franchise: she is beautiful and virtuous, exhibits some independent traits that separate her from the rest, dreams of changing her situation, and, in the end, is always dependent on her love for a man who will help her escape the clutches of the villain. In the end, a satisfying marriage is enough to sustain Esther after successfully managing to reveal her true identity to the man she loves. This satisfying marriage, though, as the end goal, also incorporates values appealing to Christian women, such as generosity, staying "true to one's self," and romantic love; these values encourage Christian women to triumph over evil.[50]

Another Christian hallmark is to de-emphasize Esther's Jewish identity and turn her godly struggle into a universal one "for such a time as this" when evangelical Christians struggle with living in secular society in the United States. An extreme example is the Christian children's series known as Veggie Tales, which created *Esther: The Girl Who Became Queen*.[51] Given its young audience, a child-friendly episode depicts banishment to the "island of perpetual tickling." Esther and her cousin Mordecai are presented as part of a family that cannot be trusted, and Haman is out to get them banished. King Xerxes loves Esther, which gives credence to his sticking up for her and Mordecai. The

[46] Ginger Garrett, *Queen Esther's Secrets of Womanhood: A Biblical Rite of Passage for Your Daughter* (Colorado Springs, CO: NavPress, 2006). Purim is not mentioned as a part of the story of Esther. Instead, Garrett describes a "national holiday" with a "big party every year" (119).

[47] Carl Ehrlich, "Esther in Film," in *The Bible in Motion: A Handbook of the Bible and Its Reception in Film*, ed. Rhonda Burnette-Bletsch, Handbooks of the Bible and Its Reception, 2 (Berlin: Walter de Gruyter, 2016), 125, 129.

[48] See Mark Pinskey, *The Gospel According to Disney: Faith, Trust, and Pixie Dust* (Louisville, KY: Westminster John Knox Press, 2004), 238–61.

[49] A Christianized Esther exists, especially heralded by the Pentecostal preacher Tommy Tenney in his popular *Hadassah: One Night with the King* from 2004. See Rebecca Phillips, "Christians Have Fallen in Love with Queen Esther" *Tablet*, March 12, 2014, http://www.tabletmag.com/jewish-life-and-religion/164916/christians-love-queen-esther.

[50] A connection also exists between faith and romance, as such Christian language reflects, discussed in Barrett, "Higher Love."

[51] *Esther: The Girl Who Became Queen*, Big Idea Entertainment, 2000. For more on this film, see Clanton, *Daring, Disreputable, and Devout*, 123ff.

episode never mentions the word "Jew" or "Jewish," let alone "Purim." Another example is Sarah Palin, a former governor of Alaska, who has been likened to Queen Esther for her conservative rise "for such a time as this."[52] The political comparisons continue, even in some gender-bending fashion, when Paula White, a televangelist and spiritual adviser to President Donald Trump, likens him to Esther. White's claim stems from considering both Esther and Trump as "unconventional choices for the roles they received" and exemplifies how evangelical Christians self-identify as those persecuted by an increasingly secular culture.[53]

But, as mentioned earlier, not all Christian authors value Esther as a moral hallmark of purity standards for women. Rachel Held Evans began a blog series on Esther after reflecting on what she learned in Sunday school: "They always made Esther out to be a biblical version of a Disney Princess—young, pretty, dressed in fine clothes, and blessed, no doubt, with a fine singing voice."[54] Held Evans recounts a sermon given by the Mars Hill Church pastor and popular evangelical preacher Mark Driscoll, who likens the virgin roundup to a season of *The Bachelor* and Esther as part of that sinful behavior.[55] Held Evans responds with a scathing review: "To ascribe sexual culpability to a girl who in a patriarchal culture had no ownership over her own body and no control over her own marriage, is as bizarre as it is disturbing." The tension Held Evans finds in biblical fiction about Esther comes with the way readers have imposed their own contemporary Christian values upon Esther's ancient Near Eastern story of Jewish survival. Even more revealing is how Jewish sources depart from these circulated Christian messages about Esther. Though by no means exhaustive, the following Jewish examples demonstrate contrasting ways to read Esther.

Modern Jewish Adaptations of Esther

Rebecca Kanner, a Jewish author, consulted *Torah of the Mothers* to write the biblical fiction *Esther: A Novel* (2015).[56] Kanner's novel opens with the violent kidnapping of Hadassah from her hut by Persian soldiers as part of the king's decree to round up

[52] Michael Joseph Gross, "Is Palin's Rise Part of God's Plan?," *Vanity Fair*, October 2010, http://www.vanityfair.com/news/2010/10/sarah-palin-as-queen-esther-201010.

[53] Colby Itkowitz, "Raised Up by God: Televangelist Paula White Compares Trump to Queen Esther," *Washington Post*, August 23, 2017, https://www.washingtonpost.com/news/acts-of-faith/wp/2017/08/23/raised-up-by-god-televangelist-paula-white-compares-trump-to-queen-esther/?utm_term=.b6cae444353e.

[54] Rachel Held Evans, "Esther Actually: Princess, Whore . . . or Something More," blog, September 10, 2012, https://rachelheldevans.com/blog/esther-introduction-princess-whore.

[55] The actual sermon by Mark Driscoll has been removed from his website but Held Evans quotes him. This is not the only reference to ABC's long-running hit show *The Bachelor*, however, since Garrett also makes this analogy in *Queen Esther's Secrets of Womanhood*: "Perhaps Xerxes' harem provided the inspiration for the television show, The Bachelor." Furthermore, she suggests that "everyone's cycle was probably synchronized" in the harem (43).

[56] Ora Wiskind Elper and Susan Handelman, eds., *Torah of the Mothers: Contemporary Jewish Women Read Classical Jewish Texts* (Jerusalem: Urim, 2006).

virgins to replace Vashti, and a long march to the palace, with flashbacks of Hadassah watching her parents die in Babylon after a Jewish rebellion by those who were exiled to Babylon from Judah. A love interest, a soldier, is introduced in the early chapters. Haman's sons wield power in the palace while they vie for their cousin Halannah, Xerxes's favorite concubine, to become queen. Halannah is likened to a demoness prowling on her competition; when the harem girls are drunk with wine she destroys their hymen and therefore ruins their chances at a virginal meeting with the king. Because Esther is strong willed and stands up to Halannah, Hegai chooses Esther as his favorite so that together they can beat Halannah's scheming. The jealousy and danger climax when Halannah poisons Esther's tea with pennyroyal, causing her to miscarry at five months of pregnancy and ruining her chances for a future pregnancy. The event causes a rift between Esther and the king. Thus this novel follows suit in constructing a villainess for Esther.

However, the characters in Kanner's novel all suffer victimization by a royal political system. Esther learns how to hide her emotions (with lots of wine) and be suspicious—to play the game of power. An older female servant advises her, "If you wish for the king to love you ... you must trick yourself into believing you are happy." Esther does not glamorize her virginity: "No matter how painful my night with the king was, at least afterward I would no longer be categorized by a tiny length of unbroken flesh."[57] As in other novels, however, Esther is attracted to the king, but unlike in other novels, her love for the king is not the central element; she does not even meet him until the halfway point of the novel. Similarly, the king admits in the end that he does not love Esther the way she deserves to be loved, but at least he loves her as much as he has any woman. In contrast, Esther loves and pines over a soldier throughout the novel, who passes Esther love-letter scrolls once a year on Purim. Fifteen years later, Esther, childless, anticipates running away with her love interest once one of the king's sons succeeds to the throne. The expectation is that Esther will have a love-filled relationship after all, just not with the king. In all the other novels I reviewed, Esther does not end up with the alternative love interest set up for her.

Kanner's author notes indicate a clear direction to give Esther "neither all-good nor all-bad" qualities because "ideals of perfection plague women and girls."[58] The ambiguities of Esther come through; in the words of Jo Carruthers, "readers will inevitably be selective in whether they privilege the stabilities or instabilities of the text" because "writers have sought above all to make this book make sense."[59]

For Jews, the book of Esther makes sense in all the ways it continues to be celebrated during Purim.[60] A rich tradition of claiming Esther for Jewish identity exists, from feminist Jewish organizations named after Hadassah to Klezmer bands. When Klezmer, traditional music of Eastern Europe adopted by Ashkenazi Jews, came to the United States, it blended with blues, jazz, and ragtime and experienced a surge of interest in the late

---

[57] Kanner, *Esther: A Novel* (New York: Howard Books, 2015), 133, 144.   [58] Ibid., 379.

[59] Carruthers, *Esther through the Centuries*, 5, 7.

[60] An essential source in this matter regarding the rich and diverse Jewish responses to Purim is Philip Goodman, ed., *The Purim Anthology* (Philadelphia, PA: Jewish Publication Society, 1973).

1970s.[61] The Queen Esther Klezmer Trio is an example of the international blend of the music as members come from Britain and Germany.[62] Klezmer remains an integral part of Purim celebrations and Jewish identity.

Humorous Purim rap videos emerge during Purim from all over the United States, many offering parodies of pop songs.[63] *Purim spiel* is Yiddish for "Purim play," a comic dramatization of the book of Esther. A modern form of comedy called Purimspiel adapts this idea into a popular form of Jewish theatrical storytelling. This form inspired Ellen Kushner's musical drama that includes Klezmer music called *Esther: The Feast of Masks*. The drama incorporates the notion of masks to unite Jews and non-Jews alike in the idea that all people engage public and private personas in their lives.[64] The rich traditions of Esther and Jewish humor, often irreverent humor, point to an element of communal survival; Esther undermines the royal system and reigning society as a way to expose its emptiness and ensure ways to survive.[65]

J. T. Waldman's graphic novel *Megillat Esther* (2005) contains the Hebrew text alongside rabbinic interpretations. The graphic novel does not portray any kind of romantic relationship between Esther and the king. In fact, some classical Jewish texts suggest that Mordecai actually married Esther (Babylonian Talmud, Megillah 13a).[66] Waldman presents Esther being taken away in Mordecai's presence and against his will. The interpretation indicates an element of discourse on Jewish masculinity in the diaspora and a challenge to assumptions of Mordecai's level of masculine passivity in the text.[67] The

---

[61] For more about Klezmer, see Henry Sapoznik, "Klezmer Music: The First One Thousand Years," in *Musics of Multicultural America*, ed. Kip Lornell and Anne K. Rasmussen (New York: Schirmer Books, 1997), 49–72.

[62] Joel E. Rubin, "'With an Open Mind and with Respect': Klezmer as a Site of the Jewish Fringe in Germany in the Early Twenty-first Century," in *Dislocated Memories: Jews, Music, and Postwar German Culture*, ed. Tina Frühauf and Lily E. Hirsch (New York: Oxford University Press, 2014), 31–56.

[63] One such example is a parody of "Ex's and Oh's" by Elle King called "Esther's a Jew" from the Manhattan Jewish Experience and Erez Cohen in March 2016, in which they sing about the king, "He's got no clue, Esther's a Jew" (https://www.youtube.com/watch?v=c39menj1dBI).

[64] Ellen Kushner, *Esther: The Feasts of Masks* summary and link to listen to the full show is available online at http://www.ellenkushner.com/writing/drama/esther-the-feast-of-masks/.

[65] See Kathleen M. O'Connor, "Humour, Turnabouts and Survival in the Book of Esther," in *Are We Amused? Humour about Women in the Biblical Worlds*, ed. Athalya Brenner (New York: T & T Clark International, 2003), 52–64.

[66] For more on this tradition, see Barry Dov Walfish, "Kosher Adultery? The Mordecai-Esther-Ahasuerus Triangle in Talmudic, Medieval, and Sixteenth-Century Exegesis," in *The Book of Esther in Modern Research*, ed. Leonard Greenspoon and Sidnie White Crawford (London: T & T Clark International, 2003), 111–36.

[67] See Matt Reingold, "Jewish Sexualities in J. T. Waldman's Megillat Esther," in *Visualizing Jewish Narrative: Jewish Comics and Graphic Novels*, ed. Derek Parker Royal (New York: Bloomsbury, 2016), 41–54. Esther challenges the assumption of a long-standing Jewish passive display of masculinity, perhaps not in Mordeai's depiction but in the violence that ensues at the end of the book. Certainly in the name of Purim, many Jews have engaged in violence and many Christians have as well, as studied by Horowitz in *Reckless Rites*. See also Jackson Katz, "Not-So-Nice Jewish Boys: Notes on Violence and the Construction of Jewish-American Masculinity in the Late 20th and Early 21st Centuries," in *Brother Keepers: New Perspectives on Jewish Masculinity*, ed. Harry Brod and Shawn Israel Zevit (Harriman, TN: Men's Studies Press, 2010), 57–74.

sexual politics of Esther come through in the lavish illustrations of effeminate eunuchs and dramatic scenes of debauchery during the feasts. The graphic novel does not harmonize the brutality of the forces involved in Esther, including the account at the end of the many deaths of the Persians at the hands of the Jews (see ch. 9).

As this short overview demonstrates, multiple ways to express Jewish identities through Esther exist that do not come close to incorporating a Disney princess mythology. Therefore, it can be concluded that specific Christian orientations, particularly evangelical Christianity, market Esther in the frame of a Disney princess. The frame includes Esther as a virginal and religiously devout girl in a romantic relationship with the king, in which his love helps her escape the strictures of her situation while she stands up for what she thinks is right by putting her love on the line to reveal her true identity. Her biblical story is not concerned with communicating romance; the king "loved Esther more than all the other women; of all the virgins she won his favor and devotion" (2:17). The king's devotion works as motivation for her entry into the palace, which is ultimately the way the Jews triumph over Haman's plot to destroy them. The Disney frame excludes major expressions of Purim that celebrate Jewish survival in a Gentile world. Yet the biblical story presents Esther's ultimate namesake resting with the creation of Purim, as she and Mordecai "laid down for themselves and for their descendants regulations concerning their fasts and their lamentations" (9:31). Another Disney princess element not present in the biblical story is an older female antagonist who tries to stop Esther's happiness with the king. Above all, in a Disney princess mythology, her personal romantic satisfaction is key for a "happily ever after" ending for Esther the queen.

FUTURE PROSPECTS AND QUESTIONS

- This chapter analyzed several Christian novels about Esther to demonstrate an underlying Disney princess mythology at work in popular culture. What other ways, and through what other lenses, could we analyze the Esther novels discussed here?
- A universal experience of young women living in patriarchal settings and particular experiences of Jews living in a hostile world are held in tension as we continue to watch elements of Esther permeate popular culture. How did you see this tension play out in this chapter? Can you think of other areas in which this tension exists?
- Issues regarding religious identity and gender have emerged from this analysis. How could this analysis expand to include modern pop-cultural understandings of economics, race, class, and sexual identity (especially with the eunuchs) as connecting points with Esther as well?
- A young adult dystopian trilogy by Kiera Cass called *The Selection* was inspired by Esther and Cinderella, yet set in a dystopia, a difficult social and political setting,

as in *The Hunger Games*. Cass's trilogy has also been compared to *The Bachelor*. CW plans to produce *The Selection* as a television drama.[68] What values and messages regarding Esther are being produced in and marketed to popular culture in America when all of these ideas and genres collide?

Suggested Readings and Annotated Bibliography

Carruthers, Jo. *Esther through the Centuries*. Blackwell Bible Commentaries. Malden, MA: Blackwell, 2008.

Carruthers catalogs myriad ways people have interpreted Esther, capturing several important themes for understanding her in Jewish and Christian traditions.

Hancock, Rebecca. *Esther and the Politics of Negotiation: Public and Private Spaces and the Figure of the Female Royal Counselor*. Minneapolis, MN: Fortress Press, 2013.

Hancock considers Esther's role not as an exception but as a demonstration of the ways queens functioned as political figures and royal counselors in the ancient world. A helpful review of literature on Esther demonstrates the many interpretations of her role in the biblical text.

Horowitz, Elliott S. *Reckless Rites: Purim and the Legacy of Jewish Violence*. Princeton, NJ: Princeton University Press, 2008.

Although only briefly mentioned in this chapter, Horowitz's study on the use of Purim, and the book of Esther from which it came, to incite both Jewish and Christian violence is a helpful look into these dynamics.

Levenson, Jon. *Esther: A Commentary*. Old Testament Library. Louisville, KY: Westminster John Knox, 1997.

This is a comprehensive and accessible general commentary on the book of Esther that also spends time considering the differences between the Masoretic Text, the Septuagint, and the other Greek additions.

Rothschild, Sarah. *The Princess Story: Modeling the Feminine in Twentieth-Century American Fiction and Film*. Modern American Literature, 62. New York: Peter Lang, 2013.

Rothschild analyzes Disney princess movies in helpful groupings that allow for exploration of changes in the franchise over time. A comparison of non-Disney princess stories helps the reader understand what makes the Disney princess franchise unique.

---

[68] Sierra Tishgart, "Young Adult Author Kiera Cass on *The Selection*," *Teen Vogue*, April 26, 2012, http://www.teenvogue.com/story/kiera-cass-the-selection.

CHAPTER 6

....

JESUS AND POSTSOUL SATIRE ON THE SMALL SCREEN

....

ERIC THURMAN

DEPARTMENT OF RELIGIOUS STUDIES, SEWANEE, THE UNIVERSITY OF THE SOUTH

INTRODUCTION

WHAT does a short-lived cable TV show about a homeless black man who drinks, smokes pot, curses, and lives on the streets of modern-day Compton have to offer the biblical scholar *qua* biblical scholar? Especially if that man is Jesus, which is the case in Aaron McGruder's sitcom *Black Jesus*, the inspiration for and subject of this essay? Nothing and everything, it seems to me.[1]

Nothing, that is, to the academic expert whose work is defined by the constitutive divide between the production of biblical texts in their ancient contexts and all the work of reception that comes later. To such an expert, biblical scholarship worthy of the name is focused primarily or exclusively on ancient authors and original meanings, lest an interest in reception history "obscure or replace study of the New Testament itself."[2] Yet, as a representative example of popular culture, such a show has everything to offer those biblical scholars who want a more expansive way of engaging with a text beyond what the pleasures of historical problem-solving or even the hermeneutics of suspicion can provide. Everything? Yes, everything.

Popular engagements with the Bible, this essay presumes, represent the constitutive other of biblical studies as an academic field. That is, popular interpretations of the Bible

---

[1] My thanks to my student research assistant, Ryan Poole, for help with key parts of this project.

[2] Steve Walton, "What Is Progress in New Testament Studies?," *Expository Times* 124 (2013) 5:215–6.

embody everything that was, and often still is, excluded to make the discipline possible. The wild growth uprooted to clear the field for biblical studies to flourish on its own includes, on the one hand, the afterlives of biblical texts and characters, which are to be distinguished from their original forms and intended meanings, and on the other hand, the personal investment in the subjective significance and contemporary relevance of those texts and characters, a trait that is held to distinguish the nonspecialist interpreter from the more self-disciplined expert.[3] We might think of these two excluded domains as the "improper objects and affects" of biblical studies, which has its own, still vital, proper objects and affects, that have returned from time to time as sprouts in fields of biblical studies cultivated by feminist, queer, postcolonial, cultural, and reception studies.

What bears emphasizing here at the beginning, then, are the particular opportunities engaging with popular culture offers biblical scholars. "Popular forms," Stacy Takacs notes, reject a "neat bifurcation of the self [between mind and body] and, instead stimulate the mind by targeting the body. Their stories are simple, repetitive, and formulaic but also vivid, emotional, and hard-hitting. They require little concentration and even less commitment of time and energy and intellectual resources. Their pleasures are often physical—the jolt of the action film, the goosebumps of the horror story, the tears of the melodrama."[4] Or, as we will see, the laughter of the sitcom. To enter the domain of popular culture is to enter the world of these affects, that is, the world of our sensations, feelings, and attachments that affect theorists have brought to critical attention over the past twenty years. To study popular culture is thus an opportunity to vicariously experience the range of emotional responses to the biblical texts and characters the biblical scholar typically, if temporarily, represses to do their own interpretive work and make those experiences available for analytic scrutiny and affective understanding. To study the reception history of biblical texts and characters in this way may inspire that same scholar to take the full measure of what is gained and lost by working with the shopworn methodologies of biblical studies.[5]

With this perspective on popular culture in hand, this essay uses an extended commentary on McGruder's *Black Jesus* to illustrate one way, among many other useful ways, biblical scholars might approach the popular reception of biblical texts and characters and what they might gain by doing so. We begin by briefly describing the work on the cultural history of Jesus that has already been done both in and outside of biblical studies and then turn to some introductory remarks about McGruder and his place in the broader history of African American humor. After that, we move to the entertainment room, turn on the TV, and cue up the show.

---

[3] Stephen D. Moore and Yvonne Sherwood, *The Invention of the Biblical Scholar: A Critical Manifesto* (Minneapolis, MN: Fortress Press, 2011), 40, 76–81.

[4] Stacy Takacs, *Interrogating Popular Culture: Key Questions* (New York: Routledge, 2014), 171.

[5] Maia Kotrosits, *How Things Feel: Biblical Studies, Affect Theory and the (Im)Personal* (Leiden: Brill, 2016), 46–7.

OVERVIEW OF TOPIC: JESUS OF NAZARETH— FROM MESSIAH TO MEME

"We would call Jesus 'the most significant person ever.' We measure meme strength, how successfully is the idea of this person being propagated through time. With over two billion followers a full 2,000 years after his death, Jesus is an incredibly successful historical meme."[6] So say Steve Skiena and Charles Ward, authors of *Who's Bigger? Where Historical Figures Really Rank*, an elaborate effort to use quantitative data analysis to measure the influence of historical figures. Jesus of course ranks high as a pop icon as well, by almost any measure. Indeed, he has been something of a celebrity at least since Cecil B. DeMille's *King of Kings* (1927), but he went global with the mass distribution of an estimated 500 million copies of Warner Sallman's *Head of Christ* (1940) oil on canvas portrait, a work that generated an additional 500 million spinoff products with the same radiant face. The geographic and demographic reach of Sallman's shining savior has been surpassed only by the proselytizing preacher of Campus Crusade for Christ's 1979 film, *Jesus*, which allegedly has been seen by six billion people and translated into over a thousand languages.[7]

Movies and visual art fixed Jesus's star on American pop culture's walk of fame in the second half of the twentieth century, but he was put on that path over a hundred years earlier. Popular culture in America begins with "the refinement and proliferation of the printing press" in the late eighteenth century and the mass distribution of print materials beginning in the early nineteenth century.[8] A growing number of these materials put the name and face of Jesus in almanacs, newspapers, picture cards, illustrated Bibles, and evangelical tracts, like the American Tract Society's "Sin, No Trifle" (1824), whose cover was graced with "a hulking Jesus" with "huge arms, a long beard, and a head full of hair" carrying "the cross on his back."[9] Today he is easily found in virtually every form of popular media and genre, including journalism, radio, video games, social media, advertising, pop literature, comics, cooking, fashion, games, toys, kitsch, and of course television, with scholarship chasing him down paparazzi-like almost everywhere he appears.

Yet even a short list—taken only from the early twenty-first century and featuring only examples that, like McGruder's sitcom, transplant Jesus to new time periods and places—will convey the most remarked-upon feature of his presence in popular culture:

---

[6] Ryan O'Hanlon, "Jesus Christ: History's Most Successful Meme," *Salon*, December 12, 2013, https://www.salon.com/2013/12/12/jesus_is_the_most_successful_meme_of_all_time_partner/. See also Skiena and War, *Who's Bigger?*, 22, 75, 247, 253.

[7] Stephen Prothero, *American Jesus: How the Son of God Became a National Icon* (New York: Farrar, Straus and Giroux, 2003), 112–5; Edward Blum and Paul Harvey, *The Color of Christ: The Son of God and the Saga of Race in America* (Chapel Hill: University of North Carolina Press, 2012), 256–7.

[8] Jim Cullen, *The Art of Democracy: A Concise History of Popular Culture in the United States* (New York: NYU Press, 2002), 9–32, here 12.

[9] Blum and Harvey, *The Color of Christ*, 80–81.

the innumerable ways he has been remade in the image of each new cultural formation or repackaged to satisfy each new generation of consumers. Imagine, or google, if you will, a television episode like *Family Guy*'s "I Dream of Jesus" (2008); a movie like *Joshua* (2002); visual art like Jon McNaughton's *One Nation under God*; a radio show like *The Jesus Christ Show* (2008-16); a song like Nick Cave's "Jesus Alone" (2016); fiction like Venita Blackburn's short story collection, *Black Jesus and Other Superheroes* (2017); a comic like Mohammed Jones's *Jesus and Mo* (2005–); a toy like Hallmark's "My Friend Jesus" doll; a piece of jewelry like "What Would Jesus Do?" bracelets; humor like *Funny or Die*'s "Prop 8: The Musical" video (2008); an internet meme like "Jesus is a Jerk" (2004); kitsch like St. Patrick's Guild's "Jesus is My Coach" football figurine; or food like Chocolate Deities' "Sacred Heart" candy (2006).

In his essay "Here, There, Everywhere: Images of Jesus in American Popular Culture," one of the first overviews by a biblical scholar, Dan W. Clanton, Jr. wonders "why so many people are still so interested in doing things with Jesus." He concludes that, despite the predominance of Christianity in American culture and history, "Jesus functions as an empty shell into which various meanings or significations can be poured."[10] This is a key observation, but it prompts an equally important question, one that Clanton does not raise directly: What are the historical conditions that made it possible for Jesus to become such a bright star in the constellations of popular culture? We might look for an answer in four key historical developments highlighted in recent cultural histories of the Bible: the reconfiguration of the Bible's authority in terms of its cultural significance in post-Enlightenment Europe; the rise of "culture" itself as a central component of nationalism as a political project in eigteenth- and ninetheenth-century Europe and America; the disestablishment of Christianity and resultant rise of religious entrepreneurship and competition in eighteenth- and nineteenth-century America; and the technological and commercial evolution of mass media in America from the late eighteenth to the late twentieth century.

As George Aichele has suggested in *Simulating Jesus: Reality Effects in the Gospels*, perhaps the most ambitious and sophisticated approach to theorizing the figure of Jesus in popular culture to date, these are the changing material, economic, and social conditions that made it possible for the hermeneutical potential of the biblical texts to be realized in novel ways. With new forms of technological dissemination—from the printing press to the internet and new ideological networks of readers and intertexts—generated by the commodification of the Bible, unauthorized adaptations of the gospels and afterlives of Jesus could successfully compete for attention, for the first time in history, in the market for religious instruction and entertainment, alongside the institutional apparatus of the post-Constantinian church or outside the reach of ecclesial authority altogether.[11]

---

[10]   Dan W. Clanton, Jr., "'Here, There, Everywhere': Images of Jesus in American Popular Culture," in *The Bible and/in Popular Culture* (Atlanta: Society of Biblical Literature, 2010), 41–60, here 57.

[11]   George Aichele, *Simulating Jesus: Reality Effects in the Gospels* (London: Equinox, 2011), 3–23.

Most scholarship on the "cultural Jesus" that emerged from these historical processes tracks his movements within discrete genres and media forms or across religious and ethnic boundaries. Here, for our purposes, it is a twofold takeaway from this work that is most directly relevant to the discussion of McGruder's *Black Jesus*. On the one hand, there is a hegemonic template for the visualization and characterization of Jesus in pop culture, a dominant way of depicting what he looks like and what he says and does that tends to conform to prevailing ideological positions across historical periods. Above all else, the Jesus of popular culture has tended to be white, masculine, straight, and as "good-looking" as he is morally good, which is to say he tends to be exceptional on both counts.[12] This set of ideological codes often signifies Jesus's divine qualities, if not his preexistent divine nature, when he is otherwise depicted as a mere man. Jesus's conventional good looks, for example, including his racialized physiognomy and his sex appeal, owe more to the aesthetic demands of the global entertainment and fashion industries, which still idealize Western, white, heterosexual, slender, youthful bodies as the privileged bearers of "beauty," than they do to the Publius Lentulus letter. This medieval forgery, which was well-known in nineteenth-century America, contains a verbal description of Jesus's face and hair that is instantly recognizable to most even today because it has been visualized by Sallman's *Head of Christ* and countless works before and after it.[13]

If an "ugly Jesus" is hard to find in popular culture, one must search equally far to discover a "bad Jesus."[14] No matter how much he might resemble mere mortals in other aspects of their lives, he is invariably an extraordinarily "good man," as an ethical teacher, a friend, a comforter, a liberator, a martyr, and so on. Of course, Jesus has been seen as the embodiment and origin of diverse ethical systems and cultural norms and political formations since his followers first started sharing their memories of him. Yet the distinctive emphasis placed on Jesus as an exemplar of universal moral values—itself a highly ideological claim that was epitomized early in the post-Enlightenment period by Thomas Jefferson's *The Life and Morals of Jesus of Nazareth*—arguably increased the ideological burdens he was asked to carry. With the relevance of the Bible redefined in terms of "historiography, philology, morality, and aesthetics" in response to the Enlightenment-era critique of religion, Jesus's name and likeness were more amenable to appropriation by ideological positions dictated by groups and institutions outside the Church.[15]

---

[12] See Stephen D. Moore, "On the Face and Physique of the Historical Jesus," in *God's Beauty Parlor: And Other Queer Spaces in and around the Bible* (Stanford, CA: Stanford University Press, 2001), 90–132; Blum and Harvey, *The Color of Christ*, esp. 7–26, 234–65; David Morgan, "The Likeness of Jesus," in *The Forge of Vision: A Visual History of Modern Christianity* (Berkeley: University of California Press, 2015), 168–95.

[13] Moore, "On the Face and Physique," 125–9; Blum and Harvey, *The Color of Christ*, 82–3. See also Joan Taylor, *What Did Jesus Look Like?* (New York: Bloomsbury T & T Clark, 2018), 15–25.

[14] Though see Hector Avalos, *The Bad Jesus: The Ethics of New Testament Ethics* (Sheffield, UK: Sheffield Phoenix Press, 2015).

[15] Moore and Sherwood, *The Invention of the Biblical Scholar*, 59, 65–6, though see also 46–9, drawing on Jonathan Sheehan, *The Enlightenment Bible Translation, Scholarship, Culture* (Princeton, NJ: Princeton University Press, 2007).

On the other hand, there is an increasing number of diverse representations of Jesus that proliferate alongside of and in opposition to the still reigning model. Stephen Prothero's well-known historical survey, *American Jesus: How the Son of God Became a National Icon*, is organized along these lines, as the second half deals with depictions of Jesus from "communities that operate outside the confines of white Protestantism," in whose image so many popular Jesus figures are made. "To put it another way," he says, "while Christian insiders have had the authority to dictate *that* others interpret Jesus, they have not had the authority to dictate *how* these others would do so." Key is Prothero's observation that popular Jesus figures created by groups outside the dominant circles of American society "may criticize the dominant culture rather than championing it."[16]

Here, too, Jesus is a moral exemplar, but now as a sometime radical champion of socialist or anarchist or "hippie" countercultures and multicultural gendered, racialized, and sexual identities. If, to make a somewhat obvious comparison, Sallman's *Head of Christ* exemplifies the image of Jesus that still dominates popular culture, and thus reflects and endorses the hierarchical social order in which it was made and circulated, Janet McKenzie's *Jesus of the People*, produced over half a century later, aims to speak to and for those whose bodies and identities have been marked as other by that same social order throughout most of American history, a point that Prothero himself does not develop as incisively as, say, Edward Blum and Paul Harvey in *The Color of Christ: The Son of God and the Saga of Race in America*.[17]

What Erin Runions says about "pop scripture" thus equally describes what sometimes happens when Jesus goes pop: the popular representation of Jesus "is, at the end of the day, far more complex in its dynamism and engagement with important issues of contemporary justice than is any notion of a fixed, unchanging, canonically bound Word of God."[18] Whether he escapes the canonical confines of orthodox Christology in any particular pop artifact, though, it should be clear from recent scholarship that Jesus's place in popular culture is the result of historical processes that both created and undermined easy distinctions between "religion," "secularism," and "entertainment." Likewise, it should be clear that the Jesus of popular culture remains a privileged site for expressing, negotiating, and contesting various ideologies of religion, race, nationality, gender, sexuality, class, and so on. Anyone who borrows the cultural capital that has been accumulated by his name and likeness over centuries—including, in the case to which we now turn, a cartoonist turned television show writer, Aaron McGruder—may try to reimagine the world by rewriting the story of Jesus with or without the authorization of ecclesiastical institutions.

---

[16] Prothero, *American Jesus*, 16.

[17] On McKenzie's painting alone, compare Prothero, *American Jesus*, 223–4, and Blum and Harvey, *The Color of Christ*, 246. An image of the painting, along with some reflections on the work and its reception by McKenzie herself, can be found at Janet McKenzie, "My Art Story," National Endowment for the Arts, accessed May 19, 2020, https://www.arts.gov/50th/stories/janet-mckenzie.

[18] Erin Runions, "Pop Scripture: Creating Small Spaces for Social Change," in *The Bible in/and Popular Culture*, 197–202, here 202.

SPECIFIC EXAMPLES AND/OR FOCI:
POSTSOUL SATIRE

Aaron McGruder is best known as the creator of *The Boondocks*, a nationally syndicated, and often wildly controversial, comic strip that ran from 1999 to 2006. The strip was adapted for television as an animated sitcom that ran for four seasons between 2005 and 2014 as part of the Cartoon Network's Adult Swim; this niche network has a core fan base of men eighteen to thirty-four years old that gave McGruder a younger audience.[19] His *Black Jesus* is a scripted, live-action sitcom that also ran on Adult Swim for two seasons, between 2014 and 2015, while a rumored third season has yet to be broadcast. Like *The Boondocks*, the show sparked the predictable kind of intense but short-lived controversy that caught the attention of the mainstream press before the first episode even had a chance to air. Like *The Boondocks*, the show's sitcom format finds humor in clashes between ordinary but recognizable people who live in the same place.

In *Black Jesus*, the ensemble cast is composed of a group of friends and relatives who are black or Latino/a and who live in and around an apartment complex in a working-class neighborhood in the storied city of Compton: Vic, the surly landlord; Lloyd, the homeless trickster; Fish, the struggling ex-con; Boonie, the feckless DJ; Ms. Tudi, his bossy mother; Jason, the unemployed nice guy; Diane, his Latina girlfriend and cop; Maggie, the self-absorbed millennial; and Trayvon, the awkward geek. Jesus himself is a homeless, thirtysomething, black man with long, permed hair who is dressed in dirty robes and sandals and who is "on a daily mission to spread love and kindness throughout the neighborhood with the help of his small but loyal group of downtrodden followers."[20]

Immediately after its first episode aired in August 2014, *Black Jesus* was widely criticized, most notably by the conservative American Family Association, which denounced the show as an "extremely disrespectful, blasphemous and all-around disgusting 'comedy.'"[21] Apparently the show's representation of Jesus as an African American man living on the streets of modern day Compton, California, was incompatible with the prominent evangelical organization's conception of the biblical Son of God.

---

[19]   Avi Santo, "Of Niggas and Citizens: *The Boondocks* Fans and Differentiated Black American Politics," in *Satire TV: Politics and Comedy in the Post-Network Era*, ed. Jonathan Gray, Jeffery P. Jones, and Ethan Thompson (New York: NYU Press, 2009), 252–73, here 254; Deborah Whaley, "Graphic Blackness/Anime Noir: Aaron McGruder's *The Boondocks* and the Adult Swim," in *Watching While Black: Centering the Television of Black Audiences*, ed. Beretta Smith Shomade (New Brunswick, NJ: Rutgers University Press, 2012), 187–204, here 191.

[20]   Lesley Goldberg, "'Boondocks' Creator Brings 'Black Jesus' to Adult Swim (Exclusive)," *Hollywood Reporter*, March 10, 2014, https://www.hollywoodreporter.com/live-feed/boondocks-creator-brings-black-jesus-687190.

[21]   Quotation from American Family Association, accessed July 18, 2018, http://www.afa.net/who-is-afa/press-releases/2014/08-august/offensive-and-blasphemous-black-jesus-debuts-on-cartoon-network/.

Yet the AFA and other like-minded critics have half a point about McGruder's mockery. McGruder is not out to ridicule Christian devotion to "the Lord and Savior" with his sitcom. He does aim, however, to satirize the power certain assumptions about Jesus's appearance and character have had in American religion and popular culture. More specifically, as we will see, he targets the visual representation of Jesus as a white, European male and the use of that image to give "whiteness a holy face" that goes back at least to the early nineteenth century in America.[22]

How satire works in McGruder's *Black Jesus*[23] is the focus of the rest of this essay, but it will be helpful first to clarify some concepts that set the stage for the commentary that follows. Like much of McGruder's earlier comedy, *Black Jesus*, too, is best approached as an expression of postsoul satire. To take "postsoul" first, this concept names, at minimum, "the political, social, and cultural experiences of the African-American community since the end of the civil rights and Black Power movements," though both the term and the periodization are open to some debate.[24]

"Postsoul satire," in turn, is a mode of African American art that widens both its rhetorical and formal scope to comment critically not only upon the oppressive political, economic, and social forces that still encircle African American culture in the late twentieth and early twenty-first centuries but also upon the multitude of ways in which African Americans have misused their hard-won freedoms and thereby hindered their own ascendance to equality.[25]

To better conceptualize satire itself and use it as an interpretive tool, we might turn to Dustin Griffin's more general reflections in *Satire: A Critical Reintroduction*. To oversimplify somewhat, satire on Griffin's account is the use of humor to bring into question the validity or reasonableness of accepted beliefs or practices. The key elements of satire, which can be identified in any satirical work to a greater or lesser degree, are inquiry and provocation, display and play.[26] Inquiry names the goal of satire, to raise critical questions about the status quo. Provocation prompts inquiry by using verbal or visual absurdity, incongruity, and paradox to expose and even degrade unquestioned ideas and values. Like provocation, display inspires reflection, and not mere reaction, by using the skill to entertain to direct an audience's attention to unasked questions. "Play" names the spaced cleared by provocation and display for addressing the taboo or the serious, a space of humor that is removed from moral censorship and consequences.

---

[22] Blum and Harvey, *The Color of Christ*, 8.

[23] I believe David L. Moody, *The Complexity and Progression of Black Presentation in Film and Television* (Lanham, MD: Lexington Books, 2017), 75–86, is the only academic discussion to date.

[24] Mark Anthony Neal, *Soul Babies: Black Popular Culture and the Post-Soul Aesthetic* (New York: Routledge, 2002), 3. See also Bertram D. Ashe, "Theorizing the Post-Soul Aesthetic: An Introduction," *African American Review* 41, no. 4 (2007): 609–23; Paul C. Taylor, "Post-Black, Old Black," *African American Review* 41, no. 4 (2007): 625–40.

[25] Derek C. Maus, " 'Mommy, What's a Post-Soul Satirist?': An Introduction, in *Post-Soul Satire: Black Identity After Civil Rights*, ed. Derek Maus and James J. Donahue (Jackson: University of Mississippi Press, 2014), xvii.

[26] Dustin Griffin, *Satire: A Critical Reintroduction* (Lexington: University of Kentucky Press, 1995), especially 35–94.

With this understanding of postsoul satire in hand, we enter the entertainment room, ready for the show. We begin with the first target of McGruder's inquiry, the visual representation of Jesus as a white, European male, observing along the way how the comedic display of McGruder's Jesus as a black homeless man living in modern-day Compton brings to light not just the question of how Jesus should be depicted today but also how whiteness itself continues to signify power and respectability in a supposedly postracial America. We then move to McGruder's next target, which in good postsoul fashion is a key expression of mainstream black popular culture, namely hip-hop. Again, along the way we see how the display of Jesus, now humorously framed as a gangsta or gangsta rapper, is used by McGruder to interrogate stereotypes about black masculinity associated with hip-hop culture. Next, we situate McGruder's postsoul comedy in its cultural moment, the age of Black Lives Matter. We ask what a satire that laughs at racial stereotypes has to say about systemic racism in general and police brutality in particular. Last, as the credits roll, we ponder the play of satire itself and ask if laughing at a black Jesus diffuses the power of racial stereotypes, or if laughter has a different edge and agency of its own.

"That's That Jesus Everybody Believe In"

"The history of White supremacy in the United States and the struggle against the ramifications of that history," notes Anthony Pinn, "have in part been worked out through the meaning of Jesus' physical presence on earth. And this presence involves an aesthetic of physical and spiritual beauty as well as a system of ethics ('What would Jesus do?')." "There are ways," he continues, "in which depictions of Christ—visual images of Jesus Christ—promoted a particular social cohesiveness and sense of collective identity on the cultural-political level. Yet, such images promoted more than a sociopolitical imaginary in that they also spoke to the proper 'look' of a citizen, the racially visible markers of belonging." "In this way," he concludes, "the masculine and racial matrix of 'life and liberty' in the United States had not only the force of law (and social custom) but also divine sanction based on the physical look of God's presence in the world. Said plainly, God resembles those whom God favors."[27]

Visual likenesses of Jesus are recognizable as such to the extent that they conform to a model that has long acquired the status of an unofficial archetype, a canonical blueprint. David Morgan describes this "set of characteristics—a long face, large eyes, somber expression, shoulder-length hair parted in the center, short, slightly forked beard, and a broad, uncovered forehead," as "an abiding formula for representing the face of Jesus."[28] Looking at McGruder's sitcom savior, we see a head-to-toe parody of white Jesus figures that fit this formula. The elements of his appearance that identify him as Jesus—the

---

[27] Anthony Pinn, "Putting Jesus in His Place," in *Humanism: Essays on Race, Religion and Popular Culture* (New York: Bloomsbury, 2015), 76–92, here 76, 78, 79.

[28] Morgan, "The Likeness of Jesus," 170; cf. 184.

crown of thorns; the long, straight, chestnut hair; the loose, full-length robe; and the open-toed leather sandals—are iconic, but also anachronistic. Like an ill-fitting costume, these stereotypical images from art history and pop culture are out of place in everyday American life—Lloyd says Jesus is "lookin' like the UPS man, Nigga Wan Kenobi, Taliban, the Al-Qaeda" in the series' first scene—and so draw attention to themselves as signs of aesthetic convention.[29] In this way, the viewer is alerted to the fact that depictions of Jesus do not reflect what he was "really like" but are the products of historical imagination, depictions of a white Jesus no less than the rest.

Yet it is the additional step that McGruder takes, reimagining Jesus as a homeless black man who smokes weed and swears, that moves the show from parody to satire. This reimagining draws on and exposes to critique the assumed affinity between whiteness and Jesus's godliness. It also challenges a corollary assumption, namely that Jesus would not share the attitudes and habits that pop culture deems typical of unemployed black men in urban America. Coolio, a Compton-born rap artist who makes a cameo appearance late in the first season, points to this apparent contradiction when he initially rejects Jesus's request to put on a benefit concert: "You don't even act like Jesus is supposed to act!"[30] Much of the show's humor turns on the incongruity between the white Jesus of the American imagination and a black Jesus marked by stereotypes of criminality and poverty. Over and over again the moral relationship between these two figures is implicitly inverted as a figure of black manhood is used to reflect the aesthetics and ethics of Jesus as a mediator of the divine. The occasional miracle or vision from "Pops" is complemented by more frequent moments of praying with and giving advice to his friends, which includes a vision of community celebrated as a life of "smokin', drinkin', and chillin'"—and eating vegetables.

At the same time, the presence of a black Jesus drives a broader critique of the religious, moral, and political ideals for which the white Jesus stands. White Jesus himself shows up only once in the series, in the first episode of the second season, but that appearance can be taken as a metacommentary on all the subtle but recurring jokes made about whiteness in contemporary America. After being locked up in a psychiatric hospital for six months, Jesus comes home to a party at Ms. Tudi's, where he is given a cake with a picture of a white Jesus on it. Seeing the shock on Jesus's face, Boonie consoles him: "That's that Jesus everybody believe in. But fuck him, you my man. This nigga don't never come through." White Jesus has done nothing for the Compton crew, and, as becomes clear over the course of the series, white characters and white-dominated institutions do little for them as well.

White people are as likely to appear among farmers or the homeless as they are among police officers or ordinary citizens. Yet all the people who control economic institutions and political discourse opposed to the interests of Jesus and his friends are white, from

---

[29] *Black Jesus*, "Smokin', Drinkin', and Chillin'," season 1, episode 1, directed by Mike Clattenberg, written by Aaron McGruder and Mike Clattenberg, Adult Swim, August 7, 2014. Episode information found at: https://en.wikipedia.org/wiki/List_of_Black_Jesus_episodes

[30] "Gangsta's Paradise," season 1, episode 9.

Mr. Maxwell, the apartment complex owner, to the advertising executives who use Lloyd to sell cheap liquor, to Bill O'Reilly, the conservative media personality, whom Lloyd says can "kiss my black ass."[31] Even less influential white folk are figures for clueless exploitation and appropriation, like the white teens posing as a black gang to sell fake pot to Jesus's friends, or the gentrifying hipsters willing to pay exorbitant prices to eat at Ms. Tudi's "authentic" ghetto restaurant, or the anonymous inventor of the "white lives matter" slogan Boonie ironically quotes to protect himself.[32] Lloyd might insist that only "white people" can stop a suspected terrorist attack, but only because he forgets how the tools of the "war on terror" were also deployed on the protests in Ferguson.[33] Likewise, the stained-glass image of a white God overlooks the flock of a local black church, but only to provide dubious cover for a corrupt preacher.[34] What the show's various white characters have most in common with a white Jesus, then, is not a reputation for godliness and goodness but a gross indifference to the needs of black people. The scathing satire of white Jesus and white characters is an extended exposé of the invisible authority whiteness retains in an allegedly "postracial" era.

"The Original Galilean Gangster"

As the show's title makes explicit, McGruder's Jesus is also the latest in the well-documented line of black Jesus figures constructed as critiques of a white Jesus and a white Christian culture that enslaved, lynched, segregated, incarcerated, and made second-class citizens of Americans of African descent.[35] Indeed, he seems to step right off the page of one of the seminal works of black liberation theology by the late James Cone, *Black Theology and Black Power*, which says, "Whether whites want to hear it or not, Christ is black, baby, with all the features which are so detestable to white society."[36] Or, to use a more contemporary example, McGruder's Jesus seems to be conjured straight out of Tupac Shakur's gangsta rap hymn "Black Jesus," who is

> Somebody that hurt like we hurt
> Somebody that smoke like we smoke
> Drink like we drink
> That understand where we coming from
> That's who we pray to we need help y'all.

---

[31] "Love Thy Enemy, Part 2," season 1, episode 8; "Never Say When," season 2, episode 8; "The Shit Heist," season 1, episode 3.

[32] "Smokin', Drinkin', and Chillin'"; "Tasty Tudi's," season 2, episode 5; "False Witness," season 2, episode 3.

[33] The protests in Ferguson, Missouri, that were sparked by a police shooting are discussed in the final section of this essay.

[34] "False Witness," season 2, episode 3, "Jesus Gonna Get His," season 2, episode 2.

[35] See, among other works, Kelly Brown Douglas, *The Black Christ* (Maryknoll, NY: Orbis, 1993); Prothero, *American Jesus*, 200–228; Blum and Harvey, *The Color of Christ*, 23–4, 131–2, 194–204, 218–24, 242–6.

[36] James H. Cone, *Black Theology and Black Power* (Maryknoll, NY: Orbis, 1997), 96.

Hip-hop culture has a distinctive take on Jesus that is "perhaps the most radical depiction of Jesus without whiteness" to date, according to Pinn.[37]

Hip-hop Jesus is often, to quote Pinn again, "associated with a dimension of black life troubling to whiteness and certain formations of African American identity."[38] In gangsta rap songs from Tupac's "Black Jesus" to Kayne West's "Jesus Walks," Kendrick Lamar's unreleased "Jesus Saves," and beyond, he is sometimes depicted as the leader of a crew, sometimes a "ride or die" follower, but almost always as a loyal companion. "The companion Jesus who walks and rides with rappers is usually African American," Ebony Utley observes, because this "corroborates Jesus' identity as a fellow oppressed person." In fact, "gangstas respect Jesus," she says, "because they see the parallels between his life and theirs" to such an extent that they imagine the "Jesus story is the gangsta's story" and that "Jesus was gangsta" in his own uncompromising life and state-sponsored death.[39]

Hip-hop Jesus offers help and advice to his companions but rarely passes judgment on their participation in the drug economy or other illegal or dangerous activities as ways of surviving in a postindustrial society. "Jesus rides and walks with the gangsta and not vice versa," Utley notes. "Black Jesus has no ego. He does not demand to be followed; he willingly follows the gangstas to places only their comrades would be willing to go. Like a true homie, black Jesus offers unconditional acceptance." Ultimately, the Hip-hop Jesus "is a cultural icon for resisting the rules, especially those for life and death." And by "imitating Jesus who suffered and yet emerged victorious over death, gangstas boldly appropriate Jesus' resistance as their own."[40]

Turning back to McGruder's show, its characterization of Jesus arguably offers a new twist on the Hip-hop Jesus. That is, McGruder's Jesus is affiliated with hip-hop culture and gangsta rappers over the course of two seasons, but often in ways that critique the gangsta ethos and the expression of black manhood that sustains and is sustained by that ethos. After Jesus is released from a psychiatric hospital at the beginning of season 2, for example, the association of Jesus with gangsta rap becomes even more central to his persona. He has a new plan to take his message to the streets like an old-school rapper at a neighborhood block party, and his friend Boonie goes with him. Here is Boonie, standing behind the DJ's standard two-turntable setup and introducing Jesus to crowds gathered around the crew's new food truck: "From Galilee to Gardena. Cairo to Compton. Probably seen him hanging around Rick Ross's neck. Hell, he used to be white! Give it up for Jesus Christ!" Later, he introduces Jesus again in the same way before another crowd: "It's Taco Sundays out here in the pond, and I'm about to bring to you the original Galilean gangster!"[41] Here, as in earlier scenes, McGruder's Jesus is the companion desired by Tupac and described by other hip-hop artists in their music and videos.

---

[37] Pinn, "Putting Jesus in His Place," 84.   [38] Ibid.
[39] Ebony Utley, *Rap and Religion: Understanding the Gangsta's God* (Santa Barbara, CA: Praeger, 2012), 49-69, here 50 and 49.
[40] Ibid., 50, 49, 58, 64.   [41] *Black Jesus*, "Taco Sundays," season 2, episode 6, October 2015.

Yet despite Boonie's hype, a closer look at Jesus's character shows he has little interest in the gangsta's looks or lifestyle. In fact, he is a man directly opposed to the self-interested desire for "sex, reputation, and cash" that defines the gangsta's attitude toward life. Many gangsta rap tracks, for example, are extended boasts. Lyrical boasting can be understood as an effort to affirm a sense of self-worth in a senseless world of poverty, racism, and indifference or a desire to join in the spirit of battling rivals for the title of the best MC, or both. In any case, hip-hop artists brag. A lot. Typically, their self-mythologizing stories make outlandish claims about everything from their self-made success to their sexual prowess, their rhyming skills to their street-level reputation. "Diss tracks" similarly inflate the artist's status through creative insults and intimating bravado aimed at upstart competitors, former friends, hostile police, or meddling news media. At least as much as anything else, hip-hop braggadocio is a stylized projection of male ego.[42]

Little about McGruder's Jesus shows a concern with this kind of demand for respect. Much about him demonstrates his disinterest in securing his personal reputation. Jesus may get frustrated with his friends' lack of confidence in him or their failure to follow his advice, but he never holds a grudge. Likewise, he might win a battle of insults with detractors like Vic and Lloyd, but he nevertheless always humorously reaffirms their worth to him with a line like "I still love your bitch ass. By default, fool!" Millions follow Jesus's social media accounts, and his cell phone lists Bill Gates, President Barack Obama, and the pope among his contacts, but he is uninterested in increasing his popularity. Instead, as he explains to Trayvon at one point, "I came down here to Compton to spread love. I got folks out here, and I got to spread this love with kindness. That's what I'm about."[43] Later in the series, Jesus expounds on what "love with kindness" means in practice.

In his most extensive sermon, Jesus holds up love of self and others as the only viable answer to an ego-driven society of zero-sum competition and violent payback, that is, the kind of society often depicted as the stage for the gangsta's boasts. After informing a crowd that a "hater" (Lloyd) has hacked his social media accounts, Jesus insists, "The way you stop hate is with love, otherwise you give into the destructive power of your ego," and ego, he says, "done killed more black and brown men than the police."[44] Postsoul satire, as noted earlier, has a dual focus on the "follies and self-destructive habits ... within the African American community" and the outside forces that "constrain, denigrate, or otherwise harm it in some way."[45] Here, despite the show's running critique of police brutality discussed in the next section, Jesus calls out violence in and between ethnic minority communities. This call-out strikes a jarring note in the age of Black Lives Matter. Yet it is also an implicit critique of the way vindictive violence, rhetorical or otherwise, is celebrated as a mark of credible masculinity in gangsta rap.

---

[42] Eithne Quinn, *Nuthin' but a "G" Thang: The Culture and Commerce of Gangsta Rap* (New York: Columbia University Press, 2005), 92–116.

[43] *Black Jesus*, "The Other Shoe Drops," season 1, episode 7, September 2014.

[44] *Black Jesus*, "Taco Sundays."   [45] Maus, "'Mommy, What's a Post-Soul Satirist?,'" xiii-xiv.

To bring this point home, Jesus turns to directly address a young boy in the crowd about the folly of seeking revenge for being disrespected or opposed by others. After the sermon, Jesus and crew count up the receipts from the taco truck, only to be dispirited by the meager profit earned from a long day of cooking. Just as they are about to give up on the future of the food truck altogether, the young boy from the crowd comes to the window to talk. Handing over a revolver to Jesus, the boy says the sermon made him think twice about payback and promises to "take [Jesus's] word on that."[46] Walking to Jesus and away from the temptation of violence, this young African American boy, who is addressed in familial terms as a "young brother," steps into a transformed future as the kind of man not typically depicted or celebrated in most gangsta rap. Tracts like Ice Cube's "Go to Church" in fact code religious practice as cowardice to mock rappers and other men who balk at projecting violent personas: "If you a scared motherfucker go to church." McGruder's Jesus thus seems to be as much an indirect critic of the gangsta figure as his acquiescent companion.

Ultimately, however, the critique in this scene, and by extension in the show as a whole, is at best problematic. Jesus convinces the young boy to eschew violence precisely by appealing to his ego, his desire for masculine self-affirmation. Hence Jesus's use of stereotypical sports metaphors: real men know how to play the game of life single-mindedly and successfully. Hence, too, the taunt that a man who does not fight back might be a "bitch." Jesus and the anonymous youth both end up rejecting the idea that payback is an essential part of authentic masculinity. However, they both still accept the premise that no real man would do anything considered "feminine," and this despite Jesus's affirmation of women's self-worth elsewhere.[47] McGruder's Jesus is very much part of the hip-hop culture he would reform.

Black Laughs Matter

On August 9, 2014, two days after the premiere of *Black Jesus*, an eighteen-year-old African American man, Michael Brown, was shot and killed by Officer Darren Wilson during a confrontation in Ferguson, Missouri. The two weeks of protests sparked by the incident captured the attention of national media outlets and brought the Black Lives Matter movement into national prominence.[48] As arguably the leading voice against, in their own words, "violence inflicted on Black communities by the state and vigilantes," the Black Lives Matter movement has drawn sustained attention to, among other issues, the deaths of black men and women at the hands of police and white supremacists in

[46] *Black Jesus*, "Taco Sundays."
[47] See, for example, "Thy Neighbor's Strife," season 2, episode 7.
[48] For an illuminating account of the shooting, the protests, and his own experience reporting from Ferguson for the *Washington Post*, see Wesley Lowery, *They Can't Kill Us All: Ferguson, Baltimore, and a New Era in America's Racial Justice Movement* (New York: Little, Brown, 2016), 19–69.

recent years.[49] Black Lives Matters activists and authors have put names that are familiar from news and social media—Trayvon Martin and Eric Garner, Tamir Rice and Sandra Bland, Freddie Gray and Clementa Pinckney, among others—on a nationwide map of victims of racist violence. Police shootings of black men and women around the two-plus years *Black Jesus* aired on Adult Swim—and the reporting, commentary, debates, and protests they inspired—provide an important context for thinking about the cultural politics of the show's humor, especially its satirical use of stereotypes, and the ways laughter matters in the time of Black Lives Matter.

To put the issue in the sharpest terms, McGruder invites audiences to laugh at or with stereotypes of black urban life at the same time activists protest police killings that were widely defended with many of the same stereotypes of violent, criminal black men. Many of the earliest reviews of *Black Jesus*, by commentators of diverse racial and ethnic identities, complained that the show relies on stereotypes about black men and urban life in its depiction of Jesus and his friends. Most of these pieces came out before the events of Ferguson, but reviewers scoffed at McGruder's Jesus, in part, because they saw in his character the thoughtless perpetuation of the idea that young black men are often jobless and inherently prone to criminal activity. Eddie Glaude Jr., a professor of religion at Princeton University, for example, was not the only early commentator to remark that the show's "trailer trades in a host of racial stereotypes without giving us a sense of what is the nature of Black Jesus's ministry."[50]

To be sure, this kind of criticism, that even television shows written by and for African Americans too often rely on racist caricatures for ratings or laughs, has been leveled at nearly every black sitcom to make it past a pilot episode, including McGruder's own earlier animated comedy, *The Boondocks*. Like other postsoul comics and artists, however, McGruder is animated, in the words of Mark Anthony Neal, by a "willingness to undermine or deconstruct the most negative symbols and stereotypes of black life via the use and distribution of those very symbols and stereotypes."[51] What stands out about McGruder's *Black Jesus* when framed as postsoul satire is the opportunity the show affords its audience to laugh at stereotypes of black male criminality by applying them to the respected and respectable figure of Jesus and so render them absurd. More provocatively still, the show also invites the audience to laugh at the experience of police brutal-

---

[49]   Black Lives Matter, "What We Believe," accessed September 21, 2018, https://blacklivesmatter.com/about/what-we-believe/.

[50]   Quoted in Antonia Blumberg, "Adult Swim Will Feature 'Black Jesus' but the Show May Not Do the Theology Justice," *Huffington Post*, July 21, 2014, https://www.huffingtonpost.com/2014/07/21/adult-swim-black-jesus_n_5606882.html. See also Zoe Mintz, " 'Black Jesus' Show Is 'Double Edged Sword' for African American Community," *International Business Times*, July 29, 2014, https://www.ibtimes.com/black-jesus-show-double-edged-sword-african-american-community-1642616. On the use of racist stereotypes to defend police killings of African American men in particular, see Jamelle Bouie, "Michael Brown Wasn't a Superhuman Demon," *Slate*, November 26, 2014, https://slate.com/news-and-politics/2014/11/darren-wilsons-racial-portrayal-of-michael-brown-as-a-superhuman-demon-the-ferguson-police-officers-account-is-a-common-projection-of-racial-fears.html.

[51]   Neal, *Soul Babies*, 120.

ity itself by depicting Jesus as a sometime victim of state-sanctioned harassment and racist violence.

As perverse as this may sound to some, such gallows humor has long been a part of the African American tradition of humor. "By most accounts," Glenda Carpio observes, "African American humor, like other humor that arises from oppression, has provided a balm, a release of anger and aggression, a way of coping with the painful consequences of racism."[52] Making jokes about the absurdity of living in an unjust world with a bleak future can be a form of defiance, a refusal to be defined as less than human by inhuman circumstances one has little power to change. Humor can become a momentary triumph, or at least an enjoyable escape, from fear and frustration, doubt and dread. Not for nothing, then, does the show's humor often turn on the way Jesus and his crew are routinely hassled by the police. In fact, harassment is presented less as a traumatic rupture of ordinary experience than as a regular feature of daily life in an American city. Jesus himself is arrested five times and incarcerated once for an extended period. In most of these scenes, the humor comes from the ways Jesus ultimately escapes arrest or violence, plays others, or is sometimes even played himself.

The power of satire to create a space for playing with serious issues is in full effect in these scenes, and to laugh at McGruder's Jesus is to laugh at the antics and escapades of a trickster. A familiar character of African American folklore, the trickster is a liminal figure of movement and misdirection, cunning and cleverness, deception and double meaning, who is neither a rebel with a cause nor a model of mere acquiescence. He does not, and because of his relative lack of power cannot, change the world around him. Yet he can escape the world's traps and expose its hypocrisies and injustices and sometimes temporarily reverse or undo their power.[53] Likewise, McGruder's Jesus triumphs over state institutions and racist violence more by wit, insight, evasion, endurance, and luck than any divine powers that might have been summoned on his behalf. McGruder's Jesus is not quite a "savior," even though he occasionally uses miracles to help a friend out of a jam. Nor is he exactly a "liberator," at least as liberation is often envisioned by Black Liberation theologians. McGruder's Jesus might call out violence and exploitation on an individual level, but it is his evasion of the long arm of the law that really exposes systemic racism to the satirist's mockery. Above all, this Jesus is a model of surviving and thriving in a sometimes hostile, sometimes hospitable urban American city.

As a TV trickster, McGruder's Jesus does not provide the divine answer to racist stereotypes or racism some might expect or want. Yet he undoubtedly embodies the spirit of postsoul satire in the age of Black Lives Matter. Add to his humorous scenes all the moments that expose the persistent power of whiteness and those that expose black

---

[52] Carpio, *Laughing Fit to Kill: Black Humor in the Fictions of Slavery* (New York: Oxford University Press, 2008), 5.

[53] John W. Roberts, *From Trickster to Badman: The Black Folk Hero in Slavery and Freedom* (Philadelphia: University of Pennsylvania Press, 1989), 17–64; Henry Louis Gates Jr., *The Signifying Monkey: A Theory of African-American Literary Criticism* (Oxford: Oxford University Press, 1989), 3–42; Lawrence Levine, *Black Culture and Black Consciousness: Afro-American Folk Thought from Slavery to Freedom*, 30th anniversary ed. (Oxford: Oxford University Press, 2007), 102–32, 370–85.

prejudice against Latinos, Arabs, and non-American black people, and the show's understanding of racism as both everyday reality to endure and an unending problem to address comes into clear view. The hope that all of the effects of slavery would someday come to a definitive end, according to this perspective, is as misguided as the idea that we now live in a "postracial" society. "Some might call this position cynical," Carpio notes, "yet implicit in it is a view of racial struggle that is not dependent on illusions of revolution but that nonetheless is deeply invested in fighting for freedom, both politically and artistically."[54]

Tellingly in this regard, McGruder's Jesus does not lead a movement like Black Lives Matter, which is never mentioned by name in the show. At most, the trickster Jesus, in the guise of a ride-or-die gangsta of sorts, creates a community of other noble tricksters, ordinary black folk who can live lives that matter, free from want or fear, only by working together in ordinary ways to make day-to-day life better for themselves in a world defined by racial and class inequality for the foreseeable future. McGruder's Jesus thus mostly turns out to be an ordinary man himself. He cannot make a just world by divine fiat or a direct-action campaign, but he does have an extraordinary capacity to inspire love, compassion, integrity, and self-respect in others. Of course, he also has the ability to make the TV audience at home laugh.

Humor is the dominant artistic mode of the sitcom as a genre, but, as we have seen, it is through satire that McGruder's show becomes most invested in the political fight against police brutality. Laughing at or with Jesus as a black man living in urban America may have the potential to defuse dangerous, racist stereotypes and, at its most utopian, move people toward feelings and gestures of solidarity across ideologically charged social boundaries, especially race and class. Like postsoul humor more generally, however, the invitation to laugh at or with Jesus as a victim of state-sponsored violence also speaks to something other than hope for a better world. It speaks "to a deep cultural impulse, extending beyond articulating suffering in muted tones to howling about oppression and subjugation, as well as the victories in survival and amidst strife."[55] Jesus, in other words, is "laughing mad."

FUTURE PROSPECTS AND QUESTIONS

- To date, most work on representations of Jesus in popular culture has been done by scholars outside of the field of biblical studies. Future work by biblical scholars remains to be done in this area, including reflection on the question of why the study of popular culture and reception history seems to have more traction in other fields.

---

[54] Carpio, *Laughing Fit to Kill*, 20.
[55] Bambi Haggins, *Laughing Mad: The Black Comic Persona in Post-Soul America* (New Brunswick, NJ: Rutgers University Press, 2007), 4.

- I have focused on an example of Jesus in popular culture that relocates the biblical character to a new narrative, historical, and geographical context, modern-day America, and resituates him in a new narrative genre, the sitcom, and new medium, television. Future research might benefit from drawing on the field of transmedia studies to explore what happens to familiar stories and characters when they are adapted to new modes of storytelling and appropriated for narratives that challenge the continuity of their narrative character.

- I briefly mention the role of pleasure or enjoyment in popular culture. Many academic studies of popular culture, including those done by biblical scholars, note the importance of entertainment but rarely make entertainment itself an object of inquiry. What new questions would be raised about the relationship between the Bible and popular culture if the fun and pleasure of entertainment were made more central to our inquiries or even to the way we write?

- I briefly mention the objections of some, predominantly white, conservative Christians to McGruder's depiction of Jesus. Many described the show as blasphemous or an attack on the Christian faith itself. How have scholars of religion addressed the concept of blasphemy and of provocative religious art more generally? Is there a common denominator among representations of Jesus deemed blasphemous? Or does the label say more about the perspectives and assumptions of the offended than the offense itself?

- Key to this chapter is the question of how humorous stories about Jesus reflect and respond to serious social problems created or sustained by racial inequality. McGruder's Jesus is essentially a critic of the racial formation of modern American society, however funny or kind he might be. McGruder's show thus raises some important questions that merit further reflection: In what ways, if at all, is comedy a useful mode of re-presenting the narrative character of Jesus known from the New Testament? What power, if any, does comedy itself have to address or even change entrenched social problems like racism? How else has the figure of Jesus been used to address racism in the age of Black Lives Matter? What tools and perspectives might biblical scholars *qua* biblical scholars bring to the study of popular culture when it functions as both entertainment and social critique?

Suggested Reading/Annotated Bibliography

Blum, Edward. "'Look, Baby, We Got Jesus on Our Flag': Robust Democracy and Religious Debate from the Era of Slavery to the Age of Obama." *Annals of the American Academy of Political and Social Science* 637, no. 1 (July 2011): 17–37.

Blum's essay provides one of the most up-to-date surveys of how Jesus has been represented and depicted as "black" in American culture. Though it does not discuss Hip-hop Jesus in depth, it outlines the older tradition appropriated and interrogated by gangsta rappers and provides a wide-angle political and cultural context into which the Hip-hop Jesus can be placed.

Feltmate, David. *Drawn to the Gods: Religion and Humor in* The Simpsons, South Park, *and* Family Guy. New York: New York University Press, 2017.

Along with insightful analyses of the religious theme and characters in popular animated sitcoms, Feltmate provides a smart theoretical model of how religious satire works. Key to this book are questions about what assumptions popular TV shows have about the nature of religious "others" and religion itself. Biblical scholars might be particularly interested in discussions of characters like God and Jesus.

Griffin, Dustin. *Satire: A Critical Reintroduction*. Lexington: University of Kentucky Press, 1995.

Key to Griffin's definition of satire are the elements highlighted in my essay: inquiry, provocation, display, and play. By breaking down the work of satire into these constituent parts, Griffin's theory provides a highly adaptable model, ideal for biblical scholars accustomed to close reading of the mechanics of narrative and rhetoric.

Maus, Derek, and James J. Donahue, eds. *Post-Soul Satire: Black Identity after Civil Rights*. Jackson: University of Mississippi Press, 2014.

An essential introduction to the rise of postsoul satire as a distinctive development within the long history of African American humor. McGruder's earlier work has been usefully described as postsoul, and I try to extend that claim to include *Black Jesus*.

Prothero, Stephen. *American Jesus: How the Son of God Became a National Icon*. New York: Farrar, Straus and Giroux, 2003.

This popularly pitched book is still essential reading. The breadth and variety of examples included, the taxonomy of Jesus types, and the central argument that representations of Jesus in American culture have been increasingly detached from Christian dogma and from the biblical canon itself have set the stage for subsequent discussions of the "cultural Jesus."

Siegler, Elijah. "Television." In *The Routledge Companion to Religion and Popular Culture*, ed. John C. Lyden and Eric Michael Mazur, 41–64. New York: Routledge, 2015.

One of the few overviews of religion and television published to date. Siegler's discussion of the "priestly," "prophetic," and mythological functions draw needed attention not just to the religious content of television programming but to the form itself. This essay offers some suggestive avenues into an area of popular culture biblical scholars have not much explored.

Utley, Ebony. *Rap and Religion: Understanding the Gangsta's God*. Santa Barbara, CA: Praeger, 2012.

Utley combines content analysis, ethnographic work, and theoretical reflection to discuss the central, and sometimes underappreciated, place religious symbols and themes have in hip-hop music, especially gangsta rap. The chapter "Jesus Piece" (49–68), which informed my discussion of Hip-hop Jesus, makes a compelling case for seeing Jesus in gangsta rap as a companion whose own marginal social status and experience of state-sponsored violence resonate with the self-mythologization of the gangsta rapper. Utley's work points to another area of popular culture underexplored by biblical scholars.

Yancy, George, ed. *Christology and Whiteness: What Would Jesus Do?* New York: Routledge, 2012.

As the title suggests, many of the essays in this volume approach the figure of Jesus from a theological perspective, though the racialization of Jesus in popular culture is also a recurring topic. Victor Anderson's chapter, "The Mimesis of Salvation and Dissimilitude in the Scandalous Gospel of Jesus" (196–212), is an incisive take on the devotional ideal of *imitatio Christi*, arguing in effect that historically this has meant reproducing a white Jesus. Anderson makes his point in part by looking at McGruder's representation of Jesus and Christianity in his earlier television show, *The Boondocks*.

CHAPTER 7

JUDAS IN FILMS

CAROL A. HEBRON
SCHOOL OF THEOLOGY, CHARLES STURT
UNIVERSITY, BRISBANE

INTRODUCTION

In Western culture, Judas Iscariot has become the archetype of the betrayer and villain. Reference to Judas in canonical scripture is minimal, describing him "only by slurring epithets."[1] He is portrayed as the last apostle and betrayer (Matt 10:4; Mark 3:19; Luke 6:19), a traitor (Luke 6:19), a thief (John 12:6), and as being possessed by the devil (John 13:26–27).[2] His action of handing over Jesus to the Jewish authorities has, over the past two millennia, resulted in numerous variations of representations depicting his motives; his sinister behavior, his status in the apostolic band, his relationship with Jesus—and Satan—and his suicide. These representations are documented in the writings of the early church fathers and in the creative arts. However, it is within the medium of film that the evolving and changing interpretations of the Judas Iscariot character are most obvious. In this chapter I show how the filmic Judas character has changed from being the disciple who betrayed Jesus to the one who was instrumental in bringing about salvation.

---

[1] Richard Walsh, "The Gospel According to Judas: Myth and Parable," *Biblical Interpretation* 14 (2006): 37.
[2] William Klassen questions the use of the word "betray" as opposed to the more accurate translation "to hand over." He argues that referring to Judas as the "betrayer" conveys and perpetuates negativity toward Judas. William Klassen, *Judas: Betrayer or Friend of Jesus?* (Minneapolis, MN: Fortress Press, 1996), 57. I choose to use "betray," "betrayal," and "betrayer" as I am not looking at the historical Judas but at the Judas as portrayed in films.

Overview of Topic

When studying or analyzing Jesus—and Judas—films, it is beneficial to view them in chronological order, using the dates of the film's production and release.[3] This assists in tracking the evolving and changing portrayals. One only needs to compare the Judas character in the 1905 silent Jesus film *La Vie et la Passion de Jésus Christ* to *Get Some Money* (2017) to see the vast changes in the Judas portrayals.

Silent films differ from modern films in a number of ways. There is the obvious absence of sound. The lack of dialogue requires audiences to use their imagination to decipher what the characters are saying, why they are acting in a particular manner, and even what they may be thinking. The silent actors had to compensate for the absence of sound with exaggerated actions, hand gestures, and facial expressions. Without the bonus of a musical soundtrack and sound effects to convey romance, suspense, sadness, tragedy, and similar emotions or situations, silent actors had to be acutely creative in finding ways to draw in the viewing audience to the art of visual storytelling.[4]

Changes in the way the story was told were prompted by technical advances in cinematography and cultural influences. These affected why and how filmic character portrayals developed and changed. Joseph Boggs and Dennis Petrie outline nine techniques in which a character is developed in film:[5]

1. Characterization through appearance.
2. Characterization through dialogue.
3. Characterization through external action.
4. Characterization through internal action.
5. Characterization through reactions of other characters.
6. Characterization through contrast—dramatic foils.
7. Characterization through caricature and leitmotif.
8. Characterization through choice of name—name typing.
9. Characterization through music.

I survey these nine approaches in my study of the filmic Judas. By using this approach, I show how the one-dimensional gospel figure of Judas Iscariot morphs into a multifaceted character in films. Films from the Americas, Europe, and Asia, spanning from 1905 to 2017, confirm how filmmakers have created very diverse Judas characters.

[3] Richard Stern, Clayton N. Jefford, and Guerric Debona, *Savior on the Silver Screen* (New York: Paulist Press, 1999), 4, 10.

[4] See Nicholas Chare and Liz Watkins, "Introduction: Gesture in Film," *Journal for Cultural Research* 19 (2015) 1:1–5, https://www.researchgate.net/publication/276307094_Introduction_gesture_in_film https://doi.org/10.1080/14797585.2014.920189

[5] Joseph M. Boggs and Dennis W. Petrie, *Art of Watching Films*, 7th ed. (New York: McGraw-Hill, 2008), 59–67, 298–307. These pages provide concise descriptions of these approaches as well as examples from films.

SPECIFIC EXAMPLES AND FOCI

Characterization through Appearance

Black costumes are synonymous with sinister and villainous characters. This is particularly evident in films from the silent era and western genre films. Apart from an instant identification, the black costume also helps in separating a character from the other cast members.

In *From the Manger to the Cross* (1912) Judas has black hair and beard, appropriately unkempt. To accentuate eye movement, his eyes are heavily lined with kohl. His voluminous black hood and cloak hide his body, leaving only his face and hands visible. To add to his sinister appearance Judas rubs his hands together and his eyes dart menacingly.

Judas's costume in the Italian film *Christus* (1916) is very different from the other disciples' apparel. His costume suggests he is wealthy. A satin turban adorns his head and the wide satin cummerbund around his waist is studded with gems. A full moneybag hangs from the cummerbund. His costume perpetuates the myth of Jewish avarice. The linking of this greed to the actions of Judas Iscariot and his betrayal of Jesus have fueled antisemitic interpretations of Judas.[6]

This perception of a wealthy Judas is also conveyed in the Mexican film *El mártir del Calvario* (1952). Judas is immediately recognizable in the crowd. In contrast to those around him, his costume is flamboyant. His tunic is knee-length and short-sleeved—similar to the uniforms worn by Roman centurions. He is portrayed as a lover of gold jewelry, with gold chains around his neck, garish gemmed rings and gold bangles, all suggesting he has both wealth and expensive taste. How Judas came to this wealth is unknown to the viewer. This Judas also introduces two new features to his physiology. Judas is handsome and clean-shaven and his short hair is styled with "kiss curls." The film reviewer Lucy Poems noted that he "actually looks the part of a 1950s hero."[7] The second feature is the large gold-hooped earring that he wears. In the 1950s, pirate films were popular and plentiful, so the sight of the gold earring would not faze the audience. However, pirates customarily wore the earring in their left ear; Judas wears it in his right ear.

Godspell (1973) produces a unique Judas character: a dual character of Judas and John the Baptist played by the same actor. His costume is not out of place in this hippie interpretation of the gospels. Wearing a coat with tasseled epaulettes and a rosette, a striped

---

[6] Jeremy Cohen, *Christ Killers: The Jews and the Passion from the Bible to the Big Screen* (Oxford: Oxford University Press, 2007), 257: "Judas has come to embody so many of those hateful characteristics with which Jews have been stereotyped over time."

[7] Lucy Poems, "Early Mexican Jesus Film," *Customer Reviews*, May 22, 2009, https://www.amazon.com/Martir-del-Calvario-Martyr-Calvary/dp/B000EMSM72

T-shirt with jeans, a work neck scarf, and painted tennis shoes, he bears the qualities of a circus ringleader and a politician. The reason behind the characters replacing their day-to-day clothes with colorful and mismatched garments is to set the characters apart from society and becomes an outward display of their decision to follow Jesus.[8] Judas and John wear the same costume, but the identity of John the Baptist is defined by the inclusion of a shofar. This Jewish musical instrument is appropriate for John, as he is the character responsible for calling together the disciples. Interestingly, there is no defining prop for Judas.

The low-budget film *Gospel Road* (1973) is a representation by the country and western singer Johnny Cash. The portrayal of Judas is thinly drawn, yet he is clearly distinguishable from the other disciples because during the naming of the twelve disciples, individual close-ups of each of them appear on the screen. They are all Anglo-Saxon except for Judas. From his physiology, hair, and beard we see that he is an Ashkenazi Jew. The narrator, Cash, pauses slightly between pronouncing "Judas" and "Iscariot." He seems reluctant to identify Judas as a betrayer. There is no reference to money or bargaining, no betrayal kiss, no suicide. Cash acknowledged his own transgressions and believed that God had forgiven him. Jesus died for all sinners, Judas included.[9]

The Judas character in *The Last Temptation of Christ* (1988) is interesting and somewhat radical. According to the *New York Times* film reviewer Caryn James, the director Martin Scorsese wanted to create "a stereotypical villain and then make him a hero."[10] By dressing Judas in black, Scorsese symbolically separates him from the other disciples, who are dressed in cream-colored robes. To accentuate stereotypical Jewish features, Harvey Keitel's (Judas) nose was made to look larger and curve outward. He wore a short red curly wig. This was not a flattering feature and one on which the audiences and reviewers commented.[11] Even Zebedee admits to his fellow disciple, "I don't like his hair. I've heard that his ancestor Cain had a beard like that." The implication is that Judas is a murderer in the tradition of Cain who killed his brother, Abel (Gen 4:1–16). Judas's red hair promotes further vilification. From the opening moments of the film, he is referred to as the "red devil."

---

[8] Stephen Schwartz, "Godspell Notes for Directors, Music Directors and Musicians, Producers," 1–24, 9. https://www.stephenschwartz.com/wp-content/uploads/2017/04/Godspell_Notes_for_Directors_and_Musicians.pdfcontent/uploads/2017/04/Godspell_Notes_for_Directors_and_Musicians.pdf

[9] The belief that Judas has been forgiven is echoed in Cash's song "Down There by the Train," from his 1994 album *American Recordings*. Therein Cash sings, "I saw Judas Iscariot carrying John Wilkes Booth" to "where the sinner can be washed in the blood of the lamb." These lyrics convey the image of two well-known assassins and the hope of their redemption.

[10] Caryn James, "Fascination with Faith Fuels Work by Scorsese," *New York Times*, August 8, 1988, https://www.nytimes.com/1988/08/08/movies/fascination-with-faith-fuels-work-by-scorsese.html.

[11] Michael Medved, for one, said Keitel's "wearing an orange fright wig made him look like a Biblical Bozo." Michael Medved, "Hollywood vs. Religion," *St Mark's Review* 142 (1990): 9.

Characterization through Dialogue

Characters' dialogue and delivery can reveal a great deal about them. Silent films had to rely on title cards, also known as intertitles, for dialogue and narration—much like modern-day voice-overs. These intertitles guided audiences in understanding the character.

The screen time for the Judas character in the forty-four-minute 1905 silent film *La Vie et la Passion de Jésus Christ* is a brief two minutes and thirty-five seconds. An intertitle informs the audience of the motive for Judas's betrayal: "The hatred of Judas who now sought the opportunity to betray him [Jesus]." Similarly, in *From the Manger to the Cross* (1912), the intertitles include the word "betray" and its derivative "betrayer." This not only identifies Judas as the one who betrayed Jesus but underpins his role in the narrative and film.

The title card introduces Judas in Cecil B. DeMille's epic *The King of Kings* (1927) as "Judas Iscariot, the Ambitious, who joined the Disciples in the belief that Jesus would be the Nation's King, and reward him with honor and high office." This brief description actually is quite informative. Title cards were necessarily concise as the American film audiences of the 1920s were a mixture of immigrants from Europe with limited English-language reading skills.[12]

Nicholas Ray's 1961 epic *King of Kings* presents a different and innovative interpretation of the filmic Judas. An omniscient narrator connects episodic scenes by citing scripture, explaining an event, and tying together story lines involving the main characters.[13] Any motives behind the actions of Judas are ignored, and his character bears no stereotypical Jewish traits evident in earlier films. Judas is portrayed as a "bewildered scapegoat."[14]

The rock opera *Jesus Christ Superstar* (1973)—a new genre of Jesus films—examines the last seven days of Jesus's life from the point of view of Judas. Pamela Grace observes that in the first few minutes of the film, Judas articulates more critical analysis of Christianity than most Jesus films do in two hours or more.[15] Rather than traditional dialogue, it is through the song lyrics that the characters of Judas and Jesus and other cast members are developed. Judas, played by an African American, Carl Anderson, is

---

[12] When the actor Augustus Carney asked a theater proprietor what he thought of the film *The Colleen Bawn* (1913) and how it went with the patrons, the response was "[The new film] is great—simply splendid. Those who understand it think it's one of the best ever; but the trouble is, you see, that half of my regular patrons can't read English, and, for them, the picture is spoiled by the number of leaders [intertitles]. It's well acted, of course, but what they can't get from the scenes they can't get at all." See J. Berg Esenwein and Arthur Leeds, *Writing the Photoplay* (Springfield, MA: Home Correspondence School, 1913), 172–3, https://archive.org/details/writingphotopla01leedgoog.

[13] See Paul V. M. Flesher and Robert Torry, *Religion and Film: An Introduction* (Nashville, TN: Abingdon Press, 2007), 102–3; Lloyd Baugh, *Imaging the Divine: Jesus and Christ-Figures in Film* (Franklin, WI: Sheed & Ward, 1997), 22.

[14] Roy Kinnard and Tim Davis, *Divine Images: A History of Jesus on the Screen* (New York: Carol Publishing Group, 1992), 132.

[15] Pamela Grace, *The Religious Film* (Chichester, UK: Wiley-Blackwell, 2009), 97.

the prophet who comments on the history of Roman oppression of the Jews and the similarities to modern African-Americans.[16] He reminds Jesus that they are "occupied" and asks whether Jesus has "forgotten how put down" they are. Judas warns Jesus, "They'll crush us if we go too far." Judas is the voice for the poor and oppressed and for economic justice. He also prophesies his own demonization as well as that of the Jews and Judaism. If Jesus is allowed to continue along this messianic path, great suffering will befall the Jews—"the sad solution." Judas pleads for himself in singing that he did not come to meet Caiaphas and Annas for a "reward." Nor did he come "on his own accord." He pleads, "Just don't say I'm damned for all time." Whether Judas has been damned for his betrayal of Jesus and his suicide is a question asked for nearly two millennia: Is Judas forgiven for his actions?

In *The Passion* (2008), we hear words of forgiveness. Throughout the film, there are scenes where intimate conversations take place between Judas and Jesus. Judas informs Jesus that all the disciples believe in Jesus. Perhaps already knowing that Judas has set in motion his arrest, Jesus asks Judas what he sees when he looks in his heart. Judas does not answer. Instead, he says, "Forgive me Lord." Jesus responds, "You are forgiven." Again, Jesus asks Judas what he sees "inside." Judas has no answer. Jesus then offers words of contrition: "I am sorry, Judas." In this extraordinary nonscriptural dialogue, Judas is the sinner asking for forgiveness and he receives absolution.

Characterization through External Action

Actions best depict the important traits of any character. There should be a clear relationship between a character and his or her actions. Thus the actions should evolve naturally out of the character's personality. The adage "Actions speak louder than words" is essential when applied to films. The audience is able to identify a character by what he or she does and how it is done.

There can be no mistaking that Judas in *La Vie et la Passion de Jésus Christ* (1905) did not want to partake in the Holy Communion. When Jesus hands Judas the morsel of bread, Judas turns his back on him and faces the audience, who can clearly see his actions. Judas secretively places the bread on the couch on which he is seated. When handed the cup of wine—the blood of Christ—Judas again turns his back on Jesus and the other disciples, and looking directly toward the viewing audience, pretends to drink from the cup and then tips the wine onto the floor.

Judas in *The King of Kings* (1927) shows similar contempt for the "body and blood." Having previously viewed the bread with suspicion, he takes it in his fingers and snaps off a piece. Without lifting his elbow off the table, he nonchalantly passes the bread to the disciple sitting next to him. Judas is in doubt as to what he should do it. Covering his mouth with both hands, he pretends to eat the bread. Ensuring that no one is watching

---

[16] A black actor plays Judas in *Son of Man* (2005), *Color of the Cross* (2006), and *Get Some Money: The Parable of Judas* (2017).

him, he lets the bread slip through his fingers and onto his lap. The chalice being handed to him interrupts his introspection. Again uncertainty strikes him, yet he accepts the chalice but hesitates to drink from it and in a panic returns it to the table untouched.

It is through the actions of Judas in *Christus* (1916) that we observe his rejection of Jesus and Christianity. As Jesus and his disciples make their triumphant entry into Jerusalem, Judas chooses to be an onlooker. Visibly repelled by the crowd's adoration of the Messiah, Judas breaks his staff over his knee and throws the two pieces onto the ground, where they fall in a cruciform. Horrified by this symbol, he deliberately stamps on the broken staff, symbolizing his rejection—and that of the Jews—of Jesus as the long-awaited Messiah. Judas severs himself from the gospel message. He is now an outsider.

Judas, as an outsider, is highlighted in the Last Supper scene of the French film *Golgotha* (1935). Although this is the first talking Jesus film ever made, it is in the silence—and skillful camera work and direction—that the Judas character is best developed. Having been told by Jesus, "That thou doest do quickly" (John 13:37), Judas boldly exits the upper room where the supper is being held. At this point, he stops and from the balcony watches Jesus break the bread and pour the wine. A close-up of Judas's eyes widening in amazement, followed by a look of disappointment, evokes pathos. Judas has clearly become an outsider to the apostolic group.

That Judas is no longer a member of the inner circle is evident in the 1971 Mexican film *Jesús Nuestro Señor*. During the distribution of the bread and wine in the Last Supper scene, Jesus stands and calls each disciple by name, and they in turn approach him. Each disciple breaks off a piece of bread and dips it into the wine.[17] Peter is the first to be called, then John, Andrew, James son of Zebedee, Thomas, Matthew, James son of Alphaeus, Philip, Bartholomew, Simon, and, last, Thaddeus. Jesus calls only eleven disciples. The individual naming of the disciples highlights Judas's absence and nonparticipation in the "institution of the Lord's Supper." It is almost as though Judas is dead to this group of insiders.

Judas's death and the depiction of his suicide are presented in various forms. The traditional and scriptural way—death by hanging—is the most widely used in films. However, in *The Greatest Story Ever Told* (1965), the manner of Judas's suicide is unique. Judas ascends the steps to the temple's sacrificial fire, stretches out his arms in cruciform style, and falls headlong into the blazing fire. There are various explanations as to why the director George Stevens opted for this mode of suicide. An obvious explanation is that the blazing fire signifies the fires of hell and, consequently, Judas's damnation to that place. Gerald Forshey proposes, "The Buddhist style of death suggests the depth of [Judas's] alienation from Jesus's message."[18] Richard Stern et al. argue that the action is an adaptation of Acts 1:18: "On the one hand, this action may be taken as self-sacrifice of distress made to God in the moment of a sinner's repentance. On the other hand, per-

[17] Communion by intinction is unique to this film. Intinction is the practice during Holy Communion of partly dipping the consecrated bread, or host, into the chalice of consecrated wine.

[18] Gerald E. Forshey, *American Religious and Biblical Spectaculars* (Westport, CT: Praeger), 102.

haps it is the ultimate reprisal for the betrayal of God's Son, the hurling of the deceiver into the fires of hell."[19]

Stephenson Humphries-Brook explains, "The symbol of Judas's suicide in the altar fire indicates that he is the last of the sacrifices in a temple that no longer worships God."[20] This symbolism is expanded further with W. Barnes Tatum's proposal that "Judas casts himself into the flames of the altar of sacrifice—a burnt offering, a holocaust."[21]

Another unique representation of Judas's suicide is in the Iranian film *The Messiah* (2007). In this film, the audience views two endings. The first is based on the gospels, while the second is a "continuation of events according to Islamic sources and the Gospel of Barnabas." What sets this filmic Judas apart from any other portrayal is that Judas is a sacrificial substitution: he dies in place of Jesus.

The film's alternative ending has the angel Gabriel appearing to Jesus just before he is about to be captured by the Roman soldiers. The angel informs Jesus, "Now your Lord says: 'O Son of Mary, I shall take you from this world tonight and raise you to myself.'"[22] In a blast of light, Jesus ascends into Heaven without dying. Judas witnesses the light. He screams and writhes in agony. The narrator explains, "Then the wonderful God acted wonderfully. Judas changed amazingly in speech and face into the form of Jesus." It is Judas who stands trial, is mocked and scourged, and is condemned to death. Although guilty of leading the "legion of soldiers" to Jesus, Judas claims his own innocence with his dying words from the cross: "God, why have you forsaken me, seeing the malefactor has escaped and I die unjustly?"

The 2015 French film *The Story of Judas* (*Histoire de Judas*) "takes the historical make-over a step further in suggesting that the whole traitor story was probably the fabrication of a vindictive young scribe wronged by Judas."[23] Judas is incensed when he sees a young man from Qumran taking notes as Jesus speaks. After a brief but heated exchange, Jesus tells Judas to "do what he is going to do, and do it quickly." Judas sees this as approval to burn the manuscripts of the "accursed scribe." This is quite a different understanding of what traditionally is a prediction of Judas's betrayal of Jesus!

---

[19] Stern, Jefford, and Debona, *Savior on the Silver Screen*, 139–40.

[20] Stephenson Humphries-Brook, *Cinematic Savior: Hollywood's Making of the American Christ* (Westport, CT: Praeger, 2006), 46.

[21] W. Barnes Tatum, *Jesus at the Movies: A Guide to the First Hundred Years and Beyond*, 3rd ed. (Salem, OR: Polebridge Press, 2013), 100. It is significant that the director George Stevens was part of the US Army Signal Corps, filming the liberation of Nazi concentration camps.

[22] From subtitles in the film as viewed on YouTube, accessed May 19, 2020, https://www.youtube.com/watch?v=nEjrTCRABMI. See also Geoffrey Parrinder, *Jesus in the Qur'an* (1965; Oxford: Oneworld, 2003), 105–21. The *Qur'an* states that some of the Jewish groups in Medina "said 'We have killed the Messiah, Jesus, son of Mary, the Messenger of God.' They did not kill him, nor did they crucify him, though it was made to appear like that to them; those that disagreed about him are full of doubt, with no knowledge to follow, only supposition: they certainly did not kill him—God raised him up to Himself. God is almighty and wise." Surah 4.157–8, translated by M. A. S. Abdel Haleem, *The Qur'an*, Oxford World's Classics (Oxford: Oxford University Press, 2005), 65.

[23] Deborah Young, "Story of Judas: Berlin Review," *Hollywood Reporter*, February 6, 2015, http://www.hollywoodreporter.com/review/story-judas-berlin-review-770632.

Characterization through Internal Action

Adele Reinhartz notes, "As one of the few Gospel characters who undergoes emotional development—from devotion to betrayal to remorse to suicide—Judas holds great promise for filmmakers seeking to inject passion and drama into their Jesus biopics."[24] The following scenes show how filmmakers have achieved this.

In explaining, or at least trying to understand, the reasons for Judas's suicide, filmmakers attempt to infiltrate his mind. Matthew's Gospel tells us that Judas was "filled with remorse" (27:3). As we will see, in various films this inner conflict becomes manifest in psychedelic visions and apparitions, and the influence of a Satan figure in various guises is introduced.

Alice Guy's 1906 film *La Vie du Christ* introduces a vision of the Christian interpretation of the "Suffering Servant" (Isa 52–53). This is "a masterful expression of Judas' dilemma."[25] While Jesus raises the chalice at the Last Supper, his image dissolves into that of a half-naked Jesus, wearing a crown of thorns, holding a reed scepter, and bearing the marks of crucifixion. Three angels—one on either side and one slightly above him—add authenticity to the vision. Only Judas is privy to the apparition, so when a terrified and confused Judas runs from the room, the other disciples watch his exit in bewilderment.

To avoid blame or responsibility for a wrongdoing, the claim "The devil made me do it" is a popular cliché; in some Jesus films, Judas could easily make that claim. For example, the devil/Satan—a stereotypical half-naked horned man—in *Christus* (1916) confronts Judas as he is leaving the house of Caiaphas after collecting his thirty pieces of silver. Satan provokes Judas, forcing him to take out a handful of coins from the moneybag. While staring at the coins, they "dissolve" into droplets of blood, a unique pictorial representation of the metaphoric "blood money" (Matt 27:6). It may also allude to the "blood curse": "His blood is on us and on our children!" (Matt 27:24–25). Satan reappears when Judas attempts to return the money to the chief priests and chases Judas to the tree where he hangs himself. Satan waits for Judas to enter "into the darkness where there will be weeping and gnashing of teeth" (Luke 13:28).

Satan's manipulative power influences Judas's action in the 1921 Danish film *Blade af Satans Bog*, also known by the English rendering of its title, *Leaves from Satan's Book*. Satan, in the guise of a Pharisee, is able to hide his real identity, enabling him to deceive both Judas and the Sanhedrin. Already weighed down by indecision, uncertainty, and nervousness, Judas's preoccupation with his dilemma at the Last Supper is evident by his crumbling between his fingers a piece of matzo. Satan is the one who questions Judas as to why he believes in Jesus. Satan is the one who says Jesus is "the devil's son" and that Judas has been "snared by the power of the devil." Satan is the one who instructs Judas to

---

[24] Adele Reinhartz, *Jesus of Hollywood* (Oxford: Oxford University Press, 2009), 152.
[25] Allison McMahon, *Alice Guy Blaché: Lost Visionary of the Cinema* (New York: Continuum International, 2002), 103.

identify Jesus with "the kiss of friendship." Satan is the one who pays Judas the bag of coins.

Inner voices are another ploy to express Judas's mental state. In *Golgotha* (1935), the audience hears Judas's torment and his thoughts. The voice of Jesus says, "Go and sell your house and give to the poor, then come and follow me. My kingdom is not of this world. Love thine enemies, do good to those who hate thee. If thou wouldst follow me take up your cross." As the voice develops into a loud babble, Judas's demeanor deteriorates. "They shall spit upon you. They shall scourge me. They shall put me to death. When they shall crucify me, all shall be drawn toward you. You will be persecuted for my name's sake." Judas runs off, trying to escape the voice.

As the gospels do not provide a complete and detailed Judas figure, directors and screenwriters look elsewhere to develop his character. In *The Passion of the Christ* (2004), Mel Gibson draws from legends and uses images from Anne Catherine Emmerich's *Dolorous Passion*, published in 1833. These images enhance the demonization of Judas and the moral, demonological dimension of betrayal.[26] Gibson also draws from apocryphal writings, notably the *Arabic Gospel of the Infancy of the Savior*. Based on this gospel Gibson has two boys chasing Judas through the Valley of Hinnom, the place where the people of Judah offered its children to the fire god Molech and Baal (Jer 7:31; 32:35). These two boys "morph into biting, reviling, demons." When the heavily chained Jesus is tossed over a bridge by the temple guards and falls face to face with Judas, a "screaming ghoul (resembling the figure of Munch's [painting] *Scream*) darts in and out of the darkness."[27] The ever-present voice of Satan haunts Judas to the point of madness and suicide.

Characterization through Reactions to Other Characters

Adding nonscriptural sources generally reinforces the narrative and further develops the Judas character. The director and screenwriter Giulio Antamaro includes Judas's attendance at the flagellation scene in *Christus* (1916). The focus is on Judas, not on Jesus being whipped. When Judas has seen enough, he attempts to leave, but two guards seize him and push him closer to the blood-soaked Jesus. Their gestures imply the words "Look what you have done!" Reeling back in horror, Judas falls to his knees. When a guard bends down to question him, Judas responds by kissing him on the cheek, thus admitting what he had done. An angry guard pushes Judas aside and leaves him to fight his way through the crowd of spectators, whose anger is now directed at Judas.

Judas witnessing the flagellation scene is also included in *The King of Kings* (1927). Although this is less dramatic than the *Christus* (1916) scene, it is significant. The ini-

---

[26] Scott McKnight, "The Betrayal of Jesus and the Death of Judas," in *Jesus and Mel Gibson's* The Passion of the Christ: *The Film, the Gospels and the Claims of History*, ed. Kathleen E. Corley and Robert Webb (London: Continuum, 2004), 70.

[27] Richard Walsh, *Three Versions of Judas* (London: Equinox, 2010), 104.

tially suave-looking Judas now appears possessed by a demon. Hiding behind a pillar, he watches the flogging of Jesus and flinches with the sound of each stroke of the lash. He is filled with terror as he watches the guards mock Jesus by placing the crown of thorns on his head and forcing the reed scepter into his hand. Overwhelmed with guilt, Judas leaves to return the blood money to Caiaphas.

In contrast, the Judas character in Franco Zeffirelli's *Jesus of Nazareth* (1977) is guilt-free. The screenwriter Anthony Burgess speculated that the traditional motives for Judas's betrayal—greed, ambition, jealousy, and fear—did not provide him with enough reason to betray Jesus.[28] The one guilty of betrayal is the fabricated character Zerah, a scribe who manipulates, demeans, and deceives Judas in carrying out Zerah's plan to present Jesus to the Sanhedrin. According to Zeffirelli, Zerah's actions were fueled by his ambition for power, likening him to Stalin's Yagoda, Hitler's Himmler, and Napoleon's Fouche. Zerah's actions were "part of every power system."[29] Judas is merely a pawn in the power play.

The Color of the Cross (2006) is an example of the extremes by which filmmakers deviate from the gospel texts. Judas is introduced during a discussion between members of the Sanhedrin and identified as a spy—a unique concept! Whether he is spying for the Sanhedrin or has infiltrated the Jewish court to keep it informed of attitudes toward Jesus is at this point in the narrative unclear.[30] Judas is a Zealot and holds the common purse. Fellow disciple John calls him a "thief." When the disciples scatter from the interrupted supper, one of the disciples grabs Judas from behind, holds a sword to his throat, and threatens "the traitor."

Another deviation in *The Color of the Cross* (2006) is Judas's obsession with Mary Magdalene. While a romantic love triangle between Jesus, Mary Magdalene, and Judas is not a unique concept, the actions of Judas and Mary Magdalene certainly are.[31] This relationship is different. Yes, jealousy on Judas's part is noted: "It is easier to love a messiah than a fisherman." Mary's reply to Judas's question "What is it that you see in him that is not in me?" is laced with venom: "The truth." Judas responds, "Here is my truth," and forces himself on her. Mary submits, saying, "Fine. Would you like a feast your master has not yet enjoyed?" The scene fades.

This is a vastly different image of the "twelfth disciple." The reactions of film reviewers to this scene vary. Some simply choose to ignore it. Some argue that Mary's submission is a willful "sacrificing" of her body to delay Judas's betrayal.[32] Others believe Judas rapes

---

[28] Forshey, *American Spectaculars*, 169.

[29] Franco Zeffirelli, *Franco Zeffirelli's Jesus: A Spiritual Journey* (San Francisco: Harper and Row, 1984), 104.

[30] Judas's later actions and speech suggest he is in fact an infiltrator.

[31] In the Kenyan film *Get Some Money* (2017), the love relationship between Judas Icarioti Mikwania and Magda is the driving force behind his betrayal of Jesus. See also DeMille's *The King of Kings*, the Mexican production *Maria Magdalena, pecadora de Magdala*, and *Jesus Christ Superstar*. The 2009 German animated film, *Judas & Jesus*, presents an erotic and irreverent account of this love triangle.

[32] Matt Page, "*Color of the Cross* Review," *Bible Films Blog*, January 24, 2007, http://biblefilms. blogspot.com.au/2007/01/color-of-cross-review.html.

Mary.[33] Interestingly, the *Movie Guide* review mentions Judas only once: "Judas tries to force himself on a woman."[34] That woman is not identified as Mary Magdalen, but then she is not mentioned at all in the review.

Characterization through Contrast—Dramatic Foils

The juxtaposition of characters serves a number of purposes. In *The King of Kings* (1927), Judas is compared with Peter, highlighting their differences. Judas is elevated to a higher position within the disciples: higher than Peter, who traditionally is Jesus's right-hand man. The difference between these two disciples is accentuated in the Last Supper scene. Peter, while securely holding the bread with both hands, gazes adoringly at Jesus. When handed the chalice, Peter holds it reverently, so as not to spill a drop, and while looking at Jesus takes a sip, and then presses the chalice to his heart. In contrast, Judas casually accepts the bread, looks away, and then subtly drops the bread into his lap. Judas, whose facial expression is one of contempt, takes the chalice and is hesitant about drinking from it. His act of abstinence clearly defines his behavior as dissimilar to that of the adoring Peter.

This difference is alluded to in the cleansing of the temple scene in *Jesús Nuestro Señor* (1972). While the temple priests are questioning Jesus, Judas holds Jesus's red cloak. Peter is nursing a white dove. The divergence in personalities and behaviors can be seen in these two characters and in what they are holding. The white dove symbolizes innocence, gentleness, and peace (Gen 8:8–10) while Judas's holding the red cloak prophesies future events—the fulfillment of scripture.[35] The color red is associated with passion, blood, and fire, as well as being the color of love and hate, sin and suffering, violence and death.

William Telford presents an excellent summary of the differing characters of these two apostles, Peter and Judas:

> Both Peter and Judas are shown in the New Testament to have been guilty of an act of disloyalty, treachery or denial with respect to their master, Jesus. Nevertheless, one came to be *the* great apostle, the other *the* great apostate. One is seen as the proto-typical Christian, the other the stereotypical Jew. One has come to be the supreme example of Christian discipleship, the other the universal symbol of Jewish perfidy. The one became a Pope, the other a pariah. Peter was given the keys to the kingdom of heaven, Judas was sent to eternal damnation in hell.... One was *reha-*

---

[33]   John Monaghan, "Jesus' Skin Is Least of the Issues," *Detroit Free Press*, October 27, 2006.

[34]   "Adding slightly to the Bible," *movieguide.org*. https://www.movieguide.org/reviews/color-of-the-cross.html

[35]   After Jesus was arrested, the soldiers mocked him; "They stripped him and put a scarlet robe on him" (Matt 27:28). In the Revelation of John we read, "He is clothed in a robe dripped in blood, and his name is called 'The Word of God [Jesus]'" (Rev 19:13).

bilitated after his denial of Jesus, the other *vilified* in consequence of his treachery.[36]

Judas's role in *El mártir del Calvario* (1952) is both significant and important. His final appearance in the film is paralleled with Jesus's. Where the tortured figure of Jesus carries his cross out of the city, accompanied by the sound of a beating drum, a crosscut shows Judas running through an olive grove, his hands trying to block out the sound of the drumbeats.

Judas is also portrayed as a "parallel protagonist" in *The Last Temptation of Christ* (1988).[37] He confronts Jesus and questions his actions. In an emotive scene where Jesus discloses to Judas his approaching death, both characters express confusion and uncertainty. When Jesus declares that he is "the lamb to die," Judas questions whether Jesus is the Messiah. Jesus confirms that he is the Messiah, but Judas cannot understand why Jesus has "to die on the cross." Jesus explains that he has to die so that he can "come back to judge the living and the dead." Judas protests that he will not let Jesus die. However, he is told that he does not have a choice. Neither does Jesus. Jesus further explains, "Without you, there can be no redemption." When Judas protests that God can do it "if that's what God wants," Jesus answers confidently, "He will do it, through you." Far from betraying Jesus, Judas becomes the very instrument of humanity's salvation.

Characterization through Caricature and Leitmotif

Since about the ninth century, artists have developed a variety of characteristics and motifs to distinguish Judas from the other apostles. Characteristics include exaggerated stereotypical Jewish facial features and distinctive colors for his hair and apparel.[38]

Leitmotifs include a moneybag, the iconographic trope of avarice. The moneybag is a common article of Judas's costume in films. In *Il Vangelo de secondo Matteo* (1964), Judas is seen clutching a moneybag. Sometimes he hangs the purse around his neck, symbolizing that he had already "fallen into the noose of avarice."[39] The leather purse hanging around Judas's neck in *Get Some Money* (2017) is clearly visible. To accentuate the deceitfulness of Judas and the secrecy surrounding the handing over of Jesus, Judas holds the bag behind his back or in his waistband, as in *Golgotha* (1935). Sometimes the bag is in clear view of others. In *El mártir del Calvario* (1952), Judas places the bulging

[36] William R. Telford, "The Two Faces of Betrayal: The Characterization of Peter and Judas in the Biblical Epic or Christ Film," in *Cinéma Divinité: Religion, Theology and the Bible in Film*, ed. Eric C. Christianson, Peter Francis, and William R. Telford (London: SCM Press, 2005), 214. See Mark 8:32; 14:31; 66–72; Matt 16:23; 26:57–75; Luke 22:3–6; John 18:1–11.

[37] Kaille Shilling, "Servant of the Story: Judas as Tragic Hero in Film," *Journal of Religion and Film* 8, no. 2 (2004), http://digitalcommons.unomaha.edu/jrf/vol8/iss3/3.

[38] These were described earlier in "Characterization through Appearance."

[39] Otfried Lieberknecht, "Death and Retribution: Medieval Visions of the End of Judas the Traitor," invited lecture, Saint John's University, Collegeville, MN, May 13, 1997, §4, http://www.lieberknecht.de/-diss/papers/p_judas.htm.

moneybag in front of Jesus, on the supper table! Sometimes the bag and spilled coins are situated at the base of the tree where Judas killed himself, as in *Jesus of Nazareth* (1977) and the Indian film *Karunamaydu* (1978).

Another leitmotif is a dagger. In *Jesús Nuestro Señor* (1972), Judas contemplates whether Jesus is the one who will bring armed resistance to the Roman oppressors. Judas rubs his beard with one hand and rests the other on the hilt of his sword. *The Last Temptation of Christ* (1988) also portrays Judas as a Zealot. Judas, assigned by the Zealots to assassinate Jesus, finds his chance at the monastery but puts away his knife when he realizes that his friend may indeed be a messenger from God. Judas in *The Color of the Cross* (2006) is seen sharpening his sword while the other disciples are talking. The dagger, sword, or knife helps identify the Judas character as being a threat and a Zealot. Jesus spoke of peace; these weapons express violence.[40]

Characterization through Choice of Name—Name Typing

Of the twelve disciples, only Judas is given a surname, Iscariot. The biblical commentators John R. Donahue and Daniel J. Harrington, referring to Greek and Hebrew translations, offer four possible meanings and derivatives for the name Iscariot: "the false one," "the one who handed him over," "a man from Kerioth," and "dagger-men, a group of radical Jewish assassins." Of the four proposals the second and third have the most support.[41]

The importance of a name is crucial in *The Robe* (1953). After the crucifixion of Jesus a distraught Demetrius, a freed slave of the Roman tribune Marcellus Gallio, who was in charge of the crucifixion, wanders the streets of Jerusalem. He comes across an obviously troubled man sitting on the curb muttering about why Jesus was betrayed to the Romans. The man says, "Because men are weak. Because they are cursed with envy and cowardice. Because they can dream of truth . . . but cannot live with it. So they doubt. They doubt, the fools! Why must men doubt? Tell them they must keep faith! They must keep faith!"

Demetrius begins to walk away, but intrigued, must ask, "Wait, tell who? Who are you?" The despairing man replies, "My name is Judas." For a character so integral to the plot, Judas's role is minuscule. Even the actor, Michael Ansara, is uncredited.

Similarly, Judas has a minimal role in *I Beheld His Glory* (1952). The first reference to him is in the opening scene, when Cornelius reports on the welfare of the disciples after

---

[40] In *The Kings of Kings* (1927) and the telefilm *The Day Christ Died* (1980), Peter also has a sword. This alludes to his being the disciple who cut off the right ear of the high priest's slave during the Garden of Gethsemane melee (Matt 26:51; John 18:10–11).

[41] John R. Donahue and Daniel J. Harrington, *The Gospel of Mark*, Sacra Pagina Series Volume 2. (Collegeville, MN: Liturgical Press, 2002), 125. Jerome (347–420), an early church father, argued that "no matter how you interpret it, Iscariot means money and price." See *The Homilies of Saint Jerome, Volume 1 (1–59 On the Psalms)*, trans. Sister Marie Liguori Ewald, *The Fathers of the Church: A New Translation*, 48 (Washington, DC: Catholic University of America Press, 1964), 260.

Jesus's crucifixion, "All but one is well: Judas of Kerioth who died by his own hand."[42] The audience could easily have missed the connection between "Kerioth" and "Iscariot." When Judas leaves the supper, Cornelius describes him as "the one who slipped out to betray Jesus." The name Judas Iscariot is never mentioned, and Judas is mentioned only twice. He is seen only at the Last Supper and at Gethsemane, where he speaks his only word in the film: "Master." This is when he identifies Jesus. It is in Jesus's response that we hear "Judas is it with a kiss that you betray the Son of Man?" (Luke 22:48). As in *The Robe*, the actor playing the part of Judas is not credited.

On occasion, it is not the words written—or spoken—that are important but what is omitted. In the cast list for the film *Maria Magdalena, Pecadora de Magdala* (1946) Judas has third billing—Jesus is first, followed by Maria Magdalena—which indicates Judas is a major character in the film. It is only when we read the cast listing that we realize that Judas is the only disciple who has not been granted the appellation *San* (Saint). So from the beginning of the film Judas is denounced and is separated from the apostolic group. Whether this isolation was a preproduction decision based on religious sensitivity— Mexico is predominantly Roman Catholic—is unknown.

The television miniseries *Jesus* (1999) shows Judas's first encounter with Jesus when a band of Zealots—which includes Judas—is attacking Roman soldiers offering protection to a tax collector. As Jesus walks up to Judas, he says, "Come, Judas, son of Simon Iscariot, your fate is with me." The shocked Judas asks Peter, "How did he know my name?," to which Peter replies, "Follow him and find out." This encounter between Judas and Jesus is both interesting and significant because it introduces to the narrative the theological concept of predestination. Judas was preordained by God to hand over Jesus for crucifixion, enabling salvation of the world.

Characterization through Music

Music plays an important role in creating and developing a character. It can also manipulate or guide the audience into a fuller appreciation of a character and the film's setting. The music in *Il Vangelo de secondo Matteo* (1964) provides relevant examples of how music influences characterization. The music in this film is eclectic and includes a number of musical genres. Focusing on the Judas scenes, we are able to trace and better understand Judas's actions and his emotions.

The Jewish song "Kol Nidre" is the background music during the Last Supper. Jeremy Cohen notes, "Jewish memory typically associates [this song] with the Jews of the Middle Ages."[43] This was an era when Jews were forced to convert to other religions by their oppressors or face either expulsion or execution. The melody plays again after Caiaphas offers Judas thirty pieces of silver for his impending betrayal. "Kol Nidre" adds another dimension to the gravity of Judas's action.

---

[42] Judas also introduces himself to Caiaphas as "Judas of Kerioth" in *The Day Christ Died* (1980).

[43] Cohen, *Christ Killers*, 235.

Kol nidre means "all vows" and is a prayer offered on Yom Kippur—the Day of Atonement—when one asks to be released in advance from any vows made and not kept. Although the prayer refers only to vows between the person making them and God, the director, Pier Paolo Pasolini, includes Judas's arrangement with the chief priest. Judas accepts his role in helping Jesus fulfill his own death as atonement for "the forgiveness of sins" (Matt 26:28). Judas becomes the ritualistic scapegoat in the Yom Kippur ritual, narrated in Leviticus 16, where the high priest selects two male goats. One is sacrificed to God, and the other is sent to Azazel—a supernatural being—in the wilderness, bearing the sins of Israel.

Another emotive song in *Il Vangelo de secondo Matteo* (1964) is the American gospel and blues song "Dark Was the Night, Cold Was the Ground." This song adds to the pathos when the distraught and defeated Judas makes his confession to Caiaphas, "I have sinned by betraying innocent blood" (Matt 27:4). The lyrics for this specific scene provide another perspective and introduce new insights into the character of Judas and his actions. Judas admits his "debt" (sin) and "crime" for which his "Savior paid." He asks, "How could He die to save a soul like mine?" Even though the song reinforces Judas's culpability in bringing about Jesus's death on the cross, it also includes his admission of guilt and acknowledgment that Jesus is his "Savior." More important, the lyrics allude to Judas's redemption because Jesus died "to save" his soul, clearing his "debt."

From this brief overview of the portrayal of Judas in film, it is clear that Judas not only "plays a central role in the Passion narrative" but that filmmakers have elaborated and expanded on the one-dimensional gospel character.[44] Through the manipulation of character in film, we witness the Judas character change. Judas began his screen time in the early 1900s as the twelfth apostle, keeper of the purse, thief, villain, sinner, betrayer of Jesus and damned to hell. Judas is a "gospel pawn."[45] He is portrayed as the epitome of evil. Beginning in the 1950s, filmmakers present Judas as the mouthpiece for the oppressed, a Zealot, the scapegoat, the hero, an "agent of salvation."[46]

By 2017, as seen in the Kenyan film *Get Some Money*, Judas Iscarioti Mikwanja lives in Ghetto Semane village. He is the disciples' treasurer, who begins to embezzle from their collective funds. He needs the money to spend on Magda, to woo her into marrying him. Petero, his close confidante, advises him to "sell out" Ticha (Jesus), who has a bounty on his head. Judas does just that, but overcome with remorse, he hangs himself. Judas leaves a suicide note: "Dear World, Money is power, but it also kills. I'm sorry. With all honesty. J.I." *Get Some Money* is a radical departure from the gospel accounts of Judas Iscariot, the one who betrayed Jesus.[47]

---

[44] Ibid., 255.   [45] Walsh, "The Gospel According to Judas," 38.

[46] Kim Paffenroth puts forward a convincing case that Judas is an "agent of salvation." See *Judas: Images of the Lost Disciple* (Louisville, KY: Westminster John Knox, 2001), 135–42.

[47] Winnie Njoki, the film's producer, describes *Get Some Money*: "Worth noting, apart from the fact that it is an introspective film that explores our society's obsession with money and love, it also seeks to bring to light the plight of suicidal beings in an effort to advocate for world bodies to increase awareness and speak against suicide." See Peter Chattaway, "A Kenyan Film about the Suicide of Judas Iscariot," *Patheos*, March 6, 2017, http://www.patheos.com/blogs/filmchat/2017/03/kenyan-film-suicide-judas-iscariot.html.

From the films analyzed, it is evident that the Judas character has become more than the disciple who betrayed Jesus. The primary sources for the creation of the Judas character in films are the gospels of Matthew, Mark, Luke, and John. These clearly do not have enough detail to develop the disciple's character; filmmakers need to look elsewhere for ideas, which they draw from society and its culture. "Jesus [and Judas] films have come to be understood as much more than simple adaptations of the gospel story, but as bearers of meaning and theology in their own right. These films also capture the social and cultural concerns of their time, so that the various incarnations of the celluloid Christ [and Judas] stand as artifacts of our pluralistic and diverse society."[48]

Filmmakers utilizing aspects of characterization, dialogue, and other equally important elements of film have been able to shape their own interpretation and understanding of the Judas character. Although filmmakers and directors reflect changing societal attitudes in their films, they may be shaping those attitudes more than they are reflecting them. In the filmic character of Judas we witness his evolution from damnation to redemption. In the Silent Era (1902–27) antisemitic myths are rekindled and Judas is clearly the villainous and greedy Jew. From the 1930s to 1960s, the mold of the stereotypical Jew is broken and Judas displays traits of a 1950s' hero. Although still a damned sinner in the decade of biblical epic films, the 1960s, Judas undergoes a radical metamorphosis. The 1970s and the innovative representations of Jesus provided an environment for reinterpreting the Judas character. In the decades leading into the new millennium Judas assumes the traits of a model disciple. By the second millennium, the Judas filmic character has undergone many incarnations. Judas Iscariot, previously depicted as the damned disciple, becomes the redeemed Judas.

FUTURE PROSPECTS AND QUESTIONS

- Margaret Miles in her seminal work, *Seeing and Believing: Religion and Values in Movies*, states, "What films do best…is to articulate the anxieties of a changing society."[49] How does the filmic Judas character communicate societal and cultural changes?
- There are three distinct approaches to religious criticism of popular films: theological, mythological, and ideological.[50] Theological criticism studies classic religious concerns, sensibilities, and themes and how they are expressed in films. For example, *Darkest Hour* (dir. Joe Wright, 2017) looks at ideas around leadership, sacrifice, and standing up for our values. Myth critics focus on our psychological quest for meaning

[48] Jon Rainey, "The Cinematic Savior: Jesus Films and Related Literature," *Theological Librarianship* 3, no. 2 (December 2010), 27.

[49] Margaret R. Miles, *Seeing and Believing: Religion and Values in Movies* (Boston: Beacon Press, 1996), 193.

[50] Conrad Ostwalt and Joel Martin, *Screening the Sacred: Religion, Myth, and Ideology in Popular American Film* (Boulder, CO: Westview Press, 1995), 10, 14, 16.

and aspects of our world not normally accessible through the conscious mind. The Marvel Cinematic Universal films (2007 to date) are entertaining examples. Ideological critics study the relationship of religion and society, with the underlying notion that culture and art shape and are shaped by politics. *The Post* (dir. Stephen Spielberg, 2017) tells of the battle between the press and the government. How effective are these approaches when applied to the study of Judas in film?

- No matter how a text is adapted or how a filmmaker transfers that text into images, viewers respond differently. Although a film may receive awards, it may still be a box-office flop. Consider, for example, *Moonlight* (dir. Barry Jenkins, 2017).[51] This film is a chronicle of the childhood, adolescence, and burgeoning adulthood of a young, African American, gay man growing up in a rough neighborhood of Miami. What influences diverse responses to an audience's reception of a film?
- How does film appreciation enrich theological inquiry and assist in the understanding of a dialogue between contemporary culture and theology?[52]
- A BBC spokesperson for the TV miniseries *The Passion* (2008) explained, "We are not seeking to subvert or rewrite the Gospel narrative—we are just retelling it to bring it alive for a contemporary audience."[53] What justification is there for the "retelling" of the Judas story?
- Bible films are restricted by content and rely on "notorious" events and/or Bible figures. This handicaps directors and producers who are usually tied to a profit-driven industry. Is there a future for Bible stories in the film industry? Is there even a need for Bible stories to be told? The Pew Research Center reports that the "Christian share of the [United States] population is declining, while the number of U.S. adults who do not identify with any organized religion is growing."[54] Why does Hollywood continue to film Bible stories when the population of the United States is clearly a melting pot of cultures?

SUGGESTED READINGS AND ANNOTATED BIBLIOGRAPHY

Boggs, Joseph M., and Dennis W. Petrie. *The Art of Watching Films.* 7th ed. Boston: McGraw-Hill, 2008.

Boggs and Petrie explain the complex aspects of film-art, such as the formal elements and the production process of films. This text provides guidance in how to develop the skills

---

[51] Tom Huddleston Jr., "'Moonlight' Is among the Lowest-Grossing Oscar Best Picture Winners Ever," *Fortune*, February 28, 2017, http://fortune.com/2017/02/27/moonlight-oscars-low-budget-box-office/.

[52] Christopher Deacy and Gaye Williams Ortiz, *Theology and Film: Challenging the Sacred/Secular Divide* (Malden, MA: Blackwell, 2008), viii.

[53] "BBC to Present Series Exonerating Judas, Pilate and Caiaphas," *Catholic News Agency*, March 17, 2008, http://www.catholicnewsagency.com/news/bbc_to_present_series_exonerating_judas_pilate_and_caiaphas/.

[54] "America's Changing Religious Landscape," *Pew Research Center*, May 12, 2015, http://www.pewforum.org/2015/05/12/americas-changing-religious-landscape/.

of perceptive viewing, helping students to analytically view and understand films within their historical, cultural, and social contexts. The text presents an analytical framework that can be applied to all movie genres.

Gubar, Susan. *Judas: A Biography*. New York: W. W. Norton, 2009.

Gubar's book is a valuable and informative text on the evolution of the character Judas. She explains how, throughout the ages, Judas has been represented in the arts, misrepresented and misunderstood by the church and theologians, and reinterpreted by popular culture. Gubar's scholarly metabiography is an essential text for researchers attempting to find answers to why and how this "atypical twelfth apostle in biblical times" evolved into a "venerable afterlife" in the twenty-first century.

Hebron, Carol Anne. *Judas Iscariot: Dammed or Redeemed. A Critical Examination of the Portrayal of Judas in Jesus Films (1902–2014)*. London: Bloomsbury T & T Clark, 2016.

Focusing on the Last Supper story in twenty-four Jesus films from nine countries, I analyze the changing portrayals of Judas in film and their influence on the emergence of new theologies. I use a three-lens approach. Lens 1 examines the sources and how they are used by filmmakers to construct their film of the historical Judas. Lens 2 analyzes how the filmmaker creates and communicates the content of the film. Lens 3 explains how the portrait of Judas in the film can be used as an entry point for examining the culture of the time in which the film was produced. This is a useful method for an analytical approach to studying film in that it covers textual sources, cinematic features, and cultural history.

Paffenroth, Kim. *Images of the Lost Disciple*. Louisville, KY: Westminster John Knox Press, 2001.

Paffenroth presents fourteen different images of Judas in five categories: "Judas the Obscure; the arch-sinner; the villain; the tragic hero; and, the penitent." This detailed and thorough examination of how Judas has been portrayed since the earliest traditions to the present day provides a framework for further investigation. Acknowledging the depth and complexity of Judas's character, Paffenroth makes a valuable contribution to the study of Judas by providing "a real encounter with the lost disciple."

Reinhartz, Adele. *Jesus of Hollywood*. Oxford: Oxford University Press, 2007.

Reinhartz provides a convincing argument that Jesus films reflect and influence cultural perceptions of Jesus as well as other characters in the Jesus narrative. She maintains that films transform the scriptural texts in question, rewriting and reconceptualizing them. Chapter 8 focuses on Judas Iscariot and considers his role in the movies. These include his personality, betrayal (and Satan's influence), the divine plan, and the relationship between Jesus and Judas.

Tatum, W. Barnes. *Jesus at the Movies: A Guide to the First Hundred Years and Beyond*. 3rd ed. Salem, OR: Polebridge Press, 2013.

Jesus at the Movies is a seminal reference work. Tatum provides a historical-critical perspective and uses his analyses of the films to introduce historical criticism of the gospels and the historical Jesus. Tatum's four-stage process in the history of Jesus films—"reluctance, reverence, diversity, and scandal"—provides a useful methodology in the study of Jesus (and Judas) films. His identification of the use of two scriptural trajectories—harmonizing and alternative—illustrates how the gospels have been utilized in telling the Jesus-Judas story.

FILMOGRAPHY

Christus. Dir. Giulio Antamoro. Italy, Società Italiana Cines, 1916.

The Colleen Bawn. Dir. Sydney Olcott. USA, Kalem Company, 1911.

Color of the Cross. Dir. Jeane-Claude Le Marre. USA, Nu-Light Entertainment, 2006.

The Day Christ Died. Dir. James Callen Jones. USA, 20th Century Fox Television, 1980.

El mártir del Calvario. Dir. Miguel Morayta. Mexico, Oro Films, 1952.

From the Manger to the Cross. Dir. Sidney Olcott. USA, Kalem Company, 1912.

Get Some Money: The Parable of Judas. Dir. Biko Nyongesa. Kenya, Legit Films, 2017.

Godspell: A Musical Based on the Gospel According to St. Matthew. Dir. David Greene. USA, Columbia Pictures, 1973.

Golgotha. Dir. Julien Duvivier. France, Ichtys Film, 1935.

Gospel Road: The Story of Jesus. Dir. Robert Elfstrom. USA, Twentieth Century Fox, 1973.

The Greatest Story Ever Told. Dir. George Stevens. USA, United Artists, 1965.

I Beheld His Glory. Dir. John T. Coyle. USA, Cathedral Films, 1952.

Il Vangelo de secondo Matteo. Dir. Pier Paolo Pasolini. Italy and France, Arco Film, 1964.

Jesus. Dir. Roger Young. Czechia, Italy, Denmark, USA, Antena 3 Television, 1999.

Jesus Christ Superstar. Dir. Norman Jewison. USA, Universal Pictures, 1973.

Jesús, Nuestro Señor. Dir. Miquel Zacarias. Mexico, Panorama Films, 1972.

Jesus of Nazareth. Dir. Franco Zeffirelli. Italy, UK, Incorporated Television Company, 1977.

Judas & Jesus. Dir. Olaf Eneck and Claudia Romero. Denmark, Distant Dreams Produktion, 2009.

Karunamayudu. Dir. A. Bheem Singh and Christopher Coelho. India, Dayspring International, 1978.

King of Kings. Dir. Nicholas Ray. USA, Metro-Goldwyn-Mayer, 1961.

The Kings of Kings. Dir. Cecil B. DeMille. USA, DeMille Pictures Corporation, 1927.

La Vie du Christ. Dir. Alice Guy. France, Société des Etablissments L. Gaumont, 1906.

La Vie et la Passion de Jésus Christ. Dir. Ferdinand Zecca and Lucien Nouquet. France, Pathé Frères, 1905.

The Last Temptation of Christ. Dir. Martin Scorsese. USA, Canada, Universal Pictures, 1988.

Leaves from Satan's Book, aka *Blade af Satans Bog*. Dir. Carl Theodor Dreyer. Denmark, Nordisk Film, 1921.

Maria Magdalena, pecadora de Magdala. Dir. Miguel Contreras Torres. Mexico, Hispano Continental Films, 1946.

The Messiah. Dir. Nader Talebzadeh. Iran, production company unknown, 2007.

The Passion. Dir. Michael Offer. UK, BBC, 2008.

The Passion of the Christ. Dir. Mel Gibson. USA, Icon Productions, 2004.

The Robe. Dir. Henry Koster. USA, Twentieth Century Fox, 1953.

Son of Man. Dir. Mark Dornford-May. SA, Spier Films, 2005.

The Story of Judas, aka *Histoire de Judas*. Dir. Rabah Ameur-Zaimeche. France, Sarrazink Productions, 2015.

PART III

BIBLICAL THEMES IN POPULAR CULTURE

....

CHAPTER 8

CREATION IN AMERICAN POPULAR CULTURE

....

JAMES F. MCGRATH
DEPARTMENT OF PHILOSOPHY AND RELIGION,
BUTLER UNIVERSITY

INTRODUCTION

THE 2015 album *Ill Mind of Hopsin 7* focuses in on religious themes, including direct interaction with one of the biblical creation stories, in a manner that gets directly to the heart of a number of aspects of the reception of the story in the present day:

> I hate the fact that I have to believe
> You haven't been chattin' with me like you did Adam and Eve
> And I ain't seen no fuckin' talkin' snake unravel from trees
> With an apple to eat, that shit never happens to me
> I don't know if you do or don't exist, it's drivin' me crazy.

While those familiar only with classic reverent approaches to Genesis and other creation-related material in the Bible may be surprised by or take offense at the profanity, Hopsin's lyrics engage with the text, with other elements of its reception history, and with key issues that confront the modern reader. On a literal level, the story features one human being who becomes two, a talking snake, and a divine conversation partner who comes and goes. The depiction of the forbidden fruit as an apple, while not in the biblical text, is commonplace in biblically themed artwork, and the snake unraveling from the tree(s) likewise reflects the engagement of popular culture not only "directly" with the Bible (as though unmediated interaction were in fact possible) but in the form of an interplay between the text, its prior history of reception, and contemporary issues. Contemporary readers are familiar with a great many fables in which animals talk. However, the reception of the biblical creation stories typically does not apply awareness of genre clues such as the presence of a talking animal to their framing of biblical stories, much less ask more probing questions about possible differences between ancient and modern readers and ancient and modern perceptions of genre that may be relevant to our reading of these ancient stories. This has been known to lead to the sort of crisis of faith that Hopsin speaks of, resulting from an incongruity between the ancient text and the modern approach to faith as belief in the literal truthfulness of stories such as those in Genesis 2–3. This way of defining faith, if uncritically accepted, creates issues not only (or even primarily) in connection with things like alternative data from the natural sciences but even more so in relation to the fact that everyday lived experience is at a disjuncture from the biblical narrative when treated as history. Since many modern readers have been primed to approach the text in a way that excludes its placement in a genre other than history, much discussion and debate about these stories focuses on acceptance or rejection of their literal truthfulness rather than on their symbolic potential.

Yet musical allusions to biblical imagery, however subtle, can perhaps also be useful in challenging this framework and opening those who approach the biblical creation material today to other perspectives. The 1985 hit by Mr. Mister, "Broken Wings," is not the most explicitly religious work by the band whose next hit was "Kyrie." But the lyricist John Lang was apparently inspired by Kahlil Gibran's 1959 novel *Broken Wings*, which refers in its early pages to Adam and Eve. The song in turn uses the imagery of the lover finding the beloved to be "half of the flesh and blood that makes me whole," language not far from Adam's poetic outburst about Eve as "flesh of my flesh and bone of my bone" (Gen 2:23). The Genesis story may be literally about one person becoming two, but on another level it is a symbolic story about the experience of two people becoming one, of finding another human being and experiencing them as one's "missing other half." According to Mark 10:6–8 and Matthew 19:4–6, Jesus's interpretation and application of Genesis 2 also acknowledged and focused on this symbolic level.

The reception of biblical creation material in song lyrics and elsewhere in popular culture both illustrates and at times addresses some of the most central issues of interpretation from the perspective of early twenty-first-century American readers. But the standpoint from which those readers read is shaped by a prior history of reception and reinterpretation in popular culture, which needs to be explored as well if the current trends and tendencies in reception of this material are to be clarified.

OVERVIEW OF TOPIC

Given the particular importance placed on the Genesis creation narratives in certain theological systems, it is unsurprising that these stories have figured prominently in American popular culture, not only in recent years but ever since the arrival of those stories in the Americas. Controversy over the teaching of evolution, however, made the Genesis accounts a focus of particular attention from the early twentieth century onward. But even before that, reception of biblical creation material has been framed by (or better, inextricably intertwined with) reception of developments in the natural sciences and social changes and accompanying controversies related to issues of race and gender. It is important in this context to note that "creation" in the Bible covers a much wider array of materials than simply the first chapters of Genesis, including allusions to earlier ideas about creation through the defeat of a sea monster (closely mirroring the Mesopotamian epic *Enuma Elish*). American creationists treat Genesis 1–3 as a unit, often framing it with a particular understanding of the role of Adam in Paul's epistles, and they treat the early chapters of Genesis in isolation from other creation-related material, both biblical and extrabiblical.[1] This selectivity is itself a striking and significant facet of the reception of biblical creation materials in American popular culture, precisely because it manifests within a framework that claims to be thoroughly "biblical" without leaving anything out. Popular culture's relationship to the Bible's teaching on creation is thus characterized by a particularly poignant irony. On the one hand, certain ideas are widely held to be "what the Bible says about creation," when in fact their relationship to the Bible may be at best ambiguous, and at times different or diametrically opposed. On the other hand, popular culture often reflects biblical as well as pre-biblical and extrabiblical ideas of great antiquity—without necessarily always being aware of it.

The two domains that we are talking about here—Bible and popular culture—are fluid, and their intersections multiple and multifaceted. The Bible sometimes simply *is* popular culture; at others it is *in* it; at others it may seem unrelated; and at still others it seems to stand over *against* it.[2] And yet all along the spectrum are shades of nuance and exceptions that make the reality much more complex and interwoven. We see this in relation to creation in the fact that one can find mentions of Adam and Eve alongside evolution and deep geological time throughout works of literary, visual, and musical art, with no commentary or explanation offered. Reflecting (and to some extent accounting for) this multifaceted relationship is the fact that it is not only the Bible that has influenced popular culture; ancient popular culture is sometimes presumed and sometimes polemicized against throughout the Bible, and the creation material is especially illustrative of this. The Bible includes embedded within its pages references to God's struggle with the sea monster and splitting of its body (Ps 74:13–14; 89:9–10; Isa 51:9–10). Yet we also find polemic against this idea in Genesis 1:6, where God speaks and a dome separates the waters above and below, with no hint of struggle. It is unsurprising that the Bible's relationship to popular culture in our time should be multifaceted, given that the Bible's own use of material from ancient popular culture is not uniform. Treatment of the Bible not merely at its point of intersection flowing outward into contemporary popular culture but at the inlet at which ancient popular culture enters is still quite uncommon within the context of this field, at least when articulated explicitly in those terms.

---

[1] See, e.g., the rejection of the Documentary Hypothesis in Tim Chaffey and Jason Lisle, *Old-Earth Creationism on Trial: The Verdict Is In* (Green Forest, AR: Master Books, 2008), 41–3; Ken Ham and Greg Hall, *Already Compromised* (Green Forest, AR: Master Books, 2011), 214–25.

[2] Cf. Bruce David Forbes and Jeffrey H. Mahan, *Religion and Popular Culture in America*, 3rd ed. (Oakland: University of California Press, 2017), 11–21.

Study of the Bible's use of and influence by ancient ideas, of course, is nothing new.[3] As yet, however, the insights that we gain from thinking about modern popular culture are not consistently allowed to illuminate processes involved in the texts' production and origins, nor vice versa.

This is perhaps the most crucial methodological point as it pertains to the reception of biblical creation narratives and motifs in American popular culture, or indeed any other context. Whether in ancient Gnosticism or *The Matrix*, it is not only changes in human understanding of the natural world or the realm of technology that influence and provide a framework for how Genesis and other texts are read. The social impact of changes in the realm of education, gender roles, and other areas is also of crucial importance. These constitute not mere "influences" on biblical interpretation but a domain of reception of multiple strands of human activity and culture that cannot be disentangled from the biblical text, since that text itself reflects the reception of previously existing assumptions about the natural world, gender roles, and other matters.[4]

The key theoretical insight that should be brought to bear on the examples that follow is that those who study creation in American popular culture stand entangled in the processes they seek to study, just as the biblical texts themselves cannot be shorn free of intertexts and cultural roots. Rather than being viewed as a hurdle to understanding, however, this entanglement should be appreciated as providing crucial assistance to the interpreter. We need to understand and appreciate the rootedness of the text, its socio-cultural fruit, the other elements that are part of the ecosystem in which it emerged and into which it has been transplanted, our own history of consumption of that fruit, and our ongoing influence on it through our horticultural interventions that have caused the cultivated form of Genesis 1–3 to have a different taste and appearance than it might if it grew in the wild, away from human influence. It is only in doing so that we can hope to grasp it, and potentially gain wisdom from the act of doing so.

SPECIFIC EXAMPLES AND/OR FOCI

In the 1920s several country songs reacted to the famous Scopes trial about the teaching of evolution in public schools. One such song is "The Bible's True" by Uncle Dave Macon, who famously sang, "There can't no man from anywhere, boys, make a monkey out of me."[5] That song at once reflects and perpetuates the widespread misunderstanding of

---

[3] See, e.g., Alexander Heidel, *The Babylonian Genesis: The Story of the Creation* (Chicago: University of Chicago Press, 1951), 2–3, 82–140.

[4] These emphases and texts from Genesis are also examined in Theresa Sanders's chapter in this volume.

[5] Charles Wolfe, "Bible Country: The Good Book in Country Music," in *The Bible and Popular Culture in America*, ed. Allene Stuart Phy (Philadelphia, PA: Fortress Press, 1985), 85–101, here 93–5. See also Alfred Watterson McCann, *God—Or Gorilla* (New York: Devin Adair, 1922).

biological evolution in terms of humans having come from (modern) monkeys rather than sharing a common ancestor with them. The related misunderstanding—that evolution represents a steady march of progress from primitive prehuman ancestors to modern humans—has been influenced by Rudolph Zallinger's famous illustration for the 1965 Time-Life book *Early Man* by F. Clark Howell.[6] The illustration is titled *The Road to Homo Sapiens* in the book but came to be known as *The March of Progress*, once again simultaneously reflecting and promulgating the misunderstanding. The iconic image has itself been adapted and transformed in popular culture in countless ways (including a wide array of popular memes) and often appears in antievolutionist literature that claims to be defending "biblical creation."[7] The study of biblical creation narratives in the context of American popular culture thus needs to focus on the intersection not just of the Bible with contemporary society but of *two* overlapping realms of popular culture, reflecting the perception of the natural sciences, of scripture, and of the overlap or opposition between the two.

In 1928 Roark Bradford published *Ol' Man Adam an' His Chillun*, which offered a collection of retellings of stories from Genesis in the form of African American folk tales.[8] The book would later be turned into a play by Marc Connelly, and subsequently made into a movie, under the title *The Green Pastures*. In the movie, Earth is depicted as a round globe—a detail that is of course absent from the Hebrew Bible, which takes for granted a flat Earth with a dome or "firmament" over it.[9] When the movie depicts God saying that more "firmament" needs to be added to custard that angels are making, the meaning may not be obvious to viewers.[10] In Bradford's book, however, "firmament" is said to be just a fancy name for water, which helps to clarify the film's use of the term, as well as being interesting in its own right.[11] The view that the "firmament" in Genesis 1 was a water canopy, which subsequently provided the water for Noah's flood, can still be encountered in young-earth creationist circles even today.[12] This reinterpretation of the

---

[6] F. Clark Howell and the editors of *Life*, *Early Man* (New York: Time-Life, 1965).

[7] See, e.g., the cover of Edward Humes, *Monkey Girl: Evolution, Education, Religion, and the Battle for America's Soul* (New York: Harper Collins, 2009), as well as that of the antievolutionist book by Jonathan Wells, *Icons of Evolution: Science or Myth? Why Much of What We Teach about Evolution Is Wrong* (Washington, DC: Regnery, 2002).

[8] Roard Bradford, *Ol' Man Adam an' His Chillun: Being the tales they tell about the time when the Lord walked the earth like a natural man* (New York: Harper and Brothers, 1928).

[9] Ancient people were not troubled by the shift to the Ptolemaic view of the cosmos, which envisages a spherical Earth surrounded by multiple celestial spheres, in the way that modern people have resisted new philosophical and scientific information on the basis of a supposedly literal adherence to the Bible. Nowhere has this been truer than in North America, the role of which in giving birth not just to fundamentalism in its original sense but to young-earth creationism is well-known. See George M. Marsden, *Fundamentalism and American Culture: The Shaping of Twentieth Century Evangelicalism, 1870–1925* (Oxford: Oxford University Press, 1980), 122; Eugenie Scott, *Evolution vs. Creationism: An Introduction* (Westport, CT: Greenwood Press, 2009), 105; Ronald L. Numbers, *The Creationists: From Scientific Creationism to Intelligent Design* (Cambridge, MA: Harvard University Press, 2006), 89–94.

[10] Marc Connelly, *The Green Pastures* (Madison: University of Wisconsin Press, 1979), 82.

[11] Bradford, *Ol' Man Adam*, 4.

[12] On this, see Karl W. Giberson, *Saving the Original Sinner: How Christians Have Used the Bible's*

solid dome mentioned in Genesis can be traced back at least as early as the late nineteenth century, and it has clearly influenced either Roark or his sources in the writing of his book.[13] And so *Ol' Man Adam an' His Chillun* provides a reminder that "folk tales" as popular culture do not simply exist unchanged from time immemorial, sealed off from the influence of sermons and conversations, which in turn may draw upon academic books and other such sources. Folk tales are always changing, even if they may also preserve elements over long periods of time, and they are neither composed nor transmitted in isolation from discussions that are taking place among intellectuals.[14] The connection between this retelling by and for a popular audience and speculative attempts to harmonize the Bible with modern science illustrates that, contrary to Connelly's claim in the foreword to his book, the stories do not provide evidence of a naïve literalism on the part of the tellers of the stories, much less a literalism that is predominantly found in African American churches.[15] In fact, we see on the one hand the influence of creative engagement with new scientific ideas and, on the other hand, a lighthearted approach to the stories that reworks them in fun and entertaining ways that may not always have been intended to be taken seriously, never mind literally.

Creation in the Bible has intersected with the widespread issues related to race and racism in the United States, much as it has with science denial. The cinematic rendition of *The Green Pastures* has been criticized for its all-black cast.[16] Against the backdrop of racial segregation in the context in which the movie was made and viewed, the casting clearly reflects an acceptance of that status quo. On the other hand, however, the potential is there for a depiction of God, the angels, and the first humans as having African rather than European features to serve an uplifting and subversive function. White slaveowners had believed, and taught their slaves, that black skin represented the mark of

First Man to Oppress, Inspire, and Make Sense of the World (Boston: Beacon, 2015), 155. For those who may not be familiar with it, young-earth creationism is the view that the Earth was created in six literal days less than ten thousand years ago. Valarie H. Ziegler discusses young-earth creationism in greater detail in her chapter in this volume.

[13]   See, e.g., Isaac Vail's 1874 pamphlet, *The Deluge and Its Cause* available on the Internet Archive: https://archive.org/details/delugeitscausebeoovail; J. M Woodman, *The Neptunian or Water Theory of Creation* (San Francisco: Bacon, 1888), 110–11 likewise available in the Internet Archive at https://archive.org/details/neptunianorwateroowood.

[14]   See, e.g., Barre Toelken, *The Dynamics of Folklore* (Logan: Utah State University Press, 1996), 43–4; Jack Zipes, *The Irresistible Fairy Tale: The Cultural and Social History of a Genre* (Princeton, NJ: Princeton University Press, 2012), 20.

[15]   Connelly, *Green Pastures*, xv, writes, "Unburdened by differences of more educated theologians they accept the Old Testament as a chronicle of wonders which happened to people like themselves in vague but actual places, and of rules of conduct, true acceptance of which will lead them to a tangible, three-dimensional Heaven."

[16]   Wheeler W. Dixon, *Visions of Paradise: Images of Eden in the Cinema* (New Brunswick, NJ: Rutgers University Press, 2006), refers to the all-black cast as a depiction of "an alternative universe in which racial integration is an impossibility" (147). Of related interest, see Brendan G. Carroll's biography of Erich Wolfgang Korngold, *The Last Prodigy* (Portland, OR: Amadeus Press, 1997), 260, in which he provides an amusing anecdote about the composer's reaction when he learned about American practices of segregation based on skin color while working on this film.

Cain mentioned in Genesis.[17] There is evidence that preachers among the slaves themselves already began the process of inverting the color scheme in this interpretation, so that Adam and his children were originally black, and whiteness was the mark placed on Cain.[18] The interpretation of the Bible's creation accounts in the United States in relation to the practices of slavery and segregation is notorious. Within that historical context, the way that different audiences responded to the same stories, and to the same books and movies that interpreted them, illustrates the inherent polyvalence of religious imagery related to creation.

This flexibility of possible interpretations and uses of the creation stories is also reflected in jokes about creation. Some play on the order of creation in Genesis 2 (not mirrored in the single creation of humans as male and female in Genesis 1:27), but that order is also open to a variety of interpretations. Is the creation of Adam before Eve an indication of male superiority, or a first attempt at creation improved upon in the second attempt, resulting in the creation of Eve? In one joke, God offers Adam an ideal companion who will do everything he says and practically worship him, and Adam responds by saying this sounds expensive and asking what she will cost him. God replies that she will cost him an arm and a leg, to which Adam responds by asking, "What can you give me for a rib?" Yet in Matthew Henry's famous Bible commentary, the creation of the woman from a rib is interpreted very differently, in a quote that continues to circulate widely to this day: "not made out of his head to rule over him, nor out of his feet to be trampled upon by him, but out of his side to be equal with him, under his arm to be protected, and near his heart to be beloved."[19] Whether in movies or jokes, as in the biblical narratives themselves, details ranging from the skin color of actors to the order of creation have an impact—but not always the same one irrespective of the storyteller or the audience.

This combination of power and ambivalence in the use of creation-related motifs in popular culture is also found in the utilization of the figure of Eve in advertising, which is explored in the humorously titled *Admen and Eve* by Katie Edwards.[20] Eve is a recurrent figure, appearing most frequently as a temptress or the one who gives into temptation, and as a sexual object (typically holding an apple, with a serpent nearby if not indeed

[17] For more on this topic see, e.g., Stephen R. Haynes, *Noah's Curse: The Biblical Justification of American Slavery* (Oxford: Oxford University Press, 2002).

[18] Lawrence W. Levine, *Black Culture and Black Consciousness: Afro-American Folk Thought from Slavery to Freedom* (Oxford: Oxford University Press, 2007), 84–5. See also Torin Alexander, "World/Creation in African American Theology," in *The Oxford Handbook of African American Theology*, ed. Katie G. Cannon and Anthony B. Pinn (Oxford: Oxford University Press, 2014), 185–99, here 185–6, 189–92; Emerson B. Powery and Rodney S. Sadler Jr., *The Genesis of Liberation: Biblical Interpretation in the Antebellum Narratives of the Enslaved* (Louisville, KY: Westminster John Knox, 2016), 108.

[19] Matthew Henry, *Exposition of the Old and New Testaments*, vol. 1 (London: Nisbet, 1706), 20. Cf. *Genesis Rabbah* 18.2.1.

[20] Katie B. Edwards, *Admen and Eve: The Bible in Contemporary Advertising* (Sheffield, UK: Sheffield Phoenix Press, 2012). See also Linda S. Schearing and Valarie H. Ziegler, *Enticed by Eden: How Western Culture Uses, Confuses, (and Sometimes Abuses) Adam and Eve* (Waco, TX: Baylor University Press, 2013), 111–32.

wrapped around her). Her image is used to sell items ranging from shoes and perfumes to chocolates and to promote television shows as different as *Desperate Housewives* and *Caprica*.[21] Eve's action, whether depicted reflecting a lack of willpower or too much of it, is viewed negatively from the perspective of patriarchal interpreters. Yet her decisive acquisition and mediation of knowledge has a long history of positive interpretation, at least as old as the ancient Gnostic tradition, which has itself seen a resurgence in recent years, including in popular culture, especially but not exclusively in science fiction.[22] Sometimes all it takes to call Eve to mind is for a woman to be depicted holding an apple—even though Genesis does not specify that the forbidden fruit was an apple, this being an element of popular cultural interpretation superimposed on the text. Something similar must be said of the idea that the temptation was carried out by Satan rather than (or disguised as) a talking snake. This, however, in fact represents an element that is at odds with what Genesis 3:1 explicitly says, namely that the snake or serpent was the craftiest of all the beasts of the field that God had made. Depictions in advertising of Eve with a literal snake are, in one respect, closer to the biblical text than certain other widespread reinterpretations of the story—although not inasmuch as they depict the snake entwined around her body. Factors such as evolving societal views about gender roles, the perceived selling power of images of women's bodies, the increased purchasing power of women (resulting from social changes not only in the home but in the workplace), and corresponding diversification of the range of consumer products available must all be taken into account if one is to understand the nuances of biblical reception in a realm such as marketing and sales in the United States over the course of its history. And just as the crafting of an advertisement reflects this sort of dynamic and multifaceted reception of a socially entangled Bible, so too does the reception of that reception, that is, the perception and influence of ads that utilize biblical figures and imagery.

Science fiction has its own tradition of exploration of creation, often drawing heavily on the Bible's accounts, and interacting with scientific developments in different and yet comparable ways to those we have already explored. The cribbing of details from Genesis 1–3 not only in published science fiction but in an even greater abundance of sci-fi that is rejected by editors is so commonplace and cliché that Brian Aldiss coined a term for it: "Shaggy God Stories."[23] It is not surprising that this motif should be com-

---

[21] The Hebrew name Havah, rendered as "Eve" in English, is connected to her role as the "mother of all living" (Gen 3:20), and the character who is depicted as Eve in the advertising for *Caprica* (and who plays a role in giving sentient life to the Cylons) is named Zoë, which is Greek for "life" and was often used as a translation for the Hebrew name Eve. On the related *Battlestar Galactica*, see Kevin J. Wetmore, *The Theology of* Battlestar Galactica: *American Christianity in the 2004–2009 Television Series* (Jefferson, NC: McFarland, 2012), 79–92. See also the ad campaign for Midol which featured the words "Reverse the Curse," discussed in Theresa Sanders, *Approaching Eden: Adam and Eve in Popular Culture* (Lanham, MD: Rowman & Littlefield, 2009), 118.

[22] See further James F. McGrath, *Theology and Science Fiction* (Eugene, OR: Cascade, 2016), 35–7, on Gnosticism in science fiction (as well as 41–3 on creation).

[23] He used the term in the October 1965 issue of *New Worlds* under the pseudonym Dr. Peristyle, punning on the term "shaggy dog stories." See further Sanders, *Approaching Eden*, 192–206; Brian

mon, however, given that the novel usually identified as the first work of science fiction—Mary Shelley's *Frankenstein*—is a creation story.[24] In the American science fiction TV series *Star Trek*, several episodes interact with the Adam and Eve stories from Genesis—sometimes explicitly, sometimes less so. In the episode "The Way to Eden" as well as in *Star Trek V: The Final Frontier*, the *Enterprise* is co-opted with the aim of reaching a planet that represents Eden and yet proves upon arrival to not be what those seeking it had hoped it would be. In the episode "The Apple" the crew of the *Enterprise* in essence kills the "deity" (in fact a machine) that artificially maintains a world in one vision of perfection, leading Spock to mention Genesis explicitly and the introduction of knowledge of good and evil into this garden, leading Kirk to ask whether Spock is casting him in the role of Satan.[25] In the Genesis story, Satan is not mentioned, and (as has already been mentioned) in Gnostic reinterpretations of Genesis the serpent and Eve play positive roles, providing knowledge that a malevolent deity wished to keep from humanity. Another motif in popular thought about creation is the idea that prior to the "fall" of humankind into sin, there was no death. This is viewed as "what the Bible teaches" on the subject, and yet in fact it stands diametrically opposed to the story in Genesis 2–3. In Genesis, the presence of a tree of life, the fruit of which grants immortality, makes clear that death is the rule, and only through some special intervention can it be postponed. This example highlights the fact that what many presume to be representative of biblical concepts of creation in popular culture may in fact be not merely nonbiblical but at odds with the Bible's narratives.[26]

Creation features prominently in the genre of fantasy as well as in sci-fi. In the television series *Supernatural*, the world is populated by a host of beings, many of which are drawn directly from the Bible and from extracanonical texts closely related to it. Specific stories about these beings are also drawn from those texts—for instance, the idea that God created human beings and told angels to worship them, leading to Lucifer's refusal and rebellion against God.[27] Some of the divine entities—such as God and his sister, Amara—simply existed. They in turn created other entities, and some of their creations engaged in their own acts of creation. Some entities' origin is uncertain, perhaps even to the supernatural entities themselves. The show includes elements that derive from

Attebery, *Stories about Stories: Fantasy and the Remaking of Myth* (Oxford: Oxford University Press, 2014), 102.

[24] It is interesting that Adele Reinhartz chooses *Frankenstein* and *Blade Runner* as bookends for the history of cinematic treatment of creation in her *Scripture on the Silver Screen* (Louisville, KY: Westminster John Knox, 2003), 7.

[25] The relevant episodes are surveyed in Sanders, *Approaching Eden*, 148–52.

[26] Popular knowledge of the Bible also omits things such as the presence of two rather than merely one creation account in Genesis 1–3. See Máire Byrne, "Biblical Literacy: The Irish Situation," in *Rethinking Biblical Literacy*, ed. Katie Edwards (London: Bloomsbury T & T Clark, 2015), 3–21, here 6. Some of this reflects exposure to children's versions of the creation accounts, which influences later impressions of the texts. On children's books, see Allene Stuart Phy, "The Bible as Literature for American Children," in Phy, *The Bible and Popular Culture in America*, 165–91, here 176–7.

[27] This story is found in the *Life of Adam and Eve* 14 and *Questions of Bartholomew* 54–56, as well as in the *Qurʾān* 17:61–64 and elsewhere.

extracanonical ancient sources and new elements created by the show's writers, but both kinds of material regularly seek to interpret the Genesis creation account in relation to the world as we know it, which contains evil and seems far from perfect in many of its aspects. The show depicts God as extremely powerful but not all-powerful, as not regularly involved in managing affairs on Earth, and as not encountered directly by at least some angels (to say nothing of most human beings). For some viewers, these plot elements will seem to be at odds with, perhaps even an attack on, the biblical creation stories. And yet those stories do not indicate where God comes from nor when angels and other such entities were brought into being. While there are moves within the Bible in the direction of omnipotence and omnipresence, we also find mentions of God creating through a conflict with the forces of chaos and of God dwelling or being present or absent in specific places. It is thus not surprising that ancient and modern storytellers have elaborated and expanded on what the biblical texts say, in ways that envisage not just primordial but ongoing struggle between God and other forces—which implies something other than divine omnipotence. Moreover, given that some of the stories that *Supernatural* draws upon, or at least some of the beliefs about creation reflected in them, may have roots that are older than the Bible and were never supplanted by the composition of the biblical literature, such stories illustrate the power of popular culture to preserve traditions and narratives, and to articulate theologies, that may be at odds with an "official story" or sacred text that in fact reflects—and has always reflected—the viewpoint of a small minority. Their potency and meaning should be considered in their own right, not simply measured against one particular way of interpreting the Bible that some group defines as orthodox.

Both fantasy and science fiction overlap in envisaging a world that is populated by powerful entities with abilities that seem like magic. One might expect that a difference between these two overlapping genres would be whether creation involves an instantaneous ("magical") action or a long process of (scientific) evolution, but this proves not to be the case. *Supernatural*, as we have already seen, takes evolution and the scientific view of the Earth's age for granted even while depicting God as the Creator of angels and humans. Popular culture's engagement with creation is mediated through other television genres, such as documentaries, a genre that includes shows that do not at all reflect mainstream academic knowledge, such as *Ancient Aliens*.

The abundance of artistic explorations of creation over the years continues to influence what we encounter in recent popular culture. Artists engage in a more or less direct fashion not only with the biblical creation narratives themselves but also with earlier appropriations thereof—as, for instance, in the echoing of Michelangelo's *The Creation of Adam* in a range of television and film contexts, as well as in a popular and highly varied internet meme.[28] Such reuse may or may not engage with the theme of creation per

---

[28] See also the poignant reworking of the painting by Harmonia Rosales, with both God and Adam depicted as black women. The painting bears the ambiguous title *The Creation of God*, which can be understood to be either subjective (that which God creates) or objective (humans creating God in our own image). On the one hand, much painting will be categorized as "high" rather than "popular" culture. On the other hand, visual images of creation (including icons and famous paintings in

se or do anything more than swap the figures originally depicted for humorous effect. Some of the memes, however, may be poignant, such as Dan Piraro's June 10, 2007, *Bizarro* comic, which sticks quite close to the original painting except that it has Adam busy on his laptop and phone, asking the Creator who is reaching out toward him to wait. In the process of this transformation, it becomes clear that what is depicted is no longer understood as the moment of divine creation. We see this as well in the multiple instances in which Michelangelo's *Creation of Adam* is mimicked in the television series *The Simpsons*. In one episode, Homer is shown painting his own version of this master-piece, with himself in the place of Adam and Marge in the place of God.[29] A variation on the painting appears in the Springfield Post Office (with a postal carrier in the place of God) in the episode "Blood Feud," and in the background of the title to the in-show movie *A Burns for All Seasons* in the episode "A Star Is Burns." In this last instance, Mr. Burns takes the place of Adam. There are other references to creation on *The Simpsons*, ranging from a reenactment of the Genesis account in "Simpsons Bible Stories" to an episode exploring Ned Flanders's creationism and a throwaway reference in "Everybody Hates Ned Flanders," in which, having become sick of a song he wrote that is being played everywhere, Homer says, "I've come to hate my own creation! Now I know how God feels." The sheer volume of material even within one series or franchise can be quite substantial and varied. Another reworking of Michelangelo's painting is to be found on the posters and DVD cover of the 2009 movie about the life of Charles Darwin, entitled *Creation*. These depict Darwin (played by Paul Bettany) and an orangutan with their index fingers almost touching.[30] Here too the point seems to be less one of creation (as though humans created other primates) and more one of humans acquiring quasi-divine knowledge precisely as we encounter one of our close relatives on the tree of life, opening ourselves to sources of knowledge beyond the biblical texts (as interpreters of those texts have always done, whether consciously or not, and whether willingly or not).

One of the interesting components in cinematic treatments of biblical creation mate-rial is how it is related to scientific sources of information. The 1966 movie *The Bible: In the Beginning . . .* features a narrator reading Genesis 1, with a montage of images from the world as we now know it. But the choice of those images—scenes of lava and steam-ing gases, for instance—recalls scientific depictions of Earth in its primordial form. The words of Genesis, when combined with these images, convey the idea that the Bible's creation stories and science's account of our planet and our species can go hand in

churches and museums) often influence popular culture more directly and extensively than the text itself does. See further Albert C. Labriola, "The Bible and Iconography," in *The Oxford Handbook of the Reception History of the Bible*, ed. Michael Lieb et al. (Oxford: Oxford University Press, 2011), 175–99.

[29] This occurs in the episode "The Homer of Seville." See further Sanders, *Approaching Eden*, viii; also Mark I. Pinsky, *The Gospel According to the Simpsons* (Louisville, KY: Westminster John Knox, 2007), 65, who notes another possible allusion to the famous work of art.

[30] Gaye Williams Ortiz, "Creation and Origins in Film," in *The Bible in Motion: A Handbook of the Bible and Its Reception in Film*, ed. Rhonda Burnette-Bletsch (Berlin: Walter de Gruyter, 2016), 341–54, here 343.

hand.[31] The same may be said of the Christmas Eve message the Apollo 8 astronauts sent to Earth from space in the form of a reading of Genesis 1:1–10. The imagery that accompanies a simple reading of the biblical text, and the place from which that text is read and by whom, all serve to interpret the text to the public that consumes what is broadcast.

The 2006 movie *The Fountain* envisages a quite literal "tree of life," one that is discovered by a scientist named Tommy who is trying to find a cure for his wife, Izzi, who is dying of cancer. He makes the discovery that the plant can prevent death—but not in time to save his wife's life. The movie is interspersed with scenes from the past, fragments of a story that Izzi had been writing, as well as scenes from what could be a real or an imagined future, in which Tommy has traveled far into space, sustained by the tree whose life-prolonging properties he had discovered. Before Izzi dies, she says that she wants a tree to be planted where she is buried, so that it will consume and recycle her organic material in a way that continues life. Whereas in the Genesis story the humans must ingest the fruit from the tree of life if they wish to attain personal immortality, in the movie Izzi rejects personal immortality in favor of a dissipation of her component elements back into nature—symbolized by the tree consuming her.

Within the Bible the theme of creation extends to *new creation*, and this theme is also widespread in popular culture. The 2014 movie *Noah* draws not only on Genesis but also on extracanonical expansions thereof, while taking liberties with both. It preserves several themes that are prominent in the Genesis story, among which is the idea that the flood represents an undoing and redoing of creation, a return to the time when the primordial waters covered the earth, and then a new beginning.[32] In the movie, however, Noah eventually comes to hold to a vision of a new start for the world *without humans*, considering it his family's role to help the animals survive the flood, and then to die, leaving Earth to the other living things. In the movie *Jurassic Park*, two scientists muse their way through a sequence of events related to creation and re-creation, leading up to their situation:

> DR. IAN MALCOLM: God creates dinosaurs. God destroys dinosaurs. God creates man. Man destroys God. Man creates dinosaurs.
> DR. ELLIE SATTLER: Dinosaurs eat man. Woman inherits the earth.[33]

Even if the primary role of this dialogue in the film is humor, there is an interesting engagement with biblical as well as scientific material. According to the pseudo-biblical chronology offered by young-earth creationists, dinosaurs had a place on the Ark and died off sometime well after the flood, purportedly being seen by humans and men-

---

[31] Ibid., 342.

[32] Gordon J. Wenham, *Genesis 1–15*, Word Biblical Commentary, 1 (Dallas: Word, 1987), 181.

[33] In the novel by Michael Crichton on which the movie is based, there is reference to the discoveries of dinosaur bones in the 1800s, which were assumed to be those of gigantic forms of known animals, since it was assumed that God would not allow his creations to become extinct. Michael Crichton, *Jurassic Park* (New York: Ballantine Books, 1990), 119.

tioned in Job 40:15–19 (as well as in legends about dragons from around the world).[34] *Jurassic Park* opts for the scientific timeline but includes God as Creator, depicting God making dinosaurs and eliminating them before creating humans. Humans are then said to destroy God prior to re-creating dinosaurs, which may destroy them. This coupling of the human elimination of God and the carrying out of divine prerogatives such as creating life represents what is arguably the oldest and most pervasive motif in science fiction, that of scientists playing God.[35] The coupling of man destroying God with the re-creation of dinosaurs makes the latter act one that is irreligious, as though directly in violation of some divine command (even though Genesis says nothing whatsoever about DNA, much less about the revival of extinct species through scientific means). The final twist treats the talk of "man" not as an archaic way of referring to humanity but as referring to males, and thus leaves females as the survivors of this unfolding scenario. Yet the fact that the character who offers the punch line is one of the scientists consulted on the project and is female adds an element of irony to the dialogue. It draws on the stereotype that men are scientists, and thus the ones who will arrogantly play God without attending to the ecological concerns related to their attempts to (re)create extinct life forms. It is also an implicit assumption of the dialogue that, when women rule the world after men wipe themselves out, they will do so in a more sensible way than men. One could also understand it to imply that it will take the elimination of men for women to come to hold such a position of power. Also interesting is the replacement of Genesis's language of "ruling" (Gen 1:28, a verse that has often been blamed for the exploitative approach to the natural world that human beings frequently adopt) with the language of "inheriting" the earth, drawn from the beatitude in Matthew 5:5 and its promise to the meek (which is not a word that describes the vision of the creator of Jurassic Park in the movie's story). A careful reading of film dialogue (attempts at humor) that draws on and interacts with biblical creation material can reveal inherent stereotypes that underpin its perceived meaning. In some instances, we may find that those stereotypes are drawn into the picture in order for them to be challenged. In other cases, we will find no evidence that such assumptions were noticed, much less critically interrogated.

In the realm of music, allusions to the biblical creation material are frequent, although once again they are not always focused on the act of creation or even God's role in it, as for instance in Bruce Springsteen's song "Adam Raised a Cain." Other examples involve explicit engagement with a subset of elements from the Genesis stories, such as J. Cole's "Forbidden Fruit" from his album *Born Sinner*, which draws heavily on the widespread interpretation of the Garden of Eden story in terms of illicit sex. The song also explores the act of artistic creation, and the element of ego that may be required to undertake it, as Cole situates himself as superior to other rap and hip-hop artists, boasting that God is the only man that is above him and that his word will live forever. Yet this song features a

[34] Arthur McCalla, *The Creationist Debate: The Encounter between the Bible and the Historical Mind* (New York: Bloomsbury, 2013), x.

[35] On this theme, see Alison Bright MacWilliams, "Science Playing God," in *Religion and Science Fiction*, ed. James F. McGrath (Eugene, OR: Pickwick, 2011), 80–94.

collaborating vocalist (Kendrick Lamar) and utilizes a sample from Ronnie Foster's "Mystic Brew." The tension between the lyrics and these other aspects of the song together convey a sense of the challenge for artists, who are expected to be "original" and require a high degree of confidence if not indeed arrogance to pursue a career in the realm of musical creation, and yet who never exist in a vacuum. Musical creation—like the depiction in Genesis as understood by the majority of scholarly interpreters—is not ex nihilo, and hence involves struggle to at least some degree.

One widely known example of engagement with the theology of creation and its implications in popular music is found in Lady Gaga's hit song "Born This Way":

> I'm beautiful in my way,
> 'Cause God makes no mistakes
> I'm on the right track, baby
> I was born this way.

Popular culture has engaged with issues such as same-sex attraction through the lens of creation, typically in facile ways. On the one hand there is Lady Gaga's stance, which suggests that whatever is, is good by definition—a viewpoint that is often abandoned with no sense of contradiction when people who purport to hold it are confronted with phenomena such as birth defects and deadly bacteria. On the other end of the spectrum one finds appeal to an original creation that is purportedly different from the way things are now, expressed in slogans such as "God made Adam and Eve, not Adam and Steve."[36] Neither wrestles with the underlying issues in depth. Nevertheless the treatment of the topic in the lyrics of "Born This Way" appears to be deliberately crafted to resonate with those familiar with biblical creation narratives as interpreted in American popular piety. The music video for the song begins with a prelude that crafts its own creation mythos, one that appears to draw more heavily on science fiction than the Bible. In it, a goddess—Gaga herself, referred to as "Mother Monster"—gives birth to good and evil. The traditional Creator (historically referred to by using the male pronoun highlighted in the song, which in older translations is capitalized even in the middle of sentences) plays no role.[37] As the song proper begins, the lyrics state, "It doesn't matter if you love him, or capital HIM." As so often occurs, in the very process of challenging particular traditional religious views of creation and sexual orientation, details such as pronoun choice may nevertheless default to traditional practices and norms.

Within the realm of Contemporary Christian Music, the widely sung and oft-covered song "God of Wonders," written by Steve Hindalong and Marc Byrd, refers in its opening

---

[36] On this phrase in popular culture, see further Sanders, *Approaching Eden*, 85–90. The slogan's first known appearance was on a protest sign in 1977. See Zach Schonfeld, "The Surprising History of the Phrase 'Adam and Eve, Not Adam and Steve,'" *Newsweek*, July 1, 2015, https://www.newsweek.com/surprising-history-phrase-adam-and-eve-not-adam-and-steve-348164.

[37] Courtney Weaver, "The Courage to Be…a Dirty Little Freak: Tillich, Pink, and Gaga," in *God and Popular Culture: A Behind-the-Scenes Look at the Entertainment Industry's Most Influential Figure*, ed. Stephen Butler Murray and Aimée Upjohn Light (Santa Barbara, CA: Praeger, 2015), 284–7.

lines to "all creation," expanded to "water, earth, and sky." This fits well within the frame-work of the ancient view of the cosmos reflected in the Bible. The chorus, however, speaks of God as "beyond our galaxy" and mentions "the universe," concepts that reflect modern astronomical information. Throughout popular culture we find biblical and scientific motifs being brought together. At times the relationship is harmonious, while at others it is antagonistic. More often than not, these elements are simply juxtaposed in a manner that leaves unclear what the relationship between the two is, or indeed that there might be anything worth discussing about the matter.

Popular culture's engagement with the biblical creation material is by no means always characterized by superficiality or lack of attention to detail, however. For instance, when an advertisement from Bobby's Restaurant and Bar seeks to entice one to partake of "sinfully tempting ribs" and features a photo depicting Adam and Eve after intercourse, with stitches visible on Adam's side, the engagement with Genesis and its reception history is multifaceted and thoughtful, as well as entertaining.[38] The stitches of course reflect the idea that God took a rib from Adam and made Eve from it. By layer-ing the interpretation of Genesis 3 in terms of sex and sexual temptation over the idea of barbecue spare ribs as tempting, and hinting at the verbal connection through the refer-ence to ribs, the advertisement conveys a message—and seeks to amuse—in a manner that requires careful attention to detail, and knowledge of Genesis and its interpretation, in order to get the joke and fully experience its resonances.[39] Instances of profound comprehension and creative use in popular culture will continue to appear, and will always merit attention from academics.

Since the beginning, creation has snaked its way through American popular culture's diverse genres, branching out and bearing the most fruit starting in the earliest twenti-eth century. Its waters are deep and can seem chaotic, but close study can bring light and order. Future explorations of creation in American popular culture need to take seri-ously that the wide array of influences on ancient authors and modern readers alike is not a separate part of the picture that can be removed without leaving a visible scar. These influences are part of the very flesh and bone of what Americans mean when they refer to creation in the Bible.

FUTURE PROSPECTS AND QUESTIONS

The most important points that emerge from an examination of the intersection of the Bible's creation material and popular culture also point to certain key areas around which future research and discussion may usefully focus:

---

[38] Found in Edwards, *Admen and Eve*, 16.

[39] On the sexual focus in film, see also S. Brent Plate's contribution to the entry "Adam and Eve, Story of," in *Encyclopedia of the Bible and Its Reception*, vol. 1, ed. Hans-Josef Klauck et al. (Berlin: De Gruyter, 2009), 364.

- In popular culture, one regularly encounters reference to "literal" belief in "biblical" creation, in contrast to the more nuanced "liberal" views of scholars. The points that have already been mentioned illustrate a major divide between popular and academic discourse. Careful study of the Bible reveals that there is no one biblical view of creation for readers today to accept literally. One must inevitably pick and choose from among this material. Even within one passage, such as the depiction of creation in six days found in Genesis 1, few modern readers who insist that those days must be taken literally will view in the same way the dome that holds up the waters above, into which the sun and moon are placed, and across the face of which birds fly. Large numbers of readers even today still fail to notice that there are two different creation accounts already within the early chapters of Genesis. There is room for further research on biblical equivalents of the "gorilla experiment"—that is, the way that prior prompting about what to look for when it comes to creation in the Bible causes readers to miss a great deal that features quite prominently even in Genesis 1–2.
- The academic study of popular culture's engagement with the Bible provides an important reminder of the role of readers and interpreters in making meaning and not merely finding it in these ancient sources. Scholarly engagement with creation in popular culture also carries the risk of finding underlying meanings that may reflect academics' breadth and depth of awareness of biblical and other texts and traditions, where popular knowledge is much less detailed and precise—a pitfall that awaits scholars in song lyrics as much as in scriptures. For example, given Bob Dylan's penchant for drawing on Jewish and Christian tradition in his music, it is entirely possible that his song "Everything Is Broken" reflects a Lurianic interpretation of Genesis, in which God first withdraws to make room for creation, and then sends forth the divine light, which shatters the vessels that were supposed to contain it.[40] But is the ability of interpreters to connect the language of brokenness in the song with a Jewish mystical understanding of creation in Genesis a "good" reading of the song? Might this interpretation, like the aforementioned divine light, be more than the song's lyrics can bear, liable to shatter and fragment them rather than hear them as they are? The potential of academic reception-historical work to distort rather than clarify is an area worthy of significant metalevel exploration and analysis, since rarely is reception history as an academic approach itself considered a form of biblical reception.
- Creation connects with a wide array of other biblical material. The choice of artists and other interpreters about whether to make those connections is another area that deserves further study. For instance, as noted earlier, the flood and creation are connected in multiple ways not only because both stories appear in the early chapters of Genesis, nor because "flood geology" is a major component of young-

---

[40] So, for instance, Jon Stratton, "Jews, Judaism and Popular Music," in *The Bloomsbury Handbook of Religion and Popular Music*, ed. Christopher Partridge and Marcus Moberg (New York: Bloomsbury, 2017), 125. Likewise Seth Rogovoy, *Bob Dylan: Prophet, Mystic, Poet* (New York: Scribner, 2009), 12.

earth creationism. The Genesis flood account depicts the deluge as an undoing of creation followed by a new creation, as the waters that were driven back in creation are made to cover the earth again, and then once again subside.[41] In Margaret Atwood's *MaddAddam* trilogy a "waterless flood" is the precursor to a new creation.[42] In other dystopian and apocalyptic stories and music, on the other hand (in particular heavy metal and alternative metal bands such as Disturbed), themes of destruction and messianism appear prominently, but without a comparable emphasis on a renewal (much less a restoration of paradise) that it is hoped will follow. These artistic choices—embracing doom and devastation from among biblical imagery without a counterbalancing hope and restoration of the created order—deserve further study.

Suggested Readings and Annotated Bibliography

Bielen, Kenneth G. *The Lyrics of Civility: Biblical Images and Popular Music Lyrics in American Culture*. New York: Garland, 1999.

While the present essay has sought to focus on the familiar and the classic, there is a great deal more material that is of significance, and Bielen's book discusses several examples of song lyrics that connect with biblical creation stories that are not included here.

Edwards, Katie B. *Admen and Eve: The Bible in Contemporary Advertising*. Sheffield, UK: Sheffield Phoenix Press, 2012.

Edwards surveys the appearance of Eve in advertising, focusing on the way she is depicted in ads aimed at people of different genders; whether her eyes and face are visible and, if so, where they are directed; and how cultural shifts leading up to postfeminism correlate to changes in the way Eve is interpreted.

Ortiz, Gaye Williams. "Creation and Origins in Film." In *The Bible in Motion: A Handbook of the Bible and Its Reception in Film*, edited by Rhonda Burnette-Bletsch, 341–54. Berlin: Walter de Gruyter, 2016.

Ortiz's cinematic focus includes a significant engagement with science fiction, with its depictions of aliens creating humans and humans creating artificial intelligences, including connections with themes related to environmentalism as well.

Sanders, Theresa. *Approaching Eden: Adam and Eve in Popular Culture*. Lanham, MD: Rowman & Littlefield, 2009.

A wide-ranging exploration of the two central human characters in the early chapters of Genesis. In addition to explorations of television shows, advertising, and other domains that overlap with the other two entries in this bibliography, Sanders gives significant attention to jokes and humor, cartoons, T-shirts, and much else.

[41] Gordon J. Wenham, "The Coherence of the Flood Narrative," *Vetus Testamentum* 28 (1978) 3:336–48, here 345; also Wenham, *Genesis 1–15*, 145.

[42] See in particular Margaret Atwood, *Year of the Flood* (New York: Doubleday, 2009) 11–15, 90. Atwood herself is Canadian, but this work's setting is primarily Canada's southern neighbor. In her chapter in this volume, Shayna Sheinfeld examines this trilogy in more detail.

CHAPTER 9

··

THE BIBLICAL THEME OF COVENANT AND AMERICAN POPULAR CULTURE FROM COLONIAL TIMES TO COMIC BOOKS

··

TERRY R. CLARK
DEPARTMENT OF RELIGION, GEORGETOWN COLLEGE

INTRODUCTION

··

ANY attempt to provide a comprehensive discussion, in the confines of a single chapter, of the biblical theme of covenant and the extent to which it influences American popular culture would be the epitome of hubris. Nevertheless, as is fitting for the current volume, this chapter will provide an entryway into understanding this distinctive biblical idea and its cultural influence in the United States. The concept of covenant is central to the theology of both biblical testaments and the religious traditions that lay claim to them as their most sacred scriptures. Similarly, covenant lies at the heart of a religious ideology that has pervaded national identity since before the formation of the United States of America, and such thinking persists to this day, albeit in a highly modified form. The most obvious and persistent influence derives from the covenant theology of early Puritan settlers, who imagined themselves the inheritors of ancient Israel's status as the favored people of God, a New Israel settling and taming a recently discovered wilderness full of hope and promise. In North America, Puritans sought to establish a model community in which their faith would flourish and by which they would inspire the rest of the world to mimic them, initiating a process of ushering in the Kingdom of God across the globe.

Their covenant ideal became firmly planted in the national psyche, but in ways they had not anticipated, for as the nation evolved, so did its sense of mission and purpose. The founders eventually established the principles of freedom *of* religion as well as free-dom *from* religion, the latter of which the Puritans would never have endorsed. In effect, the founders both adopted and adapted the covenant ideal promoted by the early Puritan settlers, and to a great extent the nation as a whole has followed suit. This chapter explores biblical covenant theology and several ways it has manifested in American popular culture from the founding period to the modern era. First, I trace the origins of biblical covenant thinking and discuss its core ideology. Second, I examine its influence on America during the founding period. And third, I discuss the influence of covenant ideology in the context of *Captain America* comics.

OVERVIEW OF TOPIC

The biblical concept of covenant draws upon traditions that preceded the establishment of ancient Israel and that manifested in multiple forms. All forms assume a hierarchical understanding of reality, including the way humans should ideally interact with one another and with the sacred realm. These forms include a Covenant of Peace, which is the desirable condition of harmonious relationship between the divine and human realms, as well as the so-called Sinai Covenant between Israel and their patron god, Yahweh.[1] The most likely models for the biblical Covenant of Peace, most popularly known in the story of the Great Flood in the book of Genesis (9:8–17), can be found in the earlier Baal Cycle of myths from ancient Canaan and the Mesopotamian flood myth *Atrahasis* (see also Isa 54:10; Ezek 34:25, 37:26; Hosea 2:18–25).[2] In the Canaanite text, one finds that after a period of hostility between the storm god Baal and humanity, Baal orders his consort-sister Anat to "pour peace into the heart of the earth."[3] This covenant

[1] The so-called Abrahamic Covenant of Genesis 12–17, promising to make Abram's/Abraham's progeny a great nation (12:2), the sign of which would be circumcision of all males (17:7–14), is probably a much later (sixth century BCE) development. In the Hebrew Bible as a whole, it is eclipsed in importance by the Sinai tradition.

[2] See Bernard Batto, "The Covenant of Peace: A Neglected Ancient Near Eastern Motif," *CBQ* 49 (1987): 187–211. On the Baal Cycle, see Michael D. Coogan and Mark S. Smith, eds. and trans., *Stories from Ancient Canaan*, 2nd ed. (Louisville, KY: Westminster John Knox Press, 2012), 116–9; N. Wyatt, *Religious Texts from Ugarit*, 2nd ed., Biblical Seminar 53 (New York: Sheffield Academic Press, 2003), esp. 70–78. On *Atrahasis*, see Stephanie Dalley, *Myths from Mesopotamia*, rev. ed., Oxford World's Classics (New York: Oxford University Press, 2000), 1–38; Benjamin R. Foster, *Before the Muses: An Anthology of Akkadian Literature*, 3rd ed. (Bethesda, MD: CDL Press, 2005), 227–53.

[3] Batto, "Covenant of Peace," 198, translating *CTA* 3.iii.13 (from Andrée Herdner's *Corpus tablettes alphabetiques* [Paris, 1963], an early collection of Ugaritic texts). More commonly used today is the collection *KTU* (*Keilalphabetische Texte aus Ugarit* [Cuneiform texts from Ugarit] Manfried Dietrich, Oswald Loretz, and Joachín Sanmartín, *Die keil-alphabetischen Texte aus Ugarit*, Alter Orient und Altes Testament 24/1 (Kevelaer: Verlag Butzon & Bercker / Neukirchen-Vluyn: Neukirchener Verlag, 1976).

marks the "cessation of hostility" between the divine and human realms and initiates a new beginning whereby fertility returns to the earth and its residents.[4] The somewhat fragmentary text does not clarify for today's reader the reason Heaven and Earth were at war, but one may surmise that humanity had somehow offended the divine realm through disobedience, and divine anger resulted in drought or famine. Here, peace with the gods is the necessary condition for the divinely created order to work properly, causing fertility and prosperity in the plant and animal kingdoms.

The Sinai Covenant between God and Israel, the establishment of which is explicated in the book of Exodus (19:1–31:17), is initiated by Yahweh shortly after he delivers Israel from bondage in Egypt through a series of signs and wonders (sometimes referred to as plagues) in Exodus 7–12 and dramatically concluded by the miraculous deliverance at the Red or Reed Sea, as depicted in Exodus 14–15. The covenant initiated between Yahweh and Israel upon Israel's arrival at Mt. Sinai, where the Israelite patron god is depicted as having originally resided, officially establishes Israel as Yahweh's client people and supposedly serves as the original basis for their eventual national identity in the ancient Near East. However, in the biblical tradition, Israel does not appear to actualize itself as a national entity until the later monarchy of King David, after much internal and external strife, especially witnessed in their struggle against their Philistine rivals (1–2 Sam). The Philistines, beginning in the book of Judges, compete with Israel for control over the region of Canaan (the so-called Promised Land), generally comprising the territory later referred to as Syria-Palestine, until David supposedly unites the twelve tribes of Israel into one nation.

The initiation of a monarchy in ancient Israel appears in some biblical texts to have been a matter that was highly contested (see 1 Sam 8, where it represents a rejection of Yahweh alone as king over his people). Yet the book of Deuteronomy, depicting Moses reiterating covenant law just prior to Israel's entry into Canaan, anticipates the eventual establishment of a monarchy, and, under appropriate conditions, treats it as normative and not displeasing to Yahweh, as long as the king promotes Deuteronomic law (Deut 17:14–20). The book of Exodus depicts the Sinai Covenant as having been originally established as a contractual relationship between Yahweh and all the Israelite people (imagined as a kingdom of priests; Exod 19:5–6), yet it comes to be administered to some degree through the leadership of a distinct priestly class comprising certain members of the tribe of Levi (originally led by Moses and Aaron). Later, after the establishment of David's administration, a new order of priests (represented by an originating figure named Zadok) apparently arises to challenge the Levitical line, but their origin is largely shrouded in mystery (2 Sam 8:17). Some scholars theorize that David established this new line of priests in an effort to seize more direct control over the official religious cult of the fledgling nation shortly after making the city of Jerusalem his capital.[5] It is possible that the Zadokites were the ruling priests of the native Jebusite (Canaanite) inhabit-

---

    [4] Batto, "Covenant of Peace," 187.
    [5] George E. Mendenhall, *Ancient Israel's Faith and History: An Introduction to the Bible in Context*, ed. Gary A. Herion (Louisville, KY: Westminster John Knox Press, 2001), 114–6.

ants of Jerusalem, and David brokered a deal with them in order to convince them to hand over this highly prized, well-fortified city.[6] But the Bible, for some reason, simply does not go into detail about how David acquires Jerusalem.

It is likely that during David's time we also witness the introduction of the idea, already common in the ancient Near East, that the human king was chosen and adopted as a son by the chief national deity (the divine king) and thereby endowed with the authority and responsibility to rule the nation on behalf of the deity as co-regent (see the Davidic Covenant of 2 Sam 7; also Psa 9:7–10; 29:10). With this understanding, the prosperity or success of the nation was intrinsically tied to, and to some extent dependent upon, the piety of the human king. This notion of the centrality of the king for maintaining national peace, security, and prosperity is referred to by modern scholars as royal ideology. As goes the human king, so goes the fate of the entire nation (see David's census in 2 Sam 24:1–17).

The most likely models for the Sinai Covenant are the ancient Hittite and Assyrian suzerainty treaties.[7] These treaties involved two parties of unequal power, whereby the suzerain or sovereign king establishes a political relationship with a weaker entity, often following the military conquest of the latter by the former. Mutual obligations were outlined, with the suzerain promising peace or protection and perhaps some other forms of prosperity to the vassal in return for loyalty and usually some form(s) of regularly paid tribute. In this arrangement, the imperial ruler was conceived (and/or conceived of himself) as "the Great King," who rightfully ruled by superior power over vast amounts of territory. In biblical theology, Yahweh plays the role of chief sovereign over Israel and is eventually imagined as both creator and king of the entire world.[8] In this conceptual world, which dominated thinking in the ancient Near East, religion and politics are intrinsically tied together, but admittedly, the chief benefactors were those in the highest position of power, namely, human kings.

In the ancient Near East, the institution of human kingship was authorized and promoted by the claim that it was modeled after the hierarchical and monarchical order of the heavenly realm, where the chief deity ruled supreme.[9] Even in ancient Israel, the

---

[6] As Mendenhall, *Ancient Israel's Faith and History*, notes, David's son Solomon makes Zadok "the sole priest of his regime" (126), after banishing the Levitical priest Abiathar (133; see 1 Kings 1–2). Mendenhall also points out that Judges 1 claims that Jebusites lived in Jerusalem all the way up to the time that the Deuteronomistic History was composed (121). He furthermore suggests that Nathan the prophet and Bathsheba, Solomon's mother, were both Jebusites who successfully trick David into naming Solomon his successor (132; again, see 1 Kings 1–2). For a similar view of the Jebusite origin of Zadok, see Rainer Albertz, *A History of Israelite Religion in the Old Testament Period*, vol. 1 (Louisville, KY: Westminster John Knox Press, 1994), 295. For a more recent and thorough discussion, see Deborah W. Rooke, *Zadok's Heirs: The Role and Development of the High Priesthood in Ancient Israel* (New York: Oxford University Press, 2000), 43ff.

[7] Mendenhall, *Ancient Israel's Faith and History*, 56–7, 157.

[8] J. J. M. Roberts, "The Enthronement of Yhwh and David: The Abiding Theological Significance of the Kingship Language of the Psalms," *CBQ* 64 (2002): 675–86, here 676.

[9] Keith Whitelam, "Israelite Kingship: The Royal Ideology and Its Opponents," in *The World of Ancient Israel: Sociological, Anthropological, and Political Perspectives*, ed. R. E. Clements (New York: Cambridge University Press, 1989), 119–39.

human king (at least when descended from David) was considered the adopted son of Yahweh (2 Sam 7; Psa 89). Here, religion was considered a foundational and vital component of monarchical rule because human kingship was treated as a gift from and extension of divine rule, a necessity for promoting order and prosperity in human society.[10] However, the so-called Deuteronomistic History (a scholarly name for the biblical books of Joshua through Kings) contains competing ideologies concerning Israelite monarchy.[11] In spite of its depiction of multiple sinful deeds on David's part (the adultery with or rape of Bathsheba being the one best remembered by modern readers; 2 Sam 11:1–12:23), the initiation of a Davidic dynasty still receives a surprisingly positive treatment in the Bible as a whole. The Deuteronomistic History depicts the young, unassuming shepherd-turned-king receiving the dispensation of a special covenant with Yahweh (as noted earlier), which promises a never-ending line of kings. But great ideological tensions persist. In the remainder of 1 and 2 Kings, only two of David's descendants (Hezekiah and Josiah) receive a thoroughly positive evaluation by the editors of this biblical history (2 Kings 18:3 and 22:2, respectively).

Generally speaking, in ancient Israel, national identity evolved to include (if not originated within) a matrix of the following elements: patron deity, divinely granted land, and client people, with the king primarily serving as representative of the deity (again, co-regent) before the people.[12] A critical component of national identity involved the deity granting, dwelling within, and defending a specific territory in which the client people could safely and securely reside. In this matrix, where society, politics, and religion were intrinsically intertwined, national security hinged on national piety, sometimes representatively through the piety of the king (royal ideology) and sometimes requiring the piety of the entire nation (Sinai theology). Many prophetic books implicitly critique the central importance of royal piety, instead advocating for a more egalitarian approach to national covenant fidelity and calling for a "return" to a more universal concept of righteous behavior on the part of all citizens (e.g., Amos and Hosea). Here, perhaps rather romantically conceived, the supposedly earlier Sinai Covenant is treated

[10] For a concise discussion, see Marvin A. Sweeney, "The Rights and Duties of Kingship in Israel," *Bible Odyssey*, accessed January 24, 2018, https://www.bibleodyssey.org/en/passages/related-articles/rights-and-duties-of-kingship-in-israel.

[11] Two classical works on the Deuteronomistic History are Martin Noth, *The Deuteronomistic History*, Journal for the Study of the Old Testament Supplement Series 15, 2nd ed. (Sheffield, UK: JSOT Press, 1981), and Frank Moore Cross, "The Themes of the Book of Kings and the Structure of the Deuteronomistic History," in *Canaanite Myth and Hebrew Epic: Essays in the History of the Religion of Israel* (Cambridge, MA: Harvard University Press, 1973), 274–89. For more recent treatments, see Thomas Romer, *The So-Called Deuteronomistic History: A Sociological, Historical, and Literary Introduction* (London: T & T Clark, 2006); John Van Seters, *The Biblical Saga of King David* (Winona Lake, IN: Eisenbrauns, 2009).

[12] See Daniel I. Block, *The Gods of the Nations: Studies in Ancient Near Eastern National Theology*, 2nd ed., Erfurter theologische Studien (Grand Rapids, MI: Baker, 2000), 17–33. According to what most scholars deem the oldest text of Deuteronomy 32:8–9 (following the Greek Septuagint text) is a poem suggesting that the most high god (Elyon) apportioned to each of the "Sons of God" a particular client people or nation, Yahweh receiving Israel as his allotment.

as having been the original plan for Israelite society, emphasizing social justice for all alongside singular religious allegiance to one, national deity.

However we date the concept in Israel of a religious covenant with a national deity, we might marvel at the fact that a similar concept has exerted from the beginning—and continues to exert—an enormous impact on the ideology of a modern nation like the United States. The basic concept of a divinely sponsored nation has a long and storied history not only in the ancient Near East but also in the Western world. The Roman Empire was understood to be a religio-political entity originally founded and main-tained by the patronage of Roman gods.[13] When Christianity became the official reli-gion of Rome, beginning under the influence of Emperor Constantine, what changed significantly was not the general concept of divine patronage undergirding the empire but the particular religion and/or deity or deities to which the state would pledge alle-giance. By way of contrast, the idea of politics and religion operating somewhat sepa-rately and simultaneously in the context of a secular state appears to have gained momentum in Europe in response to the works of Martin Luther, but it would arguably find its most famous expression in the Establishment and Free Exercise clauses of the fledgling United States.[14]

David Little argues that Roger Williams, the founder of the Rhode Island colony, was one of the most influential early proponents of religious liberty in America.[15] In addi-tion, Little points out that the early Puritan colonies typically established a "declaration of rights" for the members of their communities, emphasizing individual, God-given freedoms.[16] What differentiated Williams from many of his fellow Puritans in this con-text was the appropriateness of establishing one particular religion in the various colo-nies rather than upholding individual freedom of conscience in religious matters. James Madison, the "principal architect" of the Establishment Clause of the Constitution, is believed to have been influenced by the example of Williams at least as much as by European Enlightenment principles.[17] Yet it was the earlier declaration of rights among the colonies that served as the basic precursor for the US Bill of Rights, beginning with

[13] For a thorough discussion of Roman civil religion, see John Scheid, *The Gods, the State, and the Individual: Reflections on Civic Religion in Rome*, trans. Clifford Ando (Philadelphia: University of Pennsylvania Press, 2015).

[14] See Martin Luther's sermon on Matthew 22:15–22, "Christ Answers the Question, If It Were Lawful to Give Tribute unto Caesar?" For the sermon in English translation, see *The Sermons of Martin Luther*, ed. John Nicholas Lenker, trans. John Nicholas Lenker et al. (Grand Rapids, MI: Baker Book House, 1983), 5:294–306. See also Luther's treatise "On Secular Authority: To What Extent It Should Be Obeyed" (Wittenberg, 1523), in *Works of Martin Luther* (Philadelphia: A. J. Holman, 1915–6), 3:225–73. An important precursor for disestablishing religion in the US was Thomas Jefferson's 1777 "Virginia Statue for Religious Freedom." For a discussion, see Ralph Ketcham, "James Madison, Thomas Jefferson, and the Meaning of 'Establishment of Religion' in Eighteenth-Century Virginia," in *No Establishment of Religion: America's Original Contribution to Religious Liberty*, ed. T. Jeremy Gunn and John Witte Jr. (New York: Oxford University Press, 2012), 158–79.

[15] David Little, "Roger Williams and the Puritan Background of the Establishment Clause," in Gunn and Witte, *No Establishment of Religion*, 100–124.

[16] Ibid., 104.   [17] Ibid.

"The Body of Liberties of the Massachusetts Colony in New England," established in 1641.[18]

The English Puritan movement as a whole had a profound influence on the sense of identity that emerged among the founders. It revolved around a strong sense of humans living in a covenant relationship with a creator god, endowed with certain inalienable rights, and a divinely appointed mission. John Winthrop's musings during his passage to North America represent a classic example of the Puritan ideal, which included the ultimate goal of transforming the world in its own image. Winthrop's famous 1630 sermon "A Modell of Christian Charity," written aboard the ship carrying him and his followers to the New World, demonstrates the Deuteronomistic perspective from which he approached his holy mission: "Thus stands the cause between God and us. Wee are entered into Covenant with him for this worke." With due diligence to divine expectations of justice and obedience, he went on to assert, "Wee shall finde that the God of Israell is among us, when ten of us shall be able to resist a thousand of our enemies... for wee must Consider that wee shall be as a Citty upon a Hill, the eies of all people are upon us." Later in the same sermon, Winthrop makes explicit reference to Moses's farewell address to Israel in Deuteronomy 30, imagining his community as a new Israel on the verge of entering a new Promised Land, with the same opportunity to procure either blessing or curse, depending upon the degree to which they adhered to Deuteronomic principles: "Beloved there is now set before us life, and good, deathe and evill in that wee are Commanded this day to love the Lord our God, and to love one another, to walke in his ways and to keepe his Commandments and his Ordinance, and his laws, and the Articles of our Covenant."[19] The covenant theology guiding Winthrop's sense of purpose here is indisputable. But what might escape some to this day is the degree to which Puritans appropriating such a biblical mission could exert such a powerful influence on many of the more deistically minded founders to inspire a nation to idealize the values of life, liberty, and the pursuit of happiness alongside the value of full-blown religious liberty, including the freedom *from* religion, for those so inclined.

One of the more compelling explanations is that the founding period of the United States represents an example of the phenomenon that the enemy of my enemy (at least temporarily) is my friend. Founding figures from the American colonies, whether Christian or deist, believed in divine providence.[20] Most colonies had an established church, Anglicanism being the most common in the South and Congregationalism being most common in New England. Several, such as Rhode Island and Pennsylvania, had no established religion, but all were predominantly Protestant. However, in spite of these religious differences, the colonies became united in North America to face a common political foe, the king of England, who was often imagined as a new pharaoh seek-

---

[18] Ibid., 105.

[19] All quotations here come from John Winthrop, "A Modell of Christian Charity," in *God's New Israel: Religious Interpretations of American Destiny*, revised and updated ed., ed. Conrad Cherry (Chapel Hill: University of North Carolina Press, 1998), 37–41.

[20] See David L. Holmes, *The Faiths of the Founding Fathers* (New York: Oxford University Press, 2006); Cherry, *God's New Israel*, 64–5.

ing to enslave "God's chosen people" all over again. According to Conrad Cherry, "More colonists were prepared for armed resistance by the clergy's Sunday and election sermons and weekly lectures than by the books and pamphlets of a Locke or a Paine."[21] Still, tradition holds that Benjamin Franklin, a deistic member of the first committee formed to design the Great Seal of the United States of America in 1776, proposed that the reverse side of the seal depict a scene from the book of Exodus, with Pharaoh's army being drowned by the waters of the Red Sea. The motto originally proposed for this side of the seal was "Rebellion to Tyrants Is Obedience to God."[22]

Thus, in an adapted fashion, covenant thinking captured the imagination of the founding period, but with the focus shifting from explicitly Puritan Christian values to an emphasis on the God-given rights of the individual for self-determination. The biblical example of the miraculous exodus liberation, divorced from the explicit covenant requirements elaborated at Sinai (Exod 20–31) and reiterated by Moses in Deuteronomy, became the dominant vision during the Revolution and continued to exert itself in the formation of the republic and its constitution. It is true that early deists and Puritans alike worried about a society that might, with too much freedom, abandon all religious conviction and lose its way. Religion, whether traditional or deistic, was widely believed to serve an important function in promoting ethical behavior and social cohesion. To their dismay, the formal disestablishment of religion in the united colonies convinced most Puritans that their new errand into the wilderness was a failure destined to manifest destruction on the same scale as the failed nation of Israel (see 2 Kings). As the official laws of the land moved in a more secular direction, abandoning the Deuteronomic ideal of a religiously pure and religiously unified community, the New Israel was believed to be repeating the mistakes of her past, abandoning her original covenant obligations.[23] But what was not abandoned was the idea that the nation had a unique (and for some, divinely appointed) destiny to fulfill. This so-called manifest destiny to increase the nation's righteous domain seemed obvious to those who wanted to believe it. The successful conclusion to the Revolutionary War was evidence enough to inspire further westward expansion, which effectively dispossessed the native population of American Indians (the new Canaanites) of almost all landholdings.[24] Such rose-colored

---

[21] Cherry, God's New Israel, 61.

[22] On the Great Seal of the United States, see John D. MacArthur, "First Great Seal Committee: July 1776," Great Seal, accessed January 28, 2018, https://www.greatseal.com/committees/firstcomm/index.html.

[23] See, for example, the Presbyterian minister Benjamin Morgan Palmer's now infamous 1861 sermon titled "National Responsibility before God," where he describes slavery as an institution ordained by God (printed in Cherry, God's New Israel, 184–200). In his Thanksgiving sermon of November 29, 1860, Palmer described the northern states' "abolitionist spirit [as] undeniably atheistic," a clear sign that the United States had abandoned its divinely appointed mission to impose divine law upon the New World. See Cherry, God's New Israel, 165; Margaret Burr DesChamps, "Benjamin Morgan Palmer, Orator-Preacher of the Confederacy," Southern Speech Journal 9 (1953): 14–22.

[24] See Robert Allen Warrior, "A Native American Perspective: Canaanites, Cowboys, and Indians," in Voices from the Margin: Interpreting the Bible in the Third World, new ed., ed. R. S. Sugirtharajah (Maryknoll, NY: Orbis, 1995), 277–85.

vision continues to influence more modern thinking about the appropriateness of American economic, military, and even English-language expansion in the modern world, all under the banner of democracy, which for many has become equivalent to making the world better by making it more like the United States. The trajectory toward imagining liberty as the core of the nation's identity was set during the revolutionary period, but it has persisted as the "sacred" center of the nation's civil religion to the present day.

Specific Examples and/or Foci

American popular culture provides numerous examples of the continuing influence of covenant ideology, including the more traditional Jewish and Christian concept of individual humans living in a covenantal or contractual relationship with their divine creator, as well as a more secular version that undergirds American civil religion. One of the latter type will be examined here, drawn from the genre of comic books, more specifically *Captain America* comics.[25] These comics promote the idea that the United States is a special nation with a responsibility to transform the world in its image. It is as if the ancient notion of the divinely appointed king, serving as co-regent of the deity in the earthly realm (royal ideology), has been transferred to the nation as a whole. Sometimes Captain America has offered important points of critique when the nation has failed to live up to its own ideals. Yet the conviction that America is a unique collection of mostly righteous people with a special mission to fulfill—a kind of manifest destiny—persists.

Captain America comics, at times, reflect the "Captain America complex," as elaborated by Robert Jewett and John Shelton Lawrence in their book, *Captain America and the Crusade against Evil*.[26] Jewett and Lawrence focus on the way American civil religion inspires a vigilante approach to instituting justice throughout the globe. Here, the savior mentality of the Captain America superhero, which emerged in the late World War II era, becomes a lens for analyzing and challenging an American ideology that too often imagines the United States as a nation endowed with the authority and power to remake the world in its own image by exporting, through force if necessary, American democracy.

American civil religion is a topic that has been explored to a great extent in academic circles.[27] As numerous critics have observed, it carries with it a potential dark side, and

---

[25] For a more obvious example of covenant ideology in comic books, see Will Eisner, *A Contract with God* (New York: W. W. Norton, 2006). See also my own prior work, "A Contract with God? Will Eisner's Seminal Graphic Novel as Anti-Theodicy," *SBL Forum*, 2009, https://www.sbl-site.org/publications/article.aspx?ArticleId=845.

[26] Robert Jewett and John Shelton Lawrence, *Captain America and the Crusade against Evil: The Dilemma of Zealous Nationalism* (Grand Rapids, MI: Eerdmans, 2003).

[27] Several examples are Robert N. Bellah, *The Broken Covenant: American Civil Religion in Time of*

probably no other work of scholarship makes this more clear than that of Jewett and Lawrence. Published in 2003, and inspired largely by America's response to the tragedy of 9/11, *Captain America and the Crusade against Evil* traces the history of US exceptionalism, focusing especially on the comic book hero Captain America. The authors describe America's "employ[ment of] non-democratic means to achieve democratic ends" as "the Captain America complex."[28]

According to their thesis, American "superhero tales amount to a kind of mythic induction into the cultural values of America."[29] Heroic vigilantism dominates the genre of superhero comics, television, film, and video games and is inspired by a myth that "joins redemptive violence and religious piety."[30] In what Jewett and Lawrence term "the American Monomyth," vigilante heroes regularly "transcend the legal order so that the source of evil can be destroyed."[31] And no mythic character is more closely tied to American idealism than Captain America, a hero given birth in 1941, shortly before America's formal entry into World War II, by Jewish writer and artist Joe Simon and Jack Kirby. Their most famous character's secret identity was Steve Rogers, a private enlisted in the US Army. Through scientific engineering, Rogers is turned into a supersoldier and eventually equipped with an unbreakable shield brandishing the colors of the American flag.

According to Jewett and Lawrence, the chief "story line" of Captain America comics is "derived from a narrative tradition that originated in colonial times, when colonists created the 'Indian captivity narratives,'" whereby heroic cowboys would rescue innocent captives from marauding and murderous "Wild Indians."[32] In their estimation, the purpose of these tales was to justify "manifest destiny and the allegedly selfless imperialism of earlier American civil religion."[33] In a more expanded way, the tradition continues in the burgeoning of superhero films based upon Marvel and DC Comics, as well as the vast popularity of battle-based video games (see especially the Call of Duty franchise, published by Activision, with the release of the fourteenth game in late 2017: *Call of Duty WWII*). In the vast majority of these products, violent redemption is the order of the day.

Americans have long been invested in the idea of saving the world by remaking others in their own image, by force if necessary, which unfortunately is too often the case. As Jewett and Lawrence make clear, "Superheroes and -heroines exercise the powers otherwise reserved only for God in dealing with evil. They are the individuated embodiments of a civil religion that seeks to redeem the world for democracy, but by means that tran-

---

Trial, 2nd ed. (Chicago: University of Chicago Press, 1992); Cherry, *God's New Israel*; Peter Gardella, *American Civil Religion: What Americans Hold Sacred* (New York: Oxford University Press, 2013); Philip Gorski, *American Covenant: A History of Civil Religion from the Puritans to the Present* (Princeton, NJ: Princeton University, 2017); Richard T. Hughes, *Myths America Lives By* (Champaign: University of Illinois Press, 2004).

[28] Jewett and Lawrence, *Captain America*, 28.   [29] Ibid.   [30] Ibid., 27.

[31] Ibid., 29. For more on the "American monomyth," see John Shelton Lawrence and Robert Jewett, *The Myth of the American Superhero* (Grand Rapids, MI: Eerdmans, 2002).

[32] Ibid., 26–7, 55–6.   [33] Jewett and Lawrence, *Captain America*, 30–31.

scend democratic limits on the exercise of power."[34] To claim that this phenomenon represents a blind spot in the American mind is a gross understatement. But because its roots lie so deep in the history of the nation, treading upon it is considered a violation of sacred space. American exceptionalism is the wellspring from which so much national pride emanates.

While the current chapter does not allow space for a thorough review of the "Captain America complex," two of the more outstanding ironies in American civil religion are worthy of consideration. Jewett and Lawrence go so far as to label several characteristics of American thought and practice downright "fascist," including the following: (1) "Superpower held in the hands of one person can achieve more justice than the workings of democratic institutions"; and (2) "The world as a whole requires the services of American superheroism that destroys evildoers through selfless crusades."[35]

Nowhere do these claims appear to be more self-evident than in some of President George W. Bush's and his administration's responses to the terrorist attacks of September 11, 2001. These include Bush's naming of various foreign countries as a "new axis of evil," (North Korea, Iran, and Iraq);[36] his drawing a line in the sand claiming that other countries are "either with us or with the terrorists"; and the misinformed invasion of Iraq under the banner of confiscating chemical weapons, which, as it turned out, did not exist.[37] Other examples of the inability to think critically about the nation's economic, military, and political involvement in other parts of the world include "U.S. alliances with autocratic governments of the Middle East; the export of cultural materials that are deemed degrading" by other world citizens, the unlawful detention of suspected terrorists at Guantanamo Bay, Cuba, and the abrogation of the 1972 Anti-Ballistic Missile Treaty with Russia.[38]

Jewett and Lawrence explain these responses as arising from a "framework of innocence," whereby it is assumed that America could have done nothing to deserve a response of hate from any rationally thinking human being and a mindset that exempts America from playing by the same rules expected of other societies.[39] These and numerous other violations of true democratic principles throughout US history seem to confirm that the Captain America complex (so named) has a long history in US foreign relations.

However, in spite of the validity of Jewett and Lawrence's critique of superheroism in America, it is also arguably the case that Captain America comics have evolved considerably since their inception and historically have served as a place where traditional cov-

---

[34] Ibid., 35.

[35] Ibid., 42–3.

[36] State of the Union Address, January 29, 2002.

[37] Jewett and Lawrence, *Captain America*, 2, 16. For a fascinating and acute analysis of Bush-era foreign policy and rhetoric juxtaposed with the ideology of Al Qaida after 9/11, see Bruce Lincoln, *Holy Terrors: Thinking about Religion after September 11*, 2nd ed. (Chicago: University of Chicago Press, 2006), esp. appendices A–C.

[38] Jewett and Lawrence, *Captain America*, 15, 119, 320–21.

[39] Ibid., 15. See also Hughes, *Myths America Lives By*, chapter 6: "The Myth of the Innocent Nation," 153–89.

enant idealism in America sometimes comes under serious scrutiny. Certainly, the character of Captain America in the first few decades of the comics represented a less reflective, less self-critical form of US patriotism. As J. Richard Stevens points out, not only did the earliest Captain America comics depict a hero willing to use "guns and grenades" to kill his nation's political enemies (rather than merely foil their "evil" plans), but in the first several decades the comics were clearly intended to serve as propaganda, initially to drum up support for the war effort against Germany, and later to promote an anticommunist agenda.[40] National and international threats like Nazism and communism (and their local spies!) were chief concerns, both in the comics and in US society at large. Yet however much the Captain America complex eventually became ingrained in US ideology, the character of Captain America has undergone significant transformation since the Cold War thawed. In fact, one might go so far as to say that Captain America himself, especially after 9/11, may pose a potential solution to the problem of the Captain America complex.[41]

The reason for this is simple. Popular culture, like culture in general, is a dynamic site of ideological struggle, where ideas, perspectives, truth claims, and values often evolve considerably over time.[42] Captain America is no exception. As Stevens notes, "Captain America is an image that shifts over the years to fit the foreign policy climate during which his tales are presented."[43] In the world of comics, disillusionment with, and radical critical questioning of, traditional notions of superheroism began as early as the decade of the 1980s.[44] Yet Captain America's challenge to the status quo began as early as the late 1960s and 1970s, when he confronts both racial and feminist issues from a liberal perspective.[45] This has become even more noticeable in Captain America comics since the US faced ideological challenges of seismic proportions following the terrorist attack of September 11, 2001.[46] But the trajectory began much earlier.

---

[40] J. Richard Stevens, *Captain America, Masculinity, and Violence: The Evolution of a National Icon*, Television and Popular Culture Series (Syracuse, NY: Syracuse University Press, 2015), 42, 26. It is perhaps inappropriate to assume that the patriotism of Simon and Kirby (both Jews) was inspired merely by Hitler's antisemitism, which had already been well demonstrated prior to America's declaration of war against Germany. Nevertheless early *Captain America Comics* were unabashedly and explicitly used to drum up patriotic fervor both at home and abroad. One of the best examples of this is the initiation of the Sentinels of Liberty fan club, for which readers were encouraged to take a pledge to expose local spies (26). See Joe Simon and Jack Kirby, "Meet Captain America," *Captain America Comics* 1:1, March 1941.

[41] See Stevens, *Captain America*, 215.

[42] See John Storey, *Cultural Theory and Popular Culture: An Introduction*, 5th ed. (New York: Pearson, 2009), 10–11.

[43] Stevens, *Captain America*, 48.

[44] Perhaps no comic serves as a better example of this critical analysis than Alan Moore's iconic graphic novel *Watchmen*. For a short discussion, see Jason Dittmer, *Captain America and the Nationalist Superhero: Metaphors, Narratives, and Geopolitics* (Philadelphia, PA: Temple University Press, 2013), 166–70. In Dittmer's words, "*Watchmen* represents a world in which heroic violence is rarely, if ever, noble and in which the heroes are highly problematic as instruments of the status quo" (170).

[45] Stevens, *Captain America*, chapter 5, "The Liberal Crusader (1969–1979)," 98–123.

[46] See Francisco Veloso and John Bateman, "The Multimodal Construction of Acceptability: Marvel's Civil War Comic Books and the PATRIOT Act," *Critical Discourse Studies* 10, no. 4 (2013): 427–43.

Multiple authors have traced how comic books display an increase in awareness of how the US government was compromising the nation's supposedly most cherished principles of freedom and equality as early as the Reagan administration.[47] A few particular examples should suffice to demonstrate this point, as well as the significant change in tone toward American foreign policy following 9/11.

As Matthew J. Costello points out, multiple story arcs in the 1990s portray Captain America being betrayed by his own government. In the story "Superpatriot Games" beginning in March 1994, Captain America learns that the supersoldier formula, by which the government originally gave Steve Rogers his powers, is poisoning his body.[48] Rogers eventually dies and is resurrected by a blood transfusion from his perennial enemy, the Red Skull, who himself had earlier been resurrected by a body cloned from Rogers.[49] As Costello notes, the same "villainy" of the Red Skull "is represented as coursing through the veins of the icon of the American Dream."[50] In his estimation, this close connection between the Skull—the epitome of Nazi evil—and what drives America's most heroic figure calls into question America's idealistic notion of its own unique innocence, "making it impossible to draw clear lines between good and evil, us and them."[51] What drives America may be no different from what drove Hitler and his fascist allies during (and after, in the comics) World War II.

Civil War and The Death of Captain America

Two of the most important and popular of recent Captain America story arcs are found in Marvel's Civil War and The Death of Captain America.[52] In Civil War, the US government passes a Superhero Registration Act requiring all masked avengers to reveal and register their secret identity and submit to governmental control. Captain America decides to lead a resistance movement that results in all-out war between the supers. Yet, on the very verge of victory, Captain America changes course and chooses to surrender, feeling that the final battle was proving too costly to innocent civilians, a situation that

---

The authors convincingly demonstrate that, in spite of Civil War's depiction of the reasonableness of both detractors and supporters of the USA Patriot Act, ultimately the narrative "constructs a discourse of acceptability that…in the end" encourages readers to "embrace" this new governmental measure (441). Even Captain America, who initially leads a rebellion against the Superhero Registration Act (a metaphor in Civil War for the Patriot Act), eventually acquiesces for the sake of protecting innocent civilians.

[47] See Matthew J. Costello, Secret Identity Crisis: Comic Books and the Unmasking of Cold War America (New York: Continuum, 2009), chapters 5–7; Stevens, Captain America, chapters 6–7, 124–209.

[48] Costello, Secret Identity Crisis, 184–6. The story begins in Mark Gruenwald, Dave Hoover, and Danny Bulanadi, "Superpatriot Games," Captain America 425 (March 1994).

[49] Mark Waid, Ron Garney, and Denis Rodier, "Operation Rebirth," Captain America 445 (November 1995).

[50] Costello, Secret Identity Crisis, 185.   [51] Ibid.

[52] Mark Millar and Steve McNiven (illus.), Civil War (New York: Marvel Comics, 2007); Ed Brubaker and Steve Epting (illus.), The Death of Captain America: The Complete Collection (New York: Marvel Comics, 2013).

had originally prompted the registration act in the first place. This represents an attempt to gain control over an increasingly dangerous situation whereby too many different potential threats to society were being left unchecked. Captain America's surrender represents his last free act of trying to put the greater good of everyday citizens first, arguably the central justification for the existence of any government. *The Death of Captain America* then chronicles the hero's assassination and the fallout that follows upon his surrender to government authorities.

Various authors have interpreted Captain America's rebellious actions in *Civil War* as a metaphor or allegory for widespread disillusionment with US policy both foreign and domestic following 9/11, including the second Gulf War. Stevens especially sees it as an indictment of the USA Patriot Act, which forces US citizens to surrender too many of their cherished freedoms for the sake of national security.[53] Costello highlights the way the events chronicled in *Civil War* and *The Death of Captain America* signal "a loss of faith in the virtue of the nation and the government," and "may well symbolize…the death of a particular construct of the American self."[54] Stevens concludes that Captain America's death signals the end of American idealism, and we might add, the notion of American exceptionalism.[55]

Much like Bush's line in the sand shortly after 9/11, the Superhero Registration Act attempts to draw an absolute distinction between hero and villain, which Captain America cannot tolerate. With the help of Reed Richards (Mr. Fantastic), the brilliant leader of the Fantastic Four, heroes aligned with the government construct an off-world detention center (in the so-called Negative Zone, a foreign dimension) for supers who refuse to register with the government. This is an apparent analogy to the US Naval Base at Guantanamo Bay, where the US began (illegally?) detaining suspected terrorists after 9/11.[56] The first major battle between Captain America's team of antigovernment rebels and the progovernment registration team of heroes leads to the unveiling of a super-weapon (a cyborg clone of the Norse hero-god Thor constructed by Tony Stark/Iron Man and Henry Pym/Yellowjacket). It represents a marvel (no pun intended) of modern technology, but ultimately one difficult to control. Apparently it has no conscience. It kills Goliath, one of Captain America's allies, perhaps symbolizing that the US is willing to use superior lethal force against any target they deem hostile, even if that target is merely fighting for freedom from governmental hegemony.[57]

After his eventual surrender and arrest, Captain America is assassinated by a US government agent with whom he was in love, but we eventually learn that she was being mind-controlled by an ancient enemy, the Red Skull, in a plot to sow further chaos in the country. As Costello argues, the iconic hero's death represents more than just the end of the current crisis over the Registration Act. It is the end of "the myth of American virtue

---

53 Stevens, *Captain America*, 245.   54 Costello, *Secret Identity Crisis*, 230.
55 Stevens, *Captain America*, 252.   56 Costello, *Secret Identity Crisis*, 235.
57 At two points in this battle different heroes exclaim, "My God" in reference to this frighteningly powerful technological weapon (the Thor clone), the second immediately after Goliath is struck dead. One wonders if the writer is suggesting the danger of Americans placing too much faith in heartless technology (i.e., the military-industrial complex) to keep them safe from their supposed enemies.

and progress."[58] He even goes so far as to suggest that Captain America's surrender implies that "the weakened rhetoric of American national identity has been a source of the uncompromising hubris that has come to characterize the contemporary political economy."[59] In other words, America has lost her way and no longer knows what she really stands for. Central to this line of interpretation is the important government requirement that heroes unmask themselves, revealing their true identity, and agree to take orders from the government without question. And yet what is to become of a nation or a society that fails to truly understand its own identity, its history, its ideals, its motivations, its true self? Can there be progress when people no longer really understand what it is they are fighting for? Can there be true freedom and progress when one's most cherished ideals have been compromised? Where should the line be drawn between realism and idealism, liberty and security? And to what degree should the government alone be trusted to uphold the national interest of its citizens?

Marvel's *Civil War* seems to be exploring the question "What if we had collateral damage in the US like other countries face when the US acts with impunity and little to no oversight for its 'crime fighting endeavors?'"[60] The narrative also seems to assume, by analogy, that 9/11 was collateral damage or fallout from poor decision-making in American foreign policy, and therefore innocent civilians paid the price of ignorance and recklessness on the part of those in power. And finally, it suggests that the government's attempts to control mayhem may in fact be causing more aggression and terror than they are mollifying.

Such interpretation seems likely in light of precipitating events in the plot of *Civil War*. In the midst of an earlier battle between superheroes and supervillains, a villain named Nitro (with the ability to detonate his own body) causes an explosion that collapses a school building, killing a large number of innocent civilians (mostly children). This appears to be some kind of reflection upon the Twin Towers collapse on 9/11, resulting in the deaths of thousands of noncombatants. Tony Stark builds a memorial to the deceased, and the mother of one of the dead children who had idolized Tony thanks him. The emphasis here is on human collateral damage in the context of a recklessly waged war, albeit, in the case of the American superheroes, against a legitimate, domestic threat. If the analogy is pressed further, it might also suggest that the so-called good guys, in this case Captain America's team of rebel heroes, while perhaps having legitimate complaints against the US government, also exercise violence that at times threatens the well-being of American citizens. Tony Stark/Iron Man, who is allied with the US government, responds to a question about his own aggressive tactics against Captain America's team with the following statement: "There's no shame in making enemies if it means making people safer." Of course, the obvious intention of the writing here is to raise the question "Does making enemies ever really make us safer?" The answer might

---

[58] Costello, *Secret Identity Crisis*, 239.   [59] Ibid., 238.
[60] So also the film, *Captain America: Civil War*, directed by Anthony and Joe Russo, 2016. However, while attempting to make similar points, the plot of the film is only loosely based on the *Civil War* comic.

depend on whether or not one's enemies can be clearly identified and contained (or eradicated).

Civil War is laced with other provocative moments. At one point in the war between anti- and progovernment supers, the Thor clone is referred to by Captain America as a "Frankenstein's Monster," suggesting the misuse of technology and science by the government, which is apparently playing God by re-creating a god. This clone proves to be flawed, impossible to control, and frighteningly powerful. The analogy may be to US military technology, going all the way back to the Manhattan Project.

In another dangerous move, the progovernment team enlists the aid of captured villains to tip the scales in their favor against Captain America's rebels, raising the question of ends and means. This is also a likely critique of American foreign policy, which has a history of allying itself with known criminals (and dictators) in an effort to defeat their Cold War (and modern) competition. Perhaps most infamous of these was Saddam Hussein, the now deceased president of Iraq.

One of the most provocative exchanges of all in *Civil War* occurs at the moment of Captain America's surrender. When Cap realizes how much damage the rebels are doing in fighting the progovernment forces, he stops and drops his shield. Peter Parker (aka Spiderman), who had switched allegiances earlier in the struggle, responds in astonishment, "We were winning back there." Captain America replies, "Everything except the argument."

This line is a clue for deciphering the author's intentions for this rather anticlimactic end to the physical battle between the supers. It appears to be only the beginning of the more important ideological struggle taking place behind the scenes of the comic, beneath the surface of America's struggle over appropriate ends and means in her battle for a sense of national security. Is this the "argument" to which Cap refers? It is left to the reader to answer this question more precisely.

At the time of this writing, it remains unclear what the future holds for American idealism and national identity. Perhaps the Red Skull has been victorious. Chaos and entrenched factionalism appear to reign on many levels in the United States. Tensions over political and social issues both foreign and domestic are at an all-time high. Gridlock in Washington between two entrenched political parties suggests little room for progress in the near future. So how long will covenant ideology in America persist? The original Puritan mission of Christianizing the world has long since been abandoned by many. But if responses to 9/11 are any indication, in the adapted form of a mission to remake the world in its own image, the legacy appears to be alive and well.[61]

---

[61] Some early responses to the Twin Towers collapse by evangelical Christians were reminiscent of the jeremiads of an earlier era, giving credit for the disaster to divine punishment upon a Godless nation. But by and large, such expressions of Puritanical thinking were condemned in the US. See, e.g., appendix D of Lincoln's *Holy Terrors*, 104–7, a partial transcript of Pat Robertson's 700 Club interview of Jerry Falwell on September 13, 2001.

The New Deal

One of the most fascinating, and in some ways conflicted, post-9/11 Captain America stories is found in the graphic novel *Captain America: The New Deal*.[62] Here, Cap battles a foreign terrorist, only to learn that his own government is at least partially culpable for producing hatred abroad with its own reckless and violent foreign policies. In part 5, Cap claims that on 9/11 a "psychopath murdered almost three thousand defenseless human beings in an attempt to trigger World War III," revealing his conviction that such a modern-day terrorist attack is qualitatively different from prior acts of war. But as his investigation continues, he reflects upon the bombing of civilians in Dresden, Germany, by the Allies in World War II, which leads him to muse, "You didn't understand what we'd done here—until September the Eleventh. . . . History repeats itself. Like a machine gun. A **madman** lights the spark—and the **people** pay the price."

Here, terrorists like Osama bin Laden are considered analogous to Hitler—they are merely madmen. This allows their motivations to be more easily dismissed, even when they use the machinery of a government to implement their schemes. But all effects have causes. There are consequences that sometimes boomerang, and *The New Deal* spends a fair amount of time exploring 9/11, by analogy, as one outcome of the US government throwing its Cold War–era weight around in other countries, creating collateral damage in the process. Terrorists do not just manifest out of thin air.

The New Deal clearly presents a more complex and nuanced understanding of American policy and ideals. Unfortunately, in the end the story still promotes a form of American exceptionalism. Cap is depicted as fighting for the freedom and integrity of *all* innocent civilians around the world, suggesting that, somehow, this is America's guiding ethic. But is this evaluation realistic? Lying beneath this seems to be a conviction that America, as a whole, is still largely innocent, the citizens being ignorant of many policies implemented abroad by its own government. In part 6, Cap persistently draws a distinction between the government and the nation's people, claiming that America, as a whole, has learned from her mistakes and that his terrorist foe is blinded by his own personal pain, failing to realize how wrong both America and her enemies are for shedding innocent blood. The terrorist, although holding a reasonable grudge against America, has not learned from the mistakes of others and now seems to be repeating them. While placing blame squarely at the feet of the US government for inspiring terrorist retaliation, Cap exonerates the American people as a whole. And the comic never really explores whether or not civilians in a free country are accountable for the actions of their elected leaders. Julian Darius's summation is apt: "What Reiber [author of *Captain America: The New Deal*] has really done is reflect, with a conscience,

---

[62] John Ney Rieber (writer) and John Cassaday (artist), *Captain America: The New Deal* (New York: Marvel, 2010), originally published in serial form as a restart of the hero in *Captain America* 1–6 (New York: Marvel, 2002). For a fair critique of the rather messy plot and inconsistent treatment of American foreign policy that vacillates between hyperpatriotism and hypercriticism, see Julian Darius, "The Intellectual Rip-Off of Captain America's *The New Deal*," *Sequart*, April 14, 2003, http://sequart.org/magazine/1981/the-intellectual-rip-off-of-captain-americas-the-new-deal/.

the popular discourse, to encapsulate in an admittedly confused narrative the conflict-ing responses of a nation at once drawn to anti-Arab sentiment and to renewed humani-tarianism, to patriotism and to a reexamination, however lacking in subtlety, of the history of U.S. foreign policy."[63]

I am in agreement with Darius that this story exhibits a simplification of the com-plexities of history, even as it acknowledges that there may be valid reasons why some parties would want to take up arms against their perceived oppressors in the West. Ultimately, *The New Deal* writes off all violent endeavors that harm civilians as the work of madmen, or the governments run by such men. But are only madmen guilty of the death of civilians? Do only madmen commit terrorist acts? Can a supposedly free and democratic nation be considered largely innocent and sane by such a definition?

In post-9/11 Captain America comics the covenant heritage of Israel, passed down through the Puritans and adapted in the myths of American exceptionalism and inno-cence, continues to manifest, if admittedly in a highly conflicted form. The notion that the US is the world's bastion of freedom and goodness persists, even as *Civil War, The Death of Captain America,* and *The New Deal* sometimes question the integrity of our government and the appropriateness of using any means at our disposal to propagate American-style democracy. We are still, collectively and in our own minds, the "city on a hill." In spite of sometimes critically questioning America's role in eliciting terrorist plots by implementing hypocritical foreign policies that promote Western hegemony, Captain America comics retain the idea that America is somehow better than her enemies, because at heart its people are capable of overcoming self-interest for the greater good of all humanity. Yet such widespread and universal humanitarianism remains to be seen. Alongside its continued enthrallment with vigilante justice, manifest most clearly in the popular cultural form of superheroism, one continues to find in America the replication of an ancient blind spot. Much like the old Deuteronomic ethic in the Bible, American popular culture often reflects a strange blend of ingredients: an elect or exceptional sta-tus for its people; an idealistic evaluation of its own humanitarian values; and a convic-tion that America, like Israel, uniquely remains in possession of the Promised Land.[64]

The idea of American exceptionalism is the inheritance of a Puritan ethic transferred to the United States during and after the revolutionary period, which was transformed into a new mission to guarantee life, liberty, and the pursuit of happiness to US citizens. In essence, this represents a liberty and prosperity gospel at the heart of American iden-tity, initiated at the founding. The Puritans borrowed much of this ethic from the ancient Israelite tradition, combining the ideas of a chosen nation and Promised Land with a messianic mission to convert the entire world into the Kingdom of God. Ironically, the Puritans eventually came to consider this mission a dismal failure and their special cov-enant with God irreparably broken, as evidenced in the widespread preaching of

---

[63] Darius, "The Intellectual Rip-Off."

[64] It might be argued that exporting the so-called Promised Land, by force if necessary, sets the modern US apart from ancient Israel. However, texts that imagine a future where all nations stream to Israel to pay homage to Yahweh might suggest otherwise (e.g., Zec 8:22; Isa 2:2ff.; 43–5).

lament-style sermons. However, their legacy lives on, albeit more generically and secularly, in the way American civil religion continues to exhibit (often unconsciously) covenant idealism about national identity. Especially following the disaster of 9/11, both academics and pop culture products have engaged in significantly more critical thinking about American identity and America's place in an increasingly global environment. The idea of covenant, on the individual and national levels, has come under serious scrutiny, and comic books have played an important role in this phenomenon.

FUTURE PROSPECTS AND QUESTIONS

- What is the nature of heroism as imagined by biblical texts, and how does this relate to heroism as imagined in American popular culture? To what extent do comic books and films based on superhero narratives both reflect and challenge core values in American society?
- Since the founding period, there has been debate over the extent to which the United States should be considered a Christian nation (God's New Israel). How does this notion conflict with the ideas of religious freedom, separation of church and state, and attempts to export democracy?
- If Jewett and Lawrence are correct in arguing that the United States has a "Captain America complex," what responsibility might comics writers and superhero filmmakers have to provide alternatives to this way of thinking and acting? Is it appropriate for artists and writers to produce pop culture products that are politically and/or religiously motivated? Why or why not?
- To what extent should pop culture studies play a role in the study of religion and politics in America and in the rest of the world? How might a more thorough study of pop culture, religion, and violence in society lead us to rethink our interpretations (and appropriations) of sacred texts?

SUGGESTED READINGS AND ANNOTATED BIBLIOGRAPHY

In addition to, and including, some of the works already cited, the following short list of resources is recommended for further research.

Cherry, Conrad, ed. *God's New Israel: Religious Interpretations of American Destiny*. Revised and updated edition. Chapel Hill: University of North Carolina Press, 1998.

While numerous collections of historical documents about religion and politics in America abound in today's market of academic books, Cherry's collection, with meaningful short introductions to key eras of American history, remains one of the best single volumes available.

Gardella, Peter. *American Civil Religion: What Americans Hold Sacred*. New York: Oxford University Press, 2014.

This book provides a concise analysis of a wide range of historical events, ideas, monuments, music, places, and speeches that Americans hold sacred, and is therefore a good starting point for exploring American Civil Religion. What the book may lack in depth, it makes up for in breadth.

Hughes, Richard T. *Myths America Lives By*. Chicago: University of Illinois Press, 2003.

This book provides essential reading about the core components of American Civil Religion, including the myths of the "chosen nation," the "Christian nation," and the "innocent nation." Hughes takes a historical approach, spending a significant amount of time on the emergence of mythical nationalism during the founding period (broadly understood), but also addresses "mythic dimensions of American Capitalism" and the significance of the idea of the nation's innocence in the twentieth century, which continues to hold great importance after 9/11.

Lawrence, John Shelton, and Robert Jewett. *The Myth of the American Superhero*. Grand Rapids, MI: Eerdmans, 2002.

This thick text provides an engaging analysis of the emergence and ongoing role of superheroic thinking in the American psyche, with heavy, albeit selective, emphasis on the role of violence and violent redemption in modern-day films. Most of the films are rather dated now, but the concepts are easily applicable to more recent productions.

Mendenhall, George E. *Ancient Israel's Faith and History: An Introduction to the Bible in Context*. Edited by Gary A. Herion. Louisville, KY: Westminster John Knox Press, 2001.

Taking the approach that "religion is an aspect of culture" (1), Mendenhall analyzes the religion of ancient Israel from a contextualized perspective, seeking to explain it in relation to the larger cultural environment of the ancient Near East. Readers should approach the text critically, however, as Mendenhall tends to idealize ancient Israel's early covenant intentions, probably somewhat overstating its uniqueness as a revolutionary social and religious construct.

Noll, K. L. "The Patron God in the Ancient Near East." In *Canaan and Israel in Antiquity: A Textbook on History and Religion*, 182–214. 2nd edition. New York: Bloomsbury, 2013.

This chapter in Noll's book provides one of the most concise and unbiased academic discussions of ancient Israel's concept of divine-human relations, emphasizing the ways it "reflects its social, natural, economic, and political environment" (183). Noll's argument is that "the divine realm, or pantheon, presupposed by ancient Near Eastern kings mirrored the hierarchy of the human social and political world" (187), rather than the other way around. Noll demonstrates the way human religion tends to project onto the divine realm human political structures in order to lend them legitimacy.

Noll, Mark, and Luke E. Harlow, eds. *Religion and American Politics: From the Colonial Period to the Present*. 2nd edition. New York: Oxford University Press, 2007.

While taking a historical approach, this collection of well-researched, interpretive essays explores in depth the relationship between various religious and political ideologies in America. The essays emphasize how historical events and ideology coalesce in the evolution of America's unique blend of religious thinking and governmental institutions and practices.

Oropreza, B. J., ed. *The Gospel According to Superheroes: Religion and Popular Culture*. New York: Peter Lang, 2005.

> This collection of essays, written in a more popular style for a wide audience, explores the religious significance of a variety of more popular heroes, primarily emphasizing comics. The essays are divided into three parts. The first two focus on the golden and silver ages of D.C. and Marvel Comics. The last third of the book looks at what some have called the deconstructive age of superheroes (1980s forward), including two chapters on religion and film.

Whitelam, Keith W. "Israelite Kingship: The Royal Ideology and Its Opponents." In *The World of Ancient Israel: Sociological, Anthropological, and Political Perspectives*, edited by R. E. Clements, 119–39. New York: Cambridge University Press, 1989.

> Whitelam situates the ideology of kingship in ancient Israel within the larger ancient Near Eastern context, highlighting the ways religion and politics are intertwined in promoting the king as the representative of the nation's patron deity. He offers here a less biased approach than many earlier studies, which tended to emphasize the uniqueness of ancient Israelite society in comparison to neighboring nations.

CHAPTER 10

BIBLICAL PROPHECY AND POPULAR FANTASY AND SCIENCE FICTION

DAVID G. GARBER, JR.
MCAFEE SCHOOL OF THEOLOGY, MERCER
UNIVERSITY

INTRODUCTION

IN George R. R. Martin's epic fantasy series *A Game of Thrones*, Tyrion Lannister describes prophecy as a half-trained mule: "It looks as though it might be useful, but the moment you trust in it, it kicks you in the head."[1] Tyrion's description belies much of the problem with prophecy in the biblical tradition and beyond—how one interprets various cryptic sayings of the prophets. From the prophetic character of Morpheus in *The Matrix* trilogy to the prophecy of "the one who will bring balance to the Force" in the *Star Wars* prequel trilogy, prophecy and fulfillment in popular culture often take on many characteristics of biblical prophecy, including interpretive elusiveness.

OVERVIEW OF TOPIC

According to David L. Petersen, biblical prophets mediated the human and divine worlds and were "truly boundary figures, standing between the world of the sacred and

---

[1] George R. R. Martin, *A Dance with Dragons* (New York: Bantam Books, 2011), 534. Portions of this essay were adapted from David G. Garber, "Oracles of Ice and Fire: Functions of Prophecy in *Game of Thrones* and the Bible," *Oxford Biblical Studies Online*, 2016, http://global.oup.com/obso/focus/focus_on_oracles_of_ice_and_fire/.

secular."[2] Likewise, Stephen Cook describes prophets as "channelers of the transcendent," who "convey, or claim to convey, thinking or power from outside earthly, empirical reality."[3] As intermediary figures, prophets occupy a liminal space in literature. Petersen describes four role labels for the Hebrew prophets: the *rō'eh* (seer), the *'îsh hā'ĕlōhîm* (man of God), the *chōzeh* (seer), and the *nābî'* (prophet). The *rō'eh* is an urban prophet who works with the local sacrificial cult and consults on a fee basis.[4] In contrast, the *'îsh hā'ĕlōhîm* is an itinerant prophet who subsists on agriculture and alms[5] and often invokes the name of YHWH to perform miraculous demonstrations of power.[6] Petersen describes *'îsh hā'ĕlōhîm* as "dangerous, powerful, and due appropriate respect."[7] According to Petersen, the labels *chōzeh* and the *nābî'* essentially refer to one function: the central morality prophet. Such figures "speak on behalf of the values central to the society and on behalf of the god who sanctions the moral structure of society."[8] While the biblical tradition does not consider the prophets divine, their proximity to the divine realm sets them apart from normal human experience. As a result, prophets' messages are often cryptic, at times almost unintelligible. In his classic work on the prophets, Abraham J. Heschel describes the prophet as a human who "employs notes one octave too high for our ears."[9] The liminal space prophets occupy creates fodder for the human imagination, both ancient and contemporary, allowing prophets to play key roles of intrigue in literature and the arts.

Prophets in the historical books of the Bible often serve multiple functions, not least of which is granting divine approval or disapproval to the kings of Israel and Judah. Samuel offers a paradigm of prophetic functions in the biblical narrative. 1 Samuel 1 introduces the prophet by a miraculous birth to a previously childless woman, and by 1 Samuel 3 the reader has become aware of Samuel's ability to perceive divine communication despite his priestly mentor's (Eli's) apparent deafness to God's voice. As Samuel comes of age, after instructing the Israelites to put away foreign idols, he leads them to victory against the Philistines (1 Sam 7) and becomes their primary leader. The people turn to him to appoint a king over them in 1 Samuel 8, and he becomes both mentor and adviser to King Saul. After Saul disobeys his prophetic advice in two instances (1 Sam 13 and 15), Samuel demotes Saul, proclaiming that God's anointing has left the fallen king. He then anoints a new king, David, to take his place (1 Sam 16). Later prophets, such as Nathan, Ahijah the Shilonite, Elijah, and Elisha, will play similar roles in advising, validating, and condemning kings. Finally, perhaps because of their proximity to the Divine, prophets like Samuel, Elijah, and Elisha often perform miracles, sometimes

---

[2] David L. Petersen, *The Prophetic Literature: An Introduction* (Louisville, KY: Westminster John Knox Press, 2002), 7.

[3] Stephen L. Cook, "Prophets and Prophecy," in *The Oxford Encyclopedia of the Bible and Theology*, ed. Stephen L. Cook, *Oxford Biblical Studies Online*, accessed August 11, 2018, http://www.oxford biblicalstudies.com/article/opr/t467/e189.

[4] David L. Petersen, *The Roles of Israel's Prophets*, Journal for the Study of the Old Testament Supplement 17 (Sheffield, UK: JSOT Press, 1981), 51.

[5] Ibid.   [6] Ibid., 49.   [7] Petersen. *The Prophetic Literature*, 6.

[8] Petersen, *The Roles of Israel's Prophets*, 68.

[9] Abraham J. Heschel, *The Prophets: An Introduction* (New York: Harper & Row, 1962), 10.

kindly ones, like finding the lost donkeys of Saul's father (1 Sam 9), and at times horrific ones, such as Elisha's calling on bears to attack disrespectful youth (2 Kings 2:23–25).

In biblical narratives, prophets and their omens often drive the plot. For instance, in Judges 5, the prophet Deborah summons the military leader Barak and conveys God's command to him to take up a position against Sisera's army, assuring Barak of victory. Barak refuses this command unless the prophet herself accompanies him. In response, Deborah prophesies again that God will give the glory of victory to a woman instead of to Barak. This second prophecy narratively sets the stage for the fateful encounter between Sisera and Jael, the wife of Heber, in her tent, where she fulfills this prophecy by driving a tent peg through Sisera's skull (Judg 4:1–10, 17–22). Thus Deborah provides an example of a legitimate prophet according to Deuteronomy 18:22. She speaks in the name of YHWH, and what she foretells comes to pass. Her portrayal provides an example of the importance of both prophecy and fulfillment in the narratives of the Deuteronomistic History (Joshua through 2 Kings).

While works from popular culture might at times offer social commentary, their primary purpose is to entertain. In contrast, while some of the biblical narratives about prophets and prophecy are entertaining (see, for example, the narrative of Balaam and his donkey in Num 22), prophets of the Bible, particularly those in the books of classical prophecy such as Jeremiah and Micah, have a primary agenda of social and/or religious reform. Heschel portrays prophets as iconoclasts who have a "breathless impatience" with the status quo of societies that oppress the poor.[10] One might imagine that if Amos, Huldah, Deborah, Jeremiah, and Ezekiel were active today, they would employ the methods and various media of contemporary popular culture in ways similar to how they used popular culture of the time to express their messages. Ezekiel, for example, is well known for dramatizing his message (Ezek 4–5 and 12), employing songs from the culture,[11] and drawing upon iconographic imagery from the ancient world in describing his visions of God.[12]

Prophecies in the biblical tradition do not always remain constrained to their immediate narrative or historical contexts. Rather, as prophetic traditions are passed from generation to generation and received in different historical and religious circumstances, those transmitting the tradition transform them to address new audiences. The most obvious example of this process occurs with the hotly debated text and translation of Isaiah 7:14. In this text, the prophet encounters Ahaz, the king of Judah in the eighth century BCE, who is pondering what to do in response to a siege against Jerusalem by

[10] Heschel, *The Prophets*, 4.

[11] See, for example, Ezek 24:3–5, which Walther Zimmerli identifies as a parody of a popular working song. Walther Zimmerli, *Ezekiel: A Commentary on the Book of the Prophet Ezekiel, Chapters 1–24*, ed. Frank Moore Cross and Klaus Baltzer, Hermeneia (Philadelphia, PA: Fortress Press, 1983), 496.

[12] See, for example, Margaret S. Odell's discussion of Neo-Assyrian cultural influences on the book of Ezekiel in her *Ezekiel*, Smyth & Helwys Bible Commentary, 16 (Macon, GA: Smyth and Helwys, 2005), 7–9. See also Dale F. Launderville's discussions of composite beings in Ezek 1:5–25 (identified as cherubim in Ezek 10:20), Mesopotamia, and Archaic Greece: *Spirit and Reason: The Embodied Character of Ezekiel's Symbolic Thinking* (Waco, TX: Baylor University Press, 2007), 156–62.

King Rezin of Aram and King Pekah of Israel. Isaiah urges patience, suggesting that these two kings will soon pass from the scene. He even suggests that Ahaz ask for a sign to confirm the prophecy. When Ahaz refuses to ask for such a sign, Isaiah provides him one anyway, suggesting that before the young woman, who perhaps was with them at the time, gives birth to a son, and before he comes of age, the two kings' lands would be deserted, unable to harass Judah again. Judah will become as prosperous as it was before the division of the two kingdoms, centuries earlier (Isa 7:1–17). Jewish tradition and biblical scholars often identify the child as the future King Hezekiah, one of the greatest religious reformers of ancient Judah. In keeping with this interpretation, one might read the later hymn in Isaiah 9 as Hezekiah's coronation hymn.

Early Christians, however, appropriated the Isaiah prophecy for a new religious and geopolitical worldview. Taking its cue from the Septuagint translation of *ha'almāh* (the young woman) as *parthénos* (virgin), Matthew 1:22–23 suggests that the virgin birth of Christ fulfills this prophecy, transforming its meaning from its original historical context and appropriating it for the early Christian movement.[13] The complex reception history of this tradition within Christianity testifies to the doctrine of the virgin birth in Christian theology and expresses itself in various ways in popular Christian culture. The most notable reinforcement of the Isaiah tradition in popular Christian culture is the singing of George Frideric Handel's *Messiah* (1741), particularly the Alto Recitative, in many churches during the Advent season every year.[14] This is just one example of the history of reception of prophetic text and its interpretations that has permeated the thinking of successive generations and has propagated meanings throughout culture, in art, literature, and music.

SPECIFIC EXAMPLES AND/OR FOCI

Biblical prophetic tropes manifest in three primary ways in American popular culture: prophetic characters, prophecies as plot devices, and popular culture itself performing a prophetic function. An exploration of the way popular culture adopts and adapts themes from biblical prophecy may provide insight into the nature of prophecy itself and our human fascination with it. At the very least, this investigation could reveal how current creators understand, adopt, and adapt themes of biblical prophecy in their own works. In some instances, the popular culture itself can speak truth back to the power of biblical tradition as well.

---

[13] For more on the function of this text in the Gospel of Matthew, see the work of Richard B. Hays, *Reading Backwards: Figural Christology and the Fourfold Gospel Witness* (Waco, TX: Baylor University Press, 2014), 38–9: "Whatever we make of the complexities of Matthew's appropriation of Isaiah 7:14, his placement of this scriptural citation at the beginning of his narrative sounds a major keynote for the Gospel: Israel's God is now present to his people precisely in the person of Jesus."

[14] See Roger A. Bullard's analysis of Handel's use of the Isaiah and Matthew traditions in *Messiah: The Gospel According to Handel's Oratorio* (Grand Rapids, MI: Wm. B. Eerdmans, 1993), 22–7.

One might argue that Gandalf in J. R. R. Tolkien's *Lord of the Rings* trilogy is the quintessential biblical prophet in contemporary popular culture.[15] He particularly resembles prophets from the biblical books of Samuel and Kings. Like an *'ish hāĕlōhîm*, the wizard performs powerful miraculous acts, which range from magnificent fireworks and magical confrontations with ominous foes such as the Balrog to the resuscitation of King Théoden whom the evil wizard, Saruman, has poisoned in order to manipulate. Gandalf, like Samuel and Deborah, also assists or leads armies in battle as he does with Eomer at the climax of *The Two Towers*.[16]

Fleming Rutledge, in an analysis of Tolkien's source material, draws a similar comparison between Gandalf and the biblical prophet Elijah, particularly noting the similarities between Gandalf's final confrontation with Saruman and Elijah's competition with the priests of Ba'al on Mount Carmel (1 Kings 18): "In the duel on Mount Carmel, Baal is revealed to be utterly impotent, unable to do anything creative or revelatory, or indeed anything at all. In the duel between Gandalf and Saruman, it becomes apparent that Sauron's powers are fatally limited, for in the final analysis he can produce only slaves."[17] Rutledge also notes Gandalf's offer of mercy and repentance to Saruman as evidence of Gandalf's resemblance to the biblical prophets.[18] Throughout both the books and the films, Gandalf remains intricately involved in political affairs, advising kings of all the races of Middle Earth: elves, dwarves, eagles, and humans. Gandalf's long history and confrontation with death also place him in that liminal space between worlds that prophetic figures often occupy.

Prophetic characters also drive the narrative of *The Matrix* trilogy, which one might characterize as a postmodern amalgam of prophetic traditions from various religions.[19] The biblical tradition, however, is at the heart of these portrayals. Two main prophetic figures occupy the films. The first is Morpheus, a zealous figure obsessed with the prophecy of the One. Morpheus resembles two major biblical prophets in the Christian tradition,

[15] In this brief discussion of *The Lord of the Rings*, I am drawing primarily from the most accessible film versions. *The Lord of the Rings: The Fellowship of the Ring*, directed by Peter Jackson, USA, New Line Cinema, 2001; *The Lord of the Rings: The Two Towers*, directed by Peter Jackson, USA, New Line Cinema, 2002; and *The Lord of the Rings: The Return of the King*, directed by Peter Jackson, USA, New Line Cinema, 2003.

[16] Deborah reluctantly joins Barak in battle (Judg 4:9). Samuel intercedes on behalf of the Israelites by offering a sacrifice to YHWH. In response, YHWH throws the Philistines into confusion and routs them before the Israelite forces (1 Sam 7:9–11).

[17] Fleming Rutledge, *The Battle for Middle-earth: Tolkien's Divine Design in* The Lord of the Rings (Grand Rapids, MI: Wm. B. Eerdmans, 2004), 187.

[18] Ibid. This dialogue occurs in Tolkien's books, but not in Jackson's films. See, for comparison, Elijah's declaration of mercy after King Ahab's repentance in 1 Kings 21:20–29.

[19] *The Matrix*, directed by Andrew Wachowski and Laurence Wachowski, USA, Warner Bros. Pictures, 1999; *The Matrix Reloaded*, directed by Andrew Wachowski and Laurence Wachowski, USA, Warner Bros. Pictures, 2003; *The Matrix Revolutions*, directed by Andrew Wachowski and Laurence Wachowski, USA, Warner Bros. Pictures, 2003. For an analysis of the first film's gnostic Christian and Buddhist influences, see Frances Flannery-Dailey and Rachel Wagner, "Wake Up! Gnosticism and Buddhism in *The Matrix*," *Journal of Religion and Film* 5, no. 2 (October 2001), https://digitalcommons.unomaha.edu/jrf/vol5/iss2/4.

Daniel and John the Baptist. His connection with Daniel is based on two names, his own and the name of his ship. His own name derives from the Greek god of dreams, and Daniel both interprets dreams and sees visions in the book that bears his name.[20] Most notably, Daniel interprets Nebuchadnezzar's dreams in Daniel 2. This king becomes the namesake of Morpheus's ship. The creators even inserted a prophetic Easter egg on the nameplate of the ship itself. Above the name is the model number of the ship, "Mark III No. 11," seemingly a reference to a messianic passage in the New Testament: "Whenever the unclean spirits saw him, they fell down before him and shouted, 'You are the Son of God!'" (Mark 3:11).[21] The verse, when read in the context of *The Matrix* trilogy, evokes images of Neo raising his hand to projectiles (mostly bullets), which immediately fall to the ground. Similarly, in the "real" world, Neo does the same to pursuing robots, revealing his power in both realms.

Morpheus's prophetic character also resembles John the Baptist of the New Testament. Morpheus prepares the way for the coming messiah in much the same way John the Baptist does in John 1:19–27.[22] Morpheus has his own followers but is always on the lookout for the One who is greater than himself.

The second prophetic figure in *The Matrix* is, predictably, the Oracle. Much as Josiah seeks the confirmation of the law book found in 2 Kings 22 through the female prophet, Huldah, Morpheus takes Neo to the Oracle to confirm that he is indeed the One. Like most of the Hebrew prophets, the Oracle is a liminal figure. She is a program of the machines but aids humans in their quest for liberation in order to bring peace to humans and machines alike. Like Elijah and Jeremiah, who faced persecution from the kings Ahab, Jehoiakim, and Zedekiah, the Oracle is a prophet who faces great danger at the hands of the other programs. As such, she has a guardian, appropriately named Seraph, a direct reference to the Seraphim whom Isaiah encounters in his temple vision and commissioning (Isa 6). In Hebrew, the term *seraph* refers to a fiery serpent, and the verb form *saraph* means "to burn."[23] Perhaps in an intentional play on these terms, when Neo witnesses Seraph in his "matrix vision" the normal green descending characters surround the form of Seraph's characters, which are glowing in a fiery orange. In a particular scene from *The Matrix: Revolutions*, one of the guards from Club Hel describes

---

[20] Daniel is not a traditional prophetic book in the Jewish canon, nor is Daniel called a prophet in the text itself. Christian reception of the book, however, has elevated him to this status, placing the text among the prophets in most Christian canon lists. The creators of *The Matrix*, itself a postapocalyptic narrative, derive many of their references from the dominant Christian traditions that do consider Daniel a prophetic figure.

[21] All scripture citations are from the New Revised Standard Version unless otherwise noted.

[22] One might note that John's characterization as a prophet crying out in the wilderness (Mark 1:3, Matt 3:3, Luke 3:4, John 1:23) reframes another passage from Isa 40:3. The New Testament passages describe John as one roaming about in the wilderness and crying out. Isa 40:3, however, does not describe the voice being in the wilderness, but is a command for the audience to prepare a way in the wilderness. This is another example within the history of reception that shows how prophecies can morph depending on historical, religious, and literary circumstances.

[23] Ludwig Koehler, Walter Baumgartner, and Johann J. Stamm, s.v. "*srp*," in *The Hebrew and Aramaic Lexicon of the Old Testament*, 2 vols., trans. and ed. Mervyn E. J. Richardson (Leiden: Brill, 2001).

Seraph as "wingless," noting this character's difference from the typical description of Seraphim in Isaiah 6:2 as having six wings.

Unlike Huldah, who immediately answers Josiah's questions about the scroll of the Law in 2 Kings 22:15–20, *The Matrix*'s Oracle is much more cryptic. Instead, the Oracle speaks in riddles and acts more as a guide to the protagonist, who interprets his first encounter with her as confirmation that he is *not* the One. In their second encounter, the Oracle reveals that she just told him what he needed to hear at the time. While the Oracle may be less straightforward than some prophets from the biblical narrative, she does guide certain sequences in the plot and becomes a much larger player in the narrative.

Much like New Testament appropriations of Isaiah's prophecies, manifestations of prophecy in popular culture tend to limit themselves to the definition of prophecy as prediction and fulfillment, often with a bent toward the messianic. For instance, *Star Wars Episode 1: The Phantom Menace* first introduces the concept of prophecy to the cinematic space odyssey franchise as various members of the Jedi Council debate whether or not Anakin Skywalker is the one prophesied to "bring balance to the Force." While a frustration to fan culture, George Lucas also appropriated the trope of the virgin birth in his portrayal of Anakin. In *The Phantom Menace*, Shmi Skywalker tells Qui-Gon Jinn, "There was no father," leading the Jedi Master to wonder if the boy had been miraculously conceived by midichlorians, cellular agents of the Force that live in symbiosis with living beings, particularly Jedi. John D. Caputo suggests that Anakin's virgin birth testifies to the harmonious relationship between science and religion within the *Star Wars* universe and is Lucas's counterpart to the nativity narrative in the Gospel of Luke.[24] When Qui-Gon Jinn encounters the boy and notices his strong sensitivity to the Force, he claims that Anakin might be the chosen one. The first three episodes play with this notion of prophecy, consistently exhibiting both the good and evil natures of this one person who seems to embody the cosmic struggle for balance in his individual being.

While the informed audience knows from the beginning that Anakin will become Darth Vader, the villain of the original *Star Wars* trilogy, the question of whether or not he actually brings balance to the Force remains. While the original trilogy never mentioned such a prophecy, the prequel trilogy reframes the original so that subsequent viewings now often have the prophecy in mind. The interpretation of the prophecy, however, remains a mystery. Did the prophecy refer to Anakin, who eventually turns back to the light side of the Force after his son, Luke, confronts him? Or did it refer to Luke, who, after facing and overcoming his own dark side demons, eventually redeems his father? Is Rey, the protagonist of the sequel trilogy and introduced in *The Force Awakens*, now the "chosen one" of the prophecy? Caputo suggests that the messianic age of the *Star Wars* saga "depends upon the smooth and harmonious flow of the Force, while war rages when the Force is disturbed or distorted."[25] Because a world of balance

---

[24] John D. Caputo, *On Religion*, Thinking in Action (London: Routledge, 2001), 87–8.

[25] Ibid., 82. Though he published *On Religion* in 2001, Caputo also suggested that the story would take nine installments to complete and noted the financial benefits of keeping the story unresolved until they were finished (88).

within the narrative framework of the *Star Wars* universe would ultimately yield a narrative void of conflict, one might wonder if the prophecy of balance will always remain unfulfilled, or at least in question. One may liken the sequel trilogy and future productions as reinterpretations of the prophecy for new narrative contexts in a manner analogous to how the Christian tradition reframes and appropriates Hebrew Bible prophecies.

Prophecies and their fulfillment recur often in the fantasy and science fiction genres. Martin's *A Song of Ice and Fire* series, set in the fantasy world of Westeros, has a more sophisticated approach to prophecy, probably due to the series' more complex literary structure. Like multiple manuscripts of a biblical book, this popular culture artifact has two closely related but independent expressions: Martin's written novels and the HBO television series. Prophecy plays a role in both expressions. The Hebrew Bible and *Game of Thrones* each recognize the danger of prophecy and prophetic interpretations run amok. The Hebrew Bible takes great pains to restrict such prophetic interpretation:

> When you come into the land that the LORD your God is giving you, you must not learn to imitate the abhorrent practices of those nations. No one shall be found among you who makes a son or daughter pass through fire, or who practices divination, or is a soothsayer, or an augur, or a sorcerer, or one who casts spells, or who consults ghosts or spirits, or who seeks oracles from the dead.... Although these nations that you are about to dispossess do give heed to soothsayers and diviners, as for you, the LORD your God does not permit you to do so. (Deut 18:9–14)

Like Deuteronomy 18, the Faith of the Seven (the official religion of Westeros), forbids certain types of divination. This trope is most apparent in the opening scene of season 5, "The Wars to Come," a flashback to Cersei Lannister traveling with a friend to visit Maggy the Frog, a diviner who lives deep in the forest. Clearly her friend knows the two should not be in the forest and voices the forbidden nature of Cersei's quest. They reach the woman's hut and face immediate resistance.[26] While Cersei persists in her demands for prophecy, Maggy warns against it: "Everyone wants to know their future until they know their future." After Cersei insists and threatens the diviner, Maggy asks for a taste of Cersei's blood, ritually establishing the taboo nature of this inquiry. Maggy predicts Cersei's marriage to King Robert Baratheon, their childlessness together, and her children (and their death) born of her union with her brother, Jaimie Lannister. She also predicts Cersei's eventual usurper, who will be younger and more beautiful than she. While the form of the prophecy seems quite cryptic, because it is a flashback in the television series the viewer already has seen portions of its fulfillment. Cersei was queen of Westeros, became the queen mother at the death of Robert, and eventually witnessed the deaths of all three of her children. In the penultimate season of the television series, she has come face to face with another queen who may replace her.

---

[26] Michael Slovis, *Game of Thrones*, season 5, episode 1, "The Wars to Come," April 12, 2015, HBO.

Of all the prophecies in the series, this one most closely resembles a biblical narrative: King Saul's visit to the medium at Endor (1 Sam 28). Like the forbidden encounter with Maggy, Deuteronomic law (Deut 18:11) and King Saul himself forbade the medium (1 Sam 28:3). Both inquirers, Saul and Cersei, exercise authority over the medium. Both mediums are successful, Maggy by giving a straightforward fortune, and the medium at Endor by raising the prophet Samuel from Sheol to decree Saul's fate. Both oracles portray a very negative future for Saul and Cersei. While these similarities are fairly clear, the portrayal of the medium is quite distinct. In *Game of Thrones*, the producers have accentuated the mystery and danger of the medium almost to the point of caricature. In 1 Samuel 28, however, the woman at Endor, while submissive to the king's authority, acts quite compassionately, offering Saul and his men food and rest after he hears the dire word from his former friend and adviser (1 Sam 28:22–25).

While the narrative has followed Cersei's prophecy fairly closely, a second prophecy in the narrative remains more elusive. Like the woman at Endor and the prophetic enemies in Ezekiel 13, forbidden mediums in the *Game of Thrones* tend to be women. The most powerful and visible prophetic voice in the series is Melisandre, the Red Woman, a Jezebel-like figure who uses both her power as a medium and her seductiveness to sway another contender for the throne, Stannis Baratheon, away from the traditional Faith of the Seven to worship a foreign deity, the Lord of Light. Melisandre claims to read the flames, in which this god of fire shows her the future of Westeros. Whereas in the Deuteronomistic History, heroes like Elijah, Hezekiah, and Josiah are iconoclastic and radically monotheistic, Melisandre's militant and aniconic faith presents her as an enemy. She burns symbols of the Faith of the Seven in effigy as an offering to the Lord of Light in the second season opener, "The North Remembers." Melisandre intones, "Lord of Light, come to us in our darkness. We offer you these false Gods. Take them and cast your light upon us.... For the night is dark and full of terrors."

During this ritual, Melisandre also interprets, and perhaps manipulates, the prophecy of Azor Ahai, which foretells the rebirth of an ancient hero in a time of crisis: "After the long summer, darkness will fall heavy on the world. The stars will bleed.... The cold breath of winter will freeze the seas.... And the dead shall rise in the North.... In the ancient books, it's written that a warrior will draw a burning sword from the fire. And that sword shall be Lightbringer. Stannis Baratheon, warrior of light, your sword awaits you. Lord, cast your light upon us! For the night is dark and full of terrors."[27] Melisandre and Stannis have a relationship very similar to that of Jezebel and Ahab (see especially 1 Kings 21). Both narratives exhibit a fear of the influence of foreign women, and both women devise schemes to advance the power of their men, thereby increasing their own standing.

While Melisandre, the Red Woman, clearly demonstrates power and influence, she is a red herring when it comes to interpreting the Azor Ahai prophecy, particularly in light of Stannis Baratheon's death.[28] In the books, another wizened figure, Maester Aemon,

---

[27] Alan Taylor, *Game of Thrones*, season 2, episode 1, "The North Remembers," April 1, 2012, HBO.
[28] David Nutter, *Game of Thrones*, season 5, episode 10, "Mother's Mercy," June 14, 2015, HBO.

deconstructs her interpretation of the ancient prophecy: "Lady Melisandre has misread the signs. Stannis...Stannis has some of the dragon [Targaryen] blood in him, yes... I remembered that, so I allowed myself to hope...perhaps I wanted to...we all deceive ourselves, when we want to believe. Melisandre most of all, I think. The sword is wrong, she has to know that...light without heat...an empty glamor...the sword is *wrong*, and the false light can only lead us deeper into darkness....Daenerys is our hope."[29] Of course with *Game of Thrones* and *A Song of Ice and Fire* being unfinished narratives, the audience still does not know the true meaning of the prophecy, and Maester Aemon, who may have a Targaryen bias, may not have the final word. Indeed the prophetic mystery of Azor Ahai has led to an online cottage industry of speculation and fan theories, much in the same way that apparently unfulfilled biblical prophecies have generated interpretation for centuries.

The prophecies in *Game of Thrones* are mostly about driving the narrative forward, or sometimes distracting the reader with multiple possibilities to keep the mystery alive. While we have some of this function in the Deuteronomistic History, interpretations of such biblical prophecies within the canon itself do not leave as much room for the imagination. Many of the prophecies either have narrative fulfillments in close proximity to the original utterance or have been explained by successive layers of interpretation that may have been added by later redactors.[30]

In some instances popular culture's prophetic stance on justice can challenge the biblical tradition itself, particularly in terms of its patriarchal perspective. The reimagined *Battlestar Galactica* television series of the early 2000s, for example, challenges some of the misogynistic portrayals of women in prophetic literature while also asking poignant questions about what it means to be human. Before the series begins, the humans created artificially intelligent Cylons, who served humans in many capacities. The Cylons rebelled against their creators, resulting in a great human and Cylon war that ended in an armistice. The Cylons settled on another planet and ceased all communications with humankind for over forty years. During this time, the Cylons continued to evolve, introducing new, organic models that took on the image of their creators. At the beginning of the series, the Cylons finally make contact and attack the thirteen human colonies, nearly annihilating all humans save for a small fleet of spacecraft protected by the *Battlestar Galactica*.[31]

In the second season of the series, Gaius Baltar enters a cell block with Lieutenant Thorne and an apparitional version of Cylon Number Six, the tall, slender, blonde model who seduced him into betraying the entire human race, resulting in humanity's near

---

[29] George R. R. Martin, *A Feast for Crows* (New York: Bantam Books, 2011), 521–2, emphasis in original.

[30] See, for example, the symbolic actions in Ezek 4–5, where the prophet performs cryptic dramas, but the text immediately gives interpretations for the actions. In chapter 5, Ezekiel shaves off all of his hair and performs various actions on it (5:1–4). The text then explains how these actions represent different aspects of God's judgment against Jerusalem (5:5–12).

[31] Michael Rymer, *Battlestar Galactica: Miniseries*, December 8, 2003, Sci-Fi.

genocide. He sees another version of Number Six,[32] bruised and battered, wearing only a canvas sack, lying half-consciously on the floor. Immediately the viewer sees the intense pain and horror on Baltar's face as he witnesses a version of the woman with whom he fell in love lying on the cold cell floor. The viewer sees the phantom Number Six's rage, horror, and deep sadness as she witnesses a mirror of herself lying on the floor, clearly abused. In order to escape the torment, Baltar shifts from sheer terror and grief to analytical detachment as he begins to diagnose the helpless Cylon. The phantom Number Six calls him back to hear the abused Cylon's testimony: "Can't you stop being a scientist for one moment and look at the abused woman lying in front of you?"[33]

Feminist critics of the Bible have been asking this question for decades. Phyllis Trible's classic *Texts of Terror* served as a clarion call to hear the testimony of the tortured women in the biblical texts, as she memorialized Hagar, Tamar, the Levite's concubine, and Jepthah's daughter, all women terrorized by their position in a patriarchal society and narrative.[34] Renita J. Weems continued this tradition, turning her analysis to the theme of battered love and the metaphor of the promiscuous woman in the theology of the Hebrew prophets.[35] Many feminist responses to such texts of terror have followed suit, critiquing the Bible's creation of a feminine trope that has served to both testify to an ancient patriarchal system and perpetuate its biases against women as evil personified. These readings of scripture have freed the tortured woman's voice to call from the pages of the biblical text and confront a history of patriarchal readings.

Gale Yee, informed by both the realization of patriarchy and the extension of that hierarchical world into the colonization of ancient Israel and Judah, has highlighted the prophetic motif of the tortured woman as an expression of postcolonial trauma in the pornographic passage in Ezekiel 23.[36] Yee traces this theme of woman as evil throughout the Hebrew Bible. The motif has remained prominent in theological traditions, and these texts have continued to be used in certain circles to highlight the moral superiority of "valiant" men over prurient women.

One might compare the evil seductress Cylon in *Battlestar Galactica* to Nineveh, the evil seductress in Nahum 3.[37] By using this trope, the prophet dehumanizes agents of the

---

[32] Number Six is a Cylon, a cybernetic but organic being. In the reimagined series, there are twelve Cylon models with multiple copies throughout the galaxy. A phantom version of Number Six haunts Baltar. He is the only one who can see this version of the Cylon, and he has many conversations with her through the course of the series.

[33] Michael Rymer, *Battlestar Galactica*, season 2, episode 10, "Pegasus," September 23, 2005, Sci-Fi.

[34] Phyllis Trible, *Texts of Terror: Literary-Feminist Readings of Biblical Narratives*, Overtures to Biblical Theology (Philadelphia, PA: Fortress Press, 1984).

[35] Renita J. Weems, *Battered Love: Marriage, Sex, and Violence in the Hebrew Prophets*, Overtures to Biblical Theology (Minneapolis, MN: Fortress Press, 1995).

[36] Gale A. Yee, *Poor Banished Children of Eve: Woman as Evil in the Hebrew Bible* (Minneapolis, MN: Fortress Press, 2003), 111–34.

[37] The Hebrew Bible frequently employs the metaphor of a promiscuous woman for either a nation or a city. In most uses outside the book of Nahum, the metaphor points inward to refer the nation of Israel (e.g., Hosea 1–3) or the cities of Samaria and Jerusalem (e.g., Ezek 16 and 23). Ezekiel contains particularly graphic and violent imagery to describe Jerusalem's sinfulness and the punishment God metes out upon her. I have chosen Nah 3 as the intertext here because it is the primary text that

historical Assyrian Empire, personifying its capital city, Nineveh, as a harlot. In the patriarchal framework of this text, the traditional role of a woman is to remain submissive, under the authority of her husband or father and outside the realm of geopolitics. Nahum capitalizes on this patriarchal perspective of women to characterize Assyria as the reverse of this type of "good" woman. In the process, Nahum 3 plays to a male audience's vengeance fantasy by describing in detail the woman Nineveh's public and scandalous humiliation.

Nahum 3 begins in the realm of the literal acts of war before moving into the metaphorical equation of war with uncontrolled feminine sexuality:

Ah, city of crime, utterly treacherous, full of violence, where killing never stops!
Crack of whip and rattle of wheel, galloping steed and bounding chariot!
Charging horsemen, flashing swords, and glittering spears!
Hosts of slain and heaps of corpses, dead bodies without number—they stumble over bodies (Nah 3:1–3).

The prophet portrays an imperial army that has left heaps of the slain in its wake and that is about to suffer the same fate. This cry is one of vengeance, testifying to the grand horror that Nineveh has caused the people of Israel and Judah. While this depiction of Nineveh perhaps contains some embellishment, it stands as significant testimony to the ancient Israelites' embattlement with this great enemy and their subsequent vengeance fantasy. According to J. J. M. Roberts, "From Sennacherib's devastating campaign against Judah in 701 B.C. down to the revolt of Babylon against Ashurbanipal...Assyria's domination of Judah was harsh and relatively thorough."[38] Nahum declares that Nineveh's punishment will come because she has become a "gracefully alluring, mistress of sorcery, who enslaves nations through her debaucheries, and peoples through her sorcery" (Nah 3:4). By comparing Nineveh to a prostitute, the prophet has made her, as Francisco Garcia-Treto recognizes, a "quasi-demonic figure," the antithesis of the good or controllable woman.[39]

Moreover, and perhaps more dangerously, the text moves from this standpoint toward a metaphorical fantasy of vengeful torture that YHWH will enact against personified Nineveh: "I am against you, says the LORD of hosts, and will lift up your skirts over your face; and I will let nations look on your nakedness and kingdoms on your shame. I will throw filth at you and treat you with contempt, and make you a spectacle"

describes Israel's enemy as such a seductress and is more closely parallel to the use of seductive imagery in *Battlestar Galactica* to portray the conquering threat of the Cylons. The promiscuous woman imagery extends into the New Testament as well in Rev 17–18 in reference to the whore of Babylon. Interestingly, Ronald D. Moore, the executive producer of the reimagined *Battlestar Galactica* series, was also a writer on an episode of the HBO series *Carnivàle* in which the primary antagonist of the series, Reverend Crowe, drones a reading of Rev 18:2a and 18:9–10 as a narrative framework for the episode that details the rape and murder of a prostitute who is a member of the traveling carnival. Tim Hunter, *Carnivàle*, season 1, episode 5, "Babylon," October 12, 2003, HBO.

[38] J. J. M. Roberts, *Nahum, Habakkuk, and Zephaniah: A Commentary*, Old Testament Library (Louisville, KY: Westminster/John Knox Press, 1991), 38.

[39] Francisco Garcia-Treto, "The Book of Nahum," in *The New Interpreter's Bible*, 12 vols., vol. 7, ed. Leander E. Keck (Nashville, TN: Abingdon Press, 1996), 614.

(Nah 3:5–6). The judgment takes the form of a male fantasy of abuse and torture against the wanton woman. Nahum 3:7 describes the shame as follows: "Then all who see you will shrink from you and say, 'Nineveh is devastated; who will bemoan her? Where shall I seek comforters for you?'"

Just as Nahum provides a prophetic critique of the evil empire of Nineveh, the "reimagined" *Battlestar Galactica* series does not flinch from asking prophetic questions about imperialism, acts of war and terror, and the rights of the military to torture individuals for the sake of saving "humanity." During their evolution, many of the Cylons have become hypersexualized women who serve overt seductress roles in the battles that ensue. The primary evil seductress of the *Battlestar Galactica* narrative enters the scene from the very beginning of the series, which is set in a time of peace, after the first Cylon war ended in a truce forty years earlier. In the forty-year interim between conflicts, the humans have sent an ambassador to a space station built specifically to maintain human and Cylon relations, while the Cylons have sent none. In this first scene, the aging male ambassador dutifully places a picture of his wife and child (signifying the norm of the "good" woman) on the desk and waits, not expecting a Cylon emissary to arrive. When the door opens, the now organic Cylon character central to the entire series, Number Six, saunters into the room to begin "negotiations." The link between hypersexual seduction and violent intentions is immediately obvious as Number Six initiates a sexual encounter with the male ambassador, demanding that the aging man prove he is alive.[40] As Number Six initiates foreplay, the Cylon ship outside the space station levies an attack upon it, seemingly destroying both human and Cylon and initiating the final assault on humanity. The female Cylon pauses and ominously announces, "It has begun," before resuming her sexual advance. In this moment of uncontrolled feminine sexuality she literally sucks the life out of the human male as he breathes his last breath.[41]

At this point in the narrative, the Cylon model has only a number, no name. She is Cylon Number Six, a representation of modern male Western fantasy of beauty, whose primary objective includes seducing Gaius Baltar, an exceedingly ambitious and self-absorbed human scientist, so that she can gain access to the human defense network and render it useless against a Cylon attack. These opening scenes of the series take great pains to paint Number Six as a monster, leaving no doubt in the viewers' mind that it was she who initiated the near genocide of the entire human race. In an act of cyber-warfare, Number Six shuts down all human defense systems. This act of literal seduction in the series allows for the Cylon attack, resulting in the near genocide of humanity, sending a

---

[40] This scene and the plot that develops after it recalls the biblical trope of fearing the foreign woman found throughout the biblical tradition, but particularly in the book of Proverbs (e.g., 5:3–14). In fact, prior to the seduction the human male figure places photographs of his wife and family on the table in an effort to contrast the proper woman with Number Six's role as a seductress. For further reading on the biblical motif of the strange woman, see Gail Corrington Streete, *The Strange Woman: Power and Sex in the Hebrew Bible* (Louisville, KY: Westminster John Knox Press, 1997).

[41] *Battlestar Galactica: Miniseries.*

small fleet of fifty thousand survivors on the run with their only protection being the *Battlestar Galactica*.

The structure of this exodus narrative provides a framework in which the players constantly ask the question of what it means to be human. Viewers and members of the *Galactica* crew have learned, through many incidents, the desire of the Cylons to become more human, much like humans in the primeval history in Genesis 1–11 who consistently push the boundaries between humanity and divinity. Moreover, the humans in the series constantly debate about how to refer to these beings. Do they use gendered pronouns to refer to "her" or "him," or do they use the gender-neutral but dehumanizing "it"? Do they call them unnamed machines, or do they consistently call them by the human names with which they first encounter them? Throughout the series the viewer also learns that, besides the annihilation of the human race, one of the primary motivations of the Cylons is the search for their own humanity, desiring what it means to know love, to reproduce as humans do, and to find God.

This question of defining humanity comes into direct focus in the episodes "Pegasus" and "Resurrection Ship," when the fleet is surprised by the appearance of another surviving Battlestar named *Pegasus*, led by the very stern female officer Admiral Cain. Rumors of Cain's brutality and cool calculations immediately surface, bringing the question of humanity and survival to the forefront. If the prime motive of the protagonists is the saving of humanity, the show constantly asks the question, is humanity worth saving at all?

The question of the humanity of both humans and Cylons comes to the fore when Admiral Adama and Cain discuss the Cylon prisoners that each has on board their ships. Adama's prisoner is model Number Eight, whose human name is Sharon Valleri. As a "sleeper agent," Sharon infiltrated the *Galactica*'s ranks as a pilot before the genocidal attack. She is literally identified as a ticking time bomb—her pilot call sign is "Boomer"—and as she awakens to her Cylon identity she attempts to assassinate Commander Adama early in the series. Now, several episodes later, Sharon has moved into a position of remorse, solidified by her romantic relationship with a human fighter pilot that results in the birth of a human-Cylon hybrid child. In Commander Adama's brig she is treated humanely, allowed visits with her human love interest, and in return gives much information on Cylon strategy and intelligence, sometimes entering the battle against the Cylons to protect her lover and child.

Her counterpart prisoner on the *Pegasus* is a cloned version of Number Six, whose human identity is Gina. Gina does not receive the same kind of treatment on the *Pegasus*. Instead, she lies brutalized by her interrogators, who beat and rape her. The contrast in attitudes between the two crews is obvious in their very language when referring to the Cylons. On *Galactica*, Sharon is referred to by her human name or by the feminine singular pronouns "she" and "her." In contrast, Gina (Number Six) is referred to only by the impersonal terms "prisoner" and "it."[42]

---

[42] This fact is not lost on Adama in his discussions with Admiral Cain, who astutely breaks his habit of humanization and refers to Sharon as "the prisoner" or "it." In one scene, Cain considers Gina a dog, asking Baltar if he can get "it" to "sit," "roll over," or "play dead."

In the process of combining resources, Cain ironically recruits Gaius Baltar, who, through his own subtle machinations, has hidden his role in the initial genocide and become the prime adviser for Cylon intelligence on the *Galactica*, to give his advice on the *Pegasus* interrogation techniques. Baltar comes face to face with the tortured version of the woman with whom he fell in love before the initial attacks. Throughout the series, the only version of this woman that he has seen has been a mental projection of her that he believes is an expression of his unconscious desire. For the first time since the attacks, he now sees her "in the flesh," but instead of the epitome of Western beauty, Baltar witnesses a tortured and bruised Cylon who bears a resemblance to his initial obsession but who has clearly been traumatized by her experiences on board the *Pegasus*. She is still scantily clad, but now instead of designer clothes, she wears a canvas sack. Baltar asks for some privacy to analyze the prisoner and is left in the room with two versions of his lover: the phantom Number Six and Gina, who lies on the floor, unable to speak or move.

While Baltar convinces Cain to allow him to use "the carrot" to entice Gina into cooperation, Cain decides it is time to send her inquisitor, Lieutenant Thorne, to use "the stick" to coerce information from Sharon, Number Eight. In the midst of an attempted rape scene, two members of the *Galactica* crew (both of whom have been in love with Sharon), rescue her from Thorne, killing him in the process, and are sentenced to death by Cain. As Adama attempts to defend his crew members, he says they were defending Sharon from an attempted rape, at which Cain's Executive Officer Fisk asks the audience and all the players, "Can you rape a machine?" Fisk's question functions almost like the final question in the book of Jonah, the oft-cited countertext to the theology of Nahum.[43] If the viewer sympathizes with the plight of Sharon and Gina, then Gina and Sharon are no longer machines. Perhaps it is their very experience of trauma and their questioning of human motivations that has rendered them human.

The narrative of *Battlestar Galactica* surrounding the humanity of these women Cylons carries on the prophetic tradition of speaking truth to power in several ways. First, by humanizing the seductress Cylon (Number Six) and the sleeper agent Cylon (Sharon Valeri), the creators of the show are asking audience members to consider their own culture's portrayal of women as seductresses, as well as the human tendency to dehumanize military enemies. Just as the historical context of the book of Nahum plays a significant role in interpreting the original historical purpose of the trope to vilify Nineveh for its oppression of Israel and Judah, the historical context of the production of *Battlestar Galactica* gives a backdrop for the questions it poses to its audience. The episode considering the torture of two Cylon women aired on September 23, 2005, dur-

---

[43] After Jonah laments that he is angry enough to die when God sends a worm to destroy his shade bush, God challenges Jonah with the following speech: "You are concerned about the bush, for which you did not labor and which you did not grow; it came into being in a night and perished in a night. And should I not be concerned about Nineveh, that great city, in which there are more than a hundred and twenty thousand persons who do not know their right hand from their left, and also many animals?" (Jon 4:10–11). Posing the question at the end of the book invites readers to identify with Jonah and consider for themselves the humanity of the Ninevites.

ing the U.S.-Iraq War, a time in which the question of the use of torture of military prisoners was at the forefront of American consciousness. While the episodes did not conclude the argument, the powerful portrayals of the two women Cylons asked its audience to consider the humanity of enemies in much the same way that the book of Jonah, with its emphasis on the penitent Ninevites, challenges the more vengeful perspective of the book of Nahum. The series also speaks truth to the powerful reception history of women figures in religious literature as seductresses by focusing on their human characteristics, filling out their characters' motivations, and by the simple act of giving them names.

Placing popular culture's use of prophetic motifs in conversation with biblical traditions of prophecies enlightens our understandings of both modern and ancient literature. The persistence of biblical prophetic character types in popular culture highlights the human fascination with public figures that seem to have access to other-worldly wisdom and warnings. These characters from both eras remain mysterious and enigmatic. Despite their mystery, these charismatic individuals and their omens drive both biblical and contemporary narratives forward. The history of reception of the prophetic tradition, however, has sometimes reduced the function of prophecy to a purely fulfillment-driven function, rendering it a quite useful trope for popular authors and creators to drive their narratives forward, while also using the transcendent and cryptic qualities of prophecy to keep the mysteries and tensions alive, hooking their audiences into continued engagement with their media. Sometimes, and perhaps increasingly more often, creators have adopted the social function of prophecy to offer words of truth to power in both entertaining and palatable ways. At times, such as with the reimagined *Battlestar Galactica* series, they use their platform to critique the effects of biblical traditions themselves.

FUTURE PROSPECTS AND QUESTIONS

- Prophets and prophecy may be even more ubiquitous in contemporary popular culture than in the Bible. This chapter limited the scope of prophets and prophecy in popular culture to the genres of fantasy and science fiction that appear in cinema or television (though notably absent are the Harry Potter series by J. K. Rowling and subsequent movies). Even within the realm of cinema, genres could extend to include drama, the superhero genre, horror, detective mysteries, and more.
- When it comes to the third category of popular culture performing a prophetic function,[44] genre boundaries may greatly expand to include athletes, from Jackie

---

[44] See, for example, Terry Ray Clark's essay on how graphic novels function as a prophetic voice in contemporary culture: "Prophetic Voices in Graphic Novels: The 'Comic and Tragic Vision' of Apocalyptic Rhetoric in *Kingdom Come* and *Watchmen*," in *The Bible in/and Popular Culture: A Creative Encounter*, ed. Elaine M. Wainwright and Philip Culbertson, Semeia Studies, 65 (Atlanta, GA: Society of Biblical Literature, 2010), 141–56.

Robinson to Muhammad Ali, and more currently Colin Kaepernick, Serena Williams, and LeBron James. Future work may investigate the impact these athletes and their seemingly superhuman abilities have on social and political conversations.

- Like athletes, musicians tend to fall in a culturally liminal space due to their talent and influence. One might explore how Billie Holiday's performance of "Strange Fruit" functions as a contemporary prophetic lament akin to the traditions found in the book of Jeremiah. One could compare Lady Gaga's dramatic acts, Bob Dylan's folk poetry, Bono's activism, and Kendrick Lamar's rhetorical structure to those of the prophetic writings while also addressing the social visions, both ancient and modern.

- Music, cinema, and television, like prophetic works, are very fluid in terms of genre and historical reference. Lyrics may refer to a particular moment or figure in sports history. A film or television episode might use a particular musical piece in its soundtrack, transforming its message to fit the context and message of the film. One might ask, for example, how *The Matrix Trilogy* employs the music of Rage Against the Machine, and from an intertextual perspective address how each medium transforms the prophetic message of the other.

- The primary examples in this chapter explored the relationship between the Bible *and* popular culture, and I made a conscious decision not to include direct and intentional re-creations of biblical traditions *in* popular culture.[45] Such explorations that could be made range from comedic representations (e.g., Monty Python's *Life of Brian*) and period pieces (*The Ten Commandments; Exodus: Gods and Kings; The Bible; Of Kings and Prophets*) to biblical narratives retold in a modern context (the NBC one-season series *Kings*).[46] Comparisons of the ways in which, for example, *Kings, The Bible,* and *Of Kings and Prophets* treat prophetic characters such as Samuel and their function could further reveal how mainstream culture has received and understands the prophetic tradition.

SUGGESTED READINGS AND ANNOTATED BIBLIOGRAPHY

Davis, Ellen F. *Biblical Prophecy.* Louisville, KY: Westminster John Knox Press, 2014.

Davis explores the functions of prophecy and the prophetic literature in its ancient context while also suggesting implications for interpreting the prophets in light of current global

[45] Bruce David Forbes and Jeffrey H. Mahan divide their study of religion and American popular culture into four relationships: "religion in popular culture," "popular culture in religion," "popular culture as religion," and "religion and popular culture in dialogue." This suggestion for further study falls into the first category. See Bruce David Forbes, "Introduction: Finding Religion in Unexpected Places," in *Religion and Popular Culture in America, 3rd ed.,* ed. Bruce David Forbes and Jeffrey H. Mahan (Oakland: University of California Press, 2017), 1–24, especially 11–21.

[46] *The Life of Brian,* directed by Terry Jones, UK, Handmade Films and Python, 1979; *The Ten Commandments,* directed by Cecil B. DeMille, USA, Paramount Pictures, 1956; *Exodus: Of Gods and Kings,* directed by Ridley Scott,. USA, 20th Century Fox, 2014; *The Bible,* USA, LightWorkers Media, 2013; *Of Kings and Prophets,* USA, ABC Studios, 2016; *Kings,* USA, NBC, 2009.

circumstances. While she writes for Christian ministers and scholars, she gleans from other faith traditions, demonstrating a clear knowledge of Jewish tradition surrounding the biblical prophets while also confessing Jesus as the "last and greatest of the prophets" (19). Her work is extremely helpful, therefore, for investigating the Christian inheritance of the Hebrew Bible's prophetic tradition and its influence on Western culture in general.

Heschel, Abraham J. *The Prophets: An Introduction*. New York: Harper & Row, 2001.

Heschel's work on the prophets, first published in two volumes in 1962, is now considered a classic among many who study the prophets. Perhaps because of his ties to Martin Luther King Jr. and the civil rights movement in the United States, Heschel's emphasis on the prophets' messages of social justice and God's pathos for the oppressed has permeated thoughts on prophecy in both religious and secular culture.

Petersen, David L. *The Prophetic Literature: An Introduction*. Louisville, KY: Westminster John Knox Press, 2002.

As its title implies, Petersen's work offers an introduction to the prophetic tradition in the Hebrew Bible. He begins by discussing the historical and cultural context of prophets within the ancient Near East before offering commentary on each of the writing prophets. He concludes with some analyses of prophetic characters in the Pentateuch, the historical books, and writings of the Hebrew Bible.

Wetmore, Kevin J. *The Theology of* Battlestar Galactica: *American Christianity in the 2004–2009 Television Series*. Jefferson, NC: McFarland, 2012.

Wetmore identifies *Battlestar Galactica* as a theologically significant narrative. While he does not suggest that the series is a Christian narrative, he analyzes its wide range of religious expressions—atheism, fundamentalism, monotheism, and polytheism—as a reflection of a predominantly Christian culture. Chapter 7, "The Role of the Prophets," draws heavily on Heschel's framework, identifying several prophetic figures in *Battlestar Galactica*: the characters of Starbuck, Leoben Conoy (Two), D'Anna Biers (Three), Laura Roslin, Gaius Baltar, the Hybrids, and Caprica Six.

Yee, Gale A. *Poor Banished Children of Eve: Woman as Evil in the Hebrew Bible*. Minneapolis, MN: Fortress Press, 2003.

Yee uses ideological, social scientific, and literary analyses to explore the motif of woman as evil in the Hebrew Bible. She considers women figures in Genesis, Hosea, Ezekiel, and Proverbs and the impact these traditions have on perceptions of gender in Western culture. Of particular importance for the study of the reception history of prophetic motifs are her insights into how Hosea and Ezekiel offer a socioeconomic critique of colonialism while simultaneously perpetuating gender stereotypes that still affect Western culture's perception of the feminine.

CHAPTER 11

··

SCENES FROM THE END OF THE WORLD IN AMERICAN POPULAR CULTURE

··

SHAYNA SHEINFELD
SHEFFIELD INSTITUTE FOR INTERDISCIPLINARY
BIBLICAL STUDIES, THE UNIVERSITY
OF SHEFFIELD

INTRODUCTION

APOCALYPTIC and postapocalyptic movies, television series, literature, and art are currently at an all-time high in popularity. A tentative count of English-language movies between 2014 and 2019 that feature the end-time scenarios registers around seventy films, including *This Is the End* (2013), *The Book of Eli* (2010), *Legion* (2010), and even *Thor: Ragnarok* (2017), the superhero movie based on the Norse apocalypse.[1] Recent television series such as *Supernatural* (2005–2020), *The Walking Dead* (2010–), *The 100* (2014–8), and *The Leftovers* (2014–7) all also play on apocalyptic themes, as do recent novels such as *Good Omens* (Terry Pratchett and Neil Gaiman, 1990; Amazon Prime television series, 2019), *Station Eleven* (Emily St. John Mandel, 2015), and *When the English Fall* (David Williams, 2017), an apocalyptic scenario from the Amish perspective.[2] While the type of apocalypse in popular culture varies wildly—and at times is not stated at all (e.g., Cormac McCarthy's 2006 novel, *The Road*)—many utilize themes and imagery drawn directly from the biblical apocalypses, while others appropriate extra-

---

[1] See "List of Apocalyptic Films," Wikipedia, accessed November 13, 2017, https://en.wikipedia.org/wiki/List_of_apocalyptic_films#2010.E2.80.932019.

[2] For more on *The Leftovers*, see Tina Pippin's chapter in this volume.

biblical tropes for their interpretation of the apocalyptic events portrayed in their storyline.

When we talk about apocalyptic literature in the biblical canon, we are referring specifically to two texts: the book of Daniel in the Hebrew Bible (Old Testament) and the Revelation to John, which is also called the Apocalypse of John, in the New Testament; both titles are frequently shortened to Revelation or the Apocalypse (with a capital "A"). Contemporary US vernacular often refers to this text in the plural ("Revelations"), but this is a misnomer. While I will discuss both of these texts further, it is essential to establish at the beginning that while both Daniel and Revelation are the only canonical apocalypses, they were both influenced by and influenced other apocalyptic literature and the worldview called apocalypticism that are not present in the canon.[3] It will be important to at least be aware of the apocalyptic worldviews of some early Jews and Christians beyond the biblical texts since they influence the afterlives of the biblical worldview in popular culture today.

In addition to the explicit apocalypses found in the canonical Bible, other narratives from the biblical text lend themselves to the reimagining of apocalypse in popular culture. Especially prevalent in contemporary popular culture is the retelling of the flood narrative from Genesis 6–9. In Genesis 6 God regrets making humans and decides to unmake and then remake creation through a worldwide flood. However, God chooses to save Noah, the only man "righteous in his generation" (Gen 6:9; 7:1), along with his family and all the animals and birds.[4] Especially in the contemporary period, when environmental concerns are well-publicized and climate change is discussed at a national and international level, the idea of a worldwide natural catastrophe has an appeal as the premise for environmental apocalypse.[5]

OVERVIEW OF THE TOPIC

Definitions and Methodological Issues

This section briefly addresses the difficulties of defining popular culture, as well as the approach this chapter takes. Following this discussion, the chapter considers how issues

---

[3] See, for instance, *1 Enoch*, a text that is canonical in the Ethiopic Church. Of particular influence was *1 Enoch* 1–36, also called the Book of the Watchers. For an accessible translation of this text, see G. W. E. Nickelsburg and J. C. VanderKam, *1 Enoch: A New Translation, Based on the Hermeneia Commentary* (Minneapolis, MN: Fortress Press, 2004). In addition, other portions of the Jewish and Christian canons are considered by many scholars to have some apocalyptic themes, even if they are not considered apocalyptic in terms of genre. See, for instance, Isa 33, Matt 24, Mark 13, 1 Thess.

[4] All biblical quotations are taken from the New Revised Standard Version.

[5] For a recent discussion on climate change and the Bible, see Frances Flannery, "Senators, Snowballs, and Scripture: The Bible and Climate Change," in *The Bible in Political Debate*, ed. Frances Flannery and Rodney A. Werline (New York: Bloomsbury T & T Clark, 2016), 61–73.

around terms and definitions of apocalypse, apocalyptic, and apocalypticism relate to the canonical material and our analysis of apocalyptic in popular culture.

Popular Culture

While many people assume they know what is meant by "popular culture," developing a definition is challenging. Some difficulty arises in the fact that the words "popular" and "culture" are not easily definable. For the purposes of this essay we will consider popular culture to be mainstream materials (e.g., texts, literature, film, music), rituals and practices, and ideas that are widely accessible to an extensive variety of people through a shared and complex system.[6] While still a problematic definition, my hope is that this working definition attempts to explicitly avoid creating an obvious "absent other,"[7] which John Storey argues is assumed in nearly every definition of popular culture.

Apocalypse, Apocalyptic, Apocalypticism

Contemporary portrayals of apocalypses in popular culture differ from the ancient apocalypses found in both the canonical (Daniel, Revelation) and noncanonical texts. Some scholars have referred to parts of the prophetic literature as proto-apocalyptic, although this is not general among scholars as the prophetic literature serves a different function.[8] Other portions of texts, such as Mark 13, which is referred to in scholarship as the "little apocalypse," are thought to contain strongly apocalyptic narratives and ideology. The problem is that it is often not clear what scholars mean when they use the language of "apocalypse" and "apocalyptic."[9] Also at stake is that while Daniel and Revelation are the most well-known apocalypses because of their canonical status, myriad other Jewish and Christian texts from this period that were not canonized can also be categorized as apocalypses. Add to that the apocalyptic sectarian literature produced by such groups as the Dead Sea Scrolls community, and the problems of what it is we mean when we talk about "apocalypses" or as something being "apocalyptic" become even more evident.[10]

It thus became essential to establish a base definition. According to John J. Collins, "apocalypse" can be defined as "a genre of revelatory literature with a narrative framework, in which a revelation is mediated by an otherworldly being to a human recipient, disclosing a transcendent reality which is both temporal insofar as it envisages eschatological salvation, and spatial insofar as it involves another, supernatural world."[11]

---

[6] For more discussion on the complex definitions of culture and popular culture, see John Storey, *Cultural Theory and Popular Culture: An Introduction*, 6th ed. (New York: Pearson, 2012), especially the first chapter.

[7] Ibid., 13.

[8] See, e.g., Michael Stone, *Scriptures, Sects, and Visions* (Philadelphia, PA: Fortress Press, 1980); Dereck Daschke, *City of Ruins: Mourning the Destruction of Jerusalem through Jewish Apocalypse* (Leiden: Brill, 2010).

[9] John J. Collins, *The Apocalyptic Imagination: An Introduction to Jewish Apocalyptic Literature*, 3rd ed. (Grand Rapids, MI: Eerdmans, 2016), 2.

[10] Most scholars associate this group with a sect of Judaism called the Essenes.

[11] Collins, *Apocalyptic Imagination*, 5.

Collins's definition, developed in conjunction with the Society of Biblical Literature Genres Project, was published originally in 1979 and has served as the foundation upon which subsequent studies in the field of ancient apocalypses have built.[12] This definition provided a point of departure for the study of apocalyptic literature in the ancient world; before this definition, the noun "apocalypse" and the adjective "apocalyptic" had been used within scholarship without any consistency from scholar to scholar.[13]

Collins's definition breaks down the genre of apocalypse into identifiable pieces. First, to call a text an apocalypse, it must be (1) a narrative that includes (2) revelation to (3) a human recipient through (4) an otherworldly being. This revelation must include some reflection on (5) salvation at the end times and on (6) God, angels, demons, heaven, hell, or other parts of the supernatural world. As one can see, this definition, while complex, would make it fairly painless to determine if a text in antiquity qualifies as an apocalypse. It does not, however, take into account texts that might qualify as "apocalyptic" because they reflect an "apocalyptic" ideology or contain some of the characteristics in Collins's definition but may not be formally apocalypses—such as Mark 13 and some of the Dead Sea Scrolls.

Collins's definition has been essential for the academic study of ancient apocalypses. However, while the definition is useful, it is meant to serve as a generic framework that guides scholars and students in the analysis of these ancient texts rather than to serve as a set of boxes that need to be checked in order to qualify a text as apocalypse. The definition is strictly a definition of genre and does not attempt to identify or explain the function or social settings of the ancient apocalypses.

The definition has not been without its critics.[14] For one, and most useful for our analysis here, Lorenzo DiTommaso soundly rejects the focus on the genre of apocalypse for the study of (ancient) apocalypses, and instead pushes for a focus on the worldview of apocalypticism as a starting point; he also rejects the focus on only those apocalypses found in antiquity. Instead his analysis attempts to develop an approach that considers that apocalypticism is a worldview that has had followers from *at least* as early as the earliest extant apocalyptic text (circa third century BCE) and can be found not only in ancient literature but also throughout history and different cultures, including in contemporary popular culture. DiTommaso defines apocalypticism as "a worldview, a fundamental cognitive orientation that makes axiomatic claims about time, space, and human existence."[15] This category, he argues, covers all different kinds of media, as

---

[12] John J. Collins, ed., *Semeia 14: Apocalypse, the Morphology of a Genre* (Atlanta, GA: Society of Biblical Literature, 1979).

[13] "Apocalyptic" is often used as a noun, especially in continental scholarship.

[14] For instance, see Stephen L. Cook's discussion of the problem of definition and his critique of Collins's definition in *Prophecy and Apocalypticism: The Postexilic Social Setting* (Minneapolis, MN: Augsburg Fortress, 1995), 20–35.

[15] Lorenzo DiTommaso, "Apocalypticism and Popular Culture," in *Oxford Handbook of Apocalyptic Literature*, ed. John J. Collins (Oxford: Oxford University Press, 2014), 473–509, here 474.

"[apocalypticism] is the message, not the medium."[16] DiTommaso further explains that apocalypticism

> presumes the existence of a transcendent reality, which defines the cosmos and everything in it, but remains almost entirely concealed from observation and beyond the grasp of human intellection. It contends that the present reality is constitutionally structured by two antagonistic and irreducible forces, which are typically identified with good and evil. It maintains that a final resolution of the conflict between these forces is both necessary and imminent, and that it is also redemptive, in the sense of a deliverance from the present reality. The apocalyptic worldview further assumes that the revelation of these mysteries orients existence, and gives life meaning and purpose. Together, these propositions describe an *apocalyptic minimum*, which distinguishes apocalypticism from prophecy, mysticism, divination, and other phenomena, and by which cultural expressions and social movements throughout history may be identified as apocalyptic, including those in the realm of popular culture.[17]

While Collins's definition is more useful for an analysis of the ancient Jewish and Christian apocalypses, DiTommaso's approach provides a more constructive and comprehensive definition for thinking about apocalypticism in popular culture. However, DiTommaso's definition is also limiting in its own way, as the production of popular culture labeled "apocalyptic" has exploded in the past couple of decades. With this explosion of movies, books, graphic novels, and more there has also been a turn away from the explicit dualism found in earlier works inspired by ancient apocalypticism. In fact, there has been a turn toward secular—and especially environmental—representations of apocalypses that still draw on biblical narratives that are not explicitly apocalyptic in either Collins's or DiTommaso's sense, but instead focus on eschatology and the recovery of a remnant from the events at the end time. The majority of examples of this new, secular approach, while still often relying on biblical themes, narratives, and tropes, usually hold strongly to the hope of the future, that postapocalyptic time, even if the stories themselves do not extend into this future.

Next I give a basic description of the two biblical apocalypses as well as the flood narrative from Genesis that are frequently used and adapted in contemporary apocalyptic movies and books and other forms of popular culture. This foundation will allow us to examine several examples of apocalyptic motifs in contemporary popular culture that draw on both the canonical apocalypses and the other narratives.

Overview of the Canonical Apocalypses

The canonical apocalypses of Daniel and Revelation are the most well known of the ancient apocalypses, and they have certainly had the largest influence on apocalyptic

---

[16] Ibid.   [17] Ibid.

narrative in contemporary culture, including popular culture, whether or not those portrayals are purportedly religious in nature. The rest of this section provides an overview of the books of Daniel and Revelation.

Daniel

The book of Daniel can logically be divided into two parts: chapters 1–6 are tales of Daniel and his three friends in the Babylonian court during the exile (586–39 BCE) in Babylon.[18] Chapters 7–12, with the exception of chapter 9, are three apocalypses that star Daniel as the human recipient.[19] The court tales all feature Daniel and friends remaining faithful to the Jewish God and to Torah even while faced with life-and-death situations in the polytheistic diaspora; each chapter has another situation wherein the protagonist(s) should die but manage to live and thrive due to their piety. Perhaps of greatest note in the court tales with regard to the apocalyptic elements later in the book are chapters 2, 4, and 5, where Daniel is able to understand and interpret the supernatural due to his faithfulness to God. The change is dramatic, then, when the audience reads chapter 7 and Daniel suddenly is unable to interpret his own dream and requires an angelic interpreter to explain things to him.

Chapters 7, 8, and 10–12 each constitute a distinct apocalypse[20] and in general meet the requirements laid out by Collins's definition. Of particular note is the vision of the four beasts rising from the sea (Dan 7:2–8), a traditional motif that represents earthly kingdoms (cf. Dan 2), which are judged by the "Ancient of Days"—that is, God—and followed by "one like a son of man coming with the clouds of heaven" (7:13). Since "one like a son of man" is coded language, as is most apocalyptic language, the interpretation of this figure is flexible. While this son of man likely refers to an angelic being, some later interpreters, including some early Christians, understood the "son of man" reference here in Daniel and other apocalyptic literature to refer to a messiah figure or Jesus.[21] Daniel's visions, along with those found in the book of Revelation, are commonly used by American evangelicals, such as in the popular *Left Behind* novels and movies.[22]

[18] "Court tales," like "apocalypse" is a genre of ancient literature that one finds in other biblical and apocryphal narratives as well as other Ancient Near Eastern texts. For a comparative look at Daniel's court tales, see Tawny L. Holm, *Of Courtiers and Kings: The Biblical Daniel Narratives and Ancient Story-Collections* (University Park, PA: Penn State University Press, 2013).

[19] While chapters 1–6 and 7–12 split nicely in terms of genre, the original languages of these chapters are messier. Chapters 1 and 8–12 are preserved in Hebrew, while chapters 2–7 are written in Aramaic. See Collins, *Apocalyptic Imagination*, 110–13.

[20] Daniel 9 is an interpretation of Jeremiah's prophecy of seventy weeks (Jer 25:11–12; 29:10) and a prayer following standard Deuteronomic theology which is in contrast to the predetermined nature of apocalyptic theology. See Collins, *Apocalyptic Imagination*, 134–6.

[21] See, for instance, the "little apocalypse" in Mark 13, which predicts that, after a cosmic upheaval, "the son of man [will be] coming in clouds with great power and glory" (13:26), where the reference, drawing clearly from Dan 7:13, seems to be a messianic title in the gospels. For more on this issue, see Collins, *Apocalyptic Imagination*, 126–30, 327–30; Shayna Sheinfeld, "Messianism," in *End of Days: An Encyclopedia of the Apocalypse in World Religions*, ed. Wendell G. Johnson (Santa Barbara, CA: ABC-CLIO, 2017), 236–9.

[22] For example, see Tim LaHaye and Jerry B. Jenkins, *Left Behind* series, a total of sixteen books (1995–2007; Tyndale House Publishers). The *Left Behind* series focuses on a premillennial eschatology,

Revelation

The book of Revelation contains one long revelation to an otherwise unknown John of Patmos, an island off the coast of Asia Minor in the Aegean Sea. John's revelation is of Jesus Christ, who uses John to send messages (Rev 2–3) and to spread his revelation of the end time to the seven churches in Asia Minor (4–22).[23] John's revelation is associated with two heavenly scrolls. The first has seven seals that when opened produce visions, trumpets, and catastrophes. The second—the "little scroll"—reflects more upon the social and political context that the author is critiquing. It views the Roman Empire as the major force of evil on the earth, and the author uses imagery from the book of Daniel (e.g., ch. 13) to show this. As with the book of Daniel, Revelation accepts a worldview that contains (1) the supernatural world—both good and bad—and (2) a focus on the end, when things reach their breaking point but are finally brought back to their rightful conclusion in the culmination of a new heaven and a new earth in chapter 21. Central to Revelation is, of course, the role that Jesus Christ plays, which is understandably lacking in other Jewish apocalypses, including the book of Daniel.

Daniel and Revelation are the two canonical examples of what apocalyptic looks like as biblical texts. Both the visual imagery and the ideas found within these two texts are prevalent in popular contemporary portrayals of the end of the world. Even lacking in the religious overtones or God-focus, most depictions of the end times in American pop culture in some way draw from the narratives, ideas, or themes found in the ancient Jewish and Christian apocalypses. Most important, their focus on eschatology—the end time—and the time after, when things are set right, is drawn out in contemporary portrayals.

The Flood Narrative: Genesis 6–9

With the rise of secularization and environmentalism, apocalyptic representations in contemporary pop culture have now shifted toward a secular, rather than religious, approach but still draw on biblical narratives, especially the flood narrative from Genesis 6–9. While this narrative does not meet Collins's or DiTommaso's definitions of an apocalypse or apocalypticism, the flood narrative certainly speaks about the end of the world as humans at that time knew it, and the aftermath that follows.

The flood narrative begins with God regretting having made humanity and deciding to destroy it, except for one person and his family: Noah, who, according to the text, is

---

which understands Christ's second coming as happening *before* a literal thousand-year period of peace but preceded by a time of great tribulation. This is in contrast to postmillennialism, which understands Christ's second coming as occurring *after* a thousand-year period. For more on the *Left Behind* series, see Tina Pippin's chapter in this volume.

[23] John of Patmos should not be considered the same John as the author of the Gospel of John or the Epistles of John.

righteous among his generation (Gen 6:9; 7:1). Noah follows God's instructions to build an ark that will house his family, representatives of all the animals and birds, and food to feed them all. God proceeds to partially undo creation as it is described in Genesis 1:6–9 by opening the fountains of the great deep and the windows of heaven (7:11). The world is thus cleansed by water, everything outside the ark destroyed by the water. God causes the water to recede, and eventually all the inhabitants of the ark—human and animal—exit to reestablish life on the earth (8:18–19). The flood, conceptually and literally, becomes a useful tool for secular and especially environmental representations of apocalyptic in pop culture.

Specific Examples and/or Foci

In this section I explore several examples of apocalyptic in popular culture. First I consider the novel *Good Omens* and the television series *Supernatural*, both of which draw directly from the book of Revelation. Next I consider two examples of apocalyptic in popular culture that use the flood narrative from Genesis 6–9. The first of these is Margaret Atwood's *MaddAddam* trilogy, which receives the most attention, followed by the secular environmental apocalyptic movie *2012*. These analyses highlight the shift in apocalyptic representation toward an environmental focus in contemporary popular culture.

Examples Drawing Directly from Biblical Apocalypses

Originally published in 1990, *Good Omens: The Nice and Accurate Prophecies of Agnes Nutter, Witch*, by Terry Pratchett and Neil Gaiman,[24] is a comedic telling of the end times, loosely based on the apocalyptic description in the book of Revelation and combined with other conceptions of the end times, such as the antichrist mentioned in 1 and 2 John.[25] In this novel and the subsequent television series with the same title, the prophecies of the end of the world as told by Agnes Nutter, a witch from the seventeenth century, begin to occur. Adam Young, the Antichrist, is brought up to earth from hell and subsequently misplaced due to a mix-up at the hospital. Instead of ending up with his intended family, he ends up with a normal, middle-class family in a small town in Britain. Adam receives a normal upbringing and surrounds himself with three good

[24] Terry Pratchett and Neil Gaiman, *Good Omens: The Nice and Accurate Prophecies of Agnes Nutter, Witch* (1990; London: Gollancz, 2007). The novel was also made into a television miniseries that remains fairly faithful to the book. Douglas, Mackinnon, *Good Omens*, Amazon Prime and BBC Studios. Television. 2019.

[25] The Antichrist is not named as such in the book of Revelation. Instead, references to the antichrist and antichrists can be found in 1 and 2 John and in their biblical context refer to those humans who deny Jesus.

friends (Pepper, Wensleydale, and Brian). He has no idea of his actual power or role as the Antichrist.

The angel Aziraphale (originally the guardian of the Eastern Gate of Eden) and the demon Crowley (originally the serpent from the garden) are the representations of Good/God and Evil/Devil on earth.[26] They have, over the centuries, become friendly with one another and are quite comfortable with their lives among humans. Neither one is eager for the end of the world. They decide to keep their eye on the Antichrist (who they think is a normal boy named Warlock) in order to postpone or even stop the apocalypse.

Odd signs and omens—based predominantly on Adam's reading of conspiracy theory magazines—start appearing around the world, inadvertently caused by Adam's powers. The story also introduces the Four Horsemen of the apocalypse (Rev 6), War, Death, Famine, and Pollution, who replaced Pestilence once Pestilence retired with the discovery of penicillin. At a military base near Adam's home, the Horsemen are caught by Adam and his gang, assisted by Aziraphale, Crowley, and a couple of other characters, and Adam himself stops the apocalypse by causing his human father, rather than his supernatural father, the devil, to show up.[27]

The book is a blatant and comedic retelling of the apocalyptic portions of the book of Revelation, with characters and setting adjusted to portray the contemporary (1990) world. For example, while the Four Horsemen derive directly from Revelation 6, in *Good Omens* the figure of War is portrayed as a female war correspondent who causes wars wherever she goes. Similarly the figure of Famine is a male dietician and fast-food tycoon. All the horsemen ride motorcycles rather than actual horses.

Good Omens plays on the dualism often found in apocalyptic literature by framing the characters that should be blatantly "good" or "bad" (e.g., Aziraphale, Crowley, Adam) as existing in the liminal space between good and bad, leaning heavily toward good by the end of the narrative. The story also highlights the imminent conflict of the end of the world but flips the scenario on its head by creating a situation wherein the Antichrist is able to choose not to end the world and is able to fix the catastrophic problems he causes by his naïve use of power. *Good Omens* highlights the explicit use of the book of Revelation as well as its flexibility to be translated for a contemporary audience through a comedic imagination of the end times.

The television series *Supernatural* (2005–2020)[28] follows two main characters, brothers Sam (Jared Padalecki) and Dean (Jensen Ackles) Winchester, who are hunters of evil supernatural beings. While most of the earlier episodes are self-contained, the seasons contain larger arcs that follow the brothers through various adventures. Biblical, Greek, Roman, and Ancient Near Eastern mythological references frequently appear (apocalyptic and otherwise), but in seasons 4 and 5 the Winchester brothers are on a quest to

[26] Note that the King of Hell character in *Supernatural* is named Crowley; online *Supernatural* fandom recognizes the inspiration of *Good Omens'* Crowley.

[27] Specifically Anathema Device, the descendent of Agnes Nutter, and Newton Pulsifer, one of the last members of the Witchfinder Army.

[28] Eric Kripke, *Supernatural*, USA, Warner Bros. Television, 2005–2020.

stop the sixty-six seals from being opened by the demon Lilith, who wants to release Lucifer and bring about the apocalypse.[29] Just as Revelation highlights that the end times will restore paradise on earth, most of the angelic beings in these two seasons of *Supernatural* wish to bring about the apocalypse to reach that goal, while Lucifer and other demons wish for the apocalypse in order to bring about hell on earth.

While an entire chapter could be written on the use of this imagery in *Supernatural*, I will instead focus on two particular examples. First, just as in Revelation, the Four Horsemen play a role in season 5. While in Revelation the Horsemen come from the breaking of the seals by Jesus (6:1–8), and thus bring about destruction caused by heaven on the wicked in the world, in *Supernatural* the Four Horsemen—who are portrayed as men with rings of power—are unleashed from Hell and cause the destruction of innocent humans. The Winchesters travel around in order to destroy the Horsemen with the hope of stopping the apocalypse.

A second example comes in the character of Lilith, who does not exist in any biblical apocalypse and is mentioned only in Isaiah 34:14 with a vague reference in the midst of a list of monsters. Lilith is known from Jewish mythology as the first woman created (Gen 1:27), who refused to become subservient to Adam and thus left, only after which did God create Eve from Adam's side.[30] She is associated with female demons in ancient Mesopotamia and is thought to be sexually promiscuous and to steal babies in the night. Unlike the references to the seals, to certain other angels and demons, and to the ultimate goal of paradise on earth, *Supernatural*, especially seasons 4 and 5, adapts apocalyptic language and ideas from the biblical texts but also draws liberally on other (and later) mythologies.

Examples Drawing from the Flood Narrative

The secular apocalypses portrayed in contemporary popular culture are legion. Some examples are apocalypses that are (1) environmental in nature (whether caused by humans, e.g., The CW's *The 100* or *The Hunger Games* trilogy, or caused by nature, e.g., *The Age of Miracles: A Novel* by Karen Thompson Walker); (2) pandemic or biological in origin (e.g., *Station Eleven* by Emily Saint John Mandel); (3) caused by aliens or artificial intelligence (e.g., Stephanie Meyer's *The Host*; SyFy's TV series *Battlestar Galactica*; Rick Yancey's book-turned-movie *The 5th Wave*); and, of course, (4) associated with zombies (e.g., comic-book-turned-TV series *The Walking Dead*). As with the recent surge in superhero movies, the interest in apocalyptic and dystopian popular culture derives from a population that feels insecure in their daily lives and in less control of their cir-

---

[29] Note that in Rev there are seven seals, not 66 (Rev 5–8; cf. Dan 12:4). A few gods outside these traditions do appear, such as Kali, Odin, Ganesh, Zao Shen, and Isis. However, they are not frequently cited or used in the show.

[30] See, for instance, Geoffrey W. Dennis, *The Encyclopedia of Jewish Myth, Magic and Mysticism: Second Revised, Expanded, Illustrated Edition* (Woodbury, MN: Llewellyn Worldwide, 2016), 153–6; Janet Howe Gaines, "Lilith: Seductress, Heroine or Murderer?," *Bible Review* 17, no. 5 (2001): 12–20, 43–4.

cumstances than they believe they should be. It also suggests that a large segment of the population lives with a fear of what might happen in the future. Both the superhero and the apocalyptic genre offer hope while recognizing, confronting, and usually defeating the evil in the world (extant in innumerable ways). In fact, the recent uptick in specifically *young adult* apocalyptic or dystopian genre reflects young adults' desire for control in a world in which they often have—or at least feel like they have—their voices quieted.[31]

The *MaddAddam* trilogy by Margaret Atwood[32] traces a group of characters from just before, during, and after a worldwide apocalyptic event. While the event itself is a bioengineered pandemic caused by humans—one human in particular—and is not biblical in nature, the expectation of its arrival and how to survive it, as well as other subthemes found throughout the trilogy, exemplify Atwood's use of the flood narrative to explore this human-caused pandemic.[33] One unique aspect of Atwood's *MaddAddam* trilogy is that it combines a secular and a religious approach to apocalypses in contemporary culture.

The first book in the trilogy, *Oryx and Crake*, follows the human, Snowman, in a postapocalyptic world. Snowman is the caretaker of the Crakers, a group of human-like creatures who were genetically designed by the instigator of the worldwide pandemic. Snowman takes leave of the Crakers in order to scavenge food and other supplies, including weapons. During his journey, the reader learns through flashbacks that Snowman's real name is Jimmy and that he believes himself to be the sole human survivor of the apocalypse, which was bioengineered by Jimmy's friend Crake. Crake uses Oryx, a former Asian child porn actor whom both men love, to distribute the BlyssPluss pill, which is marketed as a Viagra-type pill that protects against diseases and pregnancy and also causes extreme happiness and bliss. The pill, however, also secretly contains a bioengineered virus that eventually destroys the majority of humans around the world. The Crakers are bioengineered humanoids who contain what Crake considers the best of the animal world: they are herbivores, have specific polyandrous mating rituals that

[31] Terry Ray Clark argues for three types of apocalyptic or prophetic response to situations: apocalyptic passivity (waiting for otherworldly salvation), apocalyptic violence ("a response designed to speed up the arrival of the end, in which divine violence triumphs"), and a prophetic response that implicitly encourages humans to act in order to cause change in an apocalyptic setting, and not to do so through violence or by passively waiting on the otherworldly assistance. Terry Ray Clark, "Prophetic Voices in Graphic Novels: The 'Comic and Tragic Vision' of Apocalyptic Rhetoric in *Kingdom Come* and *Watchmen*," in *The Bible in/and Popular Culture: A Creative Encounter*, ed. P. Culbertson and E. M. Wainwright (Atlanta, GA: Society of Biblical Literature, 2010), 141–56, here 141–2. I agree with Clark in that the effect of dystopian and superhero literature may in fact act as a spur for humans to take action; my analysis is, however, a proposal about the *reason* we see the uptick in this type of genre, not about the outcome that this genre may produce.
[32] Margaret Atwood, *Oryx and Crake* (2003); *The Year of the Flood* (2009); *MaddAddam* (2013), all published by McClelland and Stewart in Toronto.
[33] I am grateful for the research assistance of Alexandra Hibbs on the religious and apocalyptic themes in Atwood's *MaddAddam* trilogy at Centre College in summer 2016. This research was funded by a grant from the Andrew W. Mellon Foundation and by the Faculty Development Committee at Centre College.

eliminate jealousy and love, they drop dead at thirty years old, and they can purr to heal minor injuries, among other "improvements." Crake designs them specifically to be incapable of symbolic language and thought in order to avoid what he considers the mistakes of humanity: religion, jealousy, old age, environmental destruction, and so on.

Corrupt corporations run the world in which Jimmy and Crake grow up. Science advances at a rapid pace, including the creation of genetic splices, such as "pigoons," which are pigs that are created to grow extra organs in order to be used for human organ transplants, and "rakunks," a new domestic pet, a cross between a skunk (without the stench) and a raccoon (without the aggression). While scientific progress is extensive, there is very little question of the ethical limitations of these experiments, including the use of natural resources and environmental pollution. It is this world that causes Crake to create the new humanoid species, and he recruits Jimmy, who is unaware of Crake's plan to wipe out the corruption of humanity, to act as the main advertiser for the BlyssPluss product. The first book ends with Jimmy/Snowman returning to the Crakers and then confronting three other survivors who visit the Crakers while he is away.

Book 2 in the *MaddAddam* series is *The Year of the Flood*, upon which my analysis will mainly focus; it overlaps with the story told in *Oryx and Crake*. It traces the storyline of two female characters joined by their shared experience in a religious sect called the God's Gardeners, led by a man called Adam One.[34] Toby is the older of the two who rides out the virus and subsequent chaos locked in the upscale AnooYoo Spa, where she was the manager. Ren is a professional dancer and sex worker locked in the "sticky room"—a secure and self-sustaining room—waiting out test results of a possible (but unlikely) exposure to a standard sexually transmitted disease. While the narrative focuses on how Toby and Ren meet up again, along with some of the other former God's Gardeners who survive, it is in this book that we learn about their ecotheology, which combines biblical ideas with science, environmentalism, and apocalyptic eschatology. God's Gardeners expect a "Waterless Flood," a human-caused pandemic that will destroy the majority of the world as well as return it to its more natural state, as God intended. The Gardeners teach their followers to create hidden "Ararats" (Gen 8:4), secret stores of preserved food and other goods in order to ride out the Waterless Flood in their own "arks." Toby does this at AnooYoo, while Ren's survival is accidental. The book ends with Ren, Toby, and some other survivors meeting up with Snowman/Jimmy, the Crakers, and some villains who reappear in the third book.

The last book of the trilogy, *MaddAddam*, focuses mainly on a Gardener named Zeb, Toby, and the other survivors, including Jimmy and the Crakers. As with the other novels in the series, flashbacks provide Zeb's (and some of Adam One's) history, while the narrative also tells of the survivors' struggles in the postapocalyptic world. Zeb and Adam One, leader of God's Gardeners (and introduced in *The Year of the Flood*) are half-

---

[34] Other adult leaders of God's Gardeners are called Adams and Eves and have numbers following their title; the number corresponds not with when they joined the sect but with their specialty for the group. Adam One's brother, Zeb, is a minor character in *The Year of the Flood* but becomes one of the key figures in *MaddAddam*.

brothers; their father is the preacher of a "petrobaptist" church, a corporate-friendly church that shunned the environmentalism that God's Gardeners eventually embraced. The brothers split up, take on separate identities, and eventually come back together to form God's Gardeners, a religious sect that also covertly undermines the major corporations.

Atwood resists the generic classification of her work as science fiction, since, in her words, science fiction describes things that "could not possibly happen."[35] Instead, she refers to her work as "speculative fiction," which covers "things that really could happen but just hadn't completely happened when the authors wrote the books."[36] We currently live in the world that Atwood builds, including the mention of the wall between TexMexico (*Year of the Flood*, 85) and the rest of the US, as well as her descriptions of genetically engineered animals, including the pigoons, who after the "Waterless Flood" become intelligent beings participating in the postapocalyptic world.[37]

While there are numerous aspects of the *MaddAddam* trilogy that are worth exploring in relation to the Bible and popular culture, I will focus on the God's Gardeners', and specifically Adam One's, use of biblical language as it relates to the expected apocalyptic event called the Waterless Flood. Apocalyptic eschatology—the expectation of an apocalyptic end time—is fundamental to the God's Gardeners theology, but for Adam One the apocalypse is tied specifically to the current environmental and ethical crises happening in their world: Adam One provides a reinterpretation and use of Genesis especially as the ideological grounding for the God's Gardeners.

Adam One's sermons highlight that the biblical text is the "human words of God" (e.g., *Year of the Flood*, 90), emphasizing that the text, while inspired, is not inerrant. This allows the space for Adam One to reinvest traditional interpretations of specific narratives with new meaning and contemporary applications. For instance, in Genesis 2:19–20, Adam names all the animals. In the first sermon by Adam One in *The Year of the Flood* (11–13), he states that the naming of the animals was a greeting or welcome between Adam and each animal. This greeting suggests to Adam One that the animals, too, have souls and thus should be treated with respect, just as the natural world is part of God's creation and thus needs to be treated with respect. Adam One then leads the congregation in a hymn where they, too, name the animals, often naming those that have gone extinct as a way of remembering God's creation.

A second example is the postdiluvian covenant between God and Noah with regard to the animals. In another sermon, Adam One reinterprets Genesis 9:2–3: "The fear and

---

[35] Margaret Atwood, *In Other Worlds: SF and the Human Imagination* (New York: Anchor Books, 2012), 6.

[36] Ibid. Although Atwood goes on to describe how Ursula Le Guin in fact uses the same definition for science fiction that Atwood uses for speculative fiction (6–7).

[37] For example, see James Rainey, "Federal Judge Whom Trump Called 'Mexican' Clears Way for Border Wall," *NBC News*, February 27, 2018, https://www.nbcnews.com/news/us-news/federal-judge-whom-trump-called-mexican-clears-way-border-wall-n851761; Jonathan Leake, "Pig Embryos to Grow Human Organs," *Times* (London), February 18, 2018, https://www.thetimes.co.uk/article/pig-embryos-to-grow-human-organs-3hzc6nw5l.

dread of you shall rest on every animal of the earth, and on every bird of the air, on everything that creeps on the ground, and on all the fish of the sea; into your hand they are delivered. Every moving thing that lives shall be food for you; and just as I gave you the green plants, I give you everything." A traditional understanding of these verses is that the animals are now to be food for humans. Adam One understands this not as God telling humans that they can destroy all the animals, but instead as God's warning to the creatures that they should "beware of Man, and of his evil heart" (91). Of course Adam One's biggest reuse of the biblical narrative is the expectation of another flood, just like the one God created at the time of Noah, except this flood will be waterless, since God promised Noah never again to use the waters of a flood to destroy the earth (Gen 9:11–12); both events are presented as an undoing and redoing of creation.

This apocalyptic event, the Waterless Flood, is the center of all that happens in the *MaddAddam* trilogy. And while it is a human-caused pandemic, it follows the basic outline of the flood in Genesis: the majority of humankind is wiped out, animals survive, and a small remnant of humans also survive, based mainly on their foresight to create the hidden Ararats of supplies that would keep them through the worst of the event. Just like *Good Omens*, Atwood's *MaddAddam* trilogy retells the story of an apocalyptic event but alters it to fit a more recent social context. In *Good Omens* it is Aziraphale and Crowley's desire to participate in contemporary society that helps stall the expected apocalyptic events as described in Revelation. In the *MaddAddam* trilogy, the events are not forestalled, and they are expected by the God's Gardeners. Thus those few can and do survive the Waterless Flood and begin to create a new world, including following God's command to "be fruitful and multiply," as seen in the numerous pregnancies during the third book.

Returning to the definitions of "apocalypse" and "apocalypticism" provided earlier, the God's Gardeners certainly support a worldview that makes claims about "time, space, and human existence."[38] While the Gardeners do not outright preach an apocalypse in the way Revelation does, their message otherwise fits the definition provided by DiTommaso: existence of a transcendent reality, dualism, imminent eschatology, conceptions of redemption, and providing reason for the meaning of the Gardeners' current existence. But as with the earlier critique of DiTommaso's definition, each individual member of the group holds disparate beliefs that accept, question, or reject some of these tenets, even while maintaining the appearance of acceptance within the group. Atwood's use of the flood as the basis for the Gardeners' apocalyptic eschatology also creates space wherein the Gardeners can actively promote environmental issues and critique the ethics of consumerism and science in the *MaddAddam* world.

The 2009 movie *2012* portrays an environmental apocalypse. In the film, scientist Adrian Helmsley (Chiwetel Ejiofor) is alerted in 2009 by his astrophysicist colleague that solar flares are causing the earth's core temperature to heat up, which will eventually lead to monumental shifts of the tectonic plates, resulting in tsunamis and other natural disasters. Helmsley reports this to the US president, following which the governments

---

[38] DiTommaso, "Apocalypticism and Popular Culture," 474.

of the world conspire to secretly build arks in the Himalayas that can carry 100,000 people as well as animals. In addition to government officials, the seats on these arks go to the highest bidders.

The protagonist of the movie, struggling author Jackson Curtis (John Cusack), discovers the imminent environmental impact through a well-timed camping trip with his two children, Noah (Liam James) and Lilly (Morgan Lily), to Yellowstone National Park. Here, Curtis meets extreme radio host Charlie Frost (Woody Harrelson), who predicts the disaster, including polar shifts, rising sea levels, and tsunamis. Curtis, who works as a chauffeur for Russian billionaire Yuri Karpov (Zlatko Buric)—who has seats on the ark for himself and his two sons—takes his family, including his ex-wife and her new husband, Gordon (Tom McCarthy), and flees Yellowstone in order to retrieve from Charlie the map with the location of the arks. They meet up with Yuri, his girlfriend, and his sons and manage to escape to China, where Yuri and his sons are picked up by the Chinese air force and taken to the arks.

In the meantime, the president of the United States chooses to remain in Washington, DC, while his daughter, Laura (Thandie Newton), along with Helmsley and others, fly to China to embark on Ark 4, the ark where the US contingent is located. Curtis, along with his family and Yuri's girlfriend, Tamara (Beatrice Rosen), attempt to stow away on Ark 4. Yuri, Tamara, and Gordon all die, and an impact driver is lodged in the gears of the ark door, which prevents the ark engines from starting. Noah and Jackson manage to dislodge the impact driver, which means that the engines start with just enough time to close the doors, and they are able to narrowly avoid hitting Mount Everest. Within twenty-seven days, the waters begin to recede and the arks approach the Cape of Good Hope on the southern tip of Africa, the continent that took the least damage during this environmental apocalypse.

While the movie *2012* utilizes the flood narrative, like the *MaddAddam* trilogy, as a way to explain an end-of-the-world scenario, the film's use of the flood is more explicit and takes the approach of a literal flooding, albeit from tsunamis rather than from God. Within the biblical text the cause of the flood is God's actual undoing of creation, opening the dome ("firmament") that God sets in the first creation narrative, in Genesis 1:6–8, so that "all the fountains of the great deep burst forth, and the windows of the heavens were opened" (7:11). *2012*'s approach is certainly secular, with scientific explanations for the extreme geological events, such as water drying up, earthquakes, and volcanic eruptions. (Compare this to Rev 16, which describes many of the same events in cosmological terms.) However, it is clear that the writers were drawing on the biblical narratives for inspiration and guidance: building arks, flooding, and even the naming of Noah, Jackson's son, who is one of the two who help save Ark 4, make the connections explicit.

We should recall at this point DiTommaso's definition of "apocalypticism," which insists on a dualism that is clearly not present in *2012* or *MaddAddam*. There are protagonists and there are villians, but most of the characters are complex in a way that reflects more realistically on the experience of contemporary audiences. In portrayals of apocalyptic in popular culture we see an acknowledgment that our lives are not black and white, not dualistic, but instead are complex, with a wide variety of shades of gray.

The question of how to define an apocalypse, or something that is "apocalyptic" or has apocalypticism as its worldview, is as complicated as the question of what constitutes (popular) culture. For this chapter, the apocalypses of Daniel and Revelation have guided the examination of the pop culture examples. However, as contemporary popular culture shifts away from a worldview based heavily in the biblical narrative, so has the portrayal of apocalyptic, at least to some degree. What has not happened, however, is the disappearance of this trope. In fact, apocalyptic literature, movies, television shows, and even artwork have become more prevalent, even as they have moved away from explicit biblical references.[39] This is apparent in the shift toward concerns about our natural environment and the subsequent adaptation of the flood narrative from Genesis 6–9 as a lens through which contemporary audiences can view an environmental apocalypse—with or without God.

FUTURE PROSPECTS AND QUESTIONS

- I argue that while traditional biblical apocalypses such as the books of Daniel and Revelation still play a role in the presentation of apocalyptic in contemporary popular culture, the shift away from a society based predominantly on religion or religious participation has shifted the presentation of apocalyptic in popular culture. Biblical language and themes are still present, such as the flood narrative from Genesis 6–9, but they are often portrayed as secular and environmentally based rather than religious. Further research might consider what other biblical narratives serve to inform the portrayal of apocalyptic in popular culture.

- At what point do renditions of the apocalypse become no longer biblical in contemporary culture? Should the movie *2012* or even the *MaddAddam* trilogy count as a portrayal of a biblical apocalypse even though they are utilizing storylines and themes found in other, non-apocalyptic parts of the Bible? Since the apocalypse in Revelation draws heavily upon the creation imagery found in Genesis, can we say that contemporary apocalyptic media that draw upon language from Genesis are clearly apocalyptic?

- What should we do with apocalyptic narratives within popular culture that are not drawing on biblical narratives at all, such as *When the English Fall*, a novel by David Williams that discusses the results on earth of solar flares accompanied by coronal mass ejection, and specifically how little direct effect these have on the Amish?[40] Or the environmental apocalyptic movie, such as *Day after Tomorrow* (2004), which describes the results of climate change and an ushering in of a new

---

[39] See, for instance, the artwork of the Kenyan-born artist Wangechi Mutu.

[40] For information on how a coronal mass ejection could affect electronics in the atmosphere and on earth, see Karen Fox, "Impacts of Strong Solar Flares," NASA, May 13, 2013, https://www.nasa.gov/mission_pages/sunearth/news/flare-impacts.html. Most Amish today do not use electricity from power lines, telephones, or motorized vehicles, and thus would not be directly affected by a CME.

ice age? Neither of these two examples of end-time popular culture draws from biblical apocalypses—nor the flood narrative—to describe the aftermath of apocalyptic catastrophe. Should these narratives, devoid of any explicit biblical content except the destruction of the world as we know it and hope for the future, be described as derivative of biblical apocalyptic?

- How do we make comparisons between biblical apocalyptic, secular apocalyptic, and other cultures (e.g. ancient Maya) and religions (e.g. Hinduism) that have apocalyptic scenarios?
- Why is there a recent surge in young adult dystopian and apocalyptic popular culture? Is it, as I posit, that along with superhero movies, this growing genre derives from a population that feels they lack control of their circumstances, and that a large segment of the population fears what will happen in the future? Is the increase in this type of genre meant to encourage its audience to take action themselves? If that is the case, are all forms of this genre acts of subversion?

SUGGESTED READINGS AND ANNOTATED BIBLIOGRAPHY

Collins, John J. *The Apocalyptic Imagination: An Introduction to Jewish Apocalyptic Literature.* 3rd edition. Grand Rapids, MI: Eerdmans, 2016.

This third edition of Collins's seminal volume explores the origins of apocalyptic literature in Second Temple Judaism and early Christianity. Collins covers the development of the definition for the genre of apocalypse as well as an overview of the content and context for ancient Jewish apocalypses. One of the highlights of this book is that Collins does not privilege canonical apocalypses, which many scholars do, but instead considers each apocalypse's influence on subsequent writings. Collins also covers some apocalyptic groups—such as the Dead Sea Scrolls community and the Early Jesus followers—who did not produce apocalypses themselves, at least initially (e.g., Revelation), and thus he minimally explores the concept of apocalypticism as a worldview.

Hicks, Heather J. *The Post-Apocalyptic Novel in the Twenty-First Century: Modernity beyond Salvage.* New York: Palgrave Macmillan, 2016.

Hicks provides an expansive exploration of contemporary postapocalyptic fiction, focusing on some of the most influential writers of this genre: Margaret Atwood, Cormac McCarthy, David Mitchell, Jeanette Winterson, Colson Whitehead, and Paolo Bacigalupi. Hicks argues that these authors utilize this genre in order to reevaluate the challenges of modernity, especially as related to politics, the environment, and the economy. Instead of giving in to despair, Hicks argues that these writers use this topic to reject postmodernism in an attempt to reengage with features of modernity such as historical thinking and nationality.

Joustra, Robert, and Alissa Wilkinson. *How to Survive the Apocalypse: Zombies, Cylons, Faith, and Politics at the End of the World.* Grand Rapids, MI: Eerdmans, 2016.

With a strong but accessible theoretical base, Joustra and Wilkinson examine contemporary apocalyptic narratives such as *Battlestar Galactica* and *The Walking Dead* and provide insight into how these narratives reflect more about the here and now than about the ancient narratives upon which they draw. The authors also suggest how Christians can live faithfully in a world filled with secular apocalyptic culture.

Kermode, Frank. *The Sense of an Ending: Studies in the Theory of Fiction*. Oxford: Oxford University Press, 2000.

Kermode's collection of essays focuses on the relationship of fiction to themes found in apocalypses, such as chaos and crisis. The collection covers traditional literature such as Shakespeare and more contemporary writers such as W. B. Yeats, Jean-Paul Sartre and Samuel Beckett and explores the similarities and differences between these writers and earlier portrayals of apocalyptic thought.

Murphy, Kelly J., and Justin Jeffcoat Schedtler, eds. *Apocalypses in Context: Apocalyptic Currents through History*. Minneapolis, MN: Fortress Press, 2016.

This edited volume gathers a series of essays, organized chronologically, that explore the historical context of different apocalyptic texts, movements, and themes, geared toward an introductory audience. While focused on the so-called Western religions (Judaism, Christianity, and Islam), the chapters also highlight such topics as zombies, environmental apocalypse, visual art, and doomsday cults.

CHAPTER 12

···

HEAVEN AFTER THE
LOSS OF HEAVEN

···

DEANE GALBRAITH
RELIGION PROGRAM, UNIVERSITY OF OTAGO

INTRODUCTION

···

THE trends observable in the depiction of heaven within American popular culture can be productively examined if we view them as responses to symbolic loss or bereavement. The present chapter examines how the heavens of US popular culture may be understood to operate as grief strategies: ways of coping with our loss of the traditional concepts of heaven.

The major encyclopedias and histories of heaven published in recent decades tend to concur that heaven, or rather our conceptions of heaven, developed more in the past two centuries than in the previous two millennia. Jeffrey Burton Russell lists consumer culture and individualism, science and technology, atheism and physicalism, deconstruction and postmodernism, the decreasing influence of Christianity in society and increasing religious syncretism as major factors that have fundamentally altered our earlier conceptions of heaven.[1] For Gary Smith, many contemporary Americans now picture heaven as the place where people get "everything they wanted," a view influenced more by "paintings, movies, songs, and novels" than "the biblical account."[2] Colleen McDannell and Bernhard Lang acknowledge that even the traditional conceptions of heaven alternated between an emphasis on its more rarified benefits (especially communion with God) and its more sensual rewards (e.g., the enjoyment of human company and fine food). Yet McDannell and Lang also identify Elizabeth Stuart Phelps's

---

[1] Jeffrey Burton Russell, *Paradise Mislaid: How We Lost Heaven—and How We Can Regain It* (New York: Oxford University Press, 2006), 133–53.

[2] Gary Scott Smith, *Heaven in the American Imagination* (Oxford: Oxford University Press, 2011), 228.

popular novel *The Gates Ajar* (1868) as marking the beginning of an innovative development: the wholesale rejection of the hope of spending one's eternity in continual worship of God (now viewed as rather boring).[3] Miriam Van Scott similarly observes that
the traditional heavenly hope for a beatific vision of God has been largely displaced by
the now-dominant hope of being reunited with loved ones.[4] While the nature of heaven
has therefore been extensively reconceived over the past two centuries, the vast majority
of Americans continue to affirm its existence—as surveys consistently find.[5] Far from
demonstrating any significant diminishment of belief, our radical reconfigurations of
heaven indicate its continued cultural significance.

One way of understanding these modern reconfigurations of heaven is that they
represent ways of responding, cognitively and emotionally, to the loss of traditional
notions of heaven. Reluctant to dispense entirely with heaven and its promises, most
Americans have renegotiated the concept, in a still ongoing dynamic of loss, transformation, and compensation. The type of loss involved in this historical process therefore constitutes what Peter Homans has termed "symbolic loss": a loss suffered not by
the physical death of a person, relative, or friend but by the loss of a cultural symbol or
ideal that had been previously essential to identity. Homans explains that, "typically,
symbolic loss refers to the loss of an attachment to a political ideology or religious
creed, or to some aspect or fragment of one, and to the inner work of coming to terms
with this kind of loss." This "coming to terms" might be "generative or creative," but
might alternatively be characterized "by disillusionment, or disappointment, or
despair."[6]

The symbolic loss of heaven necessarily involves what might be thought of as a second
level of loss, which accompanies yet goes beyond our renegotiation of the traditional
concept of heaven. In order to appreciate what I am referring to as the second level of
loss, one might compare what the Puritan leader Richard Baxter meant when he wrote
of the "loss of heaven." For Baxter, the loss of heaven was solely the fate of reprobates.
The unsaved, he warned, would fail to attain the promised future state of human perfection, which offered all Christians eternal life with God in the company of "the blessed
society of angels and saints."[7] What was lost was their access to the imagined benefits of
heaven, but not their belief in such a concept. By contrast, the contemporary loss of
heaven also incurs the loss of our "assumptive world," those central assumptions that

---

[3] Colleen McDannell and Bernhard Lang, *Heaven: A History* (New Haven, CT: Yale University
Press, 1988), xiii–xiv, 357–8, 266.

[4] Miriam Van Scott, *Encyclopedia of Heaven* (New York: St. Martin's Press, 1999), 106.

[5] The Pew Religious Survey Study (https://www.pewresearch.org/fact-tank/2015/11/10/most-
americans-believe-in-heaven-and-hell/, 2015): 72 percent believe in heaven; National Opinion Research
Center, General Social Survey (http://www.thearda.com/quickstats/qs_106.asp, 2014): 70.7 percent
believe in life after death; Gallup Poll (https://news.gallup.com/poll/193271/americans-believe-god.aspx,
2016): 71 percent believe in heaven.

[6] Peter Homans, introduction to *Symbolic Loss: The Ambiguity of Mourning and Memory at Century's
End*, ed. Peter Homans (Charlottesville: University of Virginia Press, 2000), 1–40, here 20.

[7] Richard Baxter, *The Saint's Everlasting Rest, Or, A Treatise of the Blessed State of the Saints in Their
Enjoyment of God in Heaven* (1650; Charleston, MA: Samuel T. Armstrong, 1811), 91 (chapter 5, §2[1]).

lend coherence and meaning to the world and facilitate our healthy functioning within it. We experience not only the loss of heaven but the loss of the world of meaning in which heaven is a worthy goal. This twofold loss of belief in heaven is relatively obvious in respect of disillusioned agnostics or skeptics. But even the modern fundamentalist has suffered what the theologian Marcus Borg terms the loss of "natural literalism" and its replacement with "conscious literalism": the loss of a simple premodern acceptance of heaven (because they had no reason to believe otherwise) and its replacement with a necessarily self-conscious belief in heaven (which seeks to uphold traditional views about heaven while aware of and deliberately opposing or ignoring contrary views).[8] At either extreme, traditional views of heaven are necessarily reshaped to a greater or lesser degree, and the loss of heaven also necessitates our "rearrangement or redefinition of the assumptive world."[9]

As we shall see, American popular culture has reconceived the biblical understanding of heaven in many different ways, some radical and some not, all simultaneously innovative and yet indebted to more traditional conceptions of heaven. The loss of heaven is no longer the peculiar fate of the reprobate but is felt in various degrees by the damned and saints alike as they renegotiate their conceptions of heaven and all that heaven entails, including God, life after death, and reward and punishment. As such, popular culture's reconfigurations of heaven constitute what therapists refer to as attempts "to relearn the world": attempts to deal with the loss of the traditional symbol of heaven by the creative "reworking and rebuilding of aspects of the prior world."[10]

For the purpose of contemplating its diverse modern receptions, there are many other academic stairways to pop-cultural heaven. An examination of late capitalist consumer culture would show how it has colored our pop-cultural pictures of heaven. Other productive avenues of inquiry would have included an examination of the influence of ecological concerns in raising the earth to supernal importance, or of the (originally) nineteenth-century regendering of angels from male to female and the subsequent sexualization of heaven. The pitfall to avoid in the subfield known as the reception history of the Bible is the tendency merely to catalog influences and effects of the Bible, or at most to describe and contextualize them. Also required are generative *theorizations* of the specific ways in which culture utilizes and is affected by concepts derived from the Bible. Psychological theories of loss and grief offer one such basis for theorizing American popular culture and thereby analyzing its reconfigurations of heaven.

---

[8] Marcus Borg, *Reading the Bible Again for the First Time: Taking the Bible Seriously but Not Literally* (New York: HarperCollins, 2001), 7–9. Borg adapts distinctions made in Paul Tillich, *Dynamics of Faith* (New York: Harper & Row, 1957), 51–3.

[9] John Beder, "Loss of the Assumptive World: How We Deal with Death and Loss," *OMEGA* 50, no. 4 (2004–5): 262.

[10] Darcy L. Harris, *Counting Our Losses: Reflecting on Change, Loss, and Transition in Everyday Life*, Series in Death, Dying, and Bereavement (New York: Routledge, 2011), xxi; Beder, "Loss," 262.

OVERVIEW OF TOPIC

I provide here a brief outline of the traditional conceptions of heaven, far from a univocal topic within the Bible, Judaism, and Christianity, together with a summary of the concept of heaven within American popular culture.[11]

Heaven (Heb. *šāmayim*; Gk *ouranos*) in the Bible can refer both to the sky above the earth—understood as the spheres of birds, rain, snow, hail, thunder, the moon, sun, and stars[12]—and also (at the highest level) the abode of God.[13] Heaven is therefore a physical place (or levels of places) in a layered cosmos, with the earth and underworld situated below it. The phrase "heaven and earth" is accordingly used throughout the Jewish and Christian Bibles to refer to the entire universe, that is, as comprising these two realms.[14] In most of the Jewish Bible, heaven is the distinctive and supreme realm of God, the realm that separates the divine from humans, who are confined to earth during life and under the earth (the underworld) during death.[15] Yet the Bible does not picture God as existing alone in heaven; he is accompanied by a divine council, understood as lesser gods in earlier biblical texts, but as angels and other exalted creatures in later biblical texts.[16] By the second century BCE, however, the boundary between the divine and the human realms had begun to collapse: the heavens also became understood as the posthumous destination of righteous humans.[17] Daniel 12:1–3 (ca. 165 BCE) expects that, in the end times, righteous humans will rise up from their deathly underworld existence and transform into glorious heavenly beings like the stars in the dome of heaven. The belated entrance of humans into heaven caused one of the central ambiguities in Jewish and Christian traditions about heaven: sometimes the heavenly afterlife was understood as taking place in the abode of God or heavenly kingdom; sometimes in another level of the heavens, such as a heavenly Garden of Eden (Paradise); sometimes in an unspecified region of the heavens, such as the "rooms" of heaven; and sometimes it is envisioned that heaven will change and expand in the end times to bring heaven to earth (such as in

---

[11] See generally, e.g., Mitchell G. Reddish, "Heaven," in *The Anchor Bible Dictionary*, 6 vols., ed. David N. Freedman (New York: Doubleday, 1992), 3:90–1; Michael B. Hundley, "Heaven and Earth," in *The Oxford Encyclopedia of the Bible and Theology*, 2 vols., ed. Samuel E. Ballentine (Oxford: Oxford University Press, 2015), 1:451–7.

[12] For example, Gen 1.14–18, 20; Job 37:9; 38:22; Isa 55:10; Ps 135:7; Matt 6:26; Mark 13:25; Rev 11:19.

[13] For example, Gen 28:12; Deut 10:14; 1 Kings 8:27; Matt 5:16; 6:9; Mark 11:25; Acts 7:49; Heb 8:11; Rev 3:12; 4:2.

[14] For example, Gen 1:1; Deut 4:26; Ps 146:6; Mark 13:31; Acts 17:24.

[15] Abode of God: Isa 6:1; 40:22; 66:1; Ps 11:4; 115:16–17; Matt 5:16; Mark 11:25; Rev 3:12; 4:2. Underworld: Gen 25:7–9; Deut 34:6; 1 Kings 2:10.

[16] As gods: Ps 82; LXX Deut 32:8. As angels: MT Deut 32:8; Isa 6:2–3.

[17] J. Edward Wright, *The Early History of Heaven* (Oxford: Oxford University Press, 2000), 85–8. See also Bart D. Ehrman, "Divine Humans in Ancient Judaism," in *How Jesus Became God: The Exaltation of a Jewish Preacher from Galilee* (New York: HarperCollins, 2014), 47–84.

Revelation, when the heavenly Jerusalem descends to earth to be populated by the righteous).[18]

What heaven looks like or what will happen there is even less clear. It is described as a place in which God's glory shines most fully and as a realm built with precious stones, crystal, and gold.[19] Heaven is also described as a place where angels continually worship God and as a place where humans will feast and enjoy themselves in ways that had brought pleasure on earth—with some resulting tension between the God-centered and human-centered functions of heaven.[20] But apart from the descriptions in Revelation, the more informative and often elaborate descriptions of heaven occur outside the Bible, in early apocalypses, as well as in later Jewish and Christian literature.[21] The second-century BCE entrance of righteous humans into the glorious realm of God is mirrored by the confinement of wicked humans to the underworld, now understood as hell, a realm of eternal suffering and contempt (Dan 12.2) and the destiny of the fallen angels and damned humanity (1 Enoch 21–22; Rev 20). The stark dualism is complicated in later Christian tradition, which imagined halfway houses between heaven and hell. The most well-known of these are *purgatory*, a place in which those destined for heaven must be cleansed from the effects of their sins before they may enter heaven, and *limbo*, a place in which unsaved deceased infants, virtuous pagans, and virtuous Old Testament patriarchs are at least initially denied the benefits of heaven but are not physically punished either, as they had committed no sin.[22]

Pop-cultural depictions of heaven often freely combine biblical descriptions of heaven with later developments in Jewish and Christian tradition. Especially influential in this regard have been Dante Alighieri's depiction of heaven in the third and final part of the *Divine Comedy, Paradiso* (1322); John Milton's portrayal of heaven and its many angelic inhabitants in *Paradise Lost* (1667) and *Paradise Regained* (1671); and Immanuel Swedenborg's Neoplatonic-influenced emphases in *Heaven and Hell* (1758) on the way in which the physical world reflects the spiritual world, on the "inner" nature of heaven, and on our ability to commune with its inhabitants during our lifetime.

Descriptions of American pop-cultural heaven are usually less ambiguous than the Bible concerning the function of heaven: it is, above all, the place for unparalleled human pleasure, enjoyment, and satisfaction of every desire.[23] Angels are ubiquitous in this heaven, but God is at best somewhere out of camera shot, if not altogether absent (e.g., the television series *Supernatural* and the comic book *Preacher*).[24] Popular culture

---

[18] Abode of God: 2 Esd 7. Lower heavens, including Paradise: 1 Enoch 24:3–5; 2 Enoch 8–9. Unspecified: John 14:2; 2 Cor 5:1–10. Heaven on earth: Rev 7:9–17; 21:1–2; 1 Thess 4:13–18.

[19] Ezek 1:26–8; 10:1; Rev 21:11, 21; 1 Enoch 14:8–23.

[20] Angels worshiping: Isa 6:2–3; Rev 5:11–12; 7:11–12; 8:3–4. Humans feasting: Isa 25:6–8; Matt 8:22.

[21] For example, 2 Enoch 8–9; Testament of Levi 8.

[22] For a historical overview of these concepts, see Henry Ansgar Kelly, "Hell with Purgatory and Two Limbos: The Geography and Theology of the Underworld," in Hell and Its Afterlife: Historical and Contemporary Perspectives, ed. Isabel Moreira and Margaret Toscano (Farnham, UK: Ashgate, 2010), 121–36.

[23] Smith, Heaven, 228, 188.

[24] Eric Kripke, Supernatural (2005–); Garth Ennis and Steve Dillon, Preacher (New York: Vertigo, 1995–2000).

extends this anthropocentric focus of the role of heaven and its angels to our earthly lives. In the television series *Highway to Heaven* (creator Michael Landon, 1984–9) and *Touched by an Angel* (creator John Masius, 1994–2003), angels are reduced to heavenly life coaches, helping people on earth, setting them free from trouble and suffering, so that they too may experience the kind of human happiness that is continually available in heaven.[25] The primary purpose of pop-cultural heaven is the enjoyment of family and friends, and even our pets, rather than the beatific enjoyment of God. In the 2012 Doritos Heaven Superbowl Commercial, for example, bikini-clad angels even grant a demon access to heaven because he brings a packet of Doritos; heaven is all about fun. On the other hand, we can detect a major change in recent decades in the characterization of the American pop-cultural heaven. In the twentieth century, angels were almost always depicted as slightly glorified humans who had "gained their wings."[26] In films such as *Michael* (dir. Nora Ephron, 1996) and *City of Angels* (dir. Brad Silberling, 1998) and in the play *Angels in America* (playwright Tony Kushner, 1991) and its television adaptation (dir. Mike Nichols, 2003), angels are sexualized and have sex; these cultural products represent the climax of the pop-cultural understanding of heaven as a place tailored for human happiness. But from the last decade of the twentieth century and into the early twenty-first century, angels have become "radically other" again, militant agents in a time of cosmic turmoil and societal disruption.[27] Heaven in contemporary popular culture has tended to one of these two extremes: a hedonistic paradise or a disruptive threat to and irruption into the earthly order.

SPECIFIC EXAMPLES AND/OR FOCI

Nonspecialists are most likely to be acquainted with the symptoms of grief outlined by Elisabeth Kübler-Ross in her Five Stage Model: denial, anger, bargaining, depression, and acceptance.[28] Yet recent scholarship on grief has exposed Kübler-Ross's neglect of nonemotional responses to loss, especially cognitive factors, and has also challenged the model's overly rigid conception of the grief process.[29] Analysts have offered in its place a

---

[25] Cf. Peter Gardella, *American Angels: Useful Spirits in the Material World* (Lawrence: University Press of Kansas, 2007), 113.

[26] Brian McHale, "What Was Postmodernism? or, The Last of the Angels," in *The Shock of the Other: Situating Alterities*, ed. Silke Horstkotte and Esther Peeren, Thamyris/Intersecting 15 (Amsterdam: Rodopi, 2007), 47.

[27] Ibid.   [28] Elisabeth Kübler-Ross, *On Death and Dying* (New York: Macmillan; 1969).

[29] George Hagman, "Beyond Decathexis: Toward a New Psychoanalytic Understanding and Treatment of Mourning," in *Meaning Reconstruction and the Experience of Loss*, ed. Robert A. Neimeyer (Washington, DC: American Psychological Association, 2001), 18; Sidney Zisook and Katherine Shear, "Grief and Bereavement: What Psychiatrists Need to Know," *World Psychiatry* 8, no. 2 (2009): 67. There is a degree of empirical support for the model's five emotional responses and for the general order in which they tend to manifest. Studies have, however, fallen short of confirming the precise sequence posited by the Five Stage Model: Paul K. Maciejewski, Baohui Zhang, Susan D. Block, and

selection of models and tools that examine typical cognitive and emotional components of grief. [30] Drawing on these newer models and recent studies, I examine five of the most distinctive cognitive and emotional elements of grief as frames to understand the transformations of heaven in American popular culture. These elements are (1) the imperative to "relearn the world" and reestablish identity following loss; (2) the paradoxical affirmation yet transformation of our symbolic bonds with the lost object, that is, heaven; (3) the intrinsically relational aspect of dealing with grief; (4) denial and the related phenomenon of misperception; (5) the experience of emotional dysphoria, including anger, bitterness, and resentment, as well as their resolution in satire.

Relearning the World, Reestablishing Identity

A major result of losing a significant individual through death is that "pre-existing assumptions are no longer viable in describing the world and functioning within it." Consequently, the work of grief that follows loss "involves a reworking and rebuilding of aspects of the prior world."[31] The grief process requires that we rewrite our life stories, establish a new sense of coherence for our lives, and, in short, reconstruct our identities. This "relearning of the world" is evident also in pop-cultural responses to the loss of heaven and its potential effects, including disillusionment, trauma, and the shattering of our collective assumptive world.[32] American pop culture has responded by reconceiving heaven as the site for the ultimate self-actualization of the subject of late capitalism.

Alice Sebold's *The Lovely Bones* (2002) and Mitch Albom's *The Five People You Meet in Heaven* (2003) were two of the most successful books featuring heaven in the early twenty-first century. *Lovely Bones* was made into a feature film (dir. Peter Jackson, 2009) and *Five People* into a television movie (dir. Lloyd Kramer, 2004). In each, God's role is conspicuously absent. Instead, heaven becomes, in effect, a celestial counseling center offering its human occupants self-fulfillment and freedom from the traumas of their past. The purpose of heaven is not worship of God but self-actualization; humans do not require God to perfect them but simply need to accept that their lives and persons are

---

Holly G. Prigerson, "An Empirical Examination of the Stage Theory of Grief," *Journal of the American Medical Association* 297, no. 7 (February 21, 2007): 716–23. See also the response in George A. Bonanno and Kathrin Boerner, "The Stage Theory of Grief," *Journal of the American Medical Association* 297, no. 24 (2007): 2693. The tendency in recent studies is to emphasize *local* emotional and cognitive responses rather than measuring an individual's grief against a one-size-fits-all period of recovery.

[30] For example, George A. Bonanno and Stacey Kaltman, "The Varieties of Grief Experience," *Clinical Psychology Review* 21, no. 5 (2001): 705–34; Nancy S. Hogan, Daryl B. Greenfield, and Lee A. Schmidt, "The Development and Validation of the Hogan Grief Reaction Checklist," *Death Studies* 25, no. 1 (2001): 1–32; Jason M. Holland et al, "The Integration of Stressful Life Experiences Scale (ISLES): Development and Initial Validation of a New Measure," *International Journal of Stress Management* 17, no. 4 (2010): 325–52; James M. Gillies, Robert A. Neimeyer, and Evgenia Milman, "The Grief and Meaning Reconstruction Inventory (GMRI): Initial Validation of a New Measure," *Death Studies* 39, no. 2 (2015): 61–74.

[31] Beder, "Loss," 262.   [32] Ibid., 258.

already meaningful and good.[33] If the sentiment reads like a Hallmark card, it is no coincidence that the filmic version of *The Five People You Meet in Heaven* was produced by Hallmark Entertainment, then a Hallmark Cards subsidiary. In that film, Eddie, a maintenance mechanic at a seaside amusement park, has at the end of his life become sad, regretful, and defeated, his youthful dreams remaining unfulfilled. At eighty-three years of age, Eddie dies trying to save a girl from getting crushed by one of the carts in the Freddy's Free Fall ride. Yet once Eddie has ascended to heaven, his regrets are gradually reversed. He becomes the star in an ethereal version of *This Is Your Life*: his wife, friends, and even relative strangers show him episodes from what he had considered a mundane life, causing Eddie to realize that he had in fact made their world a better place.

The protagonist in *Lovely Bones* is fourteen-year-old Susie Salmon, who is raped and murdered near the beginning of the story yet narrates the remainder of the story from "the in-between," a type of limbo she calls "my heaven." In order to advance to the true heaven, she, like Eddie, needs to resolve her trauma, a task that critics of the novel and film have noted she seems to achieve all too easily, given the violent horror of her final hours.[34] Throughout *Lovely Bones*, Susie seeks fulfillment by participating, as a spirit, in what she had missed out on during her earthly life. A big part of what she missed was the ongoing bonds with her other family members. As a result of ongoing posthumous contacts with her family in the course of *Lovely Bones*, these familial bonds are eventually recovered and made stronger. Above all, however, what Susie felt she had lost because of her foreshortened life was the experience of sex with her first love, Ray Singh. By assuming the body of a living girl, Ruth, Susie is able to experience "loving sex," in contrast to the sexual violence she endured at the end of her life. Loving sex brings about Susie's psychological healing, facilitating her entrance into the "wide, wide heaven"—her ultimate destination.

Heaven has the same role for the intended readers and viewers as it does for the protagonists of these two stories; it is figured as a place to "validate rather than repudiate their earthly existence."[35] The heaven of *Five People* offers positive affirmation of human actions and identity while on earth, while the heaven of *Lovely Bones* offers the fantasy that all our unsatisfied earthly desires will one day be fulfilled. As such, they intensify what Karl Marx described as heaven's offer of illusory happiness, for the hope of heaven is no longer simply the opiate that seduces us to endure the vicissitudes of the status quo before salvation is provided in the afterlife.[36] In the therapeutic heaven of *Five People* and *Lovely Bones*, heaven's happiness is already available in the here and now—so long as we grasp hold of the eternal happiness that is allegedly potentially within us and con-

---

[33]   Smith, *Heaven*, 212.

[34]   For example, Peter Bradshaw, "The Lovely Bones," *Guardian International Edition*, February 18, 2010, https://www.theguardian.com/film/2010/feb/18/the-lovely-bones-review; Roger Ebert, "After the Rape and Murder, the Really Cool Part Starts," January 13, 2010, https://www.rogerebert.com/reviews/the-lovely-bones-2010.

[35]   Smith, *Heaven*, 213.

[36]   See Karl Marx, "Contribution to the Critique of Hegel's Philosophy of Law: Introduction," in *Marx and Engels Collected Works* (1844; Moscow: Progress, 1975), 3:175.

versely passively accept our station in life or victimhood. In these books and films, the therapeutic pursuit of illusory self-fulfillment on earth has become the new sedative by which we endure rather than challenge the existing order. Indicative is the fact that the monotony of Eddie's working-class life and the sexual violence against Susie are so glibly treated in each novel. The irony is that the future heaven of the afterlife becomes functionally dispensable. For once we have realized on earth what heaven truly symbolizes—our complete self-actualization—a future heaven can offer us nothing more.

In their history of heaven, McDannell and Lang contend that the anthropocentric view of heaven "has been the most widely articulated perspective."[37] The "theocentric notion" of "eternal contemplation of God," dominant in Jewish and Christian theology during the Middle Ages, has proved difficult to sustain.[38] In American popular culture, the theocentric heaven has all but disappeared. There is a hint of a theocentric perspective in *Bill & Ted's Bogus Journey* (1991), when teenagers Bill and Ted view the white staircase leading to the throne of God and seek an audience with the Almighty. But the theocentric perspective exists only for the sake of parody: Ted greets God by saying, "Congratulations on earth, it's a most excellent planet," and the conversation quickly turns to the teenagers' material concerns, as they request advice on how to return to earth and stop the evil androids that killed them and are endangering their girlfriends. Many pop-cultural heavens are satirically human-centered. In *Happy Birthday Wanda June* (dir. Mark Robson, 1971), heaven is a fairground in which Adolf Hitler, Walt Disney, and Jesus play shuffleboard. In *Down to Earth* (dir. Chris Weitz and Paul Weitz, 2001), heaven is a packed nightclub, and at the climax of *South Park: Bigger, Longer and Uncut* (dir. Trey Parker, 1999), ten-year-old Kenny's heaven is populated by large-breasted women and naked female angels, who give Kenny his own wings and halo. In these hyper-anthropocentric views of heaven we have parodic examples of, as Wendy Brown articulates it, the reduction of morality to therapeutics and neoliberal citizens to "calculating creatures whose moral autonomy is measured by their capacity for 'self-care.'" In the neoliberal heaven, the body politic ceases to exist; it survives only as "a group of individual entrepreneurs and consumers."[39]

Pop-cultural heaven's role in realizing and affirming every human desire reaches its acme with the tailor-made, individualized heaven. A number of books and films envisage that each good person will receive a separate heaven, the fulfillment of their individual tastes, preferences, and dreams—the ultimate late-capitalist consumer-culture fantasy. For example, in *What Dreams May Come* (dir. Vincent Ward, 1998), the recently deceased Dr. Chris Nielsen learns that his surroundings in heaven are determined by whatever he imagines—based on preferences and desires formed during his earthly existence. As his son informs him, heaven is "big enough for everyone to have their own private universe." His daughter transforms into the likeness of a fifteen-year-old girl she once saw on earth and thought was attractive—an eternal perpetuation of teenage

---

[37] McDannell and Lang, *Heaven*, xiii–xiv.   [38] Ibid., xiv.

[39] Wendy Brown, *Edgework: Critical Essays on Knowledge and Politics* (Princeton, NJ: Princeton University Press, 2005), 42, 43.

American infatuation with body image. In *Supernatural*, the happy memories that human souls experienced on earth are reified into their personal heavens. A structure containing long white corridors provides access to the individualized heavens of every soul, each with a name plaque on the door. In the comedy *The Good Place* (creator Michael Schur, 2016–2020), each inhabitant of a heaven-like utopia is told that they have been perfectly matched with their soul mate, to live eternally in an especially designed suburban neighborhood. Each person receives a house to match their distinct personality, and there is an abundance of frozen yogurt restaurants, each with thousands of flavors on offer. *The Good Place*, however, ultimately critiques the conception of the self-centered, individualized heaven as illusory, extolling communal good over the pursuit of personal reward. With apparent influence from Sartre's play *No Exit* (1944), *The Good Place* reproaches neoliberalism's model citizen whose overriding moral imperative is to strategize social, political, and economic activities for optimal individual benefit.

Continued yet Transformed Symbolic Bonds

Recent studies of loss following individual death have rejected the earlier view that successful grief involves the gradual withdrawal of connections with the deceased.[40] Rather, studies show that continued symbolic bonds with the deceased should be viewed as healthy.[41] While some dimensions of the relationship (in particular its physicality) of necessity come to an end with death, other dimensions (e.g., symbolic, internalized, imagined) "remain, and continue to evolve and change."[42] The American pop-cultural response to the loss of the traditional heaven likewise demonstrates an enduring bond with the idea of heaven. Popular culture has continued to yearn for heaven, even as it has reinterpreted heaven's design, purpose, and inhabitants.

For example, in the popular culture of the second half of the twentieth century, angels were largely reduced to figures assigned by heaven as guardians of individual humans. Their role was to rescue humans from life's troubles, steer them onto the right course, give their lives meaning, and guarantee their happiness. Angels were rarely seen in other traditional roles, such as praise and worship of God, fighting in wars against evil powers, binding demons, or revealing cosmic mysteries. Heaven's mandate, according to the popular culture of the post–World War II era, was for individual humans to be happy and flourish, reflecting the heightened optimism, prosperity, and individualism of those

---

[40] Hagman, "Beyond Decathexis," 19. The earlier view originates with Sigmund Freud, "Mourning and Melancholia" (1914), in *Essential Papers on Object Loss*, ed. Rita V. Frankiel (New York: New York University Press, 1951), 38–51.

[41] Robert Gaines, "Detachment and Continuity: The Two Tasks of Mourning," *Contemporary Psychoanalysis* 33, no. 4 (1997): 549–71; Dennis Klass, Phyllis R. Silverman, and Steven L. Nickman, eds., *Continuing Bonds: New Understandings of Grief* (New York: Routledge, 1996).

[42] Sidney Zisook and Katherine Shear, "Grief and Bereavement: What Psychiatrists Need to Know," *World Psychiatry* 8, no. 2 (2009): 68.

years. The paradigmatic film to champion these themes was *It's a Wonderful Life* (dir. Frank Capra, 1946), which was for decades afterward and even today has remained a Christmas television staple. Facing financial ruin on Christmas Eve, kindhearted businessman George Bailey contemplates suicide by jumping off a bridge into the icy river below, but is saved by the hapless angel Clarence Odbody, sent on the mission by two senior angels in heaven. After Clarence introduces himself as "your guardian angel," George tells him he wishes he had never been born. So Clarence gives him "a chance to see what the world would be like without" him, by temporarily granting this wish. But the world is a much worse place without George: his brother, Harry, drowned because George was not there to save him; the bank in which he would have worked was forced to close; the replacement banker embezzled funds; and George's wife married an alcoholic. George learns the lesson that "each man's life touches so many other lives," so "when he isn't around he leaves an awful hole." Peter Gardella notes that the film not only presents humans as interconnected but shows the human and heavenly worlds as somehow bound to each other.[43] For example, the occupants of heaven have aspirations for upward mobility and promotion that differ little from the aspirations of earth's inhabitants. So on earth George is saved, and in heaven Clarence earns his angelic wings for saving him. The angels are no more than exalted humans, replicating earthly class differences in the celestial realms. The lowly, wingless angel Clarence is described as a former "clock-maker," while the "head angel," Franklin, is Benjamin Franklin.[44] Higher status in heaven reflects higher status on earth. The rule in *It's a Wonderful Life* is that the first shall be *first*—so long as they have conducted their business with kindness. The film also portrays heaven as an office bureaucracy, in common with contemporary films such as *The Horn Blows at Midnight* (dir. Raoul Walsh, 1945) and *For Heaven's Sake* (dir. George Seaton, 1950), thereby accentuating heaven's continuity with George's earthly world of business and competition. The film's plot and depiction of heaven clearly promote the American ideal that hard work, tempered by a degree of kindness and charity, guarantees success.

In many other films from the post–World War II era, heaven and its angelic agents serve primarily to guarantee American middle-class goals and aspirations. In *A Guy Named Joe* (dir. Victor Fleming, 1943), World War II bomber pilot Pete Sandidge dies and becomes the guardian angel of another pilot, Ted Randall. He descends from the clouds to teach him what he has learned as a pilot, and even how to romance his own ex-girlfriend Dorinda Durston. The angels in *For Heaven's Sake* are portrayed as heavenly social workers who try to rescue a married couple who are drifting apart. The angel Charles descends to earth, taking human form to help the couple reconcile, in particular because there is a "cherub" in heaven waiting to be born to the couple. In *Here Comes Mr. Jordan* (dir. Alexander Hall, 1951), boxer Joe Pendleton dies in a plane crash and is rescued by his guardian angel, "Messenger 7013." But it transpires that the over-officious

---

[43] Gardella, *American Angels*, 90.

[44] As identified in an earlier version of the script: Michael Willian, *The Essential* It's a Wonderful Life: *A Scene-by-Scene Guide to the Classic Film* (Chicago: Chicago Review Press, 2006), 4.

angel took his soul too soon, as the heavenly records show that Joe should have lived for a further fifty years. Heaven feels obliged to offer Joe a career that is as successful as he would have had if he had lived. So the angels first give him the body of a wealthy banker and then the body of a heavyweight fighter. Joe goes on to win a championship fight, reunite with his former girlfriend Miss Logan, and in the closing moments walks off with Miss Logan on his arm. The 1978 remake of the film (*Heaven Can Wait*, dir. Warren Beatty and Buck Henry) changes Joe Pendleton to a football quarterback about to lead his team to the Super Bowl. Similarly, in *Angels in the Outfield* (dir. Clarence Brown, 1951), a group of angels who are deceased baseball greats help the Pittsburgh Pirates win the National League pennant. The film was remade in 1994 with the California Angels; it spawned two sequels, *Angels in the Endzone* (dir. Gary Nadeau, 1997) and *Angels in the Infield* (dir. Robert King, 2000). Heaven in these films offers the realization of the American Dream: a successful career, prosperity, upward mobility, a loving marriage, children, and even a winning baseball or football team. With all these material benefits on offer from one's guardian angel, it is little wonder that the 2008 Baylor Religion Survey found that 55 percent of Americans believe that, at some point in their lives, their guardian angel has actively protected them from harm.[45]

By the Reagan era, the mandate of pop-cultural angels as guarantors of individual happiness and well-being met its apotheosis in the Care Bears. These brightly colored, miniature bears originated as characters on American Greetings cards, which had long employed angels to express similar sentiments. The Care Bears were then incarnated as plush teddy bears, and soon after starred in children's animated television and film. The Care Bears were portrayed as living in the clouds, descending to earth whenever children needed their help. The abstract on the VHS cover of the first Care Bears film makes clear their angel-like role: "Way up high where the clouds and rainbows live, the Care Bears watch over the Earth and make sure everyone is kind and friendly to one another."[46]

By contrast, in the final decade of the twentieth century and early twenty-first century, US popular culture reasserted the darker side of heaven and angelic beings: their supernatural, transcendent, inexplicable, and chaotic characteristics, as well as the military function of angels in the ongoing battle against evil. All of these features are present in *Supernatural*, the longest running American fantasy TV series. The show follows two brothers, Dean and Sam Winchester, as they hunt supernatural fiends. For the first three seasons, *Supernatural*'s material was drawn overwhelmingly from urban legends about such supernatural monsters as vengeful spirits, poltergeists, ghosts, werewolves, wendigos, shape-shifters, witches, trickster gods, people with telekinetic abilities, changelings, and vampires, all accompanied by a veritable legion of demons. But from the fourth season, after the deceased Dean is pulled out of hell by the angel Castiel, the two brothers get caught up in the War in Heaven between God's angels and the fallen angels (includ-

---

[45] Rodney Stark, *What Americans Really Believe: New Findings from the Baylor Surveys of Religion* (Waco, TX: Baylor University Press, 2008), 57.

[46] *The Care Bears Movie*, dir. Arna Selznick (1985), in Gardella, *American Angels*, 28.

ing Lucifer/Satan), a conflict ongoing since the creation of humanity. The existence of a conflict in heaven traces back to Jewish tradition from the third century BCE in the *Book of Watchers* (*1 Enoch* 1–36), which narrates the actions of two hundred fallen angels, including a leader named Azazel—who also features prominently in *Supernatural*.[47] The tradition of Satan's expulsion from heaven with other fallen angels, and their responsibility for the existence of demons, was preserved especially in Christian tradition. There are several different accounts of the rebellion in heaven, but *Supernatural* favors the version in which Satan/Lucifer became jealous or resentful after God had created humans and exalted humanity above angels in the cosmic hierarchy.[48]

The Apocalypse in *Supernatural* is based foremost on the depiction of the final war between the devil and angels in the biblical book of Revelation (ch. 12). Yet, reflecting contemporary American loss of faith in moral absolutes, government, institutions, grand narratives, and political and religious ideologies, the show deconstructs the stark opposition between good and evil found in Revelation. In *Supernatural*, God, angels, and heaven become at best morally ambiguous. Allegedly good angels, it turns out, are not following God's commands. The angels under the leadership of the archangel Michael even try to free Lucifer and bring about the Apocalypse. It transpires that God himself is absent from heaven, having departed sometime in the distant past. The *deus otiosus* in *Supernatural* acts as a metaphor for widespread contemporary dissatisfaction with the world and God's purported governance of it. Heaven itself in *Supernatural* provides a mirror of contemporary societal disorder, marked by strife and competing factions, with angels vying for supremacy and the hostilities erupting into a civil war between the forces of Raphael and Castiel. The angel Metatron later casts all of the angels out of heaven, effectively making every angel except himself a fallen angel. In addition, both Castiel and Metatron claim at various points to be the new God in heaven.

Supernatural reverses the traditional role of heaven as an abode of perfect peace and tranquility under the governance of God; heaven becomes instead an anarchic and chaotic realm where war is a continual threat. Heaven is still a place of hope, but not in the sense of freedom from earthly conflict and imperfection. Rather, heaven is the place where earthly travails receive meaning simply by participating in a more profound and higher dimension of chaos and conflict. Heaven invests Dean and Sam's actions with eternal significance, even if it can no longer bring about the Apocalypse that will terminate all earthly conflict. Resigned to the inevitability of conflict and disorder, *Supernatural* offers a heaven that is in many ways the opposite of the therapeutic heaven of the post–World War II and Reagan eras, yet that finds its sociopolitical homology in the age of neoconservative military aggression, the post-9/11 perpetual War on Terror, and intensified class inequality and racial hostilities.

---

[47] Although the fall of Satan traditions derive from Enochic Judaism, texts such as Isa 14:12–15 and Ezek 28:1–9 are later interpreted as referring to the fall of Satan (e.g., Origin, *Against Celsus* 6.43; *On First Principles* 1.5.5; Tertullian, *Against Marcion* 2.10). Such a meaning is foreign to the original contexts.

[48] *Life of Adam and Eve* 12–16; *2 Enoch* 29.4–5; *Questions of Bartholomew* 4.53–7.

Social and Relational

Recent studies have emphasized that dealing with loss is not simply an internal, private process but involves one's family, friends, and social networks.[49] Grief is typically experienced within a community. This is why the loss of heaven can be so traumatic—it threatens the very relational support structures by which we deal with loss itself. One of the main attractions of heaven in American popular culture concerns just this aspect: that it will be the place where we are reunited with all our loved ones. The almost exclusive focus on this anthropocentric view of heaven acts as compensation for the almost complete loss of the theocentric view of heaven (in which the worship of God is our primary hope and enjoyment). In the music video for "I Ain't Mad at Cha" (1995), 2Pac (Tupac Shakur) meets his heroes in heaven, including Jimi Hendrix, Bob Marley, Nat King Cole, Miles Davis, Marvin Gaye, Billie Holiday, and Sammy Davis Jr. The music video also depicts 2Pac's return to earth as an angel to help his friend. Similarly, Puff Daddy's tribute to The Notorious B.I.G., "I'll Be Missing You" (1997), imagines Biggie "smilin' down" from heaven and looks forward to "that day, when I see your face again." The dying protagonist of Audioslave's "Like a Stone" (2002) has a "pagan" belief in a plurality of "gods and angels," any of whom might take him to heaven. The song's protagonist, vocalized by Chris Cornell, implicitly rejects the possibility of a heavenly encounter with a monotheistic God, instead looking forward to meeting some unnamed person from their past, possibly a loved one. In "Heaven and Hell" (2010), Kendrick Lamar juxtaposes a long list of natural and human-made evils on earth—"exactly what Hell look like"—with a list of what he hopes to find in heaven. At the top of his list are *people*: Malcolm X and Martin Luther King laughing, The Notorious B.I.G. and 2Pac rapping, and Gregory Hines tap-dancing.

With 62 percent of US households owning a pet and 70 percent of owners regularly carrying a photograph of their pet on their person,[50] it is not surprising that deceased animals also have a prominent place in pop-cultural heaven. Grief over the loss of a pet can be similar in nature and intensity to the grief experienced after the loss of a family member.[51] In *All Pets Go to Heaven: The Spiritual Lives of the Animals We Love*, the best-selling psychic and author Sylvia Browne looks for evidence that animals have souls and spirits—a traditional prerequisite for going to heaven. In the children's book *Dog Heaven* by Cynthia Rylant, "canine spirits find comfortable cloud beds, delicious dog treats, and never-ending fetch games."[52] Jim Warren's widely reprinted painting *All Dogs Go to Heaven*, from his "Stairway to Heaven" series, portrays a stairway bordered by brightly

[49]   Robert A. Neimeyer, introduction to Neimeyer, *Meaning Reconstruction*, 3.

[50]   Allen R. McConnell et al., "Friends with Benefits: On the Positive Consequences of Pet Ownership," *Journal of Personality and Social Psychology* 101, no. 6 (1997): 1239; John Archer, "Why Do People Love Their Pets?," *Evolution and Human Behavior* 18, no. 4 (1997): 237–59.

[51]   Claire White and Daniel M. T. Fessler, "Evolutionizing Grief: Viewing Photographs of the Deceased Predicts the Misattribution of Ambiguous Stimuli by the Bereaved," *Evolutionary Psychology* 11, no. 5 (2013): 1091.

[52]   Van Scott, *Encyclopedia of Heaven*, 62–3.

colored flowers, with a recently deceased dog bathed in light at the bottom and the faces of happy, heavenly dogs in the white clouds above. In the film *All Dogs Go to Heaven* (dir. Don Bluth and Gary Goldman, 1989), even gangster dog Charlie B. Barkin enters heaven because, unlike humans, all dogs go to heaven. Examples such as these show that, in American pop-cultural heaven, you are far more likely to encounter dog than God. The theocentric view of heaven may have been lost, but its replacement is not strictly *anthropo*centric; American pop-cultural heaven is a place to be reunited with friends, relatives, *and* pets.

Denial and Misperception

A common initial reaction to loss is denial or disbelief, resulting from shock, and usually most intensely felt soon after learning of the loss. This stage, according to the psychologist John Bowlby, is followed by an attempt to retrieve the lost object, which can sometimes involve moments of denial that the loss will be permanent, even while one is rationally aware that this is not so.[53] Misperceptions of the deceased, or "false recognitions" such as hearing the deceased's footsteps on the stairs, are also common and are reported across cultures.[54] Such misperceptions are linked to the continuing bonds with the deceased and the bereaved's ongoing yearning for them. Accounts of near-death experiences (NDEs) and transhumanist techno-fantasies are two ways in which popular culture attempts to deny the loss of heaven.

Popular books about NDEs have regularly been on bestseller lists since Raymond Moody's *Life after Life* (1975), in which the term was first employed.[55] The most common contents of an NDE, according to Mally Cox-Chapman, are "feelings of peace and quiet; feeling oneself out of the body; going through a dark tunnel; meeting others, including one or more Beings of Light; a life review; coming to a border or limit; coming back; seeing life differently; and having new views of death."[56]

The burgeoning literature on NDEs, which contains vivid descriptions of the beauty and peacefulness of heaven combined with scientific-sounding explanations, provides a modern form of reassurance for those who might struggle with the traditional picture of the heavenly realm. The NDE heaven is typically blissful and open to all who experience it. Cox-Chapman notes that, in contrast to medieval Christian visionary experiences of

---

[53] John Bowlby, "The Process of Mourning." *International Journal of Psychoanalysis* 42 (1961): 317–40; "Pathological Mourning and Childhood Mourning," *Journal of the American Psychoanalytic Association* 11 (1963): 500–41.

[54] Claire White and Daniel M. T. Fessler, "An Evolutionary Account of Vigilance in Grief," *Evolution, Medicine, and Public Health* 2018, no. 1 (2018): 36; P. Richard Olson et al., "Hallucinations of Widowhood," *Journal of the American Geriatrics Society* 33, no. 8 (1985): 543–7.

[55] Raymond A. Moody, *Life after Life: The Investigation of a Phenomenon, Survival of Bodily Death* (1975; New York: HarperCollins, 2015); Van Scott, *Encyclopedia of Heaven*, 195.

[56] Mally Cox-Chapman, *The Case for Heaven: Near-Death Experiences as Evidence of the Afterlife* (New York: Putnam, 1995), 6.

the otherworld, "frightening experiences are rare in the near-death literature."[57] Hellfire and clawing demons have become passé. Cox-Chapman argues, "It may be that the message of forgiveness and unconditional love is the message needed in our time. As a source of contemporary revelation, near-death experiencers receive the message we most need to hear."[58] Leaving aside her implication that these experiences are somehow conveying a message from the other side, Cox-Chapman has made a cogent point here. NDEs retain that aspect of heaven that fits perfectly with contemporary late-capitalist therapeutic desires about what heaven can do for us. Notably, it is only the *therapeutic* character of heaven that is retained and that becomes the subject matter of the NDE. Far more Americans believe they are going to heaven than to hell, and a significant percentage do not believe in hell even if they believe in heaven.[59] Unsurprisingly, then, this is precisely the vision of heaven most NDE experiencers report, on the basis of their altered state of consciousness. Those who experience an NDE also typically report that it leaves them with a change of perspective that closely mirrors the reassuring benefits of consumer capitalism: they come out of the experience with improvements to "their self-image, their relationships, and their work," an openness to the marketplace of religions rather than specific doctrines, and a tendency to "believe any religious path leads to God."[60]

In *A.I. Artificial Intelligence* (dir. Steven Spielberg, 2001), a gigolo robot named Joe is not only able to provide sexual satisfaction to customers but can also play recorded romantic music. Whenever Joe twitches, we hear the song lyrics "Heaven, I'm in heaven, and my heart beats so that I can hardly speak!" The future possibility that humans will be able to upload their minds to a computer has become a common sci-fi trope.[61] Mind uploading first became popular in 1950s sci-fi but was popularized in William Gibson's *Neuromancer* (1984) and features in films such as *Avatar* (dir. James Cameron, 2009) and the television series *Altered Carbon* (series creator Laeta Kalogridis, 2018–). Mind uploading, sometimes referred to as "the Singularity," offers individuals one of the primary benefits of the traditional notion of heaven: eternal life. There are also real-life equivalents. The Terasem movement, for example, offers to store "mindfiles" of its members, in the hope that future technology will allow their consciousness to be re-created digitally. According to Gabriel Rothblatt, a pastor at Terasem and the son of the Terasem movement founder, "Heaven could be a virtual reality world hosted on a computer server somewhere."[62]

---

[57] Ibid., 57.   [58] Ibid., 58.

[59] CBS News Poll, "Thinking about Death and Mortality," *CBS News*, April 27, 2014, https://www.cbsnews.com/htdocs/pdf/CBSNewsPoll_Apr2014c_Death.pdf; Aleksandra Sandstrom, "If the U.S. Had 100 People: Charting Americans' Religious Beliefs and Practices," Pew Research Center, December 1, 2016, https://www.pewresearch.org/fact-tank/2016/12/01/if-the-u-s-had-100-people-charting-americans-religious-beliefs-and-practices/.

[60] Cox-Chapman, *Case for Heaven*, 8.

[61] Austin Busch, "Heaven; VI. Literature," in *Encyclopedia of the Bible and Its Reception*, vol. 11: *Halah—Hizquni*, ed. Hans-Josef Klauck et al. (Berlin: de Gruyter, 2015), 566.

[62] Anthony Cuthbertson, "Virtual Reality Heaven: How Technology Is Redefining Death and the Afterlife," *International Business Times*, December 9, 2015, https://www.ibtimes.co.uk/virtual-reality-heaven-how-technology-redefining-afterlife-1532429.

A related trope in sci-fi novels and films is immersive virtual reality, or immersion, which combines heaven's freedom from death with the potential satisfaction of our every desire. Modern faith in technology thus compensates for the loss of the traditional concept of heaven by offering all of its advantages, with the exception that humans themselves will be heaven's gods. Robert M. Geraci demonstrates the prevalence of the theme of "techno-salvation" throughout popular science books on robotics and artificial intelligence. Just as apocalyptic theology promises a future transformation of humanity, "Apocalyptic AI" promises a "transcendent digital world" in which "we will upload our conscious minds into robots and computers, which will provide us with the limitless computational power and effective immortality."[63] But popular science and science fiction do not only foresee relief from the travails, limitations, and mortality of material existence and the enhancement of our intellectual potential. They also anticipate unforeseen heights of human morality, the end of tribalism and warfare during a millennium-like period of peace, and physical matter transcended as life becomes completely virtual.[64] For AI advocate Ray Kurzweil, "the Singularity will ultimately infuse the universe with spirit" and "will make life more than bearable; it will make life truly meaningful."[65] In popular science's anticipated culmination of our transition to pure mind or spirit, "heaven will absorb Earth and the rest of the cosmos, spreading infinitely in all directions and providing a home to resurrected, reconstituted, and immortal minds."[66]

Anger, Resentment, Bitterness

Pop-cultural parodies and satires of heaven rarely simply dismiss the existence of heaven. Their goal is typically more subtle: to critique what are seen as the more problematic aspects of the traditional conception of God's dwelling place. This tendency fits with Linda A. Morris's observation that, in satire, "often the humor builds upon a sense of authorial indignation targeted at any number of possible human and/or institutional shortcomings.... Most satire, in spite of the anger that may lie behind it, depends for its success upon a...sense that there is some hope that exposing society's excesses might lead to reform."[67] Psychological studies have affirmed that anger, along with other forms of dysphoric emotion (e.g., irritability, hostility, sadness, fear, guilt), are widely experienced after loss and may result in blame in an attempt at resolution.[68] The anger or

---

[63] Robert M. Geraci, *Apocalyptic AI: Visions of Heaven in Robotics, Artificial Intelligence, and Virtual Reality* (Oxford: Oxford University Press, 2010), 1.

[64] Ibid., 31–6.

[65] Ray Kurzweil, *The Singularity Is Near: When Humans Transcend Biology* (New York: Penguin Books, 2005), 389, 372, in Geraci, *Apocalyptic AI*, 35.

[66] Geraci, *Apocalyptic AI*, 36.

[67] Linda A. Morris, "American Satire: Beginnings through Mark Twain," in *A Companion to Satire: Ancient and Modern*, ed. Ruben Quintero (Malden, MA: Blackwell, 2007), 377.

[68] Bonanno and Kaltman, "Varieties of Grief Experience," 715; Mary S. Cerney and James R. Buskirk, "Anger: The Hidden Part of Grief," *Bulletin of the Menninger Clinic* 55, no. 2 (1991): 228–37.

indignation that often drives satire also results from a similar sense of loss or deficiency; for this reason, satirical critique makes it clear who is to blame for societal problems and what is required to rectify matters.

Garth Ennis and Steve Dillon's *Preacher* unleashes one of the most unrestrained assaults on the traditional understanding of heaven to be found in US popular culture. The comic series (1995–2000), together with its AMC television adaptation (2016–2019), feature gritty West Texas preacher Jesse Custer, his badass girlfriend Tulip, and the Irish vampire Cassidy, who are united in a hunt for God—the Almighty having recently abandoned heaven. The plot device of a God missing from heaven is not difficult to decode: God has evidently deserted the American towns and cities to which Custer and his friends travel on the road trip that is at the heart of *Preacher*. God's absence is manifested in the ubiquitous decay, deviance, violence, and crime that pervade these towns and cities.[69] God's absence also unleashes chaos in the heavenly realms. As the angels known as Adephi succinctly summarize, "The Kingdom of God is fucked."[70] In *Preacher*, comments Mike Grimshaw, "God is either absent or neglectful" and so "needs to be called to account."[71] But rather than abandon all hope, the main protagonist wants answers from God. God's abandonment of heaven does not lead Custer to abandon religion or belief but to his "search for meaning and purpose" in the towns and cities of America.[72] Possessed by the hybrid offspring of a demon and angel, a superlatively powerful being called Genesis, Custer believes that he has sufficient strength to confront God and ask him why he has not been "facin' up to his responsibilities."[73]

With its demons, angels, vampires, and spirit possessions, *Preacher* is typical of many contemporary comics and graphic novels in bringing a mishmash of beings to life from popular supernatural lore and drawing on fringe traditions within contemporary Christianity and the history of Western esotericism. In the world of *Preacher*, a "UFO fanatic" who has an "obsession with weird shit"[74] is a more dependable guide to finding God than is the pope or any other established religious authority. The demon-angel hybrid Genesis who possesses Custer is another source of secret knowledge within the comic. Genesis escapes heaven in order to unite himself with the soul of a man and to teach him "the secret ways of paradise"[75]—a plot reminiscent of the Jewish tradition of the fallen angels who first taught technology and magic to humankind (1 Enoch 8). Genesis, as his name suggests, provides the potential for a new beginning in the Kingdom of Heaven, one without the irresponsible Creator of humankind. However, *Preacher's* deliberately blasphemous plot, punk-like antiestablishmentism, and vendetta against God never become purely atheistic. Custer just wants God to be a better deity. As Custer writes to Tulip, God's abandonment of heaven and his provocation of a war between the angels in heaven were "not the actions of a loving God." Instead, "they are

---

[69] Mike Grimshaw, "On *Preacher* (Or, the Death of God in Pictures)," in *Graven Images: Religion in Comic Books and Graphic Novels*, ed. A. David Lewis and Christine Hoff Kraemer (New York: Continuum, 2010), 152.

[70] Ennis and Dillon, *Preacher* #3 (June 1995).   [71] Grimshaw, "On *Preacher*," 153.

[72] Ibid., 152.   [73] Ennis and Dillon, *Preacher* #5 (August 1995).   [74] Ibid.

[75] Ennis and Dillon, *Preacher* #1 (April 1995).

the fucked-up twisted machinations of a being dangerously set on being adored."[76] The only solution, for Custer, is that "humanity must be freed of him, if we're to have any chance of making it at all."[77] Free of God, yes; free of all gods, no. At the comic series' denouement, another supernatural being sits down on the throne of God, with no guarantee that things will be better than before, but at least offering that possibility.

Since the mid-twentieth century, the changing depictions of American pop-cultural heaven have mirrored the socioeconomic shift from prosperity to decline within late or consumer capitalism. In the post–World War II and Reagan eras, American pop-cultural heaven typically offered to satisfy the ever-increasing desires generated by consumerism, as the valorized individual largely replaced God as the most important being in heaven. From approximately the 1990s, responding to growing disillusionment with the American Dream, pop-cultural heaven recovered its violent side, as the scene of battle against the encroaching forces of evil—God no longer merely out-of-scene but the absent cause of evil on earth. Yet most American consumers of popular culture have continued to believe in heaven, and so this chapter has proposed that their renegotiations of the nature of heaven may also be accounted for as responses to loss, as grief strategies employed to deal with the loss of traditional notions of heaven. Pop-cultural films, television, comics, books, and songs have incorporated the individualism of consumer culture into the notion of heaven, turning it into a realm of ultimate self-actualization. Our enduring bond with the idea of heaven has been paradoxically preserved by de-emphasizing its theocentric elements and conversely emphasizing its fulfillment of middle-class values or, in more recent decades, its guarantee of meaning despite the seeming chaos of increased American militancy abroad and economic uncertainty at home. Grief is also a relational process, and portrayals of pop-cultural heaven have duly emphasized the future expectation of being reunited with loved ones, including family, friends, and pets. In addition, fantasies of NDEs and transhumanism have sustained belief in a future heavenly existence by giving heaven new guises, just as we find in psychological studies of denial and misperception following loss. Lastly, the growing tendency to satirize heaven and its inhabitants reflects the ubiquity of dysphoric emotion following loss, together with its attempted resolution. Heaven in American popular culture continues to offer a powerful symbol of hope, but only by renegotiating and reformulating the lost hopes of the past.

FUTURE PROSPECTS AND QUESTIONS

- It is productive to study pop-cultural heavens as forms of response to loss. Some indications of the historical transformations of this loss were provided in this chapter, such as the shift from post–World War II prosperity to late-capitalist

---

[76] Ennis and Dillon, *Preacher* #66 (October 2000).   [77] Ibid.

consumer culture and the impoverishment of the US lower class. What other historical, political, social, and economic trends have influenced pop-cultural depictions of heaven during this period? How do these trends shape the various pop-cultural heavens?

- I apply a range of psychological studies of loss to the issue of the developing pop-cultural conception of heaven. I have only selected some of the more prominent symptoms of grief. How might other studies and aspects of loss and grief be applied to the study of the transformations of heaven in popular culture?

- To what extent, if any, does this analysis of grief and American pop-cultural heaven apply to other cultures? How might their experiences and symptoms of grief differ? How do contemporary conceptions of heaven (or any comparable concepts) differ in other cultures? How could the analysis differ in cultures that do not have a dominant Christian population, as does the United States? How might it differ in minority cultures within the United States?

- Does the psychological analysis of human responses to loss provide a generative analytical lens for examining the reception of other biblical and religious concepts? How do studies of the dynamics of loss elucidate, as examples, the effects of the Babylonian exile on the development of Judaism, modern transformations in the conception of God, the evolution of religious communities, the conception of the morally good life, the existence of evil, and the recent increase in experiential forms of religion (e.g., Pentecostalism, Hasidism and Jewish Renewal, Sufism)?

Suggested Readings and Annotated Bibliography

Gardella, Peter. *American Angels: Useful Spirits in the Material World*. Lawrence: University Press of Kansas, 2007.

An engaging study of the roles of angels in contemporary America, based especially on their uses within popular culture. Gardella posits the thesis that angels represent a distinctly American deviation from monotheistic religion, what he terms "transtheism": a layperson-led, anticlerical belief in "many spiritual forces that come together in an underlying unity" (97).

Geraci, Robert M. *Apocalyptic AI: Visions of Heaven in Robotics, Artificial Intelligence, and Virtual Reality*. Oxford: Oxford University Press, 2010.

An informative examination of the utopian expectations of the proponents of transhumanist technologies. Geraci provides an anthropological study of popular-science writers and their communities.

Homans, Peter, ed. *Symbolic Loss: The Ambiguity of Mourning and Memory at Century's End*. Charlottesville: University Press of Virginia, 2000.

A collection of historical studies examining how the processes of mourning elucidate culture, history, groups, and symbols. Studies examine the symbolic losses suffered, for example, by Germany after the collapse of Nazism, by the French Communist Party subsequent to their discovery in 1956 of Stalin's crimes, by Philippe Ariès after his loss of Catholic faith, and by Michel Vovelle after his disillusionment with Marxism.

McDannell, Colleen, and Bernhard Lang. *Heaven: A History*. 2nd edition. New Haven, CT: Yale University Press, 2001.

A history of major eras in the history of heaven, from the ancient world to contemporary Christianity. Chapters include studies on heaven in the ancient world, first-century Christianity, Irenaeus and Augustine, the Middle Ages, the Renaissance, the Reformation and Counter-Reformation, Swedenborg, and various developments since the nineteenth century in literature, the arts, and popular culture.

Smith, Gary Scott. *Heaven in the American Imagination*. Oxford: Oxford University Press, 2011.

A wide-ranging, largely chronological survey of the ways Americans have imagined heaven, from Puritanism to postmodernity. While predominantly concerned with theological trends, Scott integrates popular opinion and media where available, in particular in sections from the mid-twentieth century onward.

Van Scott, Miriam. *Encyclopedia of Heaven*. New York: St. Martin's Press, 1999.

An engrossing encyclopedia aimed at the general reader, surveying topics related to heaven (and comparable concepts) from a wide range of religions and regions, from antiquity to the present, although with a weighting in favor of Christian, Jewish, and American material. The work includes discussion of a large selection of twentieth-century films, art, and literature.

CHAPTER 13

....

HELL AND THE DEVIL

....

KATHRYN GIN LUM
RELIGIOUS STUDIES, STANFORD UNIVERSITY

INTRODUCTION

"A culture gets the devil it deserves," writes W. Scott Poole in *Satan in America: The Devil We Know*.[1] Much recent scholarship has shed light on how Americans have "gotten" a devil they can use to scapegoat their enemies, along with a horrifying hell of eternal fire and brimstone to which they can consign them. George Ratliff's 2001 documentary, *Hell House*, introduced viewers to a fundamentalist subculture of condemnation, in which haunted houses are transformed into gory morality plays showing the consequences of—among other things—drug use, homosexuality, and abortion. Red-faced devils cackling with voice-enhanced audio slip in and out of scenes, dragging screaming teenagers to the fiery pit. Scholars have parsed the political and cultural ramifications of such manifestations of hell and the devil.[2] As Poole puts it, "Satan has always been someone in the story of American history," and in the age of the culture wars, that "someone" has often been political opponents, particularly those who advocate things like a woman's right to choose and same-sex marriage.

But hell and the devil are not just epiphenomenal manifestations of a culture's open cultural wounds and political sores, though they can and have certainly operated as such in America. The concepts also carry real moral weight for believers and developed as ways of justifying an eternal God to mortal, perishing humans living in a flawed world. In other words, they developed as ways of addressing the problem of evil, both without and within. The concepts have also increasingly been used for play and entertainment,

---

[1] W. Scott Poole, *Satan in America: The Devil We Know* (Lanham, MD: Rowman & Littlefield, 2009), xx.

[2] As Alan Segal puts it in *Life after Death: A History of the Afterlife in the Religions of the West* (New York: Doubleday, 2004), "The lines of causation between our current lives and our hopes for the future are bidirectional. Our current lives affect our notions of the afterlife; our notions of the afterlife affect our behavior in this one" (10).

whether for shock value in horror films or for didactic fun, such as in the hell houses that remain popular. Moreover, hell and the devil have been appropriated by countercultural movements that have identified with God's opponents in order to challenge the status quo. To understand their history in America—as external menaces, internal threats, and playful freaks—requires beginning with their origins as theodicy and their development in theology.

OVERVIEW OF TOPIC

Hell and the devil are not unique to the Christian tradition, but it is Christianity that has provided most of the imagery and ideas related to their development in the American context. Christian ideas about the afterlife drew from and expanded upon ancient traditions, primarily from the Middle East and the Hellenistic world. According to Colleen McDannell and Bernhard Lang in *Heaven: A History*, the ancient Jews had no concept of heaven as a place of rewards or hell as a place of punishment, but rather conceived of "an upper realm of the gods (heaven), a middle human world given to us by those gods (earth), and a lower part consisting of a great cave situated deep below the surface of the earth (the netherworld or Sheol)."[3] Sheol was the place to which all the dead went. The ancient Greeks similarly conceived of one shadowy realm for the dead: Hades.

The concepts of hell and the devil arose to provide ethical nuance, even if today, in the American context, they can seem like political bludgeons that are anything but nuanced. The afterlife and God became "twinned," as scholar Jeffrey Burton Russell puts it, in response to the perception that a good God could not be responsible for evil and that injustices in this life deserved recompense in the life to come. That is to say, the devil and hell emerged out of a sense of unfairness: why should everyone end up in the same eternal state if some lived upright lives on earth and others cheated, plundered, and murdered? And why should humans worship a God or Creator who made a world that was so unequal and unjust?

In biblical traditions, the messages of Ecclesiastes and Job raise these problems most directly, while Proverbs offers reassurance that human actions have appropriate consequences. The "accuser" (*ha-satan*) in Job has often been interpreted as an agent of God rather than his adversary, provoking Job with God's consent. Such an interpretation preserves the monotheistic omnipotence of God. By contrast, the Persian prophet Zoroaster was among the first to systematically proffer a dualistic version of God's nature, from a Janus-like deity that combined both good and evil qualities to a good principle (Ahura Mazda) engaged in cosmic battle with an evil one (Ahriman).[4] Zoroaster also posited

---

[3] Colleen McDannell and Bernhard Lang, *Heaven: A History* (1988; New Haven, CT: Yale University Press, Yale Nota Bene, 2001), 3. The following discussion of Jewish beliefs about the afterlife also primarily draws from McDannell and Lang, chapter 1, "The Dawn of Heaven," except where noted.

[4] Jeffrey Burton Russell, *The Devil: Perceptions of Evil from Antiquity to Early Christianity* (Ithaca, NY: Cornell University Press, 1977), chapter 3: "The Devil East and West."

that individual judgments sent the dead either to heavenly rewards or to punishments in hell rather than to a single shady abode.[5]

Meanwhile, Greek philosophers were beginning to conceive of life after death as non-physical: the soul was immortal, while matter was illusory and impermanent. Those who recognized this would ultimately return to the pure realm of eternal, unchanging, perfect ideals from which all souls initially sprang and for which they all ultimately longed, while those who did not would keep reincarnating until they learned better. Such a philosophical afterlife was not entirely satisfying for all, though, so those more interested in material rewards conceived of earthly paradises of pleasure and recreation—the Elysian Fields and Isles of the Blest—for the noblest of mortals closest to the gods and heroes. Over time, the ranks of the blessed expanded to include not just the nobly born but also the righteous and good. As the good were taken out of Hades, the wicked and vile were sent down to be tortured in Tartarus, a dark and dungeon-like realm of the underworld lower even than Hades itself.

A similar movement toward a differentiated afterlife occurs in the later biblical literature. Toward the end of the Hebrew Bible, and especially in the apocalyptic literature, hints emerge of an escape from Sheol to bodily resurrection in a joyful afterlife for the pious, while the wicked suffer in the underworld after death.[6] Jewish prophets drew from Zoroaster's teachings and from Hellenistic influences, sometimes suggesting communal resurrection for an exiled people and at other times implying individual resurrection for the righteous. Yahweh, an ambivalent deity who combined the principles of goodness and revenge, was similarly "twinned," albeit incompletely, into the good Lord and a demonic counterpart who was not equal to the Lord (Judaism remained monotheistic without capitulating to absolute dualism) but whom the Lord would one day vanquish.

All of these ideas contributed to early Christian formulations of hell and the devil.[7] Early Christianity retained Judaism's "creative tension" between monism and dualism, between a good God and an oppositional evil being who could tempt humans to sin and who was responsible for the presence of suffering and death in the world. It would fall to the early leaders of the Church to solidify these ideas into accepted doctrines. They did so by defining their position against the teachings of groups like the Monarchians, who taught that God is one rather than a Trinity, and the Gnostics, who taught a much more absolute dualism not only between good and evil but also between spirit and matter.

---

[5] McDannell and Lang, *Heaven*, 12.

[6] See Jan N. Bremmer, *The Rise and Fall of the Afterlife* (London: Routledge, 2002); Mark Finney, *Resurrection, Hell, and the Afterlife: Body and Soul in Antiquity, Judaism, and Christianity* (London: Routledge, 2016); Rachel S. Hallote, *Death, Burial, and Afterlife in the Biblical World: How the Israelites and Their Neighbors Treated the Dead* (New York: Rowman & Littlefield, 2001); Kevin L. Madigan and Jon D. Levenson, *Resurrection: The Power of God for Christians and Jews* (New Haven, CT: Yale University Press, 2008), F. Dorie Mansen, *The Unremembered Dead: The Non-Burial Motif in the Hebrew Bible* (Piscataway, NJ: Gorgias, 2018); Matthew Suriano, *A History of Death in the Hebrew Bible* (New York: Oxford University Press, 2018).

[7] Jeffrey Burton Russell, *A History of Heaven: The Singing Silence* (Princeton, NJ: Princeton University Press, 1997), chapter 3: "The Heaven of the Early Christians."

Painting such groups as agents of the devil, the leaders of the early Christian church—most prominently, Irenaeus, Tertullian, and especially Augustine—instead suggested that God retained complete power over evil; that humanity's choice of evil was a result of free will, but a free will whose choices were foreseen by God; that evil was privation rather than reality; that there would be an intermediate state between death and God's ultimate vanquishing of the forces of evil, led by Satan, who by now had become prince of hell; and that prayers for the dead in this intermediate state could be efficacious in ameliorating their sufferings.[8]

Within this consensus, "heretics" like the Gnostics and, later, the Cathars, continued to propose dualistic schemes, while others, like Clement of Alexandria and Origen, took the idea of God's ultimate destruction of evil to a logical extreme: the universalistic doctrine that all creation will eventually return to its Creator and that hell is but a temporary state of punishment for sinners between death and the end of time.[9] Such thinkers stressed God's mercy, whereas the orthodoxy argued that sinning against an infinite Creator necessitated an infinite punishment to fulfill divine justice.

Medieval scholastics expanded on the teachings of the early Church.[10] But hell and the devil also flourished in popular culture in the Middle Ages, as laypeople combined church teachings with folk beliefs and pagan practices. In popular religion, evil was not a philosophical absence of good but was personified as a demonic trickster or tempter, leader of witches and wizards, and master of the dark arts. The tradition of associating oppositional groups with the devil continued in the Middle Ages but expanded beyond heretics who proposed "wrong" versions of Christianity to also include Jews and Muslims. As George Fredrickson explains in *Racism: A Short History*, the Crusades "stirred up ... rhetoric" that was used not only to "redeem the Holy Land from Muslims" but also to scapegoat "local Jews." Where Jews and Muslims had previously coexisted relatively peacefully in European towns as traders and merchants, "by the thirteenth and fourteenth centuries, a folk mythology had taken root that could put Jews [and Muslims] outside the pale of humanity by literally demonizing them." Muslims presented a "political and military threat to Christendom," while Jews presented a "spiritual threat": "like Satan himself they seemingly knew very well that Christ was the Son of God but nonetheless arrayed themselves against him."[11] Conspiracy theories arose connecting Jews to the devil and to witches; this led to massacres and expulsion of Jews and laid the foundation for the later demonization and violent expulsion of other "others" whose commitment to their own religious traditions presented a challenge to Christianity.[12]

---

[8] This summary is taken from Russell, *The Devil* and *A History of Heaven*, and Elaine Pagels, *The Origin of Satan* (New York: Random House, 1995).

[9] Russell, *A History of Heaven*, chapter 4: "Returning to God." Also Jeffrey Burton Russell, *Satan: The Early Christian Tradition* (Ithaca, NY: Cornell University Press, 1981), chapter 5: "Mercy and Damnation: The Alexandrians."

[10] See the descriptions of the scholastics and Aquinas in Russell, *A History of Heaven*, and Russell, *Lucifer: The Devil in the Middle Ages* (Ithaca, NY: Cornell University Press, 1984).

[11] George Fredrickson, *Racism: A Short History* (Princeton, NJ: Princeton University Press, 2002).

[12] See Jeremy Cohen, ed., *From Witness to Witchcraft: Jews and Judaism in Medieval Christian Thought* (Wiesbaden: Harrassowitz Verlag, 1996).

While Jews and Muslims became unquestionably bound for hell in the popular medieval Christian imagination, the other significant development of the Middle Ages was the "birth of purgatory," to use Jacques Le Goff's titular phrase. Purgatory gave the vast majority of ordinary medieval women and men a third afterlife option for those who were neither so good as to merit heaven immediately nor so bad as to deserve eternal hell. But purgatory also added more quandaries to already complicated ideas about the afterlife. The connections between the living and the dead, first definitively articulated by Augustine when he suggested that prayers for the dead could be efficacious, blossomed into an elaborate systematization of different types of sins and the punishments they would incur, as well as the various remedies—indulgences, masses, charitable almsgiving—that could shorten those punishments. But what number of masses or indulgences corresponded to what length of time in purgatory? What sins accrued what types and durations of punishment? Who was doing the punishing, if Satan was lord of the inferno and Christ the Lord of paradise? Of what salvific purpose was Christ's sacrifice on the cross if sinners could pay for their own salvation with purgation after death?

Questions like these drove Protestant reformers to argue that purgatory was a hollow, scripturally insupportable doctrine, since it seemed to posit a means of salvation (purgation from sins) that diminished the importance of Christ's sacrifice. Reformers argued that justification by faith alone should release people from worries about whether they were performing enough penances themselves and prayers for their dead. But for ordinary people in Protestant countries, the "death of purgatory," to use Peter Marshall's phrase, could promote fear, since hell now stood as the only alternative for those who did not merit heaven.[13] The power of the devil to tempt Christians away from the straight and narrow path and usher them straight into hell became magnified with the death of purgatory. Though reformers like John Calvin were staunch monists, the day-to-day challenges of believing in a God who could doubly predestine some to salvation and others to damnation could lend credence to the concept of the Devil as equal contributor to man's destruction by tempting the will to turn from God. Because reformers also abolished priestly confession and exorcism, the solitary Protestant was left "alone in his closet with his Bible, pondering his sins, unsure of his faith, fearful of the power of the tempter."[14]

It was in the context of Reformation-era debates over hell and the devil that European colonizers launched their invasion of the Americas. Catholics and Protestants alike feared the devil and sought to avoid ending up in his dominion. Catholic and Protestant colonizers also each saw the devil lurking in the "New World." And in their competition for gold and souls, Catholics and Protestants consigned each other to the place of fire and brimstone. The colonial experience convinced Europeans that the devil remained a

---

[13] See Peter Marshall, *Beliefs and the Dead in Reformation England* (Oxford: Oxford University Press, 2002).

[14] Jeffrey Burton Russell, *Mephistopheles: The Devil in the Modern World* (Ithaca, NY: Cornell University Press, 1986), 30–1.

force within their own hearts and communities, as well as an external menace, who had made the "New World" into his principality.[15]

Specific Examples and/or Foci: The American Context

Initial reactions to the "New World" and its previously unknown (to Europeans) inhabitants sparked debate about whether they were descendants of the Lost Tribes of Israel, innocents who had wandered off and were awaiting the gospel, or agents of the devil surreptitiously amassing their strength while Europeans fought each other. The famous debates between Bartolomé de las Casas and Juan Ginés de Sepúlveda at Valladolid modulated between these extremes; Las Casas famously defended the NATIVES as "gentle lambs," while Sepúlveda dubbed them "impious servants of the Devil."[16]

When early efforts at missionization gave way to violence and competition for resources, demonization was the likely result. By the late sixteenth century, the theory proffered by the Spanish Jesuit José de Acosta in his *Natural and Moral History of the Indies* (1590) became most influential. Acosta explained that the NATIVE people had likely wandered from Europe on a land bridge long ago; they were not innately demonic but in the "New World" had become susceptible to the wiles of the devil, who had "retired to the most remote places" of the world after "idolatry was rooted out" of Europe. According to Acosta, the devil operated by inverting and mimicking true Christianity. The devil encouraged people to worship him instead of God, to sacrifice themselves or others instead of believing in Christ's sacrifice, and to drink the blood and eat the flesh of those they sacrificed in a perversion of Holy Communion.[17]

English Protestants also engaged in the demonization of NATIVE people, especially when they refused to accede to European demands, both for their material goods and for their souls. Mary Rowlandson's famous captivity narrative accused her NATIVE captors of being devils who brought hell to earth. "Oh the roaring, and singing and dancing, and yelling of those black creatures in the night, which made the place a lively resemblance of hell," she wrote. "So like were these barbarous creatures to him who was a lyar from the beginning."[18] Not surprisingly, such characterizations of indigenous people facilitated continued violence against them. During King William's War (1689–97), for instance, Cotton Mather offered a sermon to soldiers ("Souldiers Counseled and

---

[15] See Jorge Cañizares-Esguerra, *Puritan Conquistadors: Iberianizing the Atlantic, 1550–1700* (Stanford, CA: Stanford University Press, 2006).

[16] See Inga Clendinnen, *Ambivalent Conquests: Maya and Spaniard in Yucatan, 1517–1570* (New York: Cambridge University Press, 1987).

[17] See Anthony Pagden, *The Fall of Natural Man* (New York: Cambridge University Press, 1982).

[18] Mary Rowlandson, *The Sovereignty and Goodness of God, Together with the Faithfulness of His Promises Displayed: Being a Narrative of the Captivity and Restoration of Mrs. Mary Rowlandson and Related Documents*, ed. Neil Salisbury (Boston: Bedford/St. Martin's Press, 1997), 89.

Comforted"), equating them to righteous Israelites and NATIVE enemies to "Tawny Pagans," Amalekites, and "Barbarians" who, "by their Diabolical Charms, keep our Dogs from Hurting of them, but they shall not so keep our Swords from coming at them."[19]

But Puritans did not only fear the devil in others; they also feared his presence in and among themselves, even as they worried about the state of their souls. As David Stannard has pointed out, "if the Puritans' sense of *national* mission was infused with an over-whelming and single-minded confidence, their sense of *individual* salvation was beset with agonizing insecurity."[20] Strict Calvinists, they believed that after the Fall, everyone merited eternal hell and that the predestination of the elect was a stunning concession by an omnipotent, omniscient, and sovereign God to His disobeying creatures. But the Puritans were not just dour theologians obsessed with balancing a sense of God's mercy in electing some with His justice in condemning everyone else. They were also steeped in folk traditions about devils and witches, evil spirits and magic amulets, much like the Africans and Native Americans with whom they interacted on a daily basis and with whom they shared healing strategies.

Medicine and magic were not separate realms in the colonies, and in the witchcraft scares that shook New England in the late seventeenth century women known as healers came under particular suspicion, especially if they were widows or otherwise unmar-ried. Feared as witches who could sway teenage girls and bring them under their domin-ion, they were believed to be the agents of an active devil who wanted to destroy the Puritan "city on a hill." Women in general were believed to be more easily tempted than men, as Eve had supposedly been first to capitulate to the wiles of the snake in the Garden of Eden. As Elizabeth Reis puts it in *God*, "Derogatory cultural images of women fueled witchcraft accusations and proceedings, and women's guilt over their perceived spiritual inadequacies could even lead them to confess to specific transgressions they apparently had not committed. Puritans—men as well as women—lived a roller-coaster life, alternately assured of their salvation and convinced of their depravity."[21] Witch pan-ics occurred when the unsteady balance between assurance and anxiety tipped in the direction of the latter.

The psychological weight of such uncertainty is often illustrated by Jonathan Edwards's famous (or infamous) sermon, "Sinners in the Hands of an Angry God," delivered and published in 1741.[22] "There is nothing that keeps wicked men, at any one moment, out of hell, but the mere pleasure of God," Edwards intoned. For God "is not only able to cast wicked men into hell, but he can most *easily* do it." Edwards's sermon

[19] Cotton Mather, "Souldiers Counseled and Comforted: A Discourse Delivered unto Some Part of the Forces Engaged in the Just War of New-England against the Northern and Eastern Indians" (Boston: Samuel Green, 1689).

[20] David E. Stannard, *The Puritan Way of Death: A Study in Religion, Culture, and Social Change* (New York: Oxford University Press, 1977), 41.

[21] Elizabeth Reis, *Damned Women: Sinners and Witches in Puritan New England* (Ithaca, NY: Cornell University Press, 1997), xv.

[22] Jonathan Edwards, "Sinners in the Hands of an Angry God" (1741), in *A Jonathan Edwards Reader*, ed. John Smith, Harry Stout, and Kenneth Minkema (New Haven, CT: Yale University Press, 1995).

has been remembered for the vivid imagery he used to convey the perilous condition of the unrepentant sinner, at whom a righteous God is justifiably angry: "The wrath of God burns against them, their damnation don't slumber, the pit is prepared, the fire is made ready, the furnace is now hot, ready to receive them, the flames do now rage and glow." Devils, clearly subservient to God, wait for Him to give them the souls of the damned, "like greedy hungry lions that see their prey, and expect to have it, but are for the present kept back." Humans are like "a spider, or some loathsome insect" compared to the perfect God; having sinned against his perfection and infinitude, they can expect nothing less than eternal condemnation. Edwards cautions that "God is not altogether such an one as themselves, though they may imagine him to be so": "he is of purer eyes than to bear to have you in his sight; you are ten thousand times so abominable in his eyes as the most hateful venomous serpent is in ours."

As much as Edwards's God might seem terrifying to modern readers, though, Edwards was also careful to show Him as a God of mercy and love. For if sinners deserved to be burned in the flames of hell and tormented by devils, it was only the grace of God that kept them out of it (for now). Yes, He might be dangling humans over the pit, but He had not yet let go. This meant that sinners still had time to repent, and no excuse not to do so. And so, for Edwards, "Sinners" also operated as a kind of altar call, an important transition from earlier Puritan theology. "And now you have an extraordinary opportunity," he urged, "a day wherein Christ has flung the door of mercy wide open, and stands in the door calling and crying with a loud voice to poor sinners." Edwards took on the issue of how belief in predestination could possibly provoke conversions if sinners were told that their eternal status was determined by God. Defending the revivals in Northampton and elsewhere, he offered a theological compromise. All humans were born with the moral inability to repent; it was God's grace alone that changed some people's hardened hearts. But all humans (at least in a Christian setting) had the natural ability to repent, especially if nothing physical got in the way of their doing so. In a revival setting, there was absolutely nothing standing in the way of people repenting—and indeed, they knew they *had* to repent, given ministers' altar calls—except their own stubbornness and intransigence. So God was justified in dropping them into hell if they refused.

Edwards's nuancing of predestinarian theology, which affirmed total depravity, human inability, and a limited atonement, gave humans a modicum of agency in saving themselves from hell. Arminians, who critiqued predestination and emphasized free will, took the move to agency further. Populist Methodists began making inroads in the colonies in the eighteenth century and picked up converts like wildfire in the nineteenth. Free-Will Baptists, whose very name revealed their theology, also preached an Arminian theology without the administrative oversight of the Methodist connection. The itinerant preacher Lorenzo Dow put a folksy spin on Arminians' problem with Calvinist predestinarianism, alleging that it preached "We can and we can't, we shall and we shan't, you will and you won't, and you will be damned if you do, and damned if you don't." Instead, Methodists said that salvation was a matter of choosing it. But just as the individual human could now choose to be saved, so the individual human could also choose to backslide. That is, where the saints (elect) would always persevere under Calvinist theology, Arminians held that even the saved could be damned to hell if they did not stay vigilant. In practice, Calvinists too worried about staying vigilant to prove that their salvation was real and not imagined.[23]

And against whom were they to stay vigilant? The devil continued to stalk nineteenth-century Americans. Satan and his minions opposed the moral reform crusades of the nineteenth century, just as he had the Crusades of the Middle Ages. Now he was on the side of "demon rum," immigrants, and Catholics. For Americans newly empowered with a sense of their agency to choose heaven, the devil was no longer just lying in wait for God to release the damned to him in hell but was actively trying to make them stumble. Though Americans had long consumed alcohol in abundance, for instance, temperance reformers now argued that it was demonic because it inhibited individuals' ability to make clear decisions and exercise autonomy.

To make their case, reformers and clergy used the media of popular culture. As Lerone Martin explains, the "growth of America's commercial marketplace" after disestablishment, the separation of church and state, presented religious groups with a challenge and an opportunity. Religious organizations had to compete with new forms of popular culture for the time and loyalties of ordinary Americans. Those "religious traditions that thrived" after disestablishment "did so not by avoiding the 'hallmarks' of popular commercial culture, but by selectively seizing facets of the same. . . . Entrepreneurial clergy and faith communities flooded the popular culture marketplace with religious goods and experiences that mimicked popular entertainment forms," from theater, advertising, and print in the nineteenth century to radio, television, and film in the twentieth.[24]

An infamous 1830s broadside, first published in Salem and reprinted in New York City, provides a graphic illustration of the ways in which reformers used new print technologies and marshaled hell and the devil to simultaneously warn against misbehavior and entertain.[25] A series of four cartoon-like engravings shows a host of demons running "Deacon Giles's Distillery," smoke billowing from the barrels where they brew their rum. Taking a jab at professed Christians who profited from the sale of alcohol, the tract intones that "love of money lures the soul to hell," as "the tale of Deacon Amos Giles will tell." A pious man who belonged to his local Bible Society, Giles "thought he had, to heaven some pretensions, / And hell and devils were but mere inventions." But Giles unwittingly hires a crew of demons, disguised as dark-skinned, goat-like creatures wear-

[23] See Peter Thuesen, *Predestination: The American Career of a Contentious Doctrine* (New York: Oxford University Press, 2009); Kathryn Gin Lum, *Damned Nation: Hell in America from the Revolution to Reconstruction* (New York: Oxford University Press, 2014).

[24] Lerone Martin, "Religion, Race, and Popular Culture," in *The Oxford Handbook of Religion and Race in American History*, ed. Kathryn Gin Lum and Paul Harvey (New York: Oxford University Press, 2018), 112.

[25] George Barrell Cheever, "Deacon Giles' Distillery" (1835), *Alcohol, Temperance, and Prohibition Collection*, Brown Digital Repository, Brown University Library, https://repository.library.brown.edu/studio/item/bdr:33913/.

ing hats to mask their horns, to work in his distillery. After he shuts the door for the night,

> The whole distill'ry glow'd with hottest fire,
> The fiends work'd harder, as the flames rose higher,
> Some leap'd, some crawl'd, some ran, meantime the smell
> Of rum, and sulphur, rais'd a second hell.

There is a proto–Johnny Cashean sensibility to these rhyming couplets, signaling their entertainment value. At a time when lurid productions of the penny press were beginning to titillate American audiences with cheap and sensationalistic printed material, evangelicals seized the power of the press themselves and offered their own shocking tales and images.[26] The devil, death, and hell feature prominently in their productions. In "Deacon Giles's Distillery," the very rum that the demons conjure is tinctured with the remains of alcoholics:

> Stir up the cauldron, and heap on more fuel,
> More poison for this *"hell broth drunkard's gruel,"*
> Fish up these drowned corps, that liquor's zest,
> Will give a finer flavor to the rest.

Figure 13.1 shows the demons in all their naked, horn-blazing glory, dropping skeletons into giant kegs out of which the flames of hell spew.

The problem with alcohol, for nineteenth-century reformers, was that it inhibited the individual's ability to exercise moral judgment and, hence, made it impossible for them to choose the straight and narrow path to heaven. It enslaved the individual to a power outside their control, personified as the devil. Immigrants were demonized for their drinking and because many of them were Catholic. Like alcoholics, Catholics seemed (to Protestants) to be under the control of something other than themselves: the pope, himself a minion of the devil. Fears of papal conspiracies to take over America's cities and towns spread with the rising number of immigrants from Ireland, Italy, and Central Europe.[27]

Meanwhile, Catholics "brought their own, very powerful, sense of Satan to American shores," as W. Scott Poole explains. "Devotion to St. Michael the archangel proved especially strong among Irish immigrants, a devotion that included a strong conception of spiritual warfare," since "Michael had, according to scripture and church tradition,

---

[26] For another example of religious doctrine expressed and contested through new popular culture forms, see David J. Voelker's article on the "Infernal Regions" exhibit in Cincinnati, a wax museum of hell, "Cincinnati's Infernal Regions Exhibit and the Waning of Calvinist Authority," *American Nineteenth Century History* 9, no. 3 (2008): 219–39.

[27] See Maura Jane Farrelly, *Anti-Catholicism in America* (Cambridge: Cambridge University Press, 2017); Jenny Franchot, *Roads to Rome: The Antebellum Protestant Encounter with Catholicism* (Berkeley: University of California Press, 1994); Susan Griffin, *Anti-Catholicism and Nineteenth-Century Fiction* (Cambridge: Cambridge University Press, 2004).

FIGURE 13.1 Devils playing with death in the distillery of Deacon Giles. Colored wood engraving, nineteenth century. Courtesy of Wellcome Collection, Attribution 4.0 International (CC BY 4.0).

driven Lucifer and his fellow rebels from heaven." Catholic parishioners prayed to St. Michael, "Defend us in battle. Be our protection against the wickedness and snares of the devil.... Cast into hell Satan, and all evil spirits who roam throughout the world seeking to ruin souls." This prayer "remained a standard way to end Mass in most Catholic parishes in America until the Second Vatican Council of the 1960s."[28]

The notion that Satan operated by enslaving his human followers so that they could not make moral decisions on their own had obvious resonance in the crisis over the enslavement of people of African descent. William Lloyd Garrison, Theodore Dwight Weld, and the Grimké sisters were some of the white abolitionists who shifted tactics from gradual emancipation to call for the immediate end of slavery beginning in the 1820s and 1830s. One of the key criticisms they leveled against slavery was that it kept slaves shackled in moral darkness and endangered their eternal souls, since slaves were prohibited from learning to read.[29]

In response, Southern apologists ramped up a proslavery defense that held that slavery was a divinely ordained missionizing institution that could be used to rescue benighted Africans from the certain prospect of eternal hell. In his 1842 *Suggestions on the Religious Instruction of the Negroes in the Southern States*, the Presbyterian minister Charles Colcock Jones told slave owners that it was "the will of God—... [their] duty—

---

[28] Poole, *Satan in America*, 71–2.
[29] I call this the "perishing soul" motif in *Damned Nation*, chapter 5.

the great duty of the Southern Church," to raise the slaves from "ignorance" in order to bring them to "life eternal." Had they been left in Africa, proslavery apologists claimed, the slaves would have festered in heathen and hellish darkness, but now that they were in America, it was Southerners' solemn duty to train them up in the ways of God. In Southern planter paternalism, slaves needed masters to keep them from hell, and masters needed hell to keep slaves under control.[30]

Of course, enslaved people themselves, and black abolitionists, had a very different take on who belonged in hell. Slavery was "hell without fires," as one ex-slave put it years later: "This is one reason why I believe in a hell. I don't believe a just God is going to take no such man as that [her former master] into his kingdom." Slaves looked forward to the reversal of fortunes in the life to come. In his *Narrative* (1845), Frederick Douglass recalled his first exposure to the "hell of slavery" when, as a child, he watched his aunt being beaten: "It struck me with awful force. It was the blood-stained gate, the entrance to the hell of slavery, through which I was about to pass. It was a most terrible spectacle." The hell of slavery also turned slave owners into demons. Sophia Auld, Douglass's slave mistress in Baltimore, had not owned slaves previously, but her initial kindness—even teaching Douglass how to read—soon gave way to cruelty. Douglass described how Auld's once angelic face turned into "that of a demon" as she fell more and more "under the influence of slavery." Edward Covey, the slave breaker, was worse still. Douglass described him with words traditionally associated with the devil, noting his "power to deceive" and dubbing him "the snake." "Will not a righteous God visit for these things?" Douglass asked.[31]

Satan also stalked American politics, particularly as the crisis over slavery reached a boiling point. North and South accused each other of being in league with the devil. Unionists argued that "Satan was the first secessionist," leading a rebellion of angels out of heaven, much as the Confederacy was leading the South out of the Union.[32] An 1861 political cartoon (Figure 13.2) showed Jefferson Davis, Alexander Stephens, and various others consorting with Satan and his minions; Satan hands a crown and scepter to Davis and greets the Confederates with the line "Truly! Fit representatives of our Realm."[33]

---

[30] On proslavery uses of the "perishing soul motif," see Lum, *Damned Nation*, chapter 5. For general sources on the Bible and slavery, see Stephen R. Haynes, *Noah's Curse: The Biblical Justification of American Slavery* (New York: Oxford University Press, 2002); Eddie Glaude, *Exodus! Religion, Race, and Nation in Early Nineteenth-Century Black America* (Chicago: University of Chicago Press, 2000); Emerson Powery and Rodney Sadler Jr., *The Genesis of Liberation: Biblical Interpretation in the Antebellum Narratives of the Enslaved* (Louisville, KY: Westminster John Knox Press, 2016).

[31] An excellent scholarly edition of the *Narrative* is Frederick Douglass, *Narrative of the Life of Frederick Douglass, an American Slave. Written by Himself*, 2nd ed., ed. David Blight (Boston: Bedford Books, 2003).

[32] See Edward J. Blum, "'The First Secessionist Was Satan': Secession and the Religious Politics of Evil in Civil War America," *Civil War History* 60, no. 3 (2014): 234–69.

[33] Louis Haugg and L. Hough, *The Southern Confederacy a fact!!! Acknowledged by a mighty prince and faithful ally* (Philadelphia, PA: L. Hough, 1861), American Cartoon Print Filing Series, Library of Congress, https://www.loc.gov/item/2008661622/.

FIGURE 13.2 "The Southern Confederacy a Fact!!! Acknowledged by a Mighty Prince and Faithful Ally." Philadelphia, PA: L. Hough, 1861. American Cartoon Print Filing Series, Library of Congress, Prints & Photographs Division, LC-USZ62-89624 (b&w film copy neg.).

Southerners threw the same accusation back at the North for failing to read the Bible literally.[34] Nowhere did the Bible expressly condemn slavery, they argued. Abolitionism "is a trick of the evil one; and must be eschewed as a most deadly poison to the soul, or it will weigh it down to the Bottomless Pit," said a slavery apologist who went by the pen name Amor Patriae.[35] In response, abolitionists black and white contended that the spirit of the Bible was clearly opposed to slavery, since God had rescued the Israelites from bondage to Egypt. As David Walker put it, religion as practiced by "Europeans and their descendants" might lead one to "believe it was a plan fabricated by themselves and the *devils* to oppress us."[36]

[34] See Lum, *Damned Nation*, chapter 5.

[35] Amor Patriae, *The Blasphemy of Abolitionism Exposed: Servitude and the Rights of the South, Vindicated. A Bible Argument*, new ed., revised, corrected, and enlarged (New-York, 1850), 4.

[36] David Walker, *Walker's Appeal, in Four Articles; Together with a Preamble, to the Coloured Citizens of the World, but in Particular, and Very Epressly, to those of the United States of America, written in Boston, state of Massachusetts, September 28, 1829. Third and Last Edition, with Additional Notes, Corrections, &c.* (Boston: Revised and published by David Walker, 1830), 40.

The Civil War precipitated major changes but also significant continuities in American hell-talk.[37] Chaplains in the war had initially warned that soldiers who died in battle were not assured of heaven. Believing, at first, that the war would be quick and relatively mild, they saw soldiers' camps as an opportunity for missionizing among a captive audience. Their excitement at evangelizing America's men stemmed from a seismic shift in white middle-class gender roles from the Puritan days to the antebellum era. Where once women were suspected Eves who were both easily tempted by the devil and temptresses themselves, now women filled the majority of America's pews and acquired a reputation as the virtuous safeguards of America's moral heart. As household economies shifted from joint family labor to a "separation of spheres," in which men left the house to work and women managed the domestic realm, women became responsible for the piety of their families and for their salvation from hell. Women joined forces with ministers in antebellum reform movements against drinking, gambling, card playing, and the like, warning of the eternal torments that awaited the unrepentant.

At the start of the war, evangelicals complained that soldiers were enjoying a raucous good time with each other, away from the censuring eyes of their loved ones at home. But as the battles claimed more lives, and with the dawning realization that new weapon technologies made warfare more brutal while lagging medical technologies provided little defense against infection, ministers saw an opportunity. By the midpoint of the war, they noted that many soldiers were giving up their cavalier attitude toward religion and that revivals were sweeping the camps. Ministers were suddenly relevant again, with an unprecedented chance to reach men directly and forcefully, who were looking the prospect of death and damnation in the eye. "Never in all my life have I preached to men who were seemingly so anxious for the word of life," said a Union chaplain, George Phillips, in 1863.[38] The threat of hell was a helpful spur to conversion. "A man may fight and die for his country and lose his soul!" warned Chaplain A. D. Betts of the 30th North Carolina.[39] Likewise, a hospital chaplain, A. S. Billingsley, urged a soldier about to undergo an amputation, "Think of the torments of hell; of the lashings of a guilty conscience; of the gnawings of the undying worm; of the 'everlasting fire'; of the weeping, wailing, and gnashing of teeth, you will soon bring upon yourself, unless you soon repent!"[40]

By the end of the Civil War, though, such overt hell-talk largely flamed out in the public imagination, replaced with the saccharine promises of heavenly bliss. The immense scale of death forced ministers to admit that they were simply not equipped to convert so many men before the horrors of guns and gangrene claimed them. Faced with the prospect of telling families that they did not know whether or not their deceased loved

---

[37] This overview is largely drawn from Lum, *Damned Nation*, chapter 6.

[38] George Phillips to "My Dear Wife," Camp Drake, Murfreesboro TN, June 1, 1863, in Phillips (George Shane) Collection, Huntington Library, San Marino, CA, Huntington mssPhillips papers.

[39] A. D. Betts, *Experience of a Confederate Chaplain, 1861–1864* (Greenville, SC, 190-?), 73–4.

[40] A. S. Billingsley, *Christianity in the War. Containing an Account of the Sufferings, Conversions, Prayers, Dying Requests, Last Words, and Deaths of Soldiers and Officers in the Hospital, Camp, Prison, and on the Battle-Field* (Philadelphia, PA: Claxton, Remsen & Haffelfinger, 1872), 33–5.

ones were saved, many chaplains changed their tune. By the end of the war, dying for the cause became a ticket to heaven, as soldiers' sacrifices came to be equated with Christ's sacrifice on the cross. As Benjamin Babbitt put it in a eulogy for one Union soldier, Walter Raymond, "He was, on principle, devoted to the cause of his country, for which he has so heroically died. Wherefore we may trust, that through the mercy of our God in Jesus Christ, he has received the crown of life."[41] The idea that dying for one's country might save one's soul fits into the civil religion that, as Harry Stout has argued, emerged out of the crucible of war.[42]

But hell and the devil did not disappear. As the promises of emancipation gave way to the abandonment of Radical Reconstruction, disillusioned African Americans again called on a just God to right the earthly wrongs they faced.[43] The African Methodist Episcopal Church leader Henry McNeal Turner preached that hell was "populated by those persons who launched deadly assaults on the persons and rights of black Americans.... Conversely, those who spoke out on behalf of equal rights and fair treatment of people of all races would go to heaven."[44] In the 1880s, Turner also took on the colorism in Americans' assumptions about the afterlife. "We have as much right biblically and otherwise to believe that God is a Negro," he thundered, "as you buckra, or white, people have to believe that God is a fine looking, symmetrical and ornamented white man."[45] Turner's words would resonate in the liberation theologies that emerged in the 1960s and 1970s, especially in the works of the Union Seminary theologian James Cone.[46]

At the same time that Turner was calling down the fire of a just (black) God, fissures were opening in white Protestantism over the justness of hell. Theological conservatives cast their enemies—modernists, Darwinists, "infidels"—into the fires of hell, while theological liberals questioned what kind of God would create an eternal hell for the perpetual punishment of finite humans. For fundamentalists, hell raised the stakes of belief because it was one of the essential building blocks on which other doctrines rested. Take away an eternal hell, and the nature of God and of Christ's atonement changed irrevocably. Theological liberals were open to such destabilization of formerly

---

[41] Benjamin Babbitt, "A Sermon on the Death of Walter L. Raymond, a Union Soldier, Delivered on Sunday, April 3, 1865" (Andover, MA: Printed by Warren F. Draper, 1865), 9–10.

[42] See Harry Stout, *Upon the Altar of the Nation: A Moral History of the American Civil War* (New York: Viking, 2006).

[43] See Lum, *Damned Nation*, chapter 6; Kathryn Gin, "'The Heavenization of Earth': African American Visions and Uses of the Afterlife, 1863–1901," *Slavery and Abolition: A Journal of Slave and Post-Slave Studies* 31, no. 2 (2010): 207–31; Paul Harvey, "That Was about Equalization after Freedom," esp. 85, and Edward Blum, "O God of a Godless Land," esp. 95–6, both in *Vale of Tears: New Essays on Religion and Reconstruction*, ed. Edward Blum and W. Scott Poole (Macon, GA: Mercer University Press, 2005).

[44] Stephen Angell, *Bishop Henry McNeal Turner and African-American Religion in the South* (Knoxville: University of Tennessee Press, 1992), 272.

[45] Henry McNeal Turner, "God Is a Negro," in *Respect Black: The Writings and Speeches of Henry McNeal Turner*, ed. Edwin S. Redkey (New York: Arno Press and New York Times, 1971), 176, first printed in *Voice of Missions*, February 1898.

[46] See, for example, James Cone, *A Black Theology of Liberation* (Philadelphia, PA: Lippincott, 1970).

cherished beliefs, but conservatives held such destabilization to itself be a sign of the devil's tempting work on fallen humans.[47]

For modernists, hell became a sign of an illiberal, embarrassing, and antiquated religion that was incompatible with the great strides Americans had made in science and technology. As the scholar James Moorhead has shown, the fear of hell faded as the ideal of heaven became "an eternal progressive purposeful activity already begun here."[48] The desires of American audiences for future reunion with loved ones led to a seismic shift in American pulpit rhetoric. Where the threat of fire and brimstone used to be a staple of revival preaching, now preachers emphasized the promise of eternal bliss instead. The historian Jonathan M. Butler explains that Dwight Moody (1837–1899) marks this "shift from a primary emphasis on Hell to a primary emphasis on Heaven." Moody stressed God's love in order to appeal to the postbellum middle class. He and other late nineteenth-century revivalists used a domesticated heaven as a way to shore up middle-class mores, sentimentalizing mother, family, and home.[49] By 1900 an Episcopal clergyman in the *North American Review*, George Wolfe Shinn, was writing, "We hear very little about [hell] except in the profanity of the day. We do not hear it in the pulpit, nor see any religious reference to it in the religious press, nor in the modern theological book, nor is it brought up in religious conversation generally. It is tabooed by the pulpit generally."[50]

Over the course of the twentieth century and into the present day, hell and the devil increasingly became a source of entertainment, used both for horror and for humor, and by hell's defenders and detractors alike. Fundamentalists marshaled popular culture forms to fight the culture wars, using hell and the devil to condemn everything from abortion to rock music. The cartoonist Jack Chick became famous for his didactic graphic tracts that feature conniving demons and a literal hell of sulfurous scents and fiery flames. To take just one example, in a tract titled "The Last Surprise," a woman named Frances gets so angry about a preacher's fire-and-brimstone preaching that she storms out of the church. In an ironic twist, she is killed in a car accident, and the EMTs who handle her body comment on the smell of "rotten eggs" that emanates from her body. In the last frame of the cartoon, Frances is dragged down a fiery path by cackling, horned demons. She asks, "Where are you taking me?" They respond, "It's a surprise!"[51]

Hell houses function as three-dimensional, experiential versions of a Chick tract, linking moral anxiety to political fear to popular entertainment. An evangelical play on haunted houses that can be traced back to Jerry Falwell's "Scaremares" in the 1970s, hell

---

[47] See Gary Dorrien, *The Making of American Liberal Theology: Imagining Progressive Religion, 1805–1900* (Louisville, KY: Westminster John Knox Press, 2001).

[48] James Moorhead, *World without End: Mainstream American Protestant Visions of the Last Things, 1880–1925* (Bloomington: Indiana University Press, 1999), 62.

[49] Jonathan M. Butler, *Softly and Tenderly Jesus Is Calling: Heaven and Hell in American Revivalism, 1870–1920* (Brooklyn, NY: Carlson, 1991).

[50] George Wolfe Shinn, "What Has Become of Hell?," *North American Review* 170, no. 523 (June 1900): 837–49, quoted in Joshua David Wright, "'The Devil Hates That Doctrine': Hell in American Fundamentalism and Evangelicalism, 1900–2015," MA thesis, University of Colorado, 2016, 16.

[51] Jack Chick, "The Last Surprise," Chick Publications, accessed December 21, 2018, https://www.chick.com/products/tract?stk=1080.

houses take visitors through scenes of terror, gore, and death. Sinister demons and poor benighted souls (often enacted by eager youths) titillate participants with lurid details of the forbidden—sex, drugs, rock and roll, and so on—as well as terrifying them with the consequences of the same. As Jason Bivins puts it, "Through sometimes surprisingly realistic portrayals of the sins condemned, Hell Houses appropriate the tropes of genre horror and use bloody corpses, gloating demons, fiery wrecks, and weeping children to shock audiences. Each scene is written into a larger narrative about liberalism's attempt to undermine the foundations of Christian America."[52] Meanwhile, hell and the devil have also made their way into mainstream popular culture, losing their theological moorings in the process. As Greg Garrett puts it in his study of the afterlife, "Demons and devils…have become names and metaphors largely divorced from their diabolical origin," appearing on everything from roller coasters to mascots to a My Little Pony spin-off.[53] Satan sometimes functions as a joke, a punchline, and a fun signaling device that indicates one's liberation from straitlaced mores. The number of devil jokes and memes that one can find on the internet is nearly as bottomless as the bottomless pit.

The devil has also been used to sell things. Where, in the nineteenth century, Deacon Giles's Distillery served the purpose of temperance, a present-day distillery has adopted the name, the backstory, the woodcut engravings, and the visage of a devil from the original broadside to market its "Damn Righteous Spirits."[54] Demonic characters also stalk the movies, from Hannibal Lecter to Voldemort.[55] In many movies, the demonic is an externalization of evil, allowing the good to emerge victorious after adversity. As Garrett explains, "It may be that we don't all believe that Satan—an actual fallen angel who rules this world and contends with God—exists in real life. But most of us have come to accept that Satan is a logical and emotionally satisfying explanation for all that goes wrong in real life."[56] Similarly, Garrett contends that although many Americans no longer believe in hell, they need it: "Hell is horrible, the testing ground of heroes, the domain of the fallen, the home of evil and despair, but it also offers us a useful metaphor for the pain and casual violence we encounter in our own lives. None of us hopes to go to hell at the end of our life, but many of us would say that we have had some acquaintance with it."[57]

Hell on earth is a staple of the movies, whether it is wartime dramas or *The Hunger Games*.[58] An actual hell after death also occasionally appears in the movies, as in the 1998 film *What Dreams May Come*, derived from a 1978 novel by Richard Matheson.[59]

---

[52] See George Ratliff, *Hell House*, USA, Mixed Greens Media, 2001; Jason Bivins, *Religion of Fear: The Politics of Horror in Conservative Evangelicalism* (Oxford: Oxford University Press, 2008), 20 and chapter 5; Kathryn Gin Lum, "These Evangelical Haunted Houses Are Designed to Show Sinners That They're Going to Hell," *Washington Post*, October 30, 2014.

[53] Greg Garrett, *Entertaining Judgment: The Afterlife in Popular Imagination* (Oxford: Oxford University Press, 2015), 58–9. See also Garrett's chapter in this volume.

[54] Website of Deacon Giles Distillery, accessed December 22, 2018, https://www.deacongiles.com/.

[55] See, e.g., *Silence of the Lambs*, USA, Orion Pictures, 1991; *Harry Potter and the Deathly Hallows*, USA, Warner Bros., 2010–11).

[56] Garrett, *Entertaining Judgment*, 90.   [57] Ibid., 154–5.

[58] *The Hunger Games*, USA, Lionsgate, 2012.

[59] *What Dreams May Come*, USA, Polygram Filmed Entertainment through Universal Studios 1998; Richard Matheson, *What Dreams May Come* (New York: G. P. Putnam's Sons, 1978).

But this hell is not the torture chamber of an angry God; instead, it is the product of the damned's own tormented imagination. Robin Williams plays a deceased man who wakes up in heaven only to find that his wife has committed suicide and is suffering in a terrifying hell. He is determined to save her and eventually does, restoring her lost memory and lifting her from her hellish state of depression and despair. *What Dreams May Come* reflects the way hell has become psychologized as a state of mind, into which and out of which humans can go through their own agency.

This psychologizing of hell and the demonic is not exclusive to Christianity. With the relaxing of immigration quotas in 1965, Asian traditions spread in the United States and changed as Western practitioners appropriated them. To take just one example, in popular Buddhism, terrifying beings stalk the cosmic imagination. Hell and *preta* stories in ancient South Asian texts were used to shore up the authority of monks and to enforce social norms around family relations and gendered expectations. Hungry ghosts are disgusting creatures who ooze pus, blood, and fecal matter and lick the same off each other's bodies.[60] They repeatedly endure hell-like tortures, not the least of which is a gnawing starvation that can never be satisfied. As Jeff Wilson puts it in *Mindful America*, "Buddhists are warned not to commit karmic offenses, especially those involving excessive craving and attachment, lest they fall into the body of a hungry ghost after death."[61] But the appropriation of Buddhism under the form of "mindfulness" has led to the reimagining of hungry ghosts as "metaphoric images of our own mental states of desire and need ... especially common tropes in such applications as mindful addiction recovery and mindful eating."[62] Just as hell in the Christian tradition has been reinterpreted in popular culture as a state of mind, so hungry ghosts in the mindfulness movement have been reinterpreted as personal psychological hindrances that can and should be cast off.

Meanwhile, the Nation of Islam (NOI) recast demons as white people, created by a "talented but malicious scientist, Yacob, who set out six thousand years ago to create a devilish race." White devils were "weak and wicked" and "sowed discord and fomented war wherever they went."[63] They used a "science of tricknology" to "divide and control the righteous original people," Asiatic Muslims, by enslaving them and deceiving them about their true origins. According to Judith Weisenfeld, the NOI offered an apocalyptic scenario in which, as followers learned of their true identity as Asiatic Muslims and not African Americans, they would prosper, while the white devils would get their just dues.[64] The NOI held up this-worldly salvation as the goal to which followers should aspire and revised an otherworldly heaven into "the white devil's work to accommodate

---

[60] Adeana McNicholl, *Celestial Seductresses and Hungry Ghosts: Preta Narratives in Early Indian Buddhism*, PhD dissertation, Stanford University, 2019, esp. chapter 4, "Repulsive *Pretas* and the Aesthetics of Disgust."

[61] Jeff Wilson, *Mindful America: The Mutual Transformation of Buddhist Meditation and American Culture* (New York: Oxford University Press, 2014), 46–7.

[62] Ibid., 47.

[63] Judith Weisenfeld, *New World a-Coming: Black Religion and Racial Identity during the Great Migration* (New York: New York University Press, 2017), 58.

[64] Ibid., 60.

the original black people to suffering in this life." For the Nation's followers, resurrection meant rescue from the "'mental death' of ignorance and blindness to true identity."[65]

If some groups interpreted devils as this-worldly psychological or racial adversaries, others began to worship the devil himself. Satanism, defined by Ruben Van Luijk as "the *intentional, religiously motivated veneration of Satan,*"[66] arose in the nineteenth century as a romantic backlash against straitlaced Christianity and Enlightenment skepticism alike. Instead of attributing satanic qualities to one's enemies, a small group of artists and writers began to identify with the Prince of Darkness. Romantic Satanists turned to the devil as an alternative to a God who seemed to pronounce against sex, science, and freedom. The resonances of their reverence for Satan reverberated in Anton LaVey's Church of Satan, founded in 1966 in San Francisco. As Van Luijk puts it, the romantics of the nineteenth century put "in motion a cultural chain process of appropriation and rehabilitation of Satan that, through a series of diverse but interconnected stages, eventually gave birth to a religious Satanism."[67] LaVey's Church of Satan offered an alternative to the apparent secularism, on the one hand, and fundamentalism, on the other, that were polarizing the rest of society. He offered a "thoroughly sanitized" version of Satanism "for slightly wicked ladies and gentlemen," dropping "cannibalism, human sacrifice, and ritual orgies" over time.[68] Of course, even despite its sanitization, Laveyan Satanism did not sit well with America's Christians. As news media spread stories of Satanic rituals and sacrifices, related to LaVey's Church and other Satanic organizations, to heavy metal and to the Manson murders, a "Satanic panic" swept the nation, peaking in the mid-1980s and ebbing by the early 1990s.[69]

The bifurcation between people who fear hell and the devil with deadly seriousness and those who mock or identify with the embodiments of evil shows no sign of abating. A 2015 Pew Survey found that a majority of Americans (58 percent) continue to believe in hell as a place where "people who have led bad lives and die without being sorry are eternally punished." The numbers are much higher among "evangelical Protestants and members of historically Black Protestant churches"—82 percent—and roughly 76 percent among Muslim Americans. Buddhists, Hindus, and Jews are much less likely to believe in hell, with "roughly a third or less" responding to the query in the affirmative. And 27 percent of "nones" admit to such a belief.[70] Belief in the devil roughly corresponds with belief in hell, with 61 percent of Americans responding positively in a 2016 Gallup poll.[71]

The 2011 publication of *Love Wins: A Book about Heaven, Hell, and the Fate of Every Person Who Ever Lived* by the megachurch minister Rob Bell reveals the deep fissures

---

[65] Ibid., 161.

[66] Ruben Van Luijk, *Children of Lucifer: The Origins of Modern Religious Satanism*, Oxford Studies in Western Esotericism (New York: Oxford University Press, 2016), 2.

[67] Ibid., 324.   [68] Ibid., 396.   [69] Poole, *Satan in America*, 169–70.

[70] Carlyle Murphy, "Most Americans Believe in Heaven…and Hell," Pew Research Center, November 10, 2015, http://www.pewresearch.org/fact-tank/2015/11/10/most-americans-believe-in-heaven-and-hell/.

[71] Frank Newport, "Most Americans Still Believe in God," Gallup, June 29, 2016, https://news.gallup.com/poll/193271/americans-believe-god.aspx.

that continue to mark the country's infernal imagination.[72] The book offers a light universalism, asking readers to consider whether they really think Gandhi, for instance, could be in hell. Evangelical leaders rushed to condemn Bell's bestseller. *Christianity Today* called the book a "Bridge Too Far,"[73] alleging that Bell's liberalism, turning something that "offends today's current sensibilities" into "mere metaphor," makes Jesus a bland historical figure who does not inspire a passionate following. As in centuries past, hell continues to raise the stakes.

Hell has not inspired as much scholarship as some other theological ideas, largely because scholars have tended to dismiss it as "arcane," "bizarre," and illiberal. Scholarship on the devil, meanwhile, has tended to focus on how Satan is a figure used in political discourse and popular culture and to expend relatively less interpretive energy on what the devil actually means to believers. Of course, the personal is the political, the political is the personal, and both find expression in popular culture. But to better understand people's political convictions and the things by which they are haunted, horrified, and entertained, we might do well to take their "arcane" beliefs more seriously.

FUTURE PROSPECTS AND QUESTIONS

- What if we try to see hell and the devil as believers see them—as real presences that stalk their dreams and nightmares, that inspire people to action and inaction, that inflict real suffering and torment? Robert Orsi's *History and Presence* made much the same point with regard to the gods, when he urged historians and scholars of religion to be alive to the possibilities of real supernatural presence in the world.[74] If we suspend the normative assumption that hell and the devil are bizarre fictions, then how might we see and understand their real influence in the world?
- Relatedly, psychologists have recently begun to apply the work of historians on how Americans have imagined the color or race of God to contemporary experiments and studies.[75] How might the methodologies of psychology, sociology, political science, and anthropology teach us about hell and the devil's ramifications on political persuasions, voting patterns, religious affiliations, and other social formations? Are certain groups more or less likely to believe in hell and the devil than others? Why? What correlations, if any, can be drawn between region,

---

[72] Rob Bell, *Love Wins: A Book about Heaven, Hell, and the Fate of Every Person Who Ever Lived* (New York: HarperCollins, 2011).

[73] Mark Galli, "Rob Bell's Bridge Too Far," *Christianity Today*, March 14, 2011, https://www.christianitytoday.com/ct/2011/april/lovewins.html.

[74] Robert Orsi, *History and Presence* (Cambridge, MA: Harvard University Press, 2016), 8.

[75] See, for instance, Paul Harvey and Edward Blum, *The Color of Christ: The Son of God and the Saga of Race in America* (Chapel Hill: University of North Carolina Press, 2012); Steven O. Roberts et al., "God as a White man: A psychological barrier to conceptualizing Black people and women as leadership worthy," *Journal of Personality and Social Psychology* (American Psychological Association: Jan 1, 2020).

socioeconomic status, ethnic identification, age, and so on? (Historians might also do more to try to uncover such connections in earlier periods.)

- On the other hand, despite the fear and seriousness with which believers take the concepts of hell and the devil and apply them to their daily lives, hell and the devil often come across more ambiguously in popular culture. Just as the Romantic devil romanticized Satan as an alternative to God, so comic strips and films allow for demons and other hell-dwellers to become heroes or antiheroes (for instance, *Hellboy* and *Lucifer*). How are such pop-culture portrayals influencing religious ways of conceptualizing hell, not just in conservative evangelicalism's hell houses and graphic tracts but also in mainline religious cultures?

SUGGESTED READINGS AND ANNOTATED BIBLIOGRAPHY

Bivins, Jason. *Religion of Fear: The Politics of Horror in Conservative Evangelicalism*. Oxford: Oxford University Press, 2008.

This monograph provides a seminal and teachable analysis of the New Christian Right's engagement with the "politics of horror" in America: Chick tracts, antirock preaching, hell houses, and the *Left Behind* series of apocalyptic fiction. Bivins cogently explains the "religio-political" vision of conservative evangelicals and how and why it finds expression in and against popular culture.

Delbanco, Andrew. *The Death of Satan: How Americans Have Lost the Sense of Evil*. New York: Farrar, Straus and Giroux, 1995.

This is an older classic that is best read side by side with W. Scott Poole's *Satan in America: The Devil We Know*. Delbanco uses the tools of a literary historian to trace the decline of a sense of evil in America, from the Puritans to his present. His sensitive readings of Jonathan Edwards, Herman Melville, Reinhold Niebuhr, and others make this an engaging read, though it sometimes comes across as the jeremiad of a scholar who longs for a return to a deeper sense of evil.

Garrett, Greg. *Entertaining Judgment: The Afterlife in Popular Imagination*. New York: Oxford University Press, 2015.

This is the best recent publication exploring manifestations of hell, heaven, and purgatory in American popular culture. Garrett explores how the afterlife finds expression in and, indeed, makes theological points through music, art, film, television, books, graphic novels, comics, and computer and video games.

Gin Lum, Kathryn. *Damned Nation: Hell in America from the Revolution to Reconstruction*. New York: Oxford University Press, 2014.

Damned Nation asks how and why hell survived and mattered in the new United States, when other scholars have pointed to the "decline of hell" in contemporaneous Europe. Surveying sermons, diaries, and visual arts, it connects the survival of hell to unease over the end of monarchical rule, disestablishment, changing gender roles, and the slavery crisis.

Morone, James. *Hellfire Nation: The Politics of Sin in American History*. New Haven, CT: Yale University Press, 2003.

Morone's important work traces how sin and evil have been conceived in America. Morone, a political scientist, analyzes when and why sin and evil have been understood as an individual problem, and when and why they have been conceived as a social, systemic problem.

Poole, W. Scott. *Satan in America: The Devil We Know*. Lanham, MD: Rowman & Littlefield, 2009.

Poole's history of Satan in America offers an always entertaining but also ethically engaging romp through the devil's significance in the United States. Using a variety of creative sources, including fiction and film, Poole shows how the devil has always "been someone" in American history, offering a means of scapegoating enemies, explaining and conceptualizing evil, and countering injustice. In contrast to Delbanco, Poole finds the devil alive and well, writing as he is in the age of the "war on terror."

CHAPTER 14

THE RAPTURE IN AMERICAN IMAGINATION

TINA PIPPIN

RELIGIOUS STUDIES, AGNES SCOTT COLLEGE

INTRODUCTION

DREAMS of being airborne, leaving this sinful world and all its sinners behind in a cloud of chaos, is the ultimate end-time fantasy. The event comes "in the wink of an eye," but the before and after stories have infinite retellings. The story is steadfastly held by pre-millennialist, evangelical Christians who read the Rapture—which will be defined and discussed shortly—into biblical prophecy about the future of the living, and the dead, true believers. And because of this well-advertised belief, there are numerous parodies in popular culture. Both believers and nonbelievers highlight this story in fiction and film and other forms of material Christianity. Thus the Rapture spans the history of the twentieth century, often centralized in the global politics of the United States. As The Rapture Index website indicates, there are (to name a few on the list) natural disasters, epidemics, the movements of Russia and Iran and North Korea, and actions predicting the coming Antichrist that must be constantly monitored so believers can be "rapture ready."[1] The desire for heavenly flight is connected to a dystopian future of failed infra-structure and totalitarian torture. The Rapture is ultimately a violent story of people ripped from cars and homes and earth, the majority of humanity left to suffer under the rule of the Antichrist. The telling of the one story loops into other stories; thus the Rapture is prime material for popular mythmaking.

The word "rapture" does not appear in the Bible and does not get theological trac-tion until the nineteenth-century evangelical interpretations of 1 Thessalonians 4:15–17 (NRSV):

---

[1] The Rapture Ready website began in 2004. See www.raptureready.com/.

For this we declare to you by the word of the Lord, that we who are alive, who are left until the coming of the Lord, will by no means precede those who have died. For the Lord himself, with a cry of command with the archangel's call and with the sound of God's trumpet, will descend from heaven, and the dead in Christ will rise first. Then we who are alive, who are left, will be caught up in the clouds together with them to meet the Lord in the air; and so we will be with the Lord forever.

These verses are central to premillennialist Christian eschatology (the doctrine of last things). Premillennialism is the belief that Jesus will appear in the clouds *before* his thousand-year reign of peace on earth and will take the true Christian believers to heaven (unlike postmillennialism, which holds that Jesus will return only *after* a thousand-year period of peace has been established). According to premillennialist thought, once Jesus appears in the clouds, the Antichrist will arise on earth to rule those remaining in a seven-year Tribulation. Jesus appears again at the end of the Tribulation after the battle of Armageddon (Rev 16:16) and sends Satan to the lake of fire and sulfur, setting up a reign of peace for a thousand years on earth. At the end of this period, Jesus defeats Satan once and for all, ushering in the eternal New Jerusalem (aka Heaven).

According to Daniel Radosh, "In a poll conducted at the end of 2006, nearly half of white American evangelicals said Jesus was somewhat or very likely to return the following year. Pop culture may not be the cause of that belief, but it certainly contributes."[2] Barbara Rossing discusses the origins and development of this belief system, noting, "The Rapture has become embedded in American Christian culture today, but the idea of the Rapture is less than two hundred years old."[3]

[2] Daniel Radosh, *Rapture Ready! Adventures in the Parallel Universe of Christian Pop Culture* (New York: Soft Skull Press, 2010), 87. See also Angie Shumov, "How the End of the World Is Shown in Popular Culture," *The Story of God with Morgan Freeman: Apocalypse*, National Geographic Channel, April 10, 2016, https://www.nationalgeographic.com/tv/shows/the-story-of-god-with-morgan-freeman/episode-guide/season-01/episode-02-apocalypse/vdka10919237.

[3] Barbara Rossing, *The Rapture Exposed: the Message of Hope in the Book of Revelation* (Boulder, CO: Basic Books, 2007), 21. Much has been written on evangelical Christianity's premillennial, dispensational beliefs. For summaries of their beliefs in their historical context in American religious history, see Randall Balmer, *Mine Eyes Have Seen the Glory: A Journey into the Evangelical Subculture of America*, 5th ed. (Oxford: Oxford University Press, 2014); Heather Hendershot, *Shaking the World for Jesus: Media and Conservative Evangelical Culture* (Chicago: University of Chicago Press, 2004); Nicholas Guyatt, *Have a Nice Doomsday: Why Millions of Americans Are Waiting for the End of the World* (London: Ebury Press, 2007); Jon R. Stone, *A Guide to the End of the World: Popular Eschatology in America* (New York: Routledge, 1993); Timothy Weber, *Living in the Shadow of the Second Coming: American Premillennialism 1875–1882* (Chicago: University of Chicago Press, 1987); Paul Boyer, "The Growth of Fundamentalist Apocalyptic in the United States," in *The Continuum History of Apocalypticism*, ed. Bernard McGinn, John J. Collins, and Stephen J. Stein (New York: Continuum, 2003), 516–44; Grace Halsell, *Forcing God's Hand: Why Millions Pray for a Quick Rapture—and Destruction of Planet Earth* (Washington, DC: Crossroads International, 1999); Mark S. Sweetnam, "Tensions in Dispensational Eschatology," in *Expecting the End: Millennialism in Social and Historical Context*, ed. Kenneth G. C. Newport and Crawford Gribben (Waco, TX: Baylor University Press, 2006), 173–92; Matthew Avery Sutton, *American Apocalypse: A History of Modern Evangelicalism* (Cambridge, MA: Belknap Press of Harvard University Press, 2014); Robert Jewett, *Jesus against the Rapture: Seven Unexpected Prophecies* (Philadelphia, PA: Westminster Press, 1979); Kate Davis, David Heilbroner, and Franco Sacchi, dirs., *Waiting for Armageddon*, USA, First Run Features, 2009.

The Rapture does not take up much of the world's time. As people disappear (flying visibly upward or merely vanishing) and chaos ensues, the rest of the world has to cope with the mess. The crashing of cars, rampant looting, and panic tend to get more attention than the believers floating upward or the still running, suddenly abandoned lawn-mower or electric shaving razor. The focus here is on the Rapture of the church, of the truest believers. Within any believer's certainty of membership in the elite flight club there is an uncertainty, and popular narratives of the Rapture play on this fear. In material Christianity and secular parodies, the Rapture is lucrative business. Thus fundamentalist, premillennialist Christianity, and its critiques, are implanted in popular-culture visions of the way the world ends, next to zombies, alien abduction and invasion, and other imaginary (near) endings. In what follows, I give an overview of the most prominent appearances of the Rapture in American popular culture, along with the theological and political origins and connections.

OVERVIEW OF TOPIC

One of the most comprehensive investigations of the Rapture in popular culture was done by Amy Johnson Frykholm on the *Left Behind* franchise. Frykholm traces the evolution of Rapture culture in America leading to the Rapture fiction of Tim LaHaye and Jerry Jenkins. She relates, "The rapture is woven into the fabric of American culture, a part of the culture's hopes, dreams, fears, and mythology."[4] In their initial twelve books LaHaye and Jenkins follow the premillennialist timeline of the Rapture to the Glorious Appearing of Jesus to inaugurate his thousand-year reign, with a focus on the middle part, the seven-year Tribulation and reign of the Antichrist. In their prophecy outline Jesus appears two times: before and then after the seven-year Tribulation.[5] The Rapture (1 Thess 4:7) and the Glorious Appearing (Titus 2:13) are also supported by Revelation 4:1.

The idea of Rapture began as part of the dispensationalist story of the end of the world with the preacher John Nelson Darby (1800–1882), who believed that human history was divided into eras called "dispensations." At the end of the "church age" there would

---

[4] Amy Johnson Frykholm, *Rapture Culture: Left Behind in Evangelical America* (New York: Oxford University Press, 2004), 13. Catherine Keller uses the term "rapture fantasy" for dispensational theology in her *Apocalypse Now and Then: A Feminist Guide to the End of the World* (Boston: Beacon Press, 1996), 55–6. Gregory Krupey defines the Rapture as "a literal airlift of the Elect, while still alive, into Heaven." See his "The Christian Right, Zionism, and the Coming of the Penteholocaust," in *Apocalypse Culture*, ed. Adam Parfrey (Port Townsend, WA: Feral House, 1990), 286–98, here 288.

[5] Tim LaHaye and Thomas Ice, *Charting the End Times: Prophecy Study Guide* (Eugene, OR: Harvest House, 2002). In this book the authors enlist all the biblical authors possible to rally their cause. Their popular charts dominate the premillennialist scene and carry forward the tradition that began in the early twentieth-century dispensationalist movement. See also their Pre-Trib Research Center for updates on prophecy belief and the signs of the times leading to the Rapture: http://www.pre-trib.org/. See also Tim LaHaye, Thomas Ice, and Ed Hindson, eds., *The Popular Handbook on the Rapture: Experts Speak Out on End-Times Prophecy* (Eugene, OR: Harvest House, 1982).

be a "secret rapture," with the true believers meeting Jesus in the clouds.[6] Cyrus Scofield in his Scofield Reference Bible (KJV 1909, rev. 1917) used Darby's notes on the Bible, in particular the book of Revelation, thus spreading the doctrine of dispensationalism. Darby also popularized the use of the word "rapture," a Latin term from Jerome's Vulgate translation of 1 Thessalonians 4:16–17 in the late fourth century CE. Frykholm explains, "In the Vulgate translation, 'caught up' was translated *rapiemur*, from the Latin verb *rapio*. In medieval Latin, *rapio* became a noun, *rapture*, which then became in English 'rapture.' For Darby, rapture designated the event of the 'taking up' of the true church to heaven in the Last Days combined with the religious and emotional ecstasy that the word implied."[7] Dispensationalist eschatology began to spread in the late nineteenth and early twentieth centuries. Adherents remained on the margins of fundamentalist Christianity until the mid-twentieth century.

Frykholm notes, "Most scholars of American religion agree that the rapture emerged in American Protestant culture at a moment when conservative Protestants felt a decline of culture power."[8] She shows some of the uneasiness that some Christians have with the popularization (and fictionalizing) of what they believe as a basic eschatological tenet: "Readers occasionally express anxiety about the influence of secular culture and sometimes roundly condemn it, but rarely does this concern inhibit the buying, renting or consuming of popular culture in its broadest possible sense."[9] Both evangelical Christians and secularists read the *Left Behind* series, the latter as a thriller genre. Dispensationalist Rapture belief began to get a firmer foothold in popular culture with visual media, so when the *Left Behind* series was reproduced in films (a trend that began with *A Thief in the Night* in 1972), a board game, and a violent video game, this theology of the end time became immensely profitable.[10] While one intent may be to reach more

---

[6] Frykholm, *Rapture Culture*, 15.

[7] Ibid., 16–17. See also the overview of Darby and dispensationalism in Balmer, *Mine Eyes Have Seen the Glory*, 33–8.

[8] Frykholm, *Rapture Culture*, 18. She notes further "how the story of the rapture disciplines religious subjects. It brings into focus deeply rooted fears about isolation and personal failure; it plays on these fears in order to produce in even very devout people a nagging uncertainty about their own worthiness" (151).

[9] Ibid., 23.

[10] The original Rapture film was a ten-minute film for distribution to churches: *The Rapture*, dir. Carlos Baptista, USA, Scriptures Visualized Institute, 1941. The first film from the *Left Behind* series, *Left Behind: The Movie*, dir. Vic Sarin, USA, Cloud Ten, 2000, has the Rapture event. The copycat film starring Nicolas Cage does not give a religious reason for the Rapture-like event, even though the film is based on the LaHaye and Jenkins book series (*Left Behind*, dir. Vic Armstrong, USA, Sony Pictures, 2014). For an overview of rapture films, see John Wallis, "From the Rapture to *Left Behind*: The Movie and Beyond—Evangelical Christian End Times Films from 1941 to the Present," *Journal of Religion and Film* 13, no. 2 (2016), http://digitalcommons.unomaha.edu/jrf/vol13/iss2/4/; John Walliss, "Celling the End Times: The Contours of Contemporary Rapture Films," in *Reel Revelations: Apocalypse and Film*, ed. John Walliss and Lee Quinby (Sheffield, UK: Sheffield Phoenix, 2010), 91–111. Of apocalyptic films Terry Lindvall and Andrew Quiche note the exploitation of "Darby's 19th century notion of the Rapture": "This apocalyptic genre attracted an anxious and gullible audience.... These cinematic interpretations triggered fear and restlessness." Terry Lindvall and Andrew Quiche, *Celluloid Sermons: The Emergence of the Christian Film Industry, 1930–1986* (New York: New York University Press, 2011), 187.

"unsaved" people, the outcome is ultimately materialist: the financial jackpot of a long-running bestselling series.

Not only capitalist culture but (ever shifting) contemporary right-wing politics and US superiority form the backdrop of the *Left Behind* series and much of its readership. Frykholm calls the series "negotiated texts," with shifting views of the relationship of Christ and culture and of gender roles.[11] She names this re-formed Rapture culture in fiction "hybrid dispensationalism."[12]

David Morgan, a scholar of material Christianity, evaluated the Rapture belief of the mid-1800s in ways that echo current times: "The idea of the millennium allowed many evangelicals to anchor an unstable republic to an imperialistic scenario of the unfolding of the kingdom of God on American soil. Republican government thereby became yet another millennial means, a national sign of the times, and instrument to be shaped and influenced toward the higher end of divine kingship."[13] The Rapture is not really about good defeating evil. In Rapture mythologies the "good" vanish forever, leaving the "evil." Perhaps the "good" have a front-row seat to witness the Tribulation, clothed in heavenly garments, nibbling heavenly snacks, aroused by the violence on earth. The Rapture is not air tight, so to speak. The story extends beyond the Rapture, as LaHaye and Jenkins knew very well in the prequels and sequels of their *Left Behind* series.

In his discussion of the *Left Behind* series, Radosh explains that true believers can leave evangelizing material for those left behind so that they will become saved and part of the Tribulation Force in the seven-year reign of the Antichrist. This material entails the video of Tribulation instructions from the first novel that the main protagonists saw, along with a post-Rapture email sent to loved ones, from the website RaptureLetters. com.[14] The site guarantees to send letters for free to any names you submit and vows that "a letter will be sent to each of them on the first Friday after the rapture. Then they will receive another letter every Friday after that." The standard letter states, "This may come as a shock to you, but the one who sent this has been taken up to heaven."[15] Radosh observes, "Perhaps the most interesting thing about apocalyptic fiction of the early 1990s is that it is even more explicit than *Left Behind* in its political agenda."[16] Radosh's main example is Pat Robertson's novel, *The End of the Age*, which reflects Robertson's premillennialist theology.[17]

Israel and Jerusalem are central in Rapture tales, thus plugging solidly into Christian Zionism. Victoria Clark argues that belief in the Rapture "allows Christian Zionists to contemplate the wholesale horror of the End Times with a mixture of pitying resigna-

---

[11] Frykholm, *Rapture Culture*, 29–37.

[12] Ibid., 37. Frykholm quotes Anne Lamott, *Traveling Mercies: Some Thoughts on Faith* (New York: Pantheon, 1999), 60, on the series: "hard-core right-wing paranoid anti-Semitic homophobic misogynistic propaganda—not to put too fine a point on it" (177).

[13] David Morgan, *Protestants and Pictures: Religion, Visual Culture, and the Age of American Mass Production* (New York: Oxford University Press, 1999), 34.

[14] Radosh, *Rapture Ready!*, 77–8.   [15] RaptureLetters.com/letter.html.

[16] Radosh, *Rapture Ready!*, 82.   [17] Radosh, *Rapture Ready!*, 82–3.

tion and gleeful excitement."[18] On anti-Jewishness in the series Radosh explains, "Jewish characters in *Left Behind* are given three choices: join the antichrist and go to hell; resist the antichrist and go to a concentration camp (and eventually to hell); or become a Messianic Jew who believes in Jesus."[19] Jews are definitely left behind unless they convert to evangelical Christianity.

Radosh acknowledges the *Left Behind* series as "a pop culture icon" but its ongoing influence from its beginning in 1995 is waning. He writes, "As I discovered when I asked Christians about it, the secular world's continued fascination with *Left Behind* is seen as a sign of how out of touch we are with evangelical culture."[20]

Whatever the decade, premillennialist Rapture theology anticipates the violent start of God's future end game. This game begins with a jolt, the Rapture. Randall Balmer traced the theology of otherworldliness and the move from involvement in social justice in dispensationalist thought, writing, "Despite the continuation of some evangelical reform efforts, this notion relieved evangelicals of the obligation to labor for the amelioration of social ills. Evangelicals increasingly stood in judgment of culture and awaited its destruction, which would follow their translation into heaven."[21] In fact, in the *Left Behind* storyline, as well as in right-wing US politics, a fully militarized government, complete with nuclear weapons, is necessary for the coming apocalypse.

Paul Boyer summarizes the emphasis in the Rapture on escape from this world: "Belief in the Rapture—'God's rescue of all true Christians from this tortured earth'— further diluted the impetus to political activism. The redeemed would watch history's climax from the skies."[22] But Boyer is careful to point out that not all premillennialists shun social justice work.[23] Many believe in doing work "in the meantime," before the Rapture. Similarly, in Michael Northcott's analysis, "a society deeply influenced by the bad theology of the 'rapture' is a society ideologically prepared for the extreme inequality and social division that have been the consequence of the imposition of the neo-liberal 'free' market capitalism since the Reagan administrations of the 1980s."[24] Northcott acknowledges the dual modes at work in Rapture theology and ideology: "dispensationalist fatalism" and "free" market capitalism. This context sets the space for imagining "even first use nuclear weapons."[25] Northcott understands the broader implication of Rapture belief and the sullen truths behind the representations of the Rapture in popular culture (both Christian and the secular response): "Behind the walls and security guards of corporate gated communities, or in the ghettos and deracinated working-class neighborhoods of post-industrial American cities, rich and poor alike take refuge in the

---

[18] Victoria Clark, *Allies for Armageddon: The Rise of Christian Zionism* (New Haven, CT: Yale University Press, 2007), 4. See her discussion on the *Left Behind* computer game's focus on Jewish messianists making up the Tribulation Force (245).

[19] Radosh, *Rapture Ready!*, 85.   [20] Ibid., 87.

[21] Balmer, *Mine Eyes Have Seen the Glory*, 34–5. Balmer gives an overview of Darby's theology on 33–8.

[22] Boyer, *And Time Shall Be No More*, 299.   [23] See Boyer's detailed discussion (ibid., 299–304).

[24] Michael S. Northcott, *An Angel Directs the Storm: American Religion and American Empire* (London: SCM Press, 2007), 68–9.

[25] Ibid., 89.

dream that they might be included in the rapture to compensate for the failed dream of a commonwealth of liberty and democracy."[26]

Rossing gives an important response to the theology and politics implied and inspired by the *Left Behind* series and guides readers through the mess of dispensationalist prophecy belief. She maintains a hopeful reading of the last book of the Bible: "The Bible and the book of Revelation come to life most of all in life-giving experiences of hope, healing, and transformation."[27] Not all readers respond to LaHaye, Lindsey, and others with such a positive reading of biblical apocalyptic. The premillennialists have dominated popular culture, and most of the secular (liberal) response is a parody of these exaggerated, exclusivist advertisements for the End. A lot of energy has been spent responding to Rapture belief, and the effect is that the Rapture has become a prominent cultural phenomenon. Unlike popular apocalyptic tales of the near future such as *The Walking Dead*, Rapture presupposes an escape hatch for true believers. Society (mostly conceived as Western, capitalist society) slides into its final degradation, brought about by folks who do not believe in the Rapture. The novel and television show *The Leftovers* reimagines the event; the idea of a Rapture with some of the population left behind still drags with it Darby's legacy. The paranoia and neurosis of current political times—whatever the "present" is—only morphs into new forms of belief and disbelief.

The Rapture is a "floating signifier" in popular culture. According to Stephen O'Leary, the Rapture is the " 'any-moment coming' . . . a floating 'locus of the irreparable,' a temporal threshold that would cut the audience off from the chance to avoid the persecutions of the Tribulation."[28] Even so, Rapture makes every space and time apocalyptic; there is no safe refuge and no way to avoid the momentous, global event.

SPECIFIC EXAMPLES AND/OR FOCI

> Life was filled with guns and war
> And everyone got trampled on the floor....
> The children died, the days grew cold
> A piece of bread could buy a bag of gold....
> A man and wife asleep in bed
> She hears a noise and turns her head he's gone....
> There's no time to change your mind
> The Son has come and you've been left behind.[29]

---

[26] Ibid., 72.   [27] Rossing, *The Rapture Exposed*, 100.

[28] Stephen D. O'Leary, *Arguing the Apocalypse: A Theory of Millennial Rhetoric* (New York: Oxford University Press, 1994), 139. On the "secret rapture" and an overview of Hal Lindsey's premillennialist prophecy teaching, see 138–9. Lindsey refers to the rapture as "the ultimate trip" (162) and a way for believers to avoid their own physical death (139). Evan Calder Williams, *Combined and Uneven Apocalypse* (Winchester, UK: Zero Books, 2011), 149, takes a broader view: "The world is already apocalyptic. Just not all at the same time. To be overcome: the notion of apocalypse as eventual, the ground-clearing trauma that immediately founds a new *nomos* of the earth. In its place: combined and uneven apocalypse."

[29] Larry Norman, "I Wish We'd All Been Ready," *Upon This Rock*, Capitol Records, 1969.

Larry Norman's Christian rock song "I Wish We'd All Been Ready" first appeared in *A Thief in the Night* (1972), the first Christian Rapture film, and reflected the urgency of salvation. The film plays on the emotions of losing loved ones, as the opening scenes show the reactions of those left behind to the sudden disappearance of husbands, wives, and children. The film provides the setup for evangelizing and "saving souls." The point is to be "saved" and among the elect in the imminent Second Coming of Christ. Norman's album was a major entry of evangelical Christians into the genre of rock music. With the film and even more this song, premillennialist Christianity utilized the concept of the Rapture to push its urgent message of the end times.

Time magazine called *A Thief in the Night*, directed by Don. W. Thompson, a "church-basement classic," and the film has been seen by millions.[30] According to Balmer, "It is only a slight exaggeration to say that *A Thief in the Night* affected the evangelical film industry the way that sound or color affected Hollywood."[31] The story lays out the popular apocalyptic dispensational premillennialism based on Matthew 24:36–44 and 1 Thessalonians 4:16–17. Through the use of the horror genre, the drama of the film intended to shock and evoke an emotional response. The rock music by Norman, and his theme song, used a popular music genre to reach the "unsaved." This film also paved the way for the *Left Behind* franchise. And both prompted multiple spoofs of Rapture theology.

Boyer finds the Rapture in Christian kitsch that evangelizes. For example, "Salem Kirban and Leon Bates of the Texas-based Bible Believers' Evangelistic Association offered Rapture wrist watches with the words, 'one hour nearer the Lord's return' inscribed around the face... and full-color Rapture paintings, complete with crashing cars and planes."[32] The popular bumper sticker "Warning! In case of Rapture, this car will be unmanned" has provoked multiple sarcastic responses: "In case of rapture": "can I have your car?"; "you and I will still be stuck in traffic"; and "this car will be pulled off to the side of the road while I reconsider my previously amillennial eschatology." The theological debate on bumper stickers relates a much longer debate and popular parodies.

A Thief in the Night, in all its hokey, overdramatic messaging, was ripe for parody. For example, in a 2004 episode of the television series *Six Feet Under*, "In Case of Rapture," a Rapture-believing woman is listening to a Christian radio program in her car. She has the requisite "I brake for the rapture" bumper sticker. At the same time two young guys at a sex shop are putting helium-filled blow-up dolls in a net to carry to a porn film awards show. They have to brake suddenly to avoid a skateboarder, setting the netting loose and the dolls flying skyward. The devout woman mistakes the dolls for Rapturing believers; she sees them (ironically) not naked but clothed in angelic robes. In her excitement she jumps out of her car, praising Jesus and ready to join the flight, and is immediately hit and killed by an oncoming car.[33] This comic but tragic interpretation of the Rapture underscores its outrageous aspects.

---

[30] Balmer, *Mine Eyes Have Seen the Glory*, 373. Balmer discusses the film specifically on 48–70.
[31] Ibid., 65.   [32] Boyer, *And Time Shall Be No More*, 7–8.
[33] David Attias, dir., "In Case of Rapture," *Six Feet Under*, season 4, episode 2, HBO, 2004.

One of the best known Rapture interpretations in popular culture appeared on May 8, 2005. An episode of *The Simpsons*, titled "Thank God It's Doomsday," shows Homer Simpson at a Bible prophecy end-time movie called *Left Below*, an obvious play on the *Left Behind* series.[34] He is totally horrified but, believing that the end is near, goes out prophesying in Springfield. "It's the end of the world! God loves you. He's going to kill you" is the main message, despite Marge's argument that "God wouldn't spring the Rapture on us unannounced. He'd send us signs." Thereafter, the "signs" appear, after much word play. After some fancy math, Homer decides on a date and convinces the townspeople to meet on the hilltop outside of town to await the Rapture. The time passes and the people go back to their homes discouraged, leaving Homer disparaged and alone on the hill. Then the Rapture occurs and Homer is taken up to heaven. An angel gives him a tour, depositing him in his luxury hotel room with TV access to watch the Tribulation on earth. As Homer watches the torments of his family, he demands to talk to God, and he asks him "to undo the apocalypse." Reluctantly, after a destructive temper tantrum by Homer, God agrees, and Homer awakes from his "dream" and heads to Moe's Bar, his view of heaven.[35]

Following along similar lines is an episode of *American Dad* titled "Rapture's Delight."[36] The family attends their once-a-year church service at Christmas, and as the parents, Stan and Francine, have sex in the basement, the Rapture occurs. They watch a massive group of people fly naked into the air, including their two children, and Stan whines, "There's been a mistake! Lift me up, Lord!" After some endurance of the post-Rapture the family is reunited, but the main emphasis is on who is among the elect and who is left behind.

Some Hollywood films investigate a more literal reading of dispensationalist theology. For example, *The Rapture* (1991), directed by Michael Tolkin, stars Mimi Rogers as Sharon, an unbelieving woman who joins a premillennial sect.[37] She flees with her young daughter to the California desert to await the Rapture; when it fails to happen, she kills her daughter. Later, in prison, the Rapture occurs, but she is left behind because she denies God, whom she blames for the infanticide of her daughter. Thus Tolkin examines the line between prophecy and mental illness.

---

[34] "Thank God It's Doomsday," *The Simpsons*, season 16, episode 19, Fox, May 8, 2005. See the discussion of this episode in Dan W. Clanton, Jr. and Mark Roncace, "Animated Television," in *Teaching the Bible in Popular Culture and the Arts*, ed. Mark Roncace and Patrick Gray (Atlanta, GA: Society of Biblical Literature, 2007), 347.

[35] Other episodes of *The Simpsons* that depict the Rapture include "Simpsons' Bible Stories," season 10, episode 18, Fox, April 4, 1999. At the end of this episode the Simpson family does not ascend with the rest of their church (except for Lisa, whom Homer pulls down); rather they descend into the hell mouth. In "Lisa the Skeptic," season 9, episode 8, Fox, November 23, 1997, Lisa doubts that a discovered skeleton of an angel is real. See the discussion of these episodes in Mark I. Pinsky, *The Gospel according to* The Simpsons: *Bigger and Possibly Even Better! Edition* (Louisville, KY: Westminster John Knox, 2007), 24, 39, 43–5, 118–9.

[36] "Rapture's Delight," *American Dad*, season 5, episode 9, TBS, December 13, 2009.

[37] Michael Tolkin, dir., *The Rapture*, USA, Warner Bros., 1991.

Sometimes the end appears in alien form. In *Close Encounters of the Third Kind* (1977), directed by Steven Spielberg, a single mom's son is abducted by aliens in a "mother ship." Although people get returned in the end, some decide to take their chances with the aliens. Conspiracy theory about the US government and UFOs is played out in a different way than in the 1996 film *Independence Day*, for example, where the aliens are out to destroy Earth. In *Close Encounters* an alien mother ship replaces Jesus descending in the clouds.[38]

Tom Perrotta's 2011 postapocalyptic novel *The Leftovers* takes a creative, secular approach to Rapture fiction.[39] Imagining that millions of the earth's population has mysteriously disappeared into thin air, Perrotta follows the aftereffects of the remaining population dealing with such an abrupt and unexplained tragedy, known as "the Sudden Departure."[40] His focus is the suburban town of Mapleton, New York. After the departure, life continues; there is no "tribulation" period as in the *Left Behind* series, where American infrastructure crumbles under the world dictatorship of the Antichrist. The book opens with the thoughts of someone who had been left behind, Laurie Garvey, the wife of the main character and mayor of Mapleton, Kevin Garvey. She remembers learning about premillennialist thought and the rapture in a college world religions course:

> It felt like religious kitsch, as tacky as a black velvet painting, the kind of fantasy that appealed to people who ate too much fried food, spanked their kids, and had no problem with the theory that their loving God invented AIDS to punish the gays....
> And then it happened. The biblical prophecy came true, or at least partly true. People disappeared, millions of them at the same time, all over the world.... This was real. The Rapture happened in her own hometown, to her best friend's daughter, among others, while Laurie herself was in the house. God's intrusion into her life couldn't have been any clearer if He'd addressed her from a burning azalea.[41]

People deal with the departures in various ways; relationships shift. The event causes Laurie to join an apocalyptic cult, the Guilty Remnant. One key character, Nora Durst, lost her family. Perrotta's focus is not on the event of the disappearance, for he never gives an explanation for it. His interest is on the various psychological ways the survivors cope, from those with nuclear families intact to those who experience almost unbearable loss.[42] Since people of different faiths and of no faith are among the disappeared, making sense of what happened does not find a dispensationalist framework useful. No ethical framework exists for such an unexplainable event. The world looks the same in the aftermath; governments and economies continue on; that is, in a different

---

[38] Similar films that investigate the human desire to connect with intelligent life in the universe include *Contact*, dir. Robert Zemeckis, USA, Warner Bros., 1997; and *Interstellar*, dir. Christopher Nolan, USA, Paramount, 2014.

[39] Tom Perrotta, *The Leftovers: A Novel* (New York: St. Martin's Griffin, 2011). The HBO series *The Leftovers* (creator Damon Lindel, 2014–7) extended Tom Perrotta's 2011 novel: Damon Lindel, prod., "Sudden Departure," *The Leftovers*, HBO, June 24, 2014.

[40] Perrotta, *The Leftovers*, 2.   [41] Ibid.

[42] Andrew Tate, *Apocalyptic Fiction* (London: Bloomsbury Academic, 2017), 51.

way from other postapocalyptic fiction, the infrastructure of societies remains in place. Everything looks the same, but everything has changed forever. That rupture provides the eerie sense of reality—in other words, the uncanny.[43]

The novel is a study in grief and an acknowledgment of American fascination with end-times prophecies; it is also an exploration of the seductive rhetoric of fanaticism as a response to loss and a sense of powerlessness. This is a new kind of agnostic narrative: phenomena that exceed rational explanation are not dismissed or exposed as a hoax, but neither are they represented as signs to be followed into blind obedience to cult leaders or authoritarian politicians.[44]

The Rapture and its aftermath figure prominently in popular, secular representations of the apocalypse. In some ways these narratives are liberal responses to irrational visions of the future. As in Perrotta's novel, the response is to turn the idea in on itself; a Rapture-like event happens, but Jesus does not appear in the clouds, and a totally random set of humanity disappears, with many fervent prophecy believers left behind. There are multiplicities to this cruel joke; believers were duped, but the whole of humanity suffers from the sudden disappearance. Religious fanaticism (with cigarettes, since the new sect chain-smokes) is one way the left behind try to make sense of their grief. Ultimately there is no making sense of the non-sense of the event. Perrotta throws this challenge back at the premillennialists: nothing good can come of such a violent, separatist event. There is only loss, and an absent God.

In his review of the book, Stephen King points to the coincidental timing of the book's release with Harold Camping's Rapture pronouncement of May 21, 2011. King sees the plot as "the best 'Twilight Zone' episode you never saw," thus connecting the Rapture (or here, the Sudden Departure) to the uncanny.[45] The timing of Perrotta's book around Camping's radio preaching on the Rapture date is interesting. Camping's billboards were in the news; they advertised "Judgment Day May 21, 2011…The Bible Guarantees It" with a scripture reference to Jonah 3:8.[46]

The HBO television adaptation of Perrotta's book ran three seasons (2014–7) and expanded and changed the book's narrative. The Rapture-like event and what follows develops as a psychological apocalypse, especially in two of the main characters: Kevin, now a police chief, and Nora, enduring the great loss of her family. The series ends ambiguously, with Nora's story that she went through a machine to an alternate world in

---

[43] In his study of apocalyptic fiction, Tate observes, "The 'sudden disappearance…is, in part, a metafictional commentary on a culture already saturated with stories of damnation and salvation" (ibid., 49). Tate uses Slavoj Žižek's idea of the "event," a sudden happening "without discernable cause" (51); see Slavoj Žižek, *Event: Philosophy in Transit* (London: Penguin, 2014), 2.

[44] Tate, *Apocalyptic Fiction*, 60.

[45] Stephen King, "The Eerie Aftermath of a Mass Exit," *New York Times Book Review*, August 25, 2011.

[46] Jonah 3:8 reads, "Human beings and animals shall be covered with sackcloth, and they shall cry mightily to God. All shall turn from their evil ways from the violence that is in their hands" (NRSV). A documentary about Camping's eschatology traced its roots and revision after the prophesied date; Camping then preached that choosing a date was unbiblical. See Zeke Piesstrup, dir., *Apocalypse Later: Harold Camping vs the End of the World*, USA, Gravitas Ventures, 2013.

which, after a sort of Rapture, 98 percent of the population disappeared and only 2 percent survived.[47] King's thoughts on the political context of the book apply even more to the television version; he writes, "In times of real trouble, extremism trumps [no pun intended] logic and dialogue becomes meaningless. Read as a metaphor for the social and political splintering of American society after 9/11, it's a chillingly accurate diagnosis."[48]

In a similar play on the theme of sudden disappearance, Michael Grant's young adult series *Gone* (2008–13) has an unexplainable, sudden disappearance of everyone fifteen years old and older. With all the adults gone, the main teen characters slide quickly into chaos, as they morph over the nine books into superheroes or supermonsters, setting up a battle of good versus evil.[49] Dystopian science fiction is a mainstay of young adult literature, and imagining a world without adults is a cautionary tale.

The historian Nicholas Guyatt exposes the difficulties some in Bible prophecy have with selling the end times: "In the process, they've been trying to reconcile the Christian message with the demands of popular culture. Can you imagine a feel-good movie about the Rapture? If you design a video game about the Tribulation, is it okay to let people play for the Antichrist's team?"[50] The end times sells. Believers and nonbelievers alike can participate in the ultimate end-time battle of good and evil, God and Satan. The Rapture captures the imagination; the fantasy of flight away from the crises and chaos of earth into some monolithic paradise seduces.

CONCLUSION

The Rapture event serves as a dramatic opener for the drama of premillennialist, dispensational eschatology. Prophecy belief holds to biblical origins of this thinking, mainly 1 Thessalonians 4:17, where believers will be caught up into the air to meet Jesus. The proliferation of predictions and warnings about this ending will continue in material religion, fiction, film, and virtual reality (video games, etc.) in both Christian premillennial and secular forms. The Rapture is the necessary event to set off the real drama, the seven-year Tribulation. In the latter, the span from parody to more realist imaginations of mass disappearances shows how powerful the myth has become.

Popular culture has thoroughly infiltrated premillennialism; the Rapture has been "caught up" in the need for translation in secular forms.[51] As dystopian fiction and film

---

[47] Damon Lindelof and Tom Perrotta, *The Leftovers*, HBO, Film 44/Warner Bros., 2014–7.

[48] King, "The Eerie Aftermath."

[49] Michael Grant, *Gone* (repr., New York: Katherine Tegen Books, 2014).

[50] Guyatt, *Have a Nice Doomsday*, 189.

[51] See Conrad Ostwalt's discussion of the "secularization of the sacred," that is, "the tendency for religious institutions to employ secular and popular culture forms like television and movies to make religious teachings relevant to a modern audience" in his *Sacred Steeples: Popular Culture and the Religious Imagination*, 2nd ed. (London: Bloomsbury, 2012), 28.

gain in popularity, Rapture-like events will continue to fuel plot devices. Rapture sets up postcatastrophe fiction and provides a mysterious event with no clear answers.

The idea of the Rapture will continue to fuel escapist visions of the future. In an (un) certain time, depending on your belief system, the Rapture provides hope in being among the elect. Rapture also props up beliefs in the supernatural spaces of a literal heaven and hell.

In addition, the Rapture will continue to be a moneymaker, no matter how seriously or trivialized its manifestations. The Rapture will continue to be available at bookstores, grocery store Christian book racks, convenience stores at airports, and in film, fiction, games, astronomical events (e.g., Halley's comet), nuclear anxieties, and everywhere but the Bible. Will the end-time debate ever be settled? What is at stake is ultimately not souls but the need of some people to imagine a future with or without God.

FUTURE PROSPECTS AND QUESTIONS

- What is the importance of the Rapture to premillennialist Christian eschatology?
- What are the political implications of Rapture theology? In what ways has this belief in an imminent ending of the world influenced US politics, including decisions over nuclear weapons, military planning, doomsday preparations, and perceptions by some US leaders of their country's superiority in global politics?
- In what ways does Rapture theology add to the insider/outsider hierarchy in social groups? What does it mean for Christian premillennialists to be among the chosen elite?
- How do environmental occurrences (weather, climate change, extinctions, etc.) feed into prophecy beliefs about the timing of the Rapture?
- What are the major scholarly responses to Rapture theology and its cultural manifestations in material culture and media?
- What are the guidelines for formulating ethical responses to evangelical Christian end-times ideology, in terms of both the religious and political realms?

SUGGESTED READINGS AND ANNOTATED BIBLIOGRAPHY

Balmer, Randall. *Mine Eyes Have Seen the Glory: A Journey into the Evangelical Subculture in America*. 5th edition. New York: Oxford University Press, 2014.

Balmer investigates the roots of dispensationalist theology from its nineteenth-century beginnings to the twenty-first century. He shows how this theology began with Darby and gained momentum through the Scofield Reference Bible and twentieth-century Rapture films.

Boyer, Paul. *When Time Shall Be No More: Prophecy Belief in Modern American Culture*. Cambridge, MA: Harvard University Press, 1992.

Boyer offers a historian's view of the political and cultural background of Rapture and premillennialist eschatology. He explores the major players, from Darby and Scofield to Lindsey and Falwell. Interwoven into this belief system is a disregard for social justice that manifests most violently in nuclear history and continued proliferation. Boyer explores the presence of end-of-the-world prophecy in popular music (both Christian and secular), in apocalyptic fiction, and in kitschy Christian art and artifacts.

Frykholm, Amy Johnson. *Rapture Culture*: Left Behind *in Evangelical America*. New York: Oxford University Press, 2004.

Frykholm has written the central book on understanding the role of Rapture in American religion. She makes the connections between the popular *Left Behind* series and politics and culture and shows why the phenomenon of the Rapture concept is so compelling. Frykholm also studies readers of Tim LaHaye and Jerry Jenkins's *Left Behind* series. These readers may identify broadly as evangelicals, but the meaning is diverse, from a more literal fundamentalism to a looser engagement with secular culture. She describes the readers as both in the world and against the world, with the series bridging the divide. The interviews with readers expose the popularity of these books and of the desire for the Rapture.

Lindsey, Hal. *The Late Great Planet Earth*. New York: Zondervan, 1970.

Lindsey's book was the bestselling nonfiction book of the 1970s. He gives stark details of the premillennialist timeline, from the Rapture through the Tribulation. The historical and political contexts of Cold War ideology are now dated, and his original Rapture date long past, but Lindsey continues his prophecy belief on his news show *The Hal Lindsey Report* (http://www.hallindsey.com/news/). Lindsey feeds every bit of current news he can into his "prophecy belief filter" so that the Rapture is imminent.

Radosh, Daniel. *Rapture Ready! Adventures in the Parallel Universe of Christian Pop Culture*. New York: Soft Skull Press, 2010.

Radosh is a comedy writer and journalist who investigated the American evangelical subculture on Rapture theology. He met with wrestlers, creationists, punk rock evangelists, and others in popular Rapture culture. He looks into the biblical roots of a variety of Rapture enactments.

A Thief in the Night. Dir. Don W. Thompson. USA, Mark IV Pictures, 1972.

This film marked the beginning of Christian apocalyptic films aimed at a larger audience, based on 1 Thessalonians 5:2: "For you yourselves know very well that the day of the Lord will come like a thief in the night." Other films followed in this Rapture series: *A Distant Thunder* (1978), *Image of the Beast* (1981), *The Prodigal Planet* (1983). This series paved the way for subsequent films by Trinity Broadcast Network (*The Omega Code* in 1999 and *Megiddo: Omega Code 2* in 2001) and the films from the *Left Behind* series, among others. Both these films show the Tribulation and the rise of the Antichrist, but there is no Rapture due to screenplay decisions.

CHAPTER 15

THE AFTERLIFE IN THE BIBLE AND POPULAR CULTURE

GREG GARRETT

DEPARTMENT OF ENGLISH, BAYLOR UNIVERSITY

INTRODUCTION

IF religion, as many definitions would have it, is concerned with where we came from, who we are, and where we are going, then the afterlife—the fate of human souls following their earthly sojourn—is often one of the most important elements of religious faith. Many Christians read the Bible in an attempt to discover our ultimate fate. If, as Jesus tells his followers in chapter 14 of the Gospel of John, the Father's house contains many dwelling places and Jesus is departing to prepare a place for them, what are those dwelling places like? What is that place? Conversely, where are the souls of those who reject Jesus bound? What is their dwelling place to be? The faithful may pull an image from one section of the Bible, an idea from another, and construct a city paved with gold or imagine angels plucking harps (or themselves as angels plucking harps!), while the damned reside somewhere in outer darkness, where there is weeping and gnashing of teeth. Some Christians are even convinced that the Bible is a roadmap to Heaven or a travel guide to avoid Hell, since they are so taught from the pulpit, by Christian writers, or on the signs in front of churches in which certain Bible verses are indicated to be directly referring to Heaven or Hell and useful in how to reach one destination or the other.

However, a central problem in imagining the afterlife comes because, as N. T. Wright notes, the Bible does not actually contain a great deal of information about the afterlife. Many of the references to Heaven in the Christian Testament, for example, are not about a future dwelling place where the good will reside but about the Kingdom of Heaven, a new reality that Jesus has come to Earth to inaugurate.[1] So it is, Wright theorizes, that early Christians relied on the human imagination—on painting and sculpture, on tapestries and stained glass, and on the transcendent literary imaginations of great writers and poets to limn the abodes of the afterlife and the creatures who populate them. As many of us would admit if pressed, our notions of Heaven may owe more to art than to the Bible, and our visions of Hell might fall apart without Dante and John Milton. Purgatory, meanwhile, might not even exist as continuing dogma without the transcendent descriptive genius of Dante, whose *Purgatorio* was published just decades after the formal adoption of the teaching of a place called Purgatory in the First Council of Lyon (1245).[2]

These works of human imagination are only a few of the many examples of artists, writers, and other creatives taking on the mystery of what happens to us when we die. We can trace these back all the way to one of the first extant human narratives, *The Epic of Gilgamesh*, and all the way forward to the present, where the central force driving Lord Voldemort in the Harry Potter epic is his attempt to master death and avoid whatever lies beyond, and where some of our most popular television shows revolve around encounters with the walking dead, beings in the strange netherworld between this life and the next. What makes stories of the afterlife even more pervasive, however, is that they are often present even in stories not formally interested in what happens to us when we die. Stories of Heaven, Hell, and Purgatory often inform our films, TV shows, games, songs, and other forms of popular culture, helping us understand something about the lives we live now through reference to these myths about what happens to us when we die. As Terry Ray Clark has noted, popular-culture artifacts both reflect and influence how people understand religious truth, so it should not surprise us to find literature and culture simultaneously exploring and shaping religious ideas.[3]

By associating images and narratives of Heaven, Hell, Purgatory, angels, and demons with more prosaic stories, artists have found a way to elevate and explain these concepts for audiences—and at the same time, to illuminate the afterlife through reference to the events of this life. Symbols flow both ways. If, as Fred Astaire sings, dancing cheek to cheek is like Heaven, that does indeed help us understand something of the transcendent nature of romantic love. But the comparison also helps us imagine Heaven as a place filled with that kind of joy and pleasure, a place very much worth looking forward to. The intersection of religion and popular culture generates meaning of all sorts, which may explain why so many of our stories and popular-culture artifacts in some way deal with the life to come.

---

[1] N. T. Wright, *Surprised by Hope: Rethinking Heaven, the Resurrection, and the Mission of the Church* (New York: HarperOne, 2008), 18.

[2] Henry Denzinger, *The Sources of Catholic Dogma*, trans. Roy J. Deferrari (Fitzwilliam, NH: Loreto, 1955), 181.

[3] Terry Ray Clark, "Introduction: What Is Religion? What Is Popular Culture? How Are They Related?," in *Understanding Religion and Popular Culture: Theories, Themes, Products, and Practices*, ed. Terry Ray Clark and Dan W. Clanton, Jr. (London: Routledge, 2012), 9.

OVERVIEW OF TOPIC

Religions explore both how we got here and where we will go next. They help us develop a set of moral values and practices for this life, which in many beliefs are explicitly related to our fate in the afterlife. Our most consumed images, stories, and other relics also have a mythical function for us as well as an entertainment function. As Joseph Campbell, Karen Armstrong, and other writers have argued, the mythic stories we consume are perhaps not factually true (for that is not their function), but they are intended to convey some truth about those things for which objective truth can hardly be established: where we go when we die, what our encounter with a Creator might look like, and whether humans are rewarded or punished for their actions in this life in whatever life may come.[4] In Milton's *Paradise Lost*, DC Comics' Gotham City, and Belinda Carlisle's 1987 pop song "Heaven Is a Place on Earth," storytellers, artists, and musicians are exploring a myth or myths about the afterlife, and consumers of those artifacts find their own beliefs justified or expanded. If Heaven is a place on earth, then Gotham City is a Hell on earth, and readers and watchers who consume the Batman mythos are learning something about evil, its realm, and its consequences. Is Heaven actually a place on earth? Is Gotham City actually Hell? Of course not, at least not in any way that can be factually proven. But there is a mythic truth to these stories and images. They are true in all the ways that matter.

Explorations of Heaven, Hell, and Purgatory, of various stages of death or undeath, and of various affiliated characters (angels, devils, Satan) remain among our most popular narratives because they serve this mythic function. When *Sports Illustrated* uses the word "paradise" in the title of a swimsuit photo spread, it reflects our deeply held belief that Heaven must be at least as beautiful as this set of earthly visions. When a deceased character in the 1989 film *Field of Dreams* asks if a baseball field in Iowa is Heaven, he taps into our strongly expressed hope that Heaven is a place where our deepest desires will be fulfilled. When a rowdy archangel comes to earth in the movie *Michael* (1996), it affirms our desire that God (or something) is watching over us, that even though we often feel frightened or alone, a holy presence may be somewhere nearby. When we see souls in Hell in the *South Park* feature film *South Park: Bigger, Longer and Uncut* or in numerous episodes of the TV show, our conviction that those who transgress our notions of justice and fairness should be punished gets confirmed. When we encounter characters like Phil Connor (Bill Murray) in *Groundhog Day* (1993), long trapped in horrible existences, who break free with new wisdom, we see how the Purgatory ur-narrative convinces us that suffering has a transformative purpose. All of these popular-culture artifacts have a powerful mythic value, for they tell us stories that feel true to our hopes and fears about forever.

[4] Joseph Campbell, "Mythological Themes in Creative Literature and Art," in *The Mythic Dimension: Selected Essays 1959–1987*, ed. Antony Van Couvering (New York: HarperSanFrancisco, 1987), 180–2; Karen Armstrong, *The Battle for God: A History of Fundamentalism* (New York: Ballantine, 2001), xv.

But as these examples suggest, our stories of the afterlife often have more to do with our current existence than the actual attempt to explore or explain what the afterlife might be or how it might work. Our stories of the Undead—creatures in a strange state in between life and death—allow us to ask questions about what makes us human, in what cases long life is desirable, and if life is more interesting, or more complicated, than it appears. In stories about Heaven, we are trying to consider whether the universe rewards virtue and whether we might hope someday for a life or an existence more beautiful, more comfortable, or more pleasurable than the life we live now. In archetypal Heaven stories we argue that there is someplace we belong, that it is possible to be reunited with those we miss, or that somewhere there is a place where we can be safe and protected from harm. In archetypal stories of Hell, we are arguing that those who transgress moral, ethical, or societal mores will be punished, that there is genuine evil in the cosmos that must be reckoned with and, perhaps, defeated, or that perhaps we are not completely to blame for our impulses away from good. Finally, in the Purgatory archetype, we are trying to find meaning in pain, to argue that change comes only through suffering, or that all of us will be forced at some time to contend with challenges in our life. Cultural representations of the afterlife and cultural appropriations of the afterlife to tell and retell human stories are thus both notable and worthy of our own attention.

SPECIFIC EXAMPLES/FOCI

Some of the most popular tales of the afterlife in recent years paradoxically revolve around beings who have not arrived in Heaven or Hell (although in some narratives they might arguably be in Purgatory). Ghosts, zombies, and vampires all reside on earth in a strange boundary world beyond death, though short of any definitive life after death, but stories about them explore questions about the soul and about whether or not we exist in some form after we die. In most iterations of the mythos, ghosts are souls that remain on earth after their bodies perish instead of departing to their next destination. Perhaps, as in Harry Potter, they are human souls who are afraid to pass on to what is next. Perhaps, as in Charles Dickens's 1843 story *A Christmas Carol*, remade or performed year by year across America, ghosts serve the function of instructing the living and offering them the chance for radical change. Perhaps, as in *The Sixth Sense* (1999), ghosts remain behind because they have particular tasks to be accomplished before they can depart. All of these are powerful stories, and as frightening as ghosts may be to the living, we at least have the comfort of knowing that there is some existence after death, and that perhaps the spirits surrounding us mean well.

Vampires, popular both in the Bram Stoker and *Twilight* varieties, allow us the chance to see some of our culture's most powerful myths—eternal youth and eternal love—explored. In the love between Bella and Edward in the Twilight series, readers and viewers are permitted to believe in the possibility that true love can last forever. Stephanie Meyer, the author of *Twilight*, is actually bringing to life a central tenet of her Church of

Jesus Christ of Latter-day Saints (the Mormons), that those faithful united in a temple wedding are allowed to live together throughout eternity. In many vampire stories, however, particularly those drawn from the Stoker mythos, the possibility of eternal youth and love is weighed against the terrible sacrifices required to maintain those states. In various versions of the Dracula story, including Francis Ford Coppola's 1992 film *Bram Stoker's Dracula*, the true state of Dracula is a hideous old man. In the television world of *Buffy the Vampire Slayer* (1997–2003), vampires are assumed to be soulless, demons in a human body, with little memory of the people they were. In Stephen King's *Salem's Lot* (1975), they are beings with boundless hunger, willing to pervert even those they love most in their desire to feed. The Stoker vampire cautions us to be careful what we wish for—youth and eternal life may come with a startling cost. To live on in a body—but lose your soul—is, as Jesus says in Matthew 16:26 and elsewhere in the gospels, too high a price. This may look at first like Heaven, but it is probably closer to the other place.

Zombies, of course, are soulless corpses who roam in search of human flesh, and their bite transforms their victims into creatures like themselves. (In some mythos, such as *The Walking Dead* comics, TV show, and games, all who die rise as zombies, setting up a whole new set of existential questions to be explored.) The archetypal zombie George Romero introduced in his 1968 film *Night of the Living Dead* is unintelligent, incapable of speech or communication, and driven only by hunger. This may be a vision of Hell; an eternity spent as thoughtless, hungry wanderers sounds like a horrible fate. But these undead also offer us the opportunity to explore our own humanity; in Romero's *Dawn of the Dead*, in *Shaun of the Dead* (2004), and in *The Walking Dead*, the storytellers make direct correspondences between the living and the living dead. Kim Paffenroth notes that such stories "present us with a world in which humans and monsters become very hard to distinguish, and therefore the moral rules that guide our dealings with other humans . . . are discarded as irrelevant and unfeasible."[5] Our own lives, zombie tales suggest, may differ little from those of zombies if we allow ourselves to get lost in mindless repetition, unconscious consumption, and unawareness. Zombies also permit us to draw sharp contrasts with our own best lives. Humans may be susceptible to some of the things that make zombies what they are, but in many of these stories we see human beings throwing off their brute desires and achieving sacrifice and heroism for the communities they can form but zombies cannot. Perhaps, as both the TV show and the comic *The Walking Dead* suggest, "we are the walking dead," but zombie stories allow us to assert that we can be more than that.

The undead offer us ways to think about life and what follows. So too do characters that populate the locations of the afterlife: angels and devils, characters familiar to us from our culture. Heaven is the home of the angels, beings who serve the Most High as guardians, messengers, and agents. Although the Bible contains little specific information on angels (which may explain why angelology evolved into one of the most important branches of theological inquiry during the Middle Ages), they are mentioned

---

[5] Kim Paffenroth, *Gospel of the Living Dead: George Romero's Vision of Hell on Earth* (Waco, TX: Baylor University Press, 2006), 10.

approximately one hundred times in each Testament, appearing in over thirty books; so while they remain ill-defined (or open to interpretation), they clearly have a significant presence in the Bible, and an even more significant presence in our popular culture.

The Guardian Angel is perhaps the best known of these angelic manifestations in culture, represented in sacred and secular art and showing up in nursery paintings, ceramic figurines and Precious Moments products, and stories such as *Wings of Desire* (1987), the TV series *Touched by an Angel* (1994–2003), and the classic 1946 film *It's a Wonderful Life*. The Guardian Angel may shepherd children across a rickety bridge (or, in one example of popular art from the 1950s, a robed angel shields children from being backed over in the driveway as their dad heads off to work in his finned Detroit monster), or he or she may hover literally or figuratively over a character who needs guarding or guidance, as the character Angel does in his introduction in the *Buffy the Vampire Slayer* TV series.[6] Such close contact with humans often changes the angels assigned to them, and with some regularity, angels fall in love with humans and vice versa. This interspecies romance trope plays out in many of our best-known stories of angels, including the films *City of Angels* (1998) and *The Bishop's Wife* (1947). The biblical tradition contains some small warrant for this. The noncanonical book of *1 Enoch* speaks of Sons of God who intermarry with humans, and some narratives suggest that these were fallen angels, but in the actual Bible the closest to this interspecies lust can be observed when a crowd of onlookers asks that Lot send out the messengers God has sent to him in Sodom so that they can have sex with them.[7]

In many stories, angels are active characters who not only watch over humans but carry out God's wishes (or, occasionally, their own!). Milton's *Paradise Lost* contains numerous stories of angels who stand against Satan and his legions or carry information to the newly created humans. Angels may be simple messengers or major characters in a story. In *Michael*, the title character, played by John Travolta, is the archangel Michael, enjoying one last trip to Earth and trying to leave some things right in his wake. In the 2005 movie *Constantine*, Gabriel (played by Tilda Swinton) has grown tired of God's favoritism toward human beings and has set up a test to see who is worthy of God's love. In her radical stand against God, she joins the list of fallen angels, and we are permitted to see how these awesome and beautiful creatures can be powerful antagonists as well as heavenly helpers.

The best-known of these fallen angels, of course, is Satan or Lucifer, and in many stories Satan is a force of cosmic evil and an enemy to be respected and feared.[8] Little information appears on Satan (or The Satan, The Adversary) in the Bible, and many biblical scholars point out that the notion of Satan is often used by communities of faith to demonize others with whom they disagree.[9] Nonetheless an ancient evil that stands in

---

[6] Scott G. Eberle, "Solving the Mystery of the Angel of the Asphalt," *Psychology Today*, November 11, 2016, https://www.psychologytoday.com/us/blog/play-in-mind/201611/solving-the-mystery-the-angel-the-asphalt.

[7] *1 Enoch* 6–7; Gen 19:1–5.   [8] For more on Satan, see Kathryn Gin Lum's entry in this volume.

[9] The Serpent in the Garden of Eden (Genesis 3) is identified only as a snake, not as Satan or Lucifer. The Satan who appears in the Book of Job seems to function as a tester who works on behalf of

opposition to Absolute Good makes for a potent storytelling figure and a striking symbol. We can observe the familiar horned figure carrying a pitchfork in the medieval mystery plays and other art and literature of the Middle Ages, and see him all the way to U2's Bono playing a Satanic character called MacPhisto (first introduced during their Zoo TV tour to cast an ironic tinge on their earnest image) and today's *New Yorker* cartoons.[10] In some mythos, the Fallen One is renamed to make the symbol less specific to Christian belief. To wit, in "The Satan Pit," an episode featuring the tenth version of *Doctor Who* (David Tennant), this supernatural being is encountered in the interior of a planet; for well over half a century, Marvel Comics has featured diabolical villains (Nightmare, Mephisto, Dormammu) as well as the actual figure of The Satan; and DC Comics likewise offers demonic characters such as Nergal, Etrigan, The First of the Fallen, and Lucifer Morningstar as villains and, occasionally, as more nuanced protagonists. The idea of supernatural evil is a potent antagonist in many stories—and a potent idea helping to explain evil in the world.

Not all demons remain fallen. Hellboy, in comics and films, is the son of a demon prince and a human woman, and in his ongoing film and comic narrative, this demonic figure offers a powerful counterstory to that of the fallen angel. While by inclination he should be purest evil, Hellboy stands against evil and alongside human friends and lovers, offering even his life to protect the earth. Daimon Hellstrom (Marvel's "Son of Satan") and Blue Devil are other figures in comics who should incline toward the darkness yet seek the light. For their part, comic characters Daredevil (particularly in the reimagining of the character by the writer Frank Miller) and Batman are humans in devilish form who may employ fear and violence to do their work, but they stand on the side of justice. While human beings have told stories of demonic beings for thousands of years, these characters suggest that whatever their genesis, the fallen may rise and the demonic may choose good rather than evil. Unlike our biblical narrative, demons may not have to burn forever in the Lake of Fire.[11]

The Bible suggests various possible abodes where the righteous may be bound after death: Sheol (the land of the dead), Abraham's Bosom, a house with "many mansions," and a heavenly City with its gates formed of giant pearls. But it offers us no unified theory of Heaven.[12] Save for the many mentions of the Kingdom of Heaven in Jesus's cryptic kingdom teachings (in what way, precisely, would a place called Heaven be like a

God, almost like a prosecutor in a court of law. See Elaine Pagels, *The Origin of Satan: How Christians Demonized Jews, Pagans, and Heretics* (New York: Random House, 1995), for an accessible study of the development of the Satan figure in Christian thought.

[10] See Jeffrey Burton Russell, *Lucifer: The Devil in the Middle Ages* (Ithaca, NY: Cornell University Press, 1984). *Time* magazine calls MacPhisto one of the great alter egos. Dan Fletcher, "Bono/MacPhisto," *Time*, July 10, 2009, http://content.time.com/time/specials/packages/article/0,28804,1909772_1909770_1909675,00.html.

[11] "And the devil who had deceived them was thrown into the lake of fire and sulfur, where the beast and the false prophet were, and they will be tormented day and night forever and ever" (Rev 20:10, NRSV).

[12] See Thomas Francis Glasson's essay "Heaven" in *The Oxford Companion to the Bible*, ed. Bruce M. Metzger and Michael D. Coogan (New York: Oxford University Press, 1993), 270–1.

mustard seed, or like a merchant who finds a pearl of great value?), we are left with few hints as to what an enduring life with the Creator might be like following this life, if in fact there is such a life. At the time of Jesus, Jews disagreed as to whether there was life after death, and little in the Hebrew Testament can be taken to refer to Heaven; Paradise is mentioned considerably more often in the *Qur'ān* and in the hadiths and other Islamic teachings.[13]

As noted earlier, many readers of the Bible believe they receive a clear vision of Heaven through the Bible, but, as the theologian Alister McGrath argues, heaven is a prime example "of a Christian idea that is fundamentally imaginative."[14] Because the Bible gives us no clear picture of what the afterlife looks like, we fill in the gaps, leaning on images of the beautiful, the precious, and the transcendent in this life to try to describe the next. In the *South Park* mythos, Kenny McCormick and other characters have been to Heaven. At the end of the 1999 feature film *South Park: Bigger, Longer, and Uncut*, Kenny is permitted to enter Heaven, passing through a phalanx of bare-breasted female angels who fit him with wings and a halo. Shortly after 9/11, in the episode "A Ladder to Heaven," a similar vision of Heaven is depicted when the boys—and the nation of Japan—build rival ladders to reach Heaven, and Japan "claims" Heaven by planting its flag in the clouds of a stage set. The fluffy-cloud Heaven is also the setting for the Emmy-winning episode "Best Friends Forever" from 2005. After his death, Kenny is chosen to lead the angelic forces in the fight against Satan on the grounds that he has mastered a video game, *Heaven versus Hell*. When he arrives in Heaven, he enters a vision out of Christian art: a gleaming heavenly city, winged angels, the gatekeeper St. Peter, and the archangel Michael, who has taken charge of Heaven's defenses, at least until Kenny arrives.

These heavenly scenes in *South Park* parody hundreds of years of religious and cultural depictions, such as the one described by Colton Burpo, the subject of the bestselling travelog *Heaven Is for Real* (2010). During his near-death experience, four-year-old Colton sat on the lap of Jesus, who summoned winged angels and music, halos and bright colors, and a rainbow horse. In this and many other of our most traditional and sentimental visions of a Christian Heaven, a shiny, sparkling realm translates the valuable and the beautiful in this life into the next, offering us jeweled crowns, streets of gold, golden harps, giant pearls.

Heaven as Paradise is one of the most frequent depictions, from the use of the word "paradise" in songs and swimsuit spreads to John Steinbeck's use of California as an earthly paradise in the minds of the Joad family in his 1939 novel, *The Grapes of Wrath.*

---

[13] Ibid., 270; Greg Garrett, *Entertaining Judgment: The Afterlife in Popular Imagination* (New York: Oxford University Press, 2015), 104; John Kaltner, "Death and the Afterlife," in *Introducing the Qur'an: For Today's Reader* (Minneapolis, MN: Fortress Press, 2011), 215–43; Falzur Rahman, "Eschatology," in *Major Themes of the Qur'ān* (Minneapolis, MN: Bibliotheca Islamica, 1994), 106–20; Hamza Yusuf, "Death, Dying, and the Afterlife in the Quran," in *The Study Quran: A New Translation and Commentary*, ed. Seyyed Hossein Nasr et al. (New York: HarperCollins, 2015), 1819–55.

[14] Alister McGrath, *A Brief History of Heaven* (Oxford: Blackwell, 2003), 2. For more on Heaven, see Deane Galbraith's entry in this volume.

The Joads have seen a handbill advertising for hired hands to pick fruit in California and have formed an idea of the Promised Land, a Land of Milk and Honey. Grampa expresses what they all hope: that they are escaping the Dust Bowl devastation of Oklahoma to go to an earthly paradise where they can pluck grapes off a tree. The lyrics of Coldplay's Grammy-nominated 2011 song, "Paradise," juxtapose dreams of Paradise against the heaviness of this life. The lyrics, however, take us only part of the way to Paradise. Most of the song offers only "ooohs" and soaring "ohs," since no words can properly capture the ineffable reality of the world beyond. Although we cannot perhaps properly depict a place of such transcendent beauty—the narrator of Leif Enger's 2001 novel, *Peace Like a River*, likewise finds that words cannot convey the experience of that place—we do know beauty, joy, and pleasure in this life and can use those experiences to at least taste Paradise.

Heaven also appears in the guise of Zion. "Zion," a word that appears frequently in the Old and New Testaments and the Apocrypha, is an ancient name for the City of God, Jerusalem, but it is also a metaphor for something larger and nobler than any earthly dwelling place.[15] Jews—particularly those known as Zionists—think of Palestine as their holy refuge, set aside for them by the Almighty. Christians may have a similar understanding of what Zion might be; the author of the Letter to the Hebrews under-stood Zion to be a heavenly city, superior in all ways to the earthly (i.e., "Jewish") one.[16] In this understanding, Heaven becomes the ultimate gated community, a place of pro-tection and segregation from those who would harm or frighten the faithful, a place where they can rest in the company of the like-minded and like-believing. Our cultural representations also depict Zion as a place of sanctuary. In the *Matrix* films (1999–2003), Zion is the last human refuge from the machines, a place where those who have escaped the Matrix can gather with people like themselves, live, love, worship their savior (Keanu Reeves's Neo), and dance until dawn.

In many narratives, Heaven is a place of rescue and reunion. At the end of the musical *Les Miserables* (and in the 2012 film version), Jean Valjean (Hugh Jackman, in the film) is escorted to Heaven by the spirits of Fantine (Anne Hathaway) and Eponine (Samantha Banks). There, on the barricade, we see all those who have lost their lives in the course of the narrative reunited and raising their voices in a reprise of "Do You Hear the People Sing?" It is a joyous reunion for them. *Les Miserables'* Heaven, however, does not seem to have room for the story's villain, the relentless Javert (Russell Crowe). Similarly, at the conclusion of James Cameron's 1997 *Titanic*, once the top-grossing film of all time, the survivor Old Rose (Gloria Stuart) lies in bed. In dreams—or in death—she passes through the flooded halls of the wreck on the ocean floor, and then, as the scene shifts, into the lighted and restored *Titanic* itself. There, on and around the Grand Staircase, stand those who died in the disaster: passengers, crew, and Jack (Leonardo DiCaprio),

---

[15] Ben C. Ollenburger, "Zion," in Metzger and Coogan, *The Oxford Companion to the Bible*, 830.

[16] Hebrews 12:22–24. For a discussion of this conception of Zion—as well as how the author uses it to draw a (further) contrast between "Judaism" and "Christianity"—see Harold W. Attridge, *Hebrews*, Hermeneia (Philadelphia, PA: Fortress, 1989), 374–7.

Rose's great love and the man who saved her life when the ship went down. He takes her hand—and we see that in this vision (or version of Heaven)—she is Young Rose again, played by Kate Winslet. Although the Staircase was the first-class entrance on the ship, those gathered there now and applauding as Jack and Rose embrace are a cross section of the society on board, from the rich and powerful to the penniless (like Jack and his friend Fabrizio [Danny Nucci]). In this place, many are reconciled, and Rose is reunited with those she lost. And again, the bad guys—Rose's evil fiancé and her mother, who did not die on the ship, and his bodyguard, who did—are nowhere to be found. Dramatic mercy extends only so far in some stories, and there is no room in Heaven for those who made our lives hell.

Like Heaven, there is no single unified theory in the Bible of a place of eternal punishment.[17] Whether we "go down to the dust," as in the Psalms, or are thrown into outer darkness where there is weeping and gnashing of teeth, or are cast into the Lake of Fire, we are forced to construct our own hell, and in our art and literature we have done that very thing.[18] In James Joyce's 1916 novel, *A Portrait of the Artist as a Young Man*, in the paintings of Hieronymus Bosch, and in the writings of Dante and Milton, Hell comes alive before our eyes. And yet today, despite centuries of religious teaching by Christians, Jews, Muslims, and other faithful, despite these potent cultural depictions, despite my formative experiences and those of millions like me, Hell seems to be on its way out. Some consider the fiery Hell of popular culture as ridiculous as the fluffy-cloud Heaven. Hell is omitted from or irrelevant to the theology of many contemporary Christians. Even the Catholic Church that petrified Joyce and his character Stephen Daedalus with its talk of eternal punishment has downgraded Hell from everlasting flames to exile from the love of God—horrible enough, but certainly not viscerally frightening.[19]

As story, however, Hell continues to fascinate us. It is a place of driving ambition, of great conflict, of violence and abuse, and thus, naturally, of tremendous dramatic interest. As with Heaven, we find images of Hell used to flavor earthly settings and situations, while earthly analogs help us understand something about punishment and separation.

One familiar fictional setting, Gotham City, is hellish because it is full of unremitting evil, of senseless mayhem, and of violence perpetrated by or directed against its inhabitants. Despite Batman's never-ending war against crime, Gotham City remains a dark, difficult, and wretched place. Whether in comics like Frank Miller's *The Dark Knight Returns* (1986) and *Batman: Year One* (1987), or Scott Snyder's 2012–3 story, *The Joker: Death of the Family*; in the cinematic versions of Gotham brought to the screen by Tim Burton (1989's *Batman* and 1992's *Batman Returns*) and Christopher Nolan (*Batman Begins* [2005], *The Dark Knight* [2008], and *The Dark Knight Rises* [2012]), or the Gotham City with which you can interact in bestselling video games such as *Arkham*

---

[17] See Bo Reicke, "Hell," in Metzger and Coogan, *The Oxford Companion to the Bible*, 277–9.

[18] Psalms 22:29 (down to the dust); Matt 8:12, 22:13, and 25:30 (outer darkness); Rev 19:20, 20: 10, 14–15 (Lake of Fire).

[19] Gustav Niebuhr, "Hell Is Getting a Makeover from Catholics; Jesuits Call It a Painful State but Not a Sulfurous Place," *New York Times*, September 18, 1999, https://www.nytimes.com/1999/09/18/arts/hell-getting-makeover-catholics-jesuits-call-it-painful-state-but-not-sulfurous.html.

Asylum, *Arkham City*, and *Arkham Origins*—few settings in popular culture proffer so powerful a vision of Hell on earth. As in the traditional theological understandings of Hell, the residents of Gotham are far removed from God, from beauty, from justice, from peace, and from joy. Unlike Metropolis, that lovely, well-lit (we might even say heavenly) city of the future and home to the godlike Superman, Gotham feels to its inhabitants like a place of eternal punishment. Perhaps unsurprisingly, only a seemingly demonic force, that of The Batman, can prevail in the location of such evil. Only greater violence can prevent violence, greater determination overwhelm that of devilish villains like The Joker, Mr. Freeze, and Bane.

Hell is reflected throughout our literature and culture, which sometimes depicts such unspeakable evil or suffering that it strains human explanation. When Clarice Starling enters the lair of the serial murderer Jame Gumb at the end of the 1988 novel *The Silence of the Lambs*, she discovers a place of unnatural menace made more horrible by the anguished screams of his victim in the pit. In the basement bathroom, she finds a bathtub filled with plaster, from which a shriveled human hand sticks up. Jonathan Demme's 1991 film version offers this and other indelible images of horror that are difficult to reconcile with what we want to believe we understand about this world. In *Pulp Fiction* (1994), Marcellus Wallace (Ving Rhames) and Butch (Bruce Willis) are kidnapped by hillbillies who take them to a dungeon beneath their pawn shop, where they rape and kill random victims. It is inhumanity that seems inexplicable, unless we think of it as entering an anteroom of Hell. Cormac McCarthy's 2006 novel, *The Road*, offers a vision of a blasted Earth, of people chained up as livestock to be carved up joint by joint for food, of an orchard wall topped with human heads of all shapes and sizes. Suzanne Collins's *Hunger Games* series (2008–10) also offers scenes difficult for her heroine, Katniss, or for us, to accept in any world we care to recognize: contestants seemingly transformed into ravenous mutts, insects turned into murder weapons, killer monkeys, acid fog. While it might be easy for us to push away these and other inhumanities as horrible imaginings, Collins looks our inhumanity squarely in the face, and in *Mockingjay* (the final novel in the trilogy) actually questions whether our species deserves to survive.

The evocation of Hell may sometimes seem to offer us an out, a chance to duck our responsibility at the same time as it permits us some explanation of those evils we do not care to own as ours. But Hell has other uses for us than explaining the unexplainable; Hell also offers the hope of justice in a world that does not always demonstrate it, and it permits the prospect of victory over insuperable odds that makes for great stories.

The word "purgatory" does not appear in the Bible, and the concept of Purgatory has fallen somewhat out of favor (although it remains an official item of belief for Roman Catholics). Those who make a case for Purgatory rely on biblical statements seeming to call for our perfection before entering Heaven ("But nothing unclean shall enter [heaven]" [Rev 21:27], or "You [God] . . . are of purer eyes than to behold evil and cannot look on wrong" [Hab 1:13]), on prayers for the dead ("It is therefore a holy and wholesome thought to pray for the dead, that they may be loosed from sins," [2 Macc 12:46]) or forgiveness even after death (Matt 12:31-32).

Our appropriation of Purgatory may arise more from narrative need than from theological aptness, but popular culture can help us crack open even a challenging religious teaching such as Purgatory. One of the central fan theories about the 2004–10 television show *Lost*, for example, is that the strange desert island where Jack (Matthew Fox), Kate (Evangeline Lilly), John Locke (Terry O'Quinn), and the others had crashed was actually Purgatory. Certainly there seemed to be evidence in favor of this: dead people walked the island, no babies could be born there, and this gathering of people who were physically, emotionally, and spiritually lost suggested to many viewers that some form of testing or redemption was under way. All the same, the show's producers made it clear throughout the show's run that the characters on the Island were not dead and in Purgatory.[20]

That early denial, however, did not prevent them from deploying the Purgatory model of refinement and testing in the sixth and final season, when *Lost* began to feature a "Sideways World," a reality in which the crash victims lived out lives as though they had never crashed on the island. It became clear that although the island itself might not be Purgatory, this sideways world did function as a halfway station in which the characters were actively working toward their eventual salvation. The show's writer and executive producer, Damon Lindelof, has admitted that Dante's *Purgatorio* and the Bardo (the Buddhist belief in a region between death and rebirth best known perhaps from George Saunders's Man Booker–winning 2017 novel, *Lincoln in the Bardo*) both influenced his storytelling. In this sideways world, the Lostees are offered the opportunity to change and, ultimately, to be transformed into people capable of moving into the light in the final moments of the series finale.

Our movies, novels, and other forms of culture often feature stories of people who are caught in between one state and another and who are being changed for the better so that they can pass into whatever comes next for them. Sometimes this story of redemption clearly happens in the context of life after death, as in *Ghost*, *The Sixth Sense*, and other movies. In these and other stories of supernatural return, we meet ghosts or spirits who cannot move on until they accomplish something profound. But we also discover other understandings of Purgatory that emerge when characters are simply stuck in their everyday lives and seem to be unable to move forward. Take weatherman Phil Connor, the sad, self-centered soul in need of redemption in *Groundhog Day*. Unaccountably, inexplicably, Phil is stuck reliving the same day over and over again. Every morning, Sonny & Cher's "I Got You, Babe" awakens him as it blares from the clock radio in his hotel room in the small town in rural Pennsylvania where he has been sent to cover Groundhog Day. Every morning, Phil goes off to do a broadcast from the groundhog site, interacts with the locals, and attempts to get out of town.

What is one to do in the face of such a long, gray existence? The message of *Groundhog Day*—and the central narrative of many of the stories depicting Purgatory—is both dra-

---

[20] Kristin Dos Santos, "*Lost* Bosses Finally Answer: Was Everyone Really Dead the Whole Time? What Was the Show About? Find Out!," *EOnline*, March 16, 2014, https://www.eonline.com/news/521687/lost-bosses-finally-answer-were-they-really-dead-the-whole-time-what-was-the-whole-show-about.

matic and theological: If you do not like your life, if you do not like your identity, then change yourself. By the end of *Groundhog Day*, Phil has said goodbye to the hedonistic, sardonic boor he was in the opening scenes. He has transformed himself, through his own planning and hard work, into a person with realized talents and genuine compassion, and he is dramatically rewarded with the love of the lovely Rita (Andie MacDowell), who would not give the old Phil the time of day—for good reason. This redemptive and transformative storyline explains perhaps why the Purgatory narrative remains so central in our culture, despite the fact that the Protestant mainstream of American Christianity does not accept the doctrine as theology.

In all of these snapshots of the afterlife, we are learning something about how cultural representations of Heaven, Hell, and Purgatory can be used to help us understand earthly concepts like pleasure, love, joy, satisfaction, and security. We are seeing how the characters of those landscapes, whether they be lost souls or the redeemed, angels or devils, ghosts or spirits, teach us something about our own humanity. The art and culture we consume plant images and ideas in our heads about the big topics they explore in the process of entertaining us. These images of and stories about the afterlife, wherever they come from, help us to make sense of challenging concepts and along the way offer us some peace of mind.

Future Prospects and Questions

- Future research might engage the constantly shifting conceptions of Heaven, Hell, and Purgatory expressed in popular culture. In what ways are these depictions in games, books, TV, films, and other media similar to past depictions? In what ways do they demonstrate a shifting set of beliefs or narrative needs?
- As American culture becomes increasingly secular, future research might consider the uses of the afterlife, angels, and devils in literature and culture. Are they used to reinforce secular themes and meanings, or are they treated as primarily ironic and unbelievable relics of the past?
- Future research might assess the undead as a cultural trope. What needs are currently being served by stories of vampires, zombies, and ghosts? How are the undead functioning in culture at a given moment?
- N. T. Wright and others have suggested that our beliefs about the afterlife are drawn from biblical references and cultural imagination. Future research might attempt to assess the degree to which the religious are influenced by religion and culture in visioning the afterlife—and the degree to which the nonreligious are affected by biblical understandings of life after death.
- Some writers have suggested that political and cultural systems can manipulate belief in the afterlife to affect people's behavior in this life. Future research might explore how stories of the afterlife may be consciously leveraged to attempt to affect the moral and political behavior of those who consume them.

Suggested Readings and Annotated Bibliography

Casey, John. *After Lives: A Guide to Heaven, Hell, and Purgatory*. New York: Oxford University Press, 2009.

Casey's wide-ranging study examines burial practices and afterlife beliefs from prehistory, Mesopotamia, Greece, and Rome to the present. In doing so, he is also examining shifting and ever-consistent human concepts of the divine, of our understandings of our nature and existence, and of human fears, joys, and sorrows.

Clark, Terry Ray, and Dan W. Clanton, Jr. *Understanding Religion and Popular Culture*. London: Routledge, 2012.

Clark and Clanton provide a worthy introduction to the study of religion and popular culture in tandem, offering useful definitions of both and methodologies that will ease the passage of other scholars. The book explores various genres to demonstrate how such study might work and offers suggestions for further reading.

Garrett, Greg. *Entertaining Judgment: The Afterlife in Popular Imagination*. New York: Oxford University Press, 2015.

The author explores narratives about Heaven, Hell, and Purgatory by looking at a variety of art forms across centuries, but focuses most closely on literature and popular culture texts. His intent is to consider both human imaginative depictions of the afterlife, but more important, to show how our use of Heaven, Hell, and Purgatory shapes the narratives we use to define ourselves every day.

"Into Everlasting Fire." *Economist*, December 22, 2012. https://www.economist.com/christmas-specials/2012/12/22/into-everlasting-fire.

This cover article from the *Economist* considers how Hell has largely fallen out of cultural favor. Erudite yet easily accessible, "Into Everlasting Fire" is an excellent short introduction to literary, cultural, and theological stories of Hell and the uses to which human beings have put them.

Russell, Jeffery Burton. *Mephistopheles: The Devil in the Modern World*. Ithaca, NY: Cornell University Press, 1990.

In this, Russell's conclusion to a four-volume history of the diabolic figure from ancient history to the present, we see how changes in attitudes toward religion, history, and evil have led to shifts in the perception of the Devil, at the same time that the world seems to require some figure of supernatural evil.

Smith, Gary Scott. *Heaven in the American Imagination*. New York: Oxford University Press, 2011.

This cultural history of Heaven moves from the ideas of the Puritans to our current conceptions of Heaven, using sermons, art, jokes, music, and works of philosophy, sociology, liturgy, and folklore to show how America's concepts of Heaven have shifted—and what has remained constant.

Wright, N. T. *Surprised by Hope: Rethinking Heaven, the Resurrection, and the Mission of the Church*. New York: Harper One, 2008.

A renowned biblical scholar, Wright argues that most contemporary Christians have badly understood the Bible's teachings about Heaven and the Kingdom of Heaven. The Bible, he points out, says very little about the afterlife, so human imagination has been left to supply the rest for us.

PART IV

BIBLE IN POPULAR CULTURAL GENRES

CHAPTER 16

....

GENESIS 1-11 IN THE
QATSI FILM TRILOGY

....

GREGORY ALLEN ROBBINS
DEPARTMENT OF RELIGIOUS STUDIES,
UNIVERSITY OF DENVER

INTRODUCTION

....

WHEN thinking about the Bible in popular cultural genres, it is important to note that from the very advent of the medium, film has taken its inspiration from biblical narratives and characters, especially Jesus. Passion plays, themselves derived from harmonizing readings of the gospel accounts, provided dramatic impetus for cinematic renderings of the last week of Jesus's life. *La Passion* (1897), from France, has been hailed as "the first film to chronicle the life of Jesus Christ and probably the first motion picture to be based on any portion of the Bible."[1]

Following the early experiments of brothers Auguste and Louis Lumière as well as those of Thomas Edison in the waning years of the nineteenth century, Jesus films appeared regularly. The opening years of the twentieth century saw Jesus on the screen in new films produced on both sides of the Atlantic. Campbell and Pitts list thirty-five New Testament films, beginning with 1900 and before 1915, many of which take their thematic material from the Jesus story. Longer films of two reels in length with a screening time of twenty or so minutes were not uncommon. One of the most important of these was Sidney Olcott's *From the Manger to the Cross*, which was filmed on location in Egypt and Palestine. Shorter Jesus films tended to focus on specific scenes from the life of Jesus: the star over Bethlehem, the raising of Lazarus, the parable of the

---

[1] W. Barnes Tatum, *Jesus at the Movies: A Guide to the First Hundred Years* (Santa Rosa, CA: Polebridge Press, 1997), 3, citing Richard H. Campbell and Michael R. Pitts, *The Bible on Film: A Checklist* (Metuchen, NJ: Scarecrow Press, 1981), 73.

prodigal son, the betrayal of Judas. Decade by decade, Jesus films have continued to appear, keeping pace with innovations in the medium, taking advantage of the flourishing of the film industry, reflecting the culture in which they were produced, including the advent of religious studies as a discipline and the burgeoning of critical film studies.

W. Barnes Tatum, who died in 2017, began to chronicle a century of Jesus films in *Jesus at the Movies: A Guide to the First Hundred Years* in 1997. Tatum was convinced that the discussion about the historical Jesus had moved from academic circles into the public arena via that cinematic history. His three editions of *Jesus at the Movies* (1997, 2004, and 2013) alone could serve as a useful benchmark for assessing the development of our thinking about the relationship between Bible and film and the emergence of what may be characterized as an important subdiscipline of religious studies, that is, religion and film.

However, we must recognize that Jesus movies are but a subgenre of a broad-ranging category of films that may be described as "the Bible *on* film."[2] Many films, including early ones, set out explicitly to retell biblical stories in their ancient contexts. And among those, many belong to the epic genre. These historicizing films, with their extravagance and splendor, dramatize the encounter of religion and secularism in twentieth- and now twenty-first-century America. They serve to evoke a then-as-now experience for viewers who seek to confront the perennial and quintessentially human question of how to comprehend ourselves in time.

One must also reckon with "the Bible *in* film."[3] Many contemporary fictional feature films make use of the Bible, patterning fictional characters after recognizably biblical characters, quoting the Bible directly, making recognizable allusions, or drawing upon iconographic elements pertaining to the Bible (e.g., mirroring the way in which the Bible has been illustrated in the history of Western art). Biblical notions of ethics and the idea of a divinely sanctioned social and moral order make their way into fictional feature films by means of certain visual conventions.[4] The pervasive use of the Bible in feature films means that North American audiences encounter some aspect of the Bible almost every time they watch a movie. Because moviegoing, from its inception, has been inexpensive and therefore accessible to the general public—regardless of socioeconomic bracket, education, heritage, or knowledge level—film's influence is not limited to a particular class or group but extends to virtually all segments of society. For this reason, the biblical presence on the silver screen has a potential impact on a large segment of the American population, including the immigrant population (and, because of global distribution, international populations as well).

---

[2] Adele Reinhartz, *Bible and Cinema: An Introduction* (London: Routledge, 2013), 1–16.

[3] Ibid.

[4] For example, a cruciform gesture, a Eucharistic arrangement for sharing a meal, or a pietà-like embrace of a dead figure.

OVERVIEW OF TOPIC

In 1997, after five years as a special topic consultation, Religion, Film, and Visual Culture was established as a standing group within the American Academy of Religion. In the years that followed, this group served as an incubator for a good deal of the scholarly publication that has emerged in the field. That same year, the *Journal of Religion and Film* was launched by the University of Nebraska at Omaha, the first online, peer-reviewed journal in the field. In 2000 at the Society of Biblical Literature's annual meeting in Nashville, Tennessee, the Bible in Ancient and Modern Media section sponsored a session, "Jesus Movies," that included papers, formal critiques, and responses from scholars who were defining the critical parameters directed to that subgenre.

The first decade of the twenty-first century has seen a welter of increasingly sophisticated new books on religion and film and the Bible and film. Scholars like John C. Lyden, in *Film as Religion: Myths, Morals and Rituals* (2003), call for a more nuanced approach grounded in a religious studies perspective.[5] According to Lyden, popular films perform a religious function in contemporary culture. They evoke myths, create worlds to inhabit. Not unlike formal religious institutions, films provide ways to view the world. Moreover, they proffer values by which to negotiate it. The implications of this recognition for the scholar of religion and film are that it is not enough to evaluate films from a distance, *without* attending to audience reaction—real audience reaction—based on ethnographic research, hands-on analysis of what viewers themselves say they found in a film. Only by doing that difficult ethnographic work can one hope to ascertain how it may function religiously in the viewers' lives.

Lyden's work has been followed by a spate of significant, groundbreaking contributions. Melanie J. Wright, in her *Religion and Film: An Introduction* (2006), urges scholars to study films on the films' own terms, taking full account of their visual language and cinematic grammar and not simply attending to narrative or thematic treatments. Hers represents one of the earliest attempts to create a non-theological, introductory-level approach to the field.[6] Jolyon Mitchell and S. Brent Plate edited the first ever *Religion and Film Reader* (2007), remarkable not only for its international scope but also the selections in part 4, "Theological and Biblical Approaches to Analyzing Film," divided into two subsections: "Theological Dialogues" and "Biblical Connections."[7] Following closely on the heels of the *Reader* came John Lyden's massive *Routledge Companion to Religion and Film* (2009). As might be expected, the chapters by Clive Marsh and Gordon Lynch, "Audience Reception" and "Cultural Theory and Cultural Studies," respectively, are compelling, and offer a transformative vision of where the field is headed. Lynch argues that scholars must show respect to ordinary peoples' ability to

[5] John C. Lyden, *Film as Religion: Myths, Morals, and Rituals* (New York: New York University Press, 2003), especially 1–107.

[6] Melanie J. Wright, *Religion and Film: An Introduction* (London: I. B. Taurus, 2006).

[7] Jolyon Mitchell and S. Brent Plate, eds., *The Religion and Film Reader* (London: Routledge, 2007).

comment insightfully about the social and cultural contexts of their lives. Scholarship that offers purely theoretical accounts of contemporary religion are in danger of offering inadequate and, at times, straightforwardly wrong accounts of the world in which we live. Marsh contends that scholars must attend to what people are doing with film. Believers and unaffiliated viewers are watching films as part of their meaning-making. "Gauging audience reception with respect to religion and film allows scholars to understand how meanings are discovered and made in contemporary society."[8] These three works represent what scholars in the field have come to refer as the "third wave" of religion and films studies.

An important, emerging voice for commenting on the Bible and film after 2000 is that of Adele Reinhartz. A biblical scholar by training with research interests in the Gospel of John, early Jewish-Christian relations, and feminist criticism, she has become a reliable and much respected representative of the latest trends in Bible and film studies. An early work, *Scripture on the Silver Screen* (2003), constitutes a marvelous introduction to the Bible and to film. Turning not to art house films but to wildly popular ones, Reinhartz illuminates the entire canon: Law (Genesis, Exodus, Leviticus), prophets (Ezekiel), writings (Psalms, Ruth, Job), the gospels (John), epistles (1 Corinthians), and the Apocalypse. It is a perceptive, insightful *tour de force* deeply grounded in pedagogical concern to introduce student viewers to secondary reading materials that focus specifically on the use of the Bible in popular film.

From this work Reinhartz's interest in Jesus-story and Christ-figure films expanded. In 2007 she produced a counterpart to Tatum's volumes (*Jesus at the Movies*, 1997 and 2004). Like Tatum's, hers is a study of the movies made about Jesus, from the earliest silent films through to Mel Gibson's 2004 *The Passion of the Christ.*[9] Methodologically, Reinhartz is at pains to demonstrate that these movies fit into the "biopic" (biographical film) genre and that they tell the story of Jesus according to the standard biopic template. In doing so, the Jesus biopics exhibit three principal characteristics. First, they make a claim to historicity or historical authenticity. Second, and at the same time, they undermine that claim in ways that are both subtle and overt. Third, they use the Jesus story as a lens through which to view and to work out contemporary concerns, such as sexuality, ethnic identity, theology, and the relationship between religion and politics. The approach is thematic, and the chapters are organized by character, including the Holy Family (Mary, Joseph, and God), Jesus's friends and associates (Mary Magdalene and Judas), and his enemies (Pharisees, Caiaphas, and Pilate). Despite the title that seems to privilege Hollywood as the cradle from which the cinematic Jesus emerged, the book addresses films made both in the United States and elsewhere. Reinhartz's point is not to overlook the profound differences among the various national cinemas that have produced Jesus movies but to argue that all bear the imprint of the Hollywood biopic,

---

[8]   Clive Marsh, "Audience Reception," and Gordon Lynch, "Cultural Theory and Cultural Studies," both in *The Routledge Companion to Religion and Film*, ed. John Lyden (London: Routledge, 2009), 255–91.

[9]   Adele Reinhartz, *Jesus of Hollywood* (Oxford: Oxford University Press, 2009).

whether in imitation of its conventions or in conscious resistance to them. Needless to say, Reinhartz's theoretical lens and focus on characters preclude the possibility that her commentary might replicate Tatum's.

Reinhartz's latest contribution, *Bible and Cinema: An Introduction* (2013), is a mature collection of essays that explores the ways in which Hollywood movies, including but not limited to the biblical epics of the 1950s and 1960s, express, reflect, and even perpetuate particular elements of American identity.[10] Her ultimate concerns in this volume are to document, via film studies, the Bible's reception history and the Bible's role in the public square. These concerns allow her to redirect the ways we think about Jesus-story films (chapter 3) and Christ-figure films (chapter 7). Reinhartz concludes, "Christ-figure films not only depend upon our understanding of and response to the conventions, but they also have a major role in perpetuating our awareness of and sensitivity to the Christ-story and Christ-figure imagery, even if we never read the Gospels or reflect on Jesus in any meaningful way."[11] When religion classrooms are increasingly populated by "nones," this is a timely lesson.

In Reinhartz's hands we see that film is an active participant in a long and highly developed tradition of interpretation of sacred stories. But the Bible's starring role in cinema is also part of another, larger story: the Bible's role in society, culture, politics, and public discourse. Whether we are watching the Bible on film or detecting the Bible in film, such films are using the medium to reflect upon central social, cultural, and political issues, to describe human experiences and emotions, and, most important, even to create and perpetuate national identity. "As many have noted," Reinhartz claims, "Bible epics say more about mid-twentieth-century America than about ancient Israel."[12]

Most recently, film scholars increasingly see themselves as public intellectuals. They cross disciplinary boundaries. They are a regular presence at film festivals around the world. (Berlin, Toronto, and Sundance come to mind.) As a result, they publish critical reviews of independent and commercially produced films that are likely to have an impact. Scholars are talking to filmmakers. Filmmakers are talking to scholars. Some scholars have strode across the creative divide to become filmmakers themselves. Screenwriters and directors are pursuing advanced degrees in religion and film. This cross-fertilization can only bode well for the future of the subdiscipline.

SPECIFIC EXAMPLES AND/OR FOCI

While scholars who spend their waking hours pondering the Bible and the history of its interpretation and reception can easily document the cinematic use of the Bible, with some films, "the biblical elements may be apparent only to those with prior familiarity with the Bible (or, to be more precise, with its cultural interpretation)."[13] We turn to

---

[10]   Adele Reinhartz, *Bible and Cinema: An Introduction* (London: Routledge, 2013).
[11]   Ibid., 72.   [12]   Ibid., 4.   [13]   Ibid., 11.

three examples of those sorts of films, where the work of the biblical scholar can provide a genuine boon to viewers' appreciation of the ways cinema can appropriate biblical motifs and *transform* them, and how those motifs might be appropriated by the viewers. The cinematic transformations discussed here reflect the primeval history of Genesis 1–11. In contrast to what follows in Genesis, these chapters cultivate a kind of narrative that is fable-like or legendary, and sometimes residually mythic. The human actors in these stories are kept at a certain distance and seem more generalized types than individual characters with distinctive personal histories. The style tends toward formal symmetries, refrain-like repetitions, parallelisms, and other rhetorical devices of a prose that aspires to the dignity of poetry. Dialogue is less important. As Robert Alter notes, "In sum, this rapid report of the distant early stages of the human story adopts something of a distancing procedure in the style and the narrative modes with which it tells a story."[14] These stories of beginnings—cosmic ordering, the creation of the first humans (Adam and Eve), the so-called "Fall," the first fratricide (Cain's murder of his brother, Abel), angelic mating with human beings, the devolution of the created order into increasing violence and transgression of boundaries, Noah's flood, and the tower of Babel—have been endlessly evocative, marvelously generative of creative transformations, including cinematic ones. The films I discuss below are transformations in the sense that they do not merely allude to a Genesis story or touch upon it in passing. They stay with the passages to which they allude, drawing out the implications of the text, wrestling with interpretive possibilities, offering visual metamorphoses that tantalize the modern imagination. While the character of the original story remains recognizably familiar, the cinematic vesture provides dazzling transfigurations.

The stages of transformation can be delineated. In the 1950s, as S. Brent Plate explains, the aesthetician and film theorist Etienne Souriau made a scientific attempt at distinguishing several layers of "reality" when dealing with film.[15] These can assist in analyzing the process by which our selected films evoke and re-create the biblical world and draw the viewer into their reality.

1. Afilmic reality (the reality that exists independently of filmic reality).
2. Profilmic reality (the reality photographed by the camera).
3. Filmographic reality (the film as physical object, structured by techniques such as editing).
4. Scenic (or filmophanic) reality (the film as projected on a screen).
5. Diegetic reality (the fictional story world created by the film; the type of reality "supposed" by the signification of film).
6. Spectatorial reality (the spectator's perception and comprehension of a film).
7. Creational reality (the filmmaker's intentions).

[14] Robert Alter, *The Hebrew Bible: A Translation with Commentary*, vol. 1: *The Five Books of Moses* (New York: W. W. Norton, 2018), 7.

[15] S. Brent Plate, *Religion and Film: Cinema and the Re-creation of the World*, 2nd ed., Short Cuts: Introductions to Film Studies (New York: Wallflower, 2017), 12–3.

These various "realities" allow us to appreciate how the text of Genesis is refracted by the filmmaker.

The first example is the initial installment in Godfrey Reggio's *Qatsi* trilogy, *Koyaanisqatsi*. Released in 1983 after over five years of on-location shooting, it is considered by many critics to be a masterpiece. With a score by the minimalist composer Philip Glass, it reflects a perfect wedding of cinematography and music. There are no actors; there is no dialogue in the film; there is no script (mimicking that distancing mentioned above, following Alter). But the subtext is unmistakable: it is Genesis 1, and God's declaration that the created order "was very good" (1:31). The film is also a profound and profoundly disturbing meditation on the implications of what God intended when he spoke humans into existence, and blessed them, and said to them,

> Be fruitful and multiply, and fill the earth and conquer it; and hold sway over the fish of the sea and the fowl of the heavens and every beast that crawls upon the earth.... Look, I have given you every seed-bearing plant on the face of all the earth and every tree that has fruit bearing seed, yours they will be for food. And to all the beasts of the earth and to all of the fowl of the heavens and to all that crawls on the earth, which has the breath of life within it, the green plants for food. (1:28–30).[16]

The afilmic reality—the reality that exists independently of the filmic reality of *Koyaanisqatsi*—we are immediately aware of is, on the one hand, the ravishing natural beauty of the American West, vast landscapes set aside and preserved by the federal government as national parks, designated wilderness areas, and monuments. On the other hand, we are also made conscious of America's urban centers: Los Angeles, Chicago, New York City. It is the America of the late twentieth century during the presidency of Ronald Reagan. The profilmic reality, the reality photographed by the camera, reflects a juxtaposition of these two Americas. The filmographic reality, the film as physical object, structured by techniques such as editing, makes this juxtaposition in the most striking ways. The viewer is constantly aware of the location of the camera and how it moves. The film exploits both slow and fast motion (fewer or greater than twenty-four frames per second), time-lapse photography, extreme close-ups, and long tracking shots. The music is composed to match the filmographic reality frame by frame.

The opening of the film is entirely ambiguous. For the first four minutes, viewers cannot comprehend what they are witnessing. The title, in reddish ocher, drops down from a dotted, thin horizontal line that traverses the screen. Its meaning is not given. The word is vocalized and repeated in a chant, accompanied by an organ playing a four-bar passacaglia, a descending, modal theme. Shadowy cave drawings appear. At 1 minute 50 seconds, an explosion fills the screen with flame and debris. The chaos continues for two more minutes, until the screen goes white. The scene selection menu labels this sequence "Beginning." This is the "welter and waste" of Gen. 1:1.[17]

---

[16] I am relying on Alter's newly completed translation of *The Hebrew Bible*, 13.   [17] Ibid., 11.

Chaos is overcome by order. For the next fourteen minutes the viewer is treated to a cinematic paean to the primeval world. Shot in extreme slow motion, the camera treats the natural world as if it were "the first light Eden saw play" (to quote the popular, 1931 hymn by Eleanor Fajeon, 1881-1965, famously rendered by Cat Stevens in 1971). Stately buttes present themselves. Oboes create a pulse to suggest that time has been activated (Gen 1:15). The camera pans right to left, left to right. It pulls back and closes in. Cinemascope is used to great effect. A river snakes its way through the rugged terrain. Winds delicately sweep across the illuminated, selenic crescent of a sand dune. Clouds cast shadows; they roil like the sea; they mound and mount up as thunderheads. Their movement is accompanied by a quick, double-tongued trumpet ostinato. Waterfalls, the upswelling of the ocean, white caps, the breaking waves, and spray are glazed by high brass fillips. At minute 11, birds fly over the vault of a cave, a dome-shaped firmament visually echoing Genesis 1:20. An arpeggiated musical figure underscores the sheer energy at work in the creation. At minute 16, the camera, mounted on a low-flying airplane, provides a vantage point to see, at minute 17, trees and vegetation in bright array (the Central Valley in California), alluding to Genesis 1:11–12. These appear not as the product of human labor but as an organic bedecking of the world in all her glory.

This symphony of color does not last long. The musical score takes a dark, industrial turn. The earth explodes at minute 18. We are confronted with a behemothic earth mover; painted on its side are red numbers: 6 and 6. We expect to see a third 6, denoting the mark of the beast in Revelation 13:18. We are now in the world of Tubal-Cain (Gen 4:22), "who forged every tool of copper and iron."[18] During the next hour and ten minutes of the film (the total running time is eighty-six minutes), we discover that the buttes, the rivers, the sand dunes, the clouds, the waves, the birds are visual metaphors in the natural order that will be mimicked in the modern world of industry and technology. Humans create buttes for themselves in the form of skyscrapers, rivaling El Capitan, which we saw earlier. The rivers that slither through the modern hills and valleys are clogged freeway systems with cloverleafs and overpasses that bear streams of white headlights and red taillights. The intermodal transportation system, governed by traffic lights and the rhythm of the business day, harnesses the waves of cars—barely. The sliver of a sand dune is replaced with the Hoover Dam. In the canyons of modern cities, sun and moon and clouds are not seen directly but reflected in the mirroring glass skins of office towers. Birds are aped by commercial aircraft.

This brings us to consider the diegetic reality of *Koyaanisqatsi*, the fictional story world created by the film, the type of reality "supposed" by the signification of film, as well its spectatorial reality (the spectator's perception and comprehension of a film), and its creational reality, that is, the filmmaker's intentions. As *Koyaanisqatsi* unfolds, the music—and the images—become more and more frenetic, and threatening. The energizing, arpeggiated figure becomes calliope-like, then comic, then manic. There is a shot of a Boeing 747 negotiating an airport tarmac. When the plane turns to face the camera head on and continues rolling, bird-like and giant, its nose looks as if it is going to break

---

[18] Ibid., 19–20.

the plane of the screen and mow down the audience. There is a scene of a father playing a pinball game while holding his toddler son in the crook of his arm. He is totally absorbed in the game. He pays no attention to the child. The child is jostled and bounced as the pinball wizard throws more body English at the table. The music gets faster and faster. The film speed is cranked. The viewer feels nauseated. We want to scream, "Stop it!"

And, thankfully, it does stop. There is a moment of silence. The music retreats for about one minute (at 1 hour 5 minutes). The camera resumes the slow pace of the beginning of the film. But there is no return to the pristine, unadulterated world we saw there. Rather, from a height we see the grid of street lights that illuminate the western suburbs of Chicago, stretching for miles, to the vanishing point. We see the pedestrian gridlock on the streets of New York City. In one of the final sequences there is an aerial shot of Los Angeles over LAX International Airport. Then we see the same overview, shot with an infrared camera from outer space. Next we see an extreme close-up of microchips embedded in a circuit board. The director drives his point home: we are embedded, imprisoned in our technology. But that is not his sole parting shot. The final sequence also includes a ghostly image of the New York Stock Exchange. It overlays moving footage of New York sidewalks. Reggio suggests that our lives are beyond our ken, controlled by our economy, the forces of global capitalism.

Is there any escape? The ending of the film recapitulates its opening. At last we learn what we were watching with respect to the ambiguous explosion. We were watching the launch of a rocket into outer space. But the rocket never leaves the atmosphere. It suffers a catastrophic malfunction and explodes, hurling burning pieces of its hull back to earth. It is not the *Challenger* we are seeing (this was an unmanned rocket carrying a satellite), but it certainly represents a human effort to slip the surly bonds of earth—to touch the face of God.[19] The cave paintings reappear, this time illuminated. They are human figures, with eyes. They stand sentinel. The "Koyaanisqatsi" chant returns, with its somber accompaniment. We learn what it means: (1) "crazy life," (2) "life in turmoil," (3) "life out of balance," (4) "life disintegrating," and (5) "a state of life that calls for another way of living." Three Hopi prophecies, evoking that tribe's eschatological myths, are also translated immediately before the end credits roll:

> If we dig precious things from the land, we will invite disaster.
>> Near the day of Purification, there will be cobwebs spun back and forth in the sky.
>> A container of ashes might one day be thrown from the sky, which could burn the land and boil the oceans.[20]

---

[19] Alluding, of course, to the well-known sonnet by John Gillespie Magee Jr., "High Flight," written in 1941. Portions of the poem are engraved on many of the headstones in Arlington National Cemetery, and it was quoted by President Ronald Reagan in his address to the nation on January 28, 1986, after the *Challenger* disaster.

[20] Reggio became aware of these prophecies about the end of the world through his encounters with Hopi tribal representatives at Hotevilla near Santa Fe, New Mexico: David Monogyne, Ekkehart Malotki, and Michael Lomatuway'ma. See Armin W. Geertz, *The Invention of Prophecy: Continuity and Meaning in Hopi Indian Religion* (Berkeley: University of California Press, 1994).

Reggio's *Koyaanisqatsi* is an example of the sort of film Plate discusses in his chapter "Visual Mythologising." Plate asks two interrelated questions: "Firstly, what does an examination of film lend to the study of religion, specifically its myths?... Secondly, how might an understanding of religious myths and world construction challenge film critics and scholars to expand their analyses?"[21] In answering the first question, Plate argues that films can show how myths operate beyond their existence as verbal stories. Myths, like films, are created in and carried out through visual, tactile, olfactory, and other sensual modes. As noted earlier, the musical score of *Koyaanisqatsi* excites the auditory sense and serves to bring its mythological dimensions to life. Turning to the second question, Plate claims that the world's myths constitute a storehouse of grand stories that are endlessly adaptable into the audio-visual medium of film: "Because myths are inevitably 'mash-ups,' directors and screenwriters can cull from stories told through the ages, and often told again in ever-new forms. To miss the begging, borrowing and stealing that mythmakers/filmmakers do is to miss the compulsions of filmmaking in general to create new stories often by retelling old ones. And to deny the mythological origins of so many contemporary films is to risk denying something of the very humanity in the films as well. Unless film theorists and critics understand the power of myth, they will not understand the full power of film."[22] Combining as it does allusions to Genesis with Hopi prophecies, *Koyaanisqatsi* is clearly a mythic "mash-up," powerfully retooling ancient stories to convey a modern and urgent message.

The second installment of the *Qatsi* trilogy, *Powaqqatsi*, released in 1987, is a mythic mash-up as well. It, too, is a nonverbal film—and distancing. It is also complemented by a distinctive score by Glass, who traveled with the director to the twelve locations from which the scenes were gathered. Traditional religion figures prominently in this film. We see images of orthodox Jews praying at the Western Wall in Israel, views of the Alabaster Mosque in Egypt, an enormous stupa in Nepal, the Kaiser Wilhelm Gedächtniskirche in Berlin, ancient temples along the bank of the Ganges, Buddhist prayer wheels, Muslim men performing their daily prayers in a public space—and France's secular spire, the engineering wonder that is the Eiffel Tower. Like *Koyaanisqatsi*, this film, too, has a Hopi title with mythic connotations. "Powaq" means "sorcerer"; "*qatsi*," of course, "life." By extension, the definition provided in the closing moments of the film is "an entity, a way of life that consumes the life forces of other beings in order to further its own life."

However, I would argue that the controlling myth of this film is the curse of Genesis 3:17–19:

And to the human [God] said, "Because you listened to the voice of your wife and ate from the tree that I commanded you...cursed be the soil for your sake, with pangs shall you eat from it all the days of your life.

Thorn and thistle shall it sprout for you and you shall eat the plants of the field.

---

[21] Plate, *Religion and Film*, 20.   [22] Ibid., 21.

By the sweat of your brow shall you eat bread till you return to the soil, for from there were you taken, For dust you are and to dust shall you return."[23]

The opening sequence of *Powaqqatsi*, like the opening of *Koyaanisqatsi*, is ambiguous. For ten full minutes we see thousands of men, sweating men, carrying sacks of dirt up a steep and precarious incline, out of, as we come to learn, the massive Serra Pelada gold mine in northern Brazil.[24] One of the men has been knocked unconscious by a rock that has fallen from above. His coworkers put him on their backs and carry him up, pietà-like, along the ridge. The scene alerts us to observe purposive human movement in this film. It is pervasive. Humans mill grain. They separate the wheat from the chaff. They row with great effort. They cast nets into the sea with difficulty. Humans bear burdens. They convey things in their hands and on their heads. There is no purveyance without conveyance. Close attention is paid to feet. Calloused human feet. Working feet.

Unlike *Koyaanisqatsi*, which was focused on North America, *Powaqqatsi*'s profilmic reality is the Global South. It chronicles a second wave of colonialism: the arrival of technology, particularly in the form of modes of transportation—the train, the automobile, the autobus—that have a profound impact on traditional life. In Reggio's creational reality, these are the faces of the sorcerer, who is also the seducer and seductress. Other masks include mass media, advertising, commercialism, global communication, computers, and skyscrapers—with the concomitant ugliness of urban poverty, homelessness, crime, imprisonment, and pollution. Reggio's filmographic approach here, as previously, is to "engage the subject." There is no script for *Powaqqatsi*; there is no staging of a scene. The camera observes and takes advantage of the moment.[25] This is nowhere more apparent than in the scene toward the end of the film (82 minutes 30 seconds) where a young boy in traditional Indian garb walking along the side of the road is overtaken by a giant truck that totally obscures his person(hood) in exhaust and dust. There is also a haunting vision of a young girl in indigenous Peruvian garb, wiping her face and eyes, again and again and again as if to try to see the world differently. This is countered by the last scene of the movie, where a burned-out automobile, without hood or engine, sits abandoned by the side of an Egyptian road.

The need to labor does not cease. Humans work in different ways, and technology and transportation are both boon and bane to that sobering reality. The film documents the ways by which modern innovations hinder human movement, modify our behaviors, and restrict our freedoms. Three of the chapters are entitled "New Cities in Ancient Lands." They focus on China, Africa, and India. In these segments, the film explores how the resources of traditional religion are threatened by this enchantment with technology. Reggio is uniquely able to pick up on this theme because of his training as a Christian Brothers' monk. Born in 1940 in New Orleans, he entered the order at age

---

[23] Alter, *The Hebrew Bible*, 17–18.

[24] The title of the opening chapter of the film is "Serra Pelada." Both Godfrey Reggio and Philip Glass discuss the sequence in a special feature, a short video, *Impact of Progress*, which accompanies the DVD.

[25] As Reggio explains in *Impact of Progress*.

fourteen. He spent the next fourteen years immersing himself in that tradition. He moved to Santa Fe, New Mexico, in the 1960s, and in 1963 cofounded Young Citizens for Action, a community organization project that aided juvenile street gangs. In 1972 he cofounded the Institute for Regional Education in Santa Fe, a nonprofit foundation focused on media development, the arts, community organization, and research. In 1974 and 1975, with funding from the American Civil Liberties Union, Reggio co-organized a multimedia public interest campaign on the invasion of privacy and the use of technology to control behavior.[26] This leads us to a discussion of the third film in the *Qatsi* trilogy.

Naqoyqatsi (2002) comprises ten sequences. Each has a title, beginning with "Naqoyqatsi." As with the other films in the trilogy, we learn the meaning of the Hopi word only at the end of the film (at minute 82): "each other—kill many—life" (1) a life of killing each other, (2) war as a way of life, (3) (interpretation) civilized violence. The cover of the CD box offers its own rendering: "Life as War." The subsequent chapters that give expression to this sentiment are "The Primacy of Numbers," "Massman," "New World," "Religion," "Media Weather," "Old World," "Intensive Time," "Point Blank," and "The Vivid Unknown."

While the chapter titles have a mythic ring to them, the initial image of the film is clearly mythic and serves to set the tone for the viewer. It is iconic. Familiar. Unmistakable. And it is drawn from the primeval legends of Genesis 1–11. The viewer is confronted with Pieter Bruegel's 1563 painting *The Tower of Babel*, which reflects the artist's experience of seeing the architecture of the Colosseum in Rome, a citadel of hubris and of human-against-human violence. In slow motion, as the camera moves in, closer and closer, our spectatorial reality shifts. We are no longer viewing a painting. It appears as if we are going to enter the very structure itself, accompanied by the mysterious "Naqoyqatsi" chant.

We do not. The Tower of Babel is replaced by a four-minute visual tour of the exterior and the interior (especially the main concourse) of the abandoned Michigan Central Station in Detroit. We are drawn into a modern image of Babel. It, too, has a tower—thirteen stories. It is an edifice of ambitious grandiosity, and it is also decrepit, made weak by old age, dilapidated. The "Naqoykatsi" chant is replaced by a haunting dirge for cello, performed by Yo-Yo Ma. In the final moments of this segment of the opening, the camera assumes an extreme low angle, making the façade appear to be falling backward, only to be engulfed in a turbid sea like Claude Debussy's "La Cathédrale engloutie." Other tower-like structures emerge on a changing global landscape. They are buffeted by meteor showers and angry clouds. The scene concludes (at 8 minutes 20 seconds) with shadowy humans, irradiated humans, exiles, and the title as if behind bars.

Again, the mythic stories of Genesis 1–11 narrate a tale of disobedience, of the violation of boundaries, of resulting violence and destruction. As catastrophic as the flood was for the earth and humankind, it did not stanch transgressive behaviors.

---

[26] "Godfrey Reggio," Spirit of Baraka, accessed May 22, 2020, http://www.spiritofbaraka.com/reggio.aspx.

And they said, "Come let us build us a city and a tower with its top in the heavens, that we may make us a name, lest we be scattered over all the earth." And the Lord came down to see the city and the tower that the human creatures had built. And the Lord said, "As one people with one language for all, if this is what they have begun to do, now nothing they plot to do will allude them. Come let us go down and baffle their language there so that they will not understand each other's language." And the Lord scattered them from there over all the earth and they left off building the city. Therefore it is called Babel, for there the Lord made the language of all the earth babble. And from there the Lord scattered them over all the earth.[27]

Naqoykatsi presumes a global scattering. But the Babel of languages is replaced by a Babel of images. That is its profilmic reality. Unlike *Koyaanisqatsi* and *Powaqqatsi*, this film is not shot on location. For this film, we have images *as* location. Fully 80 percent of the film is made up of stock footage. Its "language" consists of iconic images, ubiquitous images, thoroughly recognizable images that have been manipulated, using every technological trick of the trade. The filmographic reality of the film depends not upon the skill of the cinematographer (like Ron Fricke, Graham Berry, and Leonidas Zourdoumis, who worked on the first two films of the trilogy) working with actors on a set or on location. The director of photography is replaced by the visual designer-cum-editor working digitally (in this case, Jon Kane). Thus the film plies the visual past—a gallery, repository, or "canon" of images—to comment on the present and to limn the future. It is as if our language is no longer capable of describing our world; a picture is literally worth a thousand words—and thousands of pictures worth hundreds of thousands more. It is the case, then, when Reggio wants to comment on globalized religion and what behaviors might be counted as religious in the modern world, he presents a montage lasting nine minutes in which he samples artsy smoke rings, the American flag, the American flag juxtaposed with the flag of the Soviet Union, a military parade, pictures of world leaders printed on their nation's currency, fans doing the wave at a football game, traders on the floor of the New York Stock Exchange, a die spinning in a roulette wheel and the rotating images of a slot machine suggesting a gambling addiction, a stash of colorful pill capsules, Hollywood stars walking the red carpet, rock stars trailed by paparazzi, astronauts being welcomed back from space, the Washington Monument and US Capitol, a gathering of veterans, a gaggle of Boy Scouts of America, the Gerber baby.

The film is abstract. Intentionally so. The demands it places upon its viewers are not inconsiderable. Reggio is also aware that this film puts the viewer in a contradictory position. *Naqoykatsi* is employing technology to critique technology. Indeed, the film as released in 2002 could not have been made much earlier. The technical elements that made it possible to bring the director's vision to the big screen were simply not available

---

[27] Alter, *The Hebrew Bible*, 38–9. Alter's commentary on this passage is as delightful as it is insightful. The fusion of similarly sounding words and repetitions reflects the striking tendency of the story as a whole to make words flow into each other. "The prose turns language itself into a game of mirrors" (38n3).

before then. Echoing the biblical theme he is exploring, Reggio says that he is employing "the vernacular of the moment we are living in, embracing the very thing we are criticizing to manifest something, to seek the truth about something."[28]

If the film exploits technology to critique technology, the musical score is decidedly retro. Glass eschews electronica in his accompaniment. With his orchestration he returns to his classical roots, to acoustic instrumentation. "I thought of the music as a bridge to the viewer." In writing as he did, including the cello solos written for Yo-Yo Ma at the beginning and end, Glass sought to provide "a voice for the film."[29] If so, it is the voice of a requiem. The humans we see in this film have no voice. According to Genesis 1, humans were originally created in God's image and likeness (1:26). What we see here is degradation perfected. A rogues' gallery if ever there was one, trapped in a life well east of Eden.

FUTURE PROSPECTS AND QUESTIONS

- The *Qatsi* trilogy was created over the course of twenty-four years. The final installment was released seventeen years ago. In light of the continued impact of technology on our lives and of climate change, do the films stand the test of time? Do they still offer a relevant perspective?
- Do you think these films are, ultimately, *misanthropic*? What are they saying about the world and human beings' place in it?
- As noted, *Koyaanisqatsi* is universally considered the masterpiece of the trilogy. *Powaqqatsi* is also widely admired, especially for the way it captures human facial expressions. Can we isolate the individual films in the trilogy? Can each film be taken on its own? Or must we view the piece as a whole?
- In the final installment, *Naqoyqatsi*, does Godfrey Reggio lose his way? Does he betray his original vision? Is he caught in a contradiction?
- Can you think of other films in which there is such a close association of image and music? How does the relationship of filmmaker and composer shape the spectatorial reality?
- What other feature-length films evoke and transform the primeval history of Genesis 1–11?
- What other feature-length films address the impacts of technology, of globalization, of overpopulation, of climate change? Do they echo biblical motifs and concerns about the created order?

---

[28] From a New York University panel discussion, chaired by John Rockwell, arts and entertainment editor of the *New York Times*, five days prior to release of the film (October 18, 2002), which included Godfrey Reggio, Jon Kane, and Philip Glass. It is included as a special feature on the DVD.

[29] From the New York University panel discussion.

Suggested Readings and Annotated Bibliography

Blizek, William L., ed. *The Bloomsbury Companion to Religion and Film*. Reprint, London: Bloomsbury Academic, 2013.

This wide-ranging volume, originally published in 2009, is designed for postgraduate students, for scholars, and as a library reference work. The first fifty pages reflect the strong voice of its fine editor, as he guides the reader in reflecting on the past and future of the subdiscipline of religion and film, how to use religion to interpret movies, and how to use film to critique religion. The text has a tripartite structure: "The Study of Religion and Film," "Religions and Film," and "Religious Themes in the Movies."

Lyden, John. C. *Film as Religion: Myths, Morals, and Rituals*. New York: New York University Press, 2003.

This volume was a game-changer when it appeared. It provided a thorough overview of religion and film scholarship at the time and argued that films function like a religion, complete with worldviews, myths, values, and rituals. Lyden's goal was to provide a new method for religion and film. He focused not only on content in films but also on viewer response. He rejected the distinction between "religion" and "culture." Lyden suggests we allow film to be "other" and to be open to self-transformation when engaging a film. The second half of the book allows him to apply his method to several genres of film (westerns and action movies, gangster films, melodramas, romantic comedies, children's films and fantasies, science fiction, thrillers and horror movies).

Lyden, John, ed. *The Routledge Companion to Religion and Film*. London: Routledge, 2009.

This useful volume brings together twenty-eight well-known scholars of religion and film to provide an overview of how the subdiscipline is developing. Divided into four parts, the *Companion* analyzes the history of the interaction of religion and film; studies religion *in* film by examining how the world's major religions, as well as postcolonial, Japanese, and new religions, are depicted by and within films; uses diverse methodologies to explore religion and film, including psychoanalytical, feminist, and audience reception theory; and highlights various religious themes in film, namely redemption, the demonic, Christ figures, heroes and superheroes.

Mitchell, Jolyon, and S. Brent Plate, eds. *The Religion and Film Reader*. London, UK: Routledge, 2007.

This was the first significant, multiauthor collection devoted to religion and film. The first two chapters are especially helpful in the way they trace the early years of cinema, gauge religious reactions, and highlight key texts in early film theory. Half of the book is devoted to short interviews with directors around the globe as well as condensed essays by filmmakers. The final two sections cover theological and biblical approaches to film analysis and include short essays by religion and film scholars.

Plate, S. Brent. *Religion and Film: Cinema and the Re-creation of the World*. London: Wallflower Press, 2009.

This brief book (144 pages), part of the Short Cuts Series, is a very creative and insightful primer in the subdiscipline of religion and film. Plate, a well-established author in the guild, argues that religions and films both operate by re-creating the known world and by presenting an alternative version to their viewers and worshippers. Like Lyden, he argues that films conjure powerful worldviews. He situates his work in the third wave of religion and film scholarship, which moves away from literary interpretations of film, engages fully film criticism and critical theory, takes seriously audience reception, and considers how the viewing of film itself is similar to participation in religious ceremonies. He is particularly interested in how films affect viewers' bodies. To test his method he turns to Hollywood blockbusters, Danish and Japanese films, cult films, avant-garde and experimental films. I consider his work invaluable for my own.

Reinhartz, Adele. *Bible and Cinema: An Introduction*. London: Routledge, 2013.

Building on her previous explorations of the intersection of Bible and film—*Scripture on the Silver Screen* (2003), *Jesus of Hollywood* (2007), *Bible and Cinema: Fifty Key Films* (2012)—this capstone volume is a comprehensive introduction to the ways in which the Bible has been used and represented in mainstream cinema. Part 1 surveys the Bible *on* film: Old Testament epics, Jesus story films, peplum movies that weave snippets of the Jesus story into broader fictional narratives ("sword-and-sandal" flicks), and biblical films that juxtapose biblical stories with modern narratives. Part 2 examines the Bible *in* film. Here Reinhartz ferrets out the Old Testament in modern guise, identifies Christ-figure films, detects traces of biblical morality, and explores biblical themes of destruction and redemption.

Settle, Zachary, and Taylor Worley, eds. *Dreams, Doubt, and Dread: The Spiritual in Film*. Eugene, OR: Cascade Books, Wipf and Stock, 2016.

This diverse group of eleven authors interprets film through the lenses of continental phenomenologists. Rather than simply use film narrative to illustrate various issues in the field of the philosophy of religion, they engage a broad array of films using continental theorists to help readers understand how representative movies affect their viewers, how films are spiritual phenomena to be experienced. With Gilles Deleuze, the volume asks, "How is it that cinema is so adept at stirring up spiritual life?" Each section of the book ("Dreams," "Doubt," and "Dread") concludes with a wide-ranging author roundtable.

Tatum, W. Barnes. *Jesus at the Movies: A Guide to the First Hundred Years*. 3rd edition. Santa Rosa, CA: Polebridge Press, 2013.

This revised and enlarged edition follows the design of its two predecessors (1997, 2004). As a viewer's guide it can be used in two related ways. The reader can approach the volume as a monograph, chronologically arranged, reading from the beginning through to the end to appreciate the arc of Jesus films' cinematic history. Or the reader can treat the volume like a reference work and read the discrete chapters on particular films as the occasion may dictate. Since each of the seventeen Jesus-story films receives a similar treatment, the reader will develop an appreciation for a film—or films—in four areas: background information on the making of the film; how the film presents the Jesus story, with special attention given to the way material from the New Testament gospels has been used in the screenplay; how the film portrays Jesus distinctively and the relation of this portrayal to other characterizations of Jesus; and the response to the film by the general public and religious groups and by critics representing the religious and secular press.

CHAPTER 17

....

TELEVISION AND THE
BIBLE IN AMERICAN
POPULAR CULTURE

....

MATTHEW A. COLLINS

DEPARTMENT OF THEOLOGY AND RELIGIOUS
STUDIES, UNIVERSITY OF CHESTER

INTRODUCTION

THE year 1928 saw the world's first public television broadcasts, from experimental television stations in Schenectady, New York (W2XB/W2XAD, now WRGB), Wheaton, Maryland (W3XK), and New York City (WRNY).[1] Though initially rather limited in terms of scope, reach, and content, one of its pioneers, Charles Francis Jenkins, described it as "the Aladdin's lamp which will enable vast audiences to see as well as hear through space," adding that "the new era will bring to the fireside a fascinating teacher and entertainer without limitation of language, literacy or age."[2] From humble beginnings, television has expanded to a global and hugely influential medium, with television sets not only becoming largely ubiquitous in households across much of the world (in 2015 an estimated 1.57 billion households worldwide owned at least one) but frequently constituting the focal point around which furniture and living space is arranged.[3] The extent of its cultural penetration has been matched only by the rise of the

[1] "What Television Offers You," *Popular Mechanics* 50, no. 5 (1928): 820–4; Gary R. Edgerton, *The Columbia History of American Television* (New York: Columbia University Press, 2007), 27–35.

[2] Cited in James N. Miller, "The Latest in Television," *Popular Mechanics* 52, no. 3 (1929): 472–6, here 475–6.

[3] Statista, "Number of TV Households Worldwide from 2010 to 2021 (in Billions)," https://www.statista.com/statistics/268695/number-of-tv-households-worldwide/.

internet, which has itself brought about significant changes in the ways we think about and access television.

Television consumption in the United States is especially prolific, with some 97 to 99 percent of households (an estimated 119.6 million in 2017) owning at least one television set (and many, two or three).[4] According to Nielsen reports, in 1985 the average American watched around 4.5 hours a day (ca. 1,642 hours a year); in 2016 that figure was 5 hours and 4 minutes (ca. 1,849 hours a year).[5] Moreover, Americans continue on average to watch more television per day than the inhabitants of any other country.[6] Diane Winston notes that "television is the most pervasive medium in American society.... On any given day, more Americans view television than listen to radio or read a newspaper."[7] Caryn James goes further, suggesting, "Anyone who does not watch television cannot possibly understand mainstream American culture.... Television provides a constantly updated chart of what mainstream America thinks."[8] But more than that: "The whole medium reflects and expresses the myths by which we live.... It takes our history and our present and interprets it to us. In a sense, television coverage of events is less concerned with history than with what the medium itself believes *ought* to be remembered. It thus becomes a kind of collective memory of our shared experiences."[9]

It is in this function as "our culture's central storyteller"[10] (as predicted by Jenkins, fulfilling a dual role of both education and entertainment) that its significance for understanding the place of the Bible in American popular culture can be found. In terms of its didactic and cultural influence, television has variously been claimed to have "superseded church" or even "replaced the Bible" itself, whether in terms of function or impact.[11] Nevertheless, it is its very popularity and prevalence that makes it a key lens

---

[4] Statista, "Number of TV Households in the United States from Season 2000–2001 to Season 2017–2018 (in Millions)," https://www.statista.com/statistics/243789/number-of-tv-households-in-the-us/.

[5] William F. Fore, *Television and Religion: The Shaping of Faith, Values, and Culture* (Minneapolis, MN: Augsburg, 1987), 16; John Koblin, "How Much Do We Love TV? Let Us Count the Ways," *New York Times*, June 30, 2016, https://www.nytimes.com/2016/07/01/business/media/nielsen-survey-media-viewing.html.

[6] Statista, "Average Daily TV Viewing Time per Person in Selected Countries Worldwide in 2016 (in Minutes)," https://web.archive.org/web/20190513004425/ https://www.statista.com/statistics/276748 /average-daily-tv-viewing-time-per-person-in-selected-countries/. See further: https://www.statista. com/statistics/276748/average-daily-tv-viewing-time-per-person-in-selected-countries/. Cf. Fore, *Television and Religion*, 17.

[7] Diane Winston, introduction to *Small Screen, Big Picture: Television and Lived Religion*, ed. Diane Winston (Waco, TX: Baylor University Press, 2009), 1–14, here 3.

[8] Caryn James, "To Get the Best View of Television, Try Using a Wide Lens," *New York Times*, October 1, 2000, http://www.nytimes.com/2000/10/01/arts/television-special-section-get-best-view-television-try-using-wide-lens.html.

[9] Fore, *Television and Religion*, 21, my italics.

[10] Jonathan Nichols-Pethick, *TV Cops: The Contemporary American Television Police Drama* (New York: Routledge, 2012), 186. Also Teresa Blythe, "Working Hard for the Money: A Faith-Based Media Literacy Analysis of the Top Television Dramas of 2000–2001," *Journal of Media and Religion* 1, no. 3 (2002): 139–51, here 140.

[11] Winston, introduction, 2; Allene Stuart Phy, "The Bible and American Popular Culture: An Overview and Introduction," in *The Bible and Popular Culture in America*, ed. Allene Stuart Phy (Philadelphia, PA: Fortress, 1985), 1–23, here 5.

through which to fruitfully explore the ongoing use, interpretation, and cultural impact of the Bible within America.

OVERVIEW OF TOPIC

Given the almost preeminent individual cultural prominence of both Bible and television, at least in the Western world, surprisingly little has been done on the intersection between the two. There is certainly plenty of work on the Bible and film.[12] However, film and television are fundamentally different. For one thing, they are experienced differently, reflecting distinct modes of engagement. Cinemas are "cathedrals of the image, where we partake in shared experiences," while televisions are "home shrines, personalized and comfortable."[13] The narratives they present are also constructed differently. That is, "Movies...are 'events'—even when watched later on TV. They generally offer 'one-time-only' opportunities to enjoy highly dramatic stories that rely more on plots than characters, and they generally have a clear resolution."[14] By contrast, a television

---

[12] See, for example, George Aichele and Richard Walsh, eds., *Screening Scripture: Intertextual Connections between Scripture and Film* (Harrisburg, PA: Trinity Press International, 2002); Rhonda Burnette-Bletsch, ed., *The Bible in Motion: A Handbook of the Bible and Its Reception in Film*, 2 vols., Handbooks of the Bible and Its Reception 2 (Berlin: De Gruyter, 2016); Laura Copier and Caroline Vander Stichele, eds., *Close Encounters between Bible and Film: An Interdisciplinary Engagement*, Semeia Studies 87 (Atlanta, GA: SBL Press, 2016); J. Cheryl Exum, ed., *The Bible in Film—The Bible and Film* (Leiden: Brill, 2006); J. Stephen Lang, *The Bible on the Big Screen: A Guide from Silent Films to Today's Movies* (Grand Rapids, MI: Baker Books, 2007); Adele Reinhartz, *Scripture on the Silver Screen* (Louisville, KY: Westminster John Knox, 2003); Adele Reinhartz, *Bible and Cinema: An Introduction* (London: Routledge, 2013); Adele Reinhartz, ed., *Bible and Cinema: Fifty Key Films* (London: Routledge, 2013); David J. Shepherd, ed., *Images of the Word: Hollywood's Bible and Beyond*, Semeia Studies 54 (Atlanta, GA: SBL Press, 2008); David J. Shepherd, *The Bible on Silent Film: Spectacle, Story and Scripture in the Early Cinema* (Cambridge: Cambridge University Press, 2013). There are also collections of essays focusing on individual films, such as Rhonda Burnette-Bletsch and Jon Morgan, eds., *Noah as Antihero: Darren Aronofsky's Cinematic Deluge* (New York: Routledge, 2017); Kathleen E. Corley and Robert L. Webb, eds., *Jesus and Mel Gibson's The Passion of the Christ* (London: Continuum, 2004); Joan E. Taylor, ed., *Jesus and Brian: Exploring the Historical Jesus and His Times via Monty Python's Life of Brian* (London: Bloomsbury T & T Clark, 2015); David Tollerton, ed., *A New Hollywood Moses: On the Spectacle and Reception of Exodus: Gods and Kings*, Biblical Reception 4 (London: Bloomsbury T & T Clark, 2017); Richard Walsh, Jeffrey L. Staley, and Adele Reinhartz, eds., *Son of Man: An African Jesus Film* (Sheffield, UK: Sheffield Phoenix Press, 2013). Other works have focused on particular characters, especially Jesus; e.g., Adele Reinhartz, *Jesus of Hollywood* (Oxford: Oxford University Press, 2007); Richard Walsh, *Reading the Gospels in the Dark: Portrayals of Jesus in Film* (Harrisburg, PA: Trinity Press International, 2003). See further Gregory Robbins's contribution to the present volume.

[13] Elijah Siegler, "Is God Still in the Box? Religion in Television Cop Shows Ten Years Later," in *God in the Details: American Religion in Popular Culture*, 2nd ed., ed. Eric Michael Mazur and Kate McCarthy (London: Routledge, 2011), 179–96, here 180.

[14] S. Elizabeth Bird, "True Believers and Atheists Need Not Apply: Faith and Mainstream Television Drama," in Winston, *Small Screen, Big Picture*, 17–41, here 36.

series has an "open narrative"[15] and is a "place of familiarity, where we interact with and get to know characters on a regular basis."[16] There is, as a result, far more opportunity for character and plot development. Roberta Pearson notes, "Since cinema's industrial conditions of production and reception preclude multi-year narratives constructed over hundreds of episodes, television may now be the superior medium, at least for some kinds of storytelling."[17] Television also lends itself to educational and informative programming in a manner largely absent from film, and as such has a far broader remit (and indeed, audience) than its cinematic cousin. Thus despite superficial similarities (and some clear overlaps) between the two, the media of film and television are markedly distinct. Consequently, the intersection between Bible and television is something worthy of examination in its own right.

Though "until recently…uneasy bedfellows,"[18] there has over the years been a steady focus on the question of *religion* and television.[19] However, work on the Bible and television has been much more limited in scope. Occasional individual essays have appeared in broader-themed volumes on the Bible and popular culture or in outlets such as the *Journal of Media and Religion* (2002–present) and *Journal of Religion and Popular Culture* (2002–present), but the collection of essays in Helen K. Bond and Edward Adams's *The Bible on Television* (2020), though predominantly concerned with documentaries and a primarily British context, is to date one of the only book-length treatments of the subject.[20]

Nevertheless, the Bible permeates television (both explicitly and implicitly), especially in the US, which is understandable given "the Bible's curious but essential role in

---

[15] Elijah Siegler, "Television," in *The Routledge Companion to Religion and Popular Culture*, ed. John C. Lyden and Eric Michael Mazur (London: Routledge, 2015), 41–64, here 54.

[16] Bird, "True Believers," 35.

[17] Roberta Pearson, "Lost in Transition: From Post-Network to Post-Television," in *Quality TV: Contemporary American Television and Beyond*, ed. Janet McCabe and Kim Akass (London: I. B. Tauris, 2007), 239–56, here 248. At the same time, technical advances and innovations "have enabled TV series to produce visual effects similar to ones that were once only seen in Hollywood movies," further rendering television "a medium that rivals film for entertainment" (Janet McCabe and Kim Akass, "Introduction: Debating Quality," in McCabe and Akass, *Quality TV*, 1–11, here 8).

[18] Siegler, "Television," 41.

[19] Here we might note, for instance, John P. Ferré, ed., *Channels of Belief: Religion and American Commercial Television* (Ames: Iowa State University Press, 1990); Fore, *Television and Religion*; Barrie Gunter and Rachel Viney, *Seeing Is Believing: Religion and Television in the 1990s* (London: John Libbey, 1994); Michael Suman, ed., *Religion and Prime Time Television* (Westport, CT: Praeger, 1997); Winston, *Small Screen, Big Picture*. See further Siegler, "Television."

[20] Helen K. Bond and Edward Adams, eds., *The Bible on Television*, Scriptural Traces 23, Library of New Testament Studies 622 (London: T & T Clark, 2020); I am very grateful indeed to the editors and authors of this volume for kindly allowing me access to the various contributions in advance of its publication. Despite its title, Peter Malone's *Screen Jesus: Portrayals of Christ in Television and Film* (Lanham, MD: Scarecrow Press, 2012) is rather more focused on film than television, while James Aston and John Walliss's edited volume *Small Screen Revelations: Apocalypse in Contemporary Television*, Bible in the Modern World 50 (Sheffield, UK: Sheffield Phoenix, 2013) is more concerned with apocalypse generally than the Bible per se.

American history and culture."[21] Accordingly, this essay concentrates primarily on the Bible in American television, focusing in particular on the twenty-first century. I suggest that there are three broad categories which may helpfully illustrate and encompass the diverse ways in which the Bible appears and/or is utilized: (1) educating about the Bible (e.g., documentaries); (2) dramatizing the Bible (renditions of biblical stories); and (3) drawing on the Bible (the impact or use of the Bible in other television programs). Examining each of these in turn, this essay highlights the prevalence of the Bible within television and thus within American popular culture more generally, as well as considering some of the myriad ways in which it has been read, used, and interpreted. In particular, it endeavors to show how the medium can function as a tool for both reflecting and promoting levels of biblical literacy among its audience.

SPECIFIC EXAMPLES AND/OR FOCI

Educating about the Bible

It is not insignificant that when *The American Bible Challenge* (GSN, 2012–2014) premiered on August 23, 2012, it had 1.7 million viewers, the Game Show Network's largest audience in its eighteen-year history.[22] This biblically themed quiz show went on to attract over 13 million total viewers in its first season. As Amy Introcaso-Davis, the channel's executive vice president, said, "The best-selling book of all time is now GSN's most viewed program of all time."[23] The program tapped into the same alluring (and lucrative) combination of Bible and television that gave rise to the success of televangelism and the "electronic church," though without any overt evangelistic agenda.[24] Instead it was presented simply as entertainment, albeit in an implicitly educational format that both rewarded and encouraged biblical literacy. Undoubtedly, however, the main means by which television has played an active role in educating its audience about the Bible is through documentaries.

---

[21] Claudia Setzer and David A. Shefferman, eds., *The Bible and American Culture: A Sourcebook* (London: Routledge, 2011), 1.

[22] John W. Kennedy, "And Then There Were Nuns (and Rabbis)! GSN's 'American Bible Challenge' Kicks Off Second Season Tonight," *Beliefnet*, March 21, 2013, http://www.beliefnet.com/columnists /faithmediaandculture/2013/03/and-then-there-were-nuns-and-rabbis-gsns-american-bible-challenge-kicks-off-second-season-tonight.html.

[23] "GSN's 'The American Bible Challenge' Debuts as the Network's Number 1 Program of All Time Delivering 2.3 Million Total Viewers," *TV by the Numbers*, August 24, 2012, http://tvbythenumbers.zap2it. com/network-press-releases/gsns-the-american-bible-challenge-debuts-as-the-networks-number-1-program-of-all-time-delivering-2-3-million-total-viewers/146227/.

[24] Perry C. Cotham, "The Electronic Church," in Phy, *The Bible and Popular Culture in America*, 103–36. See also Mark Ward, ed., *The Electronic Church in the Digital Age*, 2 vols. (Santa Barbara, CA: Praeger, 2016).

As a (sub)genre or type, the Bible documentary first came to the fore in the 1970s.[25] In line with the broader genre to which it belongs, it has since manifested in a variety of different ways. Bill Nichols identifies five key "documentary modes": expository, observational, interactive, reflexive, and performative:[26] "There is a certain historical progression of the modes, from the expository mode prominent in early documentaries, to the performative mode of a number of contemporary works. However, modes are not mutually exclusive, and the formal innovations of newly emergent modes coexist with established practices. At the same time, modes may overlap within a work and in this way a documentary may exhibit features of more than one mode."[27] To these, Keith Beattie adds the reconstructive mode, which "encompasses the increasingly prominent practice of dramatic reconstruction."[28] Though himself drawing largely upon documentary cinema, Nichols's modes (along with the reconstructive) are, to a greater or lesser extent, nevertheless all represented among Bible documentaries.

The primary function of these programs is ostensibly the dissemination of knowledge about the texts, characters, and historical context of the Bible, frequently pitched as the divulging of "new" discoveries. They are thus inherently educational in nature. Indeed, shifting degrees of biblical literacy over the past few decades means that it can no longer be assumed "that potential viewers know even the general story," and "in this new climate, documentaries are themselves often the means by which certain people gain their biblical knowledge."[29] However, the sensitive nature of the subject matter means that there is also huge potential for controversy. When *Jesus: The Evidence* (Channel 4, 1984) aired in the UK in April 1984, it was heavily informed by biblical scholarship (with eminent scholars both prominently featured in the program and involved in approving the scripts), yet its minimalist approach to the historical Jesus (though nothing new in academic circles) resulted in public outrage and calls to boycott it.[30] As Jean-Claude Bragard suggests, "broadcasters failed to anticipate the impact the Bible on TV can

[25] Richard Wallis, "Genesis of the Bible Documentary: The Development of Religious Broadcasting in the UK," in Bond and Adams, *The Bible on Television*, 16–39. See further Kenneth Wolfe, "The Bible and Broadcasting," in *Using the Bible Today: Contemporary Interpretations of Scripture*, ed. Dan Cohn-Sherbok (London: Bellew, 1991), 47–67.

[26] Bill Nichols, *Representing Reality: Issues and Concepts in Documentary* (Bloomington: Indiana University Press, 1991), 31–75; Bill Nichols, *Blurred Boundaries: Questions of Meaning in Contemporary Culture* (Bloomington: Indiana University Press, 1994), 94–5. He has since added a sixth, "the poetic mode," which precedes the expository, though being more artistic in nature this is less obviously represented among Bible documentaries. Bill Nichols, *Introduction to Documentary*, 2nd ed. (Bloomington: Indiana University Press, 2010), 31–2, 162–6.

[27] Keith Beattie, *Documentary Screens: Non-Fiction Film and Television* (New York: Palgrave Macmillan, 2004), 20.

[28] Ibid., 24.

[29] Helen K. Bond, introduction to Bond and Adams, *The Bible on Television*, 1–15, here 4.

[30] Jean-Claude Bragard, "The Bible According to TV," in Bond and Adams, *The Bible on Television*, 40–78, esp. 43–50; Geza Vermes, "A Television Documentary on Christ and the British Press: Channel 4's *Jesus: The Evidence* (April 1984)," in *Searching for the Real Jesus* (London: SCM Press, 2009), 63–9. Note similarly the reaction to *The Virgin Mary* (BBC/Discovery Channel, 2002); Helen K. Bond, "The Nativity on TV," in Bond and Adams, *The Bible on Television*, 136–59, esp. 137–46.

have."[31] In similar fashion, two seemingly innocuous Peter Jennings documentaries for ABC, *The Search for Jesus* (ABC, 2000) and *Jesus and Paul: The Word and the Witness* (ABC, 2004), provoked negative reactions and reviews from those who took exception to the scholarly findings of "experts."[32]

This suspicion of experts and scholarship more generally not only manifests where these threaten to undermine traditionally held beliefs but, conversely, can also be reflected in an increased sensationalism, whereby scholars are instead presented as the conservative guardians of tradition while the documentary purports to uncover the scandalous truth. Conservatism and sensationalism may even be combined, for instance in documentaries that claim "shocking new evidence" to support the credibility of the biblical account in the face of academic skepticism.[33] These approaches (often sidelining, minimizing, or otherwise obscuring scholarly input) have resulted in numerous program titles focused on "mysteries" or "secrets" of the Bible.[34] Like *Secrets of the Cross* (National Geographic, 2008), these claim to reveal "the conspiracies and cover-ups that have obscured the truth at each story's heart."[35] While undoubtedly successful at enticing an audience, in such presentations it can be hard to tell mainstream scholar from maverick, which may in turn raise questions about their educational value.[36] Bond suggests that the resulting diversity of documentary types encompasses "serious attempts to convey the latest scholarship to an interested public," those that adopt "a rather maverick view to reel in the audience" (even if later discredited by the program itself), and "the televisual equivalent of the tabloid press" (which "refuses to let research get in the way of a good story").[37] A brief survey of some other key Bible documentaries from the past twenty-five years will help illustrate the point.

In 1995 a three-hour documentary appeared under the relatively sober title *Who Wrote the Bible?* (A&E, 1995). Though modest in scope from an academic standpoint (examining, among other things, the view that "a number of different individuals could have written the Old and New Testaments"), it was nevertheless considered ambitious at

[31] Bragard, "The Bible According to TV," 46.

[32] Darrell Bock, "No More Hollow Jesus," *Christianity Today* 44, no. 9 (2000): 73; James W. Voelz, "The Beginnings of Christianity Are Not on Television," *Concordia Journal* 30, no. 3 (2004): 122–3.

[33] Bragard, "The Bible According to TV," 60–61; Mark Harris, "Plundering Egypt: Exodus Documentaries and the Exploitation of History," in Bond and Adams, *The Bible on Television*, 189–222, e.g., 189.

[34] Bond, introduction, 4–5; Bragard, "The Bible According to TV," 61–62. Cf. Vincent Campbell, *Science, Entertainment and Television Documentary* (London: Palgrave Macmillan, 2016), 128–31.

[35] National Geographic, "Secrets of the Cross," accessed May 26, 2020, http://www.nationalgeographic.com.au/tv/secrets-of-the-cross/.

[36] Bond, introduction, 5; Campbell, *Science*, 141–3. This has been especially noted with regard to documentaries on the Dead Sea Scrolls. See, e.g., Lawrence H. Schiffman, "Inverting Reality: The Dead Sea Scrolls in the Popular Media," *Dead Sea Discoveries* 12 (2005): 24–37; George J. Brooke, "The Scrolls in the British Media (1987–2002)," *Dead Sea Discoveries* 12 (2005): 38–51; Matthew A. Collins, "Examining the Reception and Impact of the Dead Sea Scrolls: Some Possibilities for Future Investigation," *Dead Sea Discoveries* 18 (2011): 226–46.

[37] Bond, introduction, 6. Also, Bragard, "The Bible According to TV," 40–41.

the time and involved "a plethora of scholars."[38] A year later it was repackaged and rescreened as a two-part episode within the channel's long-running series *Mysteries of the Bible* (A&E, 1994–1998), where it sat alongside episodes such as "Cities of Evil: Sodom and Gomorrah," "Apocalypse: The Puzzle of Revelation," and "The Lost Years of Jesus." Despite the series name, the approach taken throughout was not overly sensational, for the most part focusing simply on elucidating key figures and events from the Bible, with ample time given to the views of recognized scholars. The result was a fairly balanced and informed examination, albeit sometimes with a general inclination toward "cautious affirmation of the authenticity of the biblical text."[39] Highlighting the lure of Bible and television, the executive producer, Bram Roos, said, "It amazes me how successful we've been in appealing to the complete spectrum, from fundamentalists to complete agnostics and atheists."[40]

Jesus: The Complete Story (Discovery Channel, 2001)—produced in the UK as a three-part series, *Son of God* (BBC, 2001)—was shown in the US as a three-hour special coinciding with Easter Sunday. Attracting 12 million viewers, it constituted something of "a television landmark," incorporating dramatized reconstructions and capitalizing on recent developments in CGI.[41] Indeed, "the approach was so successful it would be copied time and again over the next decade by other TV genres."[42] While both popular and controversial, it remained grounded in scholarship, though took a somewhat different stance from *Jesus: The Evidence*, deciding instead to "approach the quest for the historical Jesus in a cautiously maximalist way."[43]

By way of contrast, the three-part miniseries *Walking the Bible* (PBS, 2006) was "American TV's first foray into Old Testament minimalism."[44] Presented as a travelogue, it implicitly embraced academic skepticism with regard to literal interpretations of the Bible but generally shunned scholarly interviews (along with reconstructions and CGI) in favor of a rather more personal (and indeed, literal) pilgrimage on the part of the presenter, Bruce Feiler.

Appearing the same year, *The Gospel of Judas* (National Geographic, 2006) dealt with the far more controversial topic of the discovery and publication of Codex Tchacos. Though the hype over this event no doubt served as an effective lure, the program itself was fairly academically rigorous in its execution, presenting a rather balanced unveiling of the text. The same, however, cannot necessarily be said for the various programs produced by the Israeli-Canadian filmmaker Simcha Jacobovici, including his series *The Naked Archaeologist* (Vision TV/History International, 2005–10), which ran to sixty-five episodes, *The Exodus Decoded* (History Channel, 2006), and *The Lost Tomb of Jesus* (Discovery Channel, 2007). These attempted to "prove" the historicity of biblical events, making a number of sensational and largely unsubstantiated claims along the way. The

---

[38] Connie Benesch, "A&E Asks 'Who Wrote the Bible?': Television—Scholars Present Their Theories in a 3-Hour Documentary that Premieres Sunday Night," *Los Angeles Times*, March 18, 1995, https://www.latimes.com/archives/la-xpm-1995-03-18-ca-44226-story.html.
[39] Harris, "Plundering Egypt," 193.   [40] Benesch, "A&E Asks."
[41] Bragard, "The Bible According to TV," 54–58.   [42] Ibid., 57.   [43] Ibid., 56.
[44] Ibid., 68.

latter two in particular have been heavily criticized in academic circles for their "reliance on unfounded speculation and a poor grasp of historical research," and have even been characterized as "intellectually and scientifically dishonest."[45]

Over the past decade, documentaries have increasingly (and self-consciously) adopted titles implicitly promising scandalous revelations as a means of attracting viewers; for instance, *Secrets of the Cross* (National Geographic, 2008), *The Bible's Buried Secrets* (PBS, 2008; also the title of a BBC series in 2011), *Bible Secrets Revealed* (History Channel, 2013), and *The Bible's Greatest Secrets* (AHC, 2013–2015). However, this somewhat transparent marketing ploy in fact masks a wide range of approaches to the text, with varying degrees of reasoned and measured scholarship lying behind the alluring sensationalism of the title.

Bragard suggests that, generally speaking, there has been a gradual shift "from shows that reflect the thinking of the Academy to shows that reflect the interests of television," with documentaries increasingly keen to challenge scholarship and/or tradition.[46] While remaining undeniably "educational" in nature (and implicitly marketed as such), it is "sobering then to realize that education appears to be rather low on the list of the documentary makers' priorities compared to consumer demand, sensationalism, and entertainment."[47] The nature and tone of the medium convey authority and neutrality, but the actual content is driven more by the need for "a good story." There is, as a result, an inherent interpretative selectivity at work: "The selection of scholars interviewed and the range of views expressed tends to be in the hands of the production company, whose own agenda drives the program. This makes it much harder for an unsuspecting public to discern between mainstream theories and fringe ideas, since both can be presented as equally authoritative. Indeed, such documentaries may even promote a fringe scholar or theory into the limelight, casting more mainstream academics into the role of conservative and unenlightened sideliners; a process which Lawrence H. Schiffman describes as 'inverting reality.'"[48] However, the sensational is not necessarily bad. Indeed, sensationalism and intrigue can themselves be helpful tools for promotion of the Bible (and biblical literacy) within popular culture. While often a source of irritation for scholars, the flip side of the coin is that these play a key role in ensuring the ongoing popularity of Bible documentaries and their ability to attract such large audiences. The exposure of the public to occasional ill-informed or misleading presentations is thus counterbalanced by the guarantee of a ready and eager audience beyond the academic sphere and the potential this in turn offers more reasoned scholarship for utilization of television in order to genuinely educate about the Bible.

---

[45] Harris, "Plundering Egypt," 209; Alan Cooperman, "'Lost Tomb of Jesus' Claim Called a Stunt: Archaeologists Decry TV Film," *Washington Post*, February 28, 2007, A3.

[46] Bragard, "The Bible According to TV," 64; also 40–41.   [47] Harris, "Plundering Egypt," 221.

[48] Collins, "Examining the Reception," 243. Cf. Schiffman, "Inverting Reality."

Dramatizing the Bible

In 1910, two decades before the first public television broadcasts, Rev. Herbert Jump delivered a sermon at the South Congregational Church in New Britain, Connecticut, highlighting "the religious possibilities of the motion picture."[49] Recognizing that film "could convey the biblical stories visually and hence with emotion and accessibility,"[50] he noted that "Joseph and Esther and Moses and Paul and Jesus are better known to the theatre-goers today than they ever were before, thanks to Mr Edison's invention."[51] This capacity for dramatizing the Bible was later shared by television, with the miniseries *Jesus of Nazareth* (RAI/ITV/NBC, 1977), one of the earliest and most acclaimed examples, attracting some 90 million viewers in the US alone. In recent years these have become especially prolific, with some suggesting, "The general rise in biblical illiteracy has also led to a return to simple story-telling in Bible programmes made for TV."[52]

This rise (or resurrection) of "full-scale dramas" reflects a different kind of engagement with the text. Though ostensibly uninterested in the sorts of disputes characterizing documentary programs, the very act of adaptation nevertheless still requires interpretative and exegetical choices to be made (albeit in this instance "behind the scenes" and without counterclaim or explicit justification). Translating the rather two-dimensional limitations of the text itself to *visual* media (e.g., film or television) necessitates among other things the plugging of narrative gaps (whether in plot or dialogue) and decisions about embodiment and physical representation, as well as elaboration, clarification, explanation, harmonization, and/or abridgement/omission in pursuit of a coherent narrative.[53] Dramatizations are thus never simply straightforward "performances" but are themselves acts of interpretation. Though primarily marketed as entertainment, there is accordingly some discernible overlap with documentaries (especially those of the aforementioned reconstructive mode), which often and increasingly incorporate elements of dramatization.[54]

A handful of dramatizations appeared in the 1990s and early 2000s, often featuring a prominent or all-star cast. One notable example was *The Bible Collection* (TNT, 1994–2001), a series of seventeen stand-alone television films centered upon key figures or events in the biblical narrative, from Genesis through to Revelation.[55] Around the same time, a

---

[49] Printed as a pamphlet for private distribution in December 1910 (with extracts appearing in the December 31 issue of *Moving Picture World*). The complete text is reproduced in Herbert A. Jump, "The Religious Possibilities of the Motion Picture," *Film History* 14, no. 2 (2002): 216–28.

[50] John C. Lyden, "Film," in Lyden and Mazur, *Routledge Companion*, 80–99, here 80.

[51] Jump, "Religious Possibilities," 225.

[52] Bond, introduction, 12. Also, Bragard, "The Bible According to TV," 73–78.

[53] See further Matthew A. Collins, "Depicting the Divine: The Ambiguity of Exodus 3 in *Exodus: Gods and Kings*," in Tollerton, *A New Hollywood Moses*, 9–39, esp. 11–16; Matthew A. Collins, "An Ongoing Tradition: Aronofsky's *Noah* as 21st-Century Rewritten Scripture," in Burnette-Bletsch and Morgan, *Noah as Antihero*, 8–33, esp. 19–21.

[54] Beattie, *Documentary Screens*, 24.

[55] For an examination of one of these films (*Samson and Delilah* [1996]), see Caroline Blyth's contribution to the present volume.

two-part miniseries, *In the Beginning* (NBC, 2000), focused on events from Genesis and Exodus. Though inherently involving some or all of the translational elements outlined above, these depictions tended to constitute relatively traditional renderings of biblical stories. Toward the end of the 2000s, however, a somewhat different approach was taken by the series *Kings* (NBC, 2009). This was loosely based on the story of Saul and David from 1 Samuel but set in the modern-day fictional kingdom of Gilboa. Though taking rather more liberties with the text as a result, it nevertheless remained a recognizably direct adaptation of the biblical narrative, with David Shepherd (David) singlehandedly destroying a "Goliath-class" tank and rising to prominence, thereby incurring the wrath and envy of King Silas Benjamin (Saul), the support of Rev. Ephram Samuels (Samuel), and the affections of the king's daughter, Michelle (Michal). Despite this, marketing of the series deliberately avoided highlighting its biblical nature for "fear of either backlash or marginalizing or pigeonholing," with the result that "religious America" for the most part "didn't know about it."[56] Ultimately, low ratings led to its being canceled after the first season.

More recently there has been a marked proliferation in the number of prominent television dramatizations, coinciding with the revival of the biblical epic in film (notably exemplified by *Noah* [Paramount, 2014] and *Exodus: Gods and Kings* [20th Century Fox, 2014]). Described as "a milestone in the history of the Bible on TV,"[57] the ten-part miniseries *The Bible* (History Channel, 2013) attracted over 13 million viewers for its first episode, consistently outperformed all scheduled competition throughout its run, and was nominated for three Emmy awards, as well as taking "the number one spot on iTunes for top TV show downloads."[58] As with *The Bible Collection*, it covered events from Genesis through to Revelation, though as "one story...one grand narrative" (thus, as Meg Ramey highlights, "clearly targeted for a Christian audience and [with] a Christian metanarrative").[59] In 2014 a heavily abridged version of the New Testament portions of the program received theatrical release as the film *Son of God* (20th Century Fox, 2014). The success of *The Bible* also led to a follow-up miniseries, *A.D. The Bible Continues* (NBC, 2015), consisting of twelve episodes focused specifically on events following Jesus's crucifixion from the Gospels and Acts. (Not to be confused with the network's

[56] Michael Green (creator of *Kings*), cited in Vaneta Rogers, "God Complexity: 'ELI,' KINGS, the Almighty & Network TV," *Newsarama*, May 15, 2009, https://www.newsarama.com/2905-god-complexity-eli-kings-the-almighty-network-tv.html.

[57] Bragard, "The Bible According to TV," 77.

[58] Lightworkers Media, "Roma Downey and Mark Burnett's #1 New Cable Series THE BIBLE Is Also a New York Times Best Seller, Dominating Amazon and Is #1 on iTunes and #1 on Twitter," *PR Newswire*, March 25, 2013, https://www.prnewswire.com/news-releases/roma-downey-and-mark-burnetts-1-new-cable-series-the-bible-is-also-a-new-york-times-best-seller-dominating-amazon-and-is-1-on-itunes-and-1-on-twitter-199936641.html; Erik Hayden, " 'The Bible' Earns Three Emmy Nominations," *Hollywood Reporter*, July 18, 2013, https://www.hollywoodreporter.com/live-feed/bible-earns-three-emmy-nominations-588426; Meg Ramey, "The History Channel's *The Bible*, an Epic...?," in Bond and Adams, *The Bible on Television*, 223–46, esp. 224.

[59] Eric Marrapodi, "Reality TV Goliath Takes Up Bible Miniseries Challenge, Hopes for Better Outcome," *CNN Belief Blog*, March 2, 2013, http://religion.blogs.cnn.com/2013/03/02/the-reality-of-the-bringing-the-bible-to-life/; Ramey, "The History Channel's *The Bible*," 236.

earlier five-part miniseries *A.D.* [NBC, 1985], which similarly used Acts as its spring-board.) Though effectively pitched as a sequel, it featured a different cast and overlapped significantly with the final episode of *The Bible*, expanding and retelling this part of the narrative in far greater depth. Despite apparent plans to continue through the rest of the New Testament at the same pace, *A.D. The Bible Continues* proved to be rather less successful than its forebear in terms of ratings and so was not renewed for a second season.[60]

The following year saw the arrival of yet another series, *Of Kings and Prophets* (ABC, 2016). Sharing two of the same writers as the (similarly named) big-budget blockbuster *Exodus: Gods and Kings* (20th Century Fox, 2014), it clearly intended to capitalize on the burgeoning interest in dramatizing the Bible and the resurgent success of the biblical epic in film, implicitly presenting itself as "a small screen spin-off of *Exodus*," one that might also "evoke memories of *Noah*."[61] Specifically, the series was another attempt to dramatize the story of Saul and David. Unlike the earlier series *Kings* (NBC, 2009), *Of Kings and Prophets* retained the original narrative setting, though—perhaps influenced by the wildly popular fantasy series *Game of Thrones* (HBO, 2011–2019)—placed strong emphasis on sex and violence.[62] Thus, effectively marketed as a potent blend of *The Bible* and *Game of Thrones*, it bore all the hallmarks of having the potential to succeed where *Kings* failed (perhaps even surpassing *The Bible* itself). However, it fared even worse and was canceled after just two episodes.[63] David Tollerton suggests two reasons for this. First, opposition and lobbying by the Parents Television Council (PTC) targeted advertisers, encouraging them to withdraw their support for this violent, sexualized portrayal of the biblical narrative. Given commercial television's reliance on sustained sponsorship, this tactic exploited an inherent weakness in "an economic model particularly vulnerable to targeted lobbying."[64] Yet its very format may also have been problematic. Tollerton notes that the first episode, which dealt with God's command to annihilate the Amalekites (1 Sam 15)—graphically portraying the physical and psychological horror of this divinely sanctioned genocide—echoed *Exodus: Gods and Kings* and *Noah* in its questioning of divine morality, forcing the viewer "to grapple with a morally difficult

---

[60] Cynthia Littleton, "NBC Cancels 'A.D.' as Producers Plan Digital Revival for Biblical Drama," *Variety*, July 3, 2015, https://variety.com/2015/tv/news/a-d-the-bible-continues-nbc-cancels-mark-burnett-roma-downey-1201533794/.

[61] David Tollerton, "When the Resurrected Biblical Epic Transferred to the Small Screen…and Promptly Died Again: A Critical Autopsy of the 2016 ABC Series *Of Kings and Prophets*," in Bond and Adams, *The Bible on Television*, 247–61, here 249.

[62] Bryn Elise Sandberg, "'Of Kings and Prophets' Boss Talks Sexually Explicit Bible Series: 'We're Going to Go as Far as We Can,'" *Hollywood Reporter*, January 9, 2016, https://www.hollywoodreporter.com/live-feed/kings-prophets-boss-talks-sexually-853669.

[63] Emily Yahr, "*Of Kings and Prophets* Tried to Be *Game of Thrones* and Failed: What Went Wrong?," *Washington Post*, March 9, 2016, https://www.washingtonpost.com/news/arts-and-entertainment/wp/2016/03/09/of-kings-and-prophets-tried-to-be-game-of-thrones-and-failed-what-went-wrong/.

[64] Tollerton, "Resurrected Biblical Epic," 259. Cf. Melissa Henson, "ABC's 'Of Kings and Prophets,' Broadcast TV's Version of HBO's Explicit 'Game of Thrones,'" *PTC Blog*, March 1, 2016, https://www.parentstv.org/blog/abcs-of-kings-and-prophets-broadcast-tvs-version-of-hbos-explicit-game-of-thrones.

vision of the divine."[65] But, highlighting that the number of viewers dropped significantly between episodes 1 and 2, he points out that, "The inherently episodic nature of *OKP* [*Of Kings and Prophets*] is essentially equivalent to including a vast intermission midway through screenings of *Noah* and *Exodus* in which the audience is prompted to dwell upon the horror they have witnessed and asked whether they would like to be re-immersed in that world."[66] In other words, when compared with film, there is a marked "commercial fragility" to small-screen dramatizations of the Bible, manifest not only in their reliance on continued advertiser support but also in their need "to lure viewers *back* on a consistent basis."[67] It is this which may account for the somewhat mixed fortunes witnessed by such programs.

Into this category of dramatizing the Bible would also fall a number of animated renditions, primarily aimed at a younger audience. Released first to video and later aired on TBN, Nest Family Entertainment's series *Animated Stories from the Bible* (TBN, 1992–1995) consisted of twelve short thirty-minute tales from the Hebrew Bible/Old Testament (including "Abraham and Isaac," "Joseph in Egypt," and "David and Goliath"). There was also a longer-running companion series, *Animated Stories from the New Testament* (TBN, 1987–2005), featuring twenty-four episodes. Though relatively straightforward renderings, both series were accompanied by learning materials and study resources (with Nest claiming "that education is not always entertaining, but that entertainment is always educational, especially with these young minds"),[68] thus further blurring the line between dramatizing and educating about the Bible. More recently, Big Idea Entertainment's *VeggieTales* franchise (1993–2017) fulfilled much the same role. Originally released directly to video, episodes of this computer-animated series received a couple of one-off television airings in 1998 and 2002 before being screened as a regular television program (NBC, 2006–2009; TBN, 2012–), as well as having two spin-off series on Netflix (2014–2017). Aimed at preschoolers, and with a clear educational and moralistic focus, many of these episodes retold Bible stories in a humorous (and often anachronistic) way, such as "Rack, Shack, and Benny" (about three employees in Mr. Nezzer's chocolate factory; cf. Dan 3) or "King George and the Ducky" (about a king's greedy accumulation of rubber ducks; cf. 2 Sam 11–12).[69]

---

[65] Tollerton, "Resurrected Biblical Epic," 257.   [66] Ibid., 258.

[67] Ibid., 260. Also see Bird, "True Believers," 18.

[68] Cited in R. Christopher Heard, "They're Not Just Bad, They're Stupid and Ugly, Too: The Depiction of Baal Worshippers in Nest Entertainment's *Animated Stories from the Bible*," in *Culture, Entertainment and the Bible*, ed. George Aichele, Journal for the Study of the Old Testament Supplement Series 309 (Sheffield, UK: Sheffield Academic Press, 2000), 89–103, here 103.

[69] See further Telford Work, "Veggie Ethics: What 'America's Favorite Vegetables' Say about Evangelicalism," *Theology Today* 57, no. 4 (2001): 473–83; Mark Roncace, "Youth Literature, Programming, and Entertainment," in *Teaching the Bible through Popular Culture and the Arts*, ed. Mark Roncace and Patrick Gray (Atlanta, GA: Society of Biblical Literature, 2007), 335–42, esp. 338–41. For an examination of one specific *VeggieTales* episode ("Esther: The Girl Who Became Queen"), see Dan W. Clanton, Jr., *Daring, Disreputable, and Devout: Interpreting the Bible's Women in the Arts and Music* (New York: T & T Clark, 2009), 111–41.

Targeting a somewhat older audience, equally humorous retellings of Bible stories can be found in episodes of *The Simpsons* (Fox, 1989–present). This is especially true of the episode "Simpsons Bible Stories" (1999), which contained short adaptations of Genesis 1–3, Exodus 1–16, 1 Samuel 17, and 1 Kings 3, as well as numerous references to other biblical passages.[70] Robert J. Myles suggests that "the episode functions as a surrogate Sunday school lesson in the way it similarly initiates viewers into a distorted, moralized, and simplified reading of the original biblical text."[71] He further suggests with regard to *The Simpsons*—though the same could arguably be said of similar uses of the Bible in programs such as *South Park* (Comedy Central, 1997–present) and *Family Guy* (Fox, 1999–present)—that: "*The Simpsons* has functioned, in many respects, as a foundation to biblical literacy. Its portrayal of biblical stories and allusions features as a surrogate first encounter with the text, establishing a frame of reference that influences the text's subsequent meaning and significance.... If biblical literacy concerns not only knowledge or facts about the Bible and biblical texts, but also the hermeneutical frame in which biblical material is positioned and interpolated to audiences, then *The Simpsons* can be seen to engender an Americanized, satirical, and postmodern literacy of the Bible and biblical texts."[72]

The dramatization of the Bible for television has thus had a rather checkered history. Bragard attributes the recent proliferation of such programs to a general decline in biblical literacy, such that "TV has returned to where it all began—the simple re-telling of Bible stories."[73] However, the mixed fortunes of these attempts to capitalize on the revival of the biblical epic in film demonstrate that it can be difficult to get right, highlighting the particular challenges faced by small-screen productions and further accentuating the differences between television and its cinematic cousin. Nevertheless, there are some success stories. Just as various animated renditions of Bible stories have actively encouraged biblical literacy among younger audiences (*Animated Stories from the Bible*, *VeggieTales*, etc.), Ramey highlights that "one Gallup poll taken after the series concluded reported that 11% of American adults surveyed about their Bible reading credited *The Bible* miniseries with inspiring them to read Scripture more."[74] In sum, while this "return to simple story-telling"[75] may indeed be indicative of a decline in biblical literacy, it would appear that the dramatization of the Bible itself may simultaneously play a key role in the ongoing promotion and encouragement of the same.

---

[70] See initially Robert J. Myles, "Biblical Literacy and *The Simpsons*," in *Rethinking Biblical Literacy*, ed. Katie Edwards (London: Bloomsbury T & T Clark, 2015), 143–62.

[71] Ibid., 152–3.

[72] Ibid., 143, 147. See further Dan W. Clanton, Jr. and Mark Roncace, "Animated Television," in Roncace and Gray, *Teaching the Bible*, 343–52; Todd V. Lewis, "Religious Rhetoric and the Comic Frame in *The Simpsons*," *Journal of Media and Religion* 1, no. 3 (2002): 153–65; David W. Scott, "Religiosity in *South Park*: Struggles over Institutional and Personal Piety among Residents of a 'Redneck Town,'" *Journal of Media and Religion* 10 (2011): 152–63.

[73] Bragard, "The Bible According to TV," 78.

[74] Ramey, "The History Channel's *The Bible*," 230.   [75] Bond, introduction, 12.

Drawing on the Bible

Alongside those programs specifically designed to educate about or dramatize the Bible, there are also television series which, though not biblical stories themselves, nevertheless draw heavily upon the Bible in the form of allusions to biblical episodes, characters, or themes. In some cases these are relatively explicit about their apparent biblical connection, evident from the very title of such programs as *Revelations* (NBC, 2005) and *The Book of Daniel* (NBC, 2006). The former, reminiscent of *The Omen* (20th Century Fox, 1976) and the *Left Behind* franchise, was a six-part miniseries about the end of days, the antichrist, and the second coming, which both drew upon and frequently cited biblical texts, especially Revelation.[76] *The Book of Daniel*, on the other hand, had little connection with its biblical namesake, featuring instead a modern-day Episcopal minister named Daniel who sees and talks with Jesus. Opposed by conservative Christian groups such as the American Family Association (in what Brian Kaylor terms a "cultural conflict over who gets to define Jesus"), it was canceled after just four episodes.[77] More recently, a similar fate was met by *Living Biblically* (CBS, 2018), a sitcom about a character attempting to live his life in strict accordance with biblical regulations (loosely based on A. J. Jacobs's 2007 book *The Year of Living Biblically*), which was canceled midseason after low ratings.[78]

Other programs, however, have made rather more subtle (yet in many ways, far more significant) use of the Bible. *Battlestar Galactica* (Sci-Fi/Syfy, 2003–9), a remake/reboot of the original 1970s series (ABC, 1978–1979), concerned a futuristic war between humans and a cybernetic race, the Cylons. Despite the sci-fi setting, the theme of religion featured prominently throughout (specifically the clash between the polytheism of the humans and the strict monotheism of the Cylons), and it contained significant allusions to biblical texts. Chief among these was the division of the humans into twelve colonies traveling together through space in search of a planet (Earth) known from religious scriptures. Though not simply a futuristic dramatization of the biblical story, echoes of the twelve tribes of Israel journeying to the Promised Land were reinforced through motifs such as the forty-year armistice prior to the events of the series, as well as the prophecy that the leader who would "guide the caravan of the heavens to their new homeland . . . would not live to enter the new land" (S1E10), a prophecy that indeed came

---

[76] Bird, "True Believers," 17–24. The creator, David Seltzer, was in fact also the writer of *The Omen*.

[77] Brian T. Kaylor, "Just a Little Talk with Jesus: The Portrayal of Jesus in NBC's *The Book of Daniel*," *Journal of Media and Religion* 10 (2011): 138–51, here 148; Stuart Elliott, "Few Are Booking Ads on 'The Book of Daniel,'" *New York Times*, January 11, 2006, https://www.nytimes.com/2006/01/11/business/media/few-are-booking-ads-on-the-book-of-daniel.html. An even more thoroughly modern Jesus is the subject of *Black Jesus* (Adult Swim, 2014–present); see Eric Thurman's contribution to the present volume.

[78] Jessica Pena, "*Living Biblically*: Cancelled; CBS Sitcom Pulled from Schedule," *TV Series Finale*, April 19, 2018, https://tvseriesfinale.com/tv-show/living-biblically-cancelled-cbs-sitcom-pulled-schedule/.

to pass in the final episode of the series (S4E22–23; cf. Deut 34:4).[79] Some episode titles likewise betray apparent biblical influence, including notably "Exodus, Parts 1–2" (S3E3–4), "He That Believeth in Me" (S4E3; cf. John 11:25), and "Revelations" (S4E12), as well as perhaps the choice of some prominent surnames in the series, such as Cain and Adama, or the spaceship *Gideon* and associated "*Gideon* massacre" (in S2E4–8). The overall narrative has been described as "theologically significant."[80] The character Six repeatedly insists that "God is love" (cf. 1 John 4), while the Cylons on more than one occasion cite their monotheistic god's command to procreate and "be fruitful" (S1E1; S2E5; cf. Gen 1:28).[81] The series not only utilized and alluded to the Bible but itself engaged with the question of scriptural authority and interpretation: "Both sides struggle to interpret scripture to learn the will of God/the gods. On both sides, not everyone agrees about how literally scripture should be read or to what extent scripture should be used as a template for political action."[82] Thus, while ostensibly a straightforward space-battle-centered sci-fi entertainment program, *Battlestar Galactica* was in fact loaded with biblical imagery and set in a world "in which both 'good guys' and 'bad guys' are strongly religious" and where "both sides are strongly invested in interpreting holy texts."[83]

Perhaps one of the best (and simultaneously most complex) examples of a drama series drawing on the Bible was *Lost* (ABC, 2004–10). Multi-award-winning and critically acclaimed, the program followed the survivors of a plane crash who find themselves stranded on a mysterious island. Indeed, *Lost* drew so extensively on the Bible, as well as an abundant wealth of other intertextual references to literature, philosophy, and culture, that, although by no means a "biblical" narrative, the program was nevertheless saturated throughout with biblical imagery.[84] Like *Battlestar Galactica*, a number of episode titles and character names had an apparent biblical connection; for instance, "Exodus" (S1E23–25; in which a group of survivors trek across the island toward a pillar

---

[79] Anthea D. Butler and Diane Winston, "'A Vagina Ain't a Halo': Gender and Religion in *Saving Grace* and *Battlestar Galactica*," in Winston, *Small Screen, Big Picture*, 259–86, here 264–5; C. W. Marshall and Matthew Wheeland, "The Cylons, the Singularity, and God," in *Cylons in America: Critical Studies in Battlestar Galactica*, ed. Tiffany Potter and C. W. Marshall (New York: Continuum, 2008), 91–104, here 94. "S#E##" is used here and below to indicate season and episode number.

[80] Kevin J. Wetmore Jr., *The Theology of Battlestar Galactica: American Christianity in the 2004–2009 Television Series* (Jefferson, NC: McFarland, 2012), 2.

[81] Marshall and Wheeland, "The Cylons, the Singularity, and God," 97.

[82] Heather Hendershot, "'You Know How It Is with Nuns...': Religion and Television's Sacred/Secular Fetuses," in Winston, *Small Screen, Big Picture*, 201–31, here 224.

[83] Ibid., 230. See further Douglas E. Cowan, *Sacred Space: The Quest for Transcendence in Science Fiction Film and Television* (Waco, TX: Baylor University Press, 2010), 225–60; Taneli Kukkonen, "God against the Gods: Faith and the Exodus of the Twelve Colonies," in *Battlestar Galactica and Philosophy*, ed. Jason T. Eberl (Oxford: Blackwell, 2008), 169–80; Wetmore, *The Theology of Battlestar Galactica*. See further David Garber's contribution to the present volume.

[84] See Matthew A. Collins, "Loss of the Bible and the Bible in *Lost*: Biblical Literacy and Mainstream Television," in Edwards, *Rethinking Biblical Literacy*, 71–93. For other literary and cultural allusions, see, e.g., Sarah Clarke Stuart, *Literary Lost: Viewing Television through the Lens of Literature* (London: Continuum, 2011). See further Greg Garrett's contribution to the present volume.

of smoke; cf. Exod 13:21–22), "The 23rd Psalm" (S2E10; in which Psalm 23 itself is at one point recited), and "Fire + Water" (S2E12; an episode featuring baptism, the title seemingly referencing Matt 3:11 and Luke 3:16), among others, as well as characters such as Jacob, Benjamin, Aaron, and Isaac. However, *Lost* also utilized explicit discussion of biblical passages as a narrative springboard. For instance, characters discussed the story of Abraham and Isaac (S3E17; cf. Gen 22), Josiah's discovery of the "book of the law" (S2E9; cf. 2 Kgs 22; 2 Chr 34), the baptism of Jesus (S2E12; cf. Matt 3:13–17; Mark 1:9–11; Luke 3:21–22), and the actions of Thomas (S5E6; cf. John 11:16; 20:24–29). In each case, the biblical text was used either to elucidate or provide a narrative foil to events in the episode, often cleverly intersecting with other, rather more implicit or hidden allusions, thus providing an interpretative key to the whole.[85] Indeed, in many instances "biblical themes are adopted but ultimately inverted or in some way reconfigured in the course of appropriation, reflecting an apparent degree of creativity in the use of the biblical text."[86]

One character, Eko, carves chapter and verse numbers into a staff he carries on the island (including Gen 13:14; Ps 23; Ps 144; Hab 1:3; Luke; John 3:5; Acts 4:12; Rom 6:12; Gal 3:16; Colossians; Titus 3; Rev 5:3), while Bibles themselves appear frequently (e.g., S1E19, S2E1, S2E7, S2E9, S3E1, S3E5, S3E15, S3E17, S6E9), thus depicting it not only as a book that is referenced and alluded to but one that is read. There were, moreover, numerous implicit allusions to biblical themes, characters, and motifs, including the relationship between the character Jacob and his unnamed twin brother, which appeared to draw upon and allude to a complex interweaving of three separate biblical pairings: Jacob and Esau (Gen 25:19–34; 27:1–45), Cain and Abel (Gen 4:1–16), and YHWH and "the Satan" (Job 1–2). However, notably, these dynamics are again each in some way inverted or reimagined.[87] There are also healing miracles and instances of infertility, miraculous conception, and resurrection, as well as elements such as Eko's forty days of silence (S2E7), Hurley's hallucination of "Dave" tempting him to eat and to throw himself off a cliff (S2E18; cf. Matt 4:1–11; Luke 4:1–13), the marking or branding of Juliet for having killed someone (S3E9; cf. Gen 4:15), and the frequently recurring "exodus" imagery (e.g., S1E23–25, S3E22–23, S5E15–17). The list goes on. Even promotional materials for the series were not exempt. For instance, the viral marketing website created for Ajira Airways (the fictional airline with which some of the survivors return to the island in S5E6) contained hidden references to John 3:16 throughout, revealing the flight number (and episode title) "316" to be an implicit biblical allusion to this passage.[88]

However, in the case of such oblique drawing upon the Bible, whether in *Battlestar Galactica* or *Lost*, the extent to which these biblical allusions may actually be recognized by viewers is perhaps unclear. They certainly attest to some estimable degree of biblical literacy on the part of the writers, but Adele Reinhartz (discussing the use of the Bible in

---

[85] Collins, "Loss of the Bible," 77–9.   [86] Ibid., 77.   [87] See further ibid., 82–4.

[88] Ibid., 85. In addition, both *Lost* and *Battlestar Galactica*, in promotional images for their final seasons, re-created Leonardo da Vinci's *The Last Supper* (1495–98), replacing Jesus and the disciples with characters from their respective series, in each case generating speculation as to the image's significance and meaning, while once more highlighting the underlying biblical influence. See http://lostpedia. wikia.com/wiki/The_Lost_Supper and https://en.battlestarwikiclone.org/wiki/The_Last_Supper.

film) suggests that the existence of biblical allusion on screen does not in and of itself equate to or necessitate a biblically literate audience: "One of the most difficult questions relates to whether audience knowledge of the Bible is essential, desirable, or even helpful when viewing these films. In most cases, one would guess that filmmakers do not assume that viewers will necessarily identify the biblical references."[89] Thus, while recognition of these allusions might provide "added value," thereby enabling a "deeper understanding"[90] of the show, it is not unequivocally required. Explicit references may nevertheless at least alert viewers to the potential for less obvious implicit ones, and where a series generates a sufficiently dedicated following, this may even translate to audiences actively seeking them out. In the case of *Lost*, recognizing the tendency of the writers to hide clues and "Easter eggs" throughout each episode, a vast number of dedicated websites and online forums arose, allowing fan communities to discuss theories, analyze screenshots and audio files, and consider the potential significance of every detail seen.[91] Among other things, viewers turned to the Bible in order to follow up clues (real or imagined) in the program. The scriptural references carved into Eko's staff, for instance, proved "a fertile topic of speculation for fans of the show, [their] prominence in online discussion forums attesting to the programme's apparent capacity for engendering interest in the biblical text."[92]

In this sense, "it was a history and literature lesson disguised as a television series," one actively engaged in "the promotion of literature, mythology, and history."[93] The nature of the show, together with the participatory role of its fan communities,[94] meant that "unsuspecting viewers become *accidental intellectuals*."[95] The result is that such programs can themselves become tools for promoting biblical literacy. Regardless of whether or not a biblically literate audience is anticipated, the enthusiasm of viewers to engage with a show may in such instances translate (via the wealth of explicit and implicit allusion) to enthusiasm to engage with the biblical text itself. In this manner, television programs drawing on the Bible may arguably (though perhaps unintentionally) play just as significant a role as those engaged in education or dramatization in actively encouraging and promoting biblical literacy.

Though space prohibits more detailed discussion here, the extent to which the Bible has permeated television, and indeed American popular culture as a whole, can

---

[89] Reinhartz, *Scripture on the Silver Screen*, 186.   [90] Stuart, *Literary Lost*, 3.

[91] Collins, "Loss of the Bible," 87–9. Also Will Brooker, "Television Out of Time: Watching Cult Shows on Download," in *Reading Lost: Perspectives on a Hit Television Show*, ed. Roberta Pearson (London: I. B. Tauris, 2009), 51–72; Lynn Schofield Clark, "You Lost Me: Mystery, Fandom, and Religion in ABC's *Lost*," in Winston, *Small Screen, Big Picture*, 319–41; Abby Letak, "Accidental Intellectuals: *Lost* Fandom and Philosophy," in *LOST Thought University Edition: Leading Thinkers Discuss LOST*, ed. Pearson Moore (Scotts Valley, CA: CreateSpace, 2012), 83–122.

[92] Collins, "Loss of the Bible," 79; also 88–9.

[93] Erika Olson and Jo Garfein, "Culture Disguised as Television: *Lost* in Conversation," in Moore, *LOST Thought University Edition*, 47–57, here 47.

[94] See further Dan W. Clanton, Jr.'s contribution to the present volume.

[95] Letak, "Accidental Intellectuals," 87.

be aptly illustrated by simply highlighting a few other key programs from the past decade or so that, to a greater or lesser degree, have made similar use of the Bible. Notable examples include *Firefly* (Fox, 2002), *Deadwood* (HBO, 2004–6), *Jericho* (CBS, 2006–8), *Terminator: The Sarah Connor Chronicles* (Fox, 2008–9), *The Walking Dead* (AMC, 2010–present), *Sleepy Hollow* (Fox, 2013–2017), *Luke Cage* (Netflix, 2016–2018), and *The Handmaid's Tale* (Hulu, 2017–present).[96] Given the significance of the Bible as cultural artifact, this widespread permeation should come as no surprise, confirming "the degree to which biblical narratives have shaped the ways in which Western culture tells its stories."[97] However, it can be a two-way process, with those same narratives shaped in turn by the medium through which they are retold, revisited, or reused. Accordingly, "popular culture mediates the narratives of scriptures in new ways, riffs on scriptural themes, and translates, manifests and echoes Biblical theologies in ways that are oftentimes more accessible than the original scriptures are today."[98]

Thus, as Jenkins predicted, television has become both teacher and entertainer. The three categories examined here—educating about, dramatizing, and drawing on the Bible—demonstrate the deeply ingrained prevalence of the Bible within American television, as well as helping to illustrate the diverse ways in which it appears and/or has been utilized. All three contribute to its overall accessibility, and for many contemporary viewers the Bible as mediated through television (in whatever form) might represent their first effective encounter with the text. Moreover, as has been demonstrated above, in each case the medium can function as a tool not only for reflecting but for actively encouraging and promoting levels of biblical literacy among its audience. As such, though often overshadowed in scholarly treatments by its cinematic cousin, television provides an invaluable window into the ongoing use, interpretation, and cultural impact of the Bible within America.

---

[96] See further, e.g., Kipp Davis, "Zombies in America and at Qumran: AMC's *The Walking Dead*, the Dead Sea Scrolls, and Apocalyptic Redux," *Journal of Religion and Popular Culture* 27, no. 2 (2015): 148–63; Erika Engstrom and Joseph M. Valenzano, "Religion and the Representative Anecdote: Replacement and Revenge in AMC's *The Walking Dead*," *Journal of Media and Religion* 15, no. 3 (2016): 123–35; Karl N. Jacobson, "Luke (4:18) Cage: Marvel's Most Important Work Yet," *BibPopCult*, October 5, 2016, https://bibpopcult.wordpress.com/tag/luke-cage/; Alison L. Joseph, "*The Handmaid's Tale* as a Legitimate Reading of Genesis?," *Shiloh Project*, July 9, 2017, https://shiloh-project.group.shef.ac.uk/?p=1571; cf. Larry J. Kreitzer, *Gospel Images in Fiction and Film* (London: Sheffield Academic Press, 2002), 143–71; Matthew W. Mitchell, "Some More Light on the Text: Watching HBO's *Deadwood* with and without the Apostle Paul," *Journal of Religion and Popular Culture* 25, no. 1 (2013): 110–19; Robert J. Myles, "Terminating Samson: *The Sarah Connor Chronicles* and the Rise of New Biblical Meaning," *Relegere* 1, no. 2 (2011): 329–50; Horace Newcomb, "In the Beginning...*Deadwood*," in Winston, *Small Screen, Big Picture*, 43–68; Steve A. Wiggins, "Reading the Bible in Sleepy Hollow," *Journal of Religion and Popular Culture* 28, nos. 2–3 (2016): 186–97.

[97] Reinhartz, *Scripture on the Silver Screen*, 186.

[98] Wetmore, *The Theology of Battlestar Galactica*, 2.

FUTURE PROSPECTS AND QUESTIONS

- The medium of television is undergoing tremendous changes in the digital age, witnessing a shift to online viewing, multiple platforms and devices, and increased interactivity, as well as a rise in online content and on-demand services.[99] In this "post-broadcast" era and with the blurring of the boundaries between television and internet (and indeed film), what effect will these changes have on the ways in which the Bible is both presented and engaged with or on the demographics of the audience reached?
- As witnessed, the medium faces its own particular challenges, with its reliance on sustained sponsorship, repeat audiences, and consistently high ratings resulting in a "commercial fragility." Even documentaries (typically one-off events) are adversely affected by increased commercialization.[100] To what extent might this consumer-driven model (continue to) inhibit rather more challenging presentations of the Bible?
- Does the tendency of some documentaries toward sensationalism and promotion of maverick views undermine efforts to educate about the Bible, or is this outweighed by the public interest and intrigue generated by such presentations and the opportunities this subsequently affords?
- It has been suggested that "television operates as the functional equivalent of religion in modern societies."[101] What is the functional or religious effect upon "readers" of encountering the Bible (primarily or supplementarily) as mediated through television?
- What responsibility (if any) does television have, and what opportunities might it afford, for enabling and safeguarding biblical literacy in twenty-first-century American culture?

SUGGESTED READINGS AND ANNOTATED BIBLIOGRAPHY

Bond, Helen K., and Edward Adams, eds. *The Bible on Television*. Scriptural Traces 23, Library of New Testament Studies 622. London: T & T Clark, 2020.

This edited collection is one of the only book-length treatments of the Bible and television (as opposed to religion and television, or Bible and film). It focuses mainly on documentaries but also considers some dramatizations. Despite a primarily British context, much of what is covered is more widely applicable, and many of the programs considered either originated in or have been exported to America. Though the volume as a whole is highly recommended, two contributions in particular are highlighted in more detail below.

---

[99] See, e.g., Edgerton, *Columbia History of American Television*, 410–25.

[100] Beattie, *Documentary Screens*, 207–10.

[101] Walter T. Davis Jr. et al., *Watching What We Watch: Prime-Time Television through the Lens of Faith* (Louisville, KY: Westminster John Knox, 2001), xii.

Bragard, Jean-Claude. "The Bible According to TV." In *The Bible on Television*, edited by Helen K. Bond and Edward Adams, 40–78. Scriptural Traces 23, Library of New Testament Studies 622. London: T & T Clark, 2020.

This contribution to the *Bible on Television* volume is worthy of particular mention. Bragard examines changing trends and practices in documentaries about the Bible from the 1970s to the present and notes the move toward dramatization. In doing so, he focuses especially on the vexed issue of shifting agendas and academic involvement/input.

Edwards, Katie, ed. *Rethinking Biblical Literacy*. London: Bloomsbury T & T Clark, 2015.

This collection of essays addresses and problematizes the perceived decline of biblical literacy, considering the role played by popular culture in its continued preservation and promotion. Two contributions in particular (Collins and Myles) examine the question of biblical literacy in relation to mainstream television and the ways in which it utilizes and draws upon the Bible.

Siegler, Elijah. "Television." In *The Routledge Companion to Religion and Popular Culture*, edited by John C. Lyden and Eric Michael Mazur, 41–64. London: Routledge, 2015.

Though not focused on the Bible itself, Siegler provides a helpful overview of the topic of religion and television, tracing the myriad ways in which it is utilized and engaged with across different types of program. In the process, he also highlights significant differences between television and film.

Tollerton, David. "When the Resurrected Biblical Epic Transferred to the Small Screen…and Promptly Died Again: A Critical Autopsy of the 2016 ABC Series *Of Kings and Prophets*." In *The Bible on Television*, edited by Helen K. Bond and Edward Adams, 247–61. Scriptural Traces 23, Library of New Testament Studies 622. London: T & T Clark, 2020.

Another especially noteworthy contribution to the *Bible on Television* volume, Tollerton analyzes the reasons for the commercial failure and untimely demise of the series *Of Kings and Prophets*. This has far wider implications, highlighting the particular challenges faced by small-screen productions and shedding light on the checkered history of the Bible on television.

Winston, Diane, ed. *Small Screen, Big Picture: Television and Lived Religion*. Waco, TX: Baylor University Press, 2009.

Winston gathers together an array of essays examining religion in twenty-first-century American television dramas. The volume as a whole considers the complex intersection of religion and television, suggesting that television itself is a religious text, while individual contributions examine the ways in which these programs draw upon specific religious topics or themes, including biblical texts.

CHAPTER 18

THE BIBLE IN POP AND ROCK MUSIC

MICHAEL J. GILMOUR
BIBLICAL STUDIES AND ENGLISH LITERATURE,
PROVIDENCE UNIVERSITY COLLEGE

INTRODUCTION

"Make two silver trumpets...you shall blow the trumpets...they shall serve as a reminder on your behalf before the LORD" (Num 10:2, 10).[1] So God instructs Moses. And the faithful respond to the notes those trumpets play. They are authoritative sounds. The instruments feature in the rhythms of religious ritual: "On the first day of the seventh month you shall have a holy convocation....It is a day for you to blow the trumpets" (29:1). They even accompany the people on occasions of national import: "Moses sent them to the war...along with Phinehas son of Eleazar the priest, with the vessels of the sanctuary and the trumpets for sounding the alarm in his hand" (31:6). Trumpets in the hands of priests. Music *is part of religion* as both an expression of worship and a means to communicate spiritual realities. It is a call to the faithful, the music directing the congregation to the altar.

But there are other kinds of trumpets and other kinds of audiences. For some, music itself *is religion*.[2] Gregory Reece's study of Elvis fandom observes that commemorations at Graceland (the King's birthday, the anniversary of his death, etc.) do "have many of the markings of a religious observance."[3] Rock and roll "is my religion and my law," sings

[1] Unless otherwise noted, I cite the New Revised Standard Version of the Bible.

[2] My phrasing recalls Bruce David Forbes's editorial introduction to his and Jeffrey H. Mahan's edited volume, *Religion and Popular Culture in America*, 3rd ed. (Oakland: University of California Press, 2017), 1–24, especially 11–21. They see four principal ways religion and popular culture relate: religion in popular culture; popular culture in religion; popular culture as religion; religion and popular culture in dialogue (17–19).

[3] Gregory L. Reece, *Elvis Religion: The Cult of the King* (London: I. B. Tauris, 2006), 20.

Ozzy Osbourne ("You Can't Kill Rock and Roll," *Diary of a Madman*, 1981). For Ron Sexsmith, "My song is my saviour" ("Late Bloomer," *Long Player Late Bloomer*, 2011). Audiences too find spirituality in music. Bono invites concertgoers to translate a song about political unrest into something else entirely: "If you're the prayin' kind, turn this song into a prayer" (referring to "Sunday Bloody Sunday" on the DVD *U2 Go Home: Live from Slane Castle, Ireland*, 2003). Such examples of artists and audiences finding transcendence in music are legion.

Each song just mentioned uses a sacred term ("religion," "saviour," "prayer"). Why is that? The academic study of the Bible in popular music is less often concerned with expressions of songwriters' beliefs or lack of them than in seeking to understand the reasoning behind their poetic choices. Why do secular songwriters like Osbourne and Sexsmith turn to religious concepts at all? Part of the answer lies in the pursuit of language achieving certain effects (e.g., shock) or being somehow appropriate to the subject matter. Songs expressing anger at injustice or defiance of authority or those demonstrating devotion to a lover or a manic celebration of life require terminology with suitable gravitas. Hyperbolic it may be, but sacred discourses often provide the means to say what needs to be said. This grasping after words and imagery to say the otherwise inexpressible often results in a plundering and appropriation of biblical themes, terms, and images.[4] This is somewhat counterintuitive. Rock and roll is quintessentially an oppositional art form. It is rage, hedonism, and anarchy all at once. And yet the Bible is part of it. That symbol of conservatism, hierarchy, and moral authority sounds its own trumpets in the midst of all those power chords.[5]

OVERVIEW OF TOPIC

It is not, to be sure, the Bible as a whole that resurfaces in the popular arts. To look for the Bible in film, literature, or music is to see through a glass, darkly. It is usually kaleidoscopic, piecemeal, and jumbled in re-presentation. Patterns (e.g., the heroic, self-sacrificing rescuer), stock characters (e.g., angels, devils), imagery, and meaning-laden terms (e.g., bread and wine) are what we usually refer to when discussing biblical content in novels and film. To be a biblically literate consumer of pop culture is to know something of Adam and Eve, Moses, David and Goliath, Jesus, Judas, and Peter. It is rather like the way most of us know Shakespeare—in bits and pieces. Yes, we know of Hamlet's existen-

---

[4] For numerous illustrations of ways songwriters use the Bible for their craft, see, e.g., Mark Roncace and Dan W. Clanton, Jr., "Popular Music," in *Teaching the Bible through Popular Culture and the Arts*, ed. Mark Roncace and Patrick Gray (Atlanta, GA: Society of Biblical Literature, 2007), 15–51; Michael J. Gilmour, *Gods and Guitars: Seeking the Sacred in Post-1960s Popular Music* (Waco, TX: Baylor University Press, 2009).

[5] By calling the Bible a symbol of conservatism, I mean the Bible as used within some religious communities. The Bible itself includes many instances of resistance to the status quo, not least by the prophets of ancient Israel in the Old Testament and Jesus in the New.

tial crisis and Romeo and Juliet's tragic end, but we are less likely familiar with *Coriolanus* and *Troilus and Cressida*.

But the Bible is there. It lingers in our collective memory, and this, I think, offers a partial explanation why pop songs invoke the prophets as often as they do. Songwriters and audiences *remember* it, however imperfectly and however *fragmentary* in recall. It is part of our languages and part of our cultural inheritance, constantly returning to us in film, literature, comics, painting, political discourses, and more.[6] These two principal ideas—a lingering awareness of the Bible in post-Christian, mainstream popular music, and the Bible as a fragmented text—are the focus of this chapter.

Listeners invariably associate Herman Hupfeld's 1931 classic "As Time Goes By" with Dooley Wilson's performances in the 1942 film *Casablanca*. Wilson plays the lounge piano player Sam, an employee and close friend of Rick Blaine (Humphrey Bogart). "As Time Goes By" is a symbol of an earlier whirlwind romance between Rick and Ilsa Lund (Ingrid Bergman) enjoyed before war forced their separation.

Casablanca illustrates important insights about memory and its connection to music, a connection that, Christopher Partridge argues, is "able to transform the everyday by shifting us into affective spaces that feel both familiar and unfamiliar."[7] Songs stick in our minds so that "almost immediately on hearing a familiar piece of music we enter a very particular emotional space that often merges our past and present." Music thus has the capacity to "haunt" us, and this is clearly the case for Rick and Ilsa. Songs draw us "back through ... personal histories to relationships with the lost and to places long forgotten."[8]

The film illustrates Partridge's point, namely, that music carries meanings incalculably woven into the listener's story. When Ilsa first enters the bar and before she knows Rick is nearby, she calls Sam to her table and asks him to play "As Time Goes By," but he hesitates. The boss does not allow him to perform that song in Rick's Café Américain because it conjures up painful memories of lost love. Sam also understands music's ability to transport people to other times and places. Any performance of the song, not to mention Ilsa's unexpected return, portends grief for his friend Rick. But she insists, and he plays. Sure enough, Rick storms over, angrily reminding Sam he is not to sing it. The

---

[6] Other chapters in the present volume illustrate this thoroughly. To offer but one other study of ways "biblical paradigms can be secularized and blended with steadily evolutionary forms of entertainment," see Robert Jewett and John Shelton Lawrence, "Eschatology in Pop Culture," in *The Oxford Handbook of Eschatology*, ed. Jerry L. Walls (Oxford: Oxford University Press, 2008), 667–55, here 667.

[7] Christopher Partridge, *Mortality and Music: Popular Music and the Awareness of Death*, Bloomsbury Studies in Religion and Popular Music (London: Bloomsbury Academic, 2015), 71.

[8] Ibid. Partridge defines his use of "affective spaces" at length in *The Lyre of Orpheus: Popular Music, the Sacred, and the Profane* (Oxford: Oxford University Press, 2014). In short, he means by it "the internal and social worlds of individuals." Its importance for music studies derives from the fact that "music has a fundamental relationship with emotion and, secondly, human emotionality is central to meaning making and what Jürgen Habermas has referred to as the individual's 'lifeworld'—the latent, taken-for-granted core values, beliefs, and understandings about who we are, how we relate to others, what the world is like, and how we fit into it" (38).

song carries a story (a romance), and in a similar way, popular music carries the biblical story, however vague and piecemeal it may be.

In the movie, the song segues into a flashback explaining the lovers' backstory. Consistent with Partridge's argument, music returns Rick and Ilsa to the past, to a time when their love was new. Viewers are now in Paris with them as Sam plays "As Time Goes By" during those happier days. The Nazis are nearing the city—we hear shells falling in the distance—but Rick and Ilsa's romance is carefree, even as they anticipate the looming threat of invasion. For Ilsa, the love affair is an escape. Unbeknownst to Rick, she is the wife of a leader in the Resistance, thought to be dead. In new love she finds comfort. Rick himself is also in a desperate situation. He is an American forced to leave his country, though we do not know why, and now the Nazis hunt him. The lovers plan to meet at the station before the enemy enters the city, but as the last train pulls out, before the beginning of the occupation, Ilsa is not on board. She sends a note explaining she will not come, and he must not look for her. He is heartbroken, and so too is Ilsa.

Before the flashback, in Rick's bar, Ilsa asks for the song. After the flashback, we find Rick after closing. He sits at a table drunk and despairing after seeing Ilsa again. He never thought he would. "Of all the gin joints in all the world..." Sam is there. Rick asks to hear "As Time Goes By." Again, Sam hedges. "If she can stand it, so can I," Rick yells. "Play it!"

"As Time Goes By" is sweet and simple, but its power does not reside in the lyrics, or at least the lyrics alone. Bob Dylan recorded the song for his 2017 album *Triplicate*. The Nobel laureate is one of the great songwriters of his generation, and many of his own lyrics surpass Hupfeld's in poetic complexity, and yet clearly he values the song. When asked if this album of covers from the American songbook is nostalgic, he rejects the term: "Nostalgic? No I wouldn't say that. It's not taking a trip down memory lane or longing and yearning for the good old days or fond memories of what's no more. A song like 'Sentimental Journey' is not a way back when song, it doesn't emulate the past, it's attainable and down to earth, it's in the here and now."[9]

"As Time Goes By" takes Rick and Ilsa back to Paris in memory, but the movie is actually about their own here and now, their present circumstances. It's about rediscovering their love in Casablanca. The song's power resides for them in its association with their deeply personal and unique experiences of love and loss.

Music is a form of memory, taking us into a "particular emotional space that often merges our past and present."[10] If listening to the radio we say, "They're playing our song!" or "That takes me back," we indicate meanings and associations for which lyricists and musicians are not wholly responsible. Experiences and feelings are often synonymous with sounds and words heard on an album or during a concert. If asked to define a mood or attitude, we find ourselves appealing to the "language" of pop songs for aid, just as others grasping for definition might turn to poetry or religion or nature. At the same time, those lyricists and musicians are essential to this form of emotional archiving. Their art is often the only form of speech available to us. As Jim Croce puts it,

---

[9] From a conversation with Bill Flanagan, posted at bobdylan.com on March 22, 2017.
[10] Partridge, *Mortality and Music*, 71.

"I'll have to say I love you in a song" because what I have to say "can't wait" and every time I tried to speak, "the words just came out wrong" ("I'll Have to Say I Love You in a Song," *I Got a Name*, 1973). Music fans understand this. We turn to songs that resonate with our experiences, and we use them to express that which we are unable to express ourselves. And if it is true that we depend on musicians to articulate deep feelings, it is also true that many musicians depend on sacred discourses, the Bible among them, to do the same. Music is affective. And so it is that Bruce Springsteen's "Born in the U.S.A." (*Born in the U.S.A.*, 1984), even if narrowly concerned with Vietnam veterans and the working class, and any song by The Tragically Hip, concerned as they are with a wide range of subjects, awaken patriotic pride in Americans and Canadians, respectively. To the extent songwriters use the Bible, it is part of that process of evoking and articulating the listener's inner life.

I recognize this is an odd preamble for a chapter on the Bible in popular music, but the story told in *Casablanca* serves to illustrate two pertinent ideas. First, whether we know the Bible firsthand or not, and whether we are religious or not, it is part of our cultural inheritance. It is everywhere in the arts and popular culture, including our music.[11] The Bible constantly returns to us. *We remember it.* "As Time Goes By" carries Paris and all it represents in every note, and in a similar way, many popular songs remind us of the "old, old story."[12] Second and more obviously, *Casablanca* illustrates the tendency to associate emotional experiences with music. In just one song, Ilsa and Rick relive their greatest joys and deepest sadness. The Bible—that familiar, remembered text—often provides the stuff by which songwriters explore such heights and depths of emotion. We need the sacred, the mythical, and the otherworldly to help make sense of the everyday and mundane. The Bible provides resources helping us to do this.

Specific Examples of the Bible in Popular Music

When I refer to artists needing a sacred vocabulary, I mean mainstream artists as opposed to those working within the confines of religious traditions, such as contemporary Christian music.[13] It is a distinction worth making. For the most part, the latter art-

---

[11] See, e.g., essays in Philip Culbertson and Elaine M. Wainwright, eds., *The Bible in/and Popular Culture: A Creative Encounter* (Atlanta, GA: Society of Biblical Literature, 2010).

[12] I take this phrase from Katherine Hankey's 1866 hymn "Tell Me the Old, Old Story." The old, old story she describes is the Christian gospel, the good news of "Jesus and his love."

[13] For extensive analysis of artists in this category, see Mark Allan Powell's *Encyclopedia of Contemporary Christian Music* (Peabody, MA: Hendrickson, 2002). Roy Shuker defines Christian rock or contemporary Christian music by contrasting it with and noting it is an alternative to "the mainstream 'secular' entertainment business." The term also indicates the artists' religious commitments, as opposed to, say, musical style. Roy Shuker, *Popular Music: The Key Concepts*, 2nd ed. (London: Routledge, 2005), 42.

ists approach the Bible cognizant of the strictures of the interpretive communities with which they identify. A group like the metal band Stryper (as on their albums *No More Hell to Pay*, 2013, and *Fallen*, 2015) understands the Bible in ways consistent with the generally agreed-upon conventions of evangelical confession. They adhere to a hermeneutical tradition.

By comparison, many songwriters not explicitly rehearsing a specific religious worldview employ the Bible with endless creativity. There are fewer rules of engagement because they are not beholden to creed or confession; there is no need to affirm and teach acceptable doctrines and no interest in proselytization. Stryper's near contemporaries Iron Maiden, to illustrate, also use the Bible, and almost as often, but there is very little in common between the two bands in the way they do this. Maiden uses the Bible for artistic, not religious ends. "Hallowed Be Thy Name" (*The Number of the Beast*, 1982) is the near-panicked first-person narration of a prisoner facing the gallows, and not at all concerned with the Lord's Prayer in the Authorized Version (Matt 6:9–13). It is a horror story, and the convict's appeal to an absent God—there is no indication in the song of divine intervention—adds to the terror. No help comes. Death is inevitable. Is the song satirizing religion? Possibly, but such a question asks too much of the lyrics. At minimum, "Hallowed Be Thy Name" uses the Bible to heighten the dramatic tension of the scene.

Or consider Maiden's poetically striking, even if disturbing, lines "From paper soldiers to bodies on the beach / From summer sands to Armageddon's reach" ("The Longest Day," *A Matter of Life and Death*, 2006). They refer to the troops storming the beaches on D-Day and are not directly concerned with John the Seer's vision (Rev 16:16). Like many heavy metal bands, Iron Maiden draws on the Bible's darker imagery to evoke an atmosphere of the otherworldly. It is thus only one text among many on which they rely. The Bible functions for them in ways similar to Gaston Leroux's 1909 novel *Phantom of the Opera*, as used for their album *Iron Maiden* (1980), or Samuel Taylor Coleridge's 1798 poem *The Rime of the Ancient Mariner*, featured on *Powerslave* (1984). Whether drawing on Leroux, Coleridge, or John the Seer, the fantasies created by adapting old stories free audiences from the mundane and invite the exercise of imagination. Sometimes, as in the allusion to the book of Revelation, the sparked imagination urges contemplation of real-world problems (in this case, war). Maiden's evocation of the Phantom, the Mariner, and the Bible are not completely alike, however. The first two are important influences on specific songs, whereas we find the Bible throughout the band's whole body of work.

Perhaps the most important difference between uses of the Bible in music emerging from specific religious communities and those independent of them is the degree of commitment (or not) to a grand narrative. Christian music, as Roy Shuker defines it, reflects artists' commitments to organized religion.[14] They read the Bible (and in theory, at least, the whole Bible), as revealing an all-encompassing theological story. No doubt most wearing the contemporary Christian music label agree on many points of doctrine

---

[14] See Shuker, *Popular Music*, 42.

and interpret the Scriptures in similar ways. In contrast, mainstream music's endlessly diverse uses of the Bible are usually *fragmentary*. Lyricists pick and choose, quoting and alluding to it for all kinds of reasons: Michael Jackson and Lionel Richie misquote the Gospels to help feed the poor in the charity single "We Are the World" ("God has shown us by turning stone to bread"; cf. Matt 4:3–4; Luke 4:3–4); Sheryl Crow cites the Sermon on the Mount to criticize American foreign policy ("Peace Be upon Us," *Detours*, 2008; cf. Matt 5:5); Robbie Robertson alludes to a biblical, trumpet-sounding angel when mourning a friend's death by suicide ("Fallen Angel," *Robbie Robertson*, 1987; cf., e.g., 1 Thess 4:16). Such allusions and quotations are often idiosyncratic and the songwriters' purposes for introducing them vague, whereas appeals to the Bible by contemporary Christian musicians are usually more straightforward.

Again, the Bible is broadly familiar to songwriters and audiences (to greater and lesser degrees, even if that knowledge is in decline), deeply rooted in the history of the arts, and so part of our intellectual heritage independent of religious commitments.[15] Music using the Bible taps into something *already known*, something *remembered*. When artists appeal to it as an authority, or transgress its assertions, or simply borrow its terms, they can count on an audience's (at least vague) recognition of that raw material. The Bible is, in this sense, a crucial palimpsest, a text beneath many pop-song texts, influencing our experience of the lyrics written over it. The Bible is a shared memory, however vague and however widely diverse the interpretations of songwriters and their fans.

Partridge develops Émile Durkheim's thesis about the sacred to help understand dynamics at play in audiences' engagements with popular music. Whether or not embedded in religion, the sacred "concerns those ideas which are understood to be set apart from the rest of life and which exert a profound moral claim over people's lives," whereas religion "constitutes a particular way of articulating the sacred, usually within a discourse of the supernatural. Deities, demons, heaven and hell, all become part of the rationale for submitting to and enforcing the claims of the sacred."[16] The distinction acknowledges that what some seek and find in organized religion, others find in the arts. As Robin Sylvan observes regarding the musical subcultures that are the focus of his study, "Compared to some religious traditions, these new forms [of popular religiosity] may...seem superficial and vulgar, but this makes them no less legitimate or serious as religious expressions."[17]

It is hard to tell the two apart sometimes. Religious content in mainstream music is often ironic and detached from organized religion, but this is not always the case. Given what we know of the singer, one suspects there is genuine religious sentiment behind

---

[15] For discussion of the oft-repeated claim that Bible literacy is in decline, see Katie B. Edwards, ed., *Rethinking Biblical Literacy* (London: Bloomsbury T & T Clark, 2015). As various chapters in that volume make clear, the idea of biblical literacy is a complicated one. The ubiquity of the Bible in popular culture, political discourses, and elsewhere indicates literacy of a kind different from firsthand knowledge of biblical texts.

[16] Partridge, *Lyre of Orpheus*, 4.

[17] Robyn Sylvan, *Traces of the Spirit: The Religious Dimensions of Popular Music* (New York: New York University Press, 2002), 220.

Johnny Cash's "I Came to Believe" (recorded in 1984, released on the 2014 album *Out among the Stars*): "brought down in despair / I cried for help and I felt a warm comforter there" (my transcription). On one level, it is an homage to traditional gospel music, but in this case, taking the lyrical "I" at face value, as autobiographical, seems appropriate owing to the singer's well-known religious views. Faith is a recurring theme in Cash's music.[18]

This is quite different from Robert Plant's performance of the traditional gospel song "Satan Your Kingdom Must Come Down" (*Band of Joy*, 2010). Here we also have an homage to traditional hymns but the lyrical "I" in this song seems less likely to be confessional. "I heard the voice of Jesus say," Plant sings, "Satan your kingdom must come down" (liner notes). This is an exploration of musical roots, not an expression of faith by one clinging to Jesus's words—"I watched Satan fall from heaven like a flash of lightning" (Luke 10:18)—for comfort. Plant's music often has mystical qualities but without any narrowly defined religious perspective. Furthermore, we find him exploring roots music (particularly blues and folk) throughout his career, as in his nod to the blues artist Charley Patton in "Turn It Up" (*Lullaby and… the Ceaseless Roar*, 2014). The Bible shaped those deep American musical forms, so naturally it is an indirect influence on those artists revisiting them.[19]

Bob Dylan recorded "Up to Me" in 1974 during the *Blood on the Tracks* sessions but did not release it until 1985 as part of the *Biograph* collection.[20] Like *Casablanca*, this song tells the story of a couple forced apart by unfortunate circumstances, but this time we have no backstory explaining the nature of their relationship and the exact reasons for their separation. There is, however, an intriguing reference to the Bible offering a clue about the woman's identity and the nature of their love.

The reasons for her absence are ambiguous, but there is some consolation for the heartbroken narrator of the song. In the opening stanza, he tells the absent woman, "At least I heard your bluebird sing." The image recalls Robert Frost's poem "Last Word of a Bluebird." In that poem, a crow delivers a message to a young girl on behalf of the bluebird. The crow explains to her that her little bluebird friend had to leave, owing to the onset of winter. That winter is often a symbol of death might indicate, sadly, that the separation of the bluebird and little girl is to be permanent, something not lost on Dylan's narrator, who recognizes that death keeps "following" the lovers, tracking them down. The singer longs to be reunited with his bluebird, but all efforts fail. "I would've followed you in the door but I didn't have a ticket stub." The separation is also a painful

---

[18] The unsigned entry on Johnny Cash in Colin Larkin, ed., *The Encyclopedia of Popular Music*, 5th concise ed. (New York: Omnibus, 2007) notes, "Cash often found strength and comfort in religion and went on to record many spiritual albums" (284).

[19] For a range of connections between the Bible and traditional blues, written by a biblical scholar, see Gary W. Burnett's *The Gospel According to the Blues* (Eugene, OR: Cascade, 2014). Among other things, he discusses biblical laments, particularly in the Psalms, as an important context for understanding the genre. "Though not couched in the language of the Bible," he writes, "blues songs are laments, in the same way as the spirituals" (19).

[20] For the lyrics, see Bob Dylan, *The Lyrics 1961–2012* (New York: Simon & Schuster, 2016), 348–9.

one: "In fourteen months I've only smiled once and I didn't do it consciously." But what is it about this mysterious woman that so haunts him, long after they part? Why is he unable to let her go?

He describes his first meeting with her as a "revelation." At first, he tried to convince himself her touch had no deep meaning, but he clearly fails. She's bewitched him, and the beguiled singer carries the memory of her wherever he goes. He meets a string of people after they part, but she continues to captivate. And the consequences of that fateful, betraying touch are troubling: things go from bad to worse; death follows them; he's only smiled once. Perhaps we ought to imagine a Bonnie-and-Clyde scenario. They have money, we are told, and he takes her picture off the wall at the post office where he works. Was it a wanted poster? Are they criminals?

He meets other women along the way, but they are uniformly uninspiring. These relationships prove unfulfilling and even tawdry. One of them has a lot to offer, but there is an unexpected fly in the ointment: "She's everything I need in love but I can't be swayed by that." What could possibly be more important than love so demanding of his allegiance? His time with Crystal is also meaningless. She is likely a prostitute. And then there is Estelle, about whom he admits there is not much to say. Another woman is currently with him behind the shades, but again the connection seems thin. She "ain't my property," he sings, suggesting there is no real tie between them.

So what does the nameless addressee, the woman whose touch was a revelation, offer the singer that all these others do not? Who is she? There are clues. She functions in the narrator's life in ways beyond the mundane. The other women in the story—Crystal, Estelle, the one behind the shades—suggest ordinary relationships, and there is something of the day-to-day, the humdrum, the routine, and the commonplace about them. But the nameless, absent woman is associated in the singer's memory with transcendence, with revelation, with the lofty and sublime. The "bluebird" of the opening stanza connects her to the poetic tradition. A reference to Jesus's Sermon on the Mount (see Matt 5–7) introduces an association with the spiritual. That Sermon is too complex, he admits, but at least they hear it together: "*We* heard the Sermon on the Mount.../ It didn't amount to anything more than what the broken glass reflects" (emphasis added). Even though its full meaning eludes them, they contemplate the flashes of light emanating from that broken glass *together*. The narrator plumbs deep mysteries *with* her, *with* this mysterious, ethereal, even ghostly woman. Presumably, many listening to "Up to Me" do not know Matthew 5–7 but are likely aware it is from the Bible. And this is enough to accomplish the intended poetic effect. By this means, by simply naming a biblical passage, Dylan introduces an element of mystery and the quasi-spiritual.

As the song ends, he still longs to be with her, but the pain resulting from her betraying touch, the heartbreak and danger he lives with as a result, provide the singer with a deep well from which his art derives. The ordinary world and its ordinary experiences, encapsulated by the ordinary relationships with Crystal and Estelle and the woman behind the shades, are all uninspiring, leaving the singer empty and unfulfilled. When he thinks of those relationships alongside the brief, fleeting, dangerous one he had with the nameless bluebird, a deep sorrow pervades all he sees and does. But the memory of that woman and their relationship, that unrequited love, is also an inspiration. From it his art flows: "My lone guitar played sweet *for you* that old-time melody. / And the harmonica around my neck, I blew it *for you*, free" (emphasis added). She is his poetic muse. To be a poet or prophet is to be compelled to speak. The Lord God hath spoken, "who can but prophesy?" says Amos in the King James Version of the Bible (3:8). "Rage— Goddess, sing of the rage of Peleus' son Achilles, murderous, doomed, that cost the Achaeans countless losses," says Homer in the opening line of the *Iliad*.[21] I blow my harmonica for you, sings Dylan's narrator. The nameless woman is the inspiration behind his distinctive creations. This is a poem about poetry, a song about songs. The writer uses the Bible to help introduce to his story something of the elusive qualities of artistic inspiration.

Umberto Eco's 1994 novel *The Island of the Day Before* tells the story of a seventeenth-century Italian nobleman named Roberto della Griva. He finds himself stranded on a disabled ship halfway around the world from his home, within sight of an island situated on the "antipodal meridian," the International Date Line, where he literally stares at yesterday. His position in the Southern Hemisphere also offers Roberto a new perspective of the stars: "He observed constellations never seen before. Those of his hemisphere he had read according to patterns others had established.... But on the *Daphne* [his ship] he had no pre-established patterns, he could join any point to any other.... Roberto did not simply gaze at the constellations: he was obliged to define them."[22] This brief scene illustrates the ways many lyricists approach the Bible when mining its imagery and concepts. As discussed, it is a broadly familiar, malleable text. For many mainstream artists, there are "no pre-established patterns," or at least fewer of them for those not beholden to church or synagogue. *Roberto did not simply gaze at the constellations: he was obliged to define them.* There are no regulating authorities imposing official interpretations on listeners either. Ilsa and Rick invest meanings and emotions in "As Time Goes By" in ways inimitable and wholly their own. Songwriters and their fans are free to connect the dots in the sky any way they choose.

This freedom allows artists to utilize biblical texts for all kinds of reasons. For instance, it lends a sense of moral authority for those addressing social ills or making political statements, as illustrated by Audioslave's self-titled debut (2002). "Set It Off" describes a political initiative organizing around a leader:

> He was standing at the rock
> Gathering the flock
> And getting there with no directions.

The gathering transforms into "a march," its leader calling his followers to "set this fucker off," presumably referring to the explosive potential of the movement. This is

---

[21] Homer, *The Iliad*, trans. Robert Fagles (London: Penguin, 1998), 77.
[22] Umberto Eco, *The Island of the Day Before*, trans. William Weaver (New York: Penguin, 1995; original Italian, 1994), 510–11.

consistent with the activist tone of the album. The liner notes provide the website address for Axis of Justice, a nonprofit organization founded by Audioslave's guitarist Tom Morello (with musician Serj Tankian). According to the description provided in the notes, it promotes grassroots activism. Its mandate: "FOR SAVING THE WORLD, FIGHTING THE POWER, ETC."

Sadly, the leader of the battle in "Set It Off" is unable to complete the fight. A bullet rips "into his heart," and he leaves the flock with a final call to "set this fucker off." Who is this leader cut down amid the movement's "march"? Martin Luther King Jr. certainly comes to mind. Perhaps it is a generic picture of heroic opposition to the forces of oppression. Challenges to hegemonic authority always invite antagonism.

The Bible is part of the story told in this song. The last verse introduces religious terminology, which offers some vague clues about the character of the leader and the movement. "Jesus," Chris Cornell sings, "is at the back door." He is behind the leader and behind the movement. This is consistent with the activist spirit of the song ("march") because Jesus spoke of caring for the needy and marginalized and defined his own work in these terms: "The Spirit of the Lord is upon me, because he has anointed me to bring good news to the poor. He has sent me to proclaim release to the captives and recovery of sight to the blind, to let the oppressed go free" (Luke 4:18, citing Isa 61:1–2; 58:6; see too Matt 25:34–40; Mark 10:21; Luke 3:11; 4:18; 6:20–21). The lyrics also assure listeners things are "all right" (there is hope yet, even if circumstances suggest otherwise) and that "revelation" remains. Here we have broad appeal to the New Testament Gospels in the service of a social-justice initiative. Cornell wrote the lyrics for *Audioslave*. On his solo albums, Morello also uses the New Testament Gospels in his calls for social justice and protest, using the moniker The Nightwatchman.[23] Here too we find alignment of political activism with Jesus's teachings, as in the song "Maximum Firepower" (*One Man Revolution*, 2007):

> I'm the triggerman, baby, tonight I'll prove
> That this machine here, well, it kills fascists too
> And don't be surprised if the "Sermon on the Mount"
> The next time is delivered in a little coffee house.

He adds the word "too" because these words refer to the singer-activist Woody Guthrie, who famously scrawled "THIS MACHINE KILLS FASCISTS" across the front of his guitar. Music (Guthrie, coffee houses) combines with Jesus's teachings about the poor (Sermon on the Mount) in a call to help those in need.

---

[23] On this, see Michael J. Gilmour, "Raging against the Machine: Tom Morello's Nightwatchman Persona and the Sound of Apocalypse-Inspired *Schadenfreude*," in *Anthems of Apocalypse: Popular Music and Apocalyptic Thought*, ed. Christopher Partridge (Sheffield, UK: Sheffield Phoenix Press, 2012), 43–54.

CONCLUSION

I close with a few remarks on Leonard Cohen's final album (*You Want It Darker*, 2016) to pull together ideas discussed in this chapter. The album's liner notes include blunt remarks about Cohen's circumstances at the time of recording. He refers to "disagreeable visitations" hindering the sessions and mentions the "medical chair" needed for him to sing. He recorded *You Want It Darker* from his deathbed. It is impossible to hear this album without thinking about this context. It is also hard to miss the conspicuous use of religious language throughout, including allusions to the Bible: "I'm ready, my Lord"; "I'm broken and lame / If thine is the glory / Then mine must be the shame" ("You Want It Darker"); "I better take my place / Lift this glass of blood / Try to say the grace" ("It Seemed the Better Way"). The artist's circumstances impose on any attempt to approach the songs objectively. As we hear them, we inevitably think of his last days. (He died about a month after the album's release.) It is an intimate collection of songs, with the poet sharing some final thoughts with his fans.

We do not find here a confession of faith constrained by religious tradition; the biblical and theological concepts in the songs seem too disjointed for that. But the appeal to the conceptual and mythic language of religion is elegant and fitting. It provides the poet a way to speak about profoundly personal and often difficult subjects. How to say goodbye? How to face the unknown? How to celebrate a life well lived? How to express love? The lofty, sacred terminology helps. It lends the needed gravitas. And like so many other songwriters, Cohen uses scattered biblical concepts (fragments) to help tell the story and trusts his audience to recognize those biblical fragments (memory).

FUTURE PROSPECTS AND QUESTIONS

- I propose the Bible lingers in the collective memory of Western cultures and that its sacred vocabulary is an important resource for the poetic expressions of many lyricists. It is also widely acknowledged that biblical literacy is in general decline. What are the implications of this for popular music, assuming this trend continues?
- Globalization, technologically facilitated connectedness, and immigration mean increasing cultural diversity. Music and the arts do not respect borders. In what ways will Western popular music change as a result? Furthermore, what religious influences will inform the music in these increasingly diverse societies? Future research into music and religion needs to be increasingly sensitive to the fact that the Christian Bible is not the only relevant sacred discourse. The *Bloomsbury Handbook of Religion and Popular Music* (2017) is an illustration of this shifting focus, with its inclusion of chapters on, among other things, music and Islam,

Judaism, Hinduism, and Buddhism, as well as Japanese, Chinese, and Caribbean religions, paganism, and the occult.

- Influence goes in both directions. Not only does religion (the Bible) shape popular music but we also find the reverse. Some church music *styles* owe more to rock and roll than time-worn chants and hymns. This is obvious from watching any number of televised church services. But do songwriters also influence the *ways we read* the Bible? Do participants in organized religion, even subconsciously, follow the lead of those lyricists whose sometimes haphazard, eclectic, and idiosyncratic uses of the Bible are heard constantly in our music-saturated world?

- Pop music is increasingly a vague category, difficult to define. Is there value in moving away from such a catchall term in studies of music and religion toward more genre-specific research? What does the use of the Bible in hip-hop look like, or in the blues or jazz?

Suggested Readings and Annotated Bibliography

Beal, Timothy, et al., eds. *The Oxford Encyclopedia of the Bible and the Arts*. 2 vols. Oxford: Oxford University Press, 2015.

There is much to explore in this wide-ranging collection. Several entries examine uses of the Bible in specific musical genres (including blues, country, folk, gospel, rap and hip-hop, and rock). Others focus on select artists, among them Leonard Cohen, Bob Dylan, and U2.

Culbertson, Philip, and Elaine M. Wainwright, eds. *The Bible in/and Popular Culture: A Creative Encounter*. Atlanta, GA: Society of Biblical Literature, 2010.

The essays in this collection illustrate the extent to which the Bible informs contemporary art and popular culture. Several chapters discuss music, including some focused on specific artists (Emmylou Harris, Nick Cave), recurring biblical imagery (e.g., Mary Magdalene), and select genres and associated subcultures (country, reggae, hip-hop).

Forbes, Bruce David, and Jeffrey H. Mahan, eds. *Religion and Popular Culture in America*. 3rd ed. Oakland: University of California Press, 2017.

Though not focused on the Bible, this is an important collection of essays helping to map out ways the sacred and the profane interact. The editors use the taxonomy mentioned in note 2 to organize the book. There are chapters on popular music throughout.

Powell, Mark Allan. *Encyclopedia of Contemporary Christian Music*. Peabody, MA: Hendrickson, 2002.

This is a particularly useful collection because Powell is both a discerning student of popular music and a careful, widely respected biblical scholar. His analyses of artists include examination of their theology, which makes it a rather unique collection. Though most entries treat music falling under the heading "Contemporary Christian" (including Stryper, mentioned in this chapter), he also treats several mainstream singers and bands whose work includes significant biblical and theological content or who have personal connections to the church. These include Alice Cooper, T Bone Burnett, Johnny Cash, Eric Clapton, Bruce Cockburn, Creed, Bob Dylan, Foreigner (Lou Gramm), Elvis Presley, Billy Preston, and U2.

Sylvan, Robin. *Traces of the Spirit: The Religious Dimensions of Popular Music*. New York: New York University Press, 2002.

> This fascinating ethnographic study explores connections between music and religion with attention to the musical subcultures associated with the Grateful Dead, dance music, heavy metal, and rap music and hip-hop. Sylvan illustrates ways the boundaries between music and something approximating religious experience are blurry.

Walsh, Brian J. *Kicking at the Darkness: Bruce Cockburn and the Christian Imagination*. Grand Rapids, MI: Brazos, 2011.

> There are many studies of the Bible in popular music focused on specific artists. Cockburn's lyrics offer a compelling example of a songwriter integrating biblical concepts into his work in sophisticated ways. As a theologian, Walsh is well positioned to explore the Cockburn catalog.

CHAPTER 19

IMPROVISING ON THE CANON THROUGH JAZZ MUSIC AND BIBLICAL INTERPRETATION IN AMERICAN POPULAR CULTURE

ANDREW MOSS
DEPARTMENT OF THEOLOGY AND RELIGION,
DURHAM UNIVERSITY

INTRODUCTION

IN 1987 a concurrent resolution of Congress designated jazz as "an indigenous American music and art form, bringing to this country and the world a uniquely American musical synthesis and culture through the African-American experience...a unifying force, bridging cultural, religious, ethnic and age differences in our diverse society...a rare and valuable national American treasure."[1] This declaration about the heritage and value of jazz in American culture is a fruitful avenue into discussions about how jazz music was shaped by and continues to mold American religious experience. If jazz can be viewed as a cultural bridge, particularly on religious grounds, then it merits consideration into how American musical and social cultures interact with this religious identity, especially within the context of biblical reception history. There are many strands that can be followed, including how jazz can be heard as a "unifying force" while at the same time being the sound of division that vocalized the margins of oppression in the African American community. Another aspect to consider is how jazz has a deeply

---

[1] "Jazz: Designation as an American National Treasure," H. Con. Res. 35, 101 Stat 2013 (1987).

rooted biblical antecedence, yet in contemporary culture is found most often within a secular rather than a sacred setting. Similar to this is how we identify jazz in popular culture, as it is increasingly apparent that what typifies jazz performers and audiences is a state of flux and communities of change. Ted Gioia is attuned to this idea when he suggests, "Jazz may have stood out as a specific local style, a certain way of playing instruments and combining aural textures, with a lineage back to New Orleans. But with the passing years, jazz has become more an attitude than a static body of practices, more an openness to the possible than a slavish devotion to the time honored."[2]

These paradoxes about jazz have not gone unnoticed by scholars and practitioners, and it may be prudent to think of jazz music in terms of "attitude" rather than "static practices" as it is this fluidity with cultural engagement that allows a deeper understanding of jazz culture in the context of biblical allusion. From the outset, a popular view that can be dispelled is one aligned to William Dean's contention that "jazz is natural to all Americans."[3] This idealistic suggestion that jazz culturally conditions the American psyche appears to neglect the more pervasive cultural tradition histories that jazz musicians produced—that for African American musical culture in particular, jazz could be recognized as a reaction *against* the cultural constraints that defined a people as "all Americans."[4] Lawrence Levine notes this dichotomy between jazz and culture: "Jazz was, or at least seemed to be, the new product of a new age; Culture was, or at least seemed to be, traditional—the creation of centuries. Jazz was raucous, discordant; Culture was harmonious, embodying order and reason. Jazz was accessible, spontaneous; Culture was exclusive, complex, available only through hard study and training."[5] If Levine's contrast between jazz and culture is adopted, it leaves us to consider what is at stake when defining how jazz artists interact with popular culture. For many avid listeners of jazz music and jazz practitioners alike, the boundaries between these terms are cloudier than Levine's description implies. This can be witnessed by the dramatic evolution of jazz throughout the twentieth century. From the genres of swing, bop, and free jazz, to current expressions of jazz as re-creations of a jazz "canon," to more avant-garde styles.[6] In certain periods of jazz history, cultural conformity has seemed to be the norm, yet at other junctures a countercultural aesthetic has dominated the music.[7] In the liner

---

[2] Ted Gioia, *The History of Jazz* (New York: Oxford University Press, 2011), 388.

[3] William D. Dean, *The American Spiritual Culture: And the Invention of Jazz, Football, and the Movies* (New York: Continuum, 2006), 118.

[4] In certain musicological circles, a similar attitude can be found in relation to improvisation—the perception that jazz improvisation involves the picking of notes out of thin air rather than a sustained process of learning, technique, and cultural assimilation. For more developed studies on jazz improvisation, see Derek Bailey, *Improvisation: Its Nature and Practice in Music* (New York: Da Capo Press, 1993); Alan Durant, "Improvisation in the Political Economy of Music," in *Music and the Politics of Culture*, ed. Christopher Norris (London: Lawrence and Wishart, 1988), 252–82.

[5] Lawrence W. Levine, "Jazz and American Culture," *Journal of American Folklore* 102, no. 403 (1989): 7.

[6] Although certain aspects of jazz history will be discussed throughout this chapter, overarching historical narratives that delve into the nature and practice of jazz are beyond the remit of this work but can be located through notable scholars, such as Gioia's *The History of Jazz* and Gunther Schuller, *Early Jazz: Its Roots and Musical Development* (New York: Oxford University Press, 1986).

[7] One need only examine jazz music produced in 1959 to recognize this movement from cultural to countercultural with the production of Miles Davis's *Kind of Blue* and Ornette Coleman's *The Shape of Jazz to Come*.

notes to the 1978 album *The History of Jazz*, Mary Lou Williams raises this tension between jazz artistry and cultural affirmation: "It has been called other names down through the years. Ragtime, Swing, Bop and Avant Garde, but whenever there's a strong beat people always want to degrade the music by calling it Jazz. And when it is called Jazz other soulful, creative and artistic aspects in the music are lost."[8]

This tension between jazz aesthetics and other popular music has been represented in jazz from the early twentieth century through to contemporary society, and it is this negotiated tension that sustains jazz's engagement with popular culture as a cultural generator, actor, and interpreter. What began as an art form expressed from the margins of American society is recognized as being (although perhaps unwittingly) a "national treasure." A similar tone to Williams's perspective is adopted by Wynton Marsalis: "Jazz music is America's past and its potential, summed up and sanctified and accessible to anybody who learns to listen to, feel, and understand it. The music can connect us to our earlier selves and to our better selves-to-come. It can remind us of where we fit in the time line of human achievement, an ultimate value of our art."[9] It is this diverse appeal of jazz—between the universal recognition of jazz as an American national treasure and the multiple forms of the jazz genre that engage with political and social norms as well as musical high and low art—that has forged jazz's place in American culture.

It is on this basis that we can construct how jazz in American popular culture interacts with some of the foremost influences on the music—that of biblical literature and images and theological principles. Compared to cultural theories, musicological analysis, and the social history of jazz in America, resonances with biblical and theological attitudes remain a neglected area of research.[10] From the religious background of some of the foremost artists to the political voicing of the oppressed for social justice, through to a pervading spirituality that was translated into the marketing of jazz albums and LPs, jazz has a significant theological and indeed biblical heritage. In American popular culture, jazz musicians have used extensive biblical imagery as a means of expressing religious identity as well as the more well-known political and social messages. From Oscar Peterson's 1984 album *Easter Suite*, an instrumental jazz trio musical interpretation of the passion and resurrection of Christ, to Charles Gayle's "Seven Days" on the 1994

[8] Mary Lou Williams, liner notes to *A History of Jazz*, Folkway Records, FW02860/FJ 2860, LP, 1978.

[9] Wynton Marsalis and Geoffrey C. Ward, *Moving to Higher Ground: How Jazz Can Change Your Life* (New York: Random House, 2009), 13. Undoubtedly numerous jazz artists may argue against Marsalis's perspective, but for the purpose of the current significance of jazz music and providing a method to discuss jazz in modern public perception, Marsalis's view connects with the American cultural value of jazz.

[10] Although there are multiple studies in relation to these topics, nearly all remain silent on the heritage of biblical literature, particularly on early jazz music. For examples of studies in the social history of jazz, as well as musicological analysis, see Ingrid T. Monson, *Saying Something: Jazz Improvisation and Interaction* (Chicago: University of Chicago Press, 1996); Paul Berliner, *Thinking in Jazz: The Infinite Art of Improvisation* (Chicago: University of Chicago Press, 1994); Daniel Fischlin and Ajay Heble, *The Other Side of Nowhere: Jazz, Improvisation, and Communities in Dialogue* (Middletown, CT: Wesleyan University Press, 2004).

album *Kingdom Come*, a free jazz improvisation on the Genesis 1 account, jazz artists have used biblical imagery in diverse and unusual ways.

To illuminate this further, two crosscurrents between jazz and biblical imagery are contemplated. The first illustrates where jazz artists use the Bible in a way that might be deemed representational, demonstrating how jazz artists use passages from the Bible and represent themes and situations located within a biblical text, and use them to create a new orientation of cultural expression. To highlight this, Philip Bohlman's historiographical approach is interwoven through his interpretation of colonial encounter, racism, nationalism, and eschatology as the defining factors of music and cultural development intertwined with biblical themes. Employing this theory, Bohlman suggests that "music represents culture in two ways, as a form of expression common to humanity, and as one of the most extreme manifestations of difference."[11] As we shall see, this tension and dissonance resonates on whether jazz musicians use the Bible as more than a hermeneutical tool and whether this representation of biblical themes and images goes beyond mere quotation of biblical narratives.

The second crosscurrent focuses on improvisation, whether the highly improvised style of the free jazz era developed in the 1960s represents a rejection of the biblical representations of jazz music or whether a broader biblical inscription that goes beyond quotation can be identified theologically in the music of artists such as John Coltrane and Sun Ra. It questions whether improvisatory jazz can be viewed as having a theological inscription that is rooted within the biblical messages of freedom and liberation.

OVERVIEW OF TOPIC

To provide a framework for how jazz musicians interacted with biblical sources is to go beyond where jazz musicians quote the biblical text. David Wilmington writes, "The major and minor figures of the first century of jazz grew up steeped in the stories, typology, conceptual and moral framework and the language of the Bible. This makes it initially confusing to realize the relative paucity of direct biblical reference in Jazz music."[12] To speak of the relationship between jazz and the Bible is more than a hermeneutical discussion of the use of biblical images or stories. Consideration of the function and use of music in the Bible may be a more fruitful methodology.

Music in the Bible is treated as an action and a participatory activity. This is reflected by Jeremy Begbie: "The music of ancient Israel and of the New Testament church, as part of the music of the ancient world, was not about works or scores; it was something made

---

[11] Philip Bohlman, "Music and Culture: Historiographies of Disjuncture," in *The Cultural Study of Music: A Critical Introduction*, ed. Martin Clayton, Trevor Herbert, and Richard Middleton (New York: Routledge, 2012), 47.

[12] David Willmington, "Jazz," in *Encyclopedia of the Bible and Its Reception* Volume 13, ed. Hans-Josef Klauck (Berlin: Walter de Gruyter, 2016), 795.

and heard."[13] Music was part of the life and active participation of ancient Israel and was used in call and response to God in distinct locations and impacts on diverse cultures. This can be most clearly seen in the Psalms, but also in Exodus 15 and Numbers 20, in the deutero-Pauline command to sing hymns and spiritual songs in Ephesians 5:19, and later in 1 Timothy 3:16. Music in biblical culture invites active participation, and this is embodied and vocalized in the lineage to jazz. To think about jazz and culture in relation to the Bible is perhaps best considered not an examination of static musical works or texts but a process of action. This is reflected in Gioia's view and in musicology in general. Christopher Small embraces this idea with the term "musicking": "The fundamental nature and meaning of music lies not in objects, not in musical works at all, but in action, in what people do. It is only by understanding what people do as they take part in a musical act that we can hope to understand its nature and the function that it fulfils in human life. Whatever that function may be, I am certain, first, that to take part in a music act is of central importance to our very humanness."[14] For our understanding of the relationship between jazz and the Bible, it is this process of action in performance that provides the interaction with cultural theories.

For American culture, the intersection between the Bible and jazz music begins with two distinct origins—one developing from the European classical tradition employing the melodies and harmonies of the classical style, the other emerging from Africa and the West Indies, particularly through rhythm and call and response.[15] America's spiritual culture is both traditionally and religiously biblically shaped and involves the active participation of the community in singing hymns and spiritual songs. Methodist and Jewish hymns, particularly the hymns of Isaac Watts and the Wesley brothers, among others, influenced jazz, as did the preachers and evangelists enriched by the Great Awakening.[16] The transmission of biblical history and narrative was also achieved through direct preaching of the Gospel, and so it is unsurprising that the biblical text translates into particularly white American culture from this source. The impact of this European inheritance is most clearly recognized in Western art criticism of music, particularly the study of classical music criticism on jazz cultures.

[13] Jeremy Begbie, *Resounding Truth: Christian Wisdom in the World of Music* (Grand Rapids, MI: Baker Academic, 2007), 60.

[14] Christopher Small, *Musicking: The Meanings of Performing and Listening* (Hanover, NH: University Press of New England, 1998), 8. This is reflected especially in John Szwed's perception of jazz as "social music": "In jazz, it is the activity itself that is as important as the result. It is a music that is learned in the doing, in the collective play: it is a social music, with some of the features of early African-American social organization still evident in execution." John Szwed, *Jazz 101: A Complete Guide to Learning and Loving Jazz* (New York: Hyperion Books, 2000), 46.

[15] For a more detailed assessment of call and response, especially in relation to theological discourse, see Bruce Ellis Benson, *Liturgy as a Way of Life* (Grand Rapids, MI: Baker Academic, 2013), 33–49.

[16] For a developed study of this, see Stephen A. Marini, "Hymnody and History: Early American Evangelical Hymns as Sacred Music," in *Music in American Religious Experience*, ed. Philip V. Bohlman, Edith Waldvogel Blumhofer, and Maria M. Chow (New York: Oxford University Press, 2006), 123–54.

In the American colonies, the Bible was used as a tool by white slave owners to convert uneducated slaves to Christianity.[17] By the nineteenth century, the focus of biblical interpretation had been inverted so that African Americans were now finding new situational meanings in the biblical text and recognizing similarities in the plight of the Israelites during the Exodus and the current situation in the American South.[18] Out of this cultural recognition and education came the birth of an Africanized version of Christianity, which led to the creation of the African American spirituals tradition.

The spirituals were a form of biblical interpretation through music, but also contained a social and political agenda encouraging identification and action.[19] "The spirituals began as a commentary not only on the experience of slavery but on the hope born of the biblical message, as that had been conveyed by the Christian churches."[20]

At the turn of the twentieth century, African American popular culture was linked to the struggle of liberation from an oppressive culture, and this is played out in the music of the spirituals. This struggle is reinforced by the biblical figures that were chosen for the genre, for example, Moses, Daniel, and Joshua as figures of the Old Testament past whose experience, sacrifice, and deliverance resonated have immanent witness among the present community. African American popular culture interpreted these Old Testament stories alongside a theology of redemption found in Christological hermeneutics: "The message of Christianity... proved more meaningful and effective than its abusive prohibitions. The Christian gospel that those who suffer on earth hold a special place with God in heaven spoke to [the community] and gave them hope. They related to this message deeply. The Black slave learned from the suffering of Jesus, and genuinely embraced Christianity saying; I want to be like Jesus."[21] The spirituals are rooted in the Old Testament, but this Old Testament basis also postulates a New Testament narrative of redemption through the suffering and death of Christ. It was this shared identity

---

[17] A study of the use of Bible on the part of slave masters and preachers from the point of view of the formerly enslaved can be found in B. Powery and Rodney S. Sadler Jr., *The Genesis of Liberation: Biblical Interpretation in the Antebellum Narratives of the Enslaved* (Louisville, KY: Westminster John Knox Press, 2016).

[18] For a discussion of the Bible and African American identity, including discussions of African American work songs in relation to the Psalms, see Vincent Wimbush, "The Bible and African Americans: An Outline of an Interpretive History," in *Stony the Road We Trod: African American Biblical Interpretation*, ed. Cain Hope Felder (Minneapolis, MN: Fortress Press, 1991), 81–97. For a more general introduction to African American religious identity in American culture, see Julius H. Bailey, *Down in the Valley: An Introduction to African American Religious History* (Minneapolis, MN: Augsburg Fortress Press, 2016), chapters 1–2.

[19] See Brian K. Blount, "The Rap against Rome: The Spiritual-Blues Impulse and the Hymns of Revelation," in *Can I Get a Witness? Reading Revelation through African American Culture* (Louisville, KY: Westminster John Knox Press, 2005), 91–117.

[20] Dean, *The American Spiritual Culture*, 127.

[21] Max Stern, *Bible and Music: Influences of the Old Testament on Western Music* (Jersey City, NJ: KTAV, 2011), 157.

among the African American community that drove the spirituals in the black churches and into the popular culture of the day.[22]

With the emergence of jazz in the early twentieth century, we encounter an inheritance of the spirituals tradition into this new genre of music production. "Jazz came into being through negotiation of the vehicles of dissemination, and with conditions it encountered in any given location."[23] For African American popular culture, the vehicle of dissemination was the spiritual. This is typified in Louis Armstrong's use of the spiritual in early jazz music.

Armstrong's religious leanings were inclined toward Baptist theology, though like many jazz musicians, he also embraced a broader religious mood. It is surprising that it is not at the beginning of Armstrong's career but rather toward the end where we find his album *Louis and the Good Book* (1958).[24] This album contains his interpretation of several well-known jazz spirituals, including the most famous example, "Go Down, Moses," an interpretation of Exodus 8:1. The black community recognized itself as the Israelites and identified with Moses, as against the white slave owners, identified as Pharaoh. Yet Armstrong's musical development of the spiritual through his own jazz aesthetic allows for an interpretation of the spiritual into popular jazz culture. His trumpet improvisation and the clarinet obligato toward the end of the track show the movement from repeating the musical theme through the phrasing (a repetition of the biblical text) through to extemporization on the theme. We therefore encounter an interpreted biblical narrative that is not constrained by the music but liberated by it. This echoes the dynamic interaction between biblical imagery and jazz in that Armstrong does not only repeat the musical material or biblical text but "sings a new song" through the music, and thus retains the social heritage of what has gone before. One could contend that the jazz improvisation reinforces the biblical and religious past of the piece by illustrating the development of the genre and the movement toward freedom and redemption in the music itself. Armstrong not only embodies the history of the culture but embraces and interprets the biblical text within the popular culture of the day.

For jazz musicians, the inheritance of the American spiritual is the most direct link between the biblical text and jazz music. This is typified by Armstrong's *Louis and the Good Book* but can also be recognized in several concerts, most notably the justly famous *From Spirituals to Swing* at Carnegie Hall in 1938–9, which shows performances of jazz and spirituals developing into improvised jazz in a concert that attempted to chart the development of jazz as a musical form indebted to and intermingling with earlier forms, like spirituals and boogie woogie.[25]

---

[22] This theme of inheritance of the theology of the black churches and its relevance for popular culture is considered further by Jon Michael Spencer (among others) in *Sacred Music of the Secular City: From Blues to Rap* (Durham, NC: Duke University Press, 1992).

[23] Bruce Johnson, "The Jazz Diaspora," in *The Cambridge Companion to Jazz*, ed. David Horn and Mervyn Cooke (Cambridge: Cambridge University Press, 2002), 39.

[24] Louis Armstrong, *Louis and the Good Book*, Decca Records, ED2618, EP, 1958.

[25] Luckily, the latter was recorded and issued as *From Spirituals to Swing—Carnegie Hall Concerts 1938/39*, Vanguard Records, VCD2-47/48, CD, 1987.

The biblical antecedents to jazz align with how the spirituals tradition developed into jazz music. However, this emerges not only from repetition of the words and phrases of the spirituals but into different genres of jazz music. As different strands of jazz were produced, sacred jazz or liturgical jazz became one such instance of how the notions of the sacred and biblical affirmation are employed in the jazz setting.

SPECIFIC EXAMPLES AND/OR FOCI

American popular culture's relationship to jazz and the Bible requires different approaches to gather a wide-ranging analysis of the use of the biblical text. One approach that has been explored is to analyze where the biblical text is encountered directly in a set number of jazz works. While this method has been a useful hermeneutical tool to understand the location of the biblical text in the music, its limitations are that citations of the biblical narrative are often erratic and decontextualized, and—as shown in our consideration of "Go Down, Moses"—heavily linked to an already established cultural interpretation of Bible passages. A more engaging approach is to identify biblical narratives through different genres of jazz. One example is the genre of sacred jazz. In this music we find scripture quoted at length and direct representations of theological attributions. These works appear both in a liturgical setting and as concert pieces, for example, Duke Ellington's *Sacred Concerts* (1965, 1968, 1973), Mary Lou Williams's *Music for Peace* (1968), and Dave Brubeck's *Psalm 23* (2010) and *Psalm 121* (1990).[26] In these compositions, we can identify representations of the biblical text. To illuminate this further, Ellington's "Come Sunday," originally on the 1958 album *Black, Brown and Beige* and included in the "Sacred Concerts" performed with Mahalia Jackson, illustrates this technique of representation and interpretation of biblical texts.[27]

The collaboration between Jackson and Ellington draws on what Albert Murray affirms as "Saturday night function meets Sunday morning church worship."[28] Toward the end of his career Ellington decided to focus on producing sacred jazz music alongside his jazz standards and in 1958 collaborated with Jackson to produce "Come Sunday."[29] The piece is saturated with biblical echoes from Psalm 108, Jeremiah 31:35, and Matthew 6:28. The lyrics have a wide resonance, with the movement of the exodus

---

[26] Brubeck's work is not confined to Psalm settings. He also composed a number of sacred choral works, including *The Gates of Justice* (1969) and *Light in the Wilderness* (1968). For an elaboration on the influences of Brubeck's religious music and its interaction with theological traditions, see Frank Burch Brown, "Lenten Practice in a Musical Mode," *Interpretation* 64, no. 1 (2010): 20–3. See also Harmon Griffith Young III, "The Sacred Choral Music of Dave Brubeck: A Historical, Analytical, and Critical Examination," PhD diss., University of Florida, 1995.

[27] Duke Ellington, *Black, Brown and Beige*, Columbia Records, CS8015, LP, 1958.

[28] Albert Murray, *Stomping the Blues* (London: Quartet Books, 1978), 136.

[29] Although a full analysis of "Come Sunday" is beyond the scope of this chapter, substantial research has been given to the cultural value of this work, including David W. Stowe, *How Sweet the Sound: Music in the Spiritual Lives of Americans* (Cambridge, MA: Harvard University Press, 2004), 196–219; Jason Bivins, *Spirits Rejoice! Jazz and American Religion* (Oxford: Oxford University Press, 2015), 96–9.

being fulfilled through the coming of Christ. At the beginning of the piece we find the lyrics "Please look down and see my people through," which resonates with Exodus 14, harking back to the Israelites' exodus from Egypt. This is resolved with "Come Sunday, oh come Sunday, that's the day," emphasizing that the exodus is bound up in the New Testament with the analogy of the Israelites obtaining freedom from Egypt with Christ breaking the bonds of death, thus redeeming humanity. For Ellington, the resolution of God's providence toward Israel is repeated in the New Testament in the incarnation; come Sunday, in the memorial of the death and resurrection of Christ, is the resolution of the new orientation of freedom experienced by the African American community. Jackson's gospel melody gives emotional force to the music. The piece is nearly entirely dominated by her narrative rather than significant jazz harmony. It is possible to read "Come Sunday" as a place of devotional space and the emphasis on the reverence that Ellington gives to the biblical narrative and to the gospel melody to convey the meaning. In the final lines Jackson sings, "Up from dawn till sunset man works all day. Come Sunday, oh come Sunday that's the day." This has a strong hermeneutic correlation between the writer of Ecclesiastes and the clamor for social justice. In Ecclesiastes 2:18–20 we read, "I hated all my toil in which I had toiled under the sun, seeing that I must leave it to those who come after me—and who knows whether they will be wise or foolish? Yet they will be master of all for which I toiled and used my wisdom under the sun. This also is vanity. So I turned and gave my heart up to despair concerning all the toil of my labours under the sun. This is also vanity" (NRSV).[30] This appears to be echoed in Ellington's music in that the toil under the sun has been witnessed during slavery, but redemption is found in "Come Sunday" in Christ's redemption once and for all. A simi-lar allegory can be found in Psalm 104:23: "Man goes forth unto his work and to his labour until the evening." The piece has wider cultural implications as an expression of the hope for freedom; in "Come Sunday" African Americans would express their yearn-ing for social rights and justice, which, if they cannot be rewarded on earth, will be rewarded in heaven. In this piece we encounter a fragment of how biblical texts in African American culture are represented in sacred jazz music. But it would be mislead-ing to imply that sacred jazz inhabited only African American culture. Indeed, the European origins of jazz also include a powerful sense of liturgical traditions, and these narratives can be identified in the development of this form of sacred jazz.

Among the iconic albums that appeared in 1959, a lesser-known LP entitled *Liturgical Jazz* was released by Ed Summerlin.[31] Grief-stricken by the terminal illness of his nine-month-old daughter, Summerlin was encouraged by his pastor to write a piece of jazz to

[30] All biblical quotations are drawn from the New Revised Standard Version (NRSV) Anglicized Edition. However it should be noted that jazz musicians accessed a variety of biblical sources and bibles (particularly the King James Version) and the usage here is to provide illustration.

[31] As mentioned previously, 1959 saw the release of *Kind of Blue*, the best-selling jazz album of all time, but also the unorthodox and challenging *The Shape of Jazz to Come* by Ornette Coleman. Other popular and persistently influential albums released in 1959 are Dave Brubeck's *Take Five*, Charles Mingus's *Mingus Ah Um*, and John Coltrane's *Giant Steps*. For more on the impact of these and other jazz in 1959, see John Szwed, "1959: Multiple Revolutions," in *Jazz 101*, 209–22, and the documentary *1959: The Year Jazz Changed*, dir. Paul Bernays, 2009).

the words and structure of the church service. The album *Liturgical Jazz* or *Requiem for Mary-Jo* was the outcome of this effort.[32] It comprises a jazz setting of morning prayer from the Sunday Morning Service of the Methodists of North America.[33] It includes an improvisation on Psalm 6, readings from the Old and New Testaments, and jazz settings of two Wesleyan hymns. This unorthodox setting for jazz music was even appraised by the theologian Paul Tillich, who wrote, "I found the program very effective, especially insofar as a liturgy was composed that seemed to be an appropriate blending of words and music."[34] *Liturgical Jazz* is the first instance in which the music of jazz is genre-defined as "sacred" within jazz studies.[35] It is the clearest interaction of jazz music, liturgy, and the Bible. The album embodies a liturgical setting and yet has very little interaction between the jazz music (mainly located in the prelude and as accompanying interjections during the liturgy) and the biblical text itself. The blending of words and music that Tillich references is more a clear articulation of the Word with jazz interpretations than of the two combined. For example, the New Testament reading from 2 Peter 1:3–11 is independent and does not have any jazz accompaniment. And yet the reading itself would allow for an interesting interpretation of sacred jazz. In 2 Peter 1:5–7 we read, "For this very reason, you must make every effort to support your faith with goodness, and goodness with knowledge, and knowledge with self-control, and self-control with endurance, and endurance with godliness, and godliness with mutual affection, and mutual affection with love." One could ponder whether this also relates to the type of jazz employed in the music, as the improvisation itself appears to be restrained rather than free, suggesting here the predominance of the words over the music.

Both Ellington's and Summerlin's versions of the biblical interpretation in their musical works represent sacred jazz in American popular culture. While the two approaches differ in their contextual frameworks, they nonetheless embody a form of representational rendering adapted to suit cultural identity and performance practice. The Bible is used as a tool to interpret the present situation, and for both pieces it expresses a displacement in history, whether it be the black community struggling for civil rights or Summerlin's loss of his daughter.

Both compositions epitomize a methodological approach seeking to illustrate a representational rendering of jazz and the Bible—of ethnographic analysis of the music-*in-culture* (of music conforming to a cultural narrative). This limited scope allows for the resonance of an analytical approach for biblical parallels within, principally, the lyrics of

---

[32] Ed Summerlin, *Liturgical Jazz—A Musical Setting of the Office of Morning Prayer*, Ecclesia Records, ER-101, LP, 1959.

[33] The Sunday Morning Service of the Methodists of North America has its authorial origin in John Wesley, who set out this new liturgy in 1784 as a revised liturgy from the 1662 Book of Common Prayer. This was adopted by the Methodist Episcopal Church. A modern version of the Office of Morning Prayer can be found in *The Methodist Worship Book* (Nashville, TN: Methodist Publishing House, 1999).

[34] Eugene Lees, ed., "Liturgical Jazz on Tour," *Down Beat*, April 14, 1960), 15.

[35] For a lengthier analysis of liturgical jazz music, with special reference to Ed Summerlin, see Derick Cordoba, "Liturgical Jazz: The Lineage of the Subgenre in the Music of Edgar E. Summerlin," A.Mus.D. diss., University of Illinois, 2017.

jazz musical works. Yet as we have seen, jazz appears to reject this kind of fixity of methodology. The openness and fluidity that jazz exudes correlate with the biblical attitude toward music to "sing to the Lord a new song, sing to the Lord all the earth" (Psalm 96:1). If jazz does indeed sing a new song, then the possibilities for how jazz might exhibit this biblical wisdom become more diverse. To develop this further, Bohlman illuminates the shift in thought from a musical perspective in terms of how music's relationship with culture develops away from a focus on representational conformity.

Bohlman contests current strands in musicology that seek to remove discussions of culture from the content of a musical work. Music and culture, he argues, "broadly or narrowly are not convenient discursive fits."[36] In recent strands of musicology, analysis of performance practices invokes a strong analytical language of representation, whether this be of notation, performance practice, or authentic works.[37] Thus identifying passages where the Bible intersects directly with certain jazz lyrics or tunes perhaps omits a greater resonance of biblical themes in jazz music and harmonizes to this analytical style. This is reflected in Daniel Chua's argument on the relationship between theology and music more generally: "Music is not some tabula rasa for theology to inscribe its wisdom; it is encrusted with a history that has to be engaged with lest we inadvertently rehearse the anti-theological discourses of the ventriloquists and so contribute the music's oscillation between the metaphysical and the physical."[38] Chua's perspective contests a structure that considers only forms of representational analysis. If we examine the Bible in jazz music only where it directly intersects with jazz standards, do we not lose some of the theological inscription and wisdom the biblical writers advance, as well as what our cultural situation necessitates?

Bohlman contends that our interpretation of culture in relation to musical understanding is important when moving away from a representational model: "While most ethnomusicologists concerned themselves with the appropriate prepositional connective between the two: music-*in*-culture, (identifying) music-*as*-culture...theorists looked beyond canonic art-music repertories, wrestled with ways of interpreting text in relation to context."[39] Bohlman introduces a method of encountering the rhetoric for music-*as*-culture in its relationship to national identity, African American social frameworks, and theological redemption history. For the topic at hand, this approach correlates with the idea of jazz-*as*-culture, with the antecedents in the colonial past; the encounter with racism and discrimination in American culture; a determination to establish the black community in America by embracing national identity; and as eschatological justification for years of suffering. The terminology jazz-*as*-culture resonates

---

[36] Bohlman, "Music and Culture," 45.

[37] For a discussion of the issues surrounding authentic musical performance, see Lydia Goehr, *The Imaginary Museum of Musical Works: An Essay on the Philosophy of Music* (Oxford: Oxford University Press, 1994).

[38] Daniel Chua, "Music as the Mouthpiece of Theology," in *Resonant Witness: Conversations between Music and Theology*, ed. Jeremy S. Begbie and Steven R. Guthrie (Grand Rapids, MI: Wm. B. Eerdmans, 2011), 159.

[39] Bohlman, "Music and Culture," 45.

with a broader perspective located within popular culture that witnesses popular culture as religion.[40] For American popular culture, jazz has a quasi-religious identity—a
community of believers and followers with aspects of religious devotion toward certain
genres or artists. As Bailey writes, "Each successive revival sees a further mining of its
history and a music once rightly described as 'the sound of surprise' is now chiefly
enjoyed as a reminder of yesteryear."[41] This repetition of tradition history and adaptation toward new meanings for jazz in contemporary culture suggests this religious cultural function. Jazz-*as*-culture provides the voicing of an eschatological narrative, the
justification for singing a new song of liberation. Jazz is witnessed as a place that uses
biblical images as a means to an end, but it also embodies through its culture something
of the transformational power of the biblical witness. When we speak of jazz, we speak
not only of representation but of openness and freedom. This new freedom to sing a new
song resonates with the attitude to music in Ephesians 5:8–9, 14, 18–19: "For once you
were darkness, but now in the Lord you are light. Live as children of light—for the fruit
of the light is found in all that is good and right and true. For everything that becomes
visible is light.... Be filled with the Spirit, as you sing psalms and hymns and spiritual
songs among yourselves, singing and making melody to the Lord in your hearts." This
command to live in light and to sing psalms, hymns, and spiritual songs is because the
light of Christ broke through the darkness of the world. The eschatological power goes
beyond representation to new orientation and new life in Christ. Thus, to speak of the
relationship between jazz music and the Bible asks us to go beyond the constituent parts
of the biblical witness in jazz music, to look at the power of jazz music as a mode of
encounter that can shape our cultural identity: "Eschatological power of music results
from both its cultural and musical sides. The former is evident in the overt use of music
to mark moments of death.... The latter resides in the temporal phenomena that shape
the ontologies of music, in other words, the power of music to calibrate and shape—as
well as negate—time."[42]

To connect the context of jazz, the Bible, and American popular culture, the potential
to recognize jazz-*as*-culture and the theological interpretation of the Bible are particularly valuable. This moves beyond simply examining how jazz music alludes to or adapts
texts from the Bible toward numerous moments of encounter that transform the very
principles that express correlation with the biblical text and seek to tease out biblical
wisdom. This involves looking over the horizon of representation to the very spiritual,

[40] Bruce David Forbes draws out the relationship between religion and popular culture by asking, "If
popular culture sometimes functions as religion, can the inverse be true as well? Can religious activity
or production not only take on the features of popular culture, but function fully as popular culture?"
See Forbes, "Introduction: Finding Religion in Unexpected Places," in *Religion and Popular Culture in
American*, 3rd ed., ed. Bruce David Forbes and Jeffrey H. Mahan (Oakland: University of California
Press, 2017), 23n15. While it is beyond the scope of this chapter to explore this claim fully, it is useful to
note that jazz music is becoming more pervasive in contemporary worship music, so perhaps this is
one method by which religions are taking on a new cultural identity. For more on this idea of "music as
religion," see Michael J. Gilmour's entry in this volume.

[41] Bailey, *Improvisation*, 49.

[42] Bohlman, "Music and Culture," 53.

religious, and cultural identity of jazz in American culture. To elucidate these ideas further requires an examination of one of the defining aspects of jazz: improvisation.

If jazz is to truly sing a new song, then this seems to be the essence of improvisation. To justify this movement toward improvisation is to suggest that improvisation is bound up with theological concerns: "Jazz exemplifies a kind of creativity that holds together the individual and community, freedom and constraint, structure and chance. Improvisation helps us to deal with the ambiguities life presents because it helps us confront the unfamiliar with the familiar, the chaotic, with order."[43] For Ann Pederson, jazz improvisation ascribes biblical wisdom as the Bible itself deals with aspects of freedom and constraint, of tension and resolution. Improvisation is part of the essence of the New Testament witness, of offer, gift, and exchange. This offer, gift, and exchange is characterized by Paul: "For if while we were enemies, we were reconciled to God through the death of his Son, much more surely, having been reconciled, will we be saved by his life. But more than that, we even boast in God through our Lord Jesus Christ, through whom we have now received reconciliation" (Rom 5:10–11).

Improvisation in jazz culture is bound up with Christological identity and active participation in this divine movement and gift. If improvisation is one aspect of what it is to be human in music-making, this itself has a theological resonance, as improvisation is bound up with the biblical witness of the church and the tradition history that flows from this: "The Church is the improvising community, living out of the expanding and limitless movement of gracious exchange which God has set in motion."[44] Resonances can also be drawn with the interaction between the assimilation of tradition history in the church and that found in the jazz culture. Kevin Vanhoozer provides a helpful inflection on this idea by suggesting, "The church always has to improvise. It does so out of a desire, not to be original, but rather to minister the gospel in new contexts, to speak and shows its understanding of the drama of redemption."[45] Improvisation in jazz says something about being bound up with this drama in that jazz musicians do not merely regurgitate a tradition history but improvise upon it. Jamie Howison notes this capacity, arguing that "to understand the tradition as something at once deeply rooted and dynamic is to acknowledge its capacity for innovation. Time will tell if such innovations become part of the organic whole, or if they simply play a temporary role in one particular time or context. Time *and* reception by musicians and listeners... will be the test of the place in the tradition of particular artists, recordings and even genres within jazz."[46]

What can be revealed in this moment is that jazz may have its antecedence in the exodus account, but the capacity for innovation allows for a voicing in new situations. The resonances with the biblical tradition history through the themes of tension and resolu-

[43] Ann Pederson, *God, Creation, and All That Jazz: A Process of Composition and Improvisation* (St. Louis, KY: Chalice Press, 2001), ix.

[44] Jeremy S. Begbie, *Theology, Music and Time* (Cambridge: Cambridge University Press, 2000), 265.

[45] Kevin Vanhoozer, *Faith Speaking Understanding: Performing the Drama of Doctrine* (Louisville, KY: Westminster John Knox Press, 2014), 190.

[46] Jamie Howison, *God's Mind in That Music: Theological Explorations through the Music of John Coltrane* (Eugene, OR: Cascade Books, 2012), 101–2.

tion, freedom and constraint allow us to explore the impact of jazz on biblical wisdom more completely. The essence of jazz to sing a new song in American culture evolves out of a cultural milieu represented by the African American community. The situational themes of displacement into a new freedom, the biblical tradition of the African American heritage to a voicing of a new song in the present is represented through jazz music in the biblical themes of freedom and liberation. The Bible is not removed or rejected but forms part of our very humanity. To improvise involves a metaphysics of participation, and as we navigate between the tension of freedom and constraint we discover that improvisation is not just about creation, repetition, or performance but is vital to our very being in and through creation. This can be affirmed through the resonances of two pieces: Coltrane's "Alabama" (1963) and Sun Ra's *Astro Black* (1973).

Coltrane epitomizes the voice of the art form. While much of the focus on his relationship to the biblical narrative has been on his seminal album *A Love Supreme*, the track "Alabama" from *Live at Birdland* illustrates the voicing of jazz beyond, but still affirming, a biblical hermeneutic.[47] "Alabama" was written in the wake of the bombing of the 16th Street Baptist Church in Birmingham by the Ku Klux Klan in September 1963. The improvisation that Coltrane employs is one of lament (a sound that has resonances with "Psalm" in *A Love Supreme*). But the improvisation is also based on the intonation of a speech given by Martin Luther King Jr. in the wake of the bombing (and in a similar way to the use in "Psalm"). The song has a double meaning in the lament of the improvisation and the recitation of the spoken narrative. "Alabama" speaks to a deeper meaning. It resonates with the community through the biblical voice of displacement in and through the improvisation. The piece characterizes Coltrane's view that improvisation speaks about God in a new way.[48] What Coltrane says about *A Love Supreme* can be applied to "Alabama" also: "I'd like to point out to people the divine in a musical language that transcends words. I want to speak to their souls."[49] Coltrane's "Alabama" emphasizes the notion of jazz-*as*-culture by creating meaning of a current situation that responds deeply to the African American community, which is then reflected in popular culture at large.

More eclectically, the emergence of Sun Ra into American popular culture reflects the tradition history that can be seen in Coltrane. Sun Ra does not achieve this by using lament in a state of disorientation; he chooses instead a reorientation of jazz liberated from the constraints of the art form to emphasize new meanings and new contexts

---

[47] See, for example, Ashley Kahn, *A Love Supreme: The Creation of John Coltrane's Classic Album* (London: Granta, 2002); Tony Whyton, *Beyond a Love Supreme: John Coltrane and the Legacy of an Album* (Oxford: Oxford University Press, 2013). For more theological studies, see Howison, *God's Mind in That Music*; Steven R. Guthrie, *Creator Spirit: The Holy Spirit and the Art of Becoming Human* (Grand Rapids, MI: Baker Academic, 2011).

[48] For more on this piece within Coltrane's oeuvre and its theological implications, see Howison's chapter on "Alabama" in *God's Mind in That Music*, 122–34. The track is found on the album *Live at Birdland*, Impulse! Records, AS-50, LP, 1964.

[49] Cited in Lewis Porter, *John Coltrane: A Life and Music* (Ann Arbor: University of Michigan Press, 1999), 232.

through the music.[50] He was fascinated with mythology of space (undoubtedly linked to the Space Race of the 1960s), but this cosmology and mythology also reflect a liberation toward a sonic and cosmic utopia. His track "Astro Black" from the album of the same name typifies this interpretation and symbolism.[51] It is linked, as Jason Bivins helpfully affirms, to "Ra's understanding of the sacred past [which] connected the dots between space travel, astrology, ancient technologies, biblical numerology and cosmic sound."[52] In "Astro Black" we recognize a move toward cosmic mythologizing and theologizing. This new orientation of cultural identity is drawn out of jazz-*as*-culture and a desire to propel culture to new understandings and new relationships. The new jazz in American popular culture therefore looked forward rather than backward, in Sun Ra's case quite literally out of space rather than back to slavery.[53] It is this liberation that Sun Ra encounters and exemplifies which transforms our biblical interpretation of jazz music toward a new religious mythology of jazz, typified by a move from the focus on the Christian story to a more pervasive and generalized spirituality.

In these pieces, we can reference an homage to the biblical themes of freedom and constraint. The Bible is not rejected but assumed into the tradition of jazz spiritual and religious culture. Jazz-*as*-culture for the American public no longer attempts to repeat biblical aspects but instead improvises on a theme. Jazz culture and study is liberated from the pervading canonical and stylistic interpretation of music analysis. The role of the Bible in American popular culture through jazz music then looks toward Bohlman's analysis of eschatology, of being liberated from the constraint of the biblical narrative and improvising in its new situation, which resonates with the cultural and social history of jazz in society.

This chapter has offered two diverse interpretations of jazz and the Bible in American popular culture. One method of approaching the Bible and jazz is to illustrate this representationally through key artists such as Duke Ellington and Ed Summerlin and their sacred jazz. The extension (or even liberation) of this has been to broaden the scope of analysis to the underpinning and liberation of jazz expression which builds on this representational aspect. There is a divergence from Dean's assessment of jazz and American culture in his affirmation "Look beneath Jazz and you will find improvisation; look beneath improvisation and you will find displacement; look beneath displacement and you will find the American story."[54] It is not the layers beneath jazz but the foundations of jazz expression, complete with the sociocultural tradition *alongside* that impact on

---

[50]   Lament, disorientation, and new orientation are referenced particularly with the Psalms. For a greater exposition of this theory, see Walter Brueggemann, *The Message of the Psalms* (Minneapolis, MN: Augsburg Publishing House, 1984).

[51]   Sun Ra, *Astro Black*, Impulse! Records, AS-9255, LP, 1973.

[52]   Bivins, *Spirits Rejoice!*, 221.

[53]   The perspective of considering jazz futures is developed by Ajay Heble and Rob Wallace by attempting to illustrate how jazz music maintains its pioneering cultural influence in society in an effort to not relegate jazz to the realm of American heritage studies. See Heble and Wallace, eds., *People Get Ready: The Future of Jazz Is Now!* (Durham, NC: Duke University Press, 2013).

[54]   Dean, *The American Spiritual Culture*, 143.

American popular culture, that tell this story. To see jazz-*as*-culture rather than only jazz-*in*-culture is the conclusion of this work.

FUTURE PROSPECTS AND QUESTIONS

- It could be argued that jazz is no longer represented in American *popular* culture. The movement of jazz into eclectic and often avant-garde forms of American life has meant that jazz is no longer one of the central focuses of American cultural production. Questions can therefore be raised about the cultural influence of jazz and whether jazz has succumbed to the canonicity of history, relying on several canonical *works* for interpretation and value.

- The interpretation of jazz here has revolved around examination of exegetical as well as theological interpretations of jazz pieces. Perhaps one model that could be adopted is a more developed examination of particularly where jazz musicians interact with texts from the Psalms and why particular Psalms are chosen by jazz artists and then how these relate back to the African American spirituals.

- One aspect that could be advanced further is whether jazz musicians take texts from the New Testament to develop into jazz pieces. Relatively few artists explicitly connect works with the Gospels or the Pauline letters, but there may be fruitful pursuits in examining pieces of modern jazz from the perspective of apocalyptic literature, especially the Book of Revelation.

- In the context of interdisciplinary research, the relationship between ethnomusicological research into jazz culture, particularly concerning African American identity, can be explored with reference to religious history. Perhaps a focus could be given to the translation of white European religious culture into jazz music and how this shaped the social history of American popular culture.

- For jazz and religion, the emergence of jazz worship services and the use of jazz in contemporary Christian music seems to suggest a revival in the style of liturgical jazz or jazz as part of the worshipping community. How jazz is used in contemporary Christian music, especially through song-writing (for example, Hillsong and other forms of particularly evangelical nondenominational forms of worship) remains an underexplored area of research.[55]

- To enhance the approach of this methodology, an international cross-cultural examination of improvisation and jazz would broaden the horizons of biblical interpretation and diversify an understanding of jazz-*as*-culture. How does jazz impact on other popular cultures, particularly in Europe, where jazz also had a lasting impact? One such example would be to examine the British saxophonist Courtney Pine's work "Deuteronomy" from the album *Europa* (2011).

[55] For an inaugural foray into this area of research, see Martyn Percy, "Jazz and Anglican Spirituality: Some Notes on Connections," in *Christian Congregational Music: Performance, Identity and Experience*, ed. Monique Ingalls, Carolyn Landau, and Tom Wagner (London: Routledge, 2016), 67–82.

- A wider theological consideration of improvisation and the nature of the spiritual and religious movements in jazz culture could also be assessed in relation to American culture. While numerous sources have alluded to these materials, a study of the relationship between the Bible and American popular *religion* would add value to the scholarship in general. This chapter has illustrated how jazz and the Bible are intertwined in American popular culture, through social and cultural history and through a new method of how we might think theologically about the liberation of the jazz style through models of representation and canonicity.

SUGGESTED READING AND ANNOTATED BIBLIOGRAPHY

Bivins, Jason. "Shadows on the Wall: Jazz Narrates American Religion." In *Spirits Rejoice! Jazz and American Religion*, 66–111. Oxford: Oxford University Press, 2015.

Bivins's work on jazz and American religion remains one of the most substantial studies in the genre. In this chapter, he illustrates how African American religious history narratives are interpreted and instilled in the cultural memory of jazz musicians. He examines how black sacred history narratives are constructed and how social-political engagement by jazz musicians shaped the music they composed and improvised on. A substantial portion of this chapter develops how "jazz has been shaped by, and partaken in, American narratives about national progress, public life, modernity and religion/secularism" (69). This is achieved by examining notable jazz artists—Charles Mingus, Archie Shepp, Abbey Lincoln, Duke Ellington, and Wynton Marsalis—and their religious or spiritual contexts. It also considers how African American sacred history has been adopted by jazz musicians and how these narratives have been used to generate new meanings through jazz expression. For scholars wishing to develop research in jazz and American culture, Bivins's work is essential reading.

Brown, David. "Blues, Musicals and Opera." In *God and Grace of Body: Sacrament in Ordinary*, 348–86. Oxford: Oxford University Press, 2007.

This chapter forms part of Brown's broader theological task "showing the range of artistic and cultural experience that theology must pay more attention to" (1). Focusing on the sphere of secular music, Brown introduces ways in which religious experience is found outside the church, particularly through the genres of blues, jazz, opera, and musical theater. Although introductory in nature, particularly in reference to jazz, Brown's seminal works on the relationship between theology and the arts are essential for deep theological engagement with contemporary issues in the discipline.

Cheetham, David. "Blues and Jazz." In *The Bloomsbury Handbook of Religion and Popular Music*, edited by Christopher Partridge and Marcus Moberg, 286–93. London: Bloomsbury, 2017.

In this chapter, Cheetham introduces the relationship between jazz and blues, particularly with engagement with the Christian liturgical tradition, contemporary Christian theology, and influences on Muslim jazz musicians. He provides a valuable overview of the origin and development of jazz and blues in both their European and African roots, in addition to the cultural influences that have shaped some of the most notable jazz musicians, including Duke Ellington, Mary Lou Williams, and Abdullah Ibrahim.

Guthrie, Steven R. "Remaking Humanity: John Coltrane and *A Love Supreme*." In *Creator Spirit: The Holy Spirit and the Art of Becoming Human*, 25–45. Grand Rapids, MI: Baker Academic, 2011.

Guthrie's chapter examines the nature of emotion and its connection to spirituality and what this may mean when constructing a theology of the Spirit. He focuses on Coltrane's album *A Love Supreme* and considers how the album succeeds as "an expression of deep passion and spirituality" (30). Guthrie combines musicological analysis of the tracks with a broader rendering of the connection between the "spiritual" character of the album and how that might engage with a deeper understanding of *Spirit*-uality (the work of the Holy Spirit) and "our own deepest and truest humanity" (34). This engagement of spirituality with humanity is developed throughout the chapter, notably using Genesis 2 and Luke 4:16–21, and offers a wider theological significance to aspects of spirituality by employing Christological hermeneutics and applying these to the value of spirituality in *A Love Supreme*.

Heble, Ajay, and Rob Wallace. Introduction to *People Get Ready: The Future of Jazz Is Now!*, 1–28. Durham, NC: Duke University Press, 2013.

This introduction to a wider collection of essays formed from the Guelph Jazz Festival Colloquium represents the status of jazz in contemporary American culture. Responding to the claim that "jazz is dead," Heble and Wallace offer a new interpretation of the nature and influence of jazz music through aesthetic, cultural, and political frameworks. They also offer introductions to critical scholars in jazz research, including Ted Gioia, John Szwed, and George E. Lewis. This book presents an innovative approach to jazz research and combats the examination of jazz culture directed only at historicized narratives.

CHAPTER 20

NONBIBLICAL COMICS ENGAGE THE BIBLE

ELIZABETH RAE COODY
MORNINGSIDE COLLEGE

INTRODUCTION

IN 1954 comics went on trial before the US Congress for corrupting the youth of America.[1] When called upon to defend his industry, the publisher William "Max" Gaines began his defense with the way comics lead "children from pictures to the printed word" and followed this closely by associating comics with the Bible.[2] While this association was probably a gambit to gain sympathy from a primarily Christian Congress, it points to the close association this largely secular medium can claim with the biblical text. Gaines's father, Max C. Gaines, had sold over a million copies of his company's *Picture Stories from the Bible*. The younger Gaines was calling on a real connection between comics and the Bible, one that remains tense but continues to run deeply through comics culture and offers a unique window into the Bible and its perception, treating comics as "instigators and/or transmitters of cultural discourses, values and mores."[3] Even when not directly interpreting the Bible, comics in America engage the Bible, the biblical, and secular and religious understandings of the Bible to tell stories of

---

[1] I follow Scott McCloud's definition of "comics" as a noun "plural in form, used with a singular verb." This precedent is followed by the large number of authors influenced by his work. The "s" helps differentiate "comics" from the comic and comedy. In the notes that follow "w" refers to the "writer" of a comic, "a" indicates the "artist." Scott McCloud (w, a), *Understanding Comics: The Invisible Art* (New York: Kitchen Sink, Harper Perennial, 1994), 9.

[2] Hearings before the Subcommittee to Investigate Juvenile Delinquency of the Committee on the Judiciary of the United States Senate, 83rd Congress, 2nd Session, pursuant to S. 190, Investigation of Juvenile Delinquency in the United States, Juvenile Delinquency (Comic Books), April 21, 22, and June 4, 1954, 97, https://archive.org/details/juveniledelinque54unit.

[3] Dan W. Clanton, Jr., ed., *The End Will Be Graphic: Apocalyptic in Comic Books and Graphic Novels*, Bible in the Modern World, 43 (Sheffield. UK: Sheffield Phoenix Press, 2012), xvi.

a mind-boggling variety including personal narrative, history, journalism, western, fantasy, science fiction, horror, romance, and even superhero.

During World War II, comics was a tremendous and growing publishing industry that dealt with a dizzying array of subjects—from the most grounded instructions to the most far-out fiction.[4] The sales of between eighty million and a hundred million copies every week did not even reflect the way issues (individual comic book magazines) were passed along or traded to between six to ten readers each.[5] Women and racial, ethnic, and social minorities who "turned to comics because they thought of themselves or their ideas as unwelcome in more reputable spheres of publishing and entertainment" found a voice and a place for their art in these near halcyon days.[6] Success attracted detractors.

In the postwar United States, the very existence of the comics industry was under siege by mainstream culture in general, and by educators and religious leaders in particular. Superhero, romance, and horror comics came under particular fire, but quickly anything recognizable as a comic book was threatened.[7] The incendiary popular psychology book *The Seduction of the Innocent* leveled accusations of corrupting the young that fueled the controversy and sometimes literal fires of book burnings. It helped to launch the congressional inquiry into the comic book industry.[8] Some religious authorities were appalled at the violent and sexual content found in too-accessible comics and went after the entire form, meaning that "comics" was blamed for corruption, not just the comics with objectionable content. The whole form gained a reputation for being suspect, far from the hallowed standing of the Bible.

In this chapter, my task is to demonstrate the relationship between the Bible and comics that do not seek to translate the Bible directly into comics form. That is, this chapter is devoted to the comics that treat biblical characters, stories, and subjects outside of the context of the Bible. I suggest that one way comics can be of use to people who study the Bible is to aid their imagination in analyzing the meanings and receptions of these complex texts. More than simply adding illustrations, comics can add new narrative structures, creative approaches, and attention to conceptual concerns in the text and in interpretations.

The categories of Bible and comics have a porous border in several ways. As a book of texts, the Bible can be translated into comics form; when done as a whole, it can be

---

[4] For example, *True Aviation Stories* detailed the key differences between Allied and Axis aircraft, while the fantasy of punching Hitler graced the cover of Captain America's magazine before America entered the war. *True Aviation Picture-Stories* #7, Parents Magazine Institute, Spring 1944, 12–13; Joe Simon (w) and Jack Kirby (a), *Captain America Comics* #1, March 1941, cover. See also Cord Scott, *Comics and Conflict: Patriotism and Propaganda from WWII through Operation Iraqi Freedom* (Annapolis, MD: Naval Institute Press, 2014).

[5] David Hajdu, *The Ten-Cent Plague: The Great Comic-Book Scare and How It Changed America* (New York: Farrar, Straus and Giroux, 2008), 5.

[6] Ibid.   [7] Ibid., 12–17 and *passim*.

[8] Fredric Wertham, *The Seduction of the Innocent* (New York: Rinehart, 1953). See also Carol L. Tilley, "Seducing the Innocent: Fredric Wertham and the Falsifications That Helped Condemn Comics," *Information & Culture: A Journal of History* 47, no. 4 (2012): 383–413.

referred to as a graphic Bible or comics Bible.[9] As texts of some authority in fan cultures, comics too can take on a biblical valence for their participants in that they function with ritual, moral, and communal meaning. Comics can also take inspiration from the biblical text, even when not directly interpreting Bible stories. My work here concentrates on this last category, where comics lend their own tendency toward what Dan Clanton calls "imaginative malleability" to the context, narrative, and characters.[10] That is, comics' tendency to allow multivocal meanings to exist in one text or character are a helpful way to understand biblical hermeneutics.

The "nonbiblical" comics under examination here are the most tenuous and controversial of the types of comics addressed in this volume. The comic strips in newspapers have largely avoided widespread modern condemnation, while direct translations of the Bible in comics form often maintain some of the distance from popular criticism enjoyed by the biblical text itself.[11] Comics or comic books have enjoyed protection by neither form nor subject. Although they share much of the vocabulary of comic strips, these are understood to be more sustained narratives, from the single-issue "floppy" of around twenty-five pages, to long-form web comics, the self-contained graphic novel, and the sweeping, generations-long saga of a single character that lasts decades and crosses many formats.

In his study of the cognitive and linguistic aspects of this language world, Neil Cohn insists, "*Comics are not a language!*…"rather, comics *are written in* visual languages in the same way that novels or magazines *are written in* English."[12] Comics translate ideas into a set of visual languages that opens up interpretive possibilities beyond text-only conversation; these possibilities extend even to the ongoing conversation with the Bible.

Every American literature engages the Bible. Comics can and do treat subjects from the mundane to the intergalactic, but the fantastical milieu of comics is particularly well-suited to supernatural stories. In suggesting this, however, I must be clear: the form of comics does not *require* certain content; it merely has room for more idiosyncratic work in both production and reception.

Comics production is more economical than most film on the whole and allows for more creative license and individual auteur control. Large publishing houses have an editorial staff that can limit comics in their labels, but there is a long history of underground "comix" that has strongly resisted censorship since being driven underground after the comics trials. Participants in the "comix" or "zine" (short for "magazine" or "fanzine") subculture reproduce by whatever available means often explicit comics about taboo topics like sex, drugs, and violence; the advent of easy access to copy machines allowed these small press publications to flourish in independent bookstores and the like. They still question powerful religious mores and figures in a way that, for

---

[9] For an examination of graphic Bibles, see Scott Elliot's chapter in this volume.

[10] Clanton, *The End Will Be Graphic*, xvi.

[11] For an examination of newspaper comic strips, see Leonard Greenspoon's chapter in this volume.

[12] Neil Cohn, *The Visual Language of Comics: Introduction to the Structure and Cognition of Sequential Images*, Bloomsbury Advances in Semiotics (New York: Bloomsbury, 2013), 2, emphasis in original.

example, Hollywood films that command large budgets and tie up vast studios simply cannot afford to do. Comix are more analogous to subculture film work using phone cameras and low to no budget, though the equipment for even the lowest budget film is more expensive than pen and paper. While the form of comics has the ability to contain any content, the fantastical milieu of comics can more easily contain experimental or fringe views of even a revered subject.

As far as their reception, comics have the capacity to give readers more visual data than a radio show or novel, while allowing more narrative specificity than more traditional art by adding text and taking place over time within various kinds of frames. As William Savage claims, comics fall somewhere between radio and screen forms: "Comic books, however accidentally, managed to split the difference. They could show whatever the artist could draw, their lines and colors directing imagination, their balloon-held texts defining time and space."[13]

The meaning-making potential of comics in the United States is located in the difficult confluence of elitism, suspicion, and outright prejudice against the unorthodox ideas of the subculture that produces them. At the meeting of the traditionally lowbrow and the sacred, comics and the Bible are at play.

OVERVIEW OF TOPIC

Scholarship on comics is often done by people from outside of the growing comics studies discipline. Although there are programs specifically in the field, most scholars come from literature, media studies, history, religion, and so on. The field of comics studies thrives on interdisciplinary methods, and methodology continues to be a concern as each brings with it "different research traditions and assumptions."[14] High-quality studies of the Bible and comics are careful not to rely only on points of plot to develop their ideas, but take the context and form of comics into account as well. Attention to the interplay of art and the text can yield complex work that adds value to readings. Scholars must find a way to theorize the visual, as has been done in the field of film studies and the history of art with which comics often share a visual vocabulary. It must matter that a particular story is told in this particular medium, or the study loses much of the depth that is possible in studying comics rather than simply studying fictional characters or stories. The medium, with its combination of pictorial and textual tools, must be understood as central to the message.

For a starting definition of comics, I follow the work of the comics scholar and creator Scott McCloud, because his work focuses on the use of the form rather than content.

[13] William W. Savage, *Commies, Cowboys, and Jungle Queens: Comic Books and America, 1945–1954* (Norman: University of Oklahoma Press, 1990), 7.

[14] Bart Beaty, Scott Bukatman, Henry Jenkins, Benjamin Woo, and Blair Davis (moderator), "Roundtable: Comics and Methodology," *INKS* 1, no. 1 (Spring 2017): 56–74.

McCloud defines comics as "juxtaposed pictorial and other images in deliberate sequence, intended to convey information and/or to produce an aesthetic response in the viewer."[15] His predecessor in comics theory, and a pioneer of the form, Will Eisner, uses the phrase "sequential art" to expand his work outside the pages of the usual comic book.[16] Eisner shows how comics are used in technical instructions, attitudinal instructions, and storyboards; he muses on the possibilities opened up by computer technology (cutting-edge thinking in 1985 that has aged particularly well).[17]

McCloud tightens Eisner's definition of comics but broadens the possible uses. His definition specifies that the sequential art images should also be "juxtaposed," which eliminates film and animation's images-in-succession from consideration.[18] He uses the word "images" rather than Eisner's "art" to avoid any perceived value judgments about content. He adds the descriptor "pictorial" to distinguish comics from text.[19] After all, written words can also be defined as simply juxtaposed images in deliberate sequence. This definition does draw a border around the form that eliminates some familiar things usually called "comics"—the single-panel comic and children's picture books, for example—but it allows McCloud to expand the origins from the usual places and times.[20]

McCloud's definition has room for improvement. Robert C. Harvey insists that this definition relies too heavily on the place of pictures and does not account for the obvious importance of the interplay of text in comics. Rather than seeing sequence at the heart of comics, Harvey sees " 'blending' verbal and visual content" as more important to comics' function as a form.[21]

Finding more social boundaries for what counts as comics helps some writers narrow down the field of study to a more manageable (although still tremendous) size. David Kunzle defines the "comic strip" more precisely for his historical work on the medium as

---

[15] McCloud, *Understanding Comics*, 9.

[16] Will Eisner, *Comics and Sequential Art* (Tamarac, FL: Poorhouse, 1985), 7.   [17] Ibid., 142–6.

[18] McCloud, *Understanding Comics*, 7.   [19] Ibid., 8.

[20] Children's books and single-panel comics are not small omissions. Without McCloud's very severe border, many children's books might be considered simply word-specific comics narratives. Popular single-panel comics include Gary Larson's *Far Side* (New York: Chronicle Features and Universal Press Syndicate, 1980–95); Bil Keane and later Jeff Keane's iconic *The Family Circus* (New York: King Features Syndicate, 1960– Present); the staggering number of single-panel comics featured over the years in the *New Yorker* magazine (New York: Condé Nast, 1925–Present); and the worldwide and long-standing popularity of single-panel political cartoons. Also of use in this discussion is Dylan Horrocks's report on McCloud's confrontation with R. C. Harvey in an interview for *Comics Journal*, in which McCloud argues that picture books cannot be comics if they are dominated by text rather than pictures. Keeping with his definition, one would expect that as long as there are two pictures in sequence, a work can be a comic. McCloud is not willing to concede the point. As Horrocks concludes, "In effect, McCloud has added an amendment to his definition: comics must not only *contain* pictorial narrative; they must be *dominated* by it." See Horrocks, "Inventing Comics: Scott McCloud's Definition of Comics," *Comics Journal*, no. 234 (2001): 29.

[21] Robert C. Harvey, "Comedy at the Juncture of Word and Image: The Emergence of the Modern Magazine Gag Cartoon Reveals the Vital Blend," in *The Language of Comics: Word and Image*, ed. Robbin Varnum and Christian T. Gibbons (Jackson: University Press of Mississippi, 2001), 76.

being a sequence, dominated by images over text, mass media, and "moral and topical" story.[22]

I hesitate to endorse his last criterion in full because of the difficulties in judging which stories are either moral or topical. Kunzle's attention to the social position of comics for his study is warranted but also reveals the complexity of positioning comics precisely over time in different social and technological contexts.

One peculiar characteristic of comics is the plethora of formats in which they come. The exact same group of a few panels can form a comic strip; a part of a comic book in an issue, trade, and digital format; and might also be classified or collected with other issues as a graphic novel. Graphic novels are bound comic books with a defined beginning and end (even if they are part of a larger story). They are usually longer than the approximately twenty-five pages of an issue and are considered part of the book trade rather than the magazine trade. They are generally (although certainly not exclusively) marketed as the more "literary" or "sophisticated" comics form, but it is difficult to make these kinds of style and content judgments when dealing with a format issue. The economies of print-based mass reproduction influence the form around page count, paper stock size, print run or edition size, color, and so on. However, meaningful content and serious skill can be packaged in even the most modest forms.

To make matters more complicated, there is no industry standard for the application of the term "graphic novel." As Hatfield explains, a graphic novel "can be almost anything: a novel, a collection of interrelated or thematically similar stories, a memoir, a travelogue or journal, a history, a series of vignettes or lyrical observations, an episode from a longer work—you name it."[23] Although it began as a name for a format, "graphic novel" is instead "an all-purpose tag for a vague new class or social object, one that, unlike the 'comic book,' need not be grounded in the exact specifications of a given physical format."[24] This uncertainty about format points to a whole other set of factors around the use of the term.

The practice of using the term "graphic novel" for a particular format sprang from comics' struggle for cultural legitimacy. Eisner used it to refer to his *Contract with God* trilogy in the first widely recognized example. It was when the phrase "a graphic novel by Will Eisner" appeared on the cover of *A Contract with God* that the term gained general use.[25] Although others had used the terms "graphic novel" and "graphic story" before, "Eisner apparently believed that he had coined a new term, out of desperation to market his book."[26] He used the term to claim a certain legitimacy for his work dealing with religious and theological topics. Some authors balk at the use of the term at all. The

---

[22] David Kunzle, *The Early Comic Strip: Narrative Strips and Picture Stories in the European Broadsheet from c. 1450 to 1825*, vol. 1 of *History of the Comic Strip* (Berkeley: University of California Press, 1973), 2.

[23] Charles Hatfield, *Alternative Comics: An Emerging Literature* (Jackson: University Press of Mississippi, 2005), 153.

[24] Ibid., 5.

[25] Will Eisner (w, a), *A Contract with God: A Graphic Novel* (New York: Baronet Books, 1978).

[26] Hatfield, *Alternative Comics*, 165.

underground comics guru Robert Fiore claims this "semantic jiggery-pokery" is "a reflection of the industry's yearning for unearned status."[27] Certainly the industry and fans have not moved to create a more exact meaning for the term, making it almost always useless in determining what kind or quality of comics a piece might be.

Questions of origins are often more useful for understanding the researcher than the actual history of comics, but there are some possibilities to consider. The prehistory of comics can show how the form functions, especially as religious. By applying his definition, McCloud traces the history of comics back to a thirty-six-foot-long, pre-Columbian screen-fold depicting the military and political exploits of the hero "Eight Deer 'Tiger's-Claw'" (made ca. 1049 CE) and the Bayeux Tapestry's presentation of the Norman Conquest (made ca. 1070 CE).[28] McCloud's interest in function means that his ideas about the first comics are concerned with how they work, using juxtaposed images in sequence to convey meaning.

Longer-form comic books have more space than newspaper strips, along with an opportunity for extended irony and metaphorical work. The Ledger Syndicate published a small broadside of their Sunday color comics on 7-by-9-inch plates in 1933. Later that year, salesman Max C. Gaines and sales manager Harry I. Wildeberg bound these into a 7½-by-10-inch book as a promotional premium for Procter and Gamble.[29] The result was *Funnies on Parade*, and the modern comic book was born. Gaines took the idea into several other early comics ventures. David Hajdu reports that Gaines was an overbearing showman who claimed that *his* comics had a direct connection to cave paintings, Sumerian mosaics, and Kozanji scrolls.[30] Gaines's short treatise on the subject, *Narrative Illustration: The Story of Comics*, was part of his promotional materials for the comic *Picture Stories from the Bible*.[31] From these early days, comics was connected to reading and reinterpreting the Bible, even if only to lend comics some of the Bible's gravitas and respectability.

Another avenue along which to pursue origins would be to trace comics from the development of the industry in North America. The industry developed into workshops and publishing houses that after some time have coalesced into a few major studios (DC, Marvel, and, lately, Image) that dwarf their more independent competition.[32] The steep

---

[27] Robert Fiore, "Comics for Beginners: Some Notes for the Newcomer," in *New Comics: Interviews from the Pages of the Comics Journal*, ed. Robert Fiore and Gary Groth (New York: Berkeley, 1988), 5.

[28] McCloud, *Understanding Comics*, 10, 12.

[29] M. Thomas Inge, *Comics as Culture* (Jackson: University Press of Mississippi, 1990), 139.

[30] Although similar claims have merit in other sources, Gaines's inflated evidence and totalizing tone make it unconvincing. For a more measured brief treatment of the relationship of comics and cave paintings, see Stephen Weiner, "Ancient Times to 1920: The Evolution of Sequentially Imaged Narratives," in *Critical Survey of Graphic Novels: History, Theme, and Technique*, ed. Bart H. Beaty and Stephen Weiner (Ipswich, MA: Salem Press, 2013), 3–6.

[31] Hajdu, *Ten-Cent Plague*, 73.

[32] Shirrel Rhoades, *A Complete History of American Comic Books* (New York: Peter Lang, 2008), 15, 33, 268.

fluctuations in profitability, often strong personalities, and hard-to-justify hiring practices have kept the industry lean and the history extremely difficult to trace accurately.[33]

Of course, accounting for the mainstream industry does not account for underground comics ("comix" or the X-rated "comixxx"). Much of the subversive possibility of comics comes from the way they escape industry and market standards. Self-publishers and independent creators still proliferate the field. In fact, web comics and self-publishing programs like Comixology Submit! have further lowered the barriers of publication. In these underground spaces, the limits are only those imposed by creators' imagination, ability, and willingness to censor themselves.

Creators can play with sacred and revered ideas with near impunity. The exceptions to this freedom often circle around explicitly forbidden religious images. Outside—or on the fringes of—the industry and major publishing houses, comics can confront whatever the creator wants. They can operate independently from their origins and restrictions. Such a scattered and unruly form does not easily fit any industry-driven definition.

Comics and religion cannot stay away from each other. This relative freedom of expression presents the opportunity for religion and comics to enter into dialogue.[34] The resulting back-and-forth is not always respectful on either side, but the conflict is both fascinating and instructive. Religion can enter comics in a scandalous way—inspiring religious ire, pillorying mainstream religious mores, or simply putting a twist on religious figures that are already established in the mainstream mind. When this happens, comics reveal the limits and borders of the religious imagination.

Appropriate to a discussion of an iconic book like the Bible, comic book art is *often* by design more "iconic" than other images. It is ill advised to make any overly general claims about the art of comics.[35] However, pictures in comics often repeat over and over to convey narratives. This repetition lends itself to simplification and symbolization, toward what is often practically called an *icon*. Like McCloud, I use the term here simply "to mean any image used to represent a person, place, thing or idea."[36] So comics are in the habit of using icons to call to mind subjects that may resemble the subjects they wish to invoke more or less. The Bible is one of the great wells of this sort of iconography for the comic book world and literature in general. The Bible itself—as icon or model for other special books, biblical plots, and biblical characters—is regular fodder for comics stories.

---

[33] Cf. Clifford Meth, *Comic Book Babylon: The Real Villains and Heroes of Comics* (Rockaway, NJ: Aardwolf, 2013); Amy Kiste Nyberg, *Seal of Approval: The History of the Comics Code* (Jackson: University of Mississippi, 1998); Hajdu, *Ten-Cent Plague, passim.*

[34] For more on popular culture and religion in dialogue, see Bruce David Forbes, "Introduction: Finding Religion in Unexpected Places," in *Religion and Popular Culture in America*, 3rd ed., ed. Bruce David Forbes and Jeffery H. Mahan (Oakland: University of California Press, 2017), 11–21.

[35] Art in comics can include any style and is not even limited to two dimensions. Chris Ware moves comic art into three dimensions in his *Building Stories* (New York: Pantheon Books, 2012).

[36] McCloud, *Understanding Comics*, 27.

First, the Bible itself as a cultural object affords a certain iconicity. From ancient Jewish and Christian art up to contemporary religious practice, the presence of the Bible is often representative of the presence of God or Jesus.[37] In secular and religious circles, a Bible can simply be taken to represent the presence of a certain understanding of an amalgamation of Christian and Jewish religions or some vague notion of the religious.

Generally, a dark, specially bound codex in a particular context can represent far more than the sacred text itself. It includes the creator's or audience's emotional and cultural understanding of the religious. Because comics work by the interplay of image and text, the image of a Bible or Bible-type book can be left to the reader's imagination, or the relationship can be spelled out in the text. In too many comics to list, Bibles appear to signal that a character has a relationship to organized religion. For example, Nightcrawler, also called Kurt Wagner, a blue-furred mutant member of the X-Men, reads from a Bible and carries a rosary to remind readers that despite his devilish appearance he has a deep religious faith.[38] More often, Bibles are simply a visual marker of certain ceremonies: weddings and funerals are almost always led by people holding a Bible. The icon is a visual mark of a widely understood culturally ceremony.

The Bible can also be used as a model for "alternative Bibles" like "Gideon's Bible," a book named after the starship whose story it tells that is constantly being stolen and retrieved from all around the Marvel Comics' Universe. It is incredibly hard to read, but it contains knowledge that—once transformed into a device called the "Wonder Toy"— helps to cure a planet of humans called the "Loonies" of madness.[39] The creators show how a difficult book can be valuable and restorative, even to a large population; the power of this Bible is understood literally. The presentation of countless books of real magic is inspired by the iconography of the Bible. In the DC series 52, the Crime Bible serves as an anti-Bible; its prophetic power for the criminal underworld inspires them to greater horrors and urges the leadership to take on Batwoman as the fulfillment of destiny. The book is made of stone, reportedly the stone that Cain used to kill Abel, and takes crime boss Bruno Manheim and his Intergang beyond crime as a means toward crime as an end in itself: "Crime is the moral standard, the universal principle, the natural successor to free market capitalism." His followers must swear on the blood-spattered Bible or die; in the introduction of the stone book to the audience, Manheim bashes a fellow villain's head on the book while it lies closed and chained on its lectern.[40] This very literal alternative Bible shows an understanding of the text as guide and ruler of

[37] Dorina Miller Parmenter, "The Bible as Icon: Myths of the Divine Origin of Scripture," in *Jewish and Christian Scripture as Artifact and Canon*, ed. Craig A. Evans and H. Daniel Zacharias, Studies in Scripture in Early Judaism and Christianity 13, Library of Second Temple Studies 70 (New York: T & T Clark, Continuum, 2009), 298–310.

[38] Given this history, it is important that he is the one who finds an alien race's "bible"—an energy crystal that tries to convert him to this alien's religious system—which is eventually used as a secret weapon to help turn back the same aliens' invasion of Earth. See Mike Carey (w), Ma Sepulveda (a), "Manifest Destiny," *Secret Invasion: X-Men* #3, Marvel, October 29, 2008.

[39] Bill Mantlo (w), Mike Mignola (a), "The Age of Enlightenment," *Rocket Raccoon* #4, Marvel, 1985.

[40] Geoff Johns (w), Grant Morrison (w), Greg Rucka (w), Mark Waid (w), and Keith Giffen (a). "Week Twenty-Five," *52*, vol. 2 (New York: DC, 2013), 252–3.

behavior. Intergang is full of people of the book with a fundamentalist fervency that the creator of the comic wishes to point out or lampoon in the followers of the Bible.

Comics may take on a "biblical aspect" with encoded typeface, format, or language. Narrative boxes can be the "voice of God"—explaining the significance or activities of characters from an omniscient perspective. This can be part of the narrative or literally quoting biblical text. In the beautifully painted comic *Kingdom Come*, generations of superheroes come into conflict before an apocalyptic event.[41] The opening narrative boxes look like torn parchment with a gothic-style typeface. They are overlaid on a ghastly collage of just what they describe: conflict, storm, a great star falling to earth, and above all, a red-washed vague "WOE." Naturally, the words are taken from the book of Revelation. Throughout, the Bible enters into the story as a guiding text, and as Terry Ray Clark argues, *Kingdom Come* serves as a prophetic and apocalyptic text. In a secular genre, it functions in practice as a sacred text that offers hope "if humanity will reject the temptation to despair or to embrace violence as the only solution to human conflict."[42] The message that humans can move forward if we focus on our commonalities gives this book characteristics of a Bible.

Many comics reimagine biblical themes and symbols in their narratives. The symbol of the cross is an easily recognizable and widely used trope. In 1982 Chris Claremont and Brent Anderson created an X-men graphic novel called *God Loves, Man Kills* that connected the crucifixion of the white male leader of the mutant X-men, Charles Xavier, and the lynching of two African American mutant children.[43] Claremont wishes the reader to recall Jesus and connect his suffering to both the children and Xavier; his caption at the start of the mutant leader's crucifixion is "And they bring him unto the place Golgotha...and they crucify him."[44] The scene is depicted in shades of red that suggest both that it is taking place in Xavier's mindscape and the horror of having a salvific figure in peril. Claremont (a white writer) made a connection between the cross and the lynching tree that black theologian James Cone shows white biblical scholars and theologians consistently fail to imagine.[45]

Using the Passion as a plot-point in another narrative here suggests the use of biblical plots in nonbiblical narratives. This has a porous border with "Bible comics"; that is, it is

---

[41] Mark Waid (w) and Alex Ross (a), *Kingdom Come*, Elseworlds, DC Comics, May 1996.

[42] Terry Ray Clark, "Prophetic Voices in Graphic Novels: The 'Comic and Tragic Vision' of Apocalyptic Rhetoric in *Kingdom Come* and *Watchmen*," in *The Bible in/and Popular Culture: A Creative Encounter*, ed. Philip Culbertson and Elaine M. Wainwright, Semeia Studies 65 (Atlanta, GA: Society of Biblical Literature, 2010), 152.

[43] For an analysis of this graphic novel in conversation with scholarship on Bible and religion and violence, see Dan W. Clanton, Jr., "'Because You Exist': Biblical Literature and Violence in the X-Men Comic Books," in *Theology and the Marvel Universe*, ed. Gregory Stevenson (Lanham, MD: Lexington Books, 2020), 55-70.

[44] Chris Claremont (w), Brent Eric Anderson (a), and Steve Oliff (i), *X-Men: God Loves, Man Kills: Special Edition* (New York: Marvel Comics Group, 1982), n.p.

[45] Clearly, one comic does not overturn Cone's point that not making this connection is a defect in the white conscience and a failure of white imagination. This is an exception that proves the rule. See James H. Cone, *The Cross and the Lynching Tree* (Maryknoll, NY: Orbis, 2011), 32.

difficult to suggest hard limits for when a comic goes from simply using a biblical plot to actually being a biblical comic or a Bible comic. Douglas Rushkoff's *Testament* is a modern sci-fi story with some obvious texts from the Bible—notably the sacrifice of Isaac (called the "Akedah" by Jews, which is also the title of the first graphic novel collection of this comics series)—woven directly into the story both narratively and visually. Gods are at play in the spaces between the panels (called "gutters"), while the stories of two fathers, Abraham and a modern scientist, being asked to sacrifice their sons run side by side, panel by panel.[46] While similar things go on in other media, only comics has the particular visual language to weave these stories in quite this way.

Comics may also contain more implicit references to biblical themes. These might be more metaphorical than literal, for example, the Marvel character Apocalypse, who employs a rotating cast of four henchmen referred to as his "Four Horsemen." Apocalypse personified is a muscular purple-blue-gray-skinned mutant. He wants to establish a world for superpowered Mutants, not a Kingdom of God, but the idea of a new world for a special people is in both stories. A more widely acknowledged example of an implicit biblical reference in comics is the many narrative parallels Superman shares with Moses, such as being sent to Earth in a spaceship and being sent down the Nile in a bulrush basket, saving everyday people from wicked crime bosses or Egyptian tyrants.[47] Like any work of literature, scholars mine these works for their religious themes whether or not the creators intended them.[48]

Biblical characters are often a literal part of the narrative. Characters who are read back into the Bible can be developed in comics and move past their origins. Lucifer or the Morningstar appears as a metaphor for the king of Babylon in Isaiah 14:12. The Accuser character (transliterated "Satan") appears in Job and Chronicles, but the character name has taken on a whole host of meanings across cultures that far outstrip its biblical references.[49] Comics allows for this development over long-form stories. In *The Sandman* (1989–96) series and the subsequent spin-off series *Lucifer* (2000–2006), Lucifer begins as the leader of hell but moves on to run a piano bar. Additionally, Samson shows up in various DC titles. The strong man has apparently escaped the temple of Dagon and has returned to his long-haired strapping persona (Judges 16:4–30). In *All-Star Superman*, for example, he pals around with Superman and Atlas and vies (unsuc-

[46] Douglas Rushkoff (w), Liam Sharp (a), *Testament* (New York: D.C. Comics, Vertigo, 2006–8).

[47] For a challenge to the idea of a Jewish Superman, see, Martin Lund, *Re-constructing the Man of Steel: Superman 1938–1941, Jewish American History, and the Invention of the Jewish-Comics Connection*, Contemporary Religion and Popular Culture (New York: Palgrave Macmillan, 2016). For more on Superman's religious valences, see, Dan W. Clanton, "The Origin(s) of Superman: Reimagining Religion in the Man of Steel," in Forbes and Mahan, *Religion and Popular Culture in America*, 33–50.

[48] See, e.g., Robert Jewett and William Sloane Coffin, *The Captain America Complex: The Dilemma of Zealous Nationalism* (Santa Fe, NM: Bear, 1984); John T. Galloway, *The Gospel According to Superman* (Philadelphia, PA: A. J. Holman, 1973); Robert L. Short, *The Gospel According to Peanuts* (1965; Louisville, KY: Westminster John Knox Press, 2000); and B. J. Oropeza, *The Gospel According to Superheroes: Religion and Pop Culture* (New York: Peter Lang, 2005).

[49] See Miguel A. De La Torre and Albert Hernández, *The Quest for the Historical Satan* (Minneapolis, MN: Fortress, 2011).

cessfully) for the love of a super Lois Lane. "By Yahweh," he vows, "I've fought the good fight across three galaxies and countless centuries, but I've never met a woman like you, Lois Lane."[50]

Some comic artists perform acts of "transvaluation"—that is, "demoting" the characters of the Bible from their religious "grandeur yet investing them with a 'texture' of common humanity" and putting them in a distinctly lowbrow format.[51] For example, the slumping, nose-picking Jesus in the series *Battle Pope* is rendered as the ne'er-do-well sidekick for the divinely superpowered, corrupt, and lecherous pontiff.[52] The series' creator, Robert Kirkman, is hardly alone in this practice of including Jesus in a nonbiblical comic; *Comic Book Religion*, a site devoted to tracking the religious affiliations of characters in comics, has identified 166 distinct comic book appearances of Jesus Christ across multiple publishers and titles.[53] Rather than delve into this as part of the overview, I want to use Jesus as an example of what nonbiblical comics can do with and for the interpretation of a biblical character.

Specific Examples and/or Foci

In order to demonstrate the mutually reinforcing process of how the Bible informs comics and then how comics can inform a view of the Bible, I will focus on the miracle-working power of Jesus. Jesus performs supernatural acts in the gospels that include various kinds of control over nature. Since the Enlightenment, however, the view of these acts in the West has split largely, though not cleanly, along liberal and conservative lines. Liberal Christianity distanced itself from "superstition" while various groups of conservatives insist on the literal truth of miracles, refitting them with scientific-sounding explanations.[54] In comics, miracles have never gone out of style.

Through comics, one can approach the ubiquity of the miraculous from several directions, but I have chosen to focus specifically on Jesus taking on the properties normally associated with superheroes. That is, when Jesus shows up in comics with miraculous

[50] Grant Morrison (w), Frank Quitely (a), Jamie Grant (i), "Sweet Dreams, Super Woman," *All-Star Superman* #3, vol. 1 (New York: DC Comics, 2007), 64.

[51] Gerard Genette, *Palimpsests: Literature in the Second Degree*, trans. Channa Newman and Claude Doubinsky (1982; Lincoln: University of Nebraska, 1997), 367.

[52] Robert Kirkman (w), Tony Moore (a), and Val Staples (l), *Battle Pope*, vol. 1: *Genesis* (Berkeley, CA: Image Comics, 2009). Kirkman is now much better known as the creator of *The Walking Dead* comics series.

[53] The site claims *Justice League of America* #40 (November 1965) as the first appearance of Jesus in US comics. This issue features historical cameos by Moses, Christ, Confucius, Mohammed, and Buddha. "The Religious Affiliation of Jesus Christ/Jesus of Nazareth," *Comic Book Religion*, accessed May 28, 2013, http://www.comicbookreligion.com/?c=888&Jesus_Christ_Jesus_of_Nazareth.

[54] For a discussion of the fight over the Bible during and after the Enlightenment, see Stephen D. Moore and Yvonne Sherwood, *The Invention of the Biblical Scholar: A Critical Manifesto* (Minneapolis, MN: Fortress, 2011), 95, *passim*.

power, I argue that those powers reveal a modern anxiety about supernatural activity and a high level of violence that further shows the trouble that is assumed when natural forces are disturbed. The visual and textual nature of comics can add layers of subversion to this anxiety.

Jesus stories all involve a Jesus, but they can do so in vastly different ways. In order to sort out the different ways these stories are told, I have drawn the language of "Jesus-story" and "Christ-figure" from film study by W. Barnes Tatum, with some modifications for this work, as well as Dan W. Clanton, Jr.'s use of Jesus in Elseworlds.[55] Outside of this scope are graphic Bibles that explicitly interpret the biblical text and would naturally have a Jesus character. The two remaining categories of comics I focus on are Jesus-story comics and Christ-figure comics.

Alternative Jesus-story comics use the character of Jesus sometimes in his own time and place and sometimes displaced into another time, place, and even body.[56] Clanton calls this "Jesus in Elseworlds" after the DC Comic Elseworlds imprint.[57] In the comics, established characters are dropped into new settings with various levels of similarity to their usual worlds and the readers' world.[58] The series makes sense even when stories start in medias res because the characters, like Superman and Batman, are so well established in the readers' minds.[59] The twist throws the character's usual attitudes and situations into relief. Jesus in Elseworlds consists of stories that take Jesus, a well-established character in the popular imagination, and throw him into new situations with familiar characteristics tweaked, exaggerated, or excised. These altered and adapted Jesus-story comics force "consumers of pop culture and perhaps even religious believers to develop...understandings of Jesus, either against them or in dialogue with them."[60]

Christ-figure stories use other characters, events, or images to "substantially recall, or resemble, the story of Jesus"; for example, the sacrificial death of Superman fits this cat-

---

[55] I use the hyphenated constructions in deference to Tatum's scheme and to keep the terms clear. See W. Barnes Tatum, *Jesus at the Movies: A Guide to the First Hundred Years*, 3rd ed. (Santa Rosa, CA: Polebridge, 2015), 315.

[56] See, for example, Jimmy Blondell (w), David Krintzman (w), and Nicholas Da Silva (a), *Black Jesus* (Coquitlam, BC, Canada: Arcana Comics, 2009); Frank Stack (w, a), *The New Adventures of Jesus: The Second Coming* (Seattle: Fantagraphics Books, 2006); Ted McKeever (w, a), *Miniature Jesus* (Berkeley, CA: Image, Shadowline, 2013); Stephen Lindsay (w), Michael Bartolotta (w), Lauren Mohardo, et al. (a), *Jesus Hates Zombies: Those Slack-Jaw Blues* (Levittown, NY: Alterna Comics, 2009); Sean Murphy (w, a), Todd Klein (l), *Punk Rock Jesus*, #1–6 (New York: Vertigo, 2013); Shawn French (w), Mortimer Glum (a), Peeter Parkker (i), Rachel Leon (l), *Escape from Jesus Island* (N.p.: Wisdum Publications, 2014–); Tim Seeley (w), Nate Bellegarde (p), Mike Norton (p), Mark Englert (i), Joseph Baker (i), Melissa S. Kaercher (i), *Loaded Bible, Book I: The Jesus vs. Vampires Gospels* (Berkeley, CA: Image Comics, 2010).

[57] Dan W. Clanton, Jr., " 'Here, There, and Everywhere': Images of Jesus in American Popular Culture," in Culbertson and Wainwright, *The Bible in/and Popular Culture*, 42.

[58] For example, Mark Waid (w) and Alex Ross (a), *Kingdom Come*, Elseworlds (New York: DC Comics, 1997); and Alan Brennert (w), Norm Breyfogle (a), Lovern Kindzierski (i), and Bill Oakley (l), *Batman: Holy Terror*, Elseworlds (New York: DC Comics, 1991).

[59] Marvel Comics has a similar series called What If? that uses their own stable of characters.

[60] Clanton, " 'Here, There, and Everywhere,' " 57.

egory.[61] The interest in the phenomenon of Christ in spandex is widespread. Superheroes take on the troubling matter of living in the world and being not quite of it in a decades-long demonstration fit for the Council of Nicaea. Umberto Eco traces the way that Superman balances the "narrative paradox" of being both a timeless myth and a person who lives in the world.[62] His powers are as plastic as any in comics—as he moves from being able to leap tall buildings in a single bound, to flight, to intergalactic and interdimensional flight, Superman's ability set evolves to defy possibilities as human abilities expand.

Comparing Jesus to Christ-figure superheroes in fiction and in criticism is an old pastime in the United States. In the February 1943 issue of *Catholic World*, Rev. Thomas E. Doyle's "What's Wrong with Comics?" makes clear that he wants comics to keep their distance from what he perceives as the domain of the church. He distrusts the otherworldliness, supernaturalism, "weird names and still weirder attributes" of popular superheroes like the Flash and Hawkman. He is troubled that their "untold power" to "defy natural laws" makes superheroes "false cartoon gods."[63] Doyle wants the church to retain control over the supernatural, but he sees it slipping into the hands of secular artists and writers. Worse, Jesus is going out of style: "Like it or not, there are plenty of American children who know more about the man-wonder Superman than they do about Christ or any of the great characters of the Bible."[64] These Christ-figure tropes are widespread.

When Jesus-story comics depict miracles, they often address the logic of "powers" or "super abilities" in the same style they would a more conventional superhero. The following counterpoint from a graphic Bible helps to show the contrast with a Jesus-story in nonbiblical comics. In the graphic Bible *The Action Bible,* the depiction is as distant from the "action" comic as is possible.[65] Jesus simply hovers as he walks on water, touches people when he heals, or waves his hands when he calms the storm without visual cues that something supernatural is happening. Rather than use the tools of the form—symbols for movement, different coloring, or perhaps simply different perspectives—this comic does nothing to *show* the miraculous. It is often difficult to tell that anything out of the ordinary has happened in this colorful yet mundane action comics setting.

In contrast, readers cannot miss the miracles in the offbeat Jesus-story comic *Jesus Christ: In the Name of the Gun.*[66] The sketchy and harsh black-and-white style suits the action-packed narrative well. Eric Peterson insists that the web comic attracted a suffi-

---

[61] Dan Jurgens (w, a), Brett Breeding (a), "Doomsday," *Superman* #75, vol. 2 (New York: DC Comics, November 1992).

[62] Umberto Eco, "The Myth of Superman" (1962), in *Arguing Comics: Literary Masters on a Popular Medium*, ed. Jeet Heer and Kent Worcester (Jackson: University Press of Mississippi, 2004), 151.

[63] Hajdu, *Ten-Cent Plague*, 81.   [64] Doyle, quoted in ibid., 82.

[65] Doug Mauss (w), Sergio Cariello (a), *The Action Bible: God's Redemptive Story* (Colorado Springs, CO: David C. Cook, 2010).

[66] Eric Peterson (w) and Ethan Nicolle (w, a), *Jesus Christ: In the Name of the Gun*, vol. 1: *A Hollow Cost* (N.p.: Bad Karma Productions, 2009).

cient "cult following" to indicate a receptive audience exists for a violent, time-traveling Jesus adventure story.[67]

Certainly there are other violent alternative Jesuses in Jesus-story comics. A. David Lewis presents those from *Battle Pope* and *Chronicles of Wormwood* as surprisingly devout presentations of Jesus, though "altogether sacrilegious works."[68] *Battle Pope* plays its Jesus as an incapable, feminized sidekick to the hypermasculine, promiscuous pontiff in their fight against demons, whereas Peterson goes hyperviolent with his savior. Peterson's cigar-chomping, foul-mouthed grump of a Jesus starts out bored, languishing in heaven with vacuous cherubim as his only company. God appears as the giant, floating head of Marlon Brando as his character Jor-El, as seen first in *Superman: The Movie* (1978).[69] He cannot answer for the tragedies of the twentieth century. Jesus expresses guilt over the failure of what he calls his "salvation thing" and decides to return to Earth to set things right, this time with guns blazing. His first idea is to kill Hitler. He goes to right human wrong, but finds that humanity's major problem is supernatural in nature: Hitler is a werewolf. Ultimate evil is not humanity's fault.

The overall voice of the comic is mocking and humorous. Although Jesus here has a seriously drawn gun and is an action hero, it is important to note how tongue-in-cheek the whole comic is. These are not the sterile action heroics as drawn in *The Action Bible*. This book is having fun with an over-the-top violent Jesus, placing a loosely drawn cartoon hypermasculine Jesus alongside a ridiculous hypermasculine Ernest Hemingway in a swashbuckling time-travel escapade for mature readers; this is not an educational tool for young Christians.

In the Name of the Gun shows how physical and natural processes can become absurd when they encounter the supernatural. This book takes the idea that heavenly miracles have earthly consequences to an uncomfortable but crudely amusing extreme. The comic takes humorous delight in the puerile and disgusting possibilities of taking the physical beyond natural bounds—both as juvenile jokes and as weapons. The first miracle in the comic is Jesus walking, or rather running, on water down a Berlin canal on his way to kill Hitler. But he does not just run on canal water. He steps up a Nazi soldier's urine stream to kick him in the face, offering a ribald action-movie-style quip while standing over his bloody face. Peterson turns each of the miracles his Jesus performs into gross weapons. By "multiply[ing] the shit out of the loaves," Jesus is able to explode a group of Nazi soldiers who have some of it in their stomachs. His blood has the power to resurrect dead people and animals and even bring to life inanimate mutant Nazi beasts, but at a cost—every time he resurrects something Jesus succumbs to what he calls "fecal incontinence." Most of the comic after this revelation is dominated by a series of battle scenes with poop jokes. This is not sophisticated humor, but it brings an element of

---

[67]   Eric Peterson, "About," *Jesus Christ Story*, 2008, accessed January 5, 2015, http://jesuschriststory.com. This site reports at one point having twenty-five thousand visitors.

[68]   A. David Lewis, "(Ir)reverence after Rapture: Mocking and Maintaining Christian Doctrine in *Battle Pope, Chronicles of Wormwood*, and *Therefore, Repent!*," in Clanton, *The End Will Be Graphic*, 44.

[69]   *Superman*, directed by Richard Donner, USA, Warner Bros., 1978.

fleshly consequences to supernatural powers. The book consistently favors considering scatology over soteriology. This depiction of miracles reveals an anxiety with the physicality of divinity that is characteristic of post-Enlightenment modernity. The miraculous here is a zero-sum game; if Jesus wants to resurrect himself, he must pay a physical price.

In the New Testament gospels, there are no visuals to aid in imagination. When Jesus walks on water, multiplies loaves, or resurrects Lazarus, there are hardly any textual clues to what this looks like. There are reactions from those around the miracles— amazement, for example (Matt 8:27, 9:33, 15:31, 21:20; Mark 2:12, 5:20)—but not much to go on. Because the pictorial nature of comics asks for some sort of depiction of the miracles, Jesus's signs and wonders require visuals. The long history of superheroes would suggest that it could be done more cleanly, but Peterson has taken the physical to the extreme in a way that does hone in on anxiety about the consequences of having a Jesus who is both human and miraculous. These are only a narrow sample of the variety of Jesus comics that treat the character outside of the Bible. Comics has a visual vocabulary for miracles that allows for uncomfortable but trenchant interpretations even in the most extreme examples.

CONCLUSION

Superhero stories, even biblical ones, are not the only subject of American comics; comics treat a diverse and varied set of subjects, genres, and tastes, including the Bible and biblical characters. The form combines the textual and the visual in a variety of formats. Scholars who study the reception of the Bible will be rewarded by new interpretive possibilities when they attend to comics outside of the strictly biblical and find the alternative perspective. Comics deal with ideas of creation, sin, judgment, redemption, sacrifice, and other theological themes in single issues, considered arcs, and generations-long character struggles. Because the form and its independent industry is open to and even encourages new and weird ideas, the study of nonbiblical comics can engage in religious ideas in fresh ways.

This study kept close to the idea of the Bible while treating the nonbiblical, but comics offers as many opportunities for literary engagement as do other forms of storytelling. Comics have been building a tremendous library in America for over one hundred years, but until recently they have not enjoyed scholarly attention in the same way as other popular forms. Comics, even nonbiblical comics, have been closely associated with the Bible from their beginning. They share the rest of American media's engagement with the Bible with an added layer of their search for artistic and cultural legitimacy. Comics are not a language, but they do insist on a way of reading that engages visual attention in fascinating ways. The study of the Word will benefit from attention to the way word and image blend in comics.

FUTURE PROSPECTS AND QUESTIONS

- What counts as a Bible in comics, and what do these Bibles do? Can this perception of the Bible change or challenge the way scholars understand relationships to the text?
- What communities accept comics that present portions of the Bible or characters from the Bible as the "real" Bible? What counts as a "real" Bible for different communities? How do the understandings of what a "real" Bible is affect the ways in which readers interpret comics that render the Bible or biblical themes?
- Are presentations of biblical material in nonbiblical comics using it as an iconic or fetish object rather than a book? Is the Bible still treated like a book in these situations? What else is it or could it be? What can the use of the biblical in these generally secular situations tell us about attitudes toward the text generally?
- The serial nature of comics, its "narrative flexibility," as Dan Clanton names it, offers insight into the way the biblical text can mean differently across time and for different communities. That opens a whole range of questions about the perception of the biblical text as both flexible and unchanging.
- Comics often function like religious texts for their devotees. The "fanboy" subculture, with its rituals and festivals (like movie openings, comic conventions, and Free Comic Book Day), moral and social codes (which when crossed cause "nerd rage"), temples (like comic book and gaming shops), and fetish objects (like certain first editions and everyday comics issues wrapped in protective layers), is ripe for scholarly investigation. Studying this religious devotion toward comics has been valuable for scholars who seek to understand the US and North American culture over the twentieth century, and there is more to be understood about what it means to take comics as a kind of sacred text that can have power over one's behavior, as the Bible purports to do for religious communities.[70]
- Comics often confront moral issues and prescribe moral codes and attitudes particularly toward nationalism, race, and women. There are many divergent views that play out in different comics, from tolerance and openness to racism and misogyny. Values come from how the medium is used, not the form itself; this form and value question has been a consistent battleground for comics creators since Fredric Wertham first came on the scene in the 1950s. Further research into the issue of moral thought in comics could address the question of where comics themselves fall on social issues and how biblical codes of law play a role or not in these moral systems.

[70] See Savage, *Commies, Cowboys, and Jungle Queens*, 3–13, 111–20; Bradford W. Wright, *Comic Book Nation: The Transformation of Youth Culture in America* (Baltimore, MD: Johns Hopkins University Press, 2001), ix–xix, 282–93; and Glen Weldon, *The Caped Crusade: Batman and the Rise of Nerd Culture* (New York: Simon and Schuster, 2016).

- Bible scholars might use the medium of comics in a constructive way by making their own comics, using the visual form to explain and interpret their own ideas about the biblical text to new audiences and transforming their pedagogy for students more comfortable with the visual mediums.
- As the field grows beyond the widely criticized show-and-tell presentation that simply introduces audiences to comics that scholars love, comics critics and scholars will delve more deeply into the world of ideas. As Benjamin Woo hopes, "we'll start seeing more interesting questions and problems that emerge *before* we pick an object to study and *before* we pick a method."[71] Comics offer scholars an imaginative treasure trove that we are only beginning to breach. These visual and textual gems can be applied to work for our ideas about the Bible and the biblical on a deeper and more profound level by new and emerging scholarship.

Suggested Readings and Annotated Bibliography

Clanton, Dan W., ed. *The End Will Be Graphic: Apocalyptic in Comic Books and Graphic Novels.* Bible in the Modern World, 43. Sheffield, UK: Sheffield Phoenix Press, 2012.

Besides being an important in-depth look at a particular genre in both biblical literature and comics, this collection of essays draws attention to comics' explanatory and creative power for the biblical scholar's imagination. Pairing both independent and mainstream comics with the study of apocalyptic literature, each piece drives home the idea that comics are a rich source of inspiration even for nuanced thought about specialized biblical topics.

Elliott, Scott. "Jesus in the Gutter: Comics and Graphic Novels." *Postscripts* 7, no. 2 (2011): 123–48.

This article offers a theory-rich discussion around the Jesus presented in two other alternative Bible comics. Elliott argues that it is the iconoclastic nature of these presentations and their resistance to orthodoxy that focuses—perhaps ironically—the subversive potential of Jesus and his story. That is, these comics lend imaginative power to the presentation of Jesus that reflects the real subversion in the biblical text.

Gamzou, Assaf, and Kenneth Koltun-Fromm, eds. *Sacred Texts and Comics: Reimagining Religion and Graphic Narratives.* Jackson: University Press of Mississippi, 2018.

This critical volume explores how comics and the sacred interweave to make robust accounts of the religious imaginary. A diverse group of nineteen academics across several methods and disciplines examines the productive intersections between religion and comics in order to critically expand the picture of the sacred in texts, bodies, and the everyday. The scholarship here is an excellent example of what moving from idea to text can offer. While generously supplied with talk of the Bible and focused on religious texts, it is not solely focused on the Bible. However, the essays across other religious texts are instructive points of comparison.

---

[71] Beaty et al., "Roundtable," 74.

Lewis, A. David, and Christine Hoff Kraemer, eds. *Graven Images: Religion in Comic Books and Graphic Novels*. New York: Continuum, 2010.

This collection of essays includes both creators and scholars from diverse disciplines all turned toward the intersection of a variety of religious traditions and attitudes with comics. It showcases the medium at its aesthetic and narrative best, while keeping the ideas of religion closely in view. They move from showing how comics give new interpretations of old religious ideas (including many from the biblical tradition), through the ways that comics rebel against religion, toward an exploration of postmodern ways of being religious in and with comics.

McCloud, Scott (w, a). *Understanding Comics: The Invisible Art*. New York: Kitchen Sink, Harper Perennial, 1994.

This is a beloved, though regularly contested, entry point for many scholars into the form of comics. This classic work of comics theory written in comics has been instrumental in bringing serious interpretation of the visuals of comics to the classroom and to many scholars from diverse fields. While McCloud's work suffers mildly from his "logophobia" that discounts much that text has to offer comics, it nevertheless is still one of the most valuable introductions to the topic available. McCloud's theory is well thought-out, but it is his talent for layout and design that makes this shine as both comic and pedagogy.

CHAPTER 21

THE BOOK OF JONAH IN GRAPHIC NOVEL ADAPTATIONS OF THE BIBLE

SCOTT S. ELLIOTT

DEPARTMENT OF PHILOSOPHY, RELIGION, AND
LEADERSHIP, ADRIAN COLLEGE

INTRODUCTION

COMICS are everywhere. We encounter them in storefronts and advertisements, on vintage T-shirts, in cinematic adaptations, and on our social media feeds. The Bible too is everywhere. It appears on billboards, church marquees, jewelry, and of course in cinematic adaptations and on our social media feeds. The fact that comics and the Bible so often occupy similar spaces begs the question of whether or to what extent they serve similar purposes and invites us to wonder about the nature of their relationship to us and of any relationship they may have to one another.

The mythic (and sometimes comedic) character of biblical narratives has been lost on many readers. Similarly, the seriousness of both the art and the social commentary of comics has been overlooked by many who regard comics as marginal, irrelevant, or juvenile. Arguably the combination of comics art and biblical narrative in graphic Bibles (i.e., works that present the sacred writings of the Jewish or Christian tradition, or some portion thereof, in the medium of comics) has the potential to draw attention to these characteristics on both sides of the equation. At their best, graphic Bibles do two things. First, they engage in close readings of the text. Graphic artists are attuned to both explicit and implicit details of the narratives they adapt, and especially to inherent gaps. Second, they often reflect an effort to respond to the narrative in kind. Biblical narrative is rife with metaphor, symbol, and imagery. That such is true also of comics should go without saying.

In the concluding paragraph of an article on graphic Bibles, Beth Davies-Stofka states:

> Scripture is a unique kind of literature. It speaks directly to us. It is multivalent, its complexity sustained by the language in which is it expressed, its meaning shifting and morphing along with the vagaries of life and changing circumstance. When translated into images, something of its complexity is lost, replaced by an encounter with an artist and a message. As seekers of truth, we might prefer the words of scripture and the open possibilities they present. But in the capable hands of a talented artist, a Bible comic may bring us closer to an equally compelling mystery. It may connect us to our humanity.[1]

Her position resembles that of Will Eisner, who argues that, "in writing with words alone, the author directs the reader's imagination. In comics the imagining is done for the reader. An image once drawn becomes a precise statement that brooks little or no further interpretation. When the two are 'mixed' the words become welded to the image and no longer serve to describe but rather to provide sound, dialogue and connective passages."[2] Words have power to conjure images in the minds of their readers, and there is truth in the adage that a picture is worth a thousand words. When words and pictures are fused together, the result might well multiply those possibilities exponentially. As one author notes, "The graphics medium expands intellectual and aesthetic possibilities rather than contracting them."[3] But it is equally possible that both will be impacted negatively. If we understand scriptures or sacred texts to be written documents deemed authoritative by a particular community for beliefs, practices, and identity they categorize as religious, then there is something terribly serious at stake for those communities in the translation and adaption of their scriptures. J. Z. Smith argues that a scriptural canon (i.e., a closed and authoritative collection of scriptures) "is best seen as one form of a basic cultural process of limitation and of overcoming that limitation through ingenuity."[4] In one sense, graphic Bibles reflect an exegetical effort to overcome the limits of canonical scriptures and ensure their perpetuation. But if, as Marshall McLuhan has suggested, message and medium are one and the same, the perceived nature of the thing itself (i.e., both scripture and the canon) is potentially destabilized and transformed.[5]

---

[1] Beth Davies-Stofka, "The Bible in Comics: Genesis," *Sacred Matters: Religious Currents in Culture,* March 5, 2014, http://sacredmattersmagazine.com/the-bible-in-comics-genesis/.

[2] Will Eisner, *Comics and Sequential Art* (Tamarac, FL: Poorhouse Press, 1985), 5.

[3] Francesca Goldsmith, "Graphic Novels," *Booklist* 94, no. 17 (May 1, 1998): 1510. She goes on to say, "Graphic novels require active, critical participation by the reader, who must not only be able to decode text but also follow its flow and grasp essentials of narrative, mood, character, or plot through images. The reader must then be able to meld the parts into a unified whole."

[4] Jonathan Z. Smith, *Imagining Religion: From Babylon to Jonestown* (Chicago: University of Chicago Press, 1982), 52.

[5] Marshall McLuhan, *Understanding Media: The Extensions of Man* (New York: McGraw-Hill, 1964).

In the following pages, we will consider precisely what constitutes comics, graphic novels, and graphic Bibles. In so doing, we will touch upon some of the fundamental characteristics and narrative techniques associated with these media. Moving on to a comparative analysis of specific examples, we will pay particular attention to the effects these aspects—especially in graphic Bibles—have on the shape and conceptualization of their source text and on the reader's experience. As with any translation or adaptation, we find that something is always lost in the process. Nevertheless, something is occasionally gained.

Overview of Topic

Graphic novels are a subcategory of comics. Scott McCloud notes that the word "comics" refers to a medium rather than an object and that a proper definition of the term requires one to separate form from content.[6] With this in mind, he ultimately arrives at the following: comics are "juxtaposed pictorial and other images in deliberate sequence, intended to convey information and/or to produce an aesthetic response in the viewer."[7] Using this definition, one might trace the origins of comics art to pre-Columbian Aztec pictograms, or beyond that to twelfth-century manga art or the eleventh-century Bayeux Tapestry, or further still to Greek vase painting, or even as far back as Egyptian hieroglyphs. Nevertheless, the sorts of productions that will come to mind for most people when they think of comics arise in the mid-nineteenth century, and comic books emerge in the early twentieth.[8]

Central to McCloud's definition is an emphasis on sequence, an emphasis he shares with Will Eisner, who described comics as "the arrangement of pictures or images and words to narrate a story or dramatize an idea."[9] Sequential organization and presentation are central components in the definition and analysis of comics because the medium functions as a form of writing and operates on the basis of a specific grammar. According to Eisner, "'Writing' for comics can be defined as the conception of an idea, the arrangement of image elements and the construction of the sequence of the narration and the composing of dialogue. It is at once a part and the whole of the medium."[10] Technically speaking, comics do not need to incorporate words.[11] However, the major-

---

[6] Scott McCloud, *Understanding Comics: The Invisible Art* (New York: Harper Perennial, 1993), 4, 5. For more on the genre of comics, see Elizabeth Rae Coody's chapter in this volume.

[7] McCloud, *Understanding Comics*, 9.

[8] For a full-scale history of comics, see David Kunzle, *The Early Comic Strip: Narrative Strips and Picture Stories in the European Broadsheet from c. 1450 to 1825* (Berkeley: University of California Press, 1973), and *The History of the Comic Strip*, vol. 2: *The Nineteenth Century* (Berkeley: University of California Press, 1990).

[9] Eisner, *Comics and Sequential Art*, 5.   [10] Ibid., 122.

[11] Contrary to most, David Carrier insists on their inclusion, arguing that "the speech balloon is a defining element of the comic because it establishes a word/image unity that distinguishes comics from pictures illustrating a text." *The Aesthetics of Comics* (University Park: Pennsylvania State University Press, 2000), 4.

ity of modern comics do include words, and those words often function as images in their own right and thereby contribute to the process of visual storytelling.[12] George Kovacs notes that "the medium of comics is usually seen and understood as a hybrid: It is not art since it contains text, nor can it be literature since it contains illustrations."[13] In fact, the unique combination of words and images that characterizes the lion's share of comics art is complex and "allows for much flexibility in the manipulation of meaning."[14] It is, in effect, a genre fundamentally characterized by hybridity. Eisner explains that "the format of the comic book presents a montage of both word and image, and the reader is thus required to exercise both visual and verbal interpretive skills. The regimens of art (e.g., perspective, symmetry, brush stroke) and the regimens of literature (e.g., grammar, plot, syntax) become superimposed upon each other. The reading of a comic book is an act of both aesthetic perception and intellectual pursuit."[15] Although Eisner recognizes the interwoven and symbiotic relationship between words and images, the function of the former seems relatively narrow and secondary to the latter. According to Eisner, "Lettering, treated 'graphically' and in service to the story, functions as an extension of the imagery. In this context, it provides the mood, a narrative bridge, and the implication of sound."[16] McCloud, on the other hand, catalogs a range of ways that words might appear in comics and function in relation to the images.[17] When words are dominant, the images serve the words primarily as illustrations. Alternatively, when words are subordinate to the images, the words often serve the images in a manner akin to a soundtrack. Often words and images work in tandem to communicate what is in essence the same message. McCloud also provides examples of "additive," "parallel," and "montage" associations wherein words and images amplify or otherwise extend one another, move in apparently different and nonintersecting directions, or appear as integrated elements of one another, respectively. He concludes his summary with "interdependent" combinations, "where words and pictures go hand in hand to convey an idea that neither could alone convey," which is the most common association in comics.[18]

When we shift from comics generally to comic books and graphic novels specifically, our definitions expand. Dan W. Clanton, Jr. describes a comic book as "a serialized piece of sequential art, often with more detail and depth of plot than a newspaper comic strip."[19] The term "graphic novel," then, would refer to "a collection of comic books or simply a novel told in the form of text and images."[20] David Burke and Lydia Lebrón-Rivera explain that graphic novels are "a type of comic book" characterized by a longer

---

[12] See Eisner, *Comics and Sequential Art*, 10–12; McCloud, *Understanding Comics*, 152–61; Carrier, *The Aesthetics of Comics*, 61–74.

[13] George Kovacs, "Comics and Classics: Establishing a Critical Frame," in *Classics and Comics*, ed. George Kovacs and C. W. Marshall (Oxford: Oxford University Press, 2011), 9.

[14] Matthew P. McAllister, Edward H. Sewell Jr., and Ian Gordon, eds., *Comics and Ideology* (New York: Peter Lang, 2001), 3.

[15] Eisner, *Comics and Sequential Art*, 8.   [16] Ibid., 10.

[17] McCloud, *Understanding Comics*, 153–5.   [18] Ibid., 155.

[19] Dan W. Clanton, Jr., "Cartoons and Comics," in *Teaching the Bible through Popular Culture and the Arts*, ed. Mark Roncace and Patrick Gray (Atlanta, GA: Society of Biblical Study, 2007), 330.

[20] Ibid.

format, "higher production values, sophisticated art, and quality papers and bindings."[21] They add that "like picture books, [graphic novels] are print materials in which pictures and narrative are joined in one interdependent format."[22] Here, they are drawing on Francisca Goldsmith. When Goldsmith refers to "narrative," it is not entirely clear whether she means words generally or the narrative as a whole that results from the combined images and words, synthesized in the mind of the reader. Nevertheless, when we consider graphic *novels*, the emphasis shifts from a discussion of medium to one of genre, and the words become a critical component.

If we narrow the discussion even further to the genre of graphic Bibles, then we are speaking of something very specific, which is in some way constrained by its content insofar as it aims to represent the Bible. Without wading into the deep and tumultuous waters that surround debates concerning what constitute translation, transmediazation, adaptation, and even the Bible itself, suffice it to say that, for the purposes of this chapter, *a graphic Bible is a work that aims to directly present Jewish or Christian scriptures as such in the medium of comics.* In other words, these works seem to say: *This* is the Bible (or biblical material) rendered as comics. Some key examples of these would be Mike Jacklin's *The Discovery Bible*;[23] Mayer, Kubert, and Redondo's *The Bible*;[24] Ruiz and Novick's *Samson: Judge of Israel*;[25] Krueger and Ruiz's *Testament*;[26] JT Waldman's *Megillat Esther*;[27] Neely's *The Gospel of Mark* and others in The Illustrated International Children's Bible series;[28] Siku, *The Manga Bible: From Genesis to Revelation*;[29] R. Crumb's *Genesis Illustrated*;[30] Basil Wolverton's *The Wolverton Bible*;[31] Mauss and Cariello's *The Action Bible: God's Redemptive Story*;[32] Siku, Richard Thomas, and Jeff Anderson's *The*

---

[21] David G. Burke and Lydia Lebrón-Rivera, "Transferring Biblical Narrative to Graphic Novel," *SBL Forum*, April 2004, http://sbl-site.org/Article.aspx?ArticleID=249.

[22] Ibid., citing Goldsmith, "Graphic Novels," 1510.

[23] Originally published as *Dècouvir la Bible* (Librarie Larousse, 1983), later translated and published by Daan Retief Publishers in 1990, and then adapted as a twenty-four-volume series by Mike Jacklin and published by Knowledge Unlimited in 1994.

[24] Sheldon Mayer, Joe Kubert, and Nestor Redondo, *The Bible* (New York: DC Comics, 1975).

[25] Mario Ruiz and Jerry A. Novick, *Samson: Judge of Israel* (New York: Metron Press, 2002).

[26] Jim Krueger and Mario Ruiz, *Testament* (New York: Metron Press, 2003).

[27] JT Waldman, *Megillat Esther* (Philadelphia, PA: Jewish Publication Society, 2005). Waldman's work is important not only with respect to graphic Bibles but in relation to the remarkable history of Jewish comics generally. See, e.g., Arie Kaplan, *From Krakow to Krypton: Jews and Comic Books* (Philadelphia, PA: Jewish Publication Society, 2008); Simcha Weinstein, *Up, Up, and Oy Vey! How Jewish History, Culture, and Values Shaped the Comic Book Superhero* (Fort Lee, NJ: Barricade Books, 2009); Derek Parker Royal, ed., *Visualizing Jewish Narrative: Jewish Comics and Graphic Novels* (New York: Bloomsbury, 2016).

[28] Keith R. Neely, David Miles, Roberta Neely, Bridget Harlow, and Thomas R. Zuber, *The Gospel of Mark*, Illustrated International Children's Bible Series (Nashville, TN: Thomas Nelson, 2006).

[29] Siku, *The Manga Bible: From Genesis to Revelation* (Colorado Springs, CO: WaterBrook Press, 2007).

[30] R. Crumb, *Genesis Illustrated* (New York: W. W. Norton, 2009).

[31] Basil Wolverton, *The Wolverton Bible* (Seattle, WA: Fantagraphics Books, 2009).

[32] Sergio Cariello and Doug Mauss, *The Adventure Bible: God's Redemptive Story* (Colorado Springs, CO: David C. Cook, 2010).

Lion Comic Book Hero Bible;[33] Rob Liefeld's *The Covenant* series;[34] and Simon Amadeus Pillario's *Word for Word Bible Comic* series.[35] These productions are distinct from comics and graphic novels that either recontextualize a biblical figure in a modern setting (e.g., Stephen Lindsay's *Jesus Hates Zombies*[36] or Frank Stack's *The New Adventures of Jesus: The Second Coming*[37]) and graphic novels that present a narrative depicting, for example, a Christ figure (e.g., Mark Millar and Peter Gross's *American Jesus Book One: Chosen*[38]).

Surveying these examples, one finds a wide variety of ways in which artists engage the biblical material, as well as a broad range in the degree to which they restrict their work to the constraints of the written text. For instance, Waldman presents the text in Hebrew but includes English translations. Crumb and the creators of the Illustrated Children's Bible series (ICB) slavishly follow their respective biblical texts (albeit in English translation), purporting to include every single word, yet there are noticeable differences between the two precisely in terms of what they mean by claiming to depict the text exactly as it is. The ICB cites chapter and verse at every turn, confines the art to small frames, and presents images that are rather restrained and add little to the words. Crumb, on the other hand, uses provocative imagery, often entailing nudity and violence, in order to interrogate and portray both explicit and implicit senses of the biblical narrative, despite referring to the project as nothing more than "a straight illustration job."[39] All of these are instances of what Gérard Genette would characterize as "intertextuality," the term he uses to describe "a relationship of copresence between two texts or among several texts: that is to say, eidetically and typically as the actual presence of one text within another."[40] In his catalog of transtextual relationships, those of the intertex-

---

[33]   Siku, Richard Thomas, and Jeff Anderson, *The Lion Comic Book Hero Bible* (Oxford: Lion Books, 2015).

[34]   Rob Liefeld, *The Covenant*, vols. 1–5 (Portland, OR: Image Comics, 2015–6).

[35]   *The Book of Judges* and *The Book of Ruth* were released in 2016, followed by *The Book of Joshua* in 2017. A Kickstarter campaign is underway to fund publication of *The Gospel of Mark*. More information is available online at https://www.wordforwordbiblecomic.com/.

[36]   Stephen Lindsay, *Jesus Hates Zombies / Lincoln Hates Werewolves*, vol. 1 (Levittown, NY: Alterna Comics, 2008).

[37]   Frank Stack, *The New Adventures of Jesus: The Second Coming* (Seattle, WA: Fantagraphics Books, 2006). The segment of this collection labeled "Stories from the Good Book" actually does match my description of graphic Bibles insofar as Stack reworks a dozen familiar episodes from the life of Jesus as recounted in the canonical gospels.

[38]   Mark Millar and Peter Gross, *American Jesus Book One: Chosen* (Berkeley, CA: Image Comics, 2009). For an analysis of *The New Adventures of Jesus* and *American Jesus* that contrasts them to more "traditional" graphic Bibles, see Scott S. Elliott, "Jesus in the Gutter: Comics and Graphic Novels Reimagining the Gospels," *Postscripts: The Journal of Sacred Texts and Contemporary Worlds* 7, no. 2 (2011): 123–48.

[39]   For a discussion of the contrasting ways in which *Genesis Illustrated* and *The Action Bible* render bodies and sexuality, and what it reflects of their artists' understandings of the Bible, see Scott S. Elliott, "Transrendering Biblical Bodies: Reading Sex in *The Action Bible* and *Genesis Illustrated*," in *Comics and Sacred Texts: Reimagining Religion and Graphic Narratives*, ed. Assaf Gamzou and Ken Koltun-Fromm (Jackson: University of Mississippi Press, 2018), 132–48.

[40]   Gérard Genette, *Palimpsests: Literature in the Second Degree*, trans. Channa Newman and Claude Doubinsky (Lincoln: University of Nebraska Press, 1997), 1–2.

tual variety are the least abstract; they reflect the most explicit and literal form of textual reworking.

In contrast are works like *Testament* and *The Action Bible*. These graphic Bibles are more selective in which biblical stories the artists choose to render. While *The Action Bible* still depicts characters and settings in ways that evoke the historical world of the Bible and provides references that direct readers to where they can find "the original" version of the stories it depicts, it paraphrases much of the biblical narrative and dialogue and often intersperses both with contemporary figures of speech. *Testament* reframes and recontextualizes the biblical material, thus creating a modern adaptation. While *The Action Bible* and *Testament* still fall safely within the boundaries of Genette's definition of an intertext, there are elements of both (especially of *Testament*) that begin to veer toward other categories Genette identifies[41] and thus signal a gentle ebbing away from the tight association one encounters in *Genesis Illustrated* and the ICB.[42]

At issue is what the creators aim to do with their graphic renditions of the Bible and what happens in the process regardless of that intention. Graphic Bibles reflect interpretive activity akin to what one encounters in collections of ancient Jewish commentaries known as the Midrashim and Targumim, which endeavor to draw out and expound upon gaps, questions, and pregnant details in the scriptural text.[43] To begin, they must of necessity make explicit that which is either implicit or simply not of concern in the written text (e.g., clothing, color, the position of speakers relative to one another). Moreover, they flesh out the often sparse details of the biblical narrative (e.g., making decisions concerning ambiguous passages of time) and are forced to engage in interpretive activity (e.g., making decisions about how to communicate tone through facial expressions and body language or how to represent divine beings). But perhaps the characteristic that is most analogous is the overarching concern with explicating the text in direct relation to the contemporary world of the reader and the seamlessness of the end product wherein graphic Bibles blur the line between text and commentary.

The bulk of McCloud's *Understanding Comics*, Eisner's *Comics and Sequential Art*, and the two important works by Thierry Groensteen, *The System of Comics*[44] and *Comics and Narration*,[45] center on the unique language of comics by exploring and explaining the fundamental mechanics of the medium. It is, in effect, a visual narratology. These

---

[41] Examples include the use of paraphrasing and of story titles in both volumes (e.g., "Cain & Abel" in *Testament* and "Brother's Blood Cry" in *The Action Bible*, in reference to Gen 4–5), and especially the frame story of *Testament* (discussed later in this chapter). In Genette's terminology, these reflect paratextual, metatextual, and, to an extent, even hypertextual associations (*Palimpsests*, 3–10).

[42] *American Jesus* and the *Testament* series by Douglas Rushkoff and Liam Sharp (New York: Vertigo, 2006–8) are excellent examples of what Genette labels hypertextuality, which characterizes a relationship in which one text is grafted onto another in a manner that is not commentary and that reflects a process of either transformation or imitation (*Palimpsests*, 5–7).

[43] See Burke and Lebrón-Rivera, "Transferring Biblical Narrative to Graphic Novel."

[44] Thierry Groensteen, *The System of Comics*, trans. Bart Beaty and Nick Nquyen (Jackson: University Press of Mississippi, 2007).

[45] Thierry Groensteen, *Comics and Narration*, trans. Ann Miller (Jackson: University Press of Mississippi, 2013).

theorists address such aspects as imagery, anatomy, iconography and representation, spatial relationships, layout, the arthrology of the frames, the role of the gutter (i.e., the space between frames), the interplay of frames and gutter to create the illusion of passing time and motion, rhythm, coloring, the role of the narrator, manipulations of affect, and the mutually enabling and reinforcing effects of pictures and words in combination to produce something that exceeds the sum of its parts. Graphic Bibles speak through the combined effect of the subtractive and additive gestures by the artist, the gap between individual frames, and the space between images and text that is created by the juxtaposition of the various elements (what McCloud refers to as the guttural language of the medium).[46] Although sequential, graphic novels are "unbounded by the presumption of linearity" and thus reflect a sort of "pictorial narratology."[47] For Mieke Bal, "pictorial narrative…becomes a secret code, a subcultural language that facilitates the production of subversive narratives."[48] She recognizes in this a political impulse that is marked by an attempt to sidestep traditional narratives wielded by official authorities to foster "proper" stories in those they govern. She states, "The political implications of the belief in a strong ontological difference, even opposition, between [verbal and visual] media become especially clear in the face of cultural objects that cannot be isolated as either verbal or visual."[49] Graphic Bibles are exemplary in this regard because there lies between frames, between words and images, and between what is subtracted from or added to "the original," a "joint where the image is not but without which it cannot be."[50]

While many graphic Bibles seem to subordinate the aesthetic dimensions of comics art to a more fundamental concern with what they perceive to be more straightforward verbal communication, understood primarily in terms of either directly transferring the Bible's perceived message to the target audience or else simply enhancing the Bible by means of illustration, there are many that are equally if not more concerned with the artistic aspects both of the comics form and of biblical literature.[51] Gale Yee, however, is right to argue that since the Bible itself was not produced as an aesthetic object the primary objective in reading it should not be interpretation.[52] According to her, the most important question concerns power: "What are the social locations of power that make meaning possible in the *production of meaning* in the text and in the *consumption of*

---

[46] McCloud, *Understanding Comics*, 85.

[47] Mieke Bal, "Figuration," *PMLA* 119 (2004): 1289. Cf. Mieke Bal, *Loving Yusef: Conceptual Travels from Present to Past* (Chicago: University of Chicago Press, 2008); Roland Barthes, *Empire of Signs*, trans. Richard Howard (New York: Hill and Wang, 1982), xi: "The text does not 'gloss' the images, which do not 'illustrate' the text. For me, each has been no more than the onset of a kind of visual uncertainty, analogous perhaps to that *loss of meaning* Zen calls a *satori*. Text and image, interlacing, seek to ensure the circulation and exchange of these signifiers: body, face, writing; and in them to read the retreat of signs" (emphases original).

[48] Bal, "Figuration," 1290.   [49] Ibid.   [50] Ibid.

[51] For an excellent study of comics in relation to aesthetics, see Carrier, *The Aesthetics of Comics*.

[52] Gale Yee, "The Author/Text/Reader and Power: Suggestions for a Critical Framework for Biblical Studies," in *Reading from This Place*, vol. 1: *Social Location and Biblical Interpretation in the U.S.*, ed. Fernando F. Segovia and Mary Ann Tolbert (Minneapolis, MN: Fortress Press, 1995), 24–7.

meaning by the reader?"[53] In other words, it is a matter of identifying the historical conditions that determine what gets to count in the construction and dissemination of meaning among readers vis-à-vis their relative positions with respect to social power.

Marshall and Kovacs suggest that comic adaptations of ancient texts must be considered in discussions regarding various appropriations of the past in relation to contemporary concerns: "What matters is the decision to use the past to make sense of the present. Sometimes these rereadings can point to something that lies dormant in the text that has not yet been isolated."[54] The editors highlight the prevalence of two-page spreads in Frank Miller's *300* as an example of how the artist signifies that "his story cannot be contained within the constraints of the standard comic-book size: The panels must somehow be larger than the medium itself."[55] Similarly, they argue that "when Barry Allen became the Flash, assuming the mantle previously worn by Jay Garrick in the Golden Age until the title was canceled in 1949, superheroes were shown to be greater than the specific narratives that contained them. They could be universalized, rewritten, mythologized: The scope of what was possible became universal."[56] There is no doubt that contemporary graphic Bibles contribute to both the (re)construction and the appropriation of the past, and they do so in complex ways. That complexity stems, in part, from the fact that the Bible is a work of literature that both contains *religious* history (i.e., history interpreted religiously) and is a historical artifact itself. Thus various graphic Bibles often reflect a mix of perspectives on and attitudes toward the biblical text and its content, and the Bible, like the ever (re)imagined past, functions as a site of conflict and rhetoric wherein meaning and purpose are repeatedly negotiated and renegotiated.

It is essential, therefore, especially in the case of graphic Bibles, to recognize and consider the ideological function of comics. To be sure, in the history of comics one will find plenty of examples that are intentionally political, particularly among so-called underground comics, or "comix." There are examples of biblical comics where this is also the case, but ideological analysis is not limited to works that are explicitly political.[57] Like Yee, the editors of *Comics and Ideology* connect ideology foremost with issues of social power, asking, "Why and how may comics challenge and/or perpetuate power differences in society? Do comics serve to celebrate and legitimize dominant values and institutions in society, or do they critique and subvert the status quo?"[58] They go on to note that "the portrayals of life found in comic art are not neutral or random images."[59] The contributors to their volume address a wide range of intersections and interactions between comics and issues of social power, such as economics, politics, gender, sex and sexuality, violence, ethnicity, and nationalism. When one considers the Bible's privileged position in the US, its involvement in the construction and contestation of group

[53] Ibid., 29, emphasis original.
[54] C. W. Marshall and George Kovacs, introduction to *Classics and Comics*, ed. George Kovacs and C. W. Marshall (Oxford: Oxford University Press, 2011), ix.
[55] Ibid., x.   [56] Ibid.
[57] See, e.g., Stack, *The New Adventures of Jesus*, and Millar and Gross, *American Jesus*.
[58] McAllister, Sewell, and Gordon, *Comics and Ideology*, 2.   [59] Ibid., 5.

identities, the role it plays in nostalgic reminiscences about our imagined past, and so on, identifying the ideological consequences of translating and transmediating it into the language of comics becomes paramount.

SPECIFIC EXAMPLES AND/OR FOCI

One approach to analyzing graphic Bibles is to compare and contrast how two or more treat the same biblical story. Hence I would like to consider briefly the similarities and differences in the presentation of Jonah among four of the graphic Bibles mentioned earlier: *Testament*, *The Manga Bible*, *The Action Bible*, and *The Lion Comic Book Hero Bible*.[60] All of these comics present Jonah in the context of the Christian biblical canon.[61] Since none of these graphic Bibles presents the entire canon but rather only a selective sample thereof, one question to arise immediately is why the artists choose to include it.

For those unfamiliar with the story of Jonah, the narrative focuses on an Israelite prophet sent by God to the city of Nineveh to "cry out against it; for their wickedness has come up before me" (Jon 1:2, NRSV). The Ninevites were part of the Assyrian Empire and were thus mortal enemies of Jonah's people, Israel. Rather than do what God had commanded, Jonah attempts to "flee . . . from the presence of the LORD" (1:3) by securing passage on a ship bound for a city a great distance away in the opposite direction. The narrator tells us that God generated a fierce storm. While everyone on the ship was terrified, cried out to their gods, and did all they could to ensure that they and the ship would survive, Jonah slept soundly below deck. Eventually it is determined that Jonah is to blame for this misfortune. On his recommendation, the crew decides to throw him overboard. As a result, the sea becomes calm and the shipmen "feared the LORD even more" (1:16). Meanwhile the reader is told that God "provided a large fish to swallow up Jonah" (1:17). Jonah remained inside the fish for three days and three nights. Finally, he prays to God for deliverance, and "then the Lord spoke to the fish, and it spewed Jonah out upon the dry land" (2:10). God recommissions Jonah, and Jonah ventures into Nineveh to deliver the following message: "Forty days more, and Nineveh shall be overthrown!" (3:4). Much to Jonah's chagrin, the people of the city are receptive and repent fervently. As a result, "God changed his mind about the calamity that he had said he would bring upon them; and he did not do it" (3:10). The final chapter depicts a deeply disgruntled Jonah lambasting God for acting kindly toward the Ninevites. God, in turn, after giving Jonah an object lesson involving a shady bush, a sultry wind, and a hungry worm, questions Jonah about his values.

---

[60] For an intriguing study of the reception history of Jonah that provides important, if indirect, context for considering renderings of the work in comics, see Yvonne Sherwood, *A Biblical Text and Its Afterlives: The Survival of Jonah in Western Culture* (Cambridge: Cambridge University Press, 2000).

[61] Although *Testament* features stories taken solely from the Hebrew Bible, it is clear from both the framing of the narrative and elements of the dialogue that the Christian Old Testament is in view.

Testament and *The Lion Comic Book Hero Bible* nicely capture, in different ways, the Bible's diversity with respect to authors, styles, genres, and so on. *The Lion Comic Book Hero Bible* does so by means of having different artists illustrate each Testament, while *Testament* goes one step further by having different artists render each individual story represented, which results in a remarkably different look and feel for each episode. The focus of the overarching frame story of *Testament* as a whole is ironic, therefore, and I think somewhat unfortunate. All of the biblical material is wrapped in the larger story of a bartender at JJ's Bar narrating the individual episode to a patron, who is none other than the reader. His message is that all of these narratives are the work of a single "Author" (viz., God), and thus the stories of creation, Noah, Moses, Saul, and so on are chapters and episodes of the larger book, and the rendering of each is fundamentally secondary to the presumed message they contain and deliver jointly. *Testament* ultimately presents a narrative theology. Nevertheless the treatment of Jonah is strikingly different from that of the other stories in the collection. Over the course of six pages, the artist (Sergio Aragonés, whose work has been featured in *MAD Magazine* for over five decades) depicts the story of Jonah like a cartoon, much like what one would expect to see in Sunday newspaper "funnies." Hence the portrayal conveys the comedic elements of the story.

The narrator's presence in *Testament*'s portrayal of Jonah is overt (as it is throughout the comic). But there is a curious tension between the even-keeled (but serious) tone of the narrating voice and the comedic portrayal of the characters and plot. On the whole, the artist and the story writers have done something quite remarkable in their use of the comics medium. *Testament* overall creatively reflects the curious hybridity of the Bible itself, which is both a book and a collection of books. And the Jonah episode creatively reflects the humorous and entertaining qualities of the book that are so often overlooked by readers who may think the Bible is too serious to ever be funny. Both of these aspects are dampened by the decision to forcefully shift the responsibility for the story to a transcendental "Author," especially when coupled with the narrator's moralizing tone. And therein lies an ironic twist: whereas the biblical story of Jonah critiques the tendency of groups to act selfishly with their gods and offers a rich exploration of the tension between God's justice and God's mercy, in the hands of the creators of *Testament* it becomes a deterministic tale that centers on the individual and on not merely the consequences of disobedience but what amounts to the inescapability of obedience.

Essentially *Testament* portrays Jonah as a bad example. The narrator begins the episode by contrasting him to Daniel, who was "willing to brave the dangers [of being God's spokesman] for the sake of the Author," and then proceeds to depict him in a manner most readers familiar with the story are accustomed to—namely, as a cantankerous curmudgeon. This is all right as far it goes, especially insofar as the book of Jonah is unique among the prophetic writings of the Hebrew Bible in its focus on the prophet rather than his message. At the same time, however, while I think *Testament*'s version is one of the better treatments of the story, teasing out aspects of the story easily overlooked by some readers as it does, it lacks the nuances of the source text. The story is flattened, and this results in a trade-off. The tension between mercy and justice, for example, is lost in favor of a more straightforward moral tale that plays to popular understandings concerning how individuals should behave in relation to God. The image of God's people wrestling with their God that begins with Jacob at the crossing of the Jabbok River in Genesis 32 and continues throughout the Hebrew Bible is reduced to an image of conflict between an all-knowing God and a naïve human being who refuses, to his own detriment, to do what he is told. There is little opportunity within the framework of *Testament* for the reader to wrestle with the text because, despite staying relatively close to the biblical narrative in its dialogue and using cartoonish illustrations to capture the biblical writer's caricature of Jonah, the reframing and recontextualization of the story positions it to be read in such a way that stifles the more complex readings afforded by the source text.

The artwork throughout *The Lion Comic Book Hero Bible* (*LCBHB*) is provocative, and much like *Testament* the work does an especially good job of capturing the epic and mythological dimensions of biblical storytelling. The Jonah episode in the *LCBHB* is titled "The Runner" and spans only two pages. Save for a single narratorial comment that frames the story as a flashback, the entire story is narrated by the protagonist himself. The opening frame portrays Jonah sprinting away from the viewer as if he has just launched off the starting block in a footrace, and the only words are "I run." It is not until the third frame that the viewer is brought into the story time of the biblical narrative. Notwithstanding the fact that he is speaking of a past event, Jonah speaks in the present tense (i.e., "I run" rather than "I ran"). Hence, for the *LCBHB*, Jonah is defined by this character trait. Despite having allowed Jonah to tell his story, the story he tells is in fact that of someone else. Not only is there his self-identification as a runner, but the *LCBHB* also ends the story of Jonah in a way that erases and supplants the probing question that concludes the biblical account. Whereas the biblical version of Jonah ends with God questioning him in a manner that invites the reader to consider her own biases and theological conceptualizations,[62] the *LCBHB* gives Jonah the final word: "And I finally got it." As noted in the discussion of *Testament*, the book of Jonah is a character-driven narrative. However, the decision to recast Jonah as a character-*narrator*, and then to have him voice his story as a parable and his identity as a runner, is an appropriation of the text that ultimately does a disservice to it. The *LCBHB* forces the character to identify with a story that is actually someone else's story about him, to tell it himself as if it represents his own perspective on his actions, and to conclude it in such a way that suggests he agrees with the writer's judgment of those actions. Rather than leaving readers to self-reflectively ponder whether or to what extent they too might be overly concerned about the wrong things or their values might be misaligned with those of God, the story is closed and its presumed lesson is handed to the reader unambiguously.

---

[62] "Then the Lord said, 'You are concerned about the bush [viz., that God caused to grow to provide Jonah with shade and then allowed a worm to destroy, provoking Jonah's anger], for which you did not labor and which you did not grow; it came into being in a night and perished in a night. And should I not be concerned about Nineveh, that great city, in which there are more than a hundred and twenty thousand persons who do not know their right hand from their left, and also many animals?'" (Jonah 4:10–11, NRSV).

In *The Manga Bible*'s version of the Jonah episode, Siku (the artist) employs a particular subgenre of manga called "Super Deformed," which the scriptwriter, Akin Akinsiku, describes as "a caricature of a caricature: massive heads and eyes."[63] Their rationale is that the departure in style from the rest of the book reflects what they perceive as the story's own departure from so much else that characterizes the Hebrew Bible. They compare their approach to Jonah with their treatment of the Psalms, stating, "It meant we could just dip in with these extra stories without stopping the flow of the bigger story." Despite the almost nonexistent use of titles elsewhere, the artists title this episode "Jonah: A Comedy Short." Together, these decisions present the episode in a manner that makes it function like an intermission.

One of the reasons I chose to focus on treatments of Jonah across these four works is because *The Manga Bible* is followed by a "Key Scenes Commentary."[64] Jonah is one of only four episodes discussed by Siku and Akinsiku. In the course of their brief conversation, both artist and writer speak of how overwhelmed they were by the seemingly endless refrain of death and destruction throughout the Hebrew Bible. Akinsiku speaks of needing "light relief" after writing so much darkness and notes, "Even though [the Bible] carries on the theme of genocide, there is redemption. You know, [laughing] it's good to remember that every once in a while people said sorry and God let them off."[65] Siku responds:

> Yeah, when I was doing Jonah's story it was quite therapeutic. After wading through all those pages of death, destruction, disobedience and wickedness, I think I made it deliberately lighter. The thing about Jonah for me was that at the beginning I wasn't really sympathetic to him. I was thinking that it was yet another tale of God's people thinking that he's their exclusive property. But when you think about it, the Assyrians were so brutal that it's not surprising that he refused to play a part in saving them.... I suppose I started to feel a bit more sympathetic towards him when I thought about it as being like the situation in the middle east today: telling a Palestinian to love their enemy is a hard thing to do, but that's what God is doing here.[66]

With a final frame depicting Jonah's head hanging in silence and the voice of God speaking from above, *The Manga Bible* ends the story of Jonah in a way that retains the wonderful abruptness and ambiguity of the biblical account.[67] Taken together, the artist and writer's decision to let the story stand that way, together with their use of the Super Deformed style to interpret the visual narrative of the overall work, may provide some readers with an opportunity to witness and reflect upon the Bible's multivocality, the self-reflexivity of its stories, and the tendency of its writers to write in dialogue with one another, thereby troubling biblical waters that are too often perceived by readers as rather tranquil. In reality, the Bible is chock-full of diverse voices and perspectives on similar issues. The book of Nahum, for instance, stands in stark contrast to Jonah on the

---

[63] Siku and Akinsiku, *The Manga Bible*, 206.   [64] Ibid., 201–8.   [65] Ibid., 205.
[66] Ibid., 205–6.   [67] See n. 63.

appropriate sentiment one should have toward one's enemy, arguing that God will indeed destroy Nineveh for its treatment of Israel.

The Action Bible does anything but upset status quo readings of the Bible. It begins the story of Jonah by making explicit the protagonist's motivations for going to Tarshish by means of a thought bubble that reads, "I'm sorry God. I can't go to such a filthy, despicable place as Nineveh," suggesting that Jonah's concerns are about purity rather than reflecting a wish for the Ninevites' destruction premised upon a desire for God's elect to receive privileged treatment, as the biblical narrative intimates. When the storm arises and the crew concludes that "someone must have angered the gods," Jonah says, "It wasn't me! I don't think," and the narrator explains that he was only refusing to admit what he knew. Even though Jonah does take responsibility for the storm in the biblical narrative, the narrator's revision in *The Action Bible* would seem to serve the interests of compounding his guilt even further by having him lie to his shipmates. The writer also adds material to Jonah's message to the Ninevites: "And when God does punish you like you deserve, don't say I didn't warn you." Throughout the story, there is a harshness to both the character of Jonah and the character of God. The latter tells Jonah, when the fish spits him out onto the shore, "Now do what I have commanded!" And God's words at the conclusion of the story are described as scolding. In this way, the Jonah episode conforms to the moralizing tone of *The Action Bible* as a whole. Consequently, it is an unintended byproduct of the overall depiction of God here and throughout *The Action Bible* that the reference to God being "true to his Holy Word" by not destroying the Ninevites when they repent seems to signal not so much God's mercifulness as God's capriciousness.

One of the most interesting things across all four of these adaptations is their handling of Jonah's prayer from inside the fish (Jon 2:2–9). In *Testament*, the narrator contextualizes and sets up Jonah's prayer, emphasizing the passing of time and Jonah's search for words, presumably in silence. Finally, with Jonah drawn in a traditional posture of prayer, he finds "the words the author always responds to" and says "I'm sorry." *LCBHB* has Jonah himself voice a summary of his prayer: "From the watery depths, I called to the Lord for help." *The Manga Bible* presents a frame showing only the fish, and we hear Jonah say from inside, "Okay God...you win!" Finally, *The Action Bible* adds a frame depicting Jonah crying out "Lord, Help me!" as he's being swallowed up by the fish after being thrown overboard, and also retains a portion of Jonah's prayer from inside the fish: "Lord, I called out to you and you saved me. The waters were all around me, but you kept me safe. You are the one who saves!"

In the biblical version, Jonah's prayer is a psalm of thanksgiving. There is no petition for either help or deliverance. The poem was quite likely an independent piece of literature at one time.[68] Repositioned within the framework of the narrative, it becomes about Jonah and anticipates his deliverance from the fish by speaking of it as a fait accompli.

---

[68] "The poem seems at odds with the surrounding material in both content and genre; these verses are likely older material incorporated anew into the Jonah narrative." Kelly J. Murphy, "Jonah," in *Women's Bible Commentary: Twentieth-Anniversary Edition*, ed. Carol A. Newsom, Sharon H. Ringe, and Jacqueline E. Lapsley (Louisville, KY: Westminster John Knox, 2012), 323.

What's more, it anticipates the deliverance of the Ninevites in the same manner (i.e., their repentance that leads to the forestalling of their destruction by God is foreshadowed in Jonah's prayer and in his subsequent release from the fish). At the same time, the entire monologue is pointedly at odds with the characterization of Jonah elsewhere in the biblical narrative. Whereas chapters 1, 3, and 4 characterize Jonah as bullheaded and tone-deaf, chapter 2 depicts him as someone who is deeply sensitive to and appreciative of the merciful nature and workings of God, and he is able to articulate those characteristics quite eloquently. This is another of the many ironies of the narrative. But the laudatory character of the prayer and the exaggerations of the story are lost (e.g., the sharp contrast between the character of Jonah reflected in the prayer and his over-the-top words and actions elsewhere) in these graphic depictions that ultimately flatten the intricacies of the biblical text in favor of something else.

Even though comics themselves demand quite a lot of their readers, it seems clear that the dominant ideology at work in all four of these graphic Bibles is one that regards the Bible itself as a relatively straightforward text. It contains a message that can be distilled and repackaged without being modified in the course of doing so. Despite the fact that most of these graphic Bibles treat the Bible as a unified work that communicates one, ongoing, and consistent story of God's efforts to save humanity (i.e., a narrative theology), the Bible is not a perfectly uniform narrative. Regarding it as such reflects a serious interpretive and rhetorical move that ultimately results in the production of something other than what the Bible actual is—namely, a disparate and sometimes fragmented collection of writings that present competing views on a host of topics and that are often in tension with one another. Ignoring this characteristic risks allowing our interpretations to supplant the text itself. Yet even then paradoxical consequences often arise. Given that Jonah is the final episode in *Testament* before returning to the frame story, and that it functions as a sort of intermission in *The Manga Bible*, it is possible that these works have inadvertently gestured toward the Bible's ability to undercut and unravel any reading of it. As noted earlier, some graphic Bibles are more attuned to these textual characteristics and attempt to capitalize on them in a way that invites the reader to wrestle with the text.[69] At the heart of the issue is how the creators of graphic Bibles regard both the comics medium and their source text in the first place.

FUTURE PROSPECTS AND QUESTIONS

- The ideology of graphic Bibles deserves further analysis. George Kovacs points out that, over the course of the past twenty years, the comics medium has gained recognition as "a legitimate artistic and literary form capable of producing work of

---

[69] See, e.g., Crumb, *Genesis Illustrated*; Stack's "Stories from the Good Book" in *The New Adventures of Jesus*; Millar and Gross, *American Jesus*; Steve Ross, *Marked* (New York: Seabury Books, 2005); Steve Ross, *Blinded: The Story of Paul the Apostle* (New York: Seabury Books, 2008); Waldman, *Megillat Esther*.

merit" and identifies two trends that have factored into this legitimization.[70] First, comics artists have extended their appeal to a broader audience by tackling more serious and more intelligent stories. Second, as seen in this chapter, a number of comics artists have turned their attention toward critical reflections on the medium that make an effort to theorize aspects of comics and the particular work that comics do. Understandably, the work of Will Eisner, Scott McCloud, Kovacs and C. W. Marshall, Thierry Groensteen, and others reflects a defense of comics art, an apology that seeks to validate them by putting them on par with other recognized (i.e., "mainline" or "traditional") forms of art. One cannot help but wonder if graphic Bibles are produced in service to this same ideology precisely because the Bible itself carries so much weight in our culture. In other words, anything that proclaims itself a representation of something that already occupies a privileged position benefits from that aura. With ideological criticism, feminist criticism, postcolonial criticism, and other approaches like them now firmly established in the field of biblical studies, there is little doubt that we can anticipate more critical work on biblical comics and graphic novels and that such work will be attuned to ideological dynamics.

- Terry Ray Clark makes the provocative suggestion that graphic novels might potentially "function as a prophetic and religious voice in our society."[71] For example, comics like *Kingdom Come* and *Watchmen* challenge the idea that humans should wait for help from some otherworldly place and should instead act now on their own behalf and in nonviolent ways. Overall, Clark makes an excellent case for the uniquely religious hope and prophetic voice of the comics medium generally, and I think his argument would hold for many underground comix in particular.[72] What I wonder is whether or to what extent this can be said of all graphic Bibles in equal measure. One can envision a situation in which comic adaptations of this iconic, revered, powerful, but also fraught literary work simultaneously critique the way the Bible has been co-opted and privileged *and* reanimate the precanonical vigor of writers and texts that themselves spoke out against such practices, precisely by exploiting the marginal and edgy position of the comics medium itself.

- It is perhaps no surprise that the vast majority of graphic Bibles favor narrative material in their selection. Arguably this creates a significant gap between "the Bible" of graphic Bibles and the Bible of Jewish and Christian traditions. It would be worthwhile to survey which stories consistently do and do not make the cut, and then to theorize what accounts for these tendencies. Are comics fundamentally limited? Why, with all the metaphorical and symbolic language they contain,

---

[70] Kovacs, "Establishing a Critical Frame," 14.

[71] Terry Ray Clark, "Apocalypse Then and Now: *Kingdom Come* and the Tradition of Imagining Armageddon," in *The End Will Be Graphic: Apocalyptic in Comic Books and Graphic Novels*, ed. Dan W. Clanton, Jr. (Sheffield, UK: Sheffield Phoenix Press, 2012), 141.

[72] See Charles Hatfield, *Alternative Comics: An Emerging Literature* (Jackson: University Press of Mississippi, 2005).

do we not see more comic renderings of prophetic oracles? Letters make up the bulk of the New Testament. What are the consequences of reducing the New Testament to the gospels, Acts, and Revelation? Crumb provided images even for genealogies in *Genesis Illustrated*. What does his decision to do so signify?

- An exploration of the didactic function of graphic Bibles with respect to decisions regarding which stories they exclude or radically alter would be illuminating, especially with regard to how this might impact students and course content were such a work used in the classroom. For example, in the case of a book like Esther, one would search in vain for a graphic Bible that pictures imperially sanctioned mass kidnapping, trafficking, and raping of young girls. By the same token, graphic Bibles could very well serve as an excellent means by which to make the case that every translation is an interpretation and every adaptation has consequences.

- It would be interesting to examine which graphic Bibles are most popular on the basis of units sold, especially in relation to the social and cultural contexts of the historical moment in which they were published. Once that information was available, it would occasion an analysis of how certain graphic Bibles reinforce specific theological positions more than others.

SUGGESTED READINGS AND ANNOTATED BIBLIOGRAPHY

Carrier, David. *The Aesthetics of Comics*. University Park: Pennsylvania State University Press, 2000.

Carrier's book is a study of comics art in relation to other visual media from the perspectives of philosophy and art history. His argument is that "to understand comics properly…we must identify the conceptual issues posed by their definition and interpretation" (3).

Clanton, Dan, Jr., ed. *The End Will Be Graphic: Apocalyptic in Comic Books and Graphic Novels*. Sheffield, UK: Sheffield Phoenix Press, 2012.

This edited collection focuses specifically on the apocalyptic so prevalent in both independent and mainstream graphic novels. Although the essays are not concerned primarily with graphic Bibles (save for one essay on *The Wolverton Bible*) and most deal with "secular" comics, the contributors demonstrate how comics and the Bible are in conversation with one another whether or not they intend to be.

Eisner, Will. *Comics and Sequential Art*. 1985; Tamarac, FL: Poorhouse Press, 2000.

Eisner is a household name among comics aficionados, and his introduction to comics art has undergone more than twenty printings since its original publication in 1985. The book presents both theory and technique. Beginning with the argument that comics reflect a particular form of reading, Eisner surveys various fundamental elements of the medium to demonstrate the dynamics of visual storytelling through the sequential art of comics.

Kovacs, George, and C. W. Marshall, eds. *Classics and Comics*. Oxford: Oxford University Press, 2011.

Kovacs's comparison of comic book readers to classics scholars in the first chapter is reason enough to recommend this volume, but the sixteen essays that follow also provide an exceptional range of models for how biblical scholars might go about analyzing not only graphic Bibles but also biblical texts in conversation with comics.

Lewis, A. David. *American Comics, Literary Theory, and Religion: The Superhero Afterlife.* New York: Palgrave Macmillan, 2014.

> Lewis weaves together perspectives on the afterlife from the field of religious studies, comics scholarship, and critical theories of the self in order to argue that "explorations of the afterlife in the comics medium offer something greater than the more 'normal' afterlife stories in other media. The superhero genre offers an alternative, nonunified version of narrative character and, in turn, alternative models of selfhood for readers" (2).

Lewis, A. David, and Christine Hoff Kraemer, eds. *Graven Images: Religion in Comic Books and Graphic Novels.* New York: Continuum, 2010.

> Nearly two dozen contributors, made up of both creators and scholars, analyze a wide range of religious tropes and themes in a variety of contemporary comics and graphic novels in order to explore the distinctive advantages of the medium for communicating religious messages, which religious messages are being communicated by comics artists and to what audiences, and the significance of traditional and innovative religious thought appearing in comics (3).

McAllister, Matthew P., Edward H. Sewell Jr., and Ian Gordon, eds. *Comics and Ideology.* New York: Peter Lang, 2001.

> Although none of the essays in this volume considers graphic Bibles specifically or religious comics generally, their analysis, from various theoretical perspectives, of the ways that numerous social groups and social issues are directly or indirectly reflected in comics art demonstrates that comics are shaped by and actively engaged in the negotiation of power. The collection highlights the need for scholars reading graphic Bibles to be cognizant of what is at stake in any decision to rework the Bible graphically.

McCloud, Scott. *Understanding Comics: The Invisible Art.* New York: Harper Perennial, 1993.

> To put it simply, this is the "Bible" of comics art analysis. McCloud uses comics art not merely to illustrate his arguments but to actually and effectively make them. After establishing a definition and providing a historical overview, the remainder of the book draws on insights from semiotics, narratology, and other dimensions of literary theory to work through all of the fundamental elements of the medium in order to explain precisely how they work in order to create and communicate meaning.

CHAPTER 22

HOW AMERICAN NEWSPAPER COMIC STRIPS PORTRAY GOD, ANGELS, AND HUMANS

LEONARD GREENSPOON
KLUTZNICK CHAIR IN JEWISH CIVILIZATION,
CREIGHTON UNIVERSITY

INTRODUCTION

I cannot remember when I first started reading comic strips. My mother says that I was an avid reader from birth. In that case, I would have digested my first comic strip and my first bottle on the same day in early December 1945.

While I am well advised never to doubt my mother or her recollections, I cannot remember reading the newspaper or anything else while I was an infant. In fact, I cannot remember when I first read a book, although I still have my copy of *The Little Fire Engine*, along with my precious (if not exactly precocious) crayon drawings to accompany the professionals' words and pictures. So I am only guessing when I suggest that I was around ten when I became a regular newspaper reader, in my case of the dailies then in circulation in Richmond, Virginia: the *News Leader* and the *Times-Dispatch*. That would have been in 1955 or 1956; at that time, among the comic strips I might have read were *Pogo, Blondie, Gasoline Alley, Li'l Abner*, and *Bringing Up Father*.[1]

---

[1] Portions of this essay first appeared as part of the editor's introduction to *Studies in Jewish Civilization 17: American Judaism in Popular Culture*, ed. Leonard J. Greenspoon and Ronald A. Simkins (Omaha, NE: Creighton University Press, 2006), ix.

OVERVIEW OF TOPIC

Most people in the Western world would have little difficulty in recognizing a comic strip. Comic strips typically consist of a series of images in frames, arranged next to each other so that we can view or read them horizontally. In this format the frames constitute a narrative or chronological sequence. In most but not all comic strips, words accompany each image. Yet some comic strips contain only a single frame, and some contain no or only rudimentary visual elements.[2]

Although elements of the comic strip existed centuries, even millennia ago, the comic strip as a mainstay of popular culture is of much more recent date, originating in the United States at the end of the nineteenth century.[3] At one time, comic strips were an essential and very popular section of printed newspapers. In this format, comic strips are far less popular in the twenty-first century than they were in the twentieth. Today just about every comic strip appears in electronic format on the internet, either exclusively or in print form as well. Popular comic strips continue to be collected in volumes published thematically or chronologically in print or online.

The term "comic strip" is uniquely American and has often been problematic in terms of the content and tenor of this format.[4] Except for the period around 1900 when the term "comic strip," or "comic," became popular, many strips have intentionally not been at all comical. In these cases, the primary audience has been adults rather than children. As we shall see, some of these noncomic strips have addressed such serious topics as homosexuality, drug overdose, and rape.

The official birth year of the comic strip in the United States as a popular cultural product is probably 1895 or 1896. It was on October 1, 1995, that the US Postal Service issued a series of stamps, drawing from twenty strips, to honor the centennial of the comic.[5] This date, while appropriate as an approximation, is inexact.

Two decades earlier some comic strips began to appear in American magazines like *Puck* and *Judge*. Even limiting our analysis exclusively to newspapers, comic strips were found several years before the date commemorated by the official centennial. A number of firsts capture the fervor of the early newspaper comic strip, which played a prominent role in the robust competition between newspapers published by Joseph Pulitzer and those under the control of William Randolph Hearst. The rewards of victory, measured in increased subscriptions and sales, were tallied with all the care and emotion of a full-scale war—which this was.

---

[2] David M. Kunzie, "Comic Strip," *Encyclopaedia Britannica Online*, accessed May 28, 2020, https://www.britannica.com/art/comic-strip. This article is regularly updated.

[3] Maurice Horn, ed., *100 Years of American Newspaper Comics* (New York: Gramercy Books, 1996), 16.

[4] Kunzie, "Comic Strip."

[5] Mike Rhode, "Comics and Stamps Have a Longer History Than You'd Expect," *Washington City Paper*, July 19, 2000, on the occasion of the issuance by the US Postal Service of another set of comics-related stamps.

In January 1894 Pulitzer's *New York World* newspaper featured a full-color, full-page comic strip for the first time. Afterward it became conventional for comics to appear in color on Sunday and in black-and-white in editions from Monday through Saturday. Almost three years later, in October 1896, rival publisher Hearst instituted the first regular weekly comic supplement in his *Morning Journal*. This eight-page feature included the work of at least one cartoonist, Richard Felton Outcault, who had up until then been employed by Pulitzer. This strip came to be known as *The Yellow Kid* after the color of the nightshirt its main character, Mickey Dugan, typically wore. The enormous popularity of this strip led to lucrative merchandising deals of everything from cigarettes to toys.

A year later, in December 1897, Hearst inspired the birth of a comic titled *Katzenjammer Kids*. Rudolph Dirks created the strip and drew it until 1913. Dirks, basing his work on a series of German children's stories from the mid-nineteenth century ("Max und Moritz"), reanimated the two boys as a pair of rebellious and rambunctious twins named Hans and Fritz. A succession of cartoonists followed Dirks, enabling the strip to continue for 109 years, until 2006. The longevity of this strip points to another element in many comics: the original cartoonist is succeeded by others (sometimes family members or close professional associates) at his retirement or death. This has allowed some strips to survive to a very old age, whether or not it was merited. One exception, and an exceptional one it is, to this practice is *Peanuts*. It died when its author, Charles Schulz, passed away on February 12, 2000.[6]

Specific Examples and/or Foci

In what follows I will discuss a variety of topics related to the Bible and the comic strip.[7] First, we will consider images of the divine (God and Jesus), which appear in a number of strips and are almost always at variance with the view that the deity is omniscient, all-powerful, and unflappable. Second, I will survey a number of strips that cite or allude to specific biblical texts in order to determine how their creators use—and sometimes abuse or misuse—these texts. Finally, I will examine strips, such as *Peanuts* and *B.C.*, that have achieved fame or infamy (sometimes both) for their handling of biblically related material as a way of discussing how strips themselves function as sites of religious identity and controversy.

---

[6] Brian Walker, *The Comics since 1945* (New York: Abrams, 2002), 283–4.

[7] I restrict this analysis to syndicated comic strips that appear in a wide variety of newspapers and other publications throughout the United States—and often beyond. I have not analyzed strips that appear solely in denominational or other specifically religious publications. This restriction has nonetheless permitted the inclusion of dozens of strips that are (or at least were) read by millions on a daily basis.

Depictions of the Divine

Within Western, in this case especially North American, cartoons, the visual portrayal of God as all-powerful, all-knowing, all-seeing, error- or emotion-free is virtually absent. Although God is almost always pictured as male, most often an older male, he is a guy who is as prone to self-doubt and second-guessing as an archetypical dad on a television sitcom. And like that human, there is no lack of naysayers and advice givers to critique every action of the divine man. While this God is certainly knocked off whatever pedestal he is thought to mount and shielded from no criticisms because of his divine nature, he nonetheless manages to retain his unique stature as a creator who somehow or other gets through the insanity and inanity of a world he shares with his creatures.

The first examples here come from *Frank and Ernest*, which was created by Tom Thaves and debuted in November 1972. Now drawn and written by his son Bob, *Frank and Ernest* is in my view one of the most literate and verbally sophisticated comics available. For the purposes of this discussion, we limit ourselves to strips in which God appears on a cloud, along with a few of his angels, viewing his creation with a combination of amazement and befuddlement. It is probably not fair to describe this deity as disheveled, but his wardrobe is far from heavenly and his beard could use some trimming.

The relevant strips in *Frank and Ernest* are almost always single panels. In one, an angel sums up the combined judgment of God and his hosts about earth (September 7, 2011): "Frankly, it's too grim for a comedy, and too silly for a tragedy." In another, with identical iconography (August 11, 2011), humans draw this judgment: "You give them free will and they spend a fortune on personal empowerment seminars!" And so it goes. God offers this advice to two obviously perplexed angels (December 25, 2005): "Let's save some time—just program history to repeat itself." Or perhaps from an earlier era, when things weren't looking so dire, an angel speaks more optimistically to God (January 20, 2016): "Neat, a start-up!" And finally God speaks (February 27, 2008): "We'll go with the tree of knowledge for now and save the internet for later."

Similar depictions abound in many other strips. Here's God the golfer, who complains (Bill Whitehead, *Free Range*, September 20, 2013), "Drat! I never should have made that Sahara sand trap so big!" Or God, hands folded over his chest, assessing his creation (Vic Lee, *Pardon My Planet*, March 8, 2006): "Intelligent design was easy. It's an intelligent maintenance program that's difficult." When God loses his keys, he tries to follow a well-advised practice (Glenn and Gary McCoy, *The Flying McCoys*, January 21, 2016): "Now think... where was I last?" But, he concludes, that's really not going to work for him: "Oh yeah—<u>everywhere</u>! Dang!" Then there's God on *Jeopardy!* taking in all the money but earning this gentle rebuke from the host (John McPherson, *Close to Home*, November 30, 2015): "Right again, God, but please wait until AFTER I ask the question to answer." "If God started tweeting," his followers could read something like this (Dan Piraro and Wayno, *Bizarro*, August 16, 2010): "Woke up omnipotent again this morning. Awesome." And what better way for God to end a busy week sorting through the "unscathed" and "scathed" files than to drink some coffee from his "Thank me it's Friday" mug (John Deering, *Strange Brew*, October 8, 2010).

In addition to these examples of the portrayal of God, I want to look at an assortment of strips that specifically portray biblical Jesus in nonbiblical contexts. Among these are queries like "What would Jesus drive?," "Where would Jesus eat?," and "What would Jesus not do?" Alas, these cartoonists provide no specific answer to any of the questions.

There's much more. For example, there is Jesus and the dinosaurs (Lalo Alcaraz, *La Cucaracha*, December 4, 2012), Jesus and Elvis (*Kudzu*, December 14, 2013), Jesus and his fifty million Twitter followers (Dave Whamond, *Reality Check*, May 14, 2009), and Jesus at the water cooler (*The Argyle Sweater*, January 28, 2015). Jesus can be counted on to (a) give fashion advice to an indecisive female in the shoe department: "Whenever I'm faced with a difficult decision, I always ask myself, 'What would Jesus do?' And as always—go with the sandal" (*Pardon My Planet*, January 5, 2009); (b) drive "the biggest, baddest F350 long-bed pickup truck he could find" (Lennie Peterson, *The Big Picture*, December 18, 2002); and (c) save his friend's seat in a crowded movie theater (Mike Baldwin, *Cornered*, May 25, 1916). On the other hand, he could not vote ("He's got no photo I.D."; *Kudzu*, September 29–30, 2012) and would certainly not burn a copy of the Qur'ān (editorial cartoon by Kirk Walters, *Toledo Blade,* 2010). And we have not even moved into controversial areas such as gun control, abortion, or the death penalty.

This figure, Jesus of the comic strips, is almost infinitely pliable. He can be made to support a practically endless list of causes and even products. This is a Jesus that humans make and remake in their own image—for better or worse.

Specific Biblical Texts

Based on almost ten years' worth of comic strips (1979–87) that appeared in the *Los Angeles Times*, Donald B. Lindsey and John Heeren constructed a statistical framework for analyzing the religious content of comics.[8] Their final and smallest category is "Biblical Texts and Contexts." In my own work, this category, subdivided into Old Testament/Hebrew Bible and New Testament, constitutes by far the largest in my collection.

In many respects, the distribution of strips among biblical topics is not surprising. For the Old Testament, it is Noah's ark that attracts most attention. But very little of that attention focuses on Noah himself. Instead, the most popular individual, in terms of comics devoted to him, is Moses, who appears under several guises: as a child, at the burning bush, crossing the Red Sea, wandering through the wilderness because he (like all males) refused to ask for directions, and receiving the Ten Commandments. (There are also a considerable number of other strips on the Ten Commandments in which Moses does not appear.) Numerically, Adam and Eve (individually or together) show up

[8]   Donald B. Lindsey and John Heeren, "Where the Sacred Meets the Profane: Religion in the Comic Strips," *Review of Religious Research* 34, no. 1 (1992): 63–77.

a bit less often, but far more than anyone except Moses and Noah. Overall, references to the five books of the Torah/Pentateuch dominate the comic strip connection with the Old Testament.

In structuring the strips from the Torah—to which can be added references to Methuselah, Cain and Abel, and Nimrod—cartoonists are assuming a body of biblical knowledge (admittedly not very wide or deep) shared by members of their target audience. Outside of the Torah, so most cartoonists correctly reason, such knowledge is rarer, as are the references. For the Prophets, only a few characters or events show up frequently. Two of them are David and Goliath (1 Samuel 17) and Beelzebub (2 Kings 1; for example v. 2 speaks of "Baal-zebub, the god of Ekron" [NRSV]). The latter of these often bears humorous fruit. For example, Dave Whamond (*Reality Check*, February 3, 2009), presents a common first-date scenario—two people meeting over drinks—with this difference: a human woman is facing a monster, to whom she complains, "So...you said you were a prince in your online profile, uh...Bee Zebub, is it?...But you left out the part about you being 'Prince of Demons.'" *Andy Capp* (Reg Smythe, May 14, 2009) features a fairly typical day in the life of the strip's eponymous antihero and his long-suffering wife, Flo. Andy comments, "I never know what to call your mother. Using her first name seems disrespectful and 'mother-in-law' is too much of a mouthful," to which Flo replies, "And yet you're comfortable with 'Beelzebub's sister.'" I admit that I was at first surprised by Beelzebub's popularity, but it is often the comic possibilities of spelling (or misspelling) his name that attract attention rather than any specific action on the part of this deity.

For Ketuvim/Writings (the third and last section into which Jews divide the Hebrew Bible; among other books it includes Psalms, Proverbs, Job, Esther, and Daniel), sporadic citations from Psalms show up, but only one expression garners multiple attestations: "My cup runneth over" from Psalm 23. In many strips, the word "cup" does not actually appear, but the reference is nonetheless clear and definite. Examples include "Your tab runneth over" (spoken by a bartender to Bung, the alcoholic court jester in Johnny Hart and Brant Parker, *The Wizard of Id*, April 6, 2011); "My coop runneth over" (Ernie to Frank as they confront a surplus of unruly chickens in *Frank and Ernest*, July 17, 2011); and "Inflation Is When Our Up Runneth Over" (Gene More, *Graffiti*, February 27, 2013).[9] In any case, it is not the Psalter but the book of Job that provides the most references from the Writings/Ketuvim. However, since about half of these are references to Behemoth (Job 40), it is not clear that most readers will connect them with this biblical book—or any book of the Bible.

When we turn to the New Testament, I should first make mention of the popularity of the nativity in certain contexts. Among these is the Christmas pageant. Fairly widespread references to the three wise men, sometimes only tangentially connected to the New Testament narrative, should also be noted. For example, in *Free Range* (December 17, 2013), drawn by Bill Whitehead, three individuals, riding on camels and clearly

---

[9] *Graffiti* can be thought of as something of a genre bender. Each single-panel strip consists of a wall as the only image, which serves as a backdrop for written words.

intended to represent the three wise men, stare at a brightly lit "CASINO" sign. One of the men exclaims to the others, "Don't tell me we've been following the wrong light!" Which earns this response, "Oh, well…since we're here…." Russ Wallace (*Natural Selection*, December 21, 2002), illustrates a second-grade Christmas play; the three kids who were supposed to appear as Magi are dressed as mini-mobsters, eliciting this reaction from their teacher: "Boys…you're supposed to be the three wise MEN…not GUYS."

Another popular category of strips that rely on biblical imagery depicts persons who had been consigned to either heaven or hell. They feature typical images of these two destinations: the heat of hell overseen by the devil and his minions; the eternally blue skies and perfect weather of heaven, populated by nearly perfect people with matching wings and halos.

For me, the most surprising element is that the denizens of hell are about as content as the inhabitants of heaven. Sure, it is hot as, well, as hot as hell. But people, being people, can overcome that with a bit of bravado and ingenuity. The fury of hell is at least bearable in the company of others, who seem no worse or better than anyone else. For sure, heaven is pleasant, its inhabitants well-fed and cared-for as they flit about. But do I not detect a touch of boredom on their part and more catty observations than necessary about mismatched wings, uneven halos, and golf and tennis games that are, well, not quite heavenly?

None of the cartoonists I have looked at seem especially eager to support the "biblical" view of heaven as an eternal place of bliss and hell as a pit of never-ending gnashing of teeth. Rather, both locales present a continuation, albeit exaggerated, of life on the terrestrial plane.[10] And who knows? These cartoonists may well be on to something. Here are several heavenly examples: St. Peter to a nervous man, cell phone in hand, just outside of the Pearly Gates: "I'm sorry, Mr. Smith, but it's a bit late to be trying to 'friend' God" (*Frank and Ernest*, May 3, 2014). In another strip, Mick Jagger, unhappy with a nearby angel, ejaculates, "Hey, you, get off of my cloud!" (John McPherson, *Close to Home*, February 18, 2014). Finally, in Eric and Bill Teitelbaum's *Bottomliners*, one haloed and winged man says to another, "And what makes things worse, the telemarketers won't stop calling me" (August 15, 2015).

From hell come the following strips. First, the devil remarks to a pizza delivery man, "You're late. So much for your 'delivered in thirty minutes or less' guarantee. Still a promise is a promise. So I can either take possession of your immortal soul or get fifty percent off my next order" (Leigh Rubin, *Rubes*, March 12, 2010). In Scott Hillburn's *The Argyle Sweater*, there is a sign in the men's room of Hell's Diner that states, "Employees Must Not Wash Hands" (December 1, 2015). Vic Lee portrays a man speaking to the devil at the entrance to hell who says, "Wow! No kidding?! You mean I get to sleep in on Sunday mornings?" (*Pardon My Planet*, May 19, 2010).

---

[10] For more on the depictions of heaven and hell in popular culture, see the chapters in this volume by Kathryn Gin Lum and Deane Galbraith, respectively.

Several times in this essay I have made reference to cartoonists' sense of what their target audience is likely to know. For the most part, those observations refer to knowledge of biblical texts or other religious data. So familiar, for example, is Noah's ark that a cartoonist can sometimes dispense with any but the most general iconography to get his or her point across. That would typically also be true with Adam and Eve, the Ten Commandments, the Burning Bush, and other well-known images.

But comic strips work at more than one level, requiring on their audiences' part more than one sort of knowledge. Let me illustrate this with cartoons about Noah's ark. One (*Free Range*, April 11, 2009) features an impatient Noah waiting for two finicky cats to decide whether or not they'll come aboard. "Well?" he asks. "Are you coming? We don't have all day, you know." "We'll think about it," one of the cats deigns to respond. "Do we get a specialized menu?" This particular cartoon has a caption: "Why We Almost Didn't Have Cats." Noah's name is not mentioned, and only a small portion of the ark appears. But readers do not really need any more than rudimentary knowledge of the story to get the point.

I would contrast this cartoon with several that portray unicorns literally missing the boat. Sometimes the male of the species tries to placate his irritated wife by assuring her that he's booked first class on the next sailing. In my view, this cartoon differs from the one on cats in that it is not self-contained. The reader needs to know that unicorns, even if they once actually existed, do not any more. From what I might term a creatively literal reading of the text, a fairly knowledgeable reader would conclude that the cartoonist attributes this lack of present-day unicorns to their failure to board the ark in a timely manner.

Another cartoon, dated October 2008—only a month or so after the largest point drop in the history of the stock market—shows a line of businessmen and women trying to board the ark. Noah turns some of them away with this remark: "Sorry. Only two corrupt CEOs per bankrupt firm" (*Bizarro*, October 27, 2008). Although readers, especially in 2008, did not need an advanced degree in economics to appreciate the significance of this cartoon, nonetheless it does require a higher level of thought than the others just mentioned. Moreover, it runs a risk of being dated that the other cartoons do not.

In short, I think that a full analysis of how a comic strip works—and for whom—requires a consideration of the types or levels of knowledge the cartoonist assumes on the part of his or her audience. For this reason, some strips work well only for a relatively small audience, which is fine if that is what the cartoonist intended.

Comic Strips as Sites of Religious Identity or Controversy

At this point I want to return to Charles Schulz so that we can examine how comic strips function as locations of religious proclamation(s), that is, as spaces in which ideologies are promulgated. Schulz is popularly and obviously associated with the inclusion of religion and religious themes in his cartoons. It is estimated that he drew almost eighteen thousand *Peanuts* strips during the fifty years that the comic ran. Of these, about 560 strips—almost a year and a half's worth of daily and Sunday strips if they had all been published one after the other—"contain a religious, spiritual, or theological reference."[11] Schulz's use of biblical citations, references, and allusions are representative of what we find in these cartoons. In a sense, he was a pioneer in almost everything he did, since most mainstream cartoonists of that era tended to shy away from any but the most general and genial references to religion.[12]

At its height, *Peanuts* appeared in over 2,500 papers in sixty-five countries, in twenty-one languages. In terms of readers, this adds up to over 350 million. When we take into account the television specials and the many themed collections of strips that appeared in book form, there is no doubt that Schulz and the characters he created were enormously significant popular culture figures. And not only "were." In terms of current volume of sales of material connected with deceased celebrities, Schulz and his crew are third, surpassed only by Elvis Presley and Michael Jackson.[13]

One characteristic of Schulz's use of biblical material is his citation, by book, chapter, and verse, of passages. This allowed him, for example, to expand his repertoire of Old Testament references far beyond the cartoon staples of the Garden of Eden, Noah's ark, and Moses. For example, one Sunday strip (December 21, 1997) pictures Sally and Charlie Brown listening to the radio. "Four calling birds" in the lyrics to a popular Christmas song leads Sally to ask what a calling bird is. Charlie, in his often unexpectedly erudite manner, identifies it with a partridge and then reads from a Bible translation, which he just happens to have on hand: "In 1 Samuel 26:20, it says, 'For the king of Israel has come out to seek my life just as though he were hunting the calling bird.'" Never one to leave well enough alone, Charlie continues, "There's a play on words here, you see. David was standing on a mountain calling, and he compared himself to a partridge being hunted." Unimpressed, Sally ignores these literary observations, preferring instead to express the hope that she doesn't get socks again as a Christmas present.

For cartoonists citing the New Testament, Jesus's Sermon on the Mount predominates. While not neglecting this rich material, Schulz goes well beyond it. My example here is also a Sunday strip, featuring another pair of siblings, Lucy and Linus van Pelt. In response to Lucy's repeated complaints that Linus's sighing is bothering her television watching, he retorts, "It's scriptural." Her incredulity is met by Linus's citation of part of Romans 8: "For likewise the spirit helps us in our weakness; for we do not know how to pray as we ought, but the spirit himself intercedes for us with sighs too deep for words."

[11] So Stephen Lind, author of *A Charlie Brown Religion: Exploring the Spiritual Life and Work of Charles M. Schulz*, Great Comics Artists Series (Jackson: University Press of Mississippi, 2015), 115.

[12] For a popular treatment of how *Peanuts* reflects a Christian worldview, see Robert Short, *The Gospel According to Peanuts* (Louisville, KY: Westminster John Knox Press, 1965). Schulz himself was not averse to talking about his faith and the impact it had on his strip. See, e.g., his short piece titled "*Peanuts* as Profession of Faith," in the collection *My Life with Charlie Brown*, ed. M. Thomas Inge (Jackson: University Press of Mississippi, 2010), 20–5.

[13] Data provided by Jonathan Merritt, "The Spirituality of Snoopy: How the Faith of Charles Schulz, Creator of the *Peanuts* Comic Strip, Shaped His Work," *Atlantic*, April 25, 2016.

As usual, Lucy has the last word, characteristically practical rather than theological: "I'm either going to have to slug him, or start going back to Sunday school."

This characteristic feature of Schulz does have parallels in many other comics that cite biblical passages, although these strips generally do not provide the biblical source and often give no indication at all that they are biblical. More along the lines of *Peanuts*, Rev. Will B. Dunn, the resident preacher in *Kudzu*, is often portrayed with Bible and biblical citation in hand when he quotes scripture.[14] But there is something wonderfully incongruous about children in *Peanuts* quoting with almost encyclopedic knowledge from the Bible.

Nowhere is this more in evidence that in another of Schulz's well-known seasonal topics, the Christmas pageant, replete with noncooperative animals and, more to the point, exceedingly lengthy biblical passages to memorize.[15] In 2007 it was Luke 2:8 that was taxing Linus's abilities: "And there were in the same country shepherds abiding in the field, keeping watch over their flock by night." Seeing Charlie Brown, Linus suggests that if none of them learns their assigned passage, there will no pageant at all. As if on cue, Charlie recites the passage perfectly, leading Linus to seek refuge on the top of Snoopy's doghouse with the refrain "This is going to be a black Christmas."

In 2008 it was a passage from the Gospel of Matthew, 2:17–18, that confronted Linus. And it was Lucy again who confronted her brother with the order to "memorize it." But, Linus contends, he needs to do research on "the 'who,' the 'where' and the 'why.'" Lucy demolishes this argument in record time: "You start memorizing right now, or you'll know **who** is going to slug you, and you'll know **where** she's going to slug you and you'll know **why** she slugged you!!!" This time Linus does get the last word in the strip, again an expanded Sunday offering, although it is none too hopeful: "Christmas is not only getting too commercial, it's getting too dangerous." He also gets the last word, or close to it, in that year's series, when, in response to one last taunt by Lucy, he recites the biblical passage perfectly. His reward from Lucy: a full-blast, "Merry Christmas, you blockhead!" (At least this time only a single explanation point punctuates her words.)

For most religious traditions, the celebration or at least commemoration of significant events or beliefs results in a calendar of holidays. Non-Christians and non-Jews are familiar with observances such as Christmas, Easter, Hanukkah, and Passover, at least in their general contours. But a holiday does not have to be "real" in order to be famous,

---

[14] Although the nominal star of *Kudzu* was sixteen-year-old Kudzu DuBose, Don Markstein notes, "The real star is Rev. Will B. Dunn, a minister who in some ways conforms to the stereotype of the Southern preacher—loud, always ready to speak his mind, and somewhat more materialistic in the eyes of others than in his own self-image. But in other ways, such as his ready sarcasm and a rather eccentric way of looking at the world, he's unique. Apparently, readers take to him more enthusiastically than they would to a more conventional fire'n'brimstone type." "Kudzu," Toonpedia, accessed May 28, 2020, http:/www.toonopedia.com/kudzu.htm. For a collection of strips featuring the Reverend, see Doug Marlette, *Preacher: The Wit and Wisdom of Reverend Will B. Dunn* (Nashville, TN: Thomas Nelson, 1984).

[15] In addition to the strips mentioned here, see also the now classic animated television special, "A Charlie Brown Christmas," which debuted on CBS, December 9, 1965. It was well received by audiences and critics, earning both an Emmy and a Peabody Award.

especially when it originates in the fertile imagination of a cartoonist like Schulz. For generations, readers of *Peanuts* have looked forward to the appearance (well, to be honest, the nonappearance) of the Great Pumpkin, who—at least according to Linus, the main (sole?) adherent of this faith—rises up out of pumpkin patches to give gifts to all good little boys and girls worldwide. This Santa substitute is active not in late December but about two months earlier, on the night of Halloween. Charlie Brown is among the naysayers who mock Linus, who misses out on the reality of Halloween candy in his elusive and never successful attempts to see the Great Pumpkin itself. In reply, Linus opines, "All right, so you believe in Santa Claus, and I'll believe in the Great Pumpkin. The way I see it, it doesn't matter what you believe just so you're sincere!"[16]

There is more than one way to interpret Linus's comment here. I see it minimally as a plea for tolerance. But it is actually more than that: it is a celebration of diversity that sweeps up a multitude of beliefs in its wake, with the proviso that belief in each of them must be sincere. And sincerity, so Schulz demonstrates repeatedly in his strips, is the result of questioning. Not certainty, but sincerity.

In this sense, I view Schulz as presenting a point of view that transcends the distinction between conservative and liberal. But not quite. For some conservatives the very act of questioning biblically related articles of faith is tantamount to denying their validity. If questioning is an attribute of a liberal perspective, then, I suppose, Schulz is a liberal.

However we come down on the best descriptor for Schulz, there is little doubt that he occupies a very different space in the cosmic comics universe than does the equally prolific and inventive Johnny Hart. Hart developed two long-running and popular strips: *B.C.*, which was first syndicated in early 1958, and *The Wizard of Id*, which first appeared in 1964. For the former, which will be the subject of our analysis in this essay, Hart both wrote and drew the strip; he also wrote *The Wizard of Id*, but Brant Parker drew it.[17]

B.C. was an essentially mainstream type of strip for its first twenty-five years, creatively mining the comic possibilities of a cast of mostly compatible humans and animals in a prehistoric setting. Beginning in the mid-1980s, Hart's faith underwent a change and so did his strip, which he began to view as his designated "ministry" to his world of readers. Although overtly religious themes were still relatively rare in frequency, they became increasingly controversial, some would say combative. Minimally, we can observe, the tone of strips such as *B.C.* is very different from what Schulz creates in *Peanuts*.

Here are a few examples chosen from the New Testament. Two strips (one from spring 2011, the other two years later) build upon the reality of Jesus's empty tomb. Admittedly the overall tone of these strips is humorous. In the first (April 24, 2011), the removal of the stone allows a salesman of burial sites to offer Jesus's now empty tomb to a prospective buyer. In the second (March 31, 2013), a caveman's accidental trip to the empty tomb

[16] See, for example, Yvonne Lai, "Never Discuss Politics, Religion or the Great Pumpkin," ABC News, October 27, 2006, http://abcnews.go.com/Entertainment/story?id=2611958&page=1.

[17] For a lengthy and generally appreciative overview of Hart's life and work, especially on *B.C.*, see R. C. Harvey, "Johnny Hart to Appear B.C.," *Comic Journal*, March 22, 2012, http://www.tcj.com/johnny-hart-to-appear-b-c/.

is, well, filled with accidents, such that he is pretty beaten up by the time he arrives there. I guess it was all worth it for him, since he declares, "Life's greatest discoveries rarely occur without pain." Lest any reader be in doubt, several nearby graves, marked incongruously with crosses, make it clear to all but the most obtuse that the empty tomb is indeed Jesus's.

Far less humorous and more overtly preacherly is a strip that features a single caveman sitting under a tree and writing (carving) a message. Perhaps inspired by the depiction of the Kingdom of God as yeast (see Matt 13:33; Luke 13), this Sunday strip begins with the image of yeast being cast out of dough, followed by "the bread of life is risen." Panel after panel displays similar sentiments, concluding with, "But now you are risen! Risen indeed! No longer dead!" Given that the image of the man writing is essentially static, these ten panels constitute nothing more—or less—than a sermon on the comic pages.

Hart did not avoid controversy, although he denies he intentionally sought it out. Whether sought or not, one of his most contentious strips appeared on Easter Sunday 2001, typically a time when Hart was at his most overt in the expression of faith. In panel after panel of this strip, the menorah, the ancient, universally recognized seven-branched symbol of Judaism, is stripped of its lights. One by one they are burned away, destroyed, in response to "the seven last words of Jesus." In the next to the last panel all that remains is a cross. The final panel pictures the empty tomb with a great boulder rolled away. The accompanying caption reads, "Do this in remembrance of me."

In my view (and I was far from alone in expressing such sentiments), this strip crossed the line by making such use of a central symbol of Judaism, in effect saying that Christianity has replaced Judaism, just as the cross takes the place of the menorah.[18] In statements issued by the distributor of his strip (Creators Syndicate), Hart vehemently denied these charges, explaining, "I believe that Replacement Theology [also referred to as supersessionism] is the stuff of lunatics and self-deluded fools. I noticed one day that the center section of the Menorah—the sacred symbol of Judaism—bore the shape of the cross. I wanted everyone to see the cross in the menorah. It was a revelation to me, that tied God's chosen people to their spiritual next-of-kin—the disciples of the Risen Christ."[19] In general, I take people at their word: Hart intended this strip to celebrate the genetic connection ("next-of-kin"), if you will, between Christianity and Judaism. But in the case of cartoonists, I also need to take into account the images they present, along with verbal accompaniment. I see little if any love or respect coming out of the panels themselves. My conclusion: whatever Hart's motives, the results he produced do not promote goodwill and mutual respect among adherents of two of the three major Western religious traditions.

It is possible for a cartoonist to take a strong theological or ideological stance without incurring the prolonged, public wrath of opponents. From a traditional stance there is

[18] Leonard Greenspoon, "Portrayal of Jews in Comics and Popular Culture in the Classroom," *SBL Forum*, October 2004, http://sbl-site.org/Article.aspx?ArticleID=329.

[19] This quotation is found in Harvey, "Johnny Hart to Appear B.C."

Bil and Jeff Keane's *Family Circus*, which has been in wide syndication since the end of February 1960.[20] Typically in the format of a single panel, the strip features a squeaky-clean suburban family of six, whose ages and mores seem frozen in time. Its approach to religion is examined in the aforementioned survey by Lindsey and Heeren and is typified by the following exchanges that feature the family's children. Upon viewing a picture of an angel, Dolly asks, "How do angels get their nightshirts on over their wings?" Another time, their mother says, "God bless you," when one of her sons, Billy, sneezes. This leads Dolly to ask, "Mommy, what's everybody in heaven say to God when He sneezes?" On another occasion, it is Billy who poses a theologically redolent question to their mother, who is always available to the children in the world of *Family Circus*: "I know what the Father and Son is, but what is the Holy Spearmint?"[21]

Bil Keane and his son Jeff have been open in acknowledging that *Family Circus* models Christian values that are conservative without being denominationally specific. The Keanes seem no less committed to their faith than Johnny Hart was to his. But what "comes out of the mouth of babes" rarely if ever has the venom that Hart's characters often articulated and exemplified. And Bil Keane never pictured himself as being on a divinely ordered mission. Quite the opposite. He said, "I never set out to be an evangelist. All I'm doing is showing the way religion touches a child's life or family life."[22] And that is undoubtedly true for some forms of religion and some configurations of family.

Taken individually or as a whole, these examples show the near impossibility of pleasing everyone when it comes to pictorial presentations of religious observance and belief among humans. It is also true that not every reader responds favorably to the depictions of the divine we looked at earlier.

Overall, this study and analysis of the Bible and comic strips reveals lines of continuity as well as unique instances of creativity. The basic structure or form of the comic strip has endured for about 120 years in the face of enormous technological changes in how comics are drawn and distributed. Even if religion, specifically the Bible, did not feature in the earliest examples of comics, cartoonists were nonetheless constantly attuned to questions related to values, the difference between right and wrong, and the struggle humans endure to make sense of our world.

For the most part, cartoonists have made use of their craft to have fun with the Bible rather than to make fun of it. Or to use references to the Bible as a means of enhancing readers' joy, critiquing their pretensions, or expanding their knowledge of Sacred Writ. In the process, cartoonists have necessarily developed some sense of how familiar or unfamiliar their audience is with the Bible. Well-known biblical accounts, such as of the Garden of Eden and Noah's ark, can be illustrated with a minimum of specificity: part of a boat with some animals or a male and female character sporting fig leaves will do. In

---

[20] For an appreciative overview, see "*Family Circus* Models Christian Values," *Thinking Out Loud*, November 24, 2011), https://paulwilkinson.wordpress.com/2011/11/24/family-circus-models-christian-values/.

[21] See the category "Religion and the World of Children" in Lindsey and Hereen, "Where the Sacred Meets the Profane," 72–3. The examples here are found on 72.

[22] As quoted in "*Family Circus* Models Christian Values."

other instances, cartoonists will explicitly include chapter and verse in order to ensure that readers catch on.

FUTURE PROSPECTS AND QUESTIONS

- How should cartoonists and their readers approach biblically related material that may be controversial and even offensive?
- What differences are cartoonists and their readers likely to face given the increasing number of strips online and their diminishing presence in traditional print newspapers?
- How can instructors use examples from the Bible in comic strips to enhance students' understanding of interpretive approaches and outcomes?
- Is it desirable to construct a set of guidelines to which cartoonists should adhere when making reference to the Bible?
- In what ways is it useful for readers to have overall knowledge of a given comic strip in order properly and fully to understand specific biblical references it contains?

SUGGESTED READINGS AND ANNOTATED BIBLIOGRAPHY

Greenspoon, Leonard J. "Jews and Judaism in Comic Strips." In *Studies in Jewish Civilization 17: American Judaism in Popular Culture*, edited by Leonard J. Greenspoon and Ronald A. Simkins, 255–70. Omaha, NE: Creighton University Press, 2006.

Although this essay deals only tangentially with specific references to the Bible, it represents a creative approach to discerning the many options cartoonists have available when dealing with topics related to religion.

Horn, Maurice, ed. *100 Years of American Newspaper Comics*. New York: Gramercy Books, 1996.

This resource is encyclopedic in coverage and in format. It is especially strong for the early period of comics. There are many illustrations, including some in full color.

Kunzie, David M. "Comic Strip." *Encyclopaedia Britannica Online*. Accessed May 28, 2020. https://www.britannica.com/art/comic-strip.

This is a concise yet comprehensive overview of the history of the comic strip and its major developments. Because it is online, this entry can be updated periodically.

Lind Stephen. *A Charlie Brown Religion: Exploring the Spiritual Life and Work of Charles M. Schulz*. Great Comics Artists Series. Jackson: University Press of Mississippi, 2015.

This well-researched monograph on Schulz's many portrayals of religion is essential reading for understanding the perennial popularity of *Peanuts*.

Lindsey, Donald B., and John Heeren. "Where the Sacred Meets the Profane: Religion in the Comic Strips." *Review of Religious Research* 34, no. 1 (1992): 63–77.

This article presents a framework for organizing and evaluating instances of religion in comic strips. Although this framework has its flaws, it remains a useful tool.

Merritt, Jonathan. "The Spirituality of Snoopy: How the Faith of Charles Schulz, Creator of the *Peanuts* Comic Strip, Shaped His Work." *Atlantic*, April 25, 2016.

A very well-written and entertaining introduction to Schulz as a person of faith committed to a pluralistic understanding of religion.

Walker, Brian. *The Comics since 1945.* New York: Abrams, 2002.

A fine decade-by-decade discussion and analysis of comic strips during the second half of the twentieth century. Illustrations appear on every page.

CHAPTER 23

THE MATERIAL DIMENSION OF THE BIBLE FROM PRINT TO DIGITAL TEXT

KATJA RAKOW

DEPARTMENT OF PHILOSOPHY AND RELIGIOUS STUDIES, UTRECHT UNIVERSITY

INTRODUCTION

THE Bible is often referred to as "the Word of God," "His Word," or "Scripture." All three terms reference the Bible as words to be read or heard and interpreted, as a text to be explored in order to discern God's will and to enable an encounter with God through His Word. To many Christians the Bible is "a material text with immaterial qualities, the latter of which are revealed as signs of God's presence in the act of reading."[1] Signifiers such as "the Word" and "Scripture" point to the textual quality of the Bible while downplaying the material dimension of words, which are made up of letters printed on pages and bound between two covers that make up the material object called a Bible. While conveying semantic meaning, the singular words of a text tend to be unseen in the actual act of reading. Although visible on the page, they tend to disappear in the process of reading. The content mediated through printed words stays with the reader and transports her, moving along a storyline or argument while the image of the words just read are already forgotten. In comparison to illustrations and pictures, the image of words on the page that have just been read is ephemeral. The eyes scan the lines of text, swiftly process the content, and fly over the pages. Sometimes the smoothness of the reading

---

[1] Matthew Engelke, "Reading and Time: Two Approaches to the Materiality of Scripture," *Ethnos* 74, no. 2 (2009): 151–74, here 151.

process is briefly interrupted when the reader stumbles over a typo and has to read again to fit the misspelled word into context in order to grasp the full meaning. The material religion scholar S. Brent Plate refers to the erasure of words in the process of reading as "words unseen," made invisible by modern typography.[2] Starting with the development of Baskerville type in the eighteenth century, which replaced the then dominant Gothic script, modern typeface was developed to reduce the distance between text and reader and to enhance legibility and readability in order to make the process of (silent) reading smoother.[3] The materiality of words is further diminished by a modernist understanding of words heavily influenced by Protestantism. Protestantism rates words higher than images, the mind higher than the body, and interiority over exteriority.[4] Words are understood as "silent, individual, immediate (i.e., 'without media'), of the spirit," and they are pitched against images, which in contrast are regarded as external, material, and visible and thereby available to a collective.[5] The perceived immediacy of the Word renders the concrete materiality of the Bible negligible to an understanding of Scripture as the immaterial presence of God.[6] But, as Plate reminds us, "regardless of their semantic meaning, words exist in and through their mediated forms and do not exist apart from their materiality. By extension, sacred texts themselves are material forms and engaged in two primary ways: through the ears and eyes."[7]

Evangelical discourse adds to the immateriality of Scripture the unchanging quality of God's Word regardless of the concrete translation or material form through which a Christian accesses the biblical text. Yet, occasionally, the materiality of Scripture becomes an issue for Christian practitioners. Take the following example of Pastor Carl Lentz from Hillsong Church, New York, addressing his audience at Hillsong Conference 2015 in Sydney: "Who has a Bible tonight? Hold it up if you do. Look to your neighbor and say, 'My Bible is so much better than yours. It's heavier; it's real.' And if your Bible is on your phone, I don't wanna see it because if you need a Word from God and, ah, your phone is dead, whatcha gonna do then? Your Bible needs to have pages."[8] Lentz expresses a preference for the printed Bible, which he regards as offering direct access to God's Word. His statement implies that a book can be opened and read at any time. In order to

---

[2] S. Brent Plate "Looking at Words: The Iconicity of the Page," in *Iconic Books and Texts*, ed. James W. Watts (Sheffield, UK: Equinox, 2013), 121.

[3] Ibid., 124–6.

[4] Colleen McDannell, *Material Christianity: Religion and Popular Culture in America* (New Haven, CT: Yale University Press, 1995), 2–15.

[5] Plate, "Looking at Words," 121.

[6] Such understandings of Scripture as the immaterial presence of God are not unique to Christianity, but can also be found in Islam, where the Qur'ān is one physical manifestation of divine revelations consisting of the *Kalam Allah*, that is, "the speech or the self-communication of God... [which] exists only in the transcendent world and not here on earth." See C. T. R. Hewer, *Understanding Islam: The First Ten Steps* (London: SCM Press, 2006), 46. Thus, the Koran as the speech of God is where God is regarded as most fully present in this world; cf. William E. Shepard, *Introducing Islam* (Abingdon, UK: Routledge, 2016), 68.

[7] Plate, "Looking at Words," 119.

[8] Carl Lentz at the Evening Rally, Hillsong Conference, Sydney, July 2, 2015. Transcript by the author.

be read, a book is not dependent on battery power or a digital screen. With its unity of pages, printed words, and binding, the book is a "real" thing that can be touched and weighs heavy in the hands of its reader. Compared to the concrete materiality of a book, the electronic text seems rather intangible. Here the printed Bible is seen as a durable and reliable material container for the immaterial Word. In contrast, the digital text on an electronic device is regarded as an unstable material carrier dependent on other external factors and thereby insufficient to act as reliable medium to the presence of God via the act of reading.[9]

At issue is the materiality of the medium through which God's Word, and thereby God, is made present to religious practitioners. It shows us that the concrete materiality of a medium matters. In spiritual questions, *matter does matter*. In this chapter, I address the material dimension of the Bible in the discourse and practice of evangelical and Pentecostal Christians.[10] First, I introduce the frame of material culture studies and the approach to materiality in the study of religion. Then I use an analytic model suggested by the material religion scholar David Morgan that lists nine aspects along which a material analysis of religious objects should be developed, and I apply it to explore the relation between Bible and materiality. The currently observable transition from print Bibles to electronic versions and Bible apps will serve as my main example to illustrate the fruitfulness of a material perspective on the Bible.

The transition from one media format to another often stirs discussions about the appropriateness of the new medium in the context of religious practices. Such discussions signal a departure from and contestation of traditional forms of communication and transmission media and point to an ongoing negotiation between the adaptability of and resistance to new forms. One historical example is the transition from Bible texts printed in Latin and mainly directed at Christian clergy to Bible scriptures published in vernacular languages and directed at common people in the context of the Protestant

---

[9] Katja Rakow, "The Bible in the Digital Age: Negotiating the Limits of 'Bibleness' of Different Bible Media," in *Christianity and the Limits of Materiality*, ed. Minna Opas and Anna Haapalainen (London: Bloomsbury, 2017), 101–21.

[10] My usage of the terms "evangelicals" and "evangelicalism" refers to a form of American Protestantism that emerged from the great revivals of the eighteenth and nineteenth centuries and, according to Randall Balmer, became quite influential to American culture. See Balmer, "Evangelicalism," in *Encyclopedia of Evangelicalism*, revised and expanded ed., ed. Randall Balmer (Waco, TX: Baylor University Press, 2004), 244–8. "Evangelicalism" as an umbrella term encompasses a diverse spectrum of churches, parachurches, organizations, and movements, which are all characterized by the following four elements: Biblicism, a view of the Bible as inspired and God's revelation to humanity; a focus on the atoning work of Jesus Christ on the cross; the centrality of the conversion experience often termed "born again" combined with a personal relationship with God through Jesus Christ; and a strong emphasis on evangelism. The terms "Pentecostals" and "Pentecostalism" as used here refer to a specific stream within American evangelicalism that developed in the beginning of the twentieth century. In addition to the aforementioned characteristics, Pentecostals emphasize the workings of the Holy Spirit in today's world and the life of the believer through signs and wonders. These beliefs also find expression through speaking in tongues and prayers for healing, deliverance, and prosperity, among other practices.

Reformation.[11] A more recent example of such a media transition is the adoption of radio and TV to broadcast the Christian message beyond the immediate church auditorium and which led some viewers and listeners to experience conversion or even healing in front of their radio transmitters or TV sets.[12] Contemporary commentators often contested the possibility of such religious experiences mediated by modern technology and media because these did not fit into the communication and practice patterns of face-to-face communication typical of church services.[13] But American evangelicals and Pentecostal Christians have a long history of being at the forefront of adopting new technologies and popular media formats.[14]

For the purpose of this chapter, I will consider digital Bibles and Bible apps provided by Bible publishers and digital content providers—whether those are commercial or nonprofit—as media that fit into the popular-culture frame (understood as referring to cultural products and related practices that are broadly disseminated through modern technology, mass media, and marketing) and that are thus widely used and appreciated by a significant number of people as indicators of their "popular status."[15] Such an understanding is easily applicable to today's ubiquity of all kinds of apps employed to organize different aspects of our daily life, ranging from managing one's bank account to monitoring fitness progress, listening to music, watching Netflix, or following a daily Bible-reading plan. If we take the increase in usage of electronic Bible media over the past years as an indicator, then we can—in extension of apps in general—also consider digital Bibles and Bible apps as popular-culture products.[16]

---

[11] Even before translating Bible scriptures into German, Martin Luther paved the way for the mass distribution of religious pamphlets and Bible texts to the common people so characteristic of the entwinement of book printing and the spread of the Protestant Reformation. Luther's translations of Psalms into vernacular German were printed as early as 1517 and consciously aimed at a wider audience. His texts were printed in the quarto format (singular sheets folded twice to produce four leaves, i.e., eight pages), which was easy to produce and cheap to acquire. The quarto became the characteristic format for many of the Reformation texts and helped to spread and circulate its theological debates widely. Cf. Mark U. Edwards, *Printing, Propaganda, and Martin Luther* (Minneapolis, MN: Fortress Press, 2005), 15–7; Andrew Pettegree, *The Book in the Renaissance* (New Haven, CT: Yale University Press, 2010), 91–106.

[12] William K. Kay, "Pentecostalism and Religious Broadcasting," *Journal of Beliefs & Values* 30, no. 3 (2009): 245–54.

[13] Shane Denson, "Faith in Technology: Televangelism and the Mediation of Immediate Experience," *Phenomenology & Practice* 5, no. 2 (2011): 96–122.

[14] For historical examples, see the study by R. Laurence Moore, *Selling God: American Religion in the Marketplace of Culture* (New York: Oxford University Press, 1994); for more contemporary examples, see Heather Hendershot, *Shaking the World for Jesus: Media and Conservative Evangelical Culture* (Chicago: University of Chicago Press, 2004).

[15] This understanding of popular culture is based on a definition provided by Terry Ray Clark, "Introduction: What Is Religion? What Is Popular Culture? How Are They Related?," in *Understanding Religion and Popular Culture*, ed. Terry Ray Clark and Dan W. Clanton (London: Routledge, 2012), 1–12, here 8.

[16] See the section "Bible Users Prefer Print, but Use Other Formats" of "The State of the Bible 2017: Top Findings," which compares the numbers from a survey in 2011 with those of the 2017 survey conducted by the Barna Group for the American Bible Society, April 4, 2017, https://www.barna.com/research/state-bible-2017-top-findings.

Overview of Topic: Material Culture and Material Religion

Materiality refers to matter, something that is concrete, substantial, physical, tangible, and real, as opposed to the immaterial, imaginary, ideal, spiritual, and intellectual dimension of human life. Usually the opposition of material/immaterial implies a hierarchy that ranks the immaterial, the spiritual, and the realm of ideas higher than the world of matter, the physical, and the corporeal. We find this notion inscribed in Protestant models of religion focusing on belief and inner conviction while downplaying religious material culture and religious practice as illustrations or reflections of beliefs and inner states of the mind. The Protestant-inflected notion of religion influenced how the category of religion was conceptualized and how religion was studied in academia. It gave precedence to religious beliefs, ideas, and concepts drawn from the authoritative sources of religious traditions while neglecting the material dimension and popular expressions of religion.[17] The reevaluation of the material dimension of religion happened in the context of a broader paradigm shift within the humanities and social sciences often referred to as "the material turn."[18] Based on the realization that material things are neither just illustrations of social facts and relations nor secondary expressions of ideas, materiality is recognized as an integral part of culture, which is shaped by humans and in turn shapes humans and the experience of their lifeworlds: "Material culture studies in various ways inevitably have to emphasize the dialectical and recursive relationship between persons and things: that persons make and use things and that the things make persons. Subjects and objects are indelibly linked. Through considering one, we find the other. Material culture is part and parcel of human culture in general."[19]

In the past two decades, more and more scholars studying religion in the past and the present have called for a "materialization" of the study of religion to counterbalance the tendency to emphasize the study of textual sources and theological or philosophical debates.[20] These scholars perceive materiality to be a—or even the—crucial element in

[17] See, for example, McDannell, *Material Christianity*, 2–8; Birgit Meyer, "Material Mediations and Religious Practices of World-Making," in *Religion across Media: From Early Antiquity to Late Modernity*, ed. Knut Lundby (New York: Peter Lang International, 2013), 1–19, here 2; David Morgan, "Introduction: The Matter of Belief," in *Religion and Material Culture: The Matter of Belief*, ed. David Morgan (London: Routledge, 2010), 1–12.

[18] Patrick Joyce and Tony Bennett, "Material Powers: Introduction," in *Material Powers: Cultural Studies, History and the Material Turn*, ed. Tony Bennett and Patrick Joyce (New York: Routledge, 2010), 1–21, here 7.

[19] Christopher Tilley, introduction to *Handbook of Material Culture*, ed. Christopher Tilley et al. (London: Sage, 2006), 1–6, here 4.

[20] See, for example, David Morgan, "Religion and Embodiment in the Study of Material Culture," in *Religion: Oxford Research Encyclopedias*, Subject: Religion in America (Oxford: Oxford University Press, 2015), doi:10.1093/acrefore/9780199340378.013.32; Birgit Meyer et al., "The Origin and Mission of Material Religion," *Religion* 40, no. 3 (2010): 207–11, here 209.

the making of religious worlds: "All religion is material religion. All religion has to be understood in relation to the media of its materiality. This necessarily includes a consideration of religious things, and also of actions and words, which are material no matter how quickly they pass from sight or sound or dissipate into the air."[21] Following the anthropologist Matthew Engelke, all religion is material because it depends on material media, such as images, objects, clothes, food, incense, liquids, spaces, but also on the acting, sensing, and experiencing human body engaging the material world the religious actors inhabit. Without the "multiple media for materializing the sacred," it would be impossible to "make the invisible visible," as Robert Orsi, a scholar of religion, puts it.[22] All these media are used to render the sacred tangible to the human senses. Media play a crucial role in bringing religious practitioners into contact with the divine and making it "sense-able"[23] in official religious rituals as well as in lived religion in the context of everyday life. Scholars studying religion through the framework of its materiality work with a broad notion of media, which does not reduce media to classic mass media formats or new forms of social media. A broad notion of media encompasses every form of materiality that is employed to mediate religion. Thus media, broadly understood, range from the world of objects to less solid substances such as sound and smell, and they include the human body, practices, performances, and spaces: "Whether as the transmission of a numinous essence to a community of believers, the self-presencing of the divine in personal experience, or the unfolding of mimetic circuits of exchange between transcendental powers and earthly practitioners, 'religion' can only be manifested through some process of mediation. Throughout history, in myriad forms, communication with and about 'the sacred' has always been enacted through written texts, ritual gestures, images and icons, architecture, music, incense, special garments, saintly relics and other objects of veneration, markings upon the flesh, wagging tongues and other body parts."[24]

In the anthropologist Birgit Meyer's conceptualization of religion as a practice of mediation—that is, the process of bringing into contact, making visible or "sense-able" the divine to the religious practitioner—media and mediation processes become the defining moment of religion and the starting point of its analysis. Central to her approach is the concept of "sensational forms," which she describes as "relatively fixed, authorized modes of invoking and organizing access to the transcendental, thereby creating and sustaining links between religious practitioners in the context of particular religious organizations. Sensational forms are transmitted and shared; they involve religious practitioners in particular practices of worship and play a central role in forming

[21] Matthew Engelke, "Material Religion," in *The Cambridge Companion to Religious Studies*, ed. Robert A. Orsi (New York: Cambridge University Press, 2012), 209.

[22] Robert Orsi, "Material Children: Making God's Presence Real through Catholic Boys and Girls," in *Religion, Media and Culture: A Reader*, ed. Gordon Lynch, Jolyon Mitchell, and Anna Strhan (New York: Routledge, 2012), 147.

[23] Birgit Meyer, "Medium," in *Key Terms in Material Religion*, ed. S. Brent Plate (London: Bloomsbury, 2015), 141.

[24] Jeremy Stolow, "Religion and/as Media," *Theory, Culture & Society* 22, no. 4 (2005): 125.

religious subjects."[25] Such sensational forms can be communally enacted religious rituals as well as individual devotional practices in which religious actors engage material objects and spaces (images, books, architecture, nature, etc.) through their body, mind, and senses. The idea of sensational forms applies to both the authorized settings of religious institutions as well as the lived religion of the daily life of religious practitioners. In both settings, collective and individual religious practices "address and involve participants in a specific manner and induce particular feelings" whereby religious experiences are enabled.[26]

Reading the Bible to discern God's will for the life of a Christian practitioner is one important sensational form in the context of American evangelicalism and Pentecostalism. This particular sensational form works on two assumptions. The first is that God is present in the Bible and thus accessible via reading His Word;[27] the second is that God's Word is unchanging but timely and thus always applicable to every situation in the life of the believer, regardless of the material container through which His Word is accessed.[28] A different sensational form concerning the Bible can be found in Pentecostal healing rituals, in which a pastor places the book on the head of an afflicted believer and declares healing in the name of the Lord, whose healing powers are mediated through the spoken declaration and the materiality of God's Word, the printed Bible. In the first example, a digital Bible on a smartphone can easily replace the printed book. For many evangelicals and Pentecostals, it does not make a difference through which medium they access the biblical text when the primary purpose is reading and interpreting. However, in the second example of the Pentecostal healing ritual, it is harder for practitioners to imagine holding an iPad above the head of a believer declaring healing in God's name.[29] These two examples illustrate the notion of "relatively fixed, authorized modes of invoking and organizing access to the transcendental" in the concept of sensational forms.[30] Thus not every medium is suitable or regarded as appropriate to mediate the presence of God within specific practice settings, and heated debates might accompany the introduction of new forms or ritual innovations.

The material turn in religious studies has recast our questions and broadened our analytical horizon. Instead of asking how elements of religious material culture such as images, architecture, symbols, and ritual objects represent and illustrate religious ideas and teachings, we now ask how religious actors create and make use of things and objects and how the engagement with things and objects simultaneously creates religious worlds and shapes religious subjects: "Materializing the study of religion means asking how religion happens materially, which is not to be confused with asking the

[25] Birgit Meyer, "Religious Sensations: Why Media, Aesthetics, and Power Matter in the Study of Contemporary Religion," in *Religion: Beyond a Concept*, ed. Hent de Vries (New York: Fordham University Press, 2008), 707.

[26] Ibid., 708.   [27] Engelke, "Reading and Time," 151.

[28] James S. Bielo, "Textual Ideology, Textual Practice: Evangelical Bible Reading in Group Study," in *The Social Life of Scriptures: Cross-Cultural Perspectives on Biblicism*, ed. James S. Bielo (New Brunswick, NJ: Rutgers University Press, 2009), 157–75.

[29] Rakow, "The Bible in the Digital Age," 113–6.   [30] Meyer, "Religious Sensations," 708.

much less helpful question of how religion is expressed in material form. A materialized study of religion begins with the assumption that things, their use, their valuation, and their appeal are not something added to a religion, but rather inextricable from it."[31] Such a material approach applied to the Bible will show that the iconic status of the Bible is "not only generated by the authority of the text and the discourse surrounding the text, but also by the Bible as an image and object employed in diverse practices that generate meaning and authority in other ways besides semantic interpretation."[32]

Specific Examples and/or Foci: Material Culture and the Bible

How can such an analysis of the material dimension of the Bible best be accomplished? David Morgan suggests a material analysis guided by nine aspects pertaining to processes of production, classification, and circulation: medium, design, manufacture, function, comparison, remediation, deployment, reception, and ideology or cultural work.[33] These nine aspects help to address the various facets of the materiality, starting with the object as such, proceeding to the handling of the object by religious practitioners and the object's function in creating and mediating religious worlds.

I will apply Morgan's nine aspects of a material analysis to sketch out the material dimension of the Bible in Christian discourse and practice. I will mainly use contemporary examples from my own research on the Bible and popular Bible media in the intersection of print culture and the digital age in contemporary evangelicalism and Pentecostalism. My observations stem from my fieldwork among evangelical and Pentecostal Christians in megachurches in the US and in Singapore, various Christian conferences in Europe and Australia, as well as an analysis of various Christian media ranging from opinion pieces to newspaper articles and blog posts over the course of the past seven years. Although part of my fieldwork was conducted outside the US, the resulting insights are easily applicable to the US context. Moreover, all churches, actors, events, and the textual products referred to in my analysis circulate within a transnational global network of evangelical and Pentecostal churches, organizations, media outlets, and publishing houses. North American Christian actors and producers of Christian Bible media can be considered important players within this global Christian network. Occasionally I will refer to historical examples, which will prevent us from regarding materiality and processes of production and consumption as characteristic of

---

[31] Meyer et al., "The Origin and Mission of Material Religion," 209.

[32] Dorina Miller Parmenter, "Iconic Books from Below: The Christian Bible and the Discourse of Duct Tape," in *Iconic Books and Texts*, ed. James W. Watts (Sheffield, UK: Equinox, 2015), 227.

[33] David Morgan, "Material Analysis and the Study of Religion," in *Materiality and the Study of Religion: The Stuff of the Sacred*, ed. Tim Hutchings and Joanne McKenzie (London: Routledge, 2017), 15.

contemporary forms or Christianity in the context of consumer capitalism. Instead, these examples will demonstrate that these processes are always part and parcel of an engagement with materiality in the context of Christian practices in particular and religious practices in general.

Production: Medium, Design, and Manufacture

The medium and its design and manufacture are aspects of the production process. The object in question is a Bible, and it can be embodied in various media formats. For many Christians today, the typical *medium* of a Bible is its iconic version as a leather-bound book. In its iconic form, the medium and the content become undistinguishable. A book with leather binding, cover and spine, and printed pages is just one way to mediate the Word of God. The Bible as such can be classified as a "transmedial" object due to the fact that it can be encountered through a range of different media such as printed book, audio format, and smartphone application. Each medium entails specific affordances, which determine the possible ways of engaging the object. For example, a digital Bible lacks physical properties of its own and exists only in the "lingua franca of bits, of ones and zeros ... embodied in magnetic impulses that require almost no physical space."[34] Further, the ones and zeros lack intrinsic meaning and need the combination of software and hardware to become accessible and meaningful to the religious actor accessing the content. Electronic devices, such as desktop computers, tablets, eBook readers, and smartphones, provide the material interface between a digital Bible and its human user. The biblical text cannot be accessed without the electronic interface and thus depends on it. The same accounts for audio formats that need additional equipment (an audio player as well as headphones or speakers) to access the biblical text and a capacity to hear in order to listen to the recording. As Tim Hutchings argues, digital objects have their own materiality and exist as images, sounds, and sometimes even vibrations mediated through the materiality of technology, users, and the context of their use.[35]

"Design is the form a medium takes," writes Morgan.[36] *Design* thus refers to the structures and configurations of an object often bearing intentionality. In Morgan's analytical schema, design is the second aspect of production and is closely interrelated with the type of medium in question, which will become obvious if we look at the available plethora of Bibles and Bible media.

On entering a Christian bookstore, one encounters several shelves full of Bibles in different shapes, translations, and brands. Although all these books share the medium of

---

[34] Roy Rosenzweig, *Clio Wired: The Future of the Past in the Digital Age* (New York: Columbia University Press, 2011), 9.

[35] Tim Hutchings, "Augmented Graves and Virtual Bibles: Digital Media and Material Religion," in Hutchings and McKenzie, *Materiality and the Study of Religion*, 87–91.

[36] Morgan, "Material Analysis," 22.

the printed page, they differ in many details: in their cover design, in the fonts used, as well as in the structure and type area of their page. In some Bibles, Jesus's words are printed in red and thereby easily distinguishable; some Bibles include illustrations or comment boxes in addition to the biblical text; other Bibles forgo the typical medium of the written text and relate the biblical content in the genre of the comic book, using sequential pictures telling the story, although often with the help of short prose descriptions.[37]

Although all these books are referred to as "the Bible," indicating an unchanging essence not bound by time or form, the differences in design are not just embellishments but actually direct and as such structure the processes of perception, reading, and interpretation. According to Walter J. Ong, printed texts in general convey "a sense of closure, a sense that what is found in a text has been finalized, has reached a state of completion."[38] It was print culture that introduced title pages, which function as labels and thereby enable "the feeling for the book as a kind of thing or object" that locks form and content into a unity between two covers connected by a spine and adorned by a title.[39] Thus printed books are supposed to convey textual content in a definite or final form that can be reproduced in the form of thousands of visual and physically consistent copies.[40]

According to Plate, the sense of closure associated with printed pages is visually created by the technology of type: perfectly regular lines and a text evenly justified at the margins to compose a visual image of the page. Thus the visual design of printed and scripted texts is not neutral but affects the emotional interaction with text as well as the cognitive interpretation of words.[41] Visual design processes therefore not only are decorative adornments that could be disregarded but "impact engagement with a text, well before readers grasp its semantic meanings."[42] How information on a page is arranged—both in digital and print media—will have consequences for accessing, seeing, grasping, and interpreting the information displayed in the visual image on a paper page or an electronic screen.

For example, the visual design and the hypertextuality of digital information enable reading, accessing, and digesting information in a nonlinear way that differs from the typical linear way of reading a Bible page from left to right and from top to bottom. Many texts displayed online or in smartphone applications still adhere to these general stylistic guidelines of print culture, although the lines on screen are usually justified on the left, displaying an uneven text on the right side and disrupting the visual sense of tidiness. In comparison, a text justified on both sides of the printed page produces a regular and tidy image of the text. Further, the colored hyperlinks open up the text, disrupt the linear flow of reading, and invite the user to venture beyond the current page. Digital media seem to open up the text and break the perceived final unity of content and form

---

[37] For an analysis of Bibles rendered into the form of sequential art, see Scott S. Elliott's chapter on graphic Bibles in this volume.

[38] Walter J. Ong, *Orality and Literacy: The Technologies of the Word* (London: Routledge, 2002), 129.

[39] Ibid., 123.   [40] Ibid., 130.   [41] Plate, "Looking at Words," 131.   [42] Ibid., 129.

by turning it into a "liquid" text filling the digital space only "for a moment," "constantly ready (and prone) to change."[43]

Manufacture refers to the actual physical process of producing an object and the skills, cultural knowledge, technologies, financial means, and human labor involved.[44] An analysis of the production of Bibles can reveal a lot about the socioreligious setting in which the manufacturing of the product happens. The historical example of the production, marketing, and selling of Victorian parlor Bibles will serve as an apt illustration of that aspect.

As Colleen McDannell has shown, the market for Bibles in nineteenth-century America was shaped by the competition between commercial and noncommercial Bible publishers and witnessed a significant growth in sales. Commercial Bible publishing houses operated along the general patterns of the book publishing industry and were similarly influenced by popular fashions shaping the emerging commodity system.[45] McDannell explains the growing Bible market by ideological changes that emphasized the importance of the Bible in the Christian household, transforming it into a precious object. In addition to being a source of religious instruction and moral guidance, the Bible became "a revered possession that activated sentiment and memory."[46] An appreciation for the Bible not just as text but as an object was the base on which the Bible as commodity could flourish.

Due to anticommercial attitudes of many nineteenth-century Christians, the Bible was portrayed as a treasured possession to be gifted or inherited but not to be sold or bought in the marketplace. In fact, Bibles were commodities designed and marketed by secular companies, who knew the tastes of their customers and fashioned their products accordingly. The result was a proliferation of Bibles—Bibles for use in church, Bibles for domestic use, and family Bibles containing supplementary materials such as family record pages, illustrations, and additional information to enhance understanding of the text. To Victorians, the religious and cultural value of the Bible was apparent; thus publishing houses focused on the physical quality of their products, such as the size of the Bible, the good quality of the leather binding, the paper and clasps, or the color and number of the illustrations, in order to entice possible buyers.[47] The choice for and the display of a family Bible in the parlor of the home was thus also a performance of taste and social status.[48]

The example of the Victorian parlor Bible also shows how medium, design, and manufacture are interrelated. Church Bibles needed no additional material and were usually simple in design and easy to carry, whereas parlor Bibles came in huge formats not made to be taken to church but to be displayed at home. In both cases, the medium is a printed book, although different in design and manufacture and ultimately different in their functionality.

---

[43] Zygmunt Bauman, *Liquid Modernities* (Cambridge: Polity Press, 2006), 2.
[44] Morgan, "Material Analysis," 23.   [45] McDannell, *Material Christianity*, 68–72.
[46] Ibid., 73.   [47] Ibid., 91.   [48] Ibid., 91, 96.

Classification: Function, Comparison, and Remediation

For a material analysis it is important to discern the *function* of an object, which in turn allows the object to be classified: what is the object, what is its purpose, how is it used and by whom, what are the effects of its use, and how is it related to other objects?[49] Coming back to the example of the Victorian parlor Bible, it is obvious that its function was not to act as medium to access the biblical text in church, as was the case with small church Bibles. The parlor Bible served a variety of functions, ranging from reading at home, recording family history, and assembling family mementos to functioning as an aesthetic cornerstone displayed in the parlor to indicate taste, status, and a good Christian home.

With regard to contemporary Bible formats, similar functional differences are observable for different Bible media. Many Christians use digital versions for Bible study and reading, appreciating the added features of electronic Bible media such as different translations of the text within one application, note-taking functions, social media sharing functions, and easy accessibility on the go. Nevertheless different studies suggest that many American Christians across the denominational landscape who engage with the Bible on a regular basis still prefer the printed book to digital devices especially for devotional, ritual, and performative practices.[50] To them, the bound Bible feels "more real" and more personal precisely due to its concrete materiality—the silky pages, the smooth leather, the personal notes scribbled in the margins—and its perceived unity of form and content.

This perceived unity of form and content of the Bible is much more ambiguous when it comes to electronic Bible media. The difference between the two media formats becomes obvious when one compares the function of various Bible media in performative ceremonies such as taking an oath of office. The *comparison* of artifacts in different media formats or of similar objects advances a material analysis significantly. It helps with tracing changes, differences, and innovations and discerning their effects in religious and social practices.

Many American presidents have taken the presidential oath of office on highly personal and symbolic Bibles. In 1989 George H. W. Bush took his oath of office on two Bibles, a family Bible and a Bible used two hundred years earlier by George Washington at his inauguration ceremony.[51] Barack Obama used two Bibles at the inauguration cer-

---

[49] Morgan, "Material Analysis," 24.

[50] See, for example, the survey "The State of the Bible 2017" and the analysis of American Bible readers by John B. Weaver, "Transforming Practice: American Bible Reading in Digital Culture," in *The Bible in American Life*, ed. Philip Goff, Arthur E. Farnsley II, and Peter J. Theusen (Oxford: Oxford University Press, 2017), 249–55. A study conducted by Tim Hutchings among evangelicals and my own content analysis of fifty-one comments on a Christian blog about digital Bibles support these conclusions; see Tim Hutchings, "E-Reading and the Christian Bible," *Studies in Religion/Sciences Religieuses* 44, no. 4 (2015): 424–5; Rakow, "The Bible in the Digital Age," 109–13. For an overview of various surveys on Bible use, see Jeffrey S. Siker, *Liquid Scripture: The Bible in a Digital World* (Minneapolis, MN: Fortress Press, 2017), 97–112.

[51] Video footage of the oath taking of George H. W. Bush on January 20, 1989 is available at AP Archive, "President George H. W. Bush Takes the Oath of Office Administered by Chief Justice William Rehnquist," YouTube, July 31, 2015, https://www.youtube.com/watch?v=HfQBxBCptcE.

emony of his second term as president of the United States: a Bible belonging to Abraham Lincoln and a Bible once used by Martin Luther King Jr.[52] In both cases, the function of the Bibles was performative, highly symbolic as well as "iconic," to use Martin E. Marty's terminology.[53] The chosen Bibles were there to be touched in the context of a ritual, but not to be read. During oath-taking ceremonies, the use of a Bible warrants the truthfulness of the oath taken and the sincerity of the speaker, and occasionally it also acts as an invocation of the divine in order to invest the speaker's status and discourse with sacred authority.[54] The performative power of "America's iconic book" hinges on the perceived unity of form and content.[55] The power of the iconic image of the Bible in which form and content are locked with each other stems from "the slipperiness between the philosophical idea of the Word of God, words on a page that convey meaning, and the Word's/words' relationship to the Book," as Dorina Miller Parmenter writes.[56] The medium of the book transforms these into a unity, a material object that seems to be unmistakably recognizable as a Bible. The same cannot be said about digital Bibles, as the following example shows.

In June 2014 Suzi Levine took the oath of office as US ambassador to Switzerland with her hand on top of a Kindle. The adoption of new technology to an established authoritative ritual of entering into a state office was widely reported in the press, showing a photograph of Levine placing her hand on the e-reader.[57] Prompted by this development, *Fox News Latino* asked, "Is a digital Bible less holy?," and subsequently posted this article on its Facebook page.[58] The author of the article remarked, "The recently tapped U.S. ambassador to Switzerland was sworn in last month with her hand not on a paper Bible but on top of a Kindle" and cites different voices that express concern about officials "choosing tablets over the printed Bible."[59] While valuing digital devices for Bible reading and study, people quoted in the article also expressed their concern about

---

[52]   David Jackson, "Obama to Use Lincoln and MLK Bibles for Inauguration," *State Journal*, January 19, 2013, 19.

[53]   Martin E. Marty, "America's Iconic Book," in *Humanizing America's Iconic Book: Society of Biblical Literature Centennial Addresses 1980*, ed. Gene M. Tucker and Douglas A. Knight (Chico, CA: Scholars Press, 1982), 8.

[54]   Frederick B. Jonassen, "'So Help Me?' Religious Expression and Artifacts in the Oath of Office and the Courtroom Oath," *Cardozo Public Law, Politics & Ethics Journal* 12, no. 303 (2014): 364; Albert D. Pionke, "'I Do Swear': Oath-Taking among the Elite Public in Victorian England," *Victorian Studies* 49, no. 4 (2007): 612.

[55]   Marty, "America's Iconic Book," 1–21.

[56]   Parmenter, "Iconic Books from Below," 233–4.

[57]   Zachary Davis Boren, "US Ambassador Suzi LeVine Sworn In Using Kindle e-reader," *Independent*, June 3, 2014, http://www.independent.co.uk/news/world/americas/usambassador-suzi-levine-sworn-in-using-kindel-ereader-9477449.html; Brian Fung, "A U.S. Ambassador Was Just Sworn In on a Kindle," *Washington Post*, June 2, 2014, https://www.washingtonpost.com/news/the-switch/wp/2014/06/02/a-u-s-ambassador-was-just-sworn-in-on-a-kindle/.

[58]   Hillary Vaughn, "Is a Digital Bible Less Holy? U.S. Officials Increasingly Sworn In on Tablets," *Fox News Latino*, July 14, 2014, http://latino.foxnews.com/latino/lifestyle/2014/07/14/isdigital-bible-less-holy-us-officials-increasingly-sworn-in-on-tablet/; the content is no longer available but was archived by the author; the related Facebook post is available at https://www.facebook.com/15704546335/posts/10152322470606336, accessed August 31, 2018.

[59]   Ibid.

the ambiguity of such devices in public ceremonies. They pointed out that a digital Bible on a Kindle is not instantly recognizable as a Bible. Some critically remarked on the multifunctionality of e-readers, as well as the fact that those most likely store diverse (and most probably secular, trivial, or even offensive) content. Facebook readers of the *Fox News Latino* post discussed similar topics. Some openly expressed their dislike of digital devices for official events, such as assuming a public office. They did not regard the swearing in on a Kindle as valid as an oath taken upon the bound book of a Bible. In this particular case, the e-reader was unable to unambiguously exhibit what Timothy Beal calls the "Bibleness" of the cultural icon, which those commentators thought to be important to warrant the sincerity and efficacy of the oath-taking ritual.[60]

The picture accompanying the *Fox News Latino* article and the related Facebook post does not allow a close-up view of the device in order to discern the text shown on its display and thus enhances the ambiguity of the medium. Shots taken from different angles published in other media reveal the interesting detail that Levine places her hand on a digital version of the US Constitution. The choice of the US Constitution and not the biblical text further supports the ambiguity of digital texts on electronic devices in ritual and performative contexts. The unity of form and content of the bound book is not available in the case of an e-reader or smartphone, which serves multiple functions unrelated to displaying and accessing the biblical text.

The difference in materiality and mediation between printed Bibles and electronic versions relates to questions of *remediation*. Reproducing an object in a different medium often places the object in question in new practice settings and interpretive contexts and thereby entails new functions, practices, and discourses in which the artifact is embedded.[61] Just as the printing revolution opened up new and more individualized ways of engaging with Scripture, the digital revolution might make the Bible more accessible for current generations, create new ways of spreading the Gospel, and result in innovative religious practices and discourses surrounding the Bible.[62] Users of Bible applications point out that the added functions offer guided reading plans with daily reminders and Bible verses popping up on the screen that help them develop and keep up a regular reading practice:

> With the digital bible I can select a reading plan based on my needs at the time and get reminders every day to read it. I also like the fact that every day I get a verse that I can read first thing in the morning when I wake up and can customize the version. I have a regular bible and have tried to read it and to me its [*sic*] not the same,

---

[60] Timothy K. Beal, "The End of the Word as We Know It: The Cultural Iconicity of the Bible in the Twilight of Print Culture," in *Iconic Books and Texts*, ed. J. W. Watts (Sheffield, UK: Equinox, 2015), 210.

[61] Morgan, "Material Analysis," 25.

[62] Paul Saenger, *Space between Words: The Origins of Silent Reading* (Stanford, CA: Stanford University Press, 1997); Peter Horsfield, *From Jesus to the Internet: A History of Christianity and Media* (Malden, MA: Wiley Blackwell, 2015).

specially [*sic*] if I want to start a reading plan. I wouldn't know where to start reading and the times I have tried, I don't follow through because I forget.[63]

One of the most downloaded Bible applications is YouVersion's freely available Bible App, which was dubbed the "digital Gideon's Bible" by *Publishers Weekly* in 2011.[64] The application was developed and funded by LifeChurch.tv in Edmond, Oklahoma, and financially supported by various donors. According to their website, YouVersion advertises its Bible app with 1,753 Bible versions and the support of 1,134 languages. The company counts every new installation of its application, which currently has over 300 million installations on smartphones and tablets worldwide.[65] Such applications offer users not only different versions of the biblical text at one swipe but a lot of additional material, such as maps, illustrations, and videos. They also offer structured reading plans and invite the user to mark passages and make notes—not only for their personal use but also for sharing and discussing with others in social networks. The smartphone or tablet, which acts as an interface between user and application, is always at hand, as people usually carry it with them wherever they go. By default, the Word of God in its different modes of digital consumption is always at hand as well, wherever they are. Accordingly, YouVersion's website used to display the slogan "The Bible is everywhere" and explained, "God is near, and so is His Word. As you wake up. While you wait. When you meet a friend. Before you go to sleep. When the Bible is always with you, it becomes a part of your daily life."[66] The producer's promise fits well with evangelicalism's emphasis of a regular Bible-reading practice as an important Christian identity marker and a practice shaping evangelical subjects.[67]

To reissue an object in a new medium or format has implications for the function of the object but also for its design and manufacture, that is, the production and the circulation. Today Bible publishers and Bible societies quite naturally offer digital versions as these make the biblical text available in a medium that has become ubiquitous in everyday life. In addition, remediation in new media formats allows producers to access new markets and reach new groups of prospective customers—or converts—and enables the distribution in missionary contexts, where the import of printed Bibles might be problematic or even dangerous.[68]

---

[63]   Comment no. 16 on the blog post "Digital Bibles: Good or Bad Idea?" by Poncho Lowder published on *Vyrso Voice: The Christian eBook Blog* (http://blog.vyrso.com) on August 5, 2013.

[64]   Marcia Z. Nelson, "Bibles and Sacred Texts 2011: As in the Rest of Publishing, It's Digital, Digital, Digital," *Publishers Weekly*, October 17, 2011, 24.

[65]   YouVersion, "The Bible App," accessed August 31, 2018, https://www.youversion.com/the-bible-app/.

[66]   Since a makeover of the website in 2018, this slogan is no longer displayed on the current version of YouVersion's web presence.

[67]   James S. Bielo, *Words upon the Word: An Ethnography of Evangelical Group Bible Study* (New York: New York University Press, 2009).

[68]   Hutchings, "E-Reading and the Christian Bible," 424–5.

Circulation: Deployment, Reception, and Ideology or Cultural Work

In Morgan's model of material analysis, *deployment* refers to the constant circulation of artifacts in the context of commercial, artistic, or public performances and private practices such as trading, collecting, displaying, and gifting.[69] Through deployment, objects might encounter new practice settings and interpretive frames that extend their original function and intent. Old illuminated Bible manuscripts become collectors' items displayed in museums for their craftsmanship and artwork. As we saw, the Bible once used by Martin Luther King Jr. becomes a symbolic object in the second-term inauguration ceremony for Barack Obama, America's first black president, on January 21, 2013, which coincided with the federal holiday in honor of the civil rights leader. In both cases, the specific design, manufacture, and history of the object influence possible deployments of the object, which are not primarily concerned with the semantic meaning of their textual content.

Reception is broadly understood as the use of objects by religious practitioners and other people who handle the artifact (e.g., traders, collectors).[70] This includes handling and practices that might differ from the original or officially intended use of the object in question. Victorian parlor Bibles were not only read but were also displayed to indicate status and express the aesthetic taste of its owners. Contemporary Bibles of devout evangelicals often are full of handwritten notes scribbled in the margins, colorful markings in the text, and sticky notes peeping out from the pages. They tell a story of intensive Bible study and a life steeped in the Word of God. Such Bibles give access to the biblical text but also function as identity marker and material repository for memories:

> My grandmother died. And on that day of her funeral my mom handed me one of the most precious treasures I've ever had in my possession—her Bible. Inside, the pages are filled with notes that capture how the Word of God was living and active for her throughout her life.... As I held it in my hands and read her secret prayers for her grandchildren written out, her bold declarations of truth, her faith in the God who saves...I knew...I had nothing of this magnitude to pass on to my own children and grandchildren. And I wouldn't if I continued to take notes on my iPad every time I studied the Bible.[71]

A Bible might function as material family memento, but the concrete materiality of a medium can limit the uses an object is put to. The lack of physical properties of digital Bible versions, which become accessible only through an electronic device and the relatively short lifespan of devices and applications before these are succeeded by updated

---

[69] Morgan, "Material Analysis," 27.   [70] Ibid., 28.

[71] Brooke McGlothlin, "Why You Should Still Read Your Bible (and Not Just Your iPad)," blog, April 25, 2013, http://brookemcglothlin.co/blog/2013/04/why-you-should-still-use-your-real-bible-and-not-just-your-ipad.

versions or a new generation, render the digital object insufficient to act as a material memento of the past.

The ninth and final aspect of Morgan's analytic model pertains to the *ideology and cultural work* an object accomplishes through all the previously mentioned aspects of its materiality, (re)mediation, deployment, and circulation. It refers to the often repetitive engagement with material culture and its function in creating, shaping, sustaining, and transforming religious worlds and subjectivities.[72] That the Bible acquired an iconic status in American culture is the result of the ideological cultural work enacted through a continuous engagement with the Bible as material object in diverse practice settings: Bible reading; the production, circulation, and consumption of Bible media; uses of the Bible in religious and public rituals; the display of Bible monuments and the encounter of biblical worlds in creation museums and Bible parks.[73]

The variety of examples illustrating the different aspects of the materiality of the Bible has shown that the Bible is more than a text to be read, interpreted, and understood. The printed Bible is a material object made of words on paper, bound pages, cover, and spine used in various ways. The biblical text itself has a material dimension that becomes obvious when looking at the visual image formed by words and typography, whether printed on pages or displayed on electronic devices. We saw that the Bible can be considered a transmedial object that is mediated and accessed through various media formats—print, digital, audio—which all come with their own affordances. Morgan's nine aspects of a material analysis point out that the material culture of the Bible relates to more than just the object as such. Thus an analysis of the materiality should always include not only the material properties of the object in question but the ways an object is used by religious practitioners, how it is deployed to create and sustain religious worlds, subjects, and communities, and how it is embedded in cultural discourses and practices.

FUTURE PROSPECTS AND QUESTIONS

- The Bible is a transmedial and transtextual object that is available in various translations, formats, and media. A material analysis guided by the nine aspects as suggested by David Morgan could be comparatively applied to different media and formats to gain insight into how different media come with different affordances and produce different effects in the context of production, circulation, and deployment of Bible media.
- Such a comparative endeavor will further our knowledge about how change and innovation in media formats affect religious discourses, practices, and identity

---

[72] Morgan, "Material Analysis," 29–30.

[73] Marty, "America's Iconic Book," 1–21; Beal, "The End of the Word," 207–24. See also the anthropologist James S. Bielo's project "Materializing the Bible," accessed July 20, 2017, http://www.materializingthebible.com/. Finally, see Bielo's essay "Theme Parks," and Valarie Ziegler's chapter on "Creationist Museums," both in this volume.

politics and thus contributes to our understanding of the ongoing transformation of religion. Such an analysis would be situated in the broader project of writing religious history as a history of religious media.[74]

- A comparative analysis of different Bible media could further focus on the question of how those media relate to each other and support, constrain, or depend on each other. This question is particularly relevant in the context of the introduction of new technologies and new media in religious contexts. The import of new media is often accompanied by processes of dispute and negotiation, of the appropriateness of such media and their ability to mediate the divine before adopting such technologies.

Suggested Readings and Annotated Bibliography

Hutchings, Tim. "Augmented Graves and Virtual Bibles: Digital Media and Material Religion." In *Materiality and the Study of Religion: The Stuff of the Sacred*, edited by Tim Hutchings and Joanne McKenzie, 85–99. London: Routledge, 2017.

The first part of this chapter applies a material approach to digital products and discusses the material dimension of digital media, showing that digital objects are produced, circulated, and consumed just like other material objects. Their specific materiality comes with certain affordances that shape and constrain the ways users engage with digital media.

Hutchings, Tim. "E-Reading and the Christian Bible." *Studies in Religion/Sciences Religieuses* 44, no. 4 (2015): 423–40.

Hutchings's article provides a good introduction to digital Bible media and how their technological properties shape the encounter and engagement with the biblical text. The article sketches user attitudes, motivations, and experiences with digital Bible media and thereby provides interesting insights into Bible practices in the digital age.

McDannell, Colleen. "Material Christianity" and "The Bible in the Victorian Home." In *Material Christianity: Religion and Popular Culture in America*, 1–16 and 67–102. New Haven, CT: Yale University Press, 1995.

The first chapter of McDannell's book argues for a materialization of the study of American Christianity and explains the main reasons for the long neglect of the material dimension of Christianity. The third chapter, on Victorian Bibles, focuses on the Bible as material artifact and the question of how the text became a precious possession and holy object in the context of the domestic sphere in the Victorian era. The volume is richly illustrated with a broad variety of historical examples.

Meyer, Birgit. "Religious Sensations: Why Media, Aesthetics, and Power Matter in the Study of Contemporary Religion." In *Religion: Beyond a Concept*, edited by Hent de Vries, 704–23. New York: Fordham University Press, 2008.

Meyer's essay is a good introduction to the material approach in studying religion. She emphasizes the crucial role of materiality, media, and religious sensations in the making and sustaining of religious worlds, subjects, and communities. She introduces her central concept of "sensational forms," a set of media and practices in which what is perceived as the divine

---

[74] Peter J. Bräunlein, "Religionsgeschichte als Mediengeschichte—Eine Skizze," *Münchner Theologische Zeitschrift* 55 (2004): 325–9; Meyer, "Material Mediations," 11.

or the transcendental becomes mediated and thus accessible and sense-able to religious practitioners.

Morgan, David. "Material Analysis and the Study of Religion." In *Materiality and the Study of Religion: The Stuff of the Sacred*, edited by Tim Hutchings and Joanne McKenzie, 14–32. London: Routledge, 2017.

Morgan's chapter introduces an analytical approach comprising nine different aspects to structure a material analysis of the various facets of the materiality of an object as well as the handling of the object by religious practitioners and the object's function in mediating religious worlds.

Parmenter, Dorina Miller. "Iconic Books from Below: The Christian Bible and the Discourse of Duct Tape." In *Iconic Books and Texts*, edited by James W. Watts, 225–38. Sheffield, UK: Equinox, 2015.

Parmenter's chapter is dedicated to more mundane and individual Bible practices, such as the worn-out and duct-taped Bibles that indicate long and heavy usage by their owners and mark them as deeply steeped in the Word of God. By studying common, noninstitutionalized, and individual Bible practices, she demonstrates that the iconic status of the Bible is produced and upheld not just by theological discourse focusing on the semantic meaning of the biblical text and official and High Church rituals but also by mundane rituals and practices of the lived religion of individual practitioners.

Plate, S. Brent. "Looking at Words: The Iconicity of the Page." In *Iconic Books and Texts*, edited by James W. Watts, 119–33. Sheffield, UK: Equinox, 2013.

In his chapter, Plate analyzes the material dimension of words, arguing that visual design influences the cognitive interpretation of texts. Using various examples, he shows how words function as images, become iconic, and shape and stimulate the process of perception long before the reader engages in deciphering the semantic meaning of the text displayed. Further, he argues that there is an intricate relationship between the typography and design of religious scriptures and related theologies or ideologies.

CHAPTER 24

APOCALYPSE AND VIDEO GAMES

RACHEL WAGNER
DEPARTMENT OF PHILOSOPHY AND RELIGION,
ITHACA COLLEGE

INTRODUCTION

THE biblical scholar John J. Collins says that Enoch's extensive "tour of the cosmos is designed to show that the destiny of humanity is not left to chance but is built into the structure of the universe."[1] Collins is referring to the otherworldly journey of a famous Jewish figure in one of the world's oldest apocalypses, *1 Enoch*. The very structure of Enoch's vision suggests that the universe as a whole is orderly. Enoch's tour of the heavens is a peek inside the programming of the cosmic machine, so to speak. The extensive descriptions of the universe and the origins of heavenly bodies in Enoch's vision are "a celebration of the order of the universe."[2] Humans crave certainty. Religious storytelling helps us to imagine worlds in which order is possible.

It might seem surprising at first, but video games can work a lot like apocalypses. Both apocalypses and games offer imaginary visits to otherworldly spaces that were designed to offer a sort of metaphysical comfort. Video games can act like otherworldly sacred spaces—massive and carefully made structures that promise something better and may even fill us with awe. As Jane McGonigal notes, instead of "traveling great distances for a single encounter with a physical cathedral, we can instantly transport ourselves there from anywhere in the world, simply by loading up a blockbuster video game."[3] To play a video game is not the same thing as inducing a supernatural vision

---

[1] John J. Collins, *The Apocalyptic Imagination: An Introduction to Jewish Apocalyptic Literature*, 3rd ed. (Grand Rapids, MI: Eerdmans, 2016), 73.

[2] Ibid., 77.

[3] Jane McGonigal, *Reality Is Broken: Why Games Make Us Better and How They Can Change the World* (New York: Penguin Press, 2011), 107.

inside an ancient temple, but it does invite us to enter into an otherworldly space that is in many ways more predictable than our own.

When we enter into programmed spaces like video games, we can usually be sure that these virtual worlds were created with an intentional design and a clear purpose. Some games even depict our own world, remade into the bits and bytes of a structured, controllable game. Games are comforting because in a game there is "no law but the algorithm."[4] The game theorist Jane McGonigal believes that video games can be viewed as a kind of "purposeful escape" that can give a "starving population a feeling of power in a powerless situation, a sense of structure in a chaotic environment."[5] But instead of depicting God as the means of control over the world, some games place the player in the position of realizing this order through the performance of violence. Even though they are actually often quite rigidly designed, the player of a shooting video game experiences a powerful sense of agency because he or she holds the gun and makes meaningful decisions about how to use it. It is this sense of *feeling* in control that I focus on here. Whereas ancient apocalypses were largely about waiting for God to intervene and violently punish one's enemies, today's games allow players to imagine *themselves* enacting vengeance. This, I argue, is one of the key differences between ancient apocalypses and contemporary gaming apocalypses: today's visionaries would rather be in charge themselves.

I have argued elsewhere that first-person shooters work a lot like apocalypses in their very design of an otherworldly, structured, imagined space.[6] First-person shooters are those video games in which the person playing views the game from a first-person perspective, as if through his or her own eyes. The only part of one's digital body visible on screen is the arm, the hand, and the weapon in the hand. The connection between ancient apocalypses and video games as apocalypses is so strong that some video game designers have successfully based games directly on existing apocalypses. *Left Behind: Eternal Forces*,[7] for example, is a real-time strategy game based in part on events portrayed in the book of Revelation. *El Shaddai: Ascension of the Metatron*[8] is based on the corpus of Jewish apocalyptic writings about the biblical figure of Enoch. In this essay, I focus primarily on *Darksiders*,[9] a game also based on the book of Revelation. Games like these use the affordances of digital technology to reinforce claims about the orderliness and predictability of the universe, revealing a surprising affinity between gaming apocalypses and biblical apocalypses. Games like *Darksiders* and *El Shaddai* depend on key narrative

---

[4] McKenzie Wark, *Gamer Theory* (Boston: Harvard University Press, 2007), 042. Wark's book is notated not by page number but by paragraph number, as it is essentially a series of numbered short observations.

[5] McGonigal, *Reality Is Broken*, 6.

[6] Rachel Wagner, "Xbox Apocalypse: Video Games and Revelatory Literature," *Society of Biblical Literature Forum* 7, no. 9 (2009), https://www.sbl-site.org/publications/article.aspx?articleId=848. See also Rachel Wagner, "Video Games and Religion," Religion, Culture, Sociology of Religion, *Oxford Handbooks Online*, September 2015, http://www.oxfordhandbooks.com/view/10.1093/oxfordhb/9780199935420.001.0001/oxfordhb-9780199935420-e-8.

[7] Inspired Media Entertainment, 2006.   [8] Ignition Tokyo and UTV Ignition Games, 2011.

[9] Vigil Games, 2010.

elements of ancient religious texts but radically increase the experience of agency for the player through a design that places the player in charge of the plot's unfolding.

There is a pronounced tension at work here; designers have predetermined what is possible in a game's storyline, but it is the player who enacts his or her chosen track within those possibilities. So even though all video games are very carefully and sometimes rigidly designed, it *feels* like the player is in control because he or she makes the decisions that allow the plot to unfold. The comfort of playing such games may partly reside, then, in the sense that the player has a knowable purpose in a world that was deliberately designed. But it is also true that we see a radical relocation of meaningful action from the godhead to the player. In the gaming rehearsal of the end times, nobody is waiting for Jesus or for angels with bowls of wrath or even for God to descend and enact the end-times narrative. Players wield weapons and use them to dispatch evil right now, all by themselves.

OVERVIEW OF TOPIC

The study of apocalypse is complicated since the texts themselves are varied in time, social context, and focus. Some apocalypses (like the book of Revelation and the apocalypse in chapters 7–12 of the book of Daniel) are well known. Others, like the *Testament of Abraham, Jubilees,* and *1 Enoch,* are less well known. A group of biblical scholars recognized the complexity inherent in these texts and wanted to create a kind of taxonomy that would help people better discuss them. So in 1979, as part of the Society of Biblical Literatures (SBL) Genre Project, they got together and produced a definition of apocalypse to aid in more precise comparisons and invite deeper study. The definition is helpful even to those who are not scholars of the Bible because it pinpoints what Collins calls "a significant cluster of traits" that can be identified across numerous texts from this ancient period and beyond. The definition is still helpful today as we recognize apocalypses in contemporary popular culture like video games.

Most of the ancient apocalyptic texts the SBL team looked at came from the intertestamental period, that is, the period of time roughly between the close of the "Old" Testament, or Tanakh (in the second century BCE), and the beginnings of the "New" Testament (in the first century CE). Certainly not all of the texts composed in the intertestamental period were apocalyptic, but many of them were, including *1 Enoch* and dozens of others, like the *Apocalypse of Abraham* and *4 Ezra.* The SBL team defines apocalypse as "a genre of revelatory literature with a narrative framework, in which a revelation is mediated by an otherworldly being to a human recipient, disclosing a transcendent reality which is both temporal, insofar as it envisages eschatological salvation, and spatial insofar as it involves another, supernatural world."[10]

---

[10] Collins, *The Apocalyptic Imagination,* 5. In her entry in this volume, Shayna Sheinfeld also engages apocalyptic literature and discusses this definition.

There are some key identifying features here: an apocalypse is a kind of narrative genre or *story* that is mediated by an *otherworldly being*. It depicts an *otherworldly location*; and it depicts an imminent *end to time*. It has a sense of urgency and purpose. Apocalypses, says Collins, are "augmented [by] a sense of determinism...by affirming that the course of history or the structure of the cosmos was determined long ago."[11] As "programs," then, apocalypses promise us that the way things are unfolding was fixed well before we engaged with the events, an experience that players of video games also experience.

The original definition of apocalypse was not intended to refer to contemporary culture, but we can certainly find lots of apocalyptic themes in films, video games, and popular media—and we find a few full-blown apocalypses as well. Collins proposes that a movement or phenomenon can reasonably be called "apocalyptic" if it also exhibits the "conceptual framework of the genre, endorsing a worldview in which supernatural revelation, the heavenly world, and eschatological judgment" play "essential parts."[12] The genre has an appeal that speaks to many people today, as we face our own anxieties about war, violence, and suffering in the world.

Joseph Dewey points to what he calls the "apocalyptic temper" as "an attempt by a culture that is genuinely puzzled and deeply disturbed to understand itself and its own time."[13] What is revealed in an apocalypse is a shift from present reality to an imminent transcendent reality—an *other*-time and *other*-space—where things are more to one's liking. By simplifying perceived chaos into a cosmic plot of rewards and punishments, apocalypse is what Elizabeth Rosen sees as "an organizing principle imposed on an overwhelming, seemingly disordered universe."[14] Apocalypses are about the way that people *wish* things could be. In apocalypses, this desire is typically expressed in an "us versus them" fashion. As Jamel Velji notes, apocalyptic movements and texts "illustrate a propensity to divide the world and its contents into absolute good and absolute evil."[15]

Apocalypticists cope with this dualism, says Velji, by imagining history as approaching its end and positing an imminent battle between these forces, predicting that evil will be "destroyed, or condemned to hell or, at best to non-existence."[16] It is not hard to see how the typical violent first-person shooter video game enacts an apocalyptically informed dualistic model, proposing that order will be reclaimed when the player (presumed good) destroys his or her enemies (presumed evil) through a series of battles. As we will see in *Darksiders*, this typical apocalyptic dualism appears, but it is subtly

---

[11] Ibid., 49.   [12] Ibid., 16.

[13] Joseph Dewey, *In a Dark Time: The Apocalyptic Temper in the American Novel of the Nuclear Age* (West Lafayette, IN: Purdue University Press, 1990), 10.

[14] Elizabeth Rosen, *Apocalyptic Transformation: Apocalypse and the Postmodern Imagination* (Lanham, MD: Lexington Books, 2008), xi.

[15] Jamel Velji, "Apocalyptic Religion and Violence," in *The Oxford Handbook of Religion and Violence*, ed. Mark Juergensmeyer, Margo Kitts, and Michael Jerryson (Oxford: Oxford University Press), 251.

[16] Ibid.

redefined: the player in *Darksiders* does not fight for "good" but simply for a restoration of balance in the universe. His or her "enemies" include anyone who gets in his or her way, and the judgment is that they will die at the player's hand.

No matter how dark their vision, apocalypses are a fictionalized attempt at certainty, a way of imagining an order that does not yet exist but that will be realized soon. Ancient apocalypticists saw purpose in the design of the world, but they were waiting for God to come reassert that order over a seemingly chaotic world. Today gamer apocalypticists do not wait for God; games are designed purposefully such that it is *the players themselves* who will reassert order over chaos. No more waiting for angels to pour bowls of wrath on their enemies. The players will take a joystick in hand and do it themselves. We see this theme of increased human agency at work explicitly in the video game *Darksiders*, which draws on the book of Revelation but places the player in the role of one of the Four Horsemen of the Apocalypse making decisions for himself or herself and fighting for a cause that only he or she understands.

SPECIFIC EXAMPLES AND/OR FOCI

Darksiders is a loosely symbolic take on the book of Revelation. The player takes on the role of War, one of the Four Horsemen of John's apocalypse. Thus in *Darksiders*, the player enacts a violent role that in the original apocalyptic text was reserved for God's supernatural agents. Indeed, in *Darksiders* God's role as creator is minimized; he has removed himself completely from the cosmos, leaving behind the Charred Council, a lesser group of divine beings whose job is simply to keep the warring factions of good and evil in "balance." The purpose of the cosmos in *Darksiders* is not the triumph of good but the uneasy coexistence of good with evil.

The game is based on the premise that a wicked angel, Abaddon, has caused a premature opening of the first six seals of the apocalypse in a bid for more personal power. When the game begins, Abaddon has already begun to sabotage the balancing work done by the Charred Council by the untimely opening of the seals and the subsequent unleashing of supernatural violence upon the earth. Unfortunately for Abaddon, one of the Four Horsemen of the Apocalypse—War personified—was also released by accident and has descended to the earth as well. The player acts as this horseman and is tasked with interrupting Abaddon's evil plan. War's purpose—known only to himself or herself in the game—is to place Abaddon in check, and thus to bring back the truce that had existed between good and evil. Unfortunately, the forces of heaven do not realize that War is innocent, and they are hunting War down to punish him or her instead. War has no choice but to fight for his or her honor against representatives of both heaven and hell. Playing as War, the player's job is—practically put—to kill as many enemies as possible in order to save the world.

In order to understand how *Darksiders* works, we have to start by looking under the hood, so to speak, at the game engine. Game engines are "assemblages of common software components and tools used to make other games."[17] Game engines are the mechanical equivalent of genres, since they form the basis upon which games are designed. But unlike film, books, or other genres, game engines even more tightly structure "individual videogames' artistic, cultural and narrative expression."[18] Genres determine how one approaches a narrative, but game engines "construe entire gameplay behaviors, facilitating functional interactions divorced from individual games."[19] Thus, when you use a preexisting game engine in the design of a new game, you have less wiggle room for play because you rely on borrowed code. Game engines powerfully "influence the kind of discourse the works can create, the ways they create them, and the ways users interact with them."[20] This means that the "us-versus-them" format of many video games is actually *programmed in* to the way game engines work. Many games are hardwired, so to speak, for the kinds of dualistic battles characteristic of apocalyptic visions.

El Shaddai: Ascension of the Metatron, for example, was made with the Gamebryo game engine used in dozens of other video games with no explicit religious influence, including *Elder Scrolls* III and IV, *Rift*, *Lego Universe*, and *Fallout: New Vegas*. *El Shaddai* opens by introducing us to Enoch in a room filled with books in huge piles on the floor. In a series of establishing scenes, Enoch is taken to a heavenly training site. For the rest of the game, the player takes on the role of Enoch and is taught by an interpreting angel, Lucifel, how to utilize the game's controls. Lucifel explains that Enoch's mission on earth is to defeat the "fallen angels" who have disobeyed God. Predictably, the game consists of a series of violent battles with these fallen angels. The borrowed narrative elements from 1 *Enoch* meld surprisingly well with the first-person shooter game engine used in *El Shaddai*, with both drawing on eschatological themes of purposeful destruction.

Darksiders was not designed using a preexisting engine. Instead, the now defunct Vigil Games developed a unique engine for the game. Nonetheless, the engine they designed recycles common game fighting tropes and draws on common expectations of game engines. One reviewer of the game summarizes these predictable components:

> Throughout *Darksiders* you'll see influences from other titles like *Halo 3* as War [the player-character] grabs heavy, fantastical versions of Bungie's turret guns, *Portal*, and, strangely enough, *Panzer Dragoon*. You get a horse named Ruin that War can ride around…and the sprint mechanic is the same as *Ocarina of Time*, only it uses little energy pellets instead of carrots. You even get the equivalent of milk jars to store powerups for use in the field. The…recycled mechanics are still fun to toy around with, particularly when fused with the combat system. *Darksiders*…can't really be described as original, but the fact that the majority of its mechanics are already proven to work and implemented well means there's certainly entertainment to be had here.[21]

---

[17] Ian Bogost, *Unit Operations: An Approach to Video Game Criticism* (Cambridge, MA: MIT Press, 2008), 55.

[18] Ibid., 56.   [19] Ibid., 57.   [20] Ibid., 64.

[21] Charles Onyett, "Darksiders Review," IGN, September 23, 2010, http://www.ign.com/articles/2010/09/23/darksiders-review.

Game engines, says Ian Bogost, "abstract" the "material requirements" or behaviors of the gameplay as their "primary—perhaps their only—formal constituent."[22] And what game engines do best is to lead the player through a series of order-making digital rituals like mazes, puzzles, carefully orchestrated defeat of numerous enemies, and other measurable, point-tallying achievements. *Darksiders* is a blend of imagery and narrative components borrowed from the book of Revelation and other ancient mythology, filtered through predictable tropes dictated by game-engine structures, inviting the player to take on a more active role in enacting the violence depicted in the biblical apocalypse.

Talmadge Wright, David Embrick, and Andrés Lukács see video games as a contemporary site for the expression of apocalyptic violence: "Apocalyptic fantasies appear in the smoldering landscape of a devastated Washington, D.C., in the game *Fallout 3*. And Washington, D.C., is destroyed again in *Call of Duty: Modern Warfare 2* as Russian troops occupy the U.S. White House. Utopian fantasies of an Ayn Rand–styled universe become a horrid nightmare in the game *Bioshock*. Utopian dreams of endless resources and castles in the sky appear in the online multiplayer game *World of Warcraft*, mixed with apocalyptic war imagery in a fantasy universe of endless fecundity."[23] *Darksiders* belongs in this list as yet another violent fantasy of earthly destruction, with the player in an active role dispensing this punishment. But unlike *Bioshock*, *Fallout*, and *Call of Duty*, *Darksiders* is designed with explicit reference to existing religious mythology. In addition to references to the Horsemen of the Apocalypse in Revelation, the game presents us with numerous religious references from Jewish, Christian, and Babylonian traditions. For example, a character named Lilith is in the entourage of hell. According to Jewish legend, Lilith was Adam's disgruntled first wife, who left him and became a demon, who medieval legend relates kills children.[24] In *Darksiders*, Lilith is a "cold, calculating temptress with an unrivaled lust for power."[25] She is also called the "Bride of Lucifer" and the "Demon Queen." In *Darksiders*, Lilith is given credit for the creation of the Nephilim, who in the game are identified as the race to which the Four Horsemen of the Apocalypse belong. In Jewish lore, the Nephilim are a giant race that was created when "watcher" angels descended to the earth and mated with human women, a crime that some religious interpretations say caused the primordial flood.[26] This kind of

---

[22] Bogost, *Unit Operations*, 57.

[23] J. Talmadge Wright, David Embrick, and Andrés Lukács, introduction to *Utopic Dreams and Apocalyptic Fantasies: Critical Approaches to Researching Video Game Play*, ed. J. Talmadge Wright, David G. Embrick, and András Lukács (Blue Ridge Summit, PA: Lexington Books, 2010), 3.

[24] One of the earliest versions of this legend is in the Jewish text called the *Alphabet of ben Sira*, from the eighth to the tenth century CE. See Louis Ginzberg's *The Legends of the Jews: From the Creation to Jacob*. Baltimore, MD: Johns Hopkins University Press, 1998, p. 65–66. This text includes an English translation of some of the Lilith stories as they appeared in Jewish midrash (a commentary on the Jewish sacred text called the Torah). In recent years, Lilith has been reclaimed by some feminist writers, who are inspired by her unwillingness to serve at Adam's whim.

[25] "Lilith," Darksiders Dungeon Wiki, October 4, 2013, http://Darksidersdungeon.net/wiki/Lilith (site currently inaccessible).

[26] This legend appears in abbreviated form in Gen 6. For an extended version in intertestamental Jewish literature, see *1 Enoch*, 12–22.

knitting together of disparate religious myths is common in *Darksiders*, where a midrash of convenience links biblical and mythic lore with newly concocted fictional elements, weaving a new and elaborate myth of violent messianic fervor.

Religious imagery abounds in *Darksiders*. For example, players will find an uncanny reproduction of Marduk's violent defeat of the goddess Tiamat. In the ancient Babylonian myth called the *Enuma Elish,* Tiamat is a babbling, conniving creator goddess whose competition with the masculine hero Marduk results in her death.[27] Her body is blown up with air, pierced with Marduk's phallic spear, then stretched to create the horizons of the earth as we know it. In *Darksiders*, Tiamat is an enormous stone-breasted creature with bat-like qualities who spits raging fireballs. She is the "boss" of the Twilight Cathedral and must be defeated in order to acquire a needed resource. The player—as War—destroys Tiamat by throwing bombs at her "ugly face" and then repeatedly slashing at her head before ripping out her still-beating heart.[28] Scholars have suggested that the testosterone-laced rape and murder of Tiamat by Marduk in the *Enuma Elish* hint at an earlier tradition of a more positively portrayed mother-goddess, a portrait that has been distorted by violent patriarchal interpretations.[29] We see the common misogyny associated with Tiamat replayed in *Darksiders* in her negative portrayal and violent annihilation.

Another character in *Darksiders*, the demon Samael, is also based on ancient Jewish lore. In one early Jewish text, Samael resides in the seventh heaven visited by Moses but is too enormous to grasp in one look. Samael is covered from head to toe in eyes, and his job is to gather up human souls from earth as a sort of ancient grim reaper.[30] He also appears in Gnostic texts like the third- or fourth-century "Hypostasis of the Archons," where he is identified as a "blind" God who does not recognize the reality of other divine forces above him.[31] He frequently shows up in rabbinic literature as "chief of evil angels."[32] In *Darksiders* too Samael is a troubling figure. He has a bad history with Abaddon because long ago, Samael had challenged Abaddon to a battle, lost, and was imprisoned as punishment. In one of the early battles in the game, War frees Samael. Samael then convinces War to help him and, as a reward, promises War access to the Black Tower, where Abaddon is hiding. Interestingly, in *Darksiders* the player exhibits

---

[27] To read the *Enuma Elish*, see Barbara C. Sproul, *Primal Myths* (New York: Harper & Row, 1979), 91–113.

[28] "Tiamat," Darksiders Wiki Guide, IGN, October 5, 2013, http://www.ign.com/wikis/darksiders/Twilight_Cathedral,_Tiamat.

[29] D. Katz, "Reconstructing Babylon: Recycling Traditions toward a New Theology," in *Babylon. Wissenskultur in Orient und Okzident, Topoi,* ed. E. Cancik-Kirschbaum, J. Marzahn, and M. van Ess, Berlin Studies in the Ancient World, 1 (Berlin: de Gruyter), 123–34.

[30] Louis Ginzberg, *The Legends of the Jews,* vol. 2 (Philadelphia, PA: Jewish Publication Society of America, 1913), 308.

[31] "The Hypostasis of the Archons" and other Gnostic texts can be found in James M. Robinson, ed., *The Nag Hammadi Library* (reprint; New York: HarperOne, 1990). On Samael as "blind," see also "3 (Hebrew Apocalypse of) Enoch," trans. and introduction by P. Alexander, in *The Old Testament Pseudepigrapha,* ed. James Charlesworth (Peabody, MA: Hendrickson, 2010), 236.

[32] See "3 (Greek Apocalypse of) Baruch," trans. and introduction by H. E. Gaylord, in Charlesworth, *The Old Testament Pseudepigrapha,* 658.

some of the characteristics of Samael from the *Ascension of Moses*, becoming a collector of "souls" who is required to use them as resources in the game.

The character Abaddon is drawn from ancient religious mythology as well. In the book of Revelation, Abaddon is identified as the "angel of the abyss," the commander of the army of locusts who will ravage the earth (Rev 9:11). In *Darksiders*, Abaddon is a bitter fallen angel, a leader of hell's forces on earth. The game ends with a dramatic battle between War and Abaddon, who appears in the form of a fierce red dragon, a clear reference to the book of Revelation's depiction of the battle between the angel Michael and the great red dragon:

> Now war arose in heaven, Michael and his angels fighting against the dragon; and the dragon and his angels fought, but they were defeated and there was no longer any place for them in heaven. And the great dragon was thrown down, that ancient serpent, who is called the Devil and Satan, the deceiver of the whole world—he was thrown down to the earth, and his angels were thrown down with him. And I heard a loud voice in heaven, saying, "Now the salvation and the power and the kingdom of our God and the authority of his Christ have come, for the accuser of our brethren has been thrown down, who accuses them day and night before our God." (Rev 12:7–10)[33]

In *Darksiders*, War, like Michael, is responding to a great heavenly war. Also like Michael, War is contending with fallen angels and must wrestle a fierce and troublesome dragon who has been "thrown down" to earth as punishment. But whereas in Revelation Michael acts on God's behalf, in *Darksiders* War fights for himself or herself and a greater purpose that nobody else understands.

The violent apocalyptic battle between the dragon and Michael is a natural fit for *Darksiders*' dualistic game engine, suggesting again the easy affinity between video games and apocalypses. The shooter video game in particular "has a history [that is] rooted in a kind of 'one-person army'" that defeats its enemies without the aid of anyone else.[34] Read metaphorically, the game proposes that once chaos has erupted, War is the only means to reestablish an uneasy "balance" between good and evil. God is gone from the scene. The Council that represents heavenly authority is out of touch and unable to assist. War alone can save the day. Such a message, implicit or not, is particularly troubling in our own post-9/11 era of seemingly endless destruction and violence.

Darksiders veers from traditional apocalypticism in situating responsibility for violent judgment on the player, who acts not *in* God's stead but *instead of* God. It is true that *Darksiders* appeals to Revelation in its use of one of the Four Horsemen of the Apocalypse to enact this violence, but it also puts the human player in *charge* of performative violence. Ancient apocalypticists were visionaries who watched cosmic violence

---

[33] All biblical passages are from the Revised Standard Version of the Bible.

[34] Gerald A. Voorhees, Josh Call, and Katie Whitlock. "Introduction: Things That Go Boom: From Guns to Griefing," in *Guns, Grenades, and Grunts: First Person Shooter Games*, ed. Gerald A. Voorhees, Josh Call, and Katie Whitlock (New York: Continuum, 2012), 4.

unfold; they almost never participated in it themselves.[35] God was in charge, and humans were tasked with waiting for God to send in his agents to put evil in its place. In Revelation, neither John nor the angel that guides him through the dark vision plays any role in the cataclysmic events that are happening in the end times. *Darksiders*, by contrast, reveals contemporary gamers' desire for a greater sense of agency, transforming an ancient literature of passive hope into contemporary literature of violent performativity.

Players today may reflexively be turning to games for imaginative spaces of greater agency over their own fates, reflecting less faith in God's control over what happens on earth. *Darksiders* is quintessentially apocalyptic in its us-versus-them structure, in its appeal to traditional apocalyptic imagery, and in its glorification of violence as the means to reestablish order in a chaotic environment. But it takes these traditional tropes and transforms them into a ritual of violent performativity that removes God while placing the player into a quasi-divine vigilante role—a "good guy with a gun." We can more closely consider this surprising kinship between video games and apocalypses by using some of the additional categories typically used in the scholarly discussion of apocalypses and applying them to games: otherworldly mediators, apocalyptic time, and the situation in which apocalypses are typically composed.

Otherworldly Mediators

In Hebrew, the word usually translated as "angel" (מַלְאָךְ/malach) literally means "messenger." Angels were the helpers God sent when he needed information or wanted to relay information to human beings, as when a messenger (angel) appears to Hagar (Gen 16:7–14) or when an angel appears to Abraham (Gen 22:11–15). In an apocalypse, the otherworldly mediator is often a messenger with an additional job: to "interpret the vision" and serve "as a guide on the otherworldly journey." The angel illuminates those elements of the vision that are "not intelligible without supernatural aid."[36] The mediator works for God and thus offers reassurance of the order in the otherworldly system the visionary is experiencing.

In many video games, there is a similar interpreting, guiding entity: an A.I.-driven NPC (nonplayer character) who serves as a "companion or helper figure." This NPC typically explains the rules of the game and in so doing reinforces the game's sense of order. For example, in *The Legend of Zelda: Twilight Princess* an entity named Midna offers guidance and encouragement, helping the player figure out what to do next. An entity named Issun guides the player in the game *Okami*. Both are similar to the functions of

---

[35] There are some exceptions to this rule. The apocalyptic community at Qumran, who wrote the Dead Sea Scrolls, did see themselves as potentially participating in a violent end-times battle. The textual apocalypses by single authors that we have from antiquity, though, almost always place the visionary in a passive position.

[36] Collins, *The Apocalyptic Imagination*, 6.

Navi in *The Ocarina of Time*, an earlier game in which the guiding A.I. trope appears.[37] In *El Shaddai*, the video game based on *1 Enoch*, the otherworldly figure of Lucifel guides the player—an odd choice, of course, since Lucifel is another name for Lucifer or Satan, but consistent with the apocalyptic theme of otherworldly guides who explain things to visionaries. In the *Halo* series, players are assisted by the A.I. entity Cortana. Cortana is a hologram and thus is part of the larger computer system, with the ability to comprehend the world in which players find themselves.

In *Darksiders*, various entities play this otherworldly guiding role—although none of them offers guidance on behalf of the creator God, a telling theological hint that in this game, the creator God is not particularly interested in the apocalyptic events unfolding on earth. Samael, for example, explains to War how to defeat the four guardians of the Black Tower, but he does so for his own selfish reasons, not to further any particular theological aim of God. Elsewhere in *Darksiders*, the angel Azrael plays a mediating role for similarly selfish purposes.[38] In *Darksiders*, Azrael is not a reliable ally since he had conspired with Abaddon to prematurely open the six seals in the first place. But War does not have much choice in trusting him, since in the game there are no reliable other-worldly guides. Azrael explains to War how the entity Straga strengthens his power through the consumption of souls. Azrael then gives War instructions for next steps in defeating Straga. Otherworldly mediators play a key role in religious apocalypses and in gaming apocalypses, where they guide participants through difficult transitions. As ambassadors of apocalypse, they are keyed into the structure the game represents, and they mirror it in their privileged awareness about what the player-visionary should do to navigate his or her way through the otherworldly journey. Noticing how these other-worldly guides both conform to apocalyptic models and challenge them (through the absence of God's direct involvement in the game) can help us to interpret games as cultural objects.

Apocalyptic Time

Revelation is not just about what the visionary sees; it is also about how time works in the world itself. In the ancient apocalyptic worldview, revelation is "transmitted from a supernatural source, through the mediation of angels" who reveal "a hidden world of angels and demons that is directly relevant to human destiny."[39] Whatever chaos the

---

[37] Steven Jones, *The Meaning of Video Games: Gaming and Textual Strategies* (New York: Routledge, 2008), 74. *Navi* is a variation on the Hebrew term *nabi*, which means "prophet," suggesting yet another way in which this in-game entity functions as a mediator between the divine and human realms.

[38] Azrael appears to be a variation of the name Asael/Azazel/Azriel. This angel appears in Jewish and Muslim traditions. For example, in the *Targum Pseudo-Jonathan* and Gen 6:1–4, Azael is associated with the fallen angels who lust after human women. And according to one Islamic tradition, Azael is an archangel of death who is covered with eyes (*'Ab. Zarah* 20b). Azael is an angel who is typically a troubling, negative figure associated with human death and sin, and thus a good fit for a contemporary game intending to complicate easy notions of good and evil.

[39] Collins, *The Apocalyptic Imagination*, 9.

reader is experiencing now, he or she can place it within the context of a larger orderly universe. Time is marching toward its inevitable transformation, and everything that happens now should be interpreted in light of the changes to come, which will benefit the visionary. This view of time is reflected in the apocalyptic notion of the "periodization" of history, which, as Collins notes, "makes it possible to locate the present in the overall schema of history" and thus increases the sense that "all is determined in advance and under divine control." Collins links the periodization of history into fixed eras, with the division of space into multiple levels of heaven. Both are a means to imagine "an ordered universe where everything proceeds in a predetermined manner."[40] The common division of games into timed quests and levels is a related echo of such ancient ordering of the universe into ascents into multiple levels of heaven, which must be achieved one by one as time moves toward its inevitable end.

People's enjoyment of first-person shooter video games, then, may be grounded in a desire to enter into an apocalyptic experience of time. The power of the programming machine is akin to the power of an externalized Godhead—even if players do not believe that God exists. As McKenzie Wark puts it, "The gamer's God is a game designer. He implants in everything a hidden algorithm. Faith is having the intelligence to intuit the parameters of this geek design and score accordingly. All that is righteous wins; all that wins is righteous. To be a loser or a lamer is the mark of damnation.... Gamers confront one another in contests of skill that reveal who has been *chosen*—chosen by the game as the one who has most fully internalized the algorithm."[41]

The primary objective of gameplay is to give oneself over to the game's structure and goals while performing tasks that display one's own power within a winnable system. Patrick Crogan points out that in games, players win not just by defeating their enemies but also by participating in the game's *own* view of inevitability. As they purposefully move through the game, players participate in the construction of "a linear, teleological sequence of play in an illusionistic *mise en scène*."[42] There are two types of confidence exhibited here: first, that the gaming universe has fixed rules (albeit violent ones) that are discoverable; second, that the player can win in this predictable, controlled cosmic game. Apocalypses and games share a conviction that the world is a knowable, competitive, structured space with a predetermined sense of time and that "winning" requires violence.

We control gameplay, but we are also controlled by what gameplay demands of us. Wark puts this tension in quasi-religious language: "Games redeem gamespace by offering a perfect unfreedom, a consistent set of constraints."[43] First-person shooter games, like apocalypses, appeal to a player's "desire to encounter the future in the form of anticipated, controllable contingencies."[44] Seen this way, video games can be viewed as an

---

[40] Ibid., 81.   [41] Wark, *Gamer Theory*, 013.

[42] "Mise-en-scène means "putting onto the stage." It consists of what viewers see onstage or on-screen and thus is part of the constructed experience being put together by the producers of games as well. Patrick Crogan, *Gameplay Mode: War, Simulation, and Technoculture* (Minneapolis: University of Minnesota Press, 2011), 75.

[43] Wark, *Gamer Theory*, 040.   [44] Ibid., 106.

"attempt to bring the future under control by representing it in terms of the present" in a form that offers a predictable, "technical means" for addressing this desire for a sense of command.[45] As Crogan notes, "In the minimal, logistical narrative of gametime, the end state is one of prevalence, literally, one of superiority, of effective dominance over the events encountered in the game. To win the game is to prevail in this sense—that is, by discovering and perfecting the means to control the events in advance of the encounter with them."[46] Winning consists of successfully managing the chaos. In the case of *Darksiders*, the player acts as a kind of self-proclaimed messiah who wreaks havoc on earth as a means of bringing an end to war. This argument—that violence is the only means to establish peace—is a frequent justification for preemptive military strikes in our own time.

Far from being about freedom, today's apocalyptic video games may be more about the wish for a purposeful sense of control over our own fate. There is an intimate relationship here between peace and war, exhibited in the confidence that the game is winnable but that the player can win only through violent means. In *Darksiders*, as War singlehandedly fights battles with bigger and more formidable enemies, their violent defeat is presented as the only path toward renewed "balance" in the world. This is a lesson clearly intended for a post-9/11 audience and brings with it some troubling ideological implications about war's purposes today.

Sitz im Leben

Biblical scholars use the term *sitz im leben* to describe the "situation in life" in which ancient apocalypses were likely written.[47] Many scholars are convinced that apocalyptic literature was meant to help people deal with perceived hardship. David Hellholm has suggested that the definition of apocalypse developed by the SBL Forum should be extended to include the phrase "intended for a group in crisis with the purpose of exhortation and/or consolation by means of divine authority."[48] In other words, apocalypses are often viewed as coping literature—they help people who feel oppressed by letting them imagine a better situation for themselves in the imminent future.

Apocalypses in antiquity comforted two communities, Jews and Christians, both suffering under the oppressive arms of authoritarian empires. For example, the apocalypse in Daniel 7–12 was likely written while living under persecution by the Syrians. The apocalypses in *4 Ezra* and *2* and *3 Baruch* may reflect grieving by Israelites about the devastating destruction of the temple in Jerusalem. The book of Revelation was written while early Christians suffered under the Roman Empire. These are all identifiable historical periods of oppression. But other texts, like the *Book of the Watchers* in the Enoch

---

[45] Ibid., 107.   [46] Ibid., 83.

[47] See Klaus Koch, *The Rediscovery of Apocalyptic* (Naperville, IL: Allenson, 1972), 21.

[48] David Hellholm, "The Problem of Apocalyptic Genre and the Apocalypse of John," in *Early Christian Apocalypticism: Genre and Social Setting*, Semeia 36, ed. Adela Yarbro Collins (Decatur, GA: Scholars Press, 1986), 27.

corpus, have no obvious "underlying crisis." The texts *may* have been a response to real historical events, but if they were, we can no longer identify what those events were.

Michael Stone proposes that even though we can never know with absolute certainty how ancient apocalypses were utilized within specific communities or "how their teachings were realized," the *actual* experience of suffering is beside the point.[49] Apocalypses need only be viewed as "crisis" literature within the eyes of the beholder, since "what is perceived as a crisis by an apocalyptic author may not have been universally so perceived."[50] Martha Himmelfarb similarly proposes that apocalypses may have been motivated by particular catastrophic events or may have been prompted simply by "ongoing discontent" in a Hellenistic age.[51] Most scholars agree that apocalypses "address some underlying problem" or at least the *perception* of such a problem.[52] An apocalyptic revelation is meant to "lend supernatural authority" to a message of a future in which things work out better for the listeners, with a "definitive resolution" to contemporary discontent.[53] Apocalypses offer cosmic comfort in the form of reassurance about the orderliness of the imagined heavenly world and, by extension, the hope for order in the real world in which their audiences lived.

We may not be able to access the specific *sitz im leben* of many ancient apocalypses, but we *can* identify the *sitz im leben* of today's gaming apocalypses: it is our own world. And while it is true that most gamers are privileged enough to enjoy games without imminent political or social crisis, today's players do face a threat to which apocalyptic video game narratives seem to respond: the shared global risks that affect us every day, from climate change and terrorism to the depletion of our earth's resources and perpetual apprehension about war. Arjun Appadurai notes that the world now "involves interactions of a new order and intensity" in a global "interactive system" that is "strikingly new" and increasingly interdependent.[54] Until very recently, he says, cultures interacted mainly through long, slow processes of military engagement or religious and cultural exchange, but these were limited due to spatial and social separations that could not easily be bridged. In the past few hundred years, more rapid modes of engagement have been possible due to facilitated modes of international trade, migration, and communications. In the past century, there has been what he calls a "technological explosion" that has introduced a "new condition of neighborliness" such that we can no longer ignore our shared fate on the planet.[55]

It is possible, then, to read video games as an apocalyptic response to the perceived threats of violence and risk that thread perniciously through the world today. Apocalypticism in popular culture is one disturbing means of envisioning survival in

---

[49]   Michael Stone, "Pseudepigraphy Reconsidered," *Review of Rabbinic Judaism* 9 (2006): 9.

[50]   Collins, *The Apocalyptic Imagination*, 47.

[51]   Martha Himmelfarb, "The Apocalyptic Vision," in *The Oxford Study Bible*, ed. M. J. Suggs, K. D. Sakenfeld, and J. R. Mueller (Oxford: Oxford University Press, 1992), 184.

[52]   Collins, *The Apocalyptic Imagination*, 51.   [53]   Ibid.

[54]   Arjun Appadurai, *Modernity at Large: Cultural Dimensions of Globalization* (Minneapolis: University of Minnesota Press, 1996), 27.

[55]   Ibid., 29.

what some see as an increasingly violent world on the brink of collapse. When read this way, our media does powerful imaginative work, much like apocalypses did for Jews and Christians in the ancient world. Appadurai describes the key role that the social imagination plays today; the media, generally speaking, is "no longer mere fantasy (opium for the masses whose real work is elsewhere), no longer simple escape (from a world defined principally by more concrete purposes and structures), no longer elite pastime (thus not relevant to the lives of ordinary people), and no longer mere contemplation (irrelevant for new forms of desire and subjectivity)."[56] Instead, the media is a powerful reflection of the social imagination. It is "an organized field of social practices, a form of work (in the sense of both labor and culturally organized practice), and a form of negotiation between sites of agency (individuals) and globally defined fields of possibility."[57] The social imagination, says Appadurai, is "the key component of the new global order."[58] Our media tells us what we fear. It sketches what the future might be like. And perhaps most disturbing, it falsely promises us that if we acquire enough deadly weapons, we can face these challenges without mutual respect or cooperation.

Reliance upon Revelation for religious imagery, then, is only part of the story. *Darksiders'* deeper apocalyptic structure is too easily mapped onto our own world, where violence and War/war are portrayed as the only means to bring about an uneasy truce among the world's raging factions. Games like *Darksiders* may comfort us by making us feel more in control, but they do so in a way that sketches a violent pattern of vigilante apocalyptic performativity. We need a hero with a gun or blade, it says, and we must play that role ourselves since it is too late for negotiation with others. When viewed in this way, games are no longer just games; they are expressions of powerful social processes that demand our critical attention.

Much more work remains to be done in making sense of the force of video games in society today—as both reflectors and as shapers of culture. Wark says that we should intentionally "trifle" with games and their forms, to resist absorbing them as declarative statements about how things should be: "You trifle with the game to understand the nature of gamespace as a world—as *the* world. You trifle with the game to discover in what way gamespace falls short of its self-proclaimed perfection."[59] In trifling with the game, we stand a better chance of trifling with reality—of finding ways of dealing with contemporary risks without retreat to violent apocalyptic scenarios.

FUTURE PROSPECTS AND QUESTIONS

- Ian Bogost proposes that we focus on the "expressive capacity of games" in order to better understand "how videogames reveal what it means to be human."[60] Do you agree with Bogost that video games reveal something about what it means to

---

[56] Ibid., 73–4.   [57] Ibid., 31.   [58] Ibid.   [59] Wark, *Gamer Theory*, 021.
[60] Bogost, *Unit Operations*, 53.

be human? What do they reveal? What do apocalyptic video games reveal? How do they reveal it?

- What do you make of the ease with which apocalypses can be transformed into contemporary video games? Why do you think these two expressive forms are so closely aligned?
- Video games are often considered a form of entertainment. They are "fun" activities meant to give us a break from our daily lives. Can apocalypses also be "fun"? Are video games that are based on violent apocalypses also just "fun"? What is at stake in asking this question?
- The dualism of friend or foe is a key characteristic of both apocalypses and many first-person shooter video games. Do video games "teach" people how to view the world this way? Why or why not? What might the implications be of repeating virtual violence in contexts in which we are expected to see the world as divided into friend and foe?
- Scholars of apocalypticism have suggested that apocalypses tend to be written when people feel oppressed, worried, and uncertain about the future. Why do you think video game apocalypses are so popular right now? What are we worried about? How do violent first-person video games express these worries?
- What do you think about games as rituals? That is to say, is there any way in which the repeated practice of dualistic storytelling might become habitual for players and bleed over into their real lives? Are violent video games (whether apocalyptic or not) dangerous?

Suggested Readings and Annotated Bibliography

Appadurai, Arjun. *Modernity at Large: Cultural Dimensions of Globalization*. Minneapolis: University of Minnesota Press, 1996.

Although written over twenty years ago, Appadurai's stunning study of globalization and media is deeply resonant with the challenges we face today. His prescient description of the challenges of global identity, and their intersection with the media we make and consume, offers poignant food for thought as we move toward an ever more precarious future.

Bogost, Ian. *Unit Operations: An Approach to Video Game Criticism*. Cambridge, MA: MIT Press, 2008.

Bogost is required reading for anyone interested in religion and video games. He intuitively recognizes the kinship between video games and religion, something he also talks about in *Persuasive Games* (Boston: MIT Press, 2010). In *Unit Operations*, he links literary theory, philosophy, and computational theory in a humanities-friendly, readable style and offers a method for the analysis of video games as a means of human expression.

Collins, John J. *The Apocalyptic Imagination: An Introduction to Jewish Apocalyptic Literature*. 3rd edition. Grand Rapids, MI: Eerdmans, 2016.

Collins's encyclopedic introduction to apocalyptic literature is written largely for the advanced scholar and focuses mainly on ancient Jewish and Christian texts. But it also contains a number of helpful insights into what apocalypticism is and how it works and is essential reading for someone deeply interested in the subject.

Huizinga, Johan. *Homo Ludens: A Study of the Play-Element in Culture.* London: Routledge, 1949.

First published in 1938, Huizinga's analysis of the role of play in human culture is still obligatory reading for those interested in the intersection between games, rituals, and religion. Religion, he proposes, is a kind of "play" comparable to theater, games, and sports. Huizinga introduces the concept of the "magic circle"—a carved-off spot in which special, ritualized activities occur—a notion that has become key to interpreting video games.

LeBlanc, Marc. "Tools for Creating Dramatic Game Dynamics." In *The Game Design Reader: A Rules of Play Anthology*, edited by Katie Salen Tekinbas and Eric Zimmerman, 438–59. Cambridge, MA: MIT Press, 2006.

This essay is a fascinating look at the design of games, especially the ways that interactive stories are programmed to create a sense of dramatic expectation. Although he never talks about religion directly, LeBlanc's analysis offers a compelling means by which to think about how game design can work in apocalyptic ways, especially in the management of time and storytelling. Also check out the other essays in the chunky *The Game Design Reader*, a must-have collection of game theory and design.

Wark, McKenzie. *Gamer Theory.* Boston: Harvard University Press, 2007.

Wark's fascinating study of the cultural and political power of games occasionally veers into explicitly religious language as he recognizes the force of gaming as a social phenomenon. The book is divided into paragraph-long observations, each numbered and each compelling in its analysis of what games mean to us as human beings.

PART V

"LIVED"/ PERFORMATIVE EXAMPLES OF THE BIBLE AND POPULAR CULTURE

CHAPTER 25

···

THEME PARKS

···

JAMES S. BIELO
DEPARTMENT OF ANTHROPOLOGY,
MIAMI UNIVERSITY OF OHIO

INTRODUCTION

THEME parks are portals to other worlds. Whereas Disney offers a nostalgic national past and optimistic global future, Sea World promises visitors a memorable encounter with nature, and Busch Gardens Williamsburg evokes idealized Western European pasts via imagineered hamlets. At biblical theme parks, the re-created world shifts to a distant past culled from the pages of scripture. Attractions imagine, materialize, and choreograph stories from Christians' sacred texts: Noah's ark, Moses's Tabernacle, Solomon's Temple, scenes from the life of Jesus, the everyday lifeworld and landscape of ancient Israelites, and many others.

For academic, popular, and theological critics alike, the idea of a biblical theme park can be troubling. Conjuring a biblical past through the register of theme park entertainment generates critique from multiple directions. For some, this brand of historical production too easily ignores or too selectively engages archaeological evidence, ultimately too prone to the elision of subaltern histories. For others, the unhesitant embrace of the modern theme park idiom and industry sullies the sacred character of scripture. And for still others, such religious entertainment is ideology-advancing capitalism run amok, cloaked as family fun: "Spectacle is politics or ideology that pretends to be entertainment; it is the theatrical figuration of capital and an expression of its excesses."[1]

Interpreting biblical theme parks with such critical frameworks has significant analytical value, but in this chapter I cultivate a different approach. First, I explore the history of the modern theme park to better understand how the biblical variety works. Second, I illustrate how biblical attractions are grounded by an immersive imperative,

---

[1] Annabel Jane Wharton, *Selling Jerusalem: Relics, Replicas, Theme Parks* (Durham, NC: Duke University Press, 2006), 190.

always oriented around a promise to heighten visitors' relation of intimacy with scripture by conjuring a scriptural past.

OVERVIEW OF TOPIC

The modern theme park was inaugurated in 1955 by the opening of Disneyland in Anaheim, California. As a genre of place, it was distinguished from related cultural forms because it posed "a new kind of cultural experiential product," in which "the carefully controlled sale of goods (souvenirs) and experiences (architecture, rides, and performances) [were] 'themed' to the corporate owner's proprietary image."[2] The strategies and technologies of theming are used to choreograph visitor experience, all the while advancing capitalist ambitions of profit-making and brand circulation. But the modern theme park did not arise in situ with no cultural forms to anticipate its arrival. Carnivals, amusement parks, World's Fair expositions, and landscape gardens are all ancestors in the theme park genealogy. Much like Disneyland, these cultural predecessors mixed consumption with leisure and education to attract, entertain, and edify a middle-class public.

The popular rise of botanical and pleasure gardens in the eighteenth century anticipated the process of imagineering. These attractions sought to create an enchanted environment, stimulating desired effects through the strategic use of material and technological forms in carefully designed spaces.[3] Nineteenth- and early twentieth-century World's Fair exhibitions elaborated the possibilities of the imagineered space by re-creating micro-scenes from distant cultures that could be consumed sequentially in a single, temporary setting.[4] When Disneyland opened in 1955, it presented the consuming public with something novel but also something familiar because it joined this rich ecology of themed environments.

The cultural resonance of the modern theme park, owing largely to the success of Disney, is wide-ranging. Airports, restaurants, museums, and urban business districts have all internalized the aim of creating "imaginary worlds that evoke a thematic coherence through architecture, landscaping, costuming, and other theatrical effects to establish a focused, integrated experience."[5] While some industries and institutions have embraced the logic of theming with gusto, others have done so more hesitantly. Living

---

[2] Susan G. Davis, *Spectacular Nature: Corporate Culture and the Sea World Experience* (Berkeley: University of California Press, 1997), 22.

[3] Terence Young and Robert Riley, *Theme Park Landscapes: Antecedents and Variations* (Washington, DC: Dumbarton Oaks Research Library and Collection, 2002). See especially chapters by Young, Harwood, and Schenker, all of which explore how eighteenth- and nineteenth-century botanical and pleasure gardens were cultural predecessors to the twentieth-century modern theme park in terms of design, placement, and visitor use.

[4] Ibid.

[5] David Chidester, *Authentic Fakes: Religion and American Popular Culture* (Berkeley: University of California Press, 2005), 146.

history museums, such as Colonial Williamsburg, self-consciously borrow tactics of visitor immersion from the likes of Disney, while adamantly asserting distance from what they consider the insult of being labeled a "theme park."[6]

The central imperative that modern theme parks inherited from predecessors like pleasure gardens and World's Fairs—and subsequently passed on to museums, restaurants, and others—is immersion.[7] The aim is to transport visitors away from the frame of everyday life and into a new experiential frame, one defined by an attraction's chosen theming. This immersive imperative capitalizes on the human capacity for and passion for play. Mobilizing the power of play—becoming physically, emotionally, and/or cognitively "caught up" in the immersive frame—has arguably become "the most influential ideological system on the planet."[8] As modern consumers, we prioritize and gravitate toward forms of leisure, gaming, and education that are interactive, participatory, and experientially compelling, not passively consumptive.

Creating immersive environments can require significant investments of time, space, money, labor, and creativity. Actors across social and institutional fields deem this significant investment worthwhile because the immersive environment promises to fulfill the ambitions of site creators. One axis of immersion's success is that it excels in generating affective attachments to the re-created world in which visitors are invited to play. Choreographed spaces testify to the power of affect, as material and sensory channels register effects on and through the bodies of visitors. Whether the aim is entertainment plus corporate loyalty and profit or entertainment plus didactic religious teaching and devotion, using immersive tactics to build affective attachment is the fuel that makes the world-making engine run.

What is true for eighteenth-century pleasure gardens and Disney World is no less true for biblically themed environments. The history of these attractions in the United States traces to 1874 and the construction of Palestine Park in Chautauqua, New York.[9] Palestine Park is a four-hundred-foot-long topographic replica of ancient Israel, which emerged from the pedagogy of the Methodist Sunday school movement. John Heyl Vincent, a cofounder of the Park, had been teaching a class on biblical Palestine in the 1850s that used material objects to immerse students in the world of scripture, which informed his design of the landscape model. Palestine Park was an early attraction at the Methodist Chautauqua Assembly (later, Chautauqua Institution) intended to help train Sunday school teachers by exploring the geography and history of biblical lands,

---

[6] Richard Handler and Eric Gable, *The New History in an Old Museum: Creating the Past at Colonial Williamsburg* (Durham, NC: Duke University Press, 1997).

[7] Scott A. Lukas, *The Themed Space: Locating Culture, Nation, and Self* (Lanham, MD: Lexington Books, 2007).

[8] Peter Stromberg, *Caught in Play: How Entertainment Works on You* (Stanford, CA: Stanford University Press, 2009), 3.

[9] This chapter focuses on biblical theme parks in the United States. However, the logic of theming and the immersive imperative to materialize the Bible are active cross-culturally. For an introduction to the global presence of biblically themed environments, see chapter 2 in James S. Bielo, *Ark Encounter: The Making of a Creationist Theme Park* (New York: NYU Press, 2018).

immersing them via miniaturized emplaced simulation.[10] Chautauqua Lake served as the Mediterranean Sea, and sculpted into and out of the earth were mountains, lakes, and the locations of cities named in scripture. Much like its nineteenth-century garden and World's Fair counterparts, Palestine Park's choreography of space and immersive invitation to imagine the past of scripture through replication anticipates the core embodied elements of the modern theme park.

The success of Palestine Park inspired other American projects geared toward transporting visitors to the Holy Land through materialized re-creations. In 1879 the Holiness Methodist camp meeting site of Ocean Grove, New Jersey, added a scale model of nineteenth-century Jerusalem and the city's surrounding landscape that measured fifty feet in diameter. A 1919 description by an Ocean Grove Camp Meeting Association trustee boasted that the model featured twelve hundred miniature trees and was "so accurate in the reproduction that scores of travelers who have visited Jerusalem have found keen delight in identifying its different sections and even individual buildings."[11] In 1904, as part of the Louisiana Purchase Exposition held in St. Louis, a roughly eleven-acre replication of Jerusalem's Old City invoked the Holy Land pilgrimage trope of "walking where Jesus walked" by immersing visitors in shrines, markets, and streets within a 1:1 scale replica.[12] Variations on the theme of Holy Land re-creation appear throughout the twentieth century, from Waterbury, Connecticut's Holy Land, USA, in 1955 (an eighteen-acre collection of miniature biblical replications) to Orlando, Florida's Holy Land Experience in 2001 (a fifteen-acre park that features replications of, among other elements, Jerusalem's Garden Tomb and a large floor model of Jerusalem, circa 66 CE).

The modern biblical theme park is exemplified by an attraction that opened to the public in July 2016. Ark Encounter is a creationist park, set on eight hundred acres in the northern Kentucky region near Cincinnati (see Figure 25.1). The park's centerpiece is a "life-sized" re-creation of Noah's ark, stretching more than five hundred feet long, containing more than 100,000 square feet of themed space, comprising more than three million board feet of timber, and costing nearly $100 million. Inside the ark, visitors explore three decks filled with a mix of sculpted animals, animatronic and static figures of Noah and family, imagined replications such as food storage containers, and teaching exhibits that integrate everyday life on board the ark with creationist theology and politics. While Ark Encounter is certainly meant to be a destination of religious entertainment, it is first and foremost a project of religious socialization and evangelism—the creationist worldview materialized, designed to convert noncreationists to creationism and challenge the authority and legitimacy of evolutionary science. The park is legally

[10]   Burke O. Long, *Imagining the Holy Land: Maps, Models, and Fantasy Travels* (Bloomington: Indiana University Press, 2003).

[11]   Quoted in Troy Messenger, *Holy Leisure: Recreation and Religion in God's Square Mile* (Philadelphia, PA: Temple University Press, 1999), 106.

[12]   Milette Shamir, "Back to the Future: The Jerusalem Exhibit at the 1904 St. Louis World's Fair," *Journal of Levantine Studies* 2, no. 1 (2012): 93–113.

FIGURE 25.1 Exterior of the re-created ark at Ark Encounter. Photo by author.

separate from, but also inextricable from, the creationist ministry Answers in Genesis, which opened the $30 million Creation Museum in northern Kentucky in 2007.

Be it the landscape of ancient Israel, Jerusalem's Old City, or re-creations of the book of Genesis as literal history, biblically themed environments have flourished on the American landscape. These attractions mobilize the power of immersion to make a promise: that visitors will find or rediscover the true meaning of scripture. They invite visitors to "experience," "encounter," "engage," "interact with," "see," and "step into" the world of the Bible. They seek to persuade visitors that they should be intimate with scripture, and the choreography of their physical, experiential environments promises to bolster that intimacy. This promised intimacy fundamentally engages the work of temporality. Biblical theme parks promise direct access to a scriptural past that is distant temporally and spatially. They promise to collapse the distance that separates the here and now from the scriptural there and then, relying on a series of devotional and peda-gogical strategies that resonate deeply with the imperatives of immersive entertainment. Objects, technology, and the human body work as channels for contacting the past world of scripture. Some focus on natural elements, such as flora named in scripture, while others focus on the art and architecture of themed environments. While the range of channels used varies widely, the organizing aim endures: to create a direct experience of scripture by engaging visitors' sensorium and imagination.

SPECIFIC EXAMPLES AND/OR FOCI

Ark Encounter vividly illustrates how the relationship among promised scriptural intimacy and immersive theming can be performed.[13] Considered from a distance, the
theme organizing the attraction might be glossed as biblical, or more precisely a fundamentalist Protestant Bible. Considered in cultural insider terms, its organizing theme is
the story of Noah and the Flood as it appears in English-language translations of Genesis
6–9. Based on my fieldwork with the Ark Encounter creative team and multiple visits to
the park, I argue that four interlaced immersive themes choreograph visitor experience:
an aesthetic centered on wood and animals; the "pre-Flood world" that provoked God's
watery judgment; the liminal existence of Noah and family on board the ark; and the
worldview (i.e., theology, history, cosmology, ideology, politics) of the modern creationist movement.

Example 1: Of Wood and Animal

Part of Ark Encounter's theming is about setting a general backdrop, a visual wash (i.e., a
what-is-in-my-visual-field-in-most-places kind of immersive effect). This theming
highlights two key forms integral to their telling of the Noah story: wood and animals.
Attractions that re-create the Holy Land frequently integrate landscape materials from
Israel-Palestine into their choreographed experience: water from the Jordan River,
stones from Jerusalem, sand or soil from the Galilee, or plants and flowers native to biblical lands. Such items function as natural conduits to the biblical past. However, because
Ark Encounter re-creates the lifeworld of Noah, not Jesus, this material tactic is unavail-
able. In the place of Holy Land dirt, rock, and liquid, Ark Encounter turns to timber.
Variations on the materiality of wood played a pivotal role in the development and actualization of the park.

Beginning with the first promotional flyers that circulated in 2011, Ark publicity
materials (print and digital), almost without exception, appear against a backdrop of
dark wood, an up-close view so the texture of grain and knots is clearly visible. Driving
into the park you are met by a three-story-tall entrance gate. At first you notice the name,
"Ark Encounter," but on second glance you realize its shape: it is modeled as an exposed

---

[13] I focus on Ark Encounter as the primary case study in this chapter because this site was the
centerpiece of a research project I conducted from 2011 to 2017. Over the course of two and a half years
I conducted ethnographic fieldwork with the creative team in charge of conceptualizing and designing
the park. In addition to my interviews with creationist visitors, observations at the park, and discourse
analysis of publicity materials, Ark Encounter triggered my comparative interest in the broader
phenomenon of materializing the Bible. This comparative interest has taken me to more than forty
biblically themed environments and instigated an archival collection of more than 800 items (e.g.,
guidebooks, souvenirs). For a detailed account of this project, see the digital scholarship project
Materializing the Bible, accessed June 19, 2020, www.materializingthebible.com/.

FIGURE 25.2 One visual field from inside the re-created ark at Ark Encounter. Photo by author.

view of construction logs and the interlocking engineering system the designers attribute to Noah.

The aesthetic of wood is most pronounced when standing inside the re-created ark (see Figure 25.2). From numerous vantage points, your visual field is drawn to the sunlight streaming down from rooftop windows and the layered depth of the large space. This is particularly striking on deck 2 as you are able to look over, down, up, and back. Tactilely your touch is drawn to the massive timbers that form the building's bones: up close, each one is utterly unique with splits, knots, and dried sap streaming out. If you are so inclined, the physicality of the space affords the visceral possibility of imagining the vessel during the Flood, perhaps just as Noah and his family experienced it.

There is no signage orchestrating this particular effect, but it was encouraged by publicity materials throughout the construction process and continuing after the park's opening. A video interview with the owner of the timber frame company that provided the construction materials was released on Ark Encounter's website and YouTube channel in December 2015.[14] Speaking in an ethical register of environmental sustainability, the owner describes with awe his experience of interacting with the large timbers:

---

[14] See Ark Encounter, "Responsible Timber Harvesting," YouTube, December 11, 2015, youtube.com/watch?v=J7Jdni8c_b0.

"Everybody who comes through [the ark] can enjoy the character and the size and the magnitude of these logs."

The significance of the wood's materiality resonated especially well with a creationist visitor I interviewed in early 2016, before the park's opening. Matt, a lifelong creationist in his early twenties, was an amateur woodworker. For birthday and Christmas gifts, he crafts presents for friends and family. For his sister's wedding, he built an arch under which the couple recited their vows. When I showed Matt the timber framing video, he said that it answered questions he had about Ark Encounter's "environmental impact" and heightened his enthusiasm for going. In contrast with other promotional videos that explained the park's design and teaching exhibits, Matt was more excited about seeing the architectural feat of the ark itself. This preference was not merely about marveling at modern construction; it was about channeling awe through the materiality of wood to access the creationist past.

To complement the representational uses of wood, there is also a prolific use of animals. The park's first television commercial, a thirty-second spot that aired nationally beginning in late 2015, featured everyday people catching amazed glimpses of various animals (elephants, rhinos, leopards) moving two-by-two, which they follow to discover a waiting ark (i.e., a digital re-creation of the then-upcoming physical ark re-creation). Transportation to the ark from the parking lot and ticketing area occurs by bus. The vehicles, reminiscent of large airport shuttles, were all purchased and refurbished by Ark Encounter. Each bus exterior is wrapped in a painted advertisement, most displaying a two-by-two collection of animals: panda bears, rhinos, kangaroos, tigers, giraffes.

Ark Encounter's general aesthetic of wood and animals is integrated in the gift shop area, located beneath deck 1 of the ark. Early in my fieldwork with the creative team, they flagged a need to both maintain consistent theming throughout the park (not just on board through exhibits) and to "surprise" visitors. During a four-hour team meeting in February 2012, they articulated this need via a discussion of the gift shop. They questioned how to manage the kind of products that would be sold. Roger, the creative director, emphasized that it must be "a style that fits in pre-Flood culture." Briefly, he and one of the administrative assistants criticized the Creation Museum on this account, noting that it resembles "any old Christian bookstore." All agreed that Ark Encounter needed to avoid this problem, extending the immersive experience to the gift shop.

In April 2015 they announced their solution through the blog portal of the park website. One half of the gift shop area would be dedicated to fair-trade products. This section would feature only handmade items from nine nations in Central America, East Africa, and Southeast Asia. The team's access to fair-trade items began with a relationship one artist had built with an evangelical ministry focused on Nicaraguan children. Between April 2015 and July 2016, three separate posts detailed the nature of fair trade commerce and why the team wanted it to be part of the experience at Ark Encounter.[15]

---

[15] For example, Ark Encounter, "Unique Fair Trade Goods Sold at Ark Encounter Benefit People around the World," July 28, 2016, arkencounter.com/blog/2016/07/28/unique-fair-trade-goods-sold-ark-encounter-benefit-people-around-world/.

The posts diligently blend multiple registers, from ethical ("We also aspire to help provide for people's physical needs around the world") to theological ("As Christians we wanted to be a part of this"), capitalist ("Since each of these products is completely handmade and unique, it will be impossible to find the same thing again"), and iconic, meaning a relation of resemblance is built between the goods and the ark itself ("[We] always wanted to have unique handmade products from around the world made with materials from nature, similar to how Noah would have made things").

As you walk through the fair-trade section of Ark Encounter's gift shop, you repeatedly encounter two representational forms: wood and animals. While not all of the handmade items are crafted from wood—one also finds recycled aluminum cans and textiles—most are. From painted bird whistles to thatched bowls, forms of sculpted lumber and reed dominate the space. Exploring the aisles also brings you in contact with animal figures in multiple forms: bird whistles that are actually shaped as birds, animal hand puppets, and stuffed animals. When first entering the space, you pass one of the more lavish souvenirs: a collectible artwork, a nearly life-size lion made from a repurposed oil drum ($3,499.00).

Example 2: Pre-Flood World

For creationists, the story of Noah and the ark is situated in scientific, historical, and theological registers. As an engagement with science, creationists treat the Flood as a literal event that occurred in history (roughly four thousand years ago) and that explains aspects of our natural world, from geologic formations to fossil distribution. Theologically this universal flood was not merely a weather event; it was God's judgment of human "wickedness."[16] For the creative team, immersing visitors into the pre-Flood world that God judged and delivered Noah from was an instrumental piece of the park's theming.

Creating a themed environment of the pre-Flood world poses at least two artistic dilemmas. First, creationists are generally quick, and pleased, to claim the mantle of biblical literalists. This identity marks their claim that the scriptural text is God's revelation to humanity and the ultimate source of authority.[17] But as an earnest biblical literalist, how do you create a theme park when the reference details are so sparse? The early chapters of Genesis offer few specifics about this time, instead emphasizing condemning descriptions of human hearts that were "only evil all the time."[18] The team's creative labor took place largely in an intertextual gap, reading between scriptural lines, faced with the task of materializing the Bible in ways that would satisfy fundamentalist audiences and make sense to nonfundamentalists. Second, much like

[16]   Genesis 6:5 (New International Version, 1973).
[17]   Christopher Toumey, *God's Own Scientists: Creationists in a Secular World* (New Brunswick, NJ: Rutgers University Press, 1994).
[18]   Genesis 6:5 (New International Version, 1973).

Disney World and other theme parks, families are a primary audience Ark Encounter relies on to purchase tickets, in particular families with children. The park must communicate to a mass public in ways deemed culturally appropriate, which means they had to critically consider how such evil hearts could be portrayed. That is, *how do you re-create the most wickedly sinful period in human history in a way that is fun for the whole family?!*

To immerse visitors in the pre-Flood world of Noah is to perform the work of world-building. As evidenced by the phenomenal success of franchises like *Star Wars*, world-building is significantly prized by our modern culture of entertainment. This makes sense in capitalist terms (world-building lends itself to an ever-expanding transmedial marketplace of tie-in commodities) but also with respect to our human capacity for play: "To invite an audience to vicariously enter another world, and then hold them there awhile is, after all, the essence of entertainment, which traces its etymology to the Latin roots *inter* meaning 'among,' and *tenere* meaning 'to hold.'"[19] A key strategy in world-building projects throughout history has been the use of maps. Visual representations of space and place from a zoomed-out vantage point are "important for establishing the imaginary world as a virtual space consistent in all its details."[20] We find this strategy of mapping worlds from Thomas More's *Utopia* in 1516 to A. A. Milne's *Winnie the Pooh* in 1926, J. R. R. Tolkien's Middle Earth in 1937, George R. R. Martin's *A Song of Ice and Fire* in 1996, and a great many others. Perhaps it is not surprising, then, that we find maps and globes of the pre-Flood world integrated into exhibits throughout the three decks on board the ark. While there are dozens of these map forms scattered throughout the ark, none is textually annotated with explanatory signage. They are simply there as immersive aids.

While this world is signified on all three decks, it is most thoroughly elaborated in a walk-through exhibit that opens deck 2, "Pre-Flood World." This winding exhibit takes visitors through a mix of dioramas, signage, painted murals, and auditory annotations that re-create events leading from the creation story to the Flood. It begins with the days of creation.

As you enter, to the left are six brightly painted panels that signify God's work on each day. To the right is a large wall mural depicting Adam and Eve in a Garden of Eden waterfall pool, surrounded by lush greenery and numerous dinosaurs. Turning a corner, the second section begins: a series of murals move from "perfect" existence in the Garden to the Fall, Exile from Eden, Cain and Abel, and the birth of Seth. Turning a corner, this scriptural play-by-play from Genesis 2–4 is followed by a multistage section depicting the spread of wickedness. A sign ("Man Abuses God-Given Abilities") frames the beginning of this section, which consists of painted panels showing scenes

---

[19] Mark J. P. Wolf, *Building Imaginary Worlds: The Theory and History of Subcreation* (London: Routledge, 2012), 17.

[20] Michael Saler, *As If: Modern Enchantment and the Literary Prehistory of Virtual Reality* (Oxford: Oxford University Press, 2012), 67.

FIGURE 25.3 Diorama scene from the Pre-Flood World exhibit at Ark Encounter. Photo by author.

from the fallen world oriented around scriptural references, such as "polygamy," "music," and "giants." The first part of this section culminates in a second large wall mural: a dramatic scene depicting a "pagan" ritual of human sacrifice, fires burning, and a crowd raging. Here the creative team's use of aurality to choreograph the immersive experience is sharply felt. Overhead, a cacophonous loop plays: fires, raucously cheering crowds, a duel of colliding and sliding swords, and human screams. There is little interpretive space to imagine anything but death by combat in view of a bloodthirsty public. It is unmistakably violent, but not more than PG. Turn a corner, and the portrayal of pre-Flood evil continues. The focal point here is two dioramas. The first is a bacchanal scene (see Figure 25.3). Small 3-D printed figures of burly men hoist chalices while draped with seductive women. One man has collapsed face down from a few too many chalices, scattering a plate of food. Musicians play and two women dance together, enticing an aroused onlooker. The second diorama presents a ritual of human sacrifice, this time shifting from the losers of deadly combat to infant babies being offered to a "false God." The Pre-Flood World exhibit concludes with a third large wall mural: a view of the ark at sea from the vantage point of unrepentant sinners stranded on rocks, soon to be consumed by a roiling ocean. Wickedness and desperation reign in the final moments just before death: scared and confused people frantically wave at the ark, while a man shoves a woman into the waters below (presumably to secure a spot on board for himself).

Example 3: Life On Board

Imagining the pre-Flood world of Noah is one form of intertextual gap-filling performed at Ark Encounter. Another explores everyday life on board the ark for Noah and family, their liminal existence between mass death and new life. This aspect of theming encompasses two kinds of immersive framing: the re-creation of the family's experience and addressing questions of historical plausibility regarding how the ark functioned.

The invitation to come and see how Noah and family lived on the ark is realized most extensively in deck 3's largest exhibit: "The Living Quarters." Several placards hanging next to the exhibit entrance explain what awaits inside, including an introduction to the eight characters. Consistent with the teaching style throughout the ark, these signs pose questions to aid visitors' imagining and present answers in the register of plausibility:

> Why are the living quarters so nice? Illustrations of Noah's Ark rarely give any consideration to the living arrangements for Noah and his family. What might their rooms have been like? Would they be simple, housing only the bare necessities, or would they have taken great care in building their rooms, just like they did with the rest of the Ark? There are many reasons to think their living quarters were quite nice. As far as we know, the Lord did not inform Noah how long they would be on the Ark, so the family would probably have prepared for an extended time inside the Ark. Also, they worked hard caring for the animals every day. Having a comfortable place to relax and refresh would be extremely beneficial for keeping up morale and energy for all the hard labor they faced.

Entering the Living Quarters, you walk by four rooms, one each for the four couples: Japheth and Rayneh, Shem and Ar'yel, Ham and Kezia, and Noah and Emzara. The rooms are flush with minute details, from beds and cushions to replications of tools and mementos and busy, lived-in workspaces. They look cozy and enjoyable, with a sufficient mix of necessities and creature comforts. The details of each room pair with imagined biographies. Rayneh, the sign explains, is "artistic" and "enjoys making crafts and adding some flair to their surroundings, such as painting intricate designs on pottery." A still life-size figure sits on the floor, enacting the scene described on the sign, surrounded by her artistic material. Her character portrayal opens further intertextual gaps, which visitors can close with their own imaginings:

> Rescued by Noah from a life-threatening situation when she was a little girl, Rayneh grew up around his family. She helped Japheth with his farming responsibilities, and the two eventually became husband and wife. She put her seamstress skills to good use during the Ark's construction, creating many of the clothes and tapestries seen on board.

The room also features numerous plant drawings and small potted plants, which mark Japheth's acumen. He stands in the corner playing a flute, perhaps delighting, perhaps annoying Rayneh with a tune. Overhead, flute music plays. The description imagines his talents and a character that is not one-dimensional:

> Japheth inherited Noah's adventurous spirit, although it is not very compatible with his agricultural work. Growing up around the Ark site has not afforded him the opportunity to explore, but he longs to set out once the Flood ends and has composed songs about these dreams. The oldest and tallest of the sons, Japheth excels in farming, just like his grandfather, Lamech. Because of this, Noah charged him with growing, preparing, and storing the food for the Ark. The plants in the room, the indoor garden, and the vast stores of grain, seeds, and nuts throughout the Ark provide evidence of his success in this area.

Just beyond the first two passengers' rooms are a series of common areas linked by the theme of food. The garden and storage area appear well-stocked and appealing, brimming with brightly colored (artificial) produce and ample supplements like streams of hanging garlic (also artificial). Display signs explain that Noah and his family were sustained by a vegetarian diet while on board. One placard shifts registers twice, from a literalist proof-text to immersive detail and then to plausibility:

> The Lord said all foods that are eaten were to be gathered (Genesis 6:21). Noah and his family probably received most of their sustenance from foods that could have been stored for the many months aboard the Ark: grains, root vegetables, legumes, and nuts. Fresh fruit was likely not on the menu, but dried and preserved fruits may have been. Conditions during the flood blocked large amounts of sunlight, but the Ark's third deck would have still received some natural light. The large window would allow the family to grow a variety of vegetables and herbs throughout the top floor to supplement their diet.

Across from the garden are the kitchen and dining areas. In each, passengers are present to lend an embodied feel to the space. For example, Ar'yel stands in the kitchen and "uses a mortar and pestle to grind tea leaves." As in the pre-Flood exhibit, an auditory annotation adds to the experience, as you hear Ar'yel working. The orchestration streams down from overhead: she hums peacefully, even delightedly, while using a knife to chop vegetables and scrape them to the side. The sounds of her contentment at work complement the intricately arranged visual scene.

The character biographies developed in The Living Quarters exhibit extend throughout the park, even to unexpected places. On my first trip to Ark Encounter I divided the time by eating lunch halfway through the visit. Emzara's Kitchen is a separate building, about fifty yards from the gift shop exit. Timber-framed, the building is made of construction materials and in a style that mimic that of the ark, only with a more house-like architecture. The space is filled with sculpted animals, each accompanied by a small placard featuring selected details about the species' history, habitat, habits, and physical characteristics. After ordering lunch, which was initially arranged in a fast-food format, I sat down to eat. Before removing the chicken sandwich, I stopped to notice that the park's theming extended even to the paper bag holding my food. One side presented a quiz reviewing small bits of information from Genesis 6–9 and on-board exhibits. Another side explained adaptations from some of the sculpted animals in the room, articulated in the register of divine creation rather than Darwinian natural selection. A third side explained the eatery's name:

> The Bible does not name Noah's wife, so the Ark Encounter used artistic license in calling her Emzara. This is based on a non-biblical book from the second century BC known as the Book of Jubilees, which states, "Noah took to himself a wife, and her name was Emzara." Emzara probably means "ancestor of Sarah," so her name was likely developed to connect her to Abraham's wife, Sarah.

As seen in these quotations from exhibit signage, matters of plausibility are interwoven with the family's re-created experience. Other exhibits flip the focus. On deck 2, exhibits present Noah's library and the sons laboring in woodworking and ironworking scenes; in each, material strategies like maps and globes of the pre-Flood world, ark blueprints, diaries, itemized manifests of food provisions, and catalogs of animals are mixed in as immersive aids with no accompanying signage. A deck 3 exhibit takes a different approach to illustrating the theme of plausibility.

"Flood Legends" addresses an oft-invoked critique of creationist history: the biblical account is merely one of many flood stories found throughout the world, so why accord any special significance to the Noah version? Of course, creationists have an answer and "Flood Legends" is their materialized rebuttal.

Stepping into the exhibit, your attention is drawn to your right, but the explanation begins on your left. Two placards voice what "critics of the Bible" might say, setting their objections up to fail. Directly in front of you is a large wall mural: a world map, intentionally not exact but still roughly to scale, which places sixteen flood legends by indigenous geographic location (e.g., Pawnee, Aztec, Norse). To your right are two features. Below is a glass case with five miniature flood vessel replicas: Epic of Gilgamesh, Vanuatu Tale, Wunambal Legend, Akkadian Tablet, and, perched above these four, The Bible. Along with the finely detailed replicas, there is a scale figure of a person and a brief sign explaining the vessel's type, size, and "problems." For example, regarding Wunambal, "People, animals, and supplies would be washed overboard. The raft would break apart if it were large enough for people, animals, and supplies." In contrast, there are no problems for the Bible's ark: "It was perfectly designed to survive the Flood." Above the miniature replicas is a digital flat screen playing a rotating animation that depicts each vessel in turn attempting to survive on rough seas. All but the ark fail, toppled over by waves. With each failure, the clip ends with an all-caps message dropping onto the screen: "NO SURVIVORS!" In contrast, the safe voyage of the ark closes with "Only the Bible tells of an Ark with size and proportions to protect its passengers from destruction." As the digital, cartoon-style comparison plays, yet another auditory shift plays overhead; it reminded me of the kind of playful tune one hears on a video game soundtrack from the 1990s, such as *Super Mario Brothers*. With the Flood Legends exhibit, theming the ark's historical plausibility is performed through a mix of museum practices (miniature replicas), creationist argumentation (the map), and video game play.

Example 4: Life on a Young Earth

The final immersive theme that helps choreograph visitor experience at Ark Encounter is the creationist worldview. This is distinct from the details of creationist history and hermeneutics because it is organized around the movement's ideological discourses of identity, namely, constructing the creationist self through the other of evolutionary science. The twin pillars of creationist identity are biblical literalism and the assertion of an evolutionary conspiracy posing a grave moral and spiritual danger to the world.[21] The unrelenting critique of evolutionary science appears throughout the ark, for example in exhibit signage that references "atheists," "skeptics," "critics of the Bible," and "secular evolutionists." This critique is perhaps most powerfully invoked by an exhibit toward the end of deck 2: "Fairy Tale Ark" (see Figure 25.4).

As you approach the exhibit, your visual field is immediately drawn upward to a series of animals lining the top of the entrance. They are certainly cartoonish, but they somehow exceed that description. In initial field notes I described them as "zany, even slightly imbalanced or crazed," signified by the design of their eyes, facial expressions, and jum-

FIGURE 25.4 Exterior of Fairy Tale Ark exhibit at Ark Encounter. Photo by author.

[21] See Toumey, *God's Own Scientists, passim.*

bled arrangement. The longer I stared at them, the more an unsettled, suspicious affect became possible.

Unlike some other exhibits, where a wooden rail bars visitors from entering the space, you must step into Fairy Tale Ark. The upbeat baseline soundtrack from the hallway shifts to a very different tune (playing on a two-minute loop). It reminded me of a dream sequence in a film, perhaps an animated film, where something terrible is about to happen. Interspersed throughout the dreamy instrumental is the sporadic sound of children laughing. The volume of their voices steadily increases, and they transform from young children playfully giggling to teenagers laughing in mockery. The exhibit's alarmist message of a secular conspiracy is simulated by this eerie auditory annotation.

Inside the small room are two dominating features. The smaller of the two, positioned on the wall to your left, is a sign encircled by a bright red snake with a dragon-like head. It reads ominously, dialogically voiced as Satan himself, "If I can convince you that the Flood was not real then I can convince you that Heaven and Hell are not real."

The primary display is positioned directly ahead, covering the entire wall. It is a collection of nearly a hundred Noah's ark–themed books written for children. Most are in English, though some are written in Spanish and French. They are arranged neatly on six rows, interspersed with other ark-themed kids' toys and games, housed directly behind panes of glass. Two textual annotations frame visitors' reading of the collection.

First, three rows up from the bottom, a series of small books are lined up side by side. They appear to be an antique collection of fables, and they present the "7 D's of Deception." For example, "Destructive for All Ages" explains, "The cute fairy tale arks are not only marketed to children, thousands of items featuring whimsical arks have been made for adults too. The abundance of these fanciful objects attacks the truthfulness of Scripture." This strategy innovates and riffs on the ministry's trademarked "7 C's of History," which is the organizing pedagogical theme of the Creation Museum and numerous ministry publications. At the center of the display is a larger book that is voiced in a rhyming, fairy tale register. It begins, "Once Upon a Time, there was an old man of god. His name was Noah and his task was quite odd. One day, the Lord said to build a little boat, 'Make it nice and cute, but who cares if it will float.'"

The cartoonish, fable-ish, and simultaneously playful-ominous aesthetic teaches a singular lesson. A literalist reading of Genesis—complete with an actual Flood, actual ark, and actual Noah and family—is lampooned every day by the ubiquitous circulation of "fairy tale" arks. This lampooning is no accident, but who is to blame? The snake-encircled sign suggests Satanic agency. The bounds of responsibility widen in the text of "Discrediting the Truth," which identifies "many atheists and other skeptics" as directly culpable. The "abundance" of unrealistic ark representations targets children, affects everyone, and is an orchestrated effort to undermine the authority and historical plausibility of literalist scripture. It is, in short, conspiracy. Here a familiar fundamentalist refrain appears as a materialized effort to expose and make obvious a taken-for-granted creationist social fact: the Bible is "under attack." The assembly of childhood artifacts performs a creationist critical discourse analysis, coaching visitors how to decode the secular antagonism to fundamentalism that circulates in secret throughout public life.

Biblical theme parks, much like secular theme parks, are portals to other worlds. Designed as choreographed spaces, both types of park invite visitors to become caught up in their immersive themes. Modern biblical theme parks, like Ark Encounter, trace their roots to nineteenth-century projects re-creating the Holy Land, projects that mobilized the power of immersion to aid religious socialization and simulate pilgrimage. Whether imagining the landscape Jesus walked in or how Noah and family lived on board the ark, these Christian-themed environments invite visitors into a particular biblical past in hopes of strengthening their intimacy with scripture. While these attractions do function as tourist destinations they are never merely about leisure.[22] Ark Encounter, for example, mobilizes the power of immersive theming to advance the ambitions of the creationist movement—to wrest authority and legitimacy from evolutionary science and reinvest public loyalties in biblical fundamentalism.

FUTURE PROSPECTS AND QUESTIONS

To close, I highlight an area of inquiry that requires dedicated empirical research to address. The analysis of Ark Encounter in this chapter emerges from my fieldwork with the creative team, my experience as a visitor to the park, limited interviewing with park visitors, and a combination of historical and ethnographic data from other biblically themed attractions. However, we can, and should, also pitch the study of biblical theme parks as part of a broader ethnography of reading. Organizing questions for this broader pitch might include the following:

- How do visitor experiences at biblical theme parks shape future acts of scripture reading, and vice versa?
- What is the feedback loop between reading the Bible and experiencing the Bible in materialized, choreographed environments?
- How might the historical imagination and forms of intertextual gap-filling performed on board Kentucky's ark inform the ways readers engage these processes as individual Bible readers or readers in social contexts such as congregational Bible study?
- How might forms of digital materializing (e.g., biblically themed video games and virtual-reality simulations) interact with textual reading and experiences with physical environments?

We can also extend this line of questioning in a more longitudinal way. Consider that by the mid-1990s, the popularity of themed attractions had begun to influence the creation of other cultural products. "Cartoons and films [were] being styled at early stages with potential theme park attractions in mind, the relevant question perhaps being 'will

---

[22] Davis, *Spectacular Nature*.

this story be good to ride?'[23] At present, it seems that biblical stories are materialized in service of existing cultural systems (e.g., Noah and creationism). But might the promise of theming and the power of entertainment have a lasting structural influence on how the Bible is engaged? Will the materializing potential of biblical stories figure into the calculus of which stories become fixed in the collective memory of religious communities? *Will this scripture be good to experience?*

SUGGESTED READINGS AND ANNOTATED BIBLIOGRAPHY

Beal, Timothy K. *Roadside Religion: In Search of the Sacred, the Strange, and the Substance of Faith.* Boston: Beacon, 2005.

Written for scholarly and popular audiences, Beal's comparative project offers close readings of ten biblically-themed sites in the United States. Each main chapter highlights one attraction, integrating interview data with founders and caretakers and his own critical observations as a visitor, all read with a nuanced understanding of the history of US Christianity. The organizing argument is that biblical attractions, from the homespun to the well-funded, constitute a distinct form of "outsider" sacred space and always reflect the religious-spiritual biography of their creator (7).

Bielo, James S. *Ark Encounter: The Making of a Creationist Theme Park.* New York: NYU Press, 2018.

In this book, I provide an extended anthropological analysis of Ark Encounter as a creationist theme park and materializing the Bible as a phenomenon. The organizing argument of the book is that the strategies and imperatives of modern entertainment structure Ark Encounter's performance of the ideology, politics, hermeneutics, and worldview of creationist culture. Throughout, the analysis highlights processes of material religion, such as the body's sensory engagement with physical forms and technologies.

Long, Burke O. *Imagining the Holy Land: Maps, Models, and Fantasy Travels.* Bloomington: Indiana University Press, 2003.

Long traces the history of American re-creations of the Holy Land from the mid-nineteenth century to the present. Most of the examples are historical—from Chautauqua's Palestine Park to stereoscopic photograph parlor shows—except for a critical reading of The Great Passion Play in Eureka Springs, Arkansas, based on a firsthand tour. Long argues that re-creations of biblical Israel, while always claiming a desired authenticity through various performative strategies, inevitably reflect the culture, religion, and politics of the re-creators.

Patterson, Sara M. *Middle of Nowhere: Religion, Art, and Pop Culture at Salvation Mountain.* Albuquerque: University of New Mexico Press, 2016.

Drawing on ethnographic and historical methods, Patterson provides a detailed analysis of Salvation Mountain, a Christian-themed attraction in the southern California desert. Using a single case study, an extended version of the smaller chapters in Beal's *Roadside*

---

[23] Susan Davis, "The Theme Park: Global Industry and Cultural Form," *Media, Culture, and Society* 18, no. 3 (1996): 407, emphasis added.

Religion, she explores the biography of the site creator, the choreography of the space itself, and the practices of diverse visitors. Patterson integrates analytical themes of sacred space, landscape, materiality, art, and devotional ritual to build a well-rounded account of this idiosyncratic destination.

Ron, Amos S., and Jackie Feldman. "From Spots to Themed Sites—the Evolution of the Protestant Holy Land." *Journal of Heritage Tourism* 4, no. 3 (2009): 201–16.

This article is an important complement to the other sources profiled here, as it illustrates how modern day Israel-Palestine is being remade in the image of Disneyesque themed environments. The authors—a cultural geographer (Ron) and an anthropologist (Feldman)—draw from decades of work as registered Israeli tour guides and empirical researchers of tourist-pilgrimage encounters in Israel and the West Bank. Analyzing attractions such as Nazareth Village, a living history museum re-creating rural life in first-century Nazareth, they argue that the strategies and imperatives of themed entertainment are actively reshaping how Holy Land attractions are designed, marketed, and consumed.

Wharton, Annabel Jane. *Selling Jerusalem: Relics, Replicas, Theme Parks.* Chicago: University of Chicago Press, 2006.

This book culminates with an analysis of the Holy Land Experience in Orlando, Florida, originally founded as a Christian Zionist theme park featuring numerous re-creations of biblical Israel. More valuable than this single analysis, however, is the book's extensive tracing of how Holy Land materials have been mobilized across time and space. Wharton begins with the early Christian church's engagement with relics and moves through various forms of Holy Land art and architecture in Western Europe and North America. Fascinating comparisons emerge, such as reading *sacri monti* replicas in northern Italy beginning in the sixteenth century alongside the growth of popular pilgrimage to Palestine in the nineteenth century. Throughout, Wharton illustrates how the Holy Land endures as a potent symbolic and ideological resource for those who reside elsewhere in the world.

CHAPTER 26

TOURING CREATION MUSEUMS, FEATURING DINOSAURS IN EDEN, PHILANDERING ALIENS, AND THE FLOOD THAT CHANGED MOLECULAR REALITY!

VALARIE H. ZIEGLER
DEPARTMENT OF RELIGIOUS STUDIES, DEPAUW
UNIVERSITY (EMERITA)

INTRODUCTION

THOUGH news about creation museums is currently dominated by the two state-of-the-art facilities in northern Kentucky run by Answers in Genesis, the Creation Museum and the Ark Encounter, creation museums in the United States come in many forms. Large, small, even mobile—some with outreach ministries at Christian camps, at fossil and dinosaur dig sites, or at geological wonders such as the Grand Canyon—creation museums function as alternative natural history museums.[1] Pointing to Genesis 1–11 as

---

[1] No one knows exactly how many creation museums exist, but two superb online resources map out the terrain. James R. Linville of the University of Lethbridge has composed a bibliography of academic sources related to creationism and provides links to sixty-two creation museums, field trips, and zoos in North America and fourteen more worldwide. See "Creation Museums, Field Trips, and Zoos," Contemporary Creationism, accessed July 16, 2017, http://contemporarycreationism.com/creation-museum. James S. Bielo of Miami University curates Materializing the Bible, a digital source

the foundation of human knowledge of both God and the natural world, their mission is to convert nonbelievers, to comfort visitors already convinced by young-earth creationism,[2] and to denounce evolutionary theory as an instrument of Satan.

Young-earth creationists argue that Genesis 1–11 should be read as literal and relatively recent history. By adding up genealogies in the Hebrew Bible, they conclude that the universe is between six to ten thousand years old, not billions of years, as evolutionists and geologists suggest. In Genesis 1, young-earth creationists argue, God created the world in six twenty-four-hour days, fashioning humankind in the divine image with dominion over the earth. The significance of the Genesis narrative, however, is not limited to its depiction of creation; Genesis 3–11 narrates a series of theological and geological catastrophes that reverberate to the present day. When the first man and woman ate the forbidden fruit in Genesis 3, God subjected all creatures to death and left humanity in need of a savior. Rampant human depravity in the generations that followed prompted God to destroy all people and land animals (except for those in Noah's Ark) through a cataclysmic global flood narrated in Genesis 6–9:17.

When the waters receded, God instructed Noah and his sons to multiply and fill the earth (Gen 9:1). But Noah's descendants preferred to stay in one location, and at Babel they built a tower that reached to the heavens. In response, God confused human language and forced humanity to scatter throughout the earth (11:1–9). The New Testament provides a plan of salvation that answers the catastrophes narrated in Genesis. The creator became incarnate in Jesus of Nazareth and died on the cross as the perfect sacrifice for human sin. In the last days, God will destroy evil altogether and institute a new heaven and earth for the faithful; the unfaithful will suffer unending damnation. Visiting a creation museum presents an opportunity to acknowledge and submit to this theological schema of creation, fall, flood, scattering, and redemption.[3]

Politically, Christians involved in creation museums see themselves as shock troops on the far right of the culture wars currently rocking the United States. Recent Gallup and Pew polls report that conservative evangelical Christians and members of the Republican Party are much more likely to be young-earth creationists than are Catholics, mainline Protestants, religiously unaffiliated Americans, political independents, and members of the Democratic Party. These polls further indicate that roughly 60 percent of Americans believe that humans evolved over time, with a bit less than 50 percent of those people asserting that God guided the evolutionary process. Thirty-four to 38 per-

project with a bibliography, virtual tours, and links to 423 regional and global Bible attractions, including creation museums, biblical history museums, biblical re-creations, and biblical gardens. See "About," Materializing the Bible, accessed July 16, 2017, http://www.materializingthebible.com/about. html, as well as Bielo's entry in this volume, "Theme Parks."

[2] For a detailed analysis of young-earth creationism, see Karl W. Giberson, *Saving Darwin: How to Be a Christian and Believe in Evolution* (New York: HarperOne, 2008); Ronald L. Numbers, *The Creationists: From Scientific Creationism to Intelligent Design*, expanded ed. (Cambridge, MA: Harvard University Press, 2006). Henry B. Morris provides an insider's perspective in his *History of Modern Creationism*, revised ed. (San Diego, CA: Institute for Creation Research, 1993).

[3] Ken Ham's illustrated *My Creation Bible: Teaching Kids to Trust the Bible from the Very First Verse* (Green Forest, AR: New Leaf, 2006), consists entirely of these five scenes.

cent of Americans are thought to be young-earth creationists.[4] Their position has high political visibility, as rejecting evolution has become de rigueur for Republican presidential candidates.

Young-earth creationism is an international powerhouse, producing an endless stream of publications, videos, sermons, lesson plans, testimonials, and even museums across the globe. There are creation museums in England, Northern Ireland, Germany, Portugal, New Zealand, and Australia, and major ark reconstruction parks are open in the Netherlands and in Hong Kong. Creationist activity has also emerged in Islam. Muslim creationism is particularly strong in Turkey, which recently removed the teaching of evolution from high school curricula. Answers in Genesis alone has outreach ministries in Central and South America, Europe, Africa, Asia, and South Asia, and its materials have been translated into many languages; thus far, more materials have been translated into Arabic than any other language.[5]

OVERVIEW OF TOPIC

Natural history museums and their displays of human origins have long been contested spaces. Henry Fairfield Osborn opened the first important permanent exhibit on human evolution at the American Museum of Natural History in New York in 1921 and resisted calls from John Roach Straton, a Baptist pastor, to give equal space to the "Bible story of creation." Straton accused Osborn of presenting evolution as a historical fact when it was actually scientific speculation.[6] A more well-known Christian attempt to provide a biblical refutation of evolution was William Jennings Bryan's testimony at the Scopes trial in 1925. Significantly, Bryan speculated that the six days of Genesis 1 were probably not actual days but ages.

[4] See Gallup, "Evolution, Creationism, Intelligent Design," accessed June 15, 2017, http://www.gallup.com/poll/21814/evolution-creationism-intelligent-design.aspx; Gallup, "In U.S., 42% Believe Creationist View of Human Origins," June 2, 2014, https://news.gallup.com/poll/170822/believe-creationist-view-human-origins.aspx; Art Swift, "In US, Belief and Creationist Views of Humans at New Low," Gallup, May 22, 2017, http://www.gallup.com/poll/210956/belief-creationist-view-humans-new-low.aspx; Pew Research Center, "Public's Views on Human Evolution," December 30, 2013, http://www.pewforum.org/2013/12/30/publics-views-on-human-evolution/; David Masci, "For Darwin Day, 6 Facts about the Evolution Debate," Pew Research Center, February 10, 2017, http://www.pewresearch.org/fact-tank/2017/02/10/darwin-day/.

[5] The best source for European developments is Stefan Blancke, Hans Henrik Hjermitslev, and Peter C. Kjaergarrd, eds., *Creationism in Europe* (Baltimore, MD: Johns Hopkins University Press, 2014).

[6] For more details, see Julie Homchick, "Objects and Objectivity: The Evolution Controversy at the American Museum of Natural History, 1915–1928," *Science and Education* 19 (2010): 485–503. Stephen T. Asma, "Risen Apes and Fallen Angels: The New Museology of Human Origins," *Curator: The Museum Journal* 54, no. 2 (2011): 141–63, highlights current practices by comparing exhibitions on origins at the Creation Museum in Kentucky, the American Museum of Natural History in New York, and the Smithsonian National Museum of Natural History in Washington, DC.

In the decades that followed, most creationists agreed with Bryan that the earth was very old. The few creationists who believed that a literal reading of Genesis demanded a young earth were stymied until 1961, when John C. Whitcomb, an evangelical biblical scholar, and Henry M. Morris, head of the civil engineering program at Virginia Polytechnic Institute, published *The Genesis Flood*. Their exposition of Genesis was driven by their theology of "biblical catastrophism." Only those who appreciated the enormity of the Fall and the Edenic curse, they argued, could understand that a cataclysmic global flood served as a corollary event to cleanse the earth of evil. The Fall and the Flood were linked events that required one another. To restore humanity to harmony with its creator demanded a catastrophe as well: Jesus's atoning death.[7]

The Genesis Flood was remarkable for the lushness of detail it provided, as its authors did not hesitate to embellish the biblical text. In the absence of any biblical evidence, Morris and Whitcomb contended, for example, that the human population of the earth in Noah's time was at least one billion (27). Dinosaurs, they said, were created with the other land animals on day 6. The Ark, Morris and Whitcomb argued, contained fewer animals than had previously been supposed because God told Noah to bring representatives of every "kind" (Gen 7:3, 7:14), not every single species. To save space, Noah probably chose juvenile animals. And when the animals came aboard, Morris and Whitcomb opined, they were fed a good meal, whereupon many went into hibernation for the duration, making less work for their human caretakers (66–74).

Morris and Whitcomb addressed earth history and flood geology at length. Borrowing from Seventh-day Adventist sources, they argued that in the original creation a vapor canopy surrounded the earth. In the Flood, God set the vapor canopy free and unloosed the "fountains of the deep" (Gen 7:11) as well. The resulting downpour from the vapor canopy, combined with earthquakes and underwater volcanoes spewing magma into the atmosphere, forever changed the earth's topography and climate. In the year Noah spent on the Ark, the vast majority of the fossil record was laid down, sedimentation occurred, and canyons and mountains were formed. When the waters receded, an ice age replaced the temperate pre-Flood climate (116–40, 240–3, 451). Moreover, Morris and Whitcomb insisted, the physical laws of the earth had changed. God's original creation was an enduring perfection, but now physical systems tended toward entropy (222–7). Minerals decayed more slowly, which explained the erroneous carbon dating that led scientists to postulate that the earth was millions or even billions of years old (352, 372). Finally, Morris and Whitcomb railed against "uniformitarianism"—the assumption that the physical nature of reality is constant throughout time. The conditions of the present, they argued, can tell us nothing about the pre-Flood world. Modern science cannot study, much less re-create, that world, since the Flood utterly destroyed it. The *only* way to access the pre-Flood world is through Scripture (213).

[7] John C. Whitcomb and Henry M. Morris, *The Genesis Flood: The Biblical Record and Its Scientific Implications*, 50th anniversary ed. (Phillipsburg, NJ: P&R, 2011), 454–7. Subsequent page references to this work will be noted parenthetically.

Morris helped establish the Creation Research Society in 1963, and in 1972 he founded the Institute for Creation Research (ICR) as a division of Christian Heritage College in San Diego. The ICR was dedicated to scientific research as well as to promoting young-earth creationism. Creation Life Publishers was developed to showcase young-earth creationist works, and in the 1970s and 1980s the ICR conducted hundreds of on-campus debates on evolution with university scientists. The ICR became an independent institution in 1980, and in 1981 it launched the ICR Graduate School in creation science.[8] In 1992 the ICR opened the four-thousand-square-foot Museum of Creation and Earth History in Santee, California. There, visitors walked through the Garden of Eden, observed dinosaurs living alongside people, and relived the Fall, Flood, and Tower of Babel narratives. They learned about flood geology. And always they were challenged to choose between the only two models of earth history possible: young-earth creationism and godless evolutionary science.[9]

An ironic result of this emphasis on flood geology (here and in subsequent creation museums) is that Adam and Eve—whom visitors might rightly expect to be the central characters of a creation museum—receded in prominence. Eve and Adam served to illustrate creation in the divine image, and their sin subjected the world to God's curse. But the real stars of the museum were the historical and geological claims. The six days of creation week established a young earth and refuted Darwinism by having God directly create all the animal kinds. Then Noah's Flood played a starring role in discrediting modern geology, with its assumptions that the earth was billions of years old. After leaving the Ark, the animals and their progeny reoccupied the earth by crossing land bridges and by "rafting."[10] Since the Ark's representative animals contained the genetic potential for their entire "kinds," as animals reproduced, they began to differentiate, developing the species known to the modern world. Drastic climate changes resulting from the Flood brought about the extinction of some animals, including most dino-

---

[8] See Morris, *History of Modern Creationism*, 270–320; Numbers, *The Creationists*, 312–20; Hee-Jong Park, "The Creation-Evolution Debate: Carving Creationism in the Public Mind," *Institute of Physics Publishing* 10 (2001): 173–86. The ICR moved to Dallas in 2008. When the ICR Graduate School was denied accreditation in Texas, it was transformed into the School of Biblical Apologetics. The ICR opened an elaborate young-earth creationist discovery center in 2019. See ICR, "The ICR Discovery Center for Science & Earth History Is Now Open!" accessed June 22, 2020, https://www.icr.org/article/icr-discovery-center-now-open.

[9] The Museum of Creation and Earth History is currently operated by the Light and Life Foundation and is open for virtual tours at http://www.creationsd.org/index.html. For a 2012 blog that provides excellent documentation of museum signage, see Monterey County Skeptics, "Creation Museum Visit," January 19, 2012, https://montereycountyskeptics.blogspot.com/2012/01/creation-museum-visit.html?view=flipcard, accessed June 20, 2020. In *Tower of Babel: The Evidence against the New Creationism* (Cambridge, MA: MIT Press, 1999), Robert T. Pennock examines the Tower of Babel exhibit at the Museum of Creation and Earth History to demonstrate that, just as young-earth creationists deny the evolution of the human race, they also reject "linguistic evolution and hold to the special creation by God of different languages at the Tower of Babel" (123).

[10] Signage at the Creation Museum in Kentucky charts land bridge and ocean routes, explaining that the Flood "must have left billions of trees floating for centuries on the ocean. These log mats served as ready-made rafts for animals to cross oceans."

saurs, though some survived, as attested in human legends of dragons and other great beasts. Finally, the Tower of Babel accounted for the scattering of people throughout the globe, with the subsequent development of distinct cultures and languages.

One of the most memorable features of this account of earth history is the insistence that people and dinosaurs coexisted. From 1992 onward, creation museums have delighted in depicting Adam and Eve hanging out with dinosaurs in Eden. To attract visitors, especially families, creation museums frequently market themselves as dinosaur sites. A simple Google search reveals that there are a lot of young-earth creationist dinosaurs out there. The pet-friendly World's Biggest Dinosaurs creation museum, featuring dinosaurs Large Marge, Mr. Rex, and Dinny, welcomes families and their dogs to the California desert.[11] At Dinosaur Encounter in Maine, or at one of its many traveling exhibitions, visitors can view one-hundred-pound "dinosaur dung" and listen to "Dino Pastor" Paul Veit prove that humans did not evolve from "primordial pond scum."[12] The Creation Evidence Museum of Texas provides photos (bogus, alas) of fossilized footprints of giant humans who lived in the pre-Flood era contemporaneously with dinosaurs. As if that were not enough, the museum's founder, Carl Baugh, exhibits a twenty-five-foot replica of Noah's Ark and a "hyperbaric biosphere" capsule in which he claims to have re-created the pre-Flood atmosphere.[13]

Field expeditions are another marketable activity, with young-earth creationist ministries eager to lead boat trips through the Grand Canyon to teach people it formed rapidly and recently. Mount St. Helens is a favorite site because the topography there changed drastically and quickly when the volcano erupted in 1980. Excursions to

[11] See the Cabazon Dinosaurs website, https://www.cabazondinosaurs.com, for site details and C. Travis Webb, "Cabazon Dinosaurs," Materializing the Bible, accessed April 12, 2018, https://www.materializingthebible.com/cabazon-dinosaurs.html for a virtual tour. The dinosaurs appeared in the 1985 film Pee-wee's Big Adventure.

[12] See the following: "The Dinosaur Encounter—Bridgton, Me," https://visitcreation.org/item/the-dinosaur-encounter-bridgton-me/. Battle Lake Alliance, "Deliberate Deceptions and Incredible Truths—Sunday August 11," August 6, 2019. https://battlelake.org/good-news/2019/8/6/tn65ejrs1104f1tz9jw8yqqf2jq4bg. "Dino Pastor to speak in Cable," Sawyer County Record, Oct, 22, 2015, https://www.apg-wi.com/sawyer_county_record/arts_and_entertainment/community_events/dino-pastor-to-speak-in-cable/article_fab35b0c-7808-11e5-8b67-a723bcb04242.html. All sites accessed June 22, 2020.

[13] See the homepage of the Creation Evidence Museum, http://www.creationevidence.org, for general information. For the museum's ark re-creation and its hyperbaric chamber, see "Noah's Ark Replica," http://www.creationevidence.org/displays/noahs_ark.php, and "Creation Model," http://www.creationevidence.org/evidence/creation_model.php, both accessed May 10, 2017. There is universal agreement that dinosaur footprints exist in this Paluxy River region of Texas, but both secular and many young-earth creationist researchers have established that no human footprints contemporaneous with dinosaurs have been discovered. Nevertheless Whitcomb and Morris, The Genesis Flood, 174–5, offers Paluxy River pictures purporting to show "contemporaneous footprints of man and dinosaur" as well as "giant human footprints" that correlate to the claim of Genesis 6:4 that in those days there were giant humans walking the earth. See Glen J. Kuban, "The Texas Dinosaur/'Man Track' Controversy," Talk Origins Archive, accessed March 15, 2018, http://www.talkorigins.org/faqs/paluxy.html. For a critique of a recent dinosaur/human footprint excursion sponsored by the Creation Evidence Museum of Texas, see Randy Moore, "Did Humans Live with Dinosaurs? Excavating 'Man Tracks' along the Paluxy River," American Biology Teacher 76, no. 4 (2014): 243–6.

unearth fossilized dinosaurs are also popular. Whether on location or in a museum, young-earth creationists' constant refrain is that the history and present condition of the earth—its atmosphere, its topography, and its organisms—can *only* be explained by a catastrophic global flood that occurred about four thousand years ago.[14]

Exploring the Ark Encounter

To explore a creation ministry and museum in depth, we turn to the most ambitious creation museum ever built: Answers in Genesis's Ark Encounter. Ken Ham, president of Answers in Genesis (AiG), describes AiG as a "content-rich, information-disseminating ministry," and anyone who has visited the Creation Museum,[15] the Ark Encounter, or the AiG website can attest that Ham did not name his organization *Answers* in Genesis in vain. From verbal inerrancy to extraterrestrial life forms, there seems to be no issue related to the Bible that AiG does not consider. AiG's creation museums bombard guests with visual and audio stimulation, and it is impossible to plumb the depths of the AiG website (https://answersingenesis.org), much less AiG's published materials, in a single lifetime.

This is very much by design. As a young science teacher in Australia, Ham struggled to reconcile evolution with his faith until he read *The Genesis Flood*. Energized by the book's vociferous rejection of evolution, he subsequently devoted his life to disseminating information about Genesis 1–11.[16] Convinced that the United States was the best platform for launching a global creationist ministry, in 1987 he left Australia to work with Henry Morris at the ICR. In 1993 Ham cofounded Answers in Genesis, currently the predominant creationist organization in the world. AiG unveiled its spectacular Creation Museum in northern Kentucky in 2007.

The Ark Encounter, which opened in July 2016, is a bookend to the Creation Museum, providing exhibits on the six days of creation and on Adam and Eve but focusing on post-Fall humanity, particularly the Noah and Babel narratives. Using *The Genesis Flood* and research by creationists John Woodmorappe, Tim Lovett, and others, the Ark Encounter's hundred-million-dollar full-size re-creation of the wooden Genesis vessel is docked in a Kentucky pasture and stretches 510 feet long, 85 feet wide, and 51 feet high.

---

[14] To see this argument in action, watch the 2017 film *Is Genesis History?* Host Del Tackett interviews young-earth creationist scientists in a variety of geologically significant locations, always concluding that only a relatively recent spectacular global flood could account for present conditions. For a response from Christian scientists who are evolutionists, see Gregg Davidson, Joel Duff, and Ken Wolgemuth, "A Geological Response to the Movie *Is Genesis History?*," BioLogos, March 1, 2017, http://biologos.org/blogs/guest/a-geological-response-to-the-movie-is-genesis-history.

[15] In "An Analysis of the Creation Museum: Hermeneutics, Language, and Information Theory," PhD diss., University of Louisville, 2014, Steven M. Watkins provides the first extensive examination of how the Creation Museum interprets the Bible. Watkins demonstrates that, though the Creation Museum claims to provide a literal interpretation of the text, it actually reads Genesis through modern scientific categories.

[16] Theresa Sanders also discusses Ken Ham and his beliefs and career in her chapter in this volume.

Its zip lines are the longest in the Midwest, and visitors can ride a camel in its petting zoo. Of course there are retail shops. Still a work in progress, the Ark Encounter will eventually boast a walled pre-Flood city, a first-century village, the Tower of Babel, a theme ride through the plagues of Egypt, and still more installations that "uphold the truth of God's Word" on its eight-hundred-acre site.[17]

For those who wonder how building or visiting a humongous wooden ship proves that God created the world in six days less than ten thousand years ago, Ham acknowledges that the Flood narrative poses many logistical questions for readers.[18] Convinced that Christians leave the church when it ignores or fails to resolve their doubts, Ham believes the Ark Encounter establishes the historicity of Genesis by offering "plausible solutions" to every question visitors might raise. Moreover, the Ark's sheer enormity is designed to catch the eyes of unbelievers. "In this secularized time," Ham argues, "I believe one of the best and most effective ways to reach tens of millions of people with the gospel message is to build another Ark—a gospel-focused life-sized Ark—and show the world that science confirms the Bible. God's word is true, and we all need to come to repentance."[19]

From their first glimpse of the Ark to entering the massive three-deck structure, visitors are meant to be stupefied. Patrick Marsh, the exhibits designer, contends, "You can't walk into the Ark without a sense of awe and 'wow.' There is a sense of godliness in the 'awe factor' and . . . we want visitors to get a sense that 'Wow, this is what Noah could have done.'"[20] As they enter the lowest of the soaring building's three decks, guests are inundated with animal sounds and music, and they wander past animal cages, storage bins, and exhibits arranged in a series of 132 portals. The exhibits require extensive reading and contain dioramas, charts, artifacts, artwork, videos, and animatronic characters. Since there are no windows, guests experience a sense of being contained within—even enveloped by—a massive wooden structure that is its own world.

If visitors are skeptical that Noah could have built such a magnificent edifice, signage at every turn proclaims that early human beings were more accomplished than their modern counterparts. Genesis records that pre-Flood individuals lived hundreds of years, giving them ample time to learn to read, write, and master technology. And because the human gene pool was not yet widely corrupted by mutations, ancient peo-

---

[17] Ark Encounter, "About the Ark," accessed July 13, 2017, https://arkencounter.com/about/. See Laura Welch, gen. ed., *Inside Noah's Ark: Why It Worked* (Green Forest, AR: Master Books, 2016), 14; Patrick Marsh, "Building of the Exhibits," in Answers in Genesis, *The Building of the Ark Encounter: By Faith the Ark Was Built* (Green Forest, AR: Master Books, 2016), 73; John Woodmorappe, *Noah's Ark: A Feasibility Study* (Dallas, TX: Institute for Creation Research, 1996); Tim Lovett, *Noah's Ark: Thinking Outside the Box* (Green Forest, AR: Master Books, 2008).

[18] Ken Ham with Jeff Kinley, research by Britt Beemer, *Ready to Return: Bringing Back the Church's Lost Generation* (Green Forest, AR: Master Books, 2015), 108.

[19] Ken Ham "The Voyage Begins Again!," Answers in Genesis, February 8, 2016, https://answersingenesis.org/ministry-news/ark-encounter/voyage-begins-again/. The claim that science proves the Bible is a frequent AiG refrain.

[20] Marsh, "Building of the Exhibits," 79.

ple were, in Ham's words, "geniuses, not brutes!"[21] Even after the Flood, early human cultures accomplished staggering feats of engineering, such as erecting the pyramids in Egypt. Signs admonish visitors not to fall prey to the evolutionary assumption that early human culture was primitive or to popular speculation that structures like the pyramids must have been designed by advanced civilizations from outer space.[22]

Though no exhibit provides the full text of Genesis 1–11, overall the Ark Encounter is intended to be a monument to biblical authority. Visitors pass by a quotation from Genesis 6:11 ("On the 17th day of the second month of Noah's 600 year, all the fountains of the great deep burst forth and the floodgates of heaven opened") before opening a door to enter the Ark, and they end their tour with the ship's largest exhibit: "Why the Bible Is True." The journey through the Bible begins on deck 2 with exhibits displaying a perfect creation, then a fall into sin, and then an eye-catching exhibit on the perversity of pre-Flood human culture. Signage explains that, since Genesis says that people grew wicked after the Fall but does not give specific examples, "this exhibit presents an artistic representation of what that world may have been like." Scenes of giants, serpent worship, child sacrifice, and lascivious drunken parties follow. The most mind-boggling diorama depicts a coliseum replete with a giant gladiator spearing a woman, other victims strewn upon the ground, a bald man screaming in agony, and—most amazingly—a man armed with only a knife facing a raging dinosaur, while spectators in tiered seats wave their arms in excitement.

After the pre-Flood world, a portal called "Kids' Spooky Animal Encounters" invites youngsters to imagine life on the Ark after dark, while the "Fairy Tale Ark" exhibit castigates children's picture book Bibles for imperiling readers' salvation by illustrating the Ark inaccurately. "The abundance of these fanciful objects attacks the truth of Scripture," a sign warns. Though Genesis is silent on these points, the deck 2 exhibits devote enormous attention to describing how Noah built and lived on the Ark. "Have you ever wondered how Noah's family fed all the animals and removed their waste?" begins one of many portals designed to show "workable models" of the operational difficulties involved in constructing the Ark and caring for its animals. A long series of installations addresses heating, ventilation, moon pools, manure management, the preservation of food, challenges presented by carnivores, and far more. Flood geology receives expansive treatment.

On deck 3, visitors meet Noah and his family. Since Genesis introduces Noah as an adult, and he never speaks a word until the Flood is long over (unlike the Ark Encounter animatronic Noah), readers know little about him other than that his three sons were born after he was five hundred years old and that he himself was righteous and obedient

---

[21] Ken Ham, "Geniuses, Not Brutes!," Answers in Genesis, December 21, 2012, https://answersingenesis.org/archaeology/ancient-technology/geniuses-not-brutes/. AiG touts *The Genius of Ancient Man: Evolution's Nightmare* (Green Forest, AR: Master Books, 2012) by Don Landis as a book-length treatment of this theme.

[22] An Ark Encounter sign titled "Alien Thinking" warns, "Popular movies and television shows have suggested that these structures were either planned or built by aliens from outer space. But, from the biblical perspective, there is no basis for believing in extraterrestrials."

to God (Gen 5:32, 6:9). Genesis does provide the names of the three sons who were with Noah on the Ark, but not the names of the wives who accompanied the four men. Since the Bible reveals so little about the Ark's inhabitants, signage explains that the museum exercised "artistic license" to invent backstories for the eight characters, "taking care not to contradict biblical details." In the "Who Was Noah?" exhibit, visitors read that Noah grew up on a farm but moved to a small port city to become a ship builder. He apprenticed with a master builder, married his master's daughter, and became proficient in metalworking. A dramatic installation takes visitors through the family's elaborate Ark living quarters, complete with the ancient equivalent of a pizza oven, Noah's library, and each couple's private apartment. Signs fill in the backstories, explaining, for example, that Noah's son Shem was particularly good at caring for animals, that son Ham was a "brilliant engineer," that daughter-in-law Kezia enjoyed "dressing up in her best," and that daughter-in-law Rayneh "was rescued by Noah from a life-threatening situation when she was a little girl." One thing we are not told is that Noah enjoyed drinking alcohol, a speculation other fictional accounts often offer, given Noah's post-Flood drunken bender in Genesis 9:21.

After the Flood, visitors proceed to the Tower of Babel. Exhibits show the peoples of earth being scattered and having their language confused; signage contends—in contradistinction to centuries of scholarly consensus that the legends of Gilgamesh and *Atrahasis* were earlier—that memories of Noah's Flood formed the basis of all the other Flood legends told around the world. Here the story of Genesis 1–11 concludes. The Ark Encounter then moves to "The Voyage of a Book," displaying artifacts on loan from the Green Collection, which stocked the recently opened Museum of the Bible in Washington, DC.[23] This exhibit traces how the Bible (like early humanity after Babel) spread from its origins in the Holy Land to the ends of the earth.

Visitors then move to the last and largest exhibit: "Why the Bible Is True." Here guests walk through a graphic novel, following two college students who wonder why anyone would believe the Bible was inerrant. After a night of drunken debauchery and a catastrophic car wreck, one of the students rejects the Bible, while the other accepts Jesus as savior. Signage confronts visitors: "Have You Entered The Door That Leads To Life? . . . There Is Only One 'Door' That Can Save Us From Eternal Judgment. Jesus Christ Is That Door." Visitors pass through one last opening to read signs summarizing why the Bible is true: it is God's Word; it is unique and unified; it has been faithfully passed down across centuries; it contains fulfilled prophecy; and it holds the key to eternal life.

---

[23] For more on the origins of the Green Collection and the Museum of the Bible, see Candida Moss and Joel Baden, *Bible Nation: The United States of Hobby Lobby* (Princeton, NJ: Princeton University Press, 2017). The museum has returned at least 17,000 unethically acquired antiquities and no longer displays fragments purportedly of the Dead Sea Scrolls that scholars have proven to be fakes. See Tom, Mashberg, "Bible Museum, Admitting Mistakes, Tries to Convert Its Critics," *New York Times*, April 5, 2020, https://www.nytimes.com/2020/04/05/arts/bible-museum-artifacts.html; Ariel Sabar, "A Biblical Mystery Unmasked at Oxford," *The Atlantic*, June 2020, https://www.theatlantic.com/magazine/archive/2020/06/museum-of-the-bible-obbink-gospel-of-mark/610576/. Both accessed June 20, 2020.

So how persuasive was the visitors' journey? The museum's designers believed that if they demonstrated the viability of the Flood narrative, showing that Noah *could* have built and maintained the Ark, they would have validated the accuracy of the Bible. The Ark Encounter overwhelms people with information, but those from outside the world of young-earth creationism typically are surprised that exhibits depend so much on extrabiblical materials. They are puzzled that the technical details about Ark construction and maintenance are purely speculative and taken aback at the wholesale fabrication of historical and biographical information. The blogger Jason Colavito, for example, argues that the pre-Flood installation is a form of "Bible fan fiction" that twists "both history and the Bible to create a Bible-adjacent pseudo-historical fantasia of what [Ham] imagines life was like before Noah's Flood."[24] Dan Phelps, a paleontologist, comments that at the Ark Encounter "details are provided by the steaming shovelful" and observes that if "anyone else invented embellished stories about anything in the Bible, AiG would have a conniption."[25] For the skeptical, then, the Ark Encounter's central presupposition—that showing how the Flood narrative *could* have happened is tantamount to proving that it *did*—is unpersuasive.

Occasionally believers also complain. A blogger named D worried that the Ark Encounter was "acting just like modern scientists trying to fill in many unknowns with hypothetical assertions." A blogger named Audrey argued that the invented historical narratives could cause visitors to confuse fact with fiction as well as make believers "look stupid among real historians."[26] But for most young-earth creationists, the Ark Encounter is a magnificent presentation of Genesis 1–11 as literal history, and they treat their visit as a pilgrimage. The very existence of the Ark strikes them as marvelous. Indeed, one person who had merely seen online pictures of the Ark gushed, "Isn't it wonderful the way it shows very clearly that the Bible is true."[27] For believers, the Ark Encounter "awe" factor functions as its own validation; seeing really is believing. It does not matter that much of what visitors encounter in the exhibits appears nowhere in the Bible. The Ark just *feels* true. In a YouTube video, Ark Encounter correspondent Jeremy Ham sums up this sensibility in a report from deck 3: "If you look at these living quarters... [at] the various rooms where they lived, or the food that they made, a lot of this is

---

[24] Jason Colavito, "Sure, It's Funny That Ken Ham Is Planning a Nephilim vs. Dinosaurs Exhibit, but Did You Read the Revealing Tweet-Storm That Followed?," blog, February 2, 2017, http://www.jasoncolavito.com/blog/sure-its-funny-that-ken-ham-is-planning-a-nephilim-vs-dinosaurs-exhibit-but-did-you-read-the-revealing-tweet-storm-that-followed.

[25] Dan Phelps, "Kentucky Gets an Ark-Shaped Second Creation 'Museum,'" National Center for Science Education, October 20, 2016, https://ncse.com/library-resource/kentucky-gets-ark-shaped-second-creation-museum.

[26] From, respectively, D at "Visiting Friends and the Ark Encounter," *As Lilies* (blog), March 12, 2017, http://asliliessewing.blogspot.com/search?q=Ark+Encounter; Audrey, July 8, 2017, at Tim Chaffey, discussing *Noah: Man of Destiny*, blog, September 30, 2016, http://midwestapologetics.org/blog/?p=1605.

[27] Elizabethd at "Visiting Friends and the Ark Encounter," *As Lilies* (blog), March 11, 2017, http://asliliessewing.blogspot.com/search?q=Ark+Encounter.

artistic license—because we don't know how it looked at all—but it is kind of creating an environment that is consistent with the Bible, and showing how they could have done it, and how the Bible is true."[28]

Experiencing "truth" in this context involves being immersed in a re-created biblical scene. The artistic license displayed in the pre-Flood world, the family living quarters, and the characters' backstories were carefully orchestrated by content manager Tim Chaffey, who oversaw every exhibit and wrote signage for many of them. After concocting Noah's backstory, Chaffey teamed up with K. Marie Adams, a member of the Ark Encounter design team, to write the Remnant Trilogy of novels about Noah.[29] The first two novels function as prequels to the Ark Encounter itself and deliberately reference events, people, and objects depicted at the museum. *Noah: Man of Resolve*, for example, depicts Noah rescuing a young girl named Rayneh and being forced to face a raging dinosaur in an amphitheater. People who have read the novel will understand the pre-Flood arena diorama and the reference to Reynah's rescue in the family living quarters.

Chaffey reports he is fascinated by the pre-Flood world of Genesis 6:1–6, describing it as a Christian Middle Earth.[30] By anyone's reading, this passage is peopled with mysterious figures: "sons of God" who produce children with human wives, "Nephilim," "giants," and warriors of "renown." Genesis 6:5 avers, moreover, that the wickedness of humanity was so great that people's thoughts were "only evil continually." For many Christians, Genesis 6:1–6 is barely a blip on the radar, but since the 1986 publication of Frank Peretti's *This Present Darkness*, fantasy fiction has depicted the characters from Genesis 6 in lurid detail.[31] Readers expect to see giants, degradation, violence, and wild adventure, just as the Remnant novels and the Ark's pre-Flood installations depict.

Nevertheless Adams and Chaffey contend that they resisted wild flights of fancy. "No pizza or aliens," quips Adams.[32] Surprisingly, that's not quite true: aliens lurk in the background of their work. In recent years, novelists and some evangelical scholars have construed the "sons of God" of Genesis 6 as fallen angels who, in mating with human wives, produced the Nephilim, thereby corrupting the human gene pool. Noah's Flood was necessary, in this reading, to wipe out all the human progeny who had been defiled. The fallen angels, however, were immortal and could not be destroyed. They reemerged throughout human history. In medieval times they were incubi and succubi, forcing their sexual attentions on sleeping humans. In the present day, the fallen angels disguise themselves as space aliens, abducting and corrupting human beings by probing them.[33]

---

[28] Ark Encounter, "*Noah: Man of Destiny* with Tim Chaffey and K. Marie Adams," YouTube, October 31, 2016, https://www.youtube.com/watch?v=BLLQSrwpSXo&t=1564s.

[29] Tim Chaffey and K. Marie Adams, *Noah: Man of Destiny* (Green Forest, AR: Master Books, 2016) and *Noah: Man of Resolve* (Green Forest, AR: Master Books, 2017).

[30] Ark Encounter, "*Noah: Man of Destiny* with Tim Chaffey and K. Mrie Adams."

[31] Frank Peretti, *This Present Darkness* (Westchester, IL: Crossway Books, 1986). Currently trending is Brian Godawa's eight-book fantasy series, *Chronicles of the Nephilim* (N.p.: Embedded Pictures Publishing, 2012–5).

[32] K. Marie Adams, "Historical Q&A: Tim Chaffey and K. Marie Adams," Family Fiction, March 9, 2017, https://www.familyfiction.com/historical-qa-tim-chaffey-k-marie-adams-noah-man-destiny/.

[33] Paul Thomas, "Meme Splicing Genesis 6:1–4 and the Apocalypse of 2012," *Journal of Religion and*

Chaffey expressed support for this view of alien abductions in his Th.M. thesis, "The Sons of God and the Nephilim."[34] And though Answers in Genesis has no official position on the identity of the sons of God of Genesis 6, the AiG *Pocket Guide to UFOs* argues that, since angels and demons (fallen angels) "are real and operate on earth and in the heavens, it is possible that some UFOs could be related to the activities of angels or demons." Observing that "there is a biblical basis for the possibility that demons can manifest themselves in appealing terms," the guide concludes that the current popularity of "the entire UFO phenomenon can be viewed as a satanic conspiracy."[35] Ark Encounter exhibits do not reference fallen angels as alien forces warring against humanity—but they easily could have. Bizarre as the pre-Flood portal is, it could have been far weirder.

Alien abductions aside, Chaffey and Adams were worried enough about readers confusing fact and fiction in their novels that they provided commentary to distinguish artistic license from the biblical text. Paradoxically Chaffey explains, "Our goal in writing fiction was to help [readers] ... discern between what is biblical and what is not."[36] But intellectually distancing oneself from a powerful story works against what the Ark Encounter is all about: making the Bible come alive. The Noah novels were written to make the Ark experience even more compelling. As Adams explains, "People have a chance to not only immerse themselves in Noah's life through the fictional account we created, but they can then feel like they're really a part of this world when they visit the Ark."[37]

For its part, AiG is unconcerned that exhibits conflate fantastical elements and the Bible. An Ark Encounter article acknowledges that Ark visitors not conversant with scripture will "likely" confuse artistic license with the biblical text, but they have only themselves to blame. "If you want to know the truth about Noah, the Ark, and the Flood," AiG advises, "read God's Word. Study it. Pray about it. Read it some more. Pay close attention to the text itself, and guard yourself against reading your own ideas into the Bible—something that seems inevitably to happen."[38] This answer ignores the reality

Popular Culture 24, no. 2 (2012): 310–325. Thomas provides a lucid introduction to recent fiction and nonfiction literature on this topic. He delineates three characteristic themes—that ancient civilizations were technologically advanced, that the Bible should be read literally, and that mainstream academia and culture are dismissive of this field—that overlap arguments presented at the Ark Encounter. There is an ancient tradition within Judaism and Christianity that interprets the "sons of God" of Genesis 6:2–4 as descended angels who led humanity into sin through illicit teaching and divine-human sexual coupling. Annette Yoshiko Reed traces this theme from antiquity through the medieval period in *Fallen Angels and the History of Judaism and Christianity* (Cambridge: Cambridge University Press, 2005).

[34] Tim Chaffey, *The Sons of God and the Nephilim* (N.p.: Midwest Apologetics, 2011), Kindle, locs. 2506, 4501. Chaffey recommends Gary Bates, *Alien Intrusion: UFOs and the Evolution Connection* (Green Forest, AR: Master Books, 2004).

[35] Danny Faulkner, *A Pocket Guide to UFOS and ETs: A Biblical and Cultural Exploration of Aliens* (Petersburg, KY: Answers in Genesis, 2015), 38–39, 60, 80.

[36] Chaffey and Adams, *Noah: Man of Destiny*, 7.

[37] Adams, "Historical Q&A."

[38] Ark Encounter, "Noah's Ark in the News," March 7, 2014, https://arkencounter.com/blog/2014/03/07/noahs-ark-in-the-news/.

that supplements to a text materially alter it, or the possibility that some biblical texts are so breviloquent that they cannot be exhibited without fabrication. Visitors inclined to be critical of artistic license may well turn the critique found in the "Fairy Tale Ark" instillation against children's picture books ("The abundance of these fanciful objects attacks the truthfulness of Scripture") back upon AiG itself.

FUTURE PROSPECTS AND QUESTIONS

Creation museums work by pitting their understanding of history and science as derived from a literal reading of the Bible against the claims of secular science. This approach raises several questions about the future:

- Creation museums go to great lengths to insist that science, when understood through scripture, validates the biblical narrative and proves that the Bible is true. Making the truth of scripture dependent upon scientific claims, however, subjects biblical interpretation to the changing nature of scientific knowledge. How will creation museums adapt when, inevitably, some of their scientific presuppositions become untenable?[39]
- Despite their claims to interpret Genesis 1–11 literally, creation museums fill in the gaps of this laconic text with flights of fancy and fantasy. Exhibits that present as fact what readers familiar with the Bible know to be speculation undermine the authority of the Bible. The reality is that the Genesis narrative simply cannot sustain a museum's worth of exhibits without being supplemented. What does this mean for the future? Is the Answers in Genesis model so well established that it will continue to set the standard for creation museums? Susan and William Trollinger, authors of an incisive study of the Creation Museum, have suggested that the future of the movement may belong to creationists who interpret the Bible more literally than AiG—groups that believe Genesis 1 promotes geocentrism, not a Copernican worldview.[40]
- As young-earth creationism has succeeded in gaining cultural influence, some scientists are actually citing Noah's Flood as historical. In 1998, for example, two scientists from Columbia University published an academic study arguing that Noah's Flood occurred in what is now known as the Black Sea about 7,600 years

[39] In July 2017 the comic strip *Non Sequitur* ran a Sunday comics mocking the relationship of science and biblical interpretation in Answers in Genesis. The first three panels depicted dinosaurs building pyramids under the direction of ancient humans. The next frame showed two of the strip's main characters (Danae and her horse) holding a scroll while sitting behind a desk labeled "The Church of Danae. Answers for Everything." When a boy standing next to the desk screams in horror, Danae pointed to the scroll and says, "That's the sound of science validating the ancient scriptures on how the pyramids were built." "Careful," her horse replies. "The ink is still wet."

[40] Susan L. Trollinger and William Vance Trollinger Jr., *Righting America at the Creation Museum* (Baltimore, MD: Johns Hopkins University Press, 2016), 144–7.

ago.[41] In May 2017, a *New York Times* article on Antarctica's melting ice sheet referenced a scientist who regards Noah's Flood as a real event.[42] Academicians in religious studies generally do not regard Noah as a historical person, and we have seen AiG supplementing the Genesis account. What are the implications of scientists interpreting Genesis more literally than scholars and self-proclaimed biblical literalists?

- Portions of the Muslim world are embracing young-earth creationism. What will young-earth creationism look like in a Muslim context? How will readings of the Qur'ān challenge or bolster the authority of the Christian Bible? What will be the political, theological, and scientific implications of this alliance of creationist Muslims and Christians?

- Both of the AiG creation museums have exhibited artifacts from the Green Collection, associated with the Museum of the Bible, a 430,000-square-foot facility opened in 2017 two blocks from the national mall in Washington, DC. Given its location, the Museum of the Bible is destined to wield enormous cultural influence. Tied to the energetic missionizing of Answers in Genesis, this is a working relationship between two Bible titans. How will young-earth creationism come to influence popular culture, politics, and the place of the Bible in American life?

SUGGESTED READINGS AND ANNOTATED BIBLIOGRAPHY

Answers in Genesis. *Journey through the Ark Encounter*. Green Forest, AR: Master Books, 2017. This lavishly illustrated book walks readers through the museum and provides a summary of its major theological arguments.

Bielo, James S. *Ark Encounter: The Making of a Creationist Theme Park*. New York: NYU Press, 2018.

Bielo, an anthropologist at Miami University, was given access to the creative team as it managed the production of the Ark Encounter. He documents how the team embraced artistic liberty and incorporated fantasy and other nonbiblical elements to provide an immersive experience for park visitors. Bielo's impressive Materializing the Bible website (https://www.materializingthebible.com/about.html) is a wondrous resource of Bible-based attractions, and anyone interested in creation museums should consult it, as well as his chapter on theme parks in this volume.

Caudill, Edward. *Intelligently Designed: How Creationists Built the Campaign against Evolution*. Champagne: University of Illinois Press, 2013.

Caudill provides an overview of creationist tactics from the Scopes trial to the Ark Encounter. He excels at showing how creationists have presented themselves as "righteous rebels fighting for individual liberty and freedom of expression." Anyone who wants to understand why creationists are winning the culture wars should start here.

---

[41] William B. F. Ryan and Walter C. Pitman, *Noah's Flood: The New Scientific Discoveries about the Event That Changed History* (New York: Simon & Schuster, 1998).

[42] Justin Gillis, *Antarctic Dispatches*, part 2, "Looming Floods, Threatened Cities," *New York Times*, May 18, 2017, https://www.nytimes.com/interactive/2017/05/18/climate/antarctica-ice-melt-climate-change-flood.html.

Ham, Ken. *Journey through the Creation Museum*. Revised and expanded edition. Green Forest, AR: Master Books, 2016.

> While the text delineates the museum's key scientific and biblical claims, the sumptuous photographs walk readers through the museum's major exhibits.

Morris, Henry M. *The New Defender's Study Bible: Understanding the Critical Issues of the Faith from a Literal Creationist Viewpoint*. Nashville, TN: World Publishing, 2006.

> Far more accessible than *The Genesis Flood*, Morris's commentary lays out his literal interpretation of Genesis in all its dizzying complexity. References, for example, to the second law of thermodynamics, demonic genetic manipulations, and subterranean pressurized reservoirs, not to mention pronouncements that Adam could have named all the animal kinds in about five hours and that pre-Flood humans were skilled in music, metallurgy, urbanization, animal husbandry, and agriculture, overwhelm the reader. Trying to keep up with the *Defenders Bible* is excellent practice for touring the Ark Encounter, which depends heavily upon Morris's commentary. Note: this Bible is also available in a Master Books edition as the *Henry Morris Study Bible*.

Numbers, Ronald L. *The Creationists: From Scientific Creationism to Intelligent Design*. Expanded edition. Cambridge, MA: Harvard University Press, 2006.

> This justly celebrated study of the institutional and intellectual development of antievolutionism among conservative Christians is the place to start to understand the players and the history of this field.

Trollinger, Susan L., and William Vance Trollinger Jr. *Righting America at the Creation Museum*. Baltimore, MD: Johns Hopkins University Press, 2016.

> This superb analysis provides a masterfully close reading of how the Creation Museum presents science, the Bible, politics, and the culture wars, as well as how it functions as a natural history museum. Chapter 3 on the Bible is particularly cogent in demonstrating how exhibits display, edit, and manipulate the text.

Welch, Laura, gen. ed. *Inside Noah's Ark: Why It Worked*. Green Forest, AR: Master Books, 2016.

> Anyone who has visited the Ark Encounter will be amazed at the intricate details it claims to know about life on board. Acknowledging that Genesis offers very little information about Noah's Ark, this book describes the myriad assumptions the Ark Encounter team made to explain the construction as well as the waste, water, food, cleaning, and animal management systems of the Ark. Much was sheer conjecture; some "creative quirks" were simply invented to help people "expand their thinking" about the flood story. The payoff, the team believed, was this: by demonstrating that the Ark story could plausibly have happened, the museum forced skeptics to grapple with the reality of God's judgment and their need for salvation.

Whitcomb, John C., and Henry M. Morris. *The Genesis Flood: The Biblical Record and Its Scientific Implications*. 50th anniversary edition. Phillipsburg, NJ: P & R, 2011.

> This book, first published in 1961 by a biblical scholar and a professor of hydraulic engineering, provided the theological and scientific impetus for young-earth creationism and for creation museums. Repudiating evolution, *The Genesis Flood* popularized flood geology and delineated the principal interpretive elements of Genesis 1–11 that remain foundational to young-earth creationism: biblical inerrancy, biblical literalism, a recent creation of the world in six twenty-four-hour days, human and animal death as a result of the Edenic fall, Noah's global cataclysmic flood as the foundation of the fossil record, the descent of all human beings from Noah's three sons and daughters-in-law, and the dispersion of humanity across the globe as God's punishment for building the Tower of Babel.

CHAPTER 27

CRUCIFIXIONS, COSPLAY, AND PARTICIPATORY FAN CULTURES

DAN W. CLANTON, JR.
DEPARTMENT OF PHILOSOPHY AND RELIGIOUS
STUDIES, DOANE UNIVERSITY

INTRODUCTION

M. Doc Geressy loves *Ghostbusters*; in fact, he estimates he has seen the 1984 film over a thousand times.[1] To express his love for the film, to *perform* his adoration, he first built a replica of the car the cinematic Ghostbusters drive. Soon after, he and some friends constructed costumes and started dressing up as the Ghostbusters, a form of fandom termed "cosplay." Geressy eventually wanted to do more to *demonstrate* his fandom, which was becoming increasingly significant to him. He and his friends formed the Carolina Ghostbusters and started making appearances at charity events and even hosting Ghostbuster-themed weddings, the proceeds going to their charitable work. Brian Ashcraft and Luke Plunkett interviewed Geressy and wrote, "For Geressy, the costume is more than fabric and props, [as he commented] 'it's a portal that allows a person to be as good-looking and as strong as the heroes they look up to and as confident and clever as the villains they admire. The costume allows a person to be someone else's hero, to make a connection with another human on a very core level, and to be the bridge that spans the gap between another person's imagination and their reality.' "[2] Geressy, in essence, found a way to integrate his fandom with his creativity and his altruism.

---

[1] It is important to note that in June 2016, Geressy was arrested for child solicitation in North Carolina. While finding this act repugnant, I have decided to use him as an example in this chapter, as his views on cosplay are still useful and on point.

[2] Brian Ashcraft and Luke Plunkett, *Cosplay World* (Munich: Prestel, 2014), 113.

In the Philippines, Eddie was worried about his son, who had a serious heart condition. No one had been able to help, so Eddie decided to make a vow (*panata*) to undergo the dangerous and physically demanding practice of self-flagellation during Holy Week in his province of Pampanga. Eddie felt this act would allow him to share (*damay*) in the pain and suffering that Christ endured and would constitute an offering to God made out of empathy (*darame*). In exchange, he hoped that God would help his son. So Eddie, along with others, constructed "material implements and clothing" to use during the ritual and proceeded to embark on their journey around their small village, their backs dripping blood.[3] Julius Bautista describes the impetus for such a religious performance: "This *darame* is not just about the penitent's sins, or about a solemn meditative pursuit of sacramental participation. The motivation for this act involves an empathetic connection between those whom the flagellant holds dear, namely God and a third party, which in [Eddie's] case is his son, but could well be another person."[4] Eddie's son survived, and Eddie believes this "is a direct result of his *darame*."[5] Through the dramatic ritual of self-flagellation, which involved his creativity and altruism, Eddie found a way to *perform* his empathy, to *demonstrate* his identification with Christ's suffering, and, in his understanding, secure health for his son.

What do Geressy and Eddie have in common? How are they and their actions different? How can people in an American context understand these performances of identity? How might the more familiar practice of cosplay we see with Geressy aid us in comprehending what Eddie does and believes? In this chapter, I address these and other questions by analyzing the practice in the Philippines of ritually reenacting the biblically based events of Christ's Passion, Crucifixion, and execution, some of which include elaborately dramatic costumes and dialogue. Like Eddie, some participants engage in self-flagellation, while others allow themselves to be ritually crucified during the celebration. As I hinted at earlier, ritual self-flagellation and crucifixion are beyond the experience of many Americans, even if they identify as religious folk. How, then, might American popular cultural practices assist in understanding these acts and their underlying motivations? In what follows, I suggest that one helpful way to understand the practice and performance of religious identity by someone like Eddie is to compare and contrast it with a kind of "participatory fan culture" prevalent in the United States that I call "enacted cosplay," like the culture in which Geressy is located. Put differently, this chapter examines various ways in which people engage in ritualized role-playing based upon characters drawn from different mythological worlds. Some draw upon the biblical world; others upon more secular mythologies, like films and comic books. By exam-

---

[3] Julius Bautista, "The Localization of Roman Catholicism: Radical Transcendence and Social Empathy in a Philippine Town," in *Routledge Handbook of Religions in Asia*, ed. Bryan S. Turner and Oscar Salemink (London: Routledge, 2015), 103.

[4] Bautista, "The Localization of Roman Catholicism," 103. Nicholas H. Barker, "The Revival of Self-Flagellation and the Birth of Crucifixion in Lowland Christian Philippines," Nagoya University Discussion Paper No. 63, Nagoya University Graduate School of International Development, 1998, 4, agrees that this self-flagellation is not primarily about penance for sins.

[5] Bautista, "The Localization of Roman Catholicism," 103.

ining these embodied practices, I will perform a comparative analysis in which I examine a secular popular-cultural practice in order to shed light on a modern-day religious practice to reveal what some people *do* with the Bible today.

OVERVIEW OF TOPIC

In order to understand what I mean by terms like "fan(s)," "fan culture," "participatory fan culture," "cosplay," and "enacted cosplay," I need to begin with some definitions. Matthew Hills writes that "fans" can be described as "individuals who have a particular liking or affection for a range of popular cultural texts, celebrities, sports (teams), or artifacts. These individuals—typically displaying an affective relationship with their fan object; that is, they are passionately interested in and committed to following their beloved pop group, sports team, or soap opera—may nevertheless not take part in socially organized fan activities."[6] Hills notes that often scholars understand larger "collective activities" to designate "fan culture," which he and others see as shaping both the identity and the practices of fans: "Fans are socialized within affective communities of fandom, and engage in subculturally distinctive fan practices such as writing their own fan fiction ('fanfic') based on characters and situations from official films and TV shows, producing their own fan magazines ('fanzines'), writing their own lyrics to popular songs or standards ('filking'), and engaging in costuming at fan conventions by making replicas of costumes worn onscreen by film or TV actors."[7]

Hills's description of "fan culture" is close to how many theorists define "participatory fan culture." For example, for Henry Jenkins et al. participatory fan cultures are groups that contain "relatively low barriers to artistic expression and civic engagement, strong support for creating and sharing one's creations," in which "members believe their contributions matter, and feel some degree of social connections with one another."[8] Many scholars focus on the artistic expressions exhibited within these groups, for example, several of the "fan practices" Hills mentions, like fan fiction.[9] However, less attention has

---

[6] See Matthew Hills, "Fans and Fan Cultures," in *The Blackwell Encyclopedia of Sociology*, ed. George Ritzer (Malden, MA: Blackwell, 2007), 1638).

[7] Ibid. For an examination of the parallels between subcultures and participatory fan cultures, see J. Patrick Williams, *Subcultural Theory: Traditions and Concepts* (Malden, MA: Polity Press, 2011), 174–84.

[8] Henry Jenkins et al., *Confronting the Challenges of Participatory Cultures: Media Education for the 21st Century*, John D. and Catherine T. MacArthur Foundation Reports on Digital Media and Learning Series (Cambridge, MA: MIT Press, 2009), xi, quoted in Aaron Delwiche and Jennifer Jacobs Henderson, "Introduction: What Is Participatory Culture?," in *The Participatory Cultures Handbook*, ed. Aaron Delwiche and Jennifer Jacobs Henderson (New York: Routledge, 2013), 3.

[9] See, e.g., Kristin M. Barton and Jonathan Malcolm Lampley, eds., *Fan CULTure: Essays on Participatory Fandom in the 21st Century* (Jefferson, NC: McFarland, 2014); Henry Jenkins, *Textual Poachers: Television Fans and Participatory Culture*, updated twentieth anniversary ed. (1992; New York: Routledge, 2013).

been paid to "enacted" fandom, which I will define below. To focus our discussion on activities like those in which Geressy engages, I will use Hills's final example of "fan practices" as a springboard to a consideration of cosplay.

Lauren Orsini defines cosplay as "the art and craft of assuming both the appearance and persona of a fictional character." She elaborates, "What differentiates cosplay and dressing-up is that cosplayers take on a theatrical persona while in costume."[10] Mark Duffett defines and describes cosplay in the context of discussing fandom, writing, "Cosplay is a diverse practice that ranges from playful fancy dress to a more profound realization of social identity than might be accepted in wider culture.... Fans adopt the garb of fiction characters as a way of extending their own participation, exploring their identities and interacting with others." He continues, "Cosplay and impersonation at fan gatherings might even now be seen as enacting virtual community in physical space."[11] Duffett here seems to be echoing the claims of Conrad Ostwalt regarding what the latter terms "communitas." Ostwalt observes that in "contemporary culture...complexity and diversity have threatened to destroy [a] sense of community.... If it is true that authentic community is vanishing, then it would not be surprising to see individuals in collectives try to re-establish community, even of the artificial or fleeting kind."[12] Ostwalt then introduces the concept of communitas to indicate "intense community feelings of solidarity, equality, and purpose, often organized around a cause that produces a sense of unity." He concludes, "If our postmodern society has produced a culture where unity is rare, it would follow that such a culture would be bereft of the transcendental potential to be achieved through communitas."[13] Popular cultural groupings such as fandom, then, have the potential to create those "community feelings" and that "sense of unity" Ostwalt describes.

To return to the issue of cosplay, there is an important difference between cosplay as it is described by Orsini and Duffett and what I mean by "enacted cosplay," namely, *the phenomenon of fandom as expressed through cosplay going beyond adoration, exploration, and fictional elaboration and entering the realms of impersonation, embodiment, and reenactment.* "Enacted cosplay," then, refers to a subculture of cosplayers who— while still practicing the elements of impersonation and embodiment—(over)emphasize the aspect of "reenactment" and as such engage in activities like charity work and community service while in costume.[14] That is to say, it is quite one thing to create a

---

[10] Lauren Orsini, *Cosplay: The Fantasy World of Role Play* (London: Carlton Books, 2015), 8.

[11] Mark Duffett, "Fan Practices," in *Understanding Fandom: An Introduction to the Study of Media Fan Culture* (New York: Bloomsbury Academic, 2013), 189–90.

[12] Conrad Ostwalt, *Secular Steeples: Popular Culture and the Religious Imagination*, 2nd ed. (London: Bloomsbury, 2012), 206.

[13] Ibid.

[14] Readers should be aware of the existence of another superhero comic book cosplay subculture, the real-life superhero movement (RLSH). As Tea Krulos writes in *Heroes in the Night: Inside the Real Life Superhero Movement* (Chicago: Chicago Review Press, 2013), 4, "The RLSH are described as a 'movement,' a 'community,' and a 'subculture,' depending on whom you talk to. They consist of mostly anonymous, costumed do-gooders trying to save the world in their own small ways. They have a wide range of missions—charity and humanitarian work, activism, and, most controversial, actual crime

Batman costume to wear at a Comic-Con, but it is quite another to drive your own Batmobile across the country to visit sick children, as one cosplayer did in Bakersfield, California, in January 2016.[15] A year earlier, another Batman cosplayer joined a fund-raiser for winter supplies for the homeless in Springfield, Missouri, and received a key to the city for his efforts.[16] Groups of cosplayers also have banded together to engage in charity and humanitarian activities, both at the local and the national level. An example of the former would be the DC Marvel League, a cosplay group that, in September 2016, attended a charity 5K run in Broken Arrow, Oklahoma, to raise awareness for non-kenotic hyperglycinemia.[17] At the national level, one finds organizations like Heartfelt Heroes, which, according to their Facebook page, is "a non-profit organization dedicated to all kinds of volunteer superhero work like visiting children in hospitals, doing crafts with kids in shelters and reading books to children in Elementary schools while dressed up as superheroes. HH also makes personalized superhero capes for special children all across the country and serves as volunteers in lots of other charitable endeavors."[18]

Maybe the most well-known example of an organized grouping of enacted cosplayers is the 501st Legion, an organization of *Star Wars* Stormtrooper cosplayers who have regularly engaged in "fundraising, charity work, and volunteerism" since 1997.[19] These examples validate my claim that there exists a cosplaying moiety that dons costumes and

fighting. Like in the comic books. But not really." Even though there is some precedent for these activities within the comic book world—for example, Mark Millar's comic book series *Kick-Ass*—there are also divergences. The two essential differences between RLSH groups and what I am calling "enacted cosplayers" is that the former (a) take the aspects of elaboration and embodiment of fandom a further step in order to create their own original and individual costumed identity, and (b) some RLSH actually engage in the physical practice of fighting crime. Krulos observes that among members of RLSH movements, there exist pockets of what he calls "costumed activists" who "do not fight crime—their superhero personas are used solely for charity, humanitarian, and sometimes activist causes. They visit children's hospitals and classrooms, hand out supplies to the homeless, do charity walks and fundraisers. And again, they are not vigilantes" (29). Even though these "costumed activists" seem to share the motivation(s) one finds among "enacted cosplayers" (see, e.g., Krulos, *Heroes in the Night*, 6, 83, 101, 106, 143, 172, 178, 231, 233), the lack of an explicit mythic model or sacred text (i.e., comic book [super]hero) within their construction of identity marks them as different enough from the phenomenon of "enacted cosplay" that I cannot discuss them in more depth here.

[15]   See Jay Jayson, "Batman Drives across the Country to Deliver Message of Hope to Kids," Comicbook, September 6, 2017, http://comicbook.com/2016/01/04/batman-drives-across-the-country-to-deliver-message-of-hope-to-k/.

[16]   See Dennis Upkins, "Batman Helps the Homeless," Comicbook, September 6, 2017, http://comicbook.com/2015/01/11/batman-helps-the-homeless/.

[17]   Jimmie Tramel, "Capes for a Cause: DC Marvel League to Appear at 5K Run," *Tulsa World*, September 10, 2016, D3.

[18]   See Heartfelt Heroes' Facebook page: https://www.facebook.com/heartfeltheroes/about/.

[19]   501st Legion, "Our Mission," accessed May 30, 2020, http://www.501st.com/mission.php. The 501st was profiled nationally in *Parade* magazine in the December 13, 2015, issue, amid a larger article on the impact *Star Wars* has had on fans (8–12). In the interest of balance, I feel I must mention that fans of *Star Trek* also perform numerous acts of community service, often while in costume. For one specific example, see the segments on Barbara Adams in the 1997 film *Trekkies*.

performs community and charitable service.[20] Put differently, there is an additional layer of enactment in the act of "extending their own participation," as Duffett puts it. In this regard, the comments of Nicolle Lamerichs are helpful. In her article "Stranger Than Fiction: Fan Identity in Cosplay," she explores the performative interplay between a cosplayer's identity and the identity of the fictional character they imitate or embody: "What we see is that the identity of the fictional character rubs off on the identity of the player. The values or features of a character are projected onto the player by the spectators and player him- or herself."[21] This interaction of identities can have profound results, as Lamerichs indicates: "When we speak of identity and identification in cosplay, we speak of two things. On the one hand, players actualize a narrative and its meaning; on the other hand, they actualize their own identities. To put it bluntly, by stating that a narrative or character is related to me—that I can identify with this particular story or person—I make a statement about myself. There is transformative potential in this ability to express who we are through fiction."[22]

As we will see, the key emphases found in enacted cosplay—(a) the reenactment of a fictional or mythic text via (b) costume and/or bodily modification in the hopes of (c) replicating or imitating the prized values, behaviors, and actions embodied by a specific character within that text for the purposes of (d) individual benefit and communal good—have obvious overlaps with the emphases in the Holy Week practices of some Filipino Christians. As such, we can fruitfully compare and contrast them simply based on these common characteristics. However, there is another, more substantive parallel between the two phenomena: in many cases, participatory fan cultures function religiously for their members; that is, *the popular culture group performs many of the same functions as religious groups do for their members.*

Scholars of religion and popular culture have long held that the aesthetic discourses of popular culture have the potential to function religiously for those who consume

---

[20] There are also numerous examples of actors from comic-book films doing charity work while in costume, as Tom Holland, the most recent actor to play Spider-Man, did in late December 2016. See Kofi Outlaw, "*Spider-Man: Homecoming*'s Tom Holland Shares Touching Video of Hospital Visit," Comicbook, September 5, 2017, http://comicbook.com/marvel/2017/01/02/spider-man-homecoming-tom-holland-hospital-visit-kids/. More recently, Gal Gadot, the Israeli actress who plays Wonder Woman in the DC Comics films, took a break from filming her second solo Wonder Woman film to visit ill children at Inova Health in Virginia in full costume. See Chelsea Cirruzzo and Stephanie Ramirez, "*Wonder Woman* Star Gal Gadot Visits Sick Kids at Virginia Hospital," *USA Today*, July 9, 2018, https://www.usatoday.com/story/life/people/2018/07/09/wonder-woman-star-gal-gadot-visits-sick-kids-virginia-hospital/768746002/.

[21] Nicolle Lamerichs, "Stranger Than Fiction: Fan Identity in Cosplay," *Transformative Works and Cultures* 7 (2011): 5.3, http://journal.transformativeworks.org/index.php/twc/article/view/246/230.

[22] Ibid., 5.4. Similarly, Jen Gunnels, "'A Jedi Like My Father before Me': Social Identity and the New York Comic Con," *Transformative Works and Cultures* 3 (2009), http://journal.transformativeworks.org/index.php/twc/article/view/161/110, notes that cosplay "isn't necessarily mere escapism. Adults engage in costume role-play to explore an identity that may not be practicable in everyday life." She continues, "Cosplay, as a performed identity, can provide a means of individual agency and social commentary on current and past social stresses" (1.3).

them.[23] Thus it is no surprise that scholars such as Julie Ingersoll and Michael Jindra argue that popular cultural groupings like Jimmy Buffett's Parrotheads and fans of *Star Trek* ("Trekkies") take on functions conventionally performed by traditional religious groups.[24] In her analysis of Parrotheads, Ingersoll discovers "many ways in which parrotheadism functions in the lives of Buffett fans that parallel aspects of traditional religion."[25] These include the positing of a "utopian paradise," ("Margaritaville") which serves as a "mythic sacred space" in which Parrotheads long to reside and at which many of their desires are aimed.[26] Second, she notes the presence of ritual practices such as "pilgrimages" to places like Key West and New Orleans—which are associated with Buffett's own biography and lyrics as well as the sites of annual gatherings of Parrotheads—and "recreational use of alcohol and drugs" as ways to prepare for and celebrate the arrival of the central ritual event of parrotheadism: a Buffett concert.[27] These concerts mark the symbolic passage from the normal, ordinariness of life into a carnival-like atmosphere in which Parrotheads don Hawaiian shirts and other festive garments, collectively chant the lyrics to songs, and share in a kind of transcendence of their normal lives.[28] Finally, Ingersoll mentions the philosophy or the discourse created by Buffett that grounds and substantiates both the utopia and the ritual.[29]

Similarly, Jindra argues that "*Star Trek* fandom . . . has features that parallel a religious movement: an origin myth, a set of beliefs, organizations, and some of the most active and creative members found anywhere."[30] Much like the undergirding philosophy of

---

[23] As Bruce David Forbes explains in "Introduction: Finding Religion in Unexpected Places," in *Religion and Popular Culture in America*, 3rd ed., ed. Bruce David Forbes and Jeffrey H. Mahan (Berkeley: University of California Press, 2017), 1–24, here 16–9. Forbes even focuses on fandom as an example of this approach to the relationship between religion and popular culture, which he characterizes as "popular culture as religion," as opposed to religion in popular culture (11–4) or popular culture in religion (14–6) or religion and popular culture in dialogue (19–21). For other works on popular culture as religion, see, e.g., the works of John C. Lyden, *Film as Religion: Myths, Morals, Rituals* (New York: New York University Press, 2003); Ostwalt, *Secular Steeples*; Robin Sylvan, *Traces of the Spirit: The Religious Dimensions of Popular Music* (New York: New York University Press, 2002).

[24] See Julie Ingersoll, "The Thin Line between Saturday Night and Sunday Morning: Meaning and Community among Jimmy Buffett's Parrotheads," in *God in the Details: American Religion in Popular Culture*, 2nd ed., ed. Eric Michael Mazur and Kate McCarthy (London: Routledge, 2011), 258–70; Michael Jindra, "It's about Faith in Our Future: *Star Trek* Fandom as Cultural Religion," in Forbes and Mahan, *Religion and Popular Culture in America*, 223–41.

[25] Ingersoll, "The Thin Line," 260.

[26] Ibid., 260–1. Many imaginings of Margaritaville echo the qualities of heaven Deane Galbraith discusses in his chapter in this volume.

[27] Ibid., 261–2. I should admit that not only have I attended five Buffett concerts, but I made a Buffett-based pilgrimage to Key West in 2002, thanks to the support of Joe Leader.

[28] For more on how music offers an experiential, integrative experience on multiple levels and can, as such, function religiously, see Sylvan, *Traces of the Spirit*, especially 19–44.

[29] Ingersoll, "The Thin Line," 262–3.

[30] Jindra, "It's about Faith in Our Future," 226. Claiming that *Trek* fandom functions as a "cultural religion" (237) is very different from claiming that religion or religious themes or issues appear within the narratives of *Star Trek* series and films. This is a fundamental analytical distinction, as Forbes explains in his "Introduction." For an analysis of religion in *Trek* (as opposed to *Trek* as religion), see Ross S. Kraemer et al., *Religions of Star Trek* (Boulder, CO: Westview Press, 2001).

parrotheadism, Jindra identifies a core set of beliefs to which Trekkies grant their assent, including an "egalitarian ideology," a "frontier" mentality, and an overwhelmingly "positive," utopian attitude toward our human future.[31] He also points out the immersive ritual role that Trek conventions and pilgrimages play in the construction of "symbolic communities."[32] That is, since many Trekkies engage in cosplay and stay "in character" for a good deal of time at these conventions, they are able to immerse themselves in the world(s) of the character they are playing. Trekkies are able to augment this immersion by visiting outdoor filming locations used in the original television series and attractions like the Star Trek Experience in the Las Vegas Hilton.[33] Jindra concludes by addressing the ways in which Trekkies "fill out" the Trek universe via their own fan creations and mythology, akin to how religious practitioners exercise their own creativity in incorporating their religious beliefs into their own lives so that it feels "real."[34]

These parallels between parrotheadism, *Star Trek* fandom, and traditional religion indicate the contribution "to both an individual sense of identity and a sense of community," as well as illuminate the ways in which popular culture can function religiously.[35] Even though some popular culture scholars are skeptical of this connection,[36] Jennifer Porter persuasively argues that fan cultures are

> an integral vehicle for the articulation and experience of something deeply meaningful—a statement about what truly matters—as filtered through and symbolized by pop culture. They are, or at least can be, a place that embodies a person's and/or community's expression of the essence of all meaning: what it means to be human, to be in community, to be in space and time, to be moral or immoral, to be finite or eternal, to simply be. As a result, pop culture fandoms are implicitly religious. Implicit religion underpins ardent pop culture fandom, just as it underpins ardent explicit religion.[37]

Porter's emphasis on "implicit religion" alongside the *functional* purpose of popular-cultural fan communities like those Ingersoll and Jindra examine points us to a holistic

---

[31] Jindra, "It's about Faith in Our Future," 227–9.   [32] Ibid., 229–31.

[33] Ibid., 232. I should admit that I visited the Star Trek Experience in 2006, thanks again to the support of Joe Leader.

[34] Ibid., 234–6.

[35] Ingersoll, "The Thin Line," 263. Obviously the examples I provide are not exhaustive. For example, in recent years we have witnessed more and more people self-identifying as "Jedi" on various censuses. The Wikipedia page "Jedi Census Phenomenon" (https://en.wikipedia.org/wiki/Jedi_census_phenomenon) provides specific figures for several countries. Adam Possamai has analyzed these curious incidents in *Religion and Popular Culture: A Hyper-Real Testament*, Gods, Humans and Religions, 7 (Brussels: Peter Lang, 2011).

[36] See, e.g., Andrew Crome, "Reconsidering Religion and Fandom: Christian Fan Works in *My Little Pony* Fandom," *Culture and Religion: An Interdisciplinary Journal* 15, no. 4 (2014): 400–2; Matthew Hills, "Fandom between Cult and Culture," in *Fan Cultures*, Sussex Studies in Culture and Communication (New York: Routledge, 2002), 117–30; Stephen Reysen, "Secular versus Religious Fans: Are They Different?," *Journal of Religion and Popular Culture* 12 (Spring 2006): n.p.

[37] Jennifer Porter, "Implicit Religion in Popular Culture: The Religious Dimensions of Fan Communities," *Implicit Religion* 12, no. 3 (2009): 277.

conception of the religious potential present in participatory fan cultures focused on popular culture discourses. This holistic conception—including as it does both *substance* and *function*, both motivation and performance—enables us to draw on understandings of popular-cultural fan groupings in order to understand better, albeit via analogy, the seemingly alien practices of self-flagellation and voluntary crucifixion by some Filipino Christians during Holy Week. It is to this understanding that I will return after I describe in more detail these Filipino rituals.

SPECIFIC EXAMPLES AND/OR FOCI

I would now like to discuss the imitative performance in the Philippines during Holy Week of ritually reenacting the events surrounding the Passion of Christ. Like Eddie, some participants engage in self-flagellation, while others allow themselves to be ritually crucified during the celebration. The reasons for accepting and inflicting harm to oneself in the context of a religious ritual are related to the mimetic nature of ritual itself. Religious studies scholars have long pointed to ritual as a way of (a) affirming the dominant values of a given community, while also (b) imitating and reenacting key events found in the myths and sacred texts preserved and interpreted by that community, in the hope of (c) both establishing or refreshing a bond and petitioning the Sacred/God(s).[38] For example, some Shi'a Muslims celebrate the holiday of Ashura, which commemorates the martyrdom of Husayn (Muhammad's grandson) in 680 CE at Karbala, by donning white garments, wielding swords, chanting, and making small cuts on their foreheads to stimulate blood flow. This ritual performance, with its blood and martial imagery, is obviously reenacting the murder of Husayn, but as Karen Armstrong asserts, it also reflects the larger Shi'a worldview, most obviously their understanding of religious leadership and their valuation of martyrdom.[39]

The ritual performance of imitative self-flagellation and crucifixion in certain Philippine Christian groups demonstrates similar emphases. Just as Ashura does with Shi'a traditions, ritual celebrations during Lent in the Philippines draw on central stories and events (myths) within the Catholic tradition.[40] In these cases, there is an obvious

---

[38] For more on the understanding of ritual in religious studies, see Lawrence S. Cunningham and John Kelsay, *The Sacred Quest: An Invitation to the Study of Religion*, 6th ed. (Upper Saddle River, NJ: Pearson, 2013), 71–84; James C. Livingston, *Anatomy of the Sacred*, 6th ed. (Upper Saddle River, NJ: Pearson Prentice Hall, 2009), 74–95. For a broader understanding of ritual in religious practice(s), see Catherine Bell, "Performance," in *Critical Terms for Religious Studies*, ed. Mark C. Taylor (Chicago: Chicago University Press, 1998), 205–24.

[39] See Karen Armstrong, *Islam: A Short History*, Modern Library Chronicle Series (New York: Random House, 2002), 43. For a more detailed examination of this celebration—including the *ta'ziya* (passion play) and bodily self-mortification practices—see Heinz Halm, *The Shi'ites: A Short History*, trans. Allison Brown, Princeton Series on the Middle East (Princeton, NJ: Markus Wiener, 2007), 41–85.

[40] For the connection between self-mortification and Catholicism, see, generally, Liz Wilson's comments in "Starvation and Self-Mutilation in Religious Traditions," in *The Oxford Handbook of*

and intrinsic connection between the myth and the ritual. During Holy Week, two inter-related events signal the significance of the biblical text for these practitioners. First, a version of the biblical account of Jesus's Passion is sung or chanted aloud, most often in a domestic setting.[41] This adaptation of the Passion is called the *pabasa*, and it sets the stage for the more public ritual celebration during Lent, the *sinakulo*, or the Passion Play.[42] This too is adapted from scriptural texts, but like the *pabasa*, it carries local flavor as well, since the most common text for the *sinakulo* was composed in 1955 by a Filipino playwright.[43] Space constraints prevent me from describing the content of these texts, but suffice it to say that both the domestic recitation of the *pabasa* and the public perfor-mance of the *sinakulo* reinforce the actualization and central importance of the biblical texts—culturally appropriated though they may be—in the "religious atmosphere" of the ritual celebration.[44]

Given the biblical basis for the mythic buttress underlying the performances of the *pabasa* and the *sinakulo*, what is the connection between these and the ritual self-mortification I described? The first thing to note is the explicit Christology found in the *pabasa* and the *sinakulo*, as well as in Filipino Catholicism more generally. Nicholas H. Barker writes, "For men in particular, the Christ of the Filipinos is pre-eminently a suffering Christ: he is the beaten, scourged, humiliated, and defeated Christ."[45] Given this understanding of Christ, some Filipinos, like Eddie, began to go beyond reenactment and impersonation—as found in the *pabasa* and more so in the *sinakulo*—to embrace embodiment through what some scholars call the *penitencia*. José M. De Mesa explains, "If the pabasa deals extensively with the suffering and death of Jesus through commemorative singing, the penitencia (physical flagellation) remembers and celebrates such passion through body language."[46] He also notes that the men who engage in the *penitencia* "find body language easier to grasp than sophisticated verbal explanations. They readily identify themselves (damay) with the beaten, scourged, and humiliated Christ."[47] Further, beginning in the 1960s, some actors in the *sinakulo* embraced the idea of a suffering Christ to the degree that they wanted to share (*damay*)

Religion and Violence, ed. Michael Jerryson, Mark Juergensmeyer, and Margo Kitts (Oxford: Oxford University Press, 2013), 245.

[41] For more on the *pabasa*, see José M. De Mesa, "Holy Week and Popular Devotions," in *Morality, Religion and the Filipino: Essays in Honor of Vitaliano R. Gorospe*, ed. René B. Javellana (Manila: Ateneo de Manila University Press, 1994), 222–3.

[42] For more on the *sinakulo*, see Anril Pineda Tiatco and Amihan Bonifacio-Ramolete, "Cutud's Ritual of Nailing on the Cross: Performance of Pain and Suffering," *Asian Theatre Journal* 25, no. 1 (2008): 61–64; Anril Pineda Tiatco, "*Libad nang Apung Iru* and *Pamamaku king Krus*: Performances of Ambivalence in Kapampangan Cultural Spectacles," *Drama Review* 54, no. 2 (2010): 92–5.

[43] Tiatco and Bonifacio-Ramolete, "Cutud's Ritual of Nailing on the Cross," 61.

[44] De Mesa, "Holy Week and Popular Devotions," 222.

[45] Barker, "The Revival of Self-Flagellation," 4. See also the more detailed examination found in Benigno P. Beltran, *The Christology of the Inarticulate: An Inquiry into the Filipino Understanding of the Jesus the Christ* (Manila: Divine Word, 1987).

[46] De Mesa, "Holy Week and Popular Devotions," 223.   [47] Ibid., 224.

in his suffering in a deeper, more physical fashion. And so began the flagellations and intermittent crucifixions for which the Pampanga province has become famous.

As we have seen, the motivation behind these corporeal practices is bound up with the concepts of *damay* and *darame*. De Mesa points out that *damay* is best understood as "compassionate solidarity" with another's suffering: "In the account of the *Pasion*, Jesus' suffering and death are commemorated as the supreme manifestations of God's damay for humankind. They are divine sympathy for our miserable situation after the fall, yes, but even more, they are also God's participation in our human condition."[48] He then explains that this empathetic participation by God moves some humans to emulate that divine sympathy via a ritual reenactment of the suffering of Christ: "The pabasa is a response to God's damay.... The singing of the *Pasion* is aimed at evoking the sentiment of compassionate solidarity with Christ.... No doubt, the penitencia graphically (bodily) reminds us of what Jesus went through for our sake. Jesus' damay with us is responded to by damay through flagellation."[49]

Given the imitative nature of religious ritual, the replication of Jesus's suffering—in this specific context, his *damay*—is not surprising. The re-creative lengths to which people like Eddie go, though, are understandable in light of their *darame*, "a form of emotional identification with another in which the verbal expression of sympathy is insufficient. The depth of compassion can only be channeled through the corporeal empathy of ritual pain."[50] Both *damay* and *darame* form the substance, the impetus for the self-inflicted physical pain participants endure, but these are only part of the ritual.

To understand these actions more fully, we need to remember the performative purpose of such acts of self-mortification. Barker observes, "Flagellation became a dramatic public spectacle, performed predominantly by lower class males as pragmatic supplication, a votive or contractual sacrifice involving literal, or highly realistic re-enactment of the passion of Jesus Christ. During the ritual process, a tangible, reciprocal relationship with the divine was created or recreated."[51] William Petersen likewise notes the importance of the relational function of these performative, mimetic actions, writing, "For the faithful, following Christ on the arduous path [to] Calvary provides complete and total sympathy (or *damay*) with the sufferings of Christ. Throughout the Philippines, Good Friday sees thousands of such processions through the streets, as individuals walk with Christ, while many enact varying degrees of suffering and mortification to complete their identification with their savior."[52] As such, one finds an actualization via ritual reenactment of a sacred myth or text—in this case, New Testament accounts of Jesus's Passion and Crucifixion—performed out of a sense of *damay*, in the hopes of securing a relationship with the Divine in order to gain an enhanced status from which one could

---

[48] Ibid., 225.   [49] Ibid., 225, 227.

[50] Bautista, "The Localization of Roman Catholicism," 105.

[51] Barker, "The Revival of Self-Flagellation," 24.

[52] William Petersen, "Holy Week in the 'Heart of the Philippines': Spirituality, Theatre, and Community in Marinduque's Moriones Festival," *Asian Theatre Journal* 24, no. 2 (2007): 323.

petition the deity "for the good of the devotee himself or herself, for a loved one (i.e., usually a sick loved one), or for the community."[53]

These ritual performances exhibit the same basic qualities we found in the phenomenon of enacted cosplay: (a) the reenactment of a fictional or mythic text via (b) costume and/or bodily modification in the hopes of (c) replicating or imitating the prized values, behaviors, and actions embodied by a specific character within that text for the purposes of (d) individual benefit and communal good. In terms of (a), it is clear that the biblical accounts of Jesus's Passion play a central role in both the *pabasa* and the *sinakulo*, which together form the mythic foundation for the dramatic reenactments I discussed. We saw that participants not only make and don costumes when partaking in the *sinakulo*, but they also engage in bodily modification or mortification via self-flagellation and, sometimes, crucifixion, all of which is reflected in (b). The motivation for doing so, or (c), is related to the concepts of *damay* and *darame* as well as the Christology found in many Filipino Catholic movements. As I noted, people like Eddie feel such empathy and compassion for Christ and his sufferings that they need to engage in a bodily, re-creative performance that displays their identification with Christ, or (c). Finally, in terms of (d), we saw that participants in these practices feel that their vow (*panata*) to undergo or ritually re-create Christ's sufferings as narrated in the *pabasa* and *sinakulo* has both individual and corporate merit. That is, these practices of bodily self-mortification "are ways of becoming Christ's intimate friend. It is nearness to Christ that is aspired to: to help 'Christ and share in his ordeal.' By establishing such a close patron-client relationship, the flagellant expects that his requests will be granted, and the crucified are sure that they will be rewarded with healing powers."[54] As such, the incentive for participation is essentially altruistic, since these requests and healings often focus on improving the lot and well-being of others.[55]

The performative and motivational parallels between enacted cosplay and the Filipino Christian devotional practices found during Holy Week should be obvious, given the four-part overlap just discussed. So how do these parallels help us to understand the

[53] Tiatco, "*Libad nang Apung Iru* and *Pamamaku king Krus*," 95. Tiatco and Bonifacio-Ramolete address the hoped-for petitionary outcome of the *panata*, or vow, made by the participant in the practice of self-crucifixion ("Cutud's Ritual of Nailing on the Cross," 70). See also Fernando N. Zialcita, "Popular Interpretations of the Passion of Christ," *Philippine Sociological Review* 34 (1986): 59.

[54] Peter J. Bräunlein, "'We Are 100% Catholic': Philippine Passion Rituals and Some Obstacles in the Study of Non-European Christianity," *Journal of Religion in Europe* 5 (2012): 395–6.

[55] Obviously, there is an individual benefit as well. When a bond is secured with the divine, one's own identity is *expanded* to include the divine within it. As Joseph Epes Brown and Emily Cousins write in *Teaching Spirits: Understanding Native American Religious Traditions* (Oxford: Oxford University Press, 2001), in performing a ritual, the participant hopes to achieve "three cumulative possibilities: purification, expansion, and identity. Purification is necessary, for that which is impure may not be united with the purity of sacred power. Expansion follows, because only that which is perfect, total, or whole can be united with absolute perfection and holiness. One must cease to be a part, an imperfect fragment; one must realize what one really is so as to expand to include the Universe within oneself. Only then, when these two conditions of purification and expansion have been actualized, may one attain the final stage, in which one's identity is grounded in a union with all that is" (111–2).

latter phenomenon, which might seem so alien to those of us in an American context? My hope is that by drawing on the presumably more familiar practice of cosplay—grounded as it is in American popular culture broadly and, in many cases, in comic-book superhero stories, which have dominated mass-distributed feature films for well over a decade now—to discuss how fans actualize and embody texts based on their identification with characters, we can see similar processes at work within the devotional mortification practices in the Philippines. The similarities I have noted not only reinforce the centrality of ritual for religious practice and cultural performance but also point to commonalities in form and intention in both phenomena. Through these parallel processes and common characteristics, we are hopefully in a better position to fulfill what Timothy K. Beal sees as the point of the academic study of religion. According to Beal, that point is to make "the strange familiar and the familiar strange. It's about encountering religious ideas, practices, traditions, and institutions that initially appear to us as 'other,' disturbingly foreign, and coming to a point where we understand how they can make sense given a certain set of circumstances. Such work requires not only critical rigor and tenacity in order to elaborate those circumstances; it also requires imagination in order to put oneself in another's situation."[56] By using the analogy of cosplay, I hope I have helped facilitate an imaginative understanding of a set of practices that might have appeared strange but now seem more familiar.

FUTURE PROSPECTS AND QUESTIONS

- In this chapter, I argue that we can understand the ritual self-mortification practices of some Filipino Christians via a comparative analogy with a kind of participatory fan culture I call "enacted cosplay." Future research might engage the implications of understanding religious groupings as participatory fan cultures—that is, just one more social grouping that performs the same functions as other fan cultures—and inquire if doing so somehow make them less "sacred."
- Conversely, what might be the implications of the claim that popular cultural fan groupings "function" religiously for those who participate therein? Is this a reductive approach to religion? Does it denigrate the "sacred" aspect of religious groupings?
- I describe the centrality of ritual for certain Filipino Christian practices, but other researchers could explore the question of whether or not participatory fan cultures engage in ritual. Key to this research would be the issue of defining both the content and the effect of these rituals.
- Obviously, texts and narratives are central for both cosplay and the Filipino Christian practices I discuss. Questions subsequent examinations could raise

[56] Timothy K. Beal, *Roadside Religion: In Search of the Sacred, the Strange, and the Substance of Faith* (Boston: Beacon Press, 2005), 12.

include the following: Do texts and narratives have a "deterministic" influence on personal, social, and/or religious identity? That is, how much influence do texts and narratives have on how we understand ourselves and/or how we explain ourselves to ourselves? What role does interpretation play in the formation and performance of identity? How do the (often creative) interpretation of texts factor into both cosplay and the Filipino Christian practices examined in this chapter?

- Are there other phenomena with which one could compare the Filipino Christian practices discussed here? I chose to examine cosplay, but are there other phenomena that would be analytically useful? If so, what are they, and why would they be useful? How would one go about investigating them and comparing them?

SUGGESTED READINGS AND ANNOTATED BIBLIOGRAPHY

Barker, Nicholas H. "The Revival of Self-Flagellation and the Birth of Crucifixion in Lowland Christian Philippines." Nagoya University Discussion Paper No. 63. Nagoya University Graduate School of International Development, 1998.

Barker's paper serves as the basis for most modern examinations of the Filipino ritual self-mortification practices I describe. He surveys the historical and theological background of these practices and pays special attention to the revival of crucifixions beginning in 1961. This is a foundational resource for understanding the issue of flagellation and crucifixion in the Philippines.

Bautista, Julius. "The Localization of Roman Catholicism: Radical Transcendence and Social Empathy in a Philippine Town." In *Routledge Handbook of Religions in Asia*, edited by Bryan S. Turner and Oscar Salemink, 96–108. London: Routledge, 2015.

In this chapter, Bautista discusses how Roman Catholic practices and beliefs are accommodated in a Filipino context. He focuses specifically on how these practices and beliefs are embodied vis-à-vis culture-specific understandings of the suffering body of Christ, as well as how ritual self-mortification and the resultant pain offers an alternative, noncolonial path to transcendence. His sections on the flagellant (102–4) and *darame* (104–5) are based on primary field research conducted in 2010 and represent an important insight into the motivations and psychology of participants in these rituals.

Bräunlein, Peter J. "'We Are 100% Catholic': Philippine Passion Rituals and Some Obstacles in the Study of Non-European Christianity." *Journal of Religion in Europe* 5 (2012): 384–413.

Bräunlein's goal is to use the example of Filipino self-flagellation and crucifixion as a case study in how the academic study of religion privileges Western norms. In the course of his article, he provides valuable insight on how the media covers and shapes understandings of these events (388–93). He also paints an "emic" picture of these practices based on fieldwork from 1996 to 1998 (393–7), as well as providing some important historical context for the presence of Catholicism in the Philippines (397–401).

Duffett, Mark. "Fan Practices." In *Understanding Fandom: An Introduction to the Study of Media Fan Culture*, 165–90. New York: Bloomsbury Academic, 2013.

This chapter from Duffett's larger introduction to fandom focuses on what fans *do* to demonstrate their adoration and engagement. Here, Duffett examines three kinds of "pleasures" in which fans engage: connection, appropriation, and innovative performance. In the context of the final kind of pleasure, Duffett highlights "impersonation and cosplay," and this section is a helpful, albeit brief, introduction to the subject. Especially recommended for beginning researchers.

Hills, Matthew. "Fans and Fan Culture." In *The Blackwell Encyclopedia of Sociology*, edited by George Ritzer, 1637–41. Malden, MA: Blackwell, 2007.

Hills published a well-received yet advanced text titled *Fan Cultures* in 2002, but this more succinct treatment is an excellent place for the neophyte student to begin. Herein Hills provides helpful definitions of both "fans" and "fan culture," as well as more technical terms he explores in his previous book, such as "performative consumption." This is possibly the best brief overview of this issue.

Lamerichs, Nicolle. "Stranger Than Fiction: Fan Identity in Cosplay." *Transformative Works and Cultures* 7 (2011). http://journal.transformativeworks.org/index.php/twc/article/view/246/230.

Investigating cosplay as a phenomenon of "appropriation" within fan culture groupings. Lamerichs helpfully examines cosplay as an example of *performance* and draws important conclusions regarding its impact on bodies and how it functions as textual elaboration and interpretation. Her article is one of the most helpful academic pieces on the subject of cosplay I have found.

Porter, Jennifer. "Implicit Religion in Popular Culture: The Religious Dimensions of Fan Communities." *Implicit Religion* 12, no. 3 (2009): 271–80.

Porter takes up a daunting question—one raised in the works of Ingersoll and Jindra I discuss in this chapter—namely, whether fan groupings organized around popular cultural products can or should be seen as "religious." After engaging five common objections to seeing fan groups as religious, Porter asserts that such groups should be understood as "implicitly religious"; that is, even though they differ from traditional religious groupings in terms of *substance* (what persons are "committed to"), their *functional* effects are similar enough for them to be classified as "implicitly religious."

Tiatco, Anril Pineda, and Amihan Bonifacio-Ramolete. "Cutud's Ritual of Nailing on the Cross: Performance of Pain and Suffering." *Asian Theatre Journal* 25, no. 1 (2008): 58–76.

This article is a very useful analysis of the practice of crucifixion from the perspective of performative criticism. The authors examine the ritual as both a "religious occasion" and a "social drama." In so doing, they include information on "the roots of the ritual" (60–4) and "the evolution of the performance" (64–70) and conclude by discussing the role of pain within the rituals and its history. An accessible introduction to the main terms and practices surrounding this ritual; this is an ideal place for the neophyte to begin.

PART VI

THE STATE OF THE FIELD

CHAPTER 28

....

THE TEN COMMANDMENTS, POSTCARDS, AND METHODOLOGICAL ISSUES AND OPPORTUNITIES

....

SCOTT M. LANGSTON
DEPARTMENT OF RELIGION, TEXAS
CHRISTIAN UNIVERSITY

INTRODUCTION

....

WITHIN academic circles, popular culture—commonly defined as "culture based on the tastes of ordinary people rather than an educated elite"—has traditionally not been given the same respect as other scholarly disciplines or cultural expressions.[1] While that assessment has changed some in recent years, ideas and insights arising from popular culture for the most part remain second-class citizens in the eyes of many. This was poignantly illustrated in a discussion that occurred on the animated program *King of the Hill*, a show airing on American television from 1997 to 2010 about a fictional community of churchgoing, beer-drinking, football-loving wage earners and their families who live in a small, central Texas town. Hank Hill, who proudly works as the assistant manager of Strickland Propane, embodies small-town values, conservatism, a strong work

---

[1] "Popular Culture," in *New Oxford American Dictionary*, ed. Angus Stevenson and Christine A. Lindberg (New York: Oxford University Press, 2010), https://www.lexico.com/definition/popular_culture.

ethic, and common sense, while being surrounded by friends and family who usually demonstrate the "lesser qualities" of the working class. In an episode that aired in 2004, Hank tries unsuccessfully to get his son, a student at Tom Landry Middle School (named after the legendary coach of the Dallas Cowboys), to stop watching so much television.[2] When his son goes to school the next day, he is placed on the school's academic quiz bowl team—not because of his academic prowess in science, math, or literature but because of his extensive knowledge of popular culture. Excited, he comes home and tells his dad, who, as is his custom, is standing in the back alley, drinking beer with his three friends. Hank is perplexed at how his son, who is no academic genius (and, according to Hank, they have the report cards to prove it), could be placed on the academic quiz bowl team. The following dialogue ensues:

HANK: Since when is popular culture considered academic?
DALE: It's serious business, Hank. You can't be a respected university these days without offering a major in commercial jingles or the films of M. Night Shyamalan.
BOOMHAUER: [Mumbles something about Oberlin College having a Phi Beta Kappa on the *Muppet Show*.]
HANK: Well, that's asinine. What kind of job can you get with a degree in popular culture?
DALE: You can be a professor—of popular culture.

OVERVIEW OF TOPIC

Many might agree with Hank Hill's assertion that it is asinine to consider popular culture an academic field of study, especially if you use the standards by which biblical studies has traditionally defined itself and carried out its business. Historically, biblical scholars have focused on the Bible's "original" meanings and contexts as its most important elements. While this has been challenged since the late twentieth century by prominent and/or vocal groups—feminists, African Americans, the "colonized," to name a few—even among these groups, the focus often remains on critiquing the "original" or traditional understandings of the text as formulated by those in power. For the most part, however, popular understandings and uses *in their own right* are rarely taken seriously in academia, which commonly dismisses them as misinterpretations or misuses of the biblical text. Even among those who are open to the study of popular culture, the subtle temptation remains to resist viewing it as legitimate. See, for instance, one reviewer's characterization of the essays in the book *The Bible in/and Popular Culture: A*

---

[2] *King of the Hill*, "Stressed for Success," season 8, episode 19, dir. Tricia Garcia and Wesley Archer, written by Tony Gama-Lobo, Rebecca May, and Wyatt Cenac, Fox Network, May 2, 2004.

Creative Encounter as interesting and amusing but in need of "more exploration of the lineaments and consequences of serious fun."[3]

Scholars, however, are more inclined to see value in popular readings when they are explored, dissected, and interpreted with academic methodologies in the service of disciplinary goals. Using a plethora of tools, scholarly work has yielded fascinating and helpful insights that further our understanding of the Bible and its relationship to popular culture. These methods, though, reflect scholarly perspectives, assumptions, and interests. This does not render these efforts meaningless or of little value, but it reminds and cautions those of us who use them that we typically engage popular readings for and with starkly different purposes and perspectives than "ordinary people." As Allene Stuart Phy observed over thirty years ago in one of the first major scholarly works on the Bible and popular culture, the latter "always reveals, sometimes innocently, the preoccupations of the people who consume it."[4] The study of the Bible and popular culture, as well as its accompanying methodologies, can tell us much about not only the "ordinary people" who produce and use these readings but also the scholars who study them. Alan Le Grys's question regarding the essays in *The Bible in/and Popular Culture: A Creative Encounter* is well-taken: "Some of the songs and books considered here might be hugely popular with academics, but do they really represent 'mainstream' experience?"[5] The role played by scholars and their methodologies in filtering and refracting popular uses of the Bible, therefore, must not be overlooked. Understanding why "ordinary people" have found a biblical text or idea useful or meaningful is just as essential as understanding how they have used it.

That scholars use a variety of technical methodologies to understand and interpret popular uses of the Bible reflects another methodological concern: it has become the domain of the well-trained specialist. The academic study of the Bible and popular culture can therefore turn into an elitist objectifying and ogling of "ordinary people's" ideas and actions rather than a dialogue between scholar and "ordinary person" based on mutual equality and respect. This is not always the case, but the risk is ever present and exacerbated by the multiplicity of technical methodologies employed by well-intentioned scholars.

Despite the large number of methodologies available to scholars, "there is as yet no systematic study of the interrelationship between the Bible and popular culture."[6] Scholars approach popular readings from many different angles, with little to unify or guide these efforts. Diversity in itself is not problematic, but it can distort our under-

[3] Richard Walsh, review of *The Bible in/and Popular Culture: A Creative Encounter*, ed. Philip Culbertson and Elaine M. Wainwright, *Biblical Interpretation* 20 (2012): 483.

[4] Allene Stuart Phy, "The Bible and American Popular Culture: An Overview and Introduction," in *The Bible and Popular Culture in America*, ed. Allene Stuart Phy (Philadelphia, PA: Fortress Press, 1985), 1–23, here 1.

[5] Alan Le Grys, review of *The Bible in/and Popular Culture: A Creative Encounter*, ed. Philip Culbertson and Elaine M. Wainwright, *Journal for the Study of the New Testament* 34, no. 5 (2012): 150.

[6] Elaine M. Wainwright, introduction to *The Bible in/and Popular Culture: A Creative Encounter*, ed. Philip Culbertson and Elaine M. Wainwright (Atlanta, GA: Society of Biblical Literature, 2010), 2.

standing of popular uses of biblical texts and ideas. When scholars slice and dice a read-ing, they can produce interesting and helpful interpretations of its component parts (such as gender, race, or ethnicity) but routinely fail to understand the reading itself in all its complexity. In other words, after the reading is taken apart, it rarely is put back together and understood in its totality. Understanding how the different elements of a particular reading function when they come in contact with each other is difficult. Yet it is necessary because the individual aspects react differently when combined with assorted elements. Two readings may contain many of the same elements, but rarely do they contain all the same elements. Each reading produces distinctive combinations that shape the biblical text. This beckons the scholar to move beyond merely under-standing individual components of a reading and to see them in context with each other.

The methodologies available to scholars, however, can inhibit this effort. Typically, scholars have engaged the Bible and popular culture through many of the same tools and approaches used in biblical studies. For instance, the book *Teaching the Bible through Popular Culture and the Arts* approaches the topic in terms of the genre and media in which biblical texts appear, something that a historical critic would do when studying the "original" contexts of biblical texts. The essays are organized according to music, film, art, literature, and "other media" (cartoons and comics, youth literature, programming, and entertainment, television, and internet websites).[7] Another anthol-ogy on the Bible and culture includes these categories, but also considers the contexts in which the Bible is used—historically (from the ancient to the modern world), religiously (Judaism and Islam), and geographically (Asia, Africa, North and Latin America, and Australasia)—as well as different disciplinary perspectives (socioeconomics, politics, ecology, psychology, gender, nationalism, postcolonialism, and postmodernism).[8] Each of these approaches emphasizes a significant aspect of how culture appropriates biblical texts and ideas, producing insightful observations regarding how they may function within a specific disciplinary category. Less often, however, do they address how the major forces that constitute a particular interpretation work collectively. Again, this does not diminish the value of these individual methods but instead highlights the need for a multidimensional understanding of the Bible and popular culture that integrates rather than isolates. The nature of popular biblical readings requires such an approach.

Popular uses of the Bible act as intersections where various components—for exam-ple, gender, race, ethnicity, and socioeconomic status—meet. To be sure, this is not unique to popular culture but characterizes any use, including scholarly and theological renderings, as well as the Bible itself. In the American context, democracy, individual-ism, human rights, capitalism, white patriarchy, and Christianity often combine with notions such as rationalism, colonialism, imperialism, American exceptionalism, mul-ticulturalism, and feminism to constitute some of the important forces that shape popu-

---

[7] Mark Roncace and Patrick Gray, eds., *Teaching the Bible through Popular Culture and the Arts* (Atlanta, GA: Society of Biblical Literature, 2007).

[8] John F. A. Sawyer, ed., *The Blackwell Companion to the Bible and Culture* (Malden, MA: Blackwell, 2006).

lar uses of the Bible. Furthermore, these elements and their meanings change over the course of American history, thereby introducing a chronological element to this interaction. The Bible, in a sense, serves as a stage on which these various components interact. The nonbiblical components, in turn, act as a filter through which biblical texts pass, with some parts of the Bible being allowed through while others are excluded. Portions of biblical texts combine with nonbiblical ingredients to form the final product. Understanding how these forces collectively act to influence biblical uses is just as important as understanding the individual strands of an interpretation.

Accomplishing this, however, is easier said than done. The sociologist Ibrahim Abraham has called for a multidisciplinary approach when studying the reception of the Bible and popular culture, exhorting academics to move beyond "methodologies designed for the study of sacred literature." Encouraging biblical scholars who study popular culture not to "restrict themselves to scholarly interpretations," Abraham argues for "methodological adaptions" that use approaches based on the social sciences. Concerned with both the disconnect between "academic experts and laity" and the need for the study of popular culture and the study of the Bible to prove their "financial viability" due to broader pressures faced by the humanities and social sciences, Abraham urges an "interdisciplinary conversation."[9] While the historian James G. Crossley agrees at many points with Abraham, he pushes back against Abraham's criticism of privileging academic interpretations over popular ones, as well as against his call to use social scientific approaches to better understand popular interpretations. Instead Crossley argues that "neither types of approaches (i.e., historical or social scientific) have an inherently superior place at the table."[10]

While both scholars make good points, this disagreement illustrates part of the challenge facing academics using precise methodologies designed to understand strands of an interpretation or to serve the needs of a particular discipline. These methodologies yield different information, but they also overlook other data and can produce incomplete interpretations. The solution does not lie in seeking a single methodology—a sort of "super-methodology"—that by itself renders a comprehensive understanding of popular uses.[11] However, being aware of and committed to producing more comprehensive analyses is a good start. Trying to answer why a particular popular reading has incorporated certain portions of the Bible and how the biblical elements interact with nonbiblical elements is the challenge. I have found reception history to be useful in this endeavor, but it is by no means the only way to accomplish it. It too can atomize a particular biblical use or interpretation.

---

[9] Ibrahim Abraham, "Would You Adam and Eve It? Social Scientific Contributions to the Study of the Reception of Scripture in Consumer Society," *Bible & Critical Theory* 10, no. 2 (2014): 32, 38–40.

[10] James G. Crossley, "On Reception History, Audiences, and Disciplinary Assumptions: A Response to Ibrahim Abraham," *Relegere: Studies in Religion and Reception* 4, no. 2 (2014): 255.

[11] Similarly, the editors of *The Bible in/and Popular Culture* acknowledge, "This volume will not be able to provide a comprehensive theoretical framework/s for the engagement with the Bible in popular culture" (4).

As John F. A. Sawyer has pointed out, even the ancient Greeks had an appreciation for a text's reception and its effect on its readers, but it has only been since the 1960s that "the notion that the reception of a text is more important than the text itself" has arisen.[12] While the term "reception history" has become commonplace, scholars still debate what its proper name and emphasis should be, starting with *Wirkungsgeschichte*, a term coined by Hans-Georg Gadamer, or *Rezeptionsaesthetik*, the term used by Hans-Robert Jauss.[13] Arising out of the social movements of the 1960s and the work in literary theory being conducted particularly at the University of Konstanz, by the early 1990s it had, according to one theorist, become common practice "to distinguish the history of effects (*Wirkungsgeschichte*) from the history of receptions (*Receptionsgeschichte*) and thus a *Wirkungsasthetik* from a *Rezeptionsasthetik*." More explicitly, "a *Wirkungsgeschichte* attempts to account for changing appreciations of what a text actually says, in terms of both its structures and its more direct messages," whereas a *Receptionsgeschichte* "stresses the creative role of the reader much more." Thus *Wirkungsgeschichte* focuses more on how textual (authorial) structures and strategies invite and control the actions of readers, while *Receptionsgeschichte* focuses on the sociohistorical conditions influencing how readers respond to texts.[14] Often those working in this field emphasize one or the other. The role of the author and that of the readers, however, constitute two sides of the same coin, both reflecting important and necessary components. For the most part, those working in reception history have rightly given attention to a text's various readers, or its afterlives, but the study of a text's "original" author and meanings should not be overlooked. Thus reception history in its broadest terms offers an opportunity to study the use, influence, and impact of the Bible in *all* its dimensions—but only if the scholar takes it up. It provides a tool for understanding and appreciating how the important aspects constituting popular uses of biblical texts work together.

Specific Examples and/or Foci

An analysis of postcards from late nineteenth- and early twentieth-century America demonstrates some of the possibilities for using reception history to understand how a

[12] John F. A. Sawyer, "The Role of Reception Theory, Reader-Response Criticism and/or Impact History in the Study of the Bible: Definition and Evaluation," paper given at the Society of Biblical Literature annual meeting, November 2004, https://drive.google.com/file/d/0BwA21tmQB0RQZHB 4eEFNSURSNjA/view.

[13] Hans-Georg Gadamer, *Wahrheit und Methode: Grundzüge einer philosophischen Hermeneutik* (Mohr: Tübingen 1960); Hans-Robert Jauss, *Toward an Aesthetic of Reception*, trans. T. Bahti (Minneapolis: University of Minnesota Press, 1982).

[14] Martyn P. Thompson, "Reception Theory and the Interpretation of Historical Meaning," *History and Theory* 32, no. 3 (October 1993): 255. Thompson ultimately concludes (271–2), "Reception History (*Receptionsgeschichte*), as I have interpreted the notion, simply pursues the implications of readers as authors and the all important observation that receptions are 'by no means the same thing' as the communication of authors' intended meanings."

reading's major biblical and nonbiblical components interact with each other. Specifically, these postcards reveal how factors such as capitalism, Victorian gender norms, American Protestant Christianity, and American exceptionalism combine to shape biblical expressions and uses. During the periods known as the Gilded Age and the Progressive Era, picture postcards, emblazoned with colorful images, became quite popular, and by 1901 a postcard craze was in full gear in Europe and, within a few years, also in the United States. (The craze appears to have ended with the end of World War I.) In 1908, for example, Americans mailed over 667 million postcards; that number rose to almost one billion by 1913. Postcards had been around since the late 1860s, but the addition of a picture seems to have created a large appetite for them, going beyond the merely utilitarian aim of sending a brief communication to appealing to the aesthetic, especially among the lower middle class and working class.[15] According to John Fraser, "The picture postcard was possibly the great vehicle for messages of the new urban proletariat between 1900 and 1914."[16] Colleen McDannell has noted that "the fad itself was part of turn-of-the-century popular culture."[17] Not only did people send these cards through the mail as means of communicating, but they also collected them, often pasting them into albums and even forming clubs; the middle class seems to have been the most avid collectors.[18] These cards became big business as secular and religious companies sought to capitalize by developing and selling various lines of religious postcards.

Depictions of biblical scenes, juxtaposed with biblical verses, commonly adorned these postcards. The scenes varied from famous works of art to the more mundane, and reflected both serious and comical sentiments. These uses reveal what biblical texts were particularly influential at the time. Among the most popular were the Ten Commandments; several editions were produced. When compared with each other, these renderings reveal the interaction between some of the important biblical and non-biblical forces. Three examples follow.

"Thou Shalt Not Kill"

The M. W. Taggart Company of New York produced in 1908 a series of ten cards, each depicting one of the Ten Commandments.[19] A scene representing the individual com-

---

[15] The first postcard was issued on October 1, 1869, in the Austro-Hungarian Empire. Britain and Ireland issued their first cards on October 1, 1870. In the 1870s in Europe, pictures began to appear on postcards, the first commercial production of these cards being allowed in 1894 in Britain and Ireland. See Séamus Kearns, "Picture Postcards as a Source for Social Historians," *Saothar* 22 (1997): 128–30.

[16] John Fraser, "Propaganda on the Picture Postcard," *Oxford Art Journal* 3, no. 2 (1980): 39, 43.

[17] Colleen McDannell, *Material Christianity: Religion and Popular Culture in America* (New Haven, CT: Yale University Press, 1995), 234.

[18] A. P. Behan, "History from Picture Postcards," *Dublin Historical Records* 46, no. 2 (1993): 129–30. A very helpful website for information on postcards is Metropostcard, http://www.metropostcard.com/index.html, accessed May 31, 2017.

[19] For an overview of the reception history of the Ten Commandments during the ancient, medieval, and modern periods, see Scott M. Langston, *Exodus through the Centuries*, Blackwell Bible Commentaries (Malden, MA: Blackwell, 2006), 186–221.

mandment covered one side of the card, accompanied by the relevant verse, while the other side was divided into two spaces, one for writing a note and one for the recipient's address and postage (one cent). In this rendering of the sixth commandment—"Thou shalt not kill"—what appears to be a representation of Cain murdering Abel (Gen 4:1–16) interprets the injunction, despite the story appearing well in advance of the command-ment in the biblical chronology. Nothing, however, specifically identifies the postcard scene with Cain and Abel. Rather, this is inferred from the presence of two altars and a shepherd's staff lying next to the slain individual, as well as sheep grazing in the background next to the altar nearest him (Abel was a "keeper of sheep")—all traits that fit the biblical description of this first murder. A biblically literate viewer might suppose from the reference to Cain that anger and jealousy motivated the murder.

The card also interprets the sixth commandment completely within a biblical context, although with a Protestant numbering (Roman Catholics count it as the fifth command-ment). While it is not altogether clear why the murder of Abel was chosen, the effect of such a presentation is to distance the viewer from the commandment by keeping it as a somewhat general ideal. Its depiction as an ancient scene makes it more a relic of history. Certainly, the viewer would affirm the sentiment, but more as a matter of principle than as something with immediate application. Such a portrayal was common, appearing on cards produced by other publishers, including Raphael Tuck and Sons (of London) and the Rose Company (of Philadelphia), and may reflect an emphasis on the Bible's status as part of America's larger cultural heritage. Emphasizing their antiquity, the command-ments are presented as ancient ideals that have stood the test of time. Thus the viewer finds value in them, in part, because of their antiquity and what they represent as a cul-tural icon. The predominance of Protestant Christianity among Americans of this period combined with its iconic representation helps turn the commandments into an expression of American values and identity and, in turn, increases the postcard's marketability.[20]

This was not the case with a postcard produced by the PFB Company, a German busi-ness in operation from 1901 to 1911 that produced postcards for the American market.[21] Like the previous depiction, this one shows a man fleeing from his slain victim. Yet there are several differences. First, the scene is made contemporary by depicting two men wearing modern clothing. The commandment no longer acts as an honored ideal from the distant past but is now a modern ethic. It is not something merely to pay homage to but something to be lived because of its contemporary relevance. Murder is an immedi-ate social concern, a current event, and the commandment is employed as a deterrent. Second, this depiction essentially connects this commandment with the eighth—"Thou

---

[20] For American uses of the Ten Commandments, see Scott M. Langston, "The Americanization of the Ten Commandments, 1880s–1920s," *Perspectives in Religious Studies* 35, no. 4 (Winter 2008): 393–410. See also Jenna Weissman Joselit, *Set in Stone: America's Embrace of the Ten Commandments* (New York: Oxford University Press, 2017).

[21] Paul Finkenrath originally founded the PFB Company, an outgrowth of Finkenrath & Grasnick, chromolitho printers in business since 1897. Its Ten Commandments postcards constituted series 8554.

shalt not steal"—suggesting that murder often begins with the desire for material goods (rather than anger and jealousy, as suggested by the Taggart card). The murderer runs away with a pistol in his hand (as opposed to the Taggart card, where the murderer holds a club) as well as a handbag, indicating that the murder was born from theft. Finally, the wording of the commandment itself—"Thou shalt do no murder"—actually comes from the King James text of Matthew 19:18 where Jesus responds to the rich young ruler's question regarding which commandments should be kept in order to obtain eternal life. This translation, along with its accompanying depiction, clearly identifies the essence of the commandment with criminal homicide, highlights it as a problem plaguing modern society rather than a relic of biblical history, and then offers a Christian solution. The sixth commandment therefore becomes a Christian effort to address a contemporary social problem, perhaps even implying that Christian ideals are the antidote to social evils.

While the previous cards depict the violation of the commandment, another one dating from at least the late 1880s gives a different presentation.[22] Following the traditional Protestant numbering, the caption reads, "The sixth commandment is, Thou shalt not kill." The artistic rendering, however, is much more abstract and serene than the previous cards. A shoreline cottage, a bird, and two red roses adorn the postcard, highlighting the peaceful and pleasant aspects of this commandment. The harsh and brutal actions associated with breaking this commandment are ignored in favor of the positive benefits of following it. For all the focus on killing that this commandment has inspired, this postcard portrays its essence as an affirmation of life and peace, resulting in a peaceful society.

All three postcards reveal the economic, religious, social, and gendered components comprising the commandment's interpretation.[23] Its commodification has helped change the way people encounter the commandment, transforming it from a black-and-white written text or invisible spoken words into a visually attractive image. Rather than being a terse legal expression or lofty moral principle, the sixth commandment is now a beautiful and colorful product that enhances the postcard's appeal. The honored status of the Ten Commandments in American society and the largely colorless nature of the available print material also contribute to the cards' marketability. The commandment's moral and religious power intertwines with its economic power to create picturesque and idealized visualizations of *male* violence (all the figures in the postcards—perpetrator and victim—are male). Nature is even incorporated into these romanticized depictions of murder. All are pictured in rural settings despite murder being a problem associated more with the period's urban areas. At the same time, though, the postcards portray the social benefits and hopes embodied in the commandment. Whereas twenty-

---

[22] This card does not identify the company that produced it, nor does it bear the date. I have estimated its date based on a handwritten note appearing on the back of the card in my possession. It includes a date of "Mar. 1889."

[23] While women do not appear in these depictions of the sixth commandment, perhaps reflecting that murder was associated primarily with male behavior, it would be interesting to know if the postcards were marketed more toward men or women and which gender was the primary purchaser.

first-century popular American culture often portrays the act of murder itself, these postcards show the aftermath, again emphasizing the benefits of keeping the commandment. These popular depictions of the sixth commandment therefore reflect how an ancient Israelite text has been transformed into a product made by and for Gilded Age Americans. Protestant Christianity and American capitalism, and more specifically, middle-class social and gender norms, have re-created and enlivened an ancient text. Its use in popular culture depends on both the ancient and modern elements.

"Thou Shalt Not Steal"

The eighth commandment was treated in similar ways to that of the sixth. An undated but early postcard with two images, one contemporary and one ancient, illustrates the prohibition against stealing. The ancient depiction portrays three "Orientals" (using the period's terminology) who have broken through a stone wall and are in the process of stealing various items, but the contemporary scene is much more innocent. A small child has been caught stealing what appears to be an apple, but once again the child as perpetrator softens the commandment's impact. In contrast, the more serious violation of the commandment is carried out by "Oriental" adult males, while the American or European violation is the product of a small boy's indiscretion. What's more, the "Orientals" appear to be getting away with their theft, but the child has been stopped, undoubtedly due to the church's influence, seen in the steeple rising up in the background. In keeping with nineteenth-century American exceptionalism, Americans commonly believed that their culture, which included Protestant Christianity, represented the highest expression of civilization. Furthermore, Americans believed it was their duty to civilize "lesser" societies, such as those of Native Americans and Asians, by converting them to Christianity and forcing upon them American ways. In the postcard, the church's civilizing influence appears to be at work among Christians but missing from non-Christian societies.

The Taggart, Tuck, and Rose postcards continue the Orientalizing of the commandment's violation. All three are quite similar, portraying an adult male dressed in "Oriental" garb fleeing with a box or boxes of valuables. The deed was committed under cover of darkness—the moon can be seen—and the individual runs through the woods, adding to the sense of treachery. In the background, a palace-type building—undoubtedly the place where the theft occurred—appears. As in previous portrayals, the American or European viewer is distanced from the condemned act, seeing it as an action taken by a cultural and chronological foreigner. Of course, no one would deny that theft existed in American or European societies, but portraying theft in an "Oriental" and even biblical context casts these cultures in a negative light and even hides the reality of theft among the more "civilized." To be fair, Taggart, Tuck, and Rose portray all ten commandments in "Oriental" fashion, with even a few in favorable scenes (such as honoring father and mother). So the intent seems aimed more at producing historically or biblically authentic renderings instead of asserting cultural superiority.

Nonetheless, this effort reinforces cultural stereotypes and portrays the commandments as historical relics rather than contemporary critiques.

PFB Publishing, however, emphasizes the modern violation with its version, portraying a brazen act of theft in a contemporary context in which a man reaches through a window into a lighted room to grab some money from an open box. It is as if the owner of the money was in the process of counting it and had briefly stepped out. While the money's owner might appear careless, the crime itself seems to be one of opportunity rather than premeditation. Whereas in the previous depictions, the thieves took the valuables while the owners were either sleeping or away, the PFB thief seems to move quickly to get what he can while the owner is gone. This thief is much more familiar than the ones appearing in the Taggart, Tuck, and Rose scenes; in many ways he looks like the viewer. The card itself seems to be warning against the kind of stealing that takes advantage of momentary lapses. The picture does not reflect an act that took a great deal of planning or stealth; an open window, a careless action, and nerve enough to reach into the room are all that is required. Yet as one considers to whom this card was being marketed—primarily the middle class—it is hard to determine what the exact message is. Is it an admonition to the viewer not to steal, or is it a middle-class statement to others not to steal their property?

Portraying and interpreting the eighth commandment in relation to its most fundamental meaning, however, was not the only way in which it was used. Two postcards use it to comment on sexual stereotypes. One shows a middle-class Victorian woman sound asleep on a hammock, vulnerable and in a position of weakness. A young man bends near to her face, but the caption, "Thou shalt not steal," reinforces Victorian boundaries between the sexes. Another comes from a series of cards entitled "The Weaker Sex." This series, in cartoon fashion, lampoons the notion that the woman is the weaker sex by showing that the woman actually exercises power over the man when it comes to romance. The woman's power is expressed in a number of ways, although stereotypically and in keeping with the period's dominant view of women. She is dressed provocatively and towers above the man, who is blindfolded. While he stands almost at attention, she bends over to kiss him. Clearly, she controls the kiss because he could never reach her. The caption is "Even when she allows you to kiss her, you're bound to feel more or less like a robber." To buttress the notion of the woman's power, a small sign states, "Thou shalt not steal kisses," or, in other words, the woman controls the situation and the man is dependent on her granting permission.

While this is clearly a secondary use of the eighth commandment, it still serves an effective purpose. Whereas the commandment's main purpose is to establish and enforce moral boundaries, particularly in regard to property, these last two cards demonstrate that it can be used to support other, previously established norms and boundaries, such as those dealing with sex and gender. In fact, it can even be used to support norms that might generally be considered at odds with the Ten Commandments. This use indicates that a biblical text's significance lies not exclusively in its fundamental meaning but also in its ability to play a supportive cultural or social role. Social and cultural forces shape and bend the biblical text to transform its meaning, while retaining its wording and basic assertion. This also reflects its cultural status because a text could not be used in this way if widespread knowledge of it did not exist. This knowledge is often used ironically, comically, or in unexpected ways, thus leaving behind the text's basic meaning. Dismissing such a use because it fails to conform to a foundational meaning, however, overlooks its power and influence. Furthermore, these popular uses demonstrate how biblical texts and economic, social, religious, gendered, and other factors shape each other.

"Thou Shalt Not Covet"

The Taggart depiction of the tenth commandment couples the King James translation of Exodus 20:17 with a picture portraying each aspect in "Oriental" terms. The complete commandment is printed at the top of the card: "Thou shalt not covet thy neighbor's house, thou shalt not covet thy neighbor's wife, nor his man-servant, nor his maid-servant, nor his ox, nor his ass, nor anything that is thy neighbor's." A man standing next to a Greek-style column gazes at another man—undoubtedly the neighbor's "man-servant"—driving a cart pulled by the neighbor's oxen, while a woman, the neighbor's "maid-servant," walks nearby, leading the neighbor's ass. In the background stands another woman—likely the neighbor's wife—and further in the distance stands the neighbor's house. Picture and text interpret each other.

The Tuck and Rose renderings also portray an "Oriental" scene, reflecting Western stereotypes of Eastern culture much more so than Taggart. Carpets, daggers, turbans, a fez, Eastern-style vases, a camel, a Turkish pipe (hookah), and a bazaar-type setting, all contribute to make this both an ancient and a foreign text. Both look more like a scene from the Ottoman Empire and as such insulate the viewer from the commandment's impact. Instead of directly confronting viewers with their own covetousness, these depictions reinforce Western stereotypes of "Orientals," particularly by portraying them as uncivilized violators of an honored code. Violence lurks in the depictions as the coveter sneaks up on the unsuspecting neighbor, brandishing a dagger. In addition, these cards clearly emphasize coveting material possessions. Following the Roman Catholic catechetical teaching, the text is given simply as "Thou shalt not covet thy neighbor's goods," avoiding any mention of the wife and therefore any connection with sexual lust. Given the "Oriental" depiction and late nineteenth- and early twentieth-century European and American imperialism and industrialism, this rendering functions as a critique of non-American and non-European culture rather than admonitions to personal behavior.

A card from PFB places the commandment in modern terms, portraying a contemporary rural scene with a man standing in front of his neighbor's house, surrounded by his neighbor's livestock. A condensed version of the text (perhaps based on the Douay-Rheims Version) reads, "Thou shalt not covet thy neighbour's house, nor his wife, nor anything that is his." The male and female servants mentioned in the biblical text do not appear, perhaps reflecting that few in the middle class could relate to having servants.

The man not only gazes upon his neighbor's wife but calls out to her with an upraised arm to get her attention. As with PFB's sixth commandment card, this depiction directly challenges the viewer. It is a pleasant and ordinary scene, demonstrating that covetousness takes on unassuming forms. Neither great wealth nor great poverty are on display, yet the man still covets and is in the process of acting on it in a way that otherwise might be considered a friendly gesture. The card visualizes middle-class covetousness and calls our attention to both the class aspects of the commandment and the seemingly innocent beginnings of covetousness.

One card, a 1905 image by Anthony Guarino published by the E. W. Gustin Company (New York), portrays a quite different aspect of coveting. It goes beyond the biblical text's emphasis on adults and their possessions and views the commandment from a child's perspective. Yet like the previous depictions, it captures the act of coveting in the gaze of the eyes, suggesting that coveting is not an act but an attitude. Here, a child with hands in pockets (not hands extended) looks desirously on a cart of apples. Taking only the first four words of the tenth commandment—"Thou shalt not covet"—this postcard gives the command its most open-ended application, even extending it to a child's desire. There is, however, nothing sinister in this depiction as in the others, no hint of theft or murder or adultery. It is a cute and sweet scene, surely causing adults to recall their childhood coveting and to sympathize with the child. In fact, one individual expressed these very sentiments in 1909 when he mailed this card with the message "I know your sympathies will be with this boy." Another person used the commandment to express her desire to be in a different place by simply writing on the front of the card underneath "Thou shalt not covet" the phrase "but I would like to be in California." In one way, the card almost invites coveting for seemingly harmless things and romanticizes the notion.

When the Gustin card is juxtaposed with previous cards, coveting's many forms become apparent, ranging from the innocent to the sinister. The popular uses of this commandment demonstrate how a variety of social and cultural factors combine to interpret the biblical commandment. American Christianity, capitalism, racial stereotypes, class, nationalism, and individual desires variously mingle with the biblical text to interpret it. They also use the biblical text to express and validate social and cultural attitudes. The commandment itself, reflecting the ancient culture from which it arose, affirms the period's patriarchy by classifying the neighbor's wife as property. The ancient and the contemporary form essential elements of these popular uses of the Bible.

FUTURE PROSPECTS AND QUESTIONS

- If we want to understand the Bible and American popular culture, we must understand the amalgam of ancient and contemporary components at work in each use. Popular culture often reflects some of the Bible's most powerful and influential uses, reminding us that the Bible is, among other things, a supremely practical book suited for use by nonspecialists. People find it useful for a variety of purposes, and these uses shape its meaning. While some of the popular presentations reflected in the postcards certainly affirm the Bible's function as an honored relic, others remind us that it functions well when it gets dirtied in the context of everyday life. Understanding these contexts in their totality represents one of the greatest methodological challenges facing those who study the Bible and American popular culture.

- Scholars can learn a lot from popular culture about the Bible and the people who use it. On the one hand, popular uses can bring out neglected aspects of the biblical text's meaning. Some of these popular innovators have a keen eye and are able to cut through centuries of interpretive traditions in order to reveal fresh insights. These often arise as biblical texts are combined and envisioned within popular notions of age, gender, ethnicity, and class. These texts therefore are particularly effective at reinforcing cultural stereotypes and asserting cultural superiority or inferiority. In the American context, the Bible acts as a conduit of American cultures and societies and is shaped by a mixture of these cultural and social forces. Methodologically, the challenge begins with realizing that these forces are not always equal, nor do they always manifest themselves in the same ways. Each unique conglomeration and its impact on the Bible must be accounted for at some point in scholarly treatments.

- On the other hand, popular culture also provides insight into the motivations involved in using certain texts. American capitalism, for example, relates to the Bible as a commodity. These postcards were created first and foremost to make a profit, and fulfilling this goal depended on their ability to appeal to large numbers of consumers. Thus they had to reflect sentiments that many people would agree with or find amusing or at least not find objectionable. Biblical texts that are used to sell products are windows into the thinking of large segments of society, revealing what these people found appealing in the Bible.[24] Americans found these texts appealing for a variety of reasons, not the least of which was what they did: affirming cultural heritage, asserting cultural superiority, commenting on cultural norms, and generating profits. Following the trails left by Americans who engaged biblical texts—and not just the ones generated by scholars—becomes a methodological imperative.

- Scholars are positioned well methodologically to achieve some of these goals. Using available methods with an eye toward braiding together and integrating their findings will help us better understand how a variety of factors function to shape biblical elements and how those elements impact American society and culture. This is a necessary step toward understanding the dynamic interrelationships

---

[24] See Linda S. Schearing and Valarie H. Ziegler, *Enticed by Eden: How Western Culture Uses, Confuses (and Sometimes Abuses) Adam and Eve* (Waco, TX: Baylor University Press, 2013), 111–32, for a discussion of how advertising finds biblical stories and symbols useful because of their status as "recognizable *cultural* artifacts."

between the Bible and American culture. The challenge will be learning to think about and understand biblical texts more holistically rather than using methods only to slice and dice them. This will call on scholars not only to expand their range of focus to see beyond the text's words and consider how the many facets related to particular uses of biblical texts function as part of the text itself, but also to accept this as part of the interpretive process.

SUGGESTED READINGS AND ANNOTATED BIBLIOGRAPHY

Abraham, Ibrahim. "Would You Adam and Eve It? Social Scientific Contributions to the Study of the Reception of Scripture in Consumer Society." *Bible & Critical Theory* 10, no. 2 (2014): 32–42.

As a sociologist of religion and contemporary culture, Abraham makes a strong argument that the study of the reception of the Bible and popular culture must use methodologies that engage the cultures that produce and consume popular culture. In doing so, he contends that biblical scholars must surrender their "privileged interpretive position." It is thought provoking!

Crossley, James G. "On Reception History, Audiences, and Disciplinary Assumptions: A Response to Ibrahim Abraham." *Relegere: Studies in Religion and Reception* 4, no. 2 (2014): 241–58.

Here, Crossley responds to an essay by Abraham that was included in a book titled *Reception History and Biblical Studies: Theory and Practice*.[25] Challenging Abraham's argument that reception history should embrace social scientific approaches over others traditionally used in biblical studies, Crossley also discusses how disciplinary assumptions influence our understanding of the reception of biblical texts. Crossley's and Abraham's articles reveal some of the important methodological issues confronting scholars of the Bible and popular culture.

Culbertson, Philip, and Elaine M. Wainwright. *The Bible in/and Popular Culture: A Creative Encounter*. Atlanta, GA: Society of Biblical Literature, 2010.

In this significant work on the Bible and popular culture, a number of important scholars working in the field showcase different ways to approach the topic. The book's overriding framework organizes the essays according to the genre and media in which biblical texts, ideas, and images are used, primarily literature, music, and "other media." Two helpful responses round out the collection focusing on the Bible's role as "pre-text" for popular culture and the phenomenon of "pop scripture."

McDannell, Colleen. *Material Christianity: Religion and Popular Culture in America*. New Haven, CT: Yale University Press, 1995.

While this book's focus is on the material aspects of American Christianity, the Bible's role and presence can be found throughout, including a chapter devoted completely to the Bible in the Victorian home. The book provides excellent methodological examples of understanding America's popular culture through its material artifacts.

---

[25] Abraham's chapter (to which Crossley is responding) is "High, Low and In-between: Reception History and the Sociology of Religion and Popular Music," in *Reception History and Biblical Studies: Theory and Practice*, ed. Emma England and William John Lyons, Scriptural Traces, 6 / Library of Hebrew Bible / Old Testament Studies, 615 (London: T&T Clark, 2015), 241-253.

Thompson, Martyn P. "Reception Theory and the Interpretation of Historical Meaning." *History and Theory* 32, no. 3 (October 1993): 248–72.

An excellent article explaining and engaging some of the foundational ideas and theories related to reception history. Thompson demonstrates the various disagreements among scholars, particularly those who emphasize the reader's role in creating meaning and those who embrace the author's or text's role. Thompson finds value in both approaches. This article will acquaint the reader with some of the fundamental theoretical issues.

CHAPTER 29

TEACHING BIBLE AND AMERICAN POPULAR CULTURE

JANE S. WEBSTER
SCHOOL OF HUMANITIES, BARTON
COLLEGE (RETIRED)

INTRODUCTION

MOST colleges and universities in America offer religious studies courses of some sort; an American Academy of Religion survey in 2005 shows that the most common focus on the biblical text.[1] Most of us who teach undergraduate religious studies courses use textbooks that deal with the Bible as an objective historical artifact, addressing questions of authorship, social context, dating, purpose, and genre.[2] While we can find common ground with most students in this way, we often overlook opportunities for subjective transformative learning, in which all our students are fully engaged in discovering, evaluating, and describing their own responses to cultural forces, comparing them to others', and creating ethical solutions or alternatives. We also miss the chance to engage students with bigger questions, such as the nature of authority, the construction of identity, and the contextualization of truth, leading them to consider ways to become more responsible citizens. Perhaps it is time to reconsider our approach to teaching the Bible.

---

[1] "AAR Undergraduate Departments Survey Shows Increases in Religious Studies," *Religious Studies News*, May 2008, 11–2; "Focus on the Undergraduate Study of Religion," http://rsnonline.org/images/pdfs/2008may.pdf; https://www.aarweb.org/common/Uploaded%20files/Data%20and%20Studies/Surveys/2008RSNMayFocusIssue(1).pdf

[2] Collin Cornell and Joel M. LeMon, "How We Teach Introductory Bible Courses: A Comparative and Historical Sampling," *Teaching Theology and Religion* 19, no. 2 (2016): 114–42.

In this chapter, I focus on teaching the Bible in dialogue with American popular culture mainly in the secular college and university setting, providing suggestions for course design specifically addressing student learning outcomes, ways to sequence learning activities, and ideas for assessment. I frame this in the language of accrediting agencies and national organizations engaged in higher education and draw generously from the scholarship of teaching and learning. Those who teach in seminaries might borrow some of these strategies and/or adapt them to their own goals, adjusting to their own accrediting agencies. Those who teach within faith communities might use the strategies to generate theological discussions, such as the nature of God or their response to ethical challenges.

OVERVIEW OF TOPIC

Teaching has undergone some remarkable developments in the past twenty years or so. At least, I hope it has! Gone are the days when we merely "profess"; now we must actually teach so that students learn. Standing at the front of the room and reading from lecture notes or PowerPoint presentations—what has been dubbed "the Sage from the Stage" model of teaching—has not received terrific learning reviews. In fact, the research shows that students might find the topic and the elucidation enthralling and captivating and even entertaining, but they are unlikely to remember much content or argument past the end of the semester; they have not experienced transformative learning.[3]

Learning how to teach has become a significant obligation for those who take up the professing profession. While some of us might receive training in pedagogy in graduate school, many more of us will pick up what we need to know while serving as teaching assistants. Unfortunately, as new faculty, we will often model our first independent forays into teaching on what we ourselves experienced as learners. What we might be forgetting—what I forgot—was that we were model students, eager to learn, to do the reading and then some, to spend hours on homework, to discuss new learning with friends and family, and to be troubled by anything but perfection. We may find that most of our students do not approach education with the same passion as we did: our students might have to care for family members, work full time, or share textbooks; they may see their college years as a rite of passage or as a ticket to a better career but certainly not as an education. Our students might not be self-directed; they might give up too easily. So often we are responsible not only for teaching biblical content but for teaching students how to learn, a job for which almost none of us has training.

---

[3] Among others, Patricia Cross, "Teaching for Learning," *AAHE Bulletin* 39, no. 8 (1987): 3–7, claims that "when students are actively involved in the learning task, they learn more than when they are passive recipients of instruction." See also, for example, Scott Freeman et al., "Active Learning Increases Student Performance in Science, Engineering, and Mathematics," *Proceedings of the National Academy of Sciences of the United States of America* 111, no. 23 (2014): 8410–5.

Furthermore, we are not always aware of what our students want to learn. In her study, Barbara Walvoord found that college students take introductory courses in religious studies to understand something about themselves and their culture, and not, as we often hope, to develop critical thinking skills.[4] Sharon Daloz Parks concurs, arguing that most college students are on a spiritual quest and seek to understand their role as an individual in their larger community.[5] The Higher Education Research Institute (HERI) at UCLA has conducted extensive studies of college students, finding that most students have "very high levels of spiritual interest and involvement. Many are actively engaged in a spiritual quest and in exploring the meaning and purpose of life.... They place great value on their college enhancing their self-understanding, helping them develop personal values, and encouraging the expression of spirituality."[6] In a later publication, HERI studies demonstrate statistically that college students who engage questions of "spiritual quest" (identity, meaning, and purpose) have more success across the curriculum: "*Spiritual growth enhances other college outcomes*, such as academic performance, psychological well-being, leadership development, and satisfaction with college."[7] How might we design a course to enable our students' spiritual quest productively and at the same time evaluate their learning? Most instructors will either focus on skills—such as critical thinking or written communication—or on religious literacy. The challenge here is to develop ways to teach the literacy and the skills but to leave space in the classroom for students to explore their own position on spiritual matters.

Students will be more likely to engage in a spiritual quest in a biblical studies classroom when they feel the space is safe. They are more likely to open themselves to learning opportunities when they feel free of ridicule or denigration, when they do not feel pressure to conform or commit to a particular religious viewpoint, and when they do not fear it is wrong or dangerous to question religious beliefs. They are more likely to engage when they are exposed to a variety of settings and have different kinds of interactions: large and small class discussions, student-led conversations, interaction with visitors, email, online forums, writing assignments with comments, office-hour conversations, and field trips. They might develop their voice by articulating their own beliefs and by taking on another role, such as listener, devil's advocate, or group facilitator.[8] When they feel it is safe to test out their understanding openly, students are more likely to engage both spiritual quest and transformative learning.

Students are more likely to engage in the study of the Bible if they understand why they should learn about it, even if they are not religiously committed. Students will learn

---

[4] Barbara Walvoord, *Teaching and Learning in College Introductory Religion Courses* (Malden MA: Blackwell, 2008).

[5] Sharon Daloz Parks, *Big Questions, Worthy Dreams: Mentoring Emerging Adults in Their Search for Meaning, Purpose, and Faith* (San Francisco: John Wiley & Sons, 2000), 10.

[6] Higher Education Research Institute, "The Spiritual Life of College Students: A National Study of College Students' Search for Meaning and Purpose," 2005, 3, https://spirituality.ucla.edu/docs/reports/Spiritual_Life_College_Students_Full_Report.pdf

[7] Alexander W. Astin, Helen S. Astin, and Jennifer A. Lindholm, *Cultivating the Spirit: How College Can Enhance Students' Inner Lives* (San Francisco: Jossey-Bass, 2011), 10, emphasis original.

[8] Walvoord, *Teaching and Learning*, 8–9.

more deeply if they know that the Bible has been instrumental in forming their society and shaping their culture. They will be more motivated if they understand that others will use biblical motifs to persuade and manipulate them; they will learn to become informed and empowered consumers of culture. They will also be informed of the biblical—and religious—forces at work in their political environment, rational or not. Students who are learning how to make decisions about their own future will have an urgent need to be able to interpret the forces that affect their choices. As many American students are immersed in a predominantly Christian culture, when they learn about the Bible they are also learning about their own tradition, making sense of the disparate facts and stories they might have absorbed from their environment. As emerging adults, they will gain biblical literacy as a relevant life skill.

We can be more effective as teachers when we tap into the intrinsic goals of students by designing courses that bring spiritual quest and biblical (religious) literacy into the forefront. But we might also integrate other learning outcomes that arise from external sources. Based on extensive input from educators and employers, the Association of American Colleges & Universities (AAC&U) identified a series of essential learning outcomes.[9] Probably the two most central outcomes for the agenda of a biblical studies course are

- Gaining "knowledge of human cultures" through focused engagement with big questions, both contemporary and enduring.
- Gaining personal and social responsibility through "intercultural knowledge and competence," anchored by active involvement with diverse communities and real-world challenges."[10]

The AAC&U challenges us to create learning opportunities that prepare all students for engagement with the subject material that goes far beyond learning content; students work with content to solve problems creatively, to reflect on ethical and social dimensions, and to develop strong communication skills.[11] We can no longer justify our course content with "You just need to know this stuff." We need to design courses that link the content to real-world application that students find meaningful, robust, and

---

[9] AAC&U, "Essential Learning Outcomes," accessed June 1, 2020, http://aacu.org/leap/essential-learning-outcomes. See also AAC&U, "College Learning for the New Global Century," 2007, https://www.aacu.org/sites/default/files/files/LEAP/GlobalCentury_final.pdf.

[10] J. M. Bennett, "Transformative Training: Designing Programs for Culture Learning," in *Contemporary Leadership and Intercultural Competence: Understanding and Utilizing Cultural Diversity to Build Successful Organizations*, ed. M. A. Moodian (Thousand Oaks, CA: Sage, 2008), 95–110. See also AAC&U, "Intercultural Knowledge and Competence VALUE Rubric," accessed June 1, 2020, https://www.aacu.org/value/rubrics/intercultural-knowledge.

[11] Carol Geary Schneider, "The LEAP Challenge: Transforming for Students, Essential for Liberal Education," *Liberal Education* 101, nos. 1–2 (Winter–Spring 2015), https://www.aacu.org/liberaleducation/2015/winter-spring/schneider; AAC&U, "The LEAP Challenge," https://www.aacu.org/leap-challenge

socially engaging. And perhaps more important, we need to use the student learning outcomes like a compass to direct students consistently to these goals.

The AAC&U also provides rubrics that we can use to assess learning.[12] Intercultural knowledge and competence, for example, should go "beyond mere exposure to culturally different others" to "meaningfully engage those others, place social justice in historical and political context, and put culture at the core of transformative learning."[13] With the rubric, they recommend a systematic way to measure the "capacity to identify our own cultural patterns, compare and contrast them with others, and adapt empathically and flexibly to unfamiliar ways of being." These are the most relevant goals of student learning in biblical studies, according to the rubric:

- Cultural self-awareness: Articulates insights into own cultural rules and biases (e.g. seeking complexity; aware of how her/his experiences have shaped these rules, and how to recognize and respond to cultural biases, resulting in a shift in self-description.)
- Knowledge of cultural worldview frameworks: Demonstrates sophisticated understanding of the complexity of elements important to members of another culture in relation to its history, values, politics, communication styles, economy, or beliefs and practices.
- Empathy: Interprets intercultural experience from the perspectives of [one's] own and more than one worldview and demonstrates ability to act in a supportive manner that recognizes the feelings of another cultural group.
- Verbal and nonverbal communication: Articulates a complex understanding of cultural differences in verbal and nonverbal communication . . . and is able to skillfully negotiate a shared understanding based on those differences.
- Curiosity: Asks complex questions about other cultures, seeks out and articulates answers to these questions that reflect multiple cultural perspectives.
- Openness: Initiates and develops interactions with culturally different others. Suspends judgment in valuing her/his interactions with culturally different others.[14]

In a course in Bible and American pop culture, students may thus be encouraged to dive deeply into cultural self-awareness, to explore "cultural rules and biases," to develop

[12] A rubric is a matrix that describes varying levels of success in multiple categories, often keyed to a grade. They are useful in evaluating work as they provide students with clear descriptions of what success looks like and gives them feedback on where they are in the continuum of success and what they need to do to improve. For templates and models, see Rubistar, rubistar.4teachers.org, or UW-Stout, "Creating and Using Rubrics for Assessment," accessed June 1, 2020, http://www.uwstout.edu/soe/profdev/rubrics.cfm.

[13] AAC&U, "Intercultural Knowledge and Competence VALUE Rubric.".https://www.aacu.org/value/rubrics/intercultural-knowledge

[14] AAC&U, "Intercultural Knowledge and Competence VALUE Rubric," accessed June 1, 2020, https://www.aacu.org/sites/default/files/files/VALUE/InterculturalKnowledge.pdf.

the ability to interpret their experience from their own worldview, to communicate it, to ask complex questions about it, to compare it to the experiences of other cultural groups, and to create socially responsible solutions or alternatives. As they learn more about themselves and their social context and reflect on what works and what does not, they become more thoughtful citizens, transformed through learning.

From these possible transformative learning outcomes we select a few target outcomes for our course, taking into consideration the level of the course (introductory, reinforced, or emphasized) and the other courses in the program of study. We then might decide what assessment will demonstrate that students have achieved that outcome—such as a cumulative project or essay—and design a rubric that will measure success at various levels. Then we "design backwards," inserting learning opportunities in sequence to lead students to success—a process called "scaffolding."[15] So if we require students to evaluate the cultural impact of a particular artifact, we may need to scaffold their learning to find an artifact, to identify it properly (cite sources, etc.), to analyze its features using language appropriate for the discipline, to identify and evaluate its ethical use, to make a personal decision about it, and to generate or propose a more ethical alternative. These learning tasks can be organized to build on one another throughout the course with measurements of learning and opportunities for recovery along the way. Consider giving frequent low-stakes formative assessments—where students can dare to fail without huge consequences—and less frequent high-stakes summative assessments that synthesize learning throughout the course. Build more complex thinking into the course design; drawing on Bloom's Revised Taxonomy, incorporate these learning skills: remember, understand, apply, analyze, evaluate, and create.[16] When all this is mapped explicitly into the course design, students will know where they are going and how they are progressing and will take responsibility for their own learning.

Studies in teaching and learning claim that students learn more when they *discover* understanding on their own rather than listening to someone *uncover* it *for* them. In *Teaching with Your Mouth Shut*, Donald L. Finkel urges us to set up students to engage the content thoroughly by themselves, to work out the issues on their own, and to reflect on what they learn in their social, emotional, and intellectual dimensions.[17] He recommends, as one example, the open-ended seminar in which all students participate in an exchange of questions and ideas without our preordained conclusions or overmanage-

---

[15] For backwards design, see Grant Wiggins and Jay McTighe, *Understanding by Design*, expanded 2nd ed. (Upper Saddle River, NJ: Prentice Hall, 2005). For backwards design in biblical studies, see G. Brooke Lester, Jane S. Webster, and Christopher M. Jones, *Understanding Bible by Design: Create Courses with Purpose* (Minneapolis, MN: Fortress, 2014).

[16] Developed by educators in conferences from 1949 to 1953 and published in 1959, 1964, and revised in 2001, Bloom's Revised Taxonomy is attributed to Benjamin Bloom, who edited the first volume of the standard text, *Taxonomy of Educational Objectives: The Classification of Educational Goals* (1956). See also Iowa State University, "Revised Bloom's Taxonomy (Flash Version)," accessed June 1, 2020, http://www.celt.iastate.edu/teaching/effective-teaching-practices/revised-blooms-taxonomy/revised-blooms-taxonomy-flash-version.

[17] Donald L. Finkel, *Teaching with Your Mouth Shut* (Portsmouth, NH: Boyton, Cook, Heinemann, 2000).

ment. We should, he suggests, sit down at the table and refrain from "telling" students; instead, we might ask, "What do you think?" or "What do you guess might be the answer?"

We advocate learning when we slow the conversation, ask questions, reclaim focus, assert civility of discourse, and summarize main ideas at the end of the class. When we refrain from telling, students will seek to make discoveries themselves: they will ask focused questions, reexamine their text, identify contradictions, apply understanding to new contexts, and test theories for coherence. Or, as Finkel claims, students can figure out for themselves "the things that matter most without consulting cultural Authorities."[18] The challenge then is to design a problem that students can solve by applying various skills to the content of the Bible. If we keep "one eye on the nature of the student population and another on the spirit of the times, [we] can usually forge a connection between actual student interests and the problem that defines the inquiry."[19] Do we need to understand the Bible today? Does the Bible matter to nonreligious people? Should the Bible be taught in a humanities program? Our role as teacher in this case is not to have solved the problem first but to be an inquirer with the student, to organize the inquiry by assigning readings or tasks, to understand how to analyze texts and cultural artifacts of any sort, to help students learn, to help students develop the tools they will need, and to assign grades.[20] Finkel also recommends that we use one main teaching strategy throughout the course to help students develop confidence in the *process* of learning. For example, we might give a series of tests or writing assignments that have the same prompt but with different content features, such as this: "Describe how [a cultural artifact] challenges or supports biblical values and why it matters." We facilitate students' learning by making the process itself explicit, asking such metacognitive questions as "What example helped you to understand that concept?" or "As you were writing about this idea, how did you develop your thesis?" or "What questions do you ask yourself when you are trying to understand the implications of your decisions?" With these teaching strategies, we shift the responsibility of learning to the students, helping them to transform themselves through self-directed inquiry.[21]

Furthermore, as we link transformative learning outcomes and assessment strategies, we might consider what meta-question our course might answer.[22] Meta-questions are

[18] Ibid., 36.   [19] Ibid., 55.

[20] Ibid., 59. For a specific example using problem-based learning in biblical studies, see Jane S. Webster, "Teaching Oppression without Oppressing the Student: A Hands-Off Approach through Problem-Based Learning," in "Teaching Oppressive Texts," by Claudia Camp, Jane S. Webster, and Rannfrid Thelle, *Teaching Theology and Religion* 16, no. 3 (2013): 256–73, here 261–7.

[21] For other excellent resources on student-centered learning, see Maryellen Weimer, *Learner-Centered Teaching: Five Key Changes to Practice*, 2nd ed. (San Francisco: Jossey-Bass, 2013); Susan A. Ambrose et al., *How Learning Works: Seven Research-Based Principles for Smart Teaching* (San Francisco: John Wiley, 2010); L. Dee Fink, *Creating Significant Learning Experiences: An Integrated Approach to Designing College Courses*, 2nd ed. (San Francisco: Jossey-Bass, 2013).

[22] See http://seminariumblog.org/general/semclass/websterj42013/; Jane S. Webster, "Teaching with Meta-Questions," in *Teaching the Bible in the Liberal Arts Classroom*, ed. Jane S. Webster and Glenn S. Holland (Sheffield, UK: Sheffield Phoenix, 2012), 217–22.

those which are open-ended and multidimensional; they can be answered and enriched when asked by different disciplines; they can be informed by research and reflection and are relevant to all inquirers. A meta-question wonders why we ask the question in the first place. Here are some examples:

> What is the nature of authority in American life?
> How does pop culture inform decisions we make today?
> How do we interpret culture?
> Who has the right to speak authoritatively about meaning?
> What is truth (truthiness)?
> What is our moral obligation to the world?
> What is an excellent life?
> What is an honorable person?
> What is integrity?
> What does it mean to be a responsible citizen?

These are age-old philosophical questions but are not often nor obviously applied in the religious studies classroom. But as a central recurring feature of course design they lend coherence and relevance to a course.

Finally, although I do not treat it separately in what follows but assume it will be brought into service as appropriate, we might consider how technology will facilitate student learning. Using online resources and applications, students can choose the time, place, and social context to engage and/or create cultural artifacts.

To summarize some principles for effective course design in biblical studies: students will often become self-motivated learners when they have a clear and urgent problem to solve, especially if they see this problem as urgent and personal for them. In this way, they are more motivated if they are given an authentic real-world task and can track their own growth. When we are explicit about the aims of the course and about how they might be accomplished and assessed, and when we encourage students to discover their own understanding, students will take more responsibility for their own learning and have a more transformative learning experience. With this framework in place, let us now turn to some of the ways to bring popular culture into dialogue with the Bible.

Specific Examples and/or Foci: Approaches to and Examples of Teaching the Bible and Popular Culture

We cannot assume our students know much about the Bible. In a 2010 Pew Forum on Religion and Public Life survey of the G-8 countries, Americans ranked first, at 58 percent, when asked if religion is important in their lives (compared to the next highest, Canada, at 29 percent). Yet in a survey of religious knowledge, a battery of questions about the Bible and Christianity, world religions, and religion in public life, scores were appallingly low across the board, with respondents averaging around 50 percent; those taking a college-level religion course scored only 3 points over the national average.[23] Therefore we will probably need to teach some basic content. For example, we might have to demonstrate how to find the assigned reading in the Bible, explaining the chapter and verse conventions. We might need to offer foundational information on the geographical and historical contexts of significant biblical narratives, characters, motifs, and genres. Or we might choose to allow students to discover their own knowledge gaps, to answer their own questions, and/or to provide instruction just when they need it.

College students may not know much about the Bible, but they probably are very familiar with some aspects of American popular culture, including but not limited to art, film, music, drama, television, literature, comics, cartoons, games, and dance. They might want to develop their cultural literacy and social capital by developing their ability to talk about popular culture with more confidence and elegance. They can tap into multiple learning preferences, such as spatial (visual, images), bodily kinesthetic, or musical, which builds confidence and thus engagement.[24] They can often acquire knowledge of popular culture effortlessly. (It is easier to watch a thirty-second advertisement than to read a few chapters of the Bible or a twenty-page academic essay.) If students are not inclined to read voraciously, they might engage reading when they find topics that interest them, and then develop good reading habits in general. Students are more likely to want to learn more deeply about things that are already on their horizon and that are easier for them to grasp and access, so bringing popular culture into dialogue with the Bible is an effective teaching strategy for transformative learning.

We can engage the Bible and American pop culture at different levels within a course. Some choose to focus on biblical literacy using occasional cultural artifacts to make it more memorable or to make a point. For example, I have used the online Brick Testament to challenge students' uncritical acceptance of Joshua's Canaanite ethnocide[25] and images of Superman to challenge understandings of Jesus.[26] Some instructors occasionally use their students' familiarity with popular culture to illuminate a biblical concept. For example, Brent A. Strawn uses the hip-hop concept of covers or sampling in music to explain biblical and Near East parallels.[27] Some instructors design courses

---

[23]   Pew Research Center, Religion and Public Life, "An Overview of the Pew Forum Survey, Results and Implications," September 28, 2010, http://www.pewforum.org/2010/09/28/us-religious-knowledge-an-overview-of-the-pew-forum-survey-results-and-implications/; Alan Levinovitz, "Americans—Not Just Liberals—Have a Religious Literacy Problem," Vox, January 5, 2017, http://www.vox.com/first-person/2017/1/5/14166366/religious-illiteracy-conservative-liberal.

[24]   See Howard Gardner, *Multiple Intelligences: The Theory in Practice* (New York: Basic, 1993) and *Intelligence Reframed: Multiple Intelligences for the 21st Century* (New York: Basic, 1999).

[25]   See the website of Brick Testament, http://www.thebricktestament.com/.

[26]   For an examination of the religious and scriptural potentialities in the origin story of Superman, see Dan W. Clanton, Jr., "The Origin(s) of Superman: Reimagining Religion in the Man of Steel," in *Religion and Popular Culture in America*, 3rd ed., ed. Bruce David Forbes and Jeffrey H. Mahan (Oakland: University of California Press, 2017), 33–50.

[27]   Brent A. Strawn, "Genesis, Gilgamesh, and 'Gettin' Jiggy Wit It': Ancient Near East Parallels, Scripture, and Hip Hop Sampling," in "Technology, Pedagogy, and Transformation in Theological Education: Five Case Studies," by Steve Delamater et al., *Teaching Theology and Religion* 10, no. 2 (2007): 64–79, here 66–9.

that focus on one type of popular culture engaging the Bible; such courses might be called Bible in Film, in Art, or in Literature, and might include skill development in film, art, and literature analysis.[28] Yet others use a theme to organize their course, such as the Bible and Women, or Violence, or Poverty, or Food, which also includes elements of popular culture. In this way, instructors use popular culture to punctuate or to organize a course.

We might also choose cultural artifacts that interact with the Bible at different levels of transparency. Some instructors use artifacts that retell biblical narratives and attempt to reproduce the "real" sociohistorical context, such as Mel Gibson's *The Passion of the Christ* or Michelangelo's *Last Supper*; they might use these types of artifacts to invite explorations of historical context and interpretive bias. Others focus on the image of the Bible as a prop (for example, *Sling Blade* or *The Scarlet Letter*) and use these artifacts to prompt students to examine the issues and nature of constructing authority. Others focus on less obvious biblical narratives, motifs and characters, such as the Christ figures in *The Truman Show* or *The Lion King*; they might lead students to discover more implicit or nuanced lines of authority in popular culture. These strategies might be used periodically throughout a course or consistently with scaffolding to lead students from explicit to more implicit cultural artifacts addressing biblical content.

Some of these cultural artifacts themselves confront the Bible differently. In some cases, cultural artifacts attempt to promote traditional biblical interpretations, such as Gustav Doré's biblical illustrations. Contemporary sword-and-sandal musicals and dramas such as *Jesus Christ Superstar*, *Godspell*, and *Jesus of Montreal*, on the other hand, critique traditional interpretations; they attempt to make Jesus more hip and invite students to identify with him and his challenges, or to wonder what Jesus would be like if he was around today. Other artifacts call the biblical story into question, such as Scorsese's *Last Temptation of Christ*, which wonders how a divine Jesus deals with human temptation, or Kevin Smith's *Dogma*, which raises a score of biblical controversies. Others disorient and subvert the message of the biblical text, calling values into question; for example, George Segal's statue *Sacrifice of Isaac* located at Princeton University calls into question American willingness to sacrifice its children in the Vietnam War. Other artifacts layer a contemporary concern over a biblical narrative to lend their agenda an aura of authority. Both *The Lion King* and *The Prince of Egypt* consecrate the quest for identity and maturity, and Cecil B. DeMille's *The Ten Commandments* eases the integration of Jews into American Christian society by making Moses look and speak more like Jesus. In other words, we can invite students to notice how popular culture approaches the Bible differently.

What do we do with these cultural artifacts in the classroom? It is important to avoid using popular culture to "fill time in the classroom," "to entertain," and to give students

---

[28]   Matthew S. Rindge urges teachers not to "proof text" films but to respect the aesthetic integrity of films, concluding that courses should be called Bible *and* Film. See his "Teaching the Bible and Film: Pedagogical Promises, Pitfalls, and Proposals," *Teaching Theology and Religion* 13, no. 2 (2010): 140–55, here 145.

"something else to do." Instead, we might consider ways to "flip the classroom," making content available online and using the class time for active learning; that is, we invite students to do something other than listen, watch, and take notes.[29] We might ask them to work in groups with some prepared discussion questions, think-pair-share, present ideas to each other, practice a skill, solve a problem, or create an artifact.[30] These strategies should be explicitly linked to the student learning outcomes and always debriefed. In other words, invite students to capture what they have learned, how they learned it, why it was important to learn, and where they need to go next. When we explicitly link every class experience to the learning outcome related to the cultural artifact, we help students stay on track, stimulate their intrinsic motivation, and set clear expectations before them. We prepare students for transformative learning.

No matter how the Bible and popular culture come together in a course, we should consider what meta-question connects the various pieces: What is the purpose or impact of examining the Bible in conversation with popular culture? Does pop culture overwhelm, actualize, or recontextualize the biblical text? How does it reconfigure its precursors? How does this new artifact affect the readings of other artifacts? Is the aura of the original lost, enhanced, or brought into new configurations? How important is context to the origin and interpretation of cultural artifacts? How does the biblical text provoke us to reconsider cultural artifacts?

In "Teaching Biblical Tourism: How Sword-and-Sandal Films Clouded My Vision," Alice Bach describes how she first used film to entice student interest but learned that she was "reaffirming the 'truthiness' of biblical narratives";[31] as a result, she shifted her focus to challenge students to be suspicious of biblical narratives communicated in film. In this way, she is moving students along Bloom's Taxonomy from remembering and understanding (paying attention to film locations, costumes, plot, characters, etc.) to analyzing (why add or omit details from the biblical account, cast this actor, etc.), evaluating (what effect do these choices make), and considering the impact of films on political and social consciousness (what does this interpretation say about current events).

To put Bach's idea to work, we might consider how Scorsese's *Last Temptation of Christ* raises thoughtful questions about Jesus's purpose and his struggle with being "fully human." Students can compare Scorsese's interpretation with the gospel accounts, note differences, interpret the value of omissions and deletions, and evaluate the overall effect of the film and how Scorsese attempts to engage contemporary American world-

---

[29] See José Antonio Bowen, *Teaching Naked: How Moving Technology Out of Your College Classroom Will Improve Student Learning* (San Francisco: John Wiley, 2012), or this TED Talk on the same subject: https://www.youtube.com/watch?v=HpdUyw_vJcU. Many students decline to purchase textbooks because of their high cost. More and more teachers are using online sources to lower student costs and increase access to primary and secondary sources.

[30] See, for example, T. A. Angelo and K. P. Cross, *Classroom Assessment Techniques: A Handbook for College Teachers*, 2nd ed. (San Francisco: Jossey-Bass, 1993).

[31] Alice Bach, "Teaching Biblical Tourism: How Sword-and-Sandal Films Clouded My Vision," in *Teaching Religion and Film*, ed. Gregory J. Watkins (New York: Oxford University Press, 2008), 57–76, here 58.

views. Is he, for example, attempting to loosen American norms of sexuality (see how even Jesus was tempted and gave in?) or to reaffirm women's primary role as seductress or nurturer? How does this speak to American self-understanding in 1988? Invite them to guess first, then to look at the significant backlash against the film when it was released. Invite students to take on the role of a film producer and write a letter to Scorsese inviting an updated version of the film to account for contemporary cultural differences: to do it "this way instead."[32] Or invite them to take the role of a school board member and write an opinion arguing for or against using *The Last Temptation* in a high school film course. Students might reflect on the role of film to shape religious, political, or social mores, values, and aspirations. Many excellent volumes are available that analyze films and draw out useful lines of inquiry. Some are organized by film, others by biblical citation or biblical character.[33]

The use of art in the classroom is often more complicated for contemporary students, usually because classic art is less familiar than contemporary films; they may need to learn the language and analytical tools of art analysis. For that very reason, it is worth experimenting with the use of art in the classroom. Again, the internet has given more students access to all sorts of art forms, and some websites organize images with very searchable categories. For example, Biblical Art on the WWW (www.biblical-art.com) lists art by biblical reference, character, artist, and by keyword; the website Art and the Bible (http://www.artbible.info/) reproduces the biblical text and inserts representational art. Art is available for high-resolution viewing through museum and gallery sites as well. Resources to interpret art are also readily available, as are volumes using art to teach biblical studies. In my Old Testament course, I invite students to act out "the short play" of Susanna and the Elders (the biblical text is the script) so they can physically experience the story. I ask them "Who is to blame?" Their ready answer is "The elders!" Then I show them a series of art titled "Susanna and the Elders" and ask them the same question. Sadly, they usually conclude, "Susanna is to be blamed." They have learned that an artist's perspective and historical context shapes an interpretation; they learn easily then that an author's rendering of a story is also shaped by their cultural context.[34] In another course, I invite students to perform an exegesis and research on a biblical

[32] Educators often use RAFT assignments to encourage students to think about various perspectives: Role of the Writer: Who are you as the writer? A movie star? The president? A plant? Audience: To whom are you writing? A senator? Yourself? A company? Format: In what format are you writing? A diary entry? A newspaper? A love letter? Topic: What are you writing about? See Cathy Allen Simon, "Using the RAFT Writing Strategy," Read Write Think, accessed June 1, 2020, http://www.readwritethink .org/professional-development/strategy-guides/using-raft-writing-strategy-30625.html. This format can also be used to assign students creative projects, such as videos, music, or games. For example, see Barnard College, "Reacting to the Past," accessed June 1, 2020, https://reacting.barnard.edu/.

[33] See the extensive bibliography in Mark Roncace and Patrick Gray, eds., *Teaching the Bible through Popular Culture and the Arts* (Atlanta, GA: Society of Biblical Literature, 2007), 92–6. A particularly useful book for teachers is Jeffrey L. Staley and Richard Walsh, *Jesus, the Gospels, and Cinematic Imagination: A Handbook to Jesus on DVD* (Louisville, KY: Westminster John Knox Press, 2007).

[34] See Jane S. Webster, "The Art of Susanna and the Elders," *Bible Odyssey*, March 9, 2017, https://www.bibleodyssey.org/en/people/related-articles/art-of-susanna-and-the-elders.aspx.

woman, identifying the bias of both the biblical text and the interpreters. They gather art forms of the character to compare interpretations of bias. Then they create their own art form, flipping the bias without departing from the biblical text: if the woman is usually portrayed as a vulnerable victim, the students might create an artistic rendering that makes her strong and resourceful. (I leave this aspect open so they can experiment; even the most unartistic student can use Photoshop or find an image they can use to make their point.) They present their findings to the class and write an essay explaining their choices. They frame their essay with a reflection on the bigger questions of the construction and evaluation of bias, biblical authority, and/or gender and how they have transformed their thinking as a result. Students thus learn the skills of exegesis, research, analysis, evaluation, written and oral communication, and innovation to explore essential meta-questions; the impact is transformative.

Another way to bring biblical ideas and American popular culture into dialogue is to use a cultural phenomenon to illuminate a biblical motif. One sensational phenomenon is Eve Ensler's *The Vagina Monologues*, a series of short first-person narratives wherein women describe their experience of and identity centered on their sexual anatomy; many colleges and universities across America feature their own students performing these monologues to raise awareness of violence against women. Several years ago, I designed a course using this play as a starting point, inviting students to generate a "Vagina Monologue" in the voice of a biblical woman. Students turned in formative writing assignments describing their research, observations of social mores and statistics at their college and local environment, and their emotional responses and the responses of others not in the course; they learned why this topic was both urgent and relevant to them. In class, they reported their findings and discussed the power of biblical authority, the construction of bias, and the need to face uncomfortable topics. As their summative assessment, they performed their original monologue before an audience, answered questions, and led discussions.[35] In this project, students learned about the Bible and its biases; they learned how to research the woman, her context in the canon, and the history of interpretation; they learned how to create something "authoritative" (because it was linked to a biblical text) that raised awareness and communicated a clear sociopolitical agenda but was also edgy; and they learned how to write effectively. All the students in the course claimed that they were transformed by this learning experience.

Note that, in these examples, students are analyzing either a biblical text or a cultural artifact, comparing interpretive choices, and evaluating the impact of those choices. When they create their own artifact, they learn more about the role of the cultural interpreter. A key to transformative learning here is to invite students to reflect on why *they* made the choices they did and what the implications of those choices might be.

---

[35] Some of these monologues were published in Kathryn Blanchard and Jane S. Webster, eds., *Lady Parts: Biblical Women and the Vagina Monologues* (Eugene, OR: Wipf & Stock, 2012).

Future Prospects and Questions

- As much as the art of professing has changed in the past few decades, we anticipate it will change again dramatically. Where I was once taught by professors lecturing to a room of students, I was expected to teach using active-learning techniques and to shut my mouth. Now I have the added challenge to develop vibrant online learning communities, meeting students literally where they are. While the basic principles of course design and learning outcomes may remain the same, as instructors we may need to develop expertise in online educational strategies, adding another layer to the skills needed to profess well. Younger faculty will, of course, be more comfortable in this new classroom and may well serve as mentors to older faculty. (May they all be humble, gentle, and gracious.) Graduate programs should now, more than ever, provide courses in instructional design for their students; educational institutions should provide appropriate training and development opportunities for their faculty.
- We are also challenged by an ever-evolving new generation of students who have different learning needs and goals. If the millennials challenged us with their internet savvy, extreme confidence, and heavily structured life, the "smartphone generation" (born between 1995 and 2012) will challenge us to find ways to make personal connections, build healthy communities, and challenge them to extend their physical horizons.[36] With each new generation, the diversity of our students will also change; we might have fewer Christians seeking to affirm their faith and more students with no religious affiliation challenging the relevance of a course on the Bible. With movements such as Black Lives Matter and #MeToo, we need to find ways to respond differently to an evolving student body. As professors, we need to attend to the research on our students and continually consider ways to create transformative learning opportunities.
- At a time when the liberal arts often must defend its place in higher education, we also need to work harder as educators both to articulate and to help students understand the relevance and urgency of their course work. Even more so, in a world where secularization has overshadowed religious commitment, and where the Bible has lost its authoritative edge for many, we must help students reflect on the nature of (religious) authority, ethics, the common good, and empathy. When we bring popular American culture into dialogue with the Bible, students can examine their own (or neighboring) religious worldview through various filters in the context of the wider cultural milieu. And rather than reauthorize scripture, we should challenge its authority and reflect on the wider questions it poses.
- One question has become more acute with each passing year: Is it time to set aside the Bible as the most popular and common course in religious studies? By giving

[36] See, for example, Jean M. Twenge, "Has the Smart Phone Destroyed a Generation?," *Atlantic*, September 2017, 58–65.

it priority of place like this in our curriculum, are we ascribing privilege to a text that is less relevant and urgent than we think it is? Do we really need to understand the Bible today? Does the Bible matter to nonreligious people? Should the Bible be taught in a humanities program? Or should we balance our biblical studies options with more comparative religion courses or interfaith courses that give students the opportunity to learn about their own traditions in a global context?[37] Given the research on the value of spiritual quest for student success, we might find better ways to create transformative learning experiences than teaching Bible and Popular Culture.

SUGGESTED READINGS AND ANNOTATED BIBLIOGRAPHY

Clines, David J. A. "Learning, Teaching, and Researching Biblical Studies, Today and Tomorrow." *Journal of Biblical Literature* 129, no. 1 (2010): 5–19.

In his presidential address to the 2009 Society of Biblical Literature annual congress, Clines urges biblical scholars to engage the task of teaching their students well. He reviews multiple theories of learning and lists student outcomes, landing on this "generic skill": "Students will be able to think like biblical scholars." More specifically, students learn best when they discover how to apply the skills of biblical scholarship to the text themselves: observation, data gathering, creating an argument, and so on.

Lester, G. Brooke, Jane S. Webster, and Christopher M. Jones. *Understanding Bible by Design: Create Courses with Purpose*. Seminarium Elements Series. Minneapolis, MN: Fortress Press, 2014.

The goal of this book is to introduce teachers to the course design promoted by Grant Wiggins and Jay McTighe in *Understanding by Design* that sets out clear student learning outcomes in the form of enduring understandings, followed by backwards design that sets in place the scaffolding necessary for effective student learning. *Understanding Bible by Design* applies these principles specifically to teaching the Bible. Examples are provided from the Hebrew Bible, the New Testament, and Jewish studies and for teaching in various contexts, both face-to-face and online.

Roncace, Mark, and Patrick Gray, eds. *Teaching the Bible: Practical Strategies for Classroom Instruction*. Atlanta, GA: Society of Biblical Literature, 2005.

Roncace, Mark, and Patrick Gray, eds. *Teaching the Bible through Popular Culture and the Arts*. Atlanta, GA: Society of Biblical Literature, 2007.

The first of these two helpful volumes collect teaching tips and strategies based on theme or biblical character, arranged canonically. The second volume includes chapters on teaching the bible in conversation with music, film, art, literature, and other media.

Teaching Theology and Religion

This journal is prepared by the Wabash Center for Teaching and Learning in Theology and Religion, providing articles that apply the scholarship of teaching and learning to teach-

---

[37] See Jane S. Webster, James J. Buckley, Tim Jensen, and Stacey Floyd-Thomas, "Responses to the AAR-Teagle White Paper: 'The Religious Studies Major in a Post 9/11 World,'" *Teaching Theology and Religion* 14, no. 1 (2011): 34–71.

ing religion in higher education, issues facing educators and students, and book reviews. Their website has a collection of syllabi for all types of religious studies courses.

Webster, Jane S., and Glenn Holland, eds. *Teaching the Bible in the Liberal Arts Classroom*. Vol. 1. Sheffield, UK: Sheffield Phoenix Press, 2012.

Webster, Jane S., and Glenn Holland, eds. *Teaching the Bible in the Liberal Arts Classroom*. Vol. 2. Sheffield, UK: Sheffield Phoenix Press, 2015.

These two volumes collect the revised papers from the Society of Biblical Literature program unit Teaching the Bible in the Undergraduate Liberal Arts Context. They address the history, issues, and principles for biblical studies courses in a secular context and identify various student learning outcomes and the potential of Bible and interdisciplinary studies. They describe the application of pedagogical theories in course design and suggest innovative and effective classroom strategies with supporting case studies.

....

CHAPTER 30

PUBLISHING IN BIBLE AND AMERICAN POPULAR CULTURE

....

ROBERT PAUL SEESENGOOD
RELIGIOUS STUDIES DEPARTMENT,
ALBRIGHT COLLEGE

INTRODUCTION

....

As the nineteenth century of biblical scholarship is synonymous with "higher criticism" among European (largely German) scholarship, the early twenty-first century, if publishing volume is any harbinger, will be known for scholarship on the Bible and popular culture (or, more broadly, "reception criticism"), particularly among Anglophone (largely North American) scholarship. Germanic higher criticism reflected larger academic and cultural values of its era, for example, a growing valuation of scientific or reasoned criticism in the humanities, assumptions about cultural evolution and social Darwinism, and the methodological refinement of supporting disciplines such as sociology, archaeology, linguistics, and philology. Scholarship on Bible and mass culture reflects our (post)modern moment through shifting assumptions of authority and semiotic and textual meaning, analysis of the cultural structures and power, and the assertion of complexity in what seems superficial and ephemeral. The study of Bible in, and, as popular culture is a hallmark of contemporary biblical scholarship.

This essay is a reflective overview of how academic publishing in the academic discipline of biblical studies has been affected by the interest in Bible and popular culture. It also asks the following: How has interest in Bible and popular culture affected academic publishing? How did these trends emerge, and what assumptions prompt them? What new journals or series or reference works have appeared that are specifically devoted to this broad topic, and what are some ways that the Bible and popular culture have been treated therein?

I want to proceed less as annotated bibliography and more as literature analysis. I will offer an overview of the field (citing some representative examples) rather than a catalog of work that pretends to be exhaustive. In review and in example, I hope to trace what I would identify as three major schools of work. First, there is classic cultural studies work, which is often heavily theoretical and draws from significant British scholarship of the late twentieth century. Second, and decidedly more American, is scholarship using various techniques of intertextual critical analysis. Third, there is work tracing the ways popular culture enacts a sort of history of interpretation and using this critical lens to dissect current ideology. I assume the current work on Bible and popular culture is a subset of reception criticism in biblical studies. Yet it is also clearly, and most directly, a scholarly trend that blends many (but by no means all) assumptions, methods, and queries from British-style cultural studies of the 1960s and 1970s, as well as American interest in mass media and internet culture. Despite some notable exceptions (which I highlight), there is disproportionate attention to film, television, and visual culture and much less on other questions common to British-style cultural studies such as material culture (or "new materialism"), race and ethnicity, food culture, civic practice, family and community studies (beyond race, class, and gender), affect criticism, or cultural ideologies. Publication and dissemination of scholarship in popular culture is, however, growing rapidly in biblical scholarship, with the support of major scholarly societies (such as the Society of Biblical Literature), the focus of several journals (many published only electronically), significant—and extremely ambitious—new reference works, and several new monograph series.

In the following, I will proceed in three general acts. First, I open with an overview of the origins of popular cultural studies, noting the broader transition of that work from the late twentieth century until today and mapping briefly the intrusion of that work into biblical studies. Second, I examine some pivotal examples of scholarship on Bible and American popular culture, and I note several current venues for the publication of similar work. Third, I trace some of the trends generally in our literature, noting some present limitations and directions for possible growth.

OVERVIEW OF THE TOPIC: DEFINING TERMS, DEVELOPING METHODOLOGIES

As we begin a study of Bible in, as, and cultural studies it is worth taking some time to define our terms. For "Bible," I am referring to the Judeo-Christian collection—what Jews refer to as the Tanakh (an acronym derived from the Hebrew words for the Law, or *Torah*; the Prophets, *Nebi'im*; and the Writings, or *Kehtubim*) and what Christians call the Old and New Testament. I certainly intend the Protestant Christian canon of sixty-six books, but I also include the extra or deuterocanonical books present in the canons of the churches of the Roman Catholic, Syriac, Ethiopic, Eastern Orthodox communities, and more.

This is, I admit, a fairly soft definition and raises a key concern: is "Bible" a simple anthology of ancient religiously oriented writings, or is it a very distinct (and sacred?) book, made uniquely significant—perhaps even made a Bible—via the process of selection, canonization, and interpretation (the reception of these ancient texts)? The question is far from trivial; its answer implies, potentially, that *all* biblical scholarship is reception criticism; that despite claims to being sacred, set apart from culture, the unique reception of the Bible in and by popular culture is, itself, what creates a Bible.

A second, critical question is what we mean by "cultural studies" and "popular/mass culture."[1] Prior to Émile Durkheim, "society" referred to the economic and political elite, "high society." Durkheim transformed this term into our more modern definition of groups with common ideologies, technologies, and so on. In a similar way, "culture" was redefined in the twentieth century. As the century dawned, "culture" referred to high-art activities—say, opera, museums, serious plays and literature. Now we understand culture to be ubiquitous, those elements of language, material, art, custom, and values that are produced by, consumed by, and defining of a given society.

The senses of both "society" and "culture" did not change overnight, nor by happenstance. Further, these transitions (fueled by a growing middle and university class after World War II) brought debates over whether there was merit (or even sense) in the scholarly analysis of "low" or popular forms of culture—items (chiefly entertainment, media, and consumables) notable for their popular appeal but deemed "lower" or less worthy of serious analysis or enjoyment by educated classes.

In the 1930s, F. R. Leavis argued (persuasively) that education should consist of cultivating "proper" leisure and exposure to the mainstays of Western literature, art, and music. The properly educated person avoided crass "mass" culture.[2] Richard Hoggart's

---

[1] A great deal of the following is outlined in Stephen D. Moore, "Between Birmingham and Jerusalem: Cultural Studies and Biblical Studies," in *In Search of the Present: The Bible through Cultural Studies*, ed. Stephen D. Moore, Semeia Studies, 82 (Atlanta, GA: Society of Biblical Literature Press, 1998), 1–32. Slightly more oriented toward historical development of the methodology would be J. Cheryl Exum and Stephen D. Moore, "Biblical Studies/Cultural Studies," in *Biblical Studies/Cultural Studies: The Third Sheffield Colloquium*, ed. J. Cheryl Exum and Stephen D. Moore, Journal for the Study of the Old Testament Supplement Series, 266, Gender, Culture, Theory, 7 (Sheffield, UK: Sheffield Academic Press, 1998), 20–45. Strong outlines of methodology, though not as oriented to history of development or as explicitly rooted in Continental thought, can also be found in John F. A. Sawyer, ed., *The Blackwell Companion to the Bible and Culture* (New York: Blackwell, 2006), 1–8. A more brief review of highlights is in Elaine Wainwright, introduction to *The Bible in/and Popular Culture: A Creative Encounter*, ed. Philip Culbertson and Elaine Wainwright, Semeia Studies, 65 (Atlanta, GA: Society of Biblical Literature, 2010), 1–12. Of significant value for the background and basic assumptions of cultural studies and the Birmingham Centre for Contemporary Cultural Studies are Simon During, ed., *The Cultural Studies Reader*, 2nd ed. (New York: Routledge, 1993); Simon During, "From the New Historicism to Cultural Studies," in *Institutions and Cultures: Theory and Practice*, ed. R. Lumsden and R. Patke (Amsterdam: Rodopi, 1996), 53–83; Stuart Hall, "Cultural Studies: Two Paradigms," *Media Culture Society* 2 (1980): 57–72; Stuart Hall, "The Rediscovery of 'Ideology': Return of the Repressed in Media Studies," in *Culture, Society and the Media*, ed. M. Gurevitch, T. Bennett, J. Curran, and J. Woolacott (London: Methuen, 1982), 56–90.

[2] F. R. Leavis, *Mass Civilization and Minority Culture* (Cambridge: Cambridge University Press, 1930).

Uses of Literacy offered an alternative perspective.[3] Hoggart analyzed how and why working-class Britons read; he challenged much of the idea and content of "high" culture, celebrating working-class values, even as he also challenged "mass culture." Raymond Williams's *Culture and Society* took the argument further, asserting that differences between "high" and "low" culture are social norms designed to perpetuate and protect class divisions and distinction.[4] Understanding "low" or mass culture, these scholars argued, was critically important, and popular or "pulp" culture was as worthy of rigorous scholarly attention as "high" culture, and in many ways more revealing.

Hoggart founded the Birmingham Centre for Contemporary Cultural Studies (CCCS) in the early 1960s to study, rigorously and seriously, mass culture as means of understanding present British society; the CCCS was led through the 1960s and 1970s by Stuart Hall.[5] In these years, general Marxist assumptions were dominant, as the Centre tended to assume elite social classes (normally, but not exclusively, the wealthy) maintained their social privilege by the exploitation of the labor and productivity of lower classes and used popular media to either create or reflect these systems.[6] Embedded within popular culture were the structures, and sometimes the mechanisms, of class distinction and social inequity. The CCCS was exploring how these social divisions were reflected in ideas of culture and how culture worked to create and perpetuate these distinctions.

The work of the neo-Marxist philosophers Antonio Gramsci[7] and Louis Althusser[8] were particularly important. Gramsci argued for what he called cultural "hegemony," whereby subdominant social groups (what he called "subaltern") participate willingly in the construction of systems that keep them oppressed (perpetuating systems of racism, gender control, religious persecution, etc.). Althusser argued that social structures called "institutions" (religion, family, the military, education) are constructed to perpetuate the social hierarchy on the whole. This of necessity means that they will perpetuate forms of social domination, and this domination was created, maintained, and mediated via the vehicle of culture, particularly mass culture.[9]

---

[3] Richard Hoggart, *The Uses of Literacy* (New York: Penguin, 1957).

[4] As argued in Raymond Williams, *Culture and Society 1780–1950* (London: Chatto & Windus, 1958). Also of interest (though also apt to points made below) is Raymond Williams, "The Future of Cultural Studies," in *What Is Cultural Studies? A Reader*, ed. John Storey (London: Arnold, 1996), 168–77.

[5] For an overview of Hall's tenure and perspective(s) on his influence, see Janice Radway, "In Honor of Stuart Hall," *Cultural Studies* 30, no. 2 (2016): 312 –21.

[6] Note, for example, the array of essays and influences in Jessica Munns and Gita Rajan, eds., *A Cultural Studies Reader: History, Theory and Practice* (New York: Longman, 1995).

[7] Particularly as represented in the collections Antonio Gramsci, *Selections from the Prison Notebooks*, ed. and trans. Q. Hoare and G. Nowell Smith (London: Lawrence & Wishart, 1971); Antonio Gramsci, *Selections from the Political Writings*, ed. and trans. Q. Hoare (London: Lawrence & Wishart, 1978); and Antonio Gramsci, *Selections from the Cultural Writings*, ed. D. Forgacs and G. Nowell Smith (London: Lawrence & Wishart, 1985).

[8] Most frequently engaging L. Althusser, *For Marx* (London: Allen Lane, 1969); and L. Althusser and E. Balibar, *Reading Capital* (London: New Left Books, 1968).

[9] Note, also T. W. Adorno, *The Culture Industry; Selected Essays on Mass Culture*, ed. J. M. Bernstein (London: Routledge, 1991), which assumes this, throughout.

In the 1980s the formal Marxist orientation of cultural studies (as practiced at the CCCS) became more tenuous, partly in conjunction with declining interest in modernist visions of social order more generally. For many, the simple equation of state versus worker or bourgeois versus proletariat was too simple. Bourgeois with respect to whom? Subaltern where? Global markets disrupted a number of conventional Marxist models. Simple Marxist systems did not work as readily in the emerging complexity of both perspective and structure that globalism created. This transition was simultaneous with postmodern or poststructuralist theory seeping from Continental (particularly French) philosophy into American thought via Yale University.[10] Uniquely adapted to the increase in global awareness and for analysis of pop culture, both argued that metanarratives should be suspect. Postmodern critique challenged traditional (often capitalist) social systems, but also "big narrative" antitraditional (and anticapitalist) systems and assertions where there are meaningful differences between "high" and "low" culture.[11] In adaptation, cultural studies began to move beyond rigid adherence to Marxism. While there is still attention to how culture produces structures of oppression and compliance for subaltern groups, how culture constructs and defends social and economic hierarchy, how culture makes rules for living, how even the idea of culture assumes some difference between the elite and the common, which really does not exist, the simple narrative of single winners and losers has been abandoned. Individuals use culture and rhetoric to define themselves ("subjectivity"). This often results in a fusion of pop-culture review and various gender, sexuality, and ethnicity studies, where the analysis of mass culture moves on to consider how it creates, subverts, or defies general assumptions about subjectivity and cultural identity. When cultural studies crossed to America, it rapidly began to lose its historic roots in Marxism and theory, even as it widely (and wildly) expanded its review of mass culture. It became a generic orientation to elements of mass culture, tuned to revelation of systems of interpretation and structures that construct social organizations.

Before returning to the topic of biblical scholarship, it is important to note one last (American) strand of critical thinking about mass culture that, in many ways, fuses mid-century work (with its interest in economics and systems of production and consumption) and late century work (with its focus on globalism and cultural ephemera). In 1984 Fredric Jameson published an article, "Postmodernity: Or, the Cultural Logic of Late Capitalism," which he later expanded and used as the central chapter of a book of the same title.[12] Jameson accepts the view of Jean-François Lyotard that postmodernity supersedes modernist optimisms. For Jameson, however, Lyotard's "suspicion of all metanarrative" is too radical a rejection of stability in its pure form. (And, to be frank, suspicion of *all* metanarrative does not happen. Postmodernity is somewhat famous for

---

[10] As argued in S. Connor, *Postmodern Culture: An Introduction to Theories of the Contemporary* (Oxford: Blackwell, 1989), 34–45.

[11] Connor, *Postmodern*, 126–34.

[12] Fredric Jameson, "Postmodernism, Or: The Cultural Logic of Late Capitalism" *New Left Review* 146 (1984): 59–92; Fredric Jameson, *Postmodernism: Or, the Cultural Logic of Late Capitalism* (Durham, NC: Duke University Press, 1991).

its tendency to reinscribe metanarratives of resistance, dissidence, hybridity.) Ideology does not cease in postmodernity; it becomes simultaneously diffuse and central.

Jameson begins with the argument of Ernst Mandel about stages of capitalism, noting that late or high capitalism marks a moment of multinational, postindustrial capitalism.[13] Capitalism, as a strategy, has two fundamentally central tenets: competition (among producers) and selection (by consumers). It does not seem entirely coincidental that capitalism expands and begins becoming global roughly contemporary with the development of ideas about natural selection and so-called social Darwinism (and, for that matter, the rise of modernity). Competition and selection determine winners and losers. Affecting the entire physical and social world surrounding us, it must, of necessity, also affect our language, cognition, and perception. For Jameson, these changes are the essential characteristics of postmodernity, though he prefers the term "late capitalism." The continuity with modernity results from capitalism's integral relationship to the products of modernism. The "post-" results in the natural breakdown of confidence and continuity resulting from the types of changes that global capitalism produces.[14] In perhaps simpler terms, Jameson is arguing that postmodernity drifts away from metanarrative via an intentional severing of any moorings. As Jameson defines it, late capitalism is, in its celebration of consumption and superficiality, effectively pop culture intellectualizing and turning its attention back toward, and feeding upon, itself.

SPECIFIC EXAMPLES AND/OR FOCI: BIBLICAL STUDIES AND CULTURAL STUDIES

To return to the study of the Bible: few books have been more massively popular (in the sense of "widely known") in Western culture. The Bible has also been used as an instrument of control and as a basis for liberation. It appears in a variety of art, dictates food customs and household practices, intrudes into folklore and custom, regulates marital and domestic relationships, alters language and proverb, espouses and is integral to political structures, and more. The Bible itself is something of a cultural item. Its presence on a lectern or living-room table defines space and communicates social location. Its symbolism is inseparable from many elements of civil life (such as courts of law or oaths of office). The Bible is inextricably mired in mass culture.[15]

What follows is an overview of work in the field. One could organize such an overview in a variety of ways: chronological, thematic, or structural. Perhaps one could think of sorting them as studies that approach the Bible in popular culture, the Bible as popular culture, or the Bible alongside popular culture. (Indeed, I will suggest in the conclu-

---

[13] Jameson, *Postmodernism*, 35. He is referring to Ernest Mandel, *Late Capitalism* (London: Verso, 1978), esp. 116–22.

[14] Jameson, *Postmodernism*, 6.

[15] Exum and Moore, "Biblical Studies/Cultural Studies," 33–35.

sion that these could be pivotal lenses for thinking about our work.) However, I am sorting works based on their justifying theory or methodology, a sort of "evolutionary tree" of work within the field. As with all such models, there will be inevitable gaps, redundancies, and oversimplifications, but, again as with all models, the simplicity of the concept map may help beginning readers. I am organizing the works around those that draw most emphatically upon classic CCCS-style work in cultural studies, those that rely upon poststructuralist models of intertextuality, and those that draw on reader-response or reception methods of analysis.

As cultural studies migrated from the United Kingdom to the United States, much of its methodological baggage was lost in transit.[16] American scholarship tended to embrace the arguments from cultural studies regarding the dissolution of "high" versus popular, formal versus mass production, and interest in cultural artifacts and general art and literature. In general, however, American approaches to cultural studies tended to avoid the hegemonic or Marxist-influenced questions driving the CCCS work. Cultural studies after the fashion of Hoggart, Hall, and others entered critical biblical scholarship in the mid- to late 1990s. Stephen D. Moore and J. Cheryl Exum noted a transition in methodological assumption between the fruit of cultural studies, particularly in America, and the original assumptions and methods of its root stock.[17] Yet they also argued that biblical criticism (particularly American) of popular culture, even as it lacked a sense of the Marxist history of the movement, was, in its growing interest in entertainment and broadcast media, well within CCCS precedent.[18]

As we will see, biblical scholarship that engages popular culture has expanded exponentially in the first decades of the twenty-first century. Stephen D. Moore and Yvonne Sherwood have argued the present turn toward cultural studies by biblicists is the natural end of postmodern literary criticism in general, and biblical studies in particular; they also assert that, as a development, it is the future of biblical scholarship.[19] Noting both the spread of the literature and the broader cultural pressures on professional academics (where an increasing number of biblical studies PhDs find themselves employed as professors, if at all, in broad, general studies–oriented interdisciplinary undergraduate departments), I would agree, and I would expand their argument by suggesting, along with Jameson, that cultural studies may well be both the fundamental basis of and the ultimate end to postmodernity.

Though he is rarely to never cited by them, much biblical scholarship on Bible and American popular culture explicitly or indirectly resonates with Jameson, particularly as it manifests in American scholarship. Scholarly trends in Bible and American popular culture, with notable exceptions (reviewed later), drift toward an examination of culture as consumable mass product (chiefly movies, television, and music) and comment on the Bible's role in or as a type of consumer good; some work remains simply descriptive

---

[16] Moore, "Between Birmingham and Jerusalem," 17–19.
[17] Exum and Moore, "Biblical Studies/Cultural Studies," 30–3.
[18] Moore, "Between Birmingham and Jerusalem," 3.
[19] Stephen D. Moore and Yvonne Sherwood, *The Invention of a Biblical Scholar: A Critical Manifesto* (Minneapolis, MN: Fortress, 2011), *passim*.

or analytical of appropriation and interpretation. Early work on Bible and popular culture drew heavily from Birmingham-style Marxism and a broad definition of "culture." As it matures, we will see, scholarship on Bible and popular culture becomes increasingly a late capitalist critique of mass media and entertainment structures even as it replicates and performs (a type of) those same structures.

A cursory review of the shifting nature of biblical criticism reveals that some sort of encounter between cultural studies and modern, academic biblical scholarship would seem inevitable.[20] Indeed, reception critical methodologies may be the capstone of modern, secular biblical criticism. Late Renaissance and early Enlightenment scholars such as Hugo de Groot and Erasmus famously read the Bible according to the norms and standards of any other book from antiquity. The Bible was not read primarily as a book opened only via divine or supernatural guidance, read solely within the protected confines of dogma and community. Instead it was subject to normal critical techniques of historical analysis and grammatical review. This seed germinated in the nineteenth century via higher criticism, whose scholars intentionally set aside allegiances to faith and read the Bible as a historical text, asking sometimes rude questions about the Bible's historical reliability, textual integrity, or even claims to authorship and authority. By the early twentieth century, these secular critiques were assumed: the Bible was a book from history, written by humans within history, and best read according to the norms of reading more generally. Scholars sought the meaning of the Bible not in spiritual revelation or disclosure but by painstaking reconstruction of content and context to disclose what the original authors most likely intended the text to mean. By the mid- to late twentieth century, these expectations had shifted again. Schooled against high modernism's intellectual overconfidence, scholars were increasingly aware of the role of the interpreter's bias in any reading—including in the reconstruction of the historical context(s) and meaning of the Bible. No longer confident a text can mean what an author intended, scholars looked more and more into analysis of how culture and bias shaped Bible readers (or how the Bible was used to construct cultures or defend biases).

Cultural studies informed biblical criticism and continues this late capitalist critique of the Bible and its influence(s). Roland Boer's *Knockin' on Heaven's Door* is an early monograph devoted to the study of the Bible in/and mass culture.[21] Boer notes that a handful of volumes preceded his own work, largely edited volumes of collected essays

---

[20] For a quick review of what follows, consult Michael Legaspi, *The Death of Scripture and the Rise of Biblical Studies*, Oxford Studies in Historical Theology (New York: Oxford University Press, 2010). Readers will note, though his survey of the history and development of modern biblical studies is quite accurate, that Legaspi, a theologian, clearly laments the loss of biblical authority resulting from the transition. Not all critics agree this loss—or perhaps better, "transformation"—is detrimental. For a manifesto for secular or political readings of the Bible unbeholden to Christian or Jewish theology, see Roland Boer, *Rescuing the Bible*, Blackwell Manifestos (London: Blackwell, 2007); Jacques Berlinerblau, *The Secular Bible: Why Nonbelievers Must Take Religion Seriously* (Cambridge: Cambridge University Press, 2005).

[21] Roland Boer, *Knockin' on Heaven's Door* (New York: Routledge, 1999). This work was, in many ways, prefaced by his *Novel Histories: The Fiction of Biblical Criticism* (Sheffield, UK: Sheffield Academic Press, 1997).

that did not engage the broader history of cultural studies. Boer is a Marxist, arguing societies are divided, hierarchically, into categories of production and consumption where higher, more altern (to use Althusser's term) groups enjoy privilege and benefit from the labor and production of subaltern groups. The subaltern communities are often exploited, though, as Gramsci has observed, often also are participating themselves, willingly, in the system(s) of exploitation.

Boer outlines the general history of cultural studies as represented by the classic CCCS literature. He notes that the academic field of religion, particularly theology and biblical studies, historically is mother to numerous other academic subfields. These fields generated cultural studies. Cultural studies was coming home. For Boer, biblical scholarship is (and always is) cultural studies. Boer seeks to undermine the "censor" of broader culture—the cultural norms (often driven by implicit metanarratives) that determine what is high and low culture, what is "vulgar" and what is "refined," what is "correct" and "incorrect" in interpretation, what is "sacred" and what is "profane"—as he reads the Bible alongside popular fiction, rock-and-roll music (including heavy metal), pornography, and the fast-food industry.

Another significant scholar—mentioned earlier—is Stephen D. Moore. Moore began his work exploring postmodern modes of reading, and as his work developed during his years on the faculty of the University of Sheffield, his interest shifted from analysis of language and theory of interpretation to exploration of popular modes of biblical appropriation and interpretation, with specific interest in cultural constructions of gender and power or hierarchy. Alongside editing two significant early collections of general scholarship on the Bible and popular culture,[22] Moore explored biblical depictions of the form or image of God and their popular appropriations in his 1996 *God's Gym*.[23] His interest was how these images inscribe gender identity for God and how this inscribed gender identity appropriated by popular culture both created and perpetuated expectations of both divine and masculine power. Moore followed this with his 1999 *God's Beauty Parlor*.[24] Many of the same themes (gender, power, cultural constructions of hierarchy) persist in this work as well. Moore's focus moves toward Jesus and toward explicit analysis of gender, sexuality, and sexual preference with a particular focus on what culture deems "queer" sexual identity. Examining queerness reveals cultural

---

[22] Exum and Moore, *Biblical Studies/Cultural Studies*; Stephen D. Moore, ed., *In Search of the Present: The Bible through Cultural Studies*, Semeia Studies, 82 (Atlanta, GA: Society of Biblical Literature, 1998).

[23] Stephen D. Moore, *God's Gym: Divine Male Bodies of the Bible* (New York: Routledge, 1996).

[24] Stephen D. Moore, *God's Beauty Parlor and Other Queer Spaces in and around the Bible*, Contraversions: Jews and Other Differences (Stanford, CA: Stanford University Press, 2001). A significant hallmark of Moore's work during this period was his use of autobiographical criticism and his interest in the emerging methodology of New Historicism. The former foregrounded the experience of the critic-as-reader in overt ways; the latter famously foregrounds the interpretive significance of popular or mass history and experience. Cultural studies, in many ways, fused these interests around questions of subjectivity and meaning. One could argue that contemporary work in affect criticism is the continuation of all these various strands. Notably, Moore is a major contributor to the development of affect theory in/and biblical scholarship.

modes of constructing "normal" identity and expression, which, in turn, reveals systems of cultural domination. Moore's work is characterized by a relentless interest in and precision toward methodology.

After the examples of Boer and Moore, the work of Erin Runions remains some of the most theoretically sophisticated and deeply informed work on Bible and popular culture. (Runions has worked as well to help shape various Society of Biblical Literature subsections on popular culture, and she is a former editorial board member of Semeia Studies.)[25] Hers is an apt example of work that fuses politico-economic theory and gendered subjectivity. Her trenchant analyses are informed by deep reading in European critical theory and revolve around issues of gender, politics, and, most recently, affect.

In American biblical criticism on popular culture and cultural studies, it would be difficult to underestimate the influence of Fernando Segovia. Writing in 1995, he defined and defended cultural studies of the Bible, grounding it within traditionally postmodern and literary approaches to biblical criticism. For Segovia, cultural studies is an opportunity for the critic to examine her own context-driven reading assumptions and investment(s): "It is the role assigned to the reader that, without doubt, most sharply differentiates cultural studies from other competing paradigms in contemporary biblical criticism. For cultural studies the reader does not and cannot remain...in the background, even if so wished and attempted, but is actively and inevitably involved in the production and meaning of 'texts' and history."[26]

Segovia argued that cultural studies readings of the Bible expose the way systems and ideologies worked to create culturally altern groups—specifically, colonial engagement and race and ethnicity. Following the work of the CCCS, biblical scholarship has maintained a principal focus on contemporary popular culture (vs. examination of ancient mass culture, as one might anticipate among biblicists).[27] In part, I would argue that this is because of the way Segovia's seminal definition justifies cultural criticism by embedding it in the experience of the (contemporary) Bible reader, but also because his rationale, within the field of biblical studies, was itself an implicit rejection of traditional historical-grammatical exegetical work (which often asserts that the reader or interpreter is merely a conduit, neutrally discerning meaning after scholarly reconstruction of both text and context).

---

[25] Note, for example, the impressive triad by Erin Runions: *Changing Subjects: Gender, Nation and Future in Micah*, Playing the Texts, 7 (Sheffield, UK: Sheffield Academic Press, 2002); *How Hysterical: Identification and Resistance in the Bible and Film* (New York: Palgrave, 2003); and *The Babylon Complex: Theopolitical Fantasies of War, Sex and Sovereignty* (New York: Fordham University Press, 2014). One can practically chart the developing sophistication of cultural studies critique across these three books.

[26] Fernando Segovia, "Cultural Studies and Contemporary Biblical Criticism: Ideological Criticism as Mode of Discourse," in *Reading from This Place*, 2 vols., ed. Fernando F. Segovia and Mary Ann Tolbert (Minneapolis, MN: Fortress, 1995), 2:12. Segovia would later refine this, writing that cultural studies is a "joint critical study of texts and readers." Fernando Segovia, *Decolonizing Biblical Studies: A View from the Margins* (Maryknoll, NY: Orbis, 2000), 30).

[27] Exum and Moore, "Biblical Studies/Cultural Studies," 39; Moore, "Between Birmingham and Jerusalem," 2–3.

The changes to cultural studies among biblical scholars, which were anticipated by Exum and Moore, have been revealed to be a combination of Segovia's interest in the location of the reader (a reader embedded in and influenced by mass culture) wedded to work also drawing from Luce Irigaray's notion of intertextuality.[28] Moving beyond the individual and her role as reader (and the attendant emphasis upon contemporary culture), a second line of scholarship has focused on reception history or "biblical afterlives," looking at systems of interpretation and ideological engagement with the Bible.

"Intertextuality," a term made most stable by Irigaray, explores the interanimation of texts. Often highly disparate works—separated from one another by varied genre, chronology, language, or purpose—reflect or reveal a mutual interest in theme, ideology, and even structure. This may be because of intentional citation or allusion, but it is often via the analysis and close reading of a reader who brings her own interests and creates her own resonances and connections. Intertextuality is intentional eisegesis via comparative reading (though most intertextual critics would argue all exegesis is, in the end, eisegetical). As intertextuality has entered cultural studies the meaning of "text" has been expanded to include recorded music, film, still image, web text, and more. Analogous to the knowledge potentially gained by comparative anatomy, the examination of moments of intertextuality can reveal "this is that" analogies and parallels exposing implicit themes, ideas, or motives in both works; it can also clarify how more transparent structures work to create meaning.[29] Intertextual approaches, rooted in scholarship of subjectivity, frequently took gender and feminist interests as a critical lens for examination of Bible in/and mass culture. Feminism has had a particular interest in the way images in general and film in particular construct and reflect popular ideas of the feminine ideal and gendered behavior, particularly asking (sometimes pointed) questions about the location of the viewer's gaze. Images of women both create and perpetuate cultural norms about feminine beauty, for example. Yet these images, as images, also draw the

[28] For early work, see Alice Bach, *Women, Seduction and Betrayal in Biblical Narrative* (Cambridge: Cambridge University Press, 1997); Alice Bach, ed., "The Bible and Popular Culture," special issue, *Biblical Interpretation* 2, no. 1 (1994). Much of this work arose from studies devoted to exploring the Bible in visual images and in film and had a notably feminist interest, as per J. Cheryl Exum, ed., "The Bible and the Arts," special issue, *Biblical Interpretation* 6, nos. 3–4 (1998); Alice Bach, *Biblical Glamour and Hollywood Glitz*, Semeia Studies, 74 (Atlanta, GA: Society of Biblical Literature, 1996); Tina Pippin, *Apocalyptic Bodies: The Biblical End of the World in Text and Image* (New York: Routledge, 1996); George Aichele and Pippin, *The Monstrous and the Unspeakable: The Bible as Fantastic Literature* (New York: Routledge, 1997). Bach's early work in advancing cultural studies and popular culture among biblical scholars is difficult to underestimate. She founded, for example, the journal *Biblicon* for this express purpose and was early, and vocally, engaged in creating space for such work at the annual meeting of the Society of Biblical Literature. On intertextuality and cultural studies readings, note in particular: George Aichele, *Culture, Entertainment and the Bible*, Library of Hebrew Bible / Old Testament Studies, 309 (Sheffield, UK: Sheffield Academic Press, 2000).

[29] Though one occasionally still runs across scholars who use the term "intertextual" to, essentially, refer to (explicit) citation of Hebrew Bible in the New Testament, in biblical or cultural studies that are truly intertextual, the Bible is read in or alongside elements of pop culture intertextually to reveal how later use exposes (or reflects or reduces or magnifies) biblical agendas and meanings.

viewer or consumer into participation in this construction. As we watch or gaze, we become collaborators with the perpetuation of these larger cultural norms.

Yvonne Sherwood's analysis of the "afterlives" of the biblical character Jonah—how Jonah's myth and image were used in later Judeo-Christian art to create or reinforce ideology of later generations—is an example and early landmark in the formal development of reception criticism.[30] Some key studies consider popular or mass cultural items from the past.[31] Reception criticism has become an increasingly broad approach to biblical criticism, generating major reference and research works, such as the Blackwell Bible Commentary[32] and the impressively ambitious *Encyclopedia of the Bible and Its Reception* published by Walter de Gruyter.[33]

Work on Bible in popular culture has expanded dramatically. The annual meeting of the Society of Biblical Literature now has several sections dedicated to popular culture, cultural studies, and the Bible in various forms of modern media. As I will discuss, several new monograph series with a focus on various aspects of Bible and popular culture or cultural studies have emerged. As this work has expanded, methodological structure has become even more diffuse, though still tending to orbit around issues of discovery of meaning and interpretation(s) of or in biblical text, the role of Bible in popular culture for the construction of identity (particularly gender), and center largely on visual images, film (including television), and music. This latter focus has foregrounded, for some, questions about the borders between work that is categorized as high and low or mass culture and the difference and similarity between professional and popular or mass interpretation.

In a survey of some contemporary work in Bible and popular culture we find elements of popular culture examined by biblical scholars vary widely but cluster (when they do) around (contemporary) mass entertainment. For example, Sawyer's *The Blackwell Companion to Bible and Culture* demonstrates the breadth of the influence of

---

[30] Yvonne Sherwood, *A Biblical Text and Its Afterlives: The Survival of Jonah in Western Culture* (Cambridge: Cambridge University Press, 2001). On reception history, see Emma England and William John Lyons, eds., *Reception History and Biblical Studies: Theory and Practice*, Library of Hebrew Bible / Old Testament Studies, 615, Critical Perspectives on the Reception and Influence of the Bible, 6 (London: T & T Clark, 2015).

[31] For example, Robert Paul Seesengood and Jennifer L. Koosed, *Jesse's Lineage: The Legendary Lives of David, Jesus and Jesse James*, Library of Hebrew Bible / Old Testament Studies, 548, Playing the Texts, 14 (London: Bloomsbury, 2013); Jennifer L. Koosed, *Gleaning Ruth: A Biblical Heroine and Her Afterlives*, Studies in Personalities of the Old Testament (Columbia: University of South Carolina Press, 2011); Dan W. Clanton, *The Good, the Bold, and the Beautiful: The Story of Susanna and Its Renaissance Interpretations*, Library of Hebrew Bible / Old Testament Studies, 430 (London: T & T Clark, 2006); or Colleen M. Conway, *Sex and Slaughter in the Tent of Jael: A Cultural History of a Biblical Story* (Oxford: Oxford University Press, 2017).

[32] Blackwell Bible Commentaries, edited by John Sawyer, Christopher Rowland, Judith Kovacs and David M. Gunn. Each of the twenty-eight individually authored volumes is subtitled *Through the Centuries*.

[33] *The Encyclopedia of the Bible and Its Reception*, edited by Christine Helmer, Steven Linn McKenzie, Thomas Chr. Römer, Jens Schröter, Barry Dov Walfish, and Eric Ziolkowski. It is published in print, but latest versions are available online at https://www.degruyter.com/view/db/ebr.

the Bible in various forms of popular culture, such as film, literature, music, and the visual arts, but also theater, architecture, and the Victorian circus.[34] Timothy K. Beal has written on the Bible as a cultural and mass publishing phenomenon[35] and has also examined the Bible and its role in American folk religion and tourism.[36] These themes echo work on the current state of popular "biblical literacy"[37] and in critique of the American Bible tourism destination without equal: the Museum of the Bible.[38] Scholars have examined the role of the Bible in popular political rhetoric in America[39] and in England.[40] The Bible's role in selling more than just political ideology; indeed, its place within the crass, very mass world of modern advertising has also received notice.[41] Much work has been devoted to the Bible in various mass entertainment media,[42] from comic books[43] to pop music,[44] but especially film.[45]

[34] Sawyer, *The Blackwell Companion to Bible and Culture*.

[35] Timothy K. Beal, *The Rise and Fall of the Bible: The Unexpected History of an Accidental Book* (New York: Mariner Books, 2012).

[36] Timothy K. Beal, *Roadside Religion: In Search of the Sacred, Strange and the Substance of Faith* (Boston: Beacon Hill, 2005).

[37] Katie Edwards, ed., *Rethinking Biblical Literacy* (London: T & T Clark, 2015). On another aspect of Bible production, see Scott S. Elliott and Roland Boer, eds., *Ideology Culture and Translation*, Semeia Studies, 69 (Atlanta, GA: Society of Biblical Literature, 2012).

[38] Joel Baden and Candida Moss, *Bible Nation: The United States of Hobby-Lobby* (Princeton, NJ: Princeton University Press, 2017); Jill Hicks-Keeton and Cavan Concannon, eds. *The Museum of the Bible: A Critical Introduction*. New York: Lexington Books / Fortress Academic Press, 2019.

[39] Jacques Berlinerblau, *Thumpin' It: The Use and Abuse of the Bible in Today's Presidential Politics* (Louisville, KY: Westminster John Knox Press, 2008).

[40] James Crossley, *Jesus in an Age of Neoliberalism: Quests, Scholarship and Ideology* (New York: Routledge, 2014); James Crossley, *Cults, Martyrs and Good Samaritans: Religion in Contemporary English Political Discourse* (London: Pluto, 2018).

[41] Katie Edwards, *Admen and Eve: The Bible in Contemporary Advertising*, Bible in the Modern World (Sheffield, UK: Sheffield Phoenix, 2012).

[42] For example: Culbertson and Wainwright, *Bible in/and Popular Culture*; Exum and Moore, *Biblical Studies/Cultural Studies*; Moore, *In Search of the Present*, and other works mentioned earlier.

[43] Dan W. Clanton, Jr., ed., *The End Will Be Graphic: Apocalyptic in Comic Books and Graphic Novels*, Bible in the Modern World, 43, Apocalypse and Popular Culture, 5 (Sheffield, UK: Sheffield Phoenix, 2012).

[44] Michael J. Gilmour, ed., *"Call Me the Seeker": Listening to Religion in Popular Music* (New York: Continuum, 2005); Michael J. Gilmour, *Gods and Guitars: Seeking the Sacred in Post-1960s Popular Music* (Waco, TX: Baylor University Press, 2009); Michael J. Gilmour, *Tangled Up in the Bible: Bob Dylan and Scripture* (New York: Continuum, 2004); Dan W. Clanton, Jr., *Daring, Disrespectful and Devout: Interpreting the Bible's Women in the Arts and Music* (New York: Continuum, 2009); Helen Leneman, *The Performed Bible: The Story of Ruth in Opera and Oratorio*, Bible in the Modern World (Sheffield, UK: Sheffield Phoenix, 2007).

[45] The study of film and television is, without serious challenge, the broadest category of work on Bible and popular culture. A very select review of recent methodology or survey-oriented work (particularly works that are multiauthor collections and good places for beginning reading) should include Rhonda Burnette-Bletsch, ed., *The Bible in Motion: A Handbook of the Bible and Its Reception in Film*, 2 vols., Handbooks of the Bible and Its Reception (Leiden: De Gruyter, 2016); Laura Copier and Caroline Vander Stichele, eds., *Close Encounters between Bible and Film: An Interdisciplinary Engagement*, Semeia Studies, 87 (Atlanta, GA: Society of Biblical Literature Press, 2016); Adele Reinhatz, *Bible and Cinema: An Introduction* (New York: Routledge, 2013); Adele Reinhatz, *Bible and Cinema: Fifty Key Films*, Routledge Key Guides (New York: Routledge, 2012); Richard Walsh, ed., *Bloomsbury Bible and Film Handbook* (New York: Bloomsbury T & T Clark, 2018).

Despite long-running interest at meetings and conferences of the Society of Biblical Literature, little of this scholarship, to date, has trickled down into the society's premier journal: the *Journal of Biblical Literature*. A number of essays, however, have appeared in the Society's monograph series Semeia Studies. Some significant journals that have been leaders in reception criticism and popular culture are *Biblical Interpretation* and *Bible and Critical Theory*. Surprisingly, much of the work on Bible and popular culture appears in various monograph series. Indeed, at the time of this writing, these are not only prominent but proliferating. Series titles include Biblical Intersections (Gorgias), The Bible and Its Reception (Society of Biblical Literature), The Bible and the Moving Image (Walter de Gruyter), Biblical Reception and The Bible in the Age of Capital (Rowan Littlefield) and The Bible in the Modern World (Sheffield Phoenix). In the late 1990s, major publishers included Routledge, T & T Clark, Continuum, and Sheffield Academic Press. Major publishers of work on Bible and popular culture or reception history, at time of this writing, are Bloomsbury, Routledge, Society of Biblical Literature, Walter de Gruyter, and Wiley-Blackwell.

FUTURE PROSPECTS AND QUESTIONS

- As studies of the Bible and popular culture have proliferated, two situations have arisen. More and more teaching scholars are discovering the pedagogic value of studies of Bible in/and pop culture.[46] How would reliance upon pop culture examples in the classroom affect biblical literacy? Would it foreground or alter what we mean by "literacy" in general?
- As we have seen, there has been a rather substantial increase in the variety of cultural elements under review. Some studies can be (at times exclusively) focused on locating and describing the appearance of the Bible in popular culture—and do not drink as deeply as one might hope from the rich, philosophically complex springs of theory and methodology that nourished cultural studies. Indirectly, then, they perpetuate a Jamesian late capitalist scholarship: like the pop culture they discuss, they become a scholarship devoid of critical weight, ephemeral, mass-accessible, entertaining, but ultimately something to consume for the moment but not longer. What is the risk of critical methodology that lacks philosophical grounding or a critical school? In what ways is a pop-culture approach to the Bible benefiting when informed by its theoretical history? What is the risk of overreliance upon methodology or a critical school? In what ways is a pop-culture approach to the Bible at its best precisely when it is evading formal schools or strict methodology?

---

[46] Mark Roncace and Patrick Gray, eds., *Teaching the Bible through Popular Culture and the Arts*, Resources for Biblical Studies, 53 (Atlanta, GA: Society of Biblical Literature, 2007). For more reflection on teaching the Bible using popular culture, see Jane S. Webster's chapter in this volume.

- The study of popular culture has three potential focal points, or lenses, for biblical criticism: the Bible *as* popular culture, the Bible *in* popular culture, and the Bible *and* popular culture.[47] Study of how the Bible has been used *in* popular culture looks at how the Bible appears in many modern venues from songs to films, formal artwork, popular tattoos, and toys, seeing each as a moment of biblical interpretation. Study of these uses reveals how popular culture is interpreting the biblical text, how the Bible is used to construct cultural types and antetypes. One may also ask, however, how the Bible *is* an element of pop culture, how the Bible itself is a pop-cultural and political icon. A third, intertextual approach is to examine how popular culture actually reveals or constructs (potential) meanings within the biblical text itself. This would be the Bible *and* popular culture. Consider: what might one expect, specifically, from a study of the Bible *in, and,* or *as* pop culture? How would these be unique? Might they ever overlap?
- Studies of Bible and popular culture have been perhaps too centered on popular entertainments and various visual media such as graphic images, illustration, television, and cinema. More needs to be done regarding material studies (and new materialism), family studies, economics and political theory, and more. Further, there is ample space to blend interests such as gender, race, economics, colonialism, ethnicity, and animal studies into popular culture critique. For example, an emerging area lies within the broadening venues of affect criticism. There is much to recommend readings that close the loop of inquiry and return, after analysis, to interrogate both popular and biblical ideas about social order, economics, ideology, and subjectivity (including race, class, sexuality, and gender). In what ways are ethnicity, gender, social status, religion, race, and other differences described (or even created) by or in popular culture? How might reading the Bible in, as, or alongside popular culture offer opportunities to reflect on these identity elements that many assume are natural and constant?

Suggested Readings and Annotated Bibliography

Culled from this chapter's review, I would recommend the following titles for both an overview of cultural studies and history of publishing on the Bible in, and, or as (American) popular culture.

Bach, Alice, ed. "The Bible and Popular Culture." Special issue of *Biblical Interpretation* 2, no. 1 (1994).

This theme issue of the journal *Biblical Interpretation* was one of the first collections of serious, critically informed work on Bible and cultural studies. It still remains paradigmatic.

---

[47] An organization similar to the one outlined in Bruce David Forbes, "Introduction: Finding Religion in Unexpected Places," in *Religion and Popular Culture in America*, 3rd ed., ed. Bruce David Forbes and Jeffrey H. Mahan (Oakland: University of California Press, 2017), 1–24, here 11–21.

Clark, Terry Ray, and Dan W. Clanton, Jr., eds. *Understanding Religion and Popular Culture*. New York: Routledge, 2012.

> More than just a nod to this volume's editors, this review is a significant reason for their reputation. An excellent review of popular culture and its influence and influences.

Culbertson, Philip, and Elaine M. Wainwright, eds. *The Bible in/and Popular Culture: A Creative Encounter*. Semeia Studies, 65. Atlanta, GA: Society of Biblical Literature, 2010.

> A nice collection of essays showcasing some of the work in popular culture and Bible around the Anglophone world.

Exum, J. Cheryl, and Stephen D. Moore, eds. *Biblical Studies/Cultural Studies: The Third Sheffield Colloquium*. Journal for the Study of the Old Testament, Supplement Series, 266, Gender, Culture, Theory, 7. Sheffield, UK: Sheffield Academic Press, 1998.

> Valuable for two reasons: the first is the essay's introduction, which outlines the growth and basic assumptions of Bible and critical study of mass culture (an essay revised by Moore and published again, most recently in his retrospective collection *The Bible in Theory: Critical and Postcritical Essays* [Atlanta, GA: SBL Press, 2010]). The second is the array of strong essays, influential on later work.

Sawyer, John F. A. *The Blackwell Companion to the Bible and Culture*. Oxford: Blackwell, 2006.

> This collection has a very good review of Bible and popular culture, with particular strength on American work. Another fine aspect of this collection is its inclusion of a variety of cultural forms and types.

Segovia, Fernando. *Decolonizing Biblical Studies: A View from the Margins*. Maryknoll, NY: Orbis, 2000.

> Significant reading for American work on Bible and popular culture. Segovia's definition of "cultural studies" has been very influential on the field. Further, this work demonstrates a critical strength of cultural studies work: the ability to move beyond the superficial and ephemeral and engage the way culture constructs and defines race, class, gender, and cultural inclusion.

Index

Note to Reader: This index has been designed to accord with our guiding principle elsewhere in the *Handbook*: usefulness. Thus, it emphasizes those authors, works, and topics discussed more substantively. Some entries will not include page references for every mention in the body of the *Handbook*, and subjects mentioned only once or in passing may not be included at all.

Note: Figures are indicated by an italic "*f*", respectively, following the page number.

SCRIPTURAL INDEX